Vikings and Goths

ALSO BY GARY DEAN PETERSON

Warrior Kings of Sweden: The Rise of an Empire in the Sixteenth and Seventeenth Centuries (McFarland, 2007)

VIKINGS AND GOTHS

A History of Ancient and Medieval Sweden

Gary Dean Peterson

McFarland & Company, Inc., Publishers
Jefferson, North Carolina

LIBRARY OF CONGRESS CATALOGUING-IN-PUBLICATION DATA

Names: Peterson, Gary Dean, 1942– author.
Title: Vikings and Goths : a history of ancient and medieval Sweden / Gary Dean Peterson.
Description: Jefferson, North Carolina : McFarland & Company, Inc., Publishers, 2016 | Includes bibliographical references and index.
Identifiers: LCCN 2016021665 | ISBN 9781476662183 (softcover : acid free paper) ∞
Subjects: LCSH: Sweden—History—To 1397. | Scandinavia—History—To 1397. | Vikings—History. | Goths—History.
Classification: LCC DL660 .P47 2016 | DDC 948.5/01—dc23
LC record available at https://lccn.loc.gov/2016021665

BRITISH LIBRARY CATALOGUING DATA ARE AVAILABLE

ISBN (print) 978-1-4766-6218-3
ISBN (ebook) 978-1-4766-2434-1

© 2016 Gary Dean Peterson. All rights reserved

No part of this book may be reproduced or transmitted in any form or by any means, electronic or mechanical, including photocopying or recording, or by any information storage and retrieval system, without permission in writing from the publisher.

Front cover image © 2016 iStock

Printed in the United States of America

McFarland & Company, Inc., Publishers
  Box 611, Jefferson, North Carolina 28640
    www.mcfarlandpub.com

To Pauline

Contents

Preface	1
Introduction	3
1. A Land Reborn	5
2. The First Settlers and Sweden's Mesolithic Age	11
3. Sweden of the Neolithic Age	23
4. Bronze Age Sweden	31
5. The Iron Age Comes to Sweden	41
6. Roman Iron Age in Sweden	49
7. Visigoths Defeat the Roman Empire	56
8. The Ostrogoths Build an Empire	64
9. Evidence of a Swedish Origin for the Goths	72
10. Sweden in the German Iron Age Migration Period (AD 400–575)	78
11. Sweden of the Vendel Period (AD 575–790)	90
12. Norwegian Vikings Assault the British Isles	102
13. Danish Vikings Invade England	106
14. Viking Raids and Conquests in Continental Europe	111
15. Viking Ships and Navigation	117
16. The Viking Search for New Lands	122
17. Danish Unification During the Viking Age	130
18. The Norwegian Struggle for Independence	134
19. The Empire of Knut the Great	138
20. William the Conqueror Invades England	145
21. Norman Kingdom of Italy and Sicily	151
22. Swedish Participation in the Western Expeditions	155

23. Swedish Unification	161
24. The Swedish People of the Viking Age	173
25. Sweden's Early Viking Expeditions to the East	190
26. The Geography and People of Eastern Europe	194
27. Swedes of the Rus Khaganate	200
28. Sweden the Great	205
29. Words Written in Stone	221
30. The Last Great Expedition to the East	227
31. End of the Viking Age	232
32. Medieval Sweden (AD 1070–1350)	235
33. Eastern Europe in the Middle Ages	253
34. Novgorod the Great, Lithuania and the Rise of Moscow	266
35. Sweden and the Black Death	271
36. St. Birgitta of Sweden	277
37. Margareta and the Kalmar Union	280
Epilogue	283
Chapter Notes	285
Bibliography	297
Index	301

Preface

Through the winter of 1631–1632, Gustav Adolf, king of Sweden, maintained his headquarters at Mainz, where he held court on the Rhine deep in German territory. At this moment in history, Gustav was the most powerful monarch in Europe. It was the height of the Thirty Years' War. Having crossed the Baltic Sea, landing in Pomerania, Gustav had advanced south and succeeded in carving out a Swedish realm in the heart of the Holy Roman Empire. At Mainz, Gustav received embassies from all over Europe, including Russia, Transylvania and the Tartars of Crimea.

During the winter months, the king and his close friend and ally, Chancellor Axel Oxenstierna, developed an administrative system for Swedish Germany. A chancery and standing council was established with an exchequer and judiciary. A system of taxation, tolls and customs was likewise implemented.

From his court on the Rhine, Gustav directed an empire that included these German holdings along with Prussia, Lithuania and Estonia, Ingria, Karelia, Finland and Sweden itself. The Baltic was a Swedish lake where Swedish fleets could swoop down and land troops when and where they were needed.

Sweden of the seventeenth century was one of the dominant military powers of Europe. Under later kings, this nation from the north would invade not just Germany but also Poland and other countries of Eastern Europe, capturing Prague and driving to the gates of Vienna. Swedish troops would overrun Novgorod, march in the streets of Moscow and carry the war with Russia into the Ukraine. This rise to power and military preeminence lasted a century and a half and was the subject of the book *Warrior Kings of Sweden* (2007). In writing that book, I was continually haunted by the question of how a relatively small nation (in terms of population), on the fringes of European geography, could evolve to become such an international power. To answer that question, I delved into the subject of Swedish ancient and medieval history. This book is a result of that investigation. What became evident in the course of my research was that Swedes had in fact been to these areas of the continent before.

Sweden's age of conquest was preceded by two outbursts of activity that shook continental Europe. One of these episodes was the invasion of the Roman Empire by the Goths. In this book, the origin of the Goths is examined for evidence of their beginnings in ancient Sweden. Crossing the Baltic, the Goths gathered strength on the Polish coast, then migrated to the Black Sea area. From there they pushed west and participated in the dismantling of the Roman Empire, creating two kingdoms of their own.

The second outburst was that of the Vikings. Sweden's involvement in the western expeditions is analyzed in order to understand the extent to which Swedish Vikings participated in the invasion and conquest of the British Isles and the plundering of continental Europe. Also, the narrative explores the role Swedes played in the discovery and settlement of the North Atlantic islands, Iceland, Greenland and ultimately North America.

Finally, there is the Swedish trading, plundering and conquest of Eastern Europe, known as "Sweden the Great." It was in this immense theater that Swedish Vikings (known as Varangians or Rus) were dominant, establishing a trade system stretching from Constantinople and Bagdad to the North Sea and the Arctic Circle. The great river road of Russia and the Ukraine was, indeed, Sweden's road to riches.

The Sweden that emerged in the sixteenth century certainly was acquainted with the territories bordering the Baltic and with the plains of Eastern Europe. The energetic nation might have even felt some claim to these areas based on past sovereignty. There can be little doubt that Sweden's rise to preeminence in the sixteenth and seventeenth centuries had its roots in the aggressive outbursts of activity in the early Christian era.

Introduction

Twenty thousand years ago, Sweden lay buried beneath millions of tons of ice, a slate wiped clean and ready to receive the imprint of flora and fauna, people and cultures, that would determine its place in history. As the glacier of the last Ice Age receded, plants, animals and humans entered this virgin territory. A variety of cultures occupied the terrain through the Stone Age, the Bronze Age and the Iron Age. This book traces the progression from barren soil to occupation by inhabitants who farmed the land and sailed the seas, raiding and trading with other people of the region.

Of special interest is the development of the instruments that made the Scandinavian people unique and created the conditions leading to the migrations and invasions that would impact ancient and medieval Europe—the longships, weapons, armor, longhouses, family structure and farm tools. All of these helped set the stage for the unleashing of the northern peoples on their southern neighbors.

As the Roman Empire collapsed, Germanic and Asiatic peoples invaded Central and Southern Europe to fill the vacuum. Among these "barbarians" were the Goths. Special attention is paid to the connection between the Goths and Sweden, as well as the latest evidence establishing Sweden as their place of origin.

Of more long-lasting significance was the Viking tidal wave that swept over Europe during the Middle Ages. The plundering and pillaging that rocked the continent from Ireland to the Urals is cataloged in detail. On the positive side was the international trade system founded by these same sea rovers, with commercial centers at Hedeby in Denmark, Birka in central Sweden and at Gotland Island. This volume examines to what degree Swedes participated in the western expeditions and the conquests in Ireland, England and continental Europe. Also investigated is the Swedish participation in the discoveries and colonization of the North Atlantic islands and the discovery of North America.

This book covers in detail the Viking penetration of Eastern Europe and the building of the great river road that crisscrossed the eastern plains. The Vikings (Varangians or Rus) built a commercial system stretching from Birka and Hedeby to Constantinople and Bagdad, with branches reaching to China and India. In the process, Swedish Vikings fostered the development of trade centers that grew into towns and then into states. Kiev and Novgorod became regional capitals under Swedish leadership and subsequently warred with one another for supremacy.

By the late Middle Ages, the Viking upheaval had subsided. By then Sweden was unified and Christian. However, the great river road to eastern riches had collapsed. Russia had turned from Sweden to Byzantium for commercial relations, adopting the Eastern Orthodox form of Christianity instead of the Latin liturgy. Finally, ties were irrevocably severed with the Mongol invasion of Russia.

Still, Sweden was not left without opportunities. There was northern Sweden yet to be tamed, and Finland was open to invasion and conquest. It was at this time that Sweden once again rose to prominence. Magnus IV of Sweden governed the largest empire in Europe. His domain included Sweden, Finland, Norway, Iceland and the colony of Greenland in which he seems to have taken a special interest. Magnus' Sweden is notable for producing St. Birgitta, the most famous Swede of her day, and for suffering the Black Death that devastated the country (as well as the rest of Europe).

The Middle Ages and this book conclude with Sweden becoming part of the Kalmar Union (along with Denmark and Norway) under Margareta, perhaps the most remarkable woman of the Middle Ages. The union protected all three countries from German intervention, but it also opened the door to domination by one of the three. In the end, Sweden would have to fight for its independence, which would lead to the country's rise as a military power.

1

A Land Reborn

It might be said that Sweden was born of ice. Beginning some 110,000 years ago, the last of the Ice Age sheets (during the epoch known as the Weichsel Glacial Stage in Scandinavia, roughly equivalent to the Wisconsin Glacial Episode in North America) spread out of the country's high mountains, gouging valleys, deepening lake beds, and detouring river courses as it moved south and east into the Swedish lowlands.[1] Granite, which underlies Sweden's geography, was polished into rounded shapes where it protruded to the surface, characteristic of the nation's cliffs and archipelagoes. Gravel, boulders, sand, and clay were moved along and then deposited in mounds and ridges of irregular moraine strata. Plants and animals that had occupied the country were forced south or eliminated altogether. While Central and Southern Europe experienced the changes in flora and fauna that occurred during the last Ice Age, the Scandinavian peninsula was buried under millions of tons of ice pressing it down into the Earth's surface.

There was life in Sweden before this last Ice Age, of course—amphibians of the Paleozoic era and dinosaurs during the Mesozoic. These were followed by the strange, sometimes truly bizarre mammals of the Tertiary Period in the early Cenozoic era. Sweden was host to the giant mammals of the early Quaternary Period, the Pleistocene Epoch during inter-glaciation. But all this was swept away. In Sweden, all life had been extinguished as a result of this last cataclysmic invasion of ice (except, perhaps, the very simplest lifeforms). By 19,000 BP, with the glacier at its maximum reach, the geographical area that is today Sweden had been smothered, brutalized, sanitized, and locked in a deep freeze, awaiting the Earth's warming and the retreat of the ice sheet.[2]

("BP" stands for "years before the present." "The present" is defined as AD 1950 by paleontologists, based on the approximate date that carbon-14 dating began to be used. The BC date is determined by subtracting 1950 from the BP date.)

Enveloped in this frozen mantle, the geographic sections of the country hibernated. At the southern tip of Sweden lie the southern plains, called Skåne or Scania, an extension of the fertile plains of Denmark and northern Germany. North of this flat lowland are the highlands of Småland, a rocky and less fertile area rising as high as 1,200 feet above sea level. Along the coasts and north of the Småland Plateau is an area of lowlands, a mostly level but fragmented landscape with granite and gneiss rock protruding in a varied terrain of meadows, hills and lakes. In these central lowlands is deposited the mineral wealth of Sweden. Here there are iron and other ores of the Bergslagen, the oldest industrial area of the country. A little further north are the copper, lead and zinc of Västerbotten and the country's iron deposits of Kiruna and Gällivare-Malmberget.

North of this low country is the watershed area of the northern three-fifths of Sweden (Norrland). Here the land slopes from the spine of the Kjölen Mountains (with peaks of 3,000–7,000 feet), which runs along the border between Sweden and Norway, down to the Gulf of Bothnia. Rolling hills and mountains cut by deep valleys dominate the landscape north to the Muonio and Tornio rivers that form Sweden's boundary with Finland. All this land slumbered in hibernation under the weight of the massive ice sheet. Of all Scandinavia, only western Jutland escaped the glacier's icy grip.

Around 19,000 BP temperatures began to warm; shortly thereafter, the southern edge of the glacier began to move north, leaving behind a virgin landscape. Ancient rivers and streams grew large with the melting ice, and new water courses were created, polishing and rounding stones and gravel bits deposited in glacial estuaries and gravely ridges. Mounds of sand were left behind, with the very finely ground material being carried to the sea coast, where it formed the fertile clay soils of the southern and central lowland plains. By 13,500 BP Scania was free of ice and became the host for plant life moving in from the south.[3]

The retreat was not linear, instead proceeding in jumps and pauses, even regressions. Paleoclimatologists divide this retreat into periods, the first being the Oldest Dryas, from about 18,000 to 15,000 BP, a stadial (cold period) that slowed or even halted deglaciation at times. Some climatologists insert an additional period before the Oldest Dryas called the Meiendorf.[4] The Oldest Dryas was interrupted by a sudden rise in temperature, marking the beginning of the Bølling Oscillation, an interstadial (warm period) during which the ice retreated well into southern Sweden. Temperatures of the time were comparable to those of today. But then deglaciation was stalled briefly (from about 14,500 to 14,000 BP) during the Older Dryas stadial of colder and drier weather.[5] A more rapid retreat of the ice sheet resumed with the Allerød Oscillation, another interstadial lasting to about 12,500 BP, during which the remainder of the Småland Plateau was uncovered; at the same time, the surrounding lowlands were inundated due to the swift rise in sea levels.[6]

One final cold snap of the Pleistocene Epoch was the Younger Dryas stadial, lasting to 11,500 BP.[7] Again deglaciation slowed and even reversed in some areas as temperatures plummeted. The end of the Younger Dryas and the termination of the Pleistocene was marked by a sharp rise in temperature: (10 ± 4°C) with a 7°C increase in as little as 50 years as measured in the Greenland ice cap.[8] Thus began the Pre-Boreal Period and the Holocene Epoch, the geological epoch we live in today. The warm Pre-Boreal Period was followed by the Boreal Period, with temperatures similar to those of today. By 10,000 BP (the beginning of the Boreal Period) the glacial ice was confined to the upper reaches of the Kjölen Mountains, though much of the lowlands were still underwater.[9] In Sweden, the last Ice Age was over.

The Boreal was followed by the Atlantic (approximately 9,000–5,800 BP), with temperatures 2.5°C above those of today.[10] This was followed by the Sub-Boreal (5,800 to 2,600 BP), a transitional period to the modern or Sub-Atlantic Period.[11]

With the weight of the Weichsel glacier removed, the Swedish land mass began to rise and is still increasing in elevation today. The coastal areas around the Gulf of Both-

1. A Land Reborn

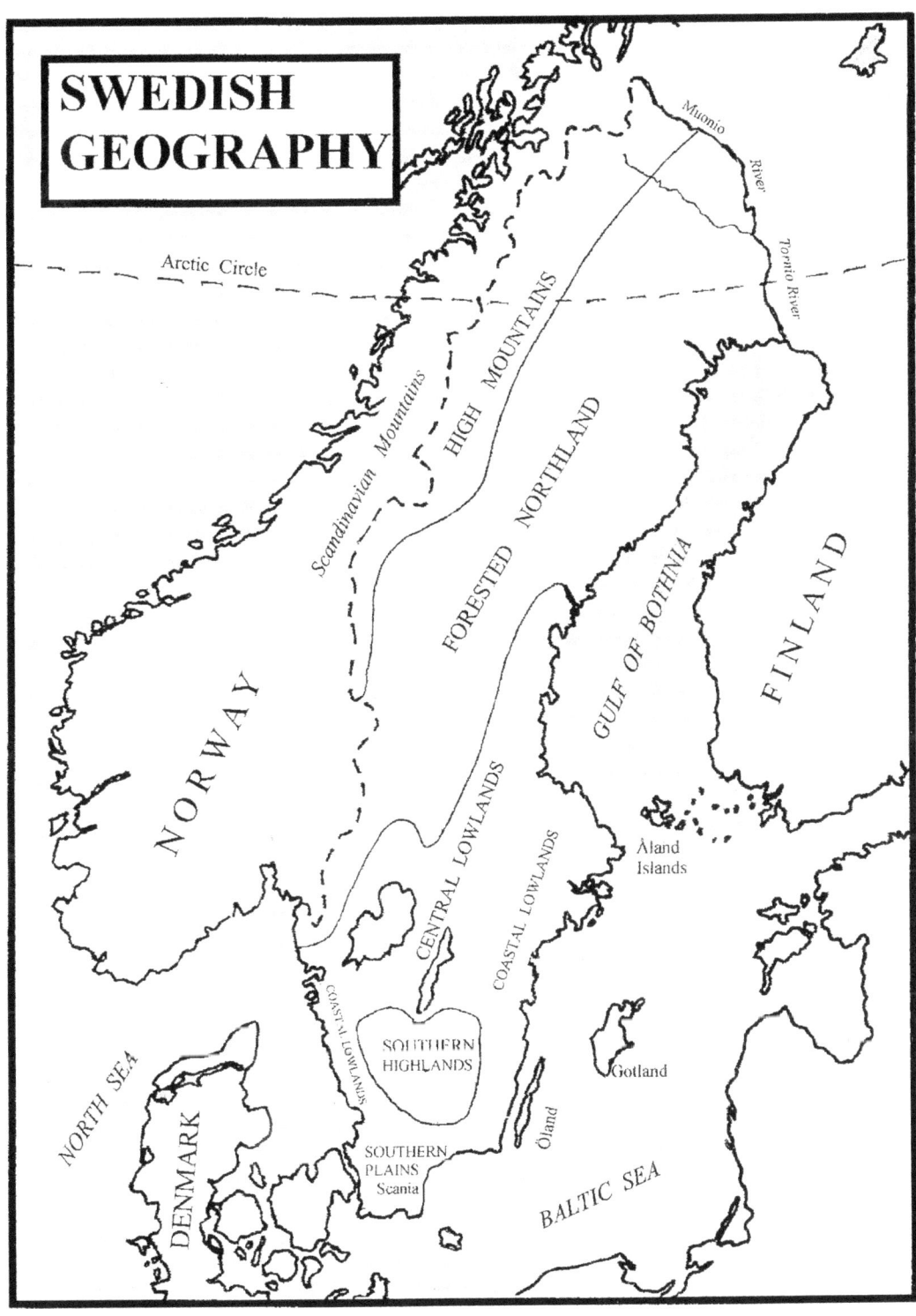

LAST OF THE ICE AGE IN SWEDEN AND THE COMING OF MAN

Geological Time	Phanerozoic Eon — Cenozoic Era — Quaternary Period
Climate Periods	Pleistocene Epoch / Holocene Epoch — Oldest Dryas, Bølling Oscillation, Older Dryas, Allerød Oscillation, Younger Dryas, Pre-Boreal, Boreal, Atlantic, Sub-Boreal (Cold Period 550-50 BC), Sub-Atlantic (Medieval Warm Period 950-1250 AD, Little Ice Age 1200-1850 AD)
Baltic Sea Stages	Baltic Ice Lake, Yoldia Sea, Ancylus Lake, Mastogloia Sea, Littorina Sea, Baltic Sea
Archaeological Periods	Nordic Paleolithic Age, Nordic Mesolithic Age, Neolithic Age, Bronze Age, Iron Age, Viking Era
Northern Sweden	Weichselian Glaciation — Suomusjärvi
Central Sweden	Weichselian Glaciation — Hensbacka — Sandarna — Lihult — Pitted-ware — Battle-axe (Corded-ware or Single-grave)
Southern Sweden	Hamburg — Federmesser? — Bromme — Ahrensburg — Maglemose — Kongemose — Ertebølle — Funnel Beaker
Age BP (Before Pres. - AD 1950)	15,000 — 13,000 — 11,000 — 10,050 — 9050 — 8050 — 7050 — 6050 — 5050 — 4050 — 3050 — 2050 — 1050 — 1000
Age BC/AD	— 15,000 — 13,000 — 11,000 — 9050 — 8000 — 7000 — 6000 — 5000 — 4000 — 3000 — 2000 — 50 BC — 950 AD

(Italics: seasonal occupation)

nia are rising at the rate of three feet per one hundred years.[12] The melting ice raised sea levels, but the uplift of the Swedish land area pushed back the coastline and eventually drained the fertile low midlands, leaving a multitude of lakes and streams.

Another geological phenomenon that will be useful in understanding the repopulation of the Swedish landscape is the creation of the Baltic Sea. As the Weichsel Glaciation waned, an ice lake formed roughly where the Baltic Sea is today.[13] With the continued melting of the glacial sheet, water overflowed and pushed through central Sweden, emptying into the North Sea, with the eastern end of the new channel near present-day Stockholm. The drainage caused the Baltic Ice Lake to drop to sea level by about 12,000 BP (10,050 BC), at which point backflow introduced salinity to the lake, making it a body of water known as the Yoldia Sea.[14] During this stage southern Sweden was connected to Germany by a land bridge through Denmark. Toward the end of the sea's existence a second channel was cut between Jutland and Sweden, emptying the water added to the Yoldia Sea from the continuing glacial melt. Thus the land bridge was severed, making migration into Sweden more difficult.

By 10,500 BP (8,550 BC), the rising Scandinavian land mass had cut off the two-way flow of both channels, forming a new body of freshwater known as the Ancylus Lake.[15] Discharge from the lake still moved through central Sweden via the Göta and Steinselva river systems, except that it was in one direction. The remains of the glacier were now confined to the mountain tops between Sweden and Norway. By 9,200 BP (7,250 BC) the lake had risen high enough to spill over the land bridge between Sweden and Denmark, cutting the Great Belt between the Danish islands of Zealand and Fyn. A connected southern Sweden and Zealand became an island for the last phase of Lake Ancylus' existence.

As the last of the glacial ice melted from the Earth's continents and seas, the ocean levels rose until they were on a par with Lake Ancylus. The northern drainage through central Sweden stopped and seawater began to penetrate the lake through the Great Belt, introducing its dissolved salts. The new brackish body of water is known as the Mastogloia Sea and is considered to have existed from about 9,500 to 8,000 BP (7,550–6,050 BC).[16] A final stage of development was the Littorina Sea, in which the brackish water, at the sea's height in about 4,500 BP (2,550 BC), was twice the volume of the present Baltic and had 26.5 percent more surface area.[17] By 3,950 BP (2,000 BC) the Baltic had very nearly taken its present shape with its extensions, the gulfs of Bothnia, Finland and Riga. The outlets to the North Sea had been formed—the Great Belt, Little Belt and, most particularly, the sound between Zealand and Skåne, which would become so important in Danish and Swedish history.

Regarding the time periods discussed in previous pages, as well as Baltic Sea evolution, climatologic, cultures, and so on, there is not complete agreement as to timing. The scientists working with carbon-14 analysis have a time sequence of events. Other scientists delving into the layers of sediment, called varves, which contain the remnants of plant spores and mollusks, have their own dating system. The same is true of those who engage in ice core sampling, tree ring analysis and other disciplines. A great deal of work has been done in an attempt to reconcile all these various branches of paleontology, but absolute agreement is still lacking. I have used the well-respected and often-cited work by Neil Roberts[18] as a basis for the dating in this and the second chapter, modified slightly by later papers, particularly those found in *The Climate Development of the North Atlantic Realm*.[19] While this is not a perfect solution, it represents a good approximation and is representative of today's thinking.

2

The First Settlers and Sweden's Mesolithic Age

As the Weichsel glacier receded, plant life sprang from the soil, with vegetation moving in from the south. These first plants were the flora of the Arctic tundra—grasses, grass-like sedges, and brush. During the Bølling Period in southern Sweden, steppe tundra took over, featuring dwarf birch and dwarf willows. By the Younger Dryas, the steppe tundra had moved north into central Sweden.[1]

Large trees and forests existed only in pockets in Southern Europe during the height of the glacial dominance. As the ice receded, these forests moved north, reaching southern Sweden during the Pre-Boreal (9500–8000 BC). First came birch-pine forestation, followed by the hazel-pine forests of the Boreal, then the linden, oak and finally beech of the Atlantic, Sub-Boreal and Sub-Atlantic, respectively.[2] Thus Sweden became the predominantly forested nation it is today.

One of the first animals known to have arrived on the peninsula was the polar bear (*Ursus maritimus*).[3] This carnivore would have preyed upon fish, sea mammals and newly arrived birds, such as divers, grebe, swans and eagles. Fish quickly populated the abundant glacial streams and rivers—turbot, grayling, roach, trout and char. Small mammals like the lemming, voles, Arctic hare and marmots were hunted by lynx, the Arctic fox and wolves.

Larger mammals soon arrived, including reindeer (*Rangifer tarandus*), ibex and wild horses (*Equus przewalskii*). Remnants of moose (*Alces alces*), wisent (European bison—*Bison bonasus*) and aurochs (wild cattle—*Bos primigenius*) have been identified from this period. Many of the great mammals of the Ice Age, like the wooly rhinoceros, had already declined toward extinction, but we know that giant deer (the Irish elk—*Megaloceros giganteus*) survived to wander into southern Sweden.[4] Perhaps the last of the mega-fauna to succumb was the woolly mammoth (*Mammuthus primigenius*), whose tusk fragments have been identified in southern and central Sweden.[5]

The rapid deglaciation of the Bølling Oscillation allowed the tundra condition to spread across the Småland southern highlands, and additional species of plants flourished in the north, including drays, mountain sorrel, wormwood and joint-fir.

Larger animals migrated northward, such as the steppe wisent (*Bison priscus*), the red deer, elk and the saiga antelope. In addition to the brown bear, there was the cave bear (*Ursus spelaeus*), the spotted hyena, the cave lion and wolverine, carnivores hunting the hare, pika, ground squirrel and jerboa. And increasing in population was the ubiquitous reindeer or caribou (*Rangifer tarandus*). So available was this game that it became the primary food source for the first humans to enter Sweden.[6]

The first hint of a human presence in Sweden comes from finds at Mölleröd in central Scania and Finja in northern Scania. These artifacts are believed to date from the late Bølling and early Older Dryas, and they are remnants of the Hamburg culture.[7] Tools characteristic of this tradition are a distinctive shouldered arrowhead and a chisel used to work horn.[8] Settlements of this culture have been identified from northern France across the Netherlands and northern Germany to Poland. Associated with these sites are slight hollows in the ground surrounded by circles of rocks thought to represent teepee rings, indicating lodgings of hide-covered wood frames. Only a few settlements have been found in southern Jutland, and the finds in Skåne are even more tentative. Archaeologists believe the Scanian artifacts represent "ephemeral exploitation"[9]—that is, these first Swedish visitors were not permanent settlers, but only seasonal hunters, traveling north across the Danish-Swedish land bridge in search of reindeer herds and retiring south when winter winds and storms began.

A second tool-making tradition that very likely had a temporary presence in Skåne following the Hamburg was the Federmesser culture. Again, this culture predominated across northern France, Belgium and Germany, with settlement sites in Jutland. Because of their proximity, members of this culture should have ventured across the land bridge into Scania; however, no artifacts have so far been discovered in Sweden. Characteristic of the Federmesser culture are small-backed flint blades and straight arrowheads. As with the Hamburg, the people of this culture would have been only temporary residents of Scania, this time during the Older Dryas and early Allerød periods.[10]

Finally, in the late Allerød and early Younger Dryas more immigrants arrived—this time to stay on a more permanent basis. These first year-round inhabitants were representatives of the Bromme culture, a tool-making tradition actually centered in northern Germany, Denmark and Scania, extending as far north as the southernmost part of Småland.[11] In Sweden this culture was first known from a settlement site at Segebro, near Malmö, but since then artifacts have been found in many parts of Scania and on the edge of the southern uplands. The stone tools these pioneers left behind are all sturdy lithic flakes used as awls, scrapers and arrowheads. The arrowheads in particular are of a more advanced design, complete with a tang (shank for mounting to the arrow or spear shaft), and are shouldered to help prevent egress of the arrow from the target animal.[12]

With the bow and arrow, these people hunted primarily reindeer. Moose, wolverines and beavers were also food sources. They lived in hide-covered lodges like the previous hunter-gatherers of the region.[13]

About the racial characteristics of the first colonizers of Sweden, we know nothing. Were they dark and stocky, a characteristic of one strain of Swedes, or were they tall, blue eyed and blond? Recent genetic studies of modern Scandinavian men suggest two possible origins for the people of the Bromme and closely associated Ahrensburg cultures. One study indicates these people came from the Dnieper-Don Valley during the Ukrainian LGM (Late Glacial Maximum) refuge between 11,000 and 5600 BC. But other studies suggest an origin in Germany. Definite conclusions are pending.[14]

SWEDISH STONE AGE IMPLEMENTS

Palaeolithic Age Artifacts

Hamburg Culture Arrowhead

Fredersmesser Culture Arrowhead

Bromme Culture Arrowhead

Ahrensburg Culture Arrowhead

Early Mesolithic Age Artifacts

Hensbacka Culture Flake Core Axe from Östergötland

Hensbacka Culture Core Axe found in Skåne

Sandarna Culture Type Flint Core Axe

The previously mentioned Ahrensburg culture followed the Bromme and is dated to the later Younger Dryas and early Pre-Boreal periods.[15] The center of this culture was further south than the related Bromme. Archaeological finds are concentrated in southern Denmark, northwestern Germany, and northern France. However, tools from this tradition have been found scattered across Scania. The artifacts consist of tanged and shouldered arrowheads, tools made of reindeer antler and a barbed harpoon.[16] This last is consistent with the shift to greater utilization of maritime game following the final extinction of the mammoths and other mega-fauna in the Allerød Period. Though

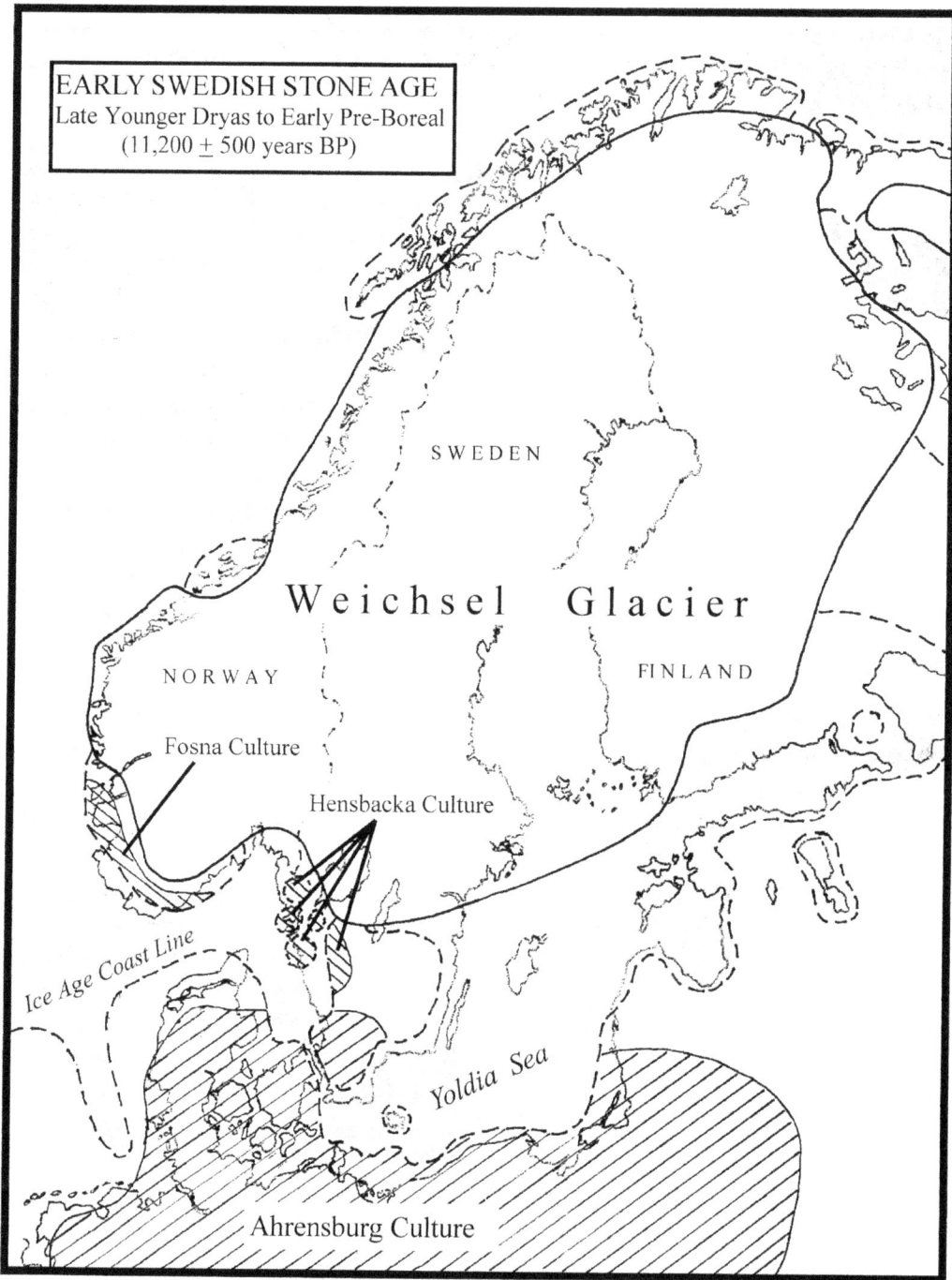

the reindeer was still a main food resource (hunted using an arrowhead very similar to that made by the Bromme), the Ahrensburg tool-making tradition was more complex, indicating a more varied diet. However, these were still hunter-gatherers living in portable skin-covered lodges. All indications are that the Ahrensburg culture was a derivative of the Bromme—very similar but more advanced. Do these two cultures represent two different peoples, one replacing the other, or was this the same population making improvements on its own or adopting new ideas from contacts to the south?

Cultures are difficult to understand if the only evidence we have are their tools. Artifacts left by tool-making traditions tell us a great deal about how people lived but almost nothing about what they looked like or what they thought. A cultural change in a geographic area may be due to population replacement, invasion and absorption, new traditions acquired from external contacts, or simply changes and improvements made by a group of people over time. Without human remains to study, answers are incomplete. DNA studies of modern-day Swedes indicate that the population has been stable for a very long time. This "population continuity [suggests that cultural changes were due to] acculturation and acceptance of new ideas rather than migration and population replacement in the Mesolithic-Neolithic transition."[17] So we might assume that, with one major exception, most cultural changes in Sweden after 5000 BC represent internal changes or the adoption of new ideas from the outside by a fairly homogeneous population. However, with these very early cultures (Paleolithic and Mesolithic), since people were widely scattered, it is likely that changes were due, at least in part, to an infiltration of new peoples from the outside bringing better implements, improved survival techniques and new DNA. We might conclude that before 6000 BC cultural changes occurred by means of either adaptation or infiltration of peoples.

An example of adaptation is the Hensbacka culture that flourished from about 8300 to 7300 BC (early Pre-Boreal to early Boreal). Artifacts from this culture have been found from the northwestern corner of Scania through Bohuslän, which was at that time made up of mostly islands. At the same time, a kindred culture, the Fosna, existed on the southwest coast of Norway. Both are considered derivatives of the Ahrensburg culture, but with even more reliance on the sea as a source of food.[18]

The Hensbacka people, in particular, are believed to have achieved an unusually high population density for a hunter-gatherer society.[19] Archaeologists think that hide-covered wooden-frame boats were used to navigate the channels between islands, in order to fish and hunt for seals. Stone tools found at settlement sites consist of the typical tanged arrowheads, lanceolate microliths and, for the first time in Swedish history, axes. Two types have been identified: the flake axe and the core axe (the latter found in Scania).[20]

The end of the Younger Dryas Period and Pleistocene Epoch in about 9600 BC was marked by a sharp temperature rise that ushered in the Pre-Boreal Period and Holocene Epoch. Increasing temperatures and humidity fostered the migration of forests, formally confined to Southern Europe, Iberia, Italy and the Balkans, into Central and eventually Northern Europe. First came the birches, quaking aspen, dwarf and shrub juniper during the Pre-Boreal. Then the pine and hazel trees spread northward. By the end of the Boreal, mixed-oak forests had supplanted the hazel-pine trees, leaving them confined to mountainsides and other higher elevations.

With the forests came new species of animals—red deer, roe deer, elk and wild pigs. Wolves, brown bear and lynx were still present, joined by the wildcat (*Felis silvestris*) hunting the European hare (*Lepus europaeus*). With the abundant wetlands came an increase in beavers and the otters. The latter dined on newly arrived fish species, northern pike and catfish, along with the marine game already present.

The reindeer hunters followed their prey into northern Sweden, eventually learning to conserve the caribou by herding instead of just hunting this precious resource. Meanwhile, the Hensbacka culture along the Swedish west coast had evolved into the Sandarna culture, still clinging to the islands and coastal areas of southwestern Sweden. From at least one archaeological find, we know these people lived in small huts housing six to nine people.[21] The culture is distinctive for two new tools: the pickaxe with biconical shaftholes and conical microblade cores. The cores were pieces of flint from which microblades were chipped. Microblades could be used as tools or further worked into microliths. Microblades and microliths were small pieces of flint that were used as tools themselves or mounted in bone or wood to be used as weapons.[22]

This microblade tradition entered Sweden from the south and quickly spread northward, perhaps by migration, but probably more by diffusion of ideas. In less than 500 years (6000–5700 BC), this tool-making practice had spread from northern Germany to Lappland in northern Sweden, a remarkably rapid migration. The Sandarna culture transitioned into the Lihult culture of Bohuslän, Sweden, which was closely related to the Nøstvet culture of southern Norway. These two Mesolithic/Neolithic cultures (7000–3200 BC) were more sedentary than their predecessors, the Fosna-Hensbacka (the Sandarna being an intermediate step between the Swedish Hensbacka and later Lihult), and grew to a significant population. The Lihult tool-making tradition was characterized by the Lihult axe, a honed axe of an advanced type, as well as microliths made from a variety of materials, flint, quartz, and quartzite.[23] The peoples of these new cultures had a varied diet that included seafowl, marine mammals, fish and land animals. They seem to have been able to adapt to the changing landscape as forests continued moving north. This staying power may have been due in part to their location on islands and along coasts and water ways where the thick forests were absent. The culture was durable, outlasting three forest cultures to the south: the Maglemose, Kongemose and Ertebølle.

In the south of Sweden, meanwhile, the first of these three new cultures appeared in Scania and Denmark, a society adept at coping with the encroaching forests. The Maglemose culture (7500–6000 BC) of the Boreal and Atlantic periods lived in the forests and wetlands by hunting and fishing, using tools of wood, bone, horn and flint microliths. They used flint microliths to edge harpoons and as spearheads and arrowheads as well as hand tools. They lived in huts made of bark instead of the hide lodges, and they had domesticated the dog. Some groups may have adopted a settled lifestyle, but most were still nomadic.[24]

They hunted large animals like the aurochs, roe deer, elk, red deer and pigs. Fur-bearing animals, including brown bears, beavers, otters, wolves, foxes, pine martins, polecats, badgers and wildcats, provided clothing and blankets. They fished for pike, tench, bream, salmon and trout. They augmented their diet by gathering hazelnuts and water lily seeds.[25]

A characteristic of the Maglemose culture, in terms of artifacts left behind, is the handle or wedge-shaped core from which the microblades were chipped. This identifiable trait came from northern Germany, indicating at least some infusion of people from the south moving with the advancing forests. This culture is unique to southern Scandinavia, however, and is therefore quite likely the result of a merging of immigrants with an established population.[26]

2. First Settlers and Sweden's Mesolithic Age

To the north in north-central Sweden (Västergötland and Värmland), which was deglaciated around 9000 BC, artifacts from the Hensbacka and Fosna cultures have been found, indicating seasonal occupation of hunting and fishing expeditions. By the middle of the Mesolithic Period, more permanent colonization is evidenced by larger numbers of finds from the Sandarna culture (pickaxes with biconical shaft holes and conical microblade cores). Even more prevalent are Lihult axes, implying heavy trade with (if not outright invasion by) the Lihult/Nøstvet culture of southwestern Sweden

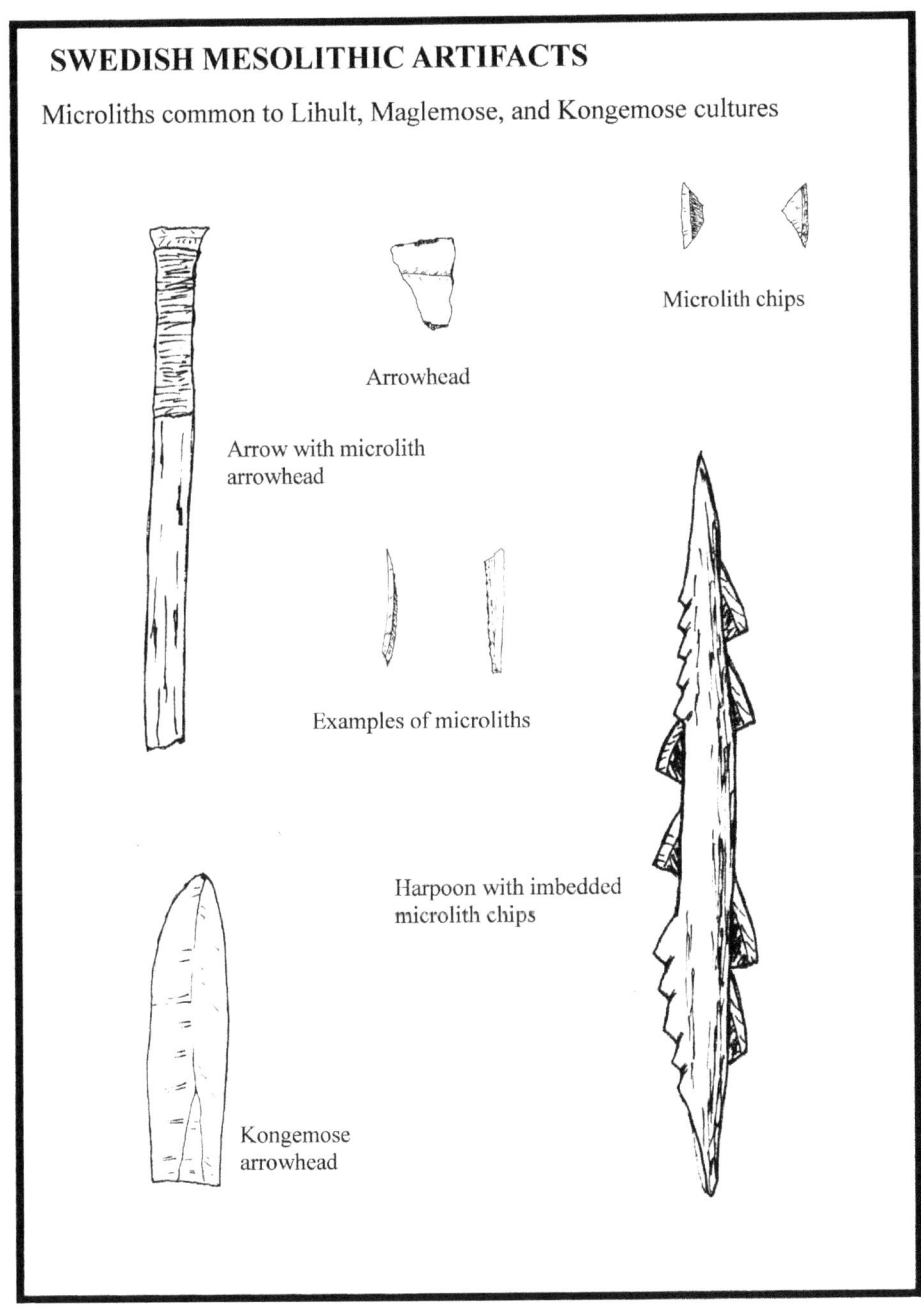

SWEDISH MESOLITHIC ARTIFACTS

Microliths common to Lihult, Maglemose, and Kongemose cultures

Microlith chips

Arrowhead

Arrow with microlith arrowhead

Examples of microliths

Harpoon with imbedded microlith chips

Kongemose arrowhead

and Norway. Handle cores and wedge-shaped cores have also been found, suggesting a connection with the Maglemose forest dwellers of Scania. This wedge-shaped core tool tradition has been found in northern Sweden into Lappland, but in northern Sweden other artifacts have also been found that are from eastern traditions. These are the double-edged slate knives (or possibly spear points) and leaf-shaped slate points.[27]

Slate, used as a tool-making material, was a tradition of the Suomusjärvi culture of Finland.[28] The practice is believed to have reached northern Finland in about 5000 BC. Northernmost Sweden (Lappland) was finally deglaciated around 7500 BC, with tundra conditions developing within a few hundred years. Populations were poised to invade from both the south and the east, and that is what appears to have happened. The slate tool tradition spread west into Sweden from Finland and then south into the Kjölen watershed area, perhaps by a mixing of peoples, but certainly through an infusion of ideas.

Returning to southern Sweden of the Mesolithic, we find the Maglemose culture was replaced by the Kongemose (ca. 6000–5200 BC), another true forest-dwelling people.[29] Their tool-making tradition consisted of long flint flakes used to make the culture's characteristic rhombic arrowheads, scarpers, drills, awls, and toothed blades. The Kongemose people made stone axes and other tools of horn and bone. They also chipped tiny microliths that were embedded on the edges of bone daggers. Some of these knives may have been status symbols or ceremonial pieces, as they were decorated with geometric designs. Whether the Kongemose were an outgrowth of the Maglemose culture or a parallel but independent development has not been determined.[30]

The Kongemose hunted and gathered much the same fish, game and vegetation as the people of the Maglemose culture, but they added some new sources of food. Sea fish, particularly cod, become important in their diets, along with sea mammals, such as seals and porpoises. Water fowl was increasingly relied upon—ducks, cranes and white-tailed eagles. Refuse of shellfish, oysters, cockles and clams likewise become more plentiful. This was a successful hunting and fishing society that spread north until limited by the Lihult tribes.[31]

By 5000 BC, the southern Swedish landscape was being invaded from the south by oak and alder forests, replacing the pine-hazel forestation. With the warmer temperatures of the Atlantic Period (warmer and moister than today's climate), the forests became dense and impenetrable, forcing out the last of the large mammals (moose, aurochs and wisents) and confining human settlements to coasts, islands, lakes and waterways. The Kongemose culture was replaced by the Ertebølle (or Kitchen Midden in Denmark), a culture we know a great deal about because of several sites that have been explored.

It is believed that the change in cultures was primarily an adaptation by an indigenous people using new ideas to deal with the changing environment stimulated by some migration from the south, where the jungle-like forests were already established. The tool-making tradition is of high quality and a unified standard. Flint was used in making flake axes, arrowheads and long flakes for scrapers and knives. Wood, bone and antler were also used in tool making by these people.[32]

Now, for the first time in Swedish history, we find pottery manufactured indigenously. Native clays tempered with sand, crushed granite, quartzite and sandstone were

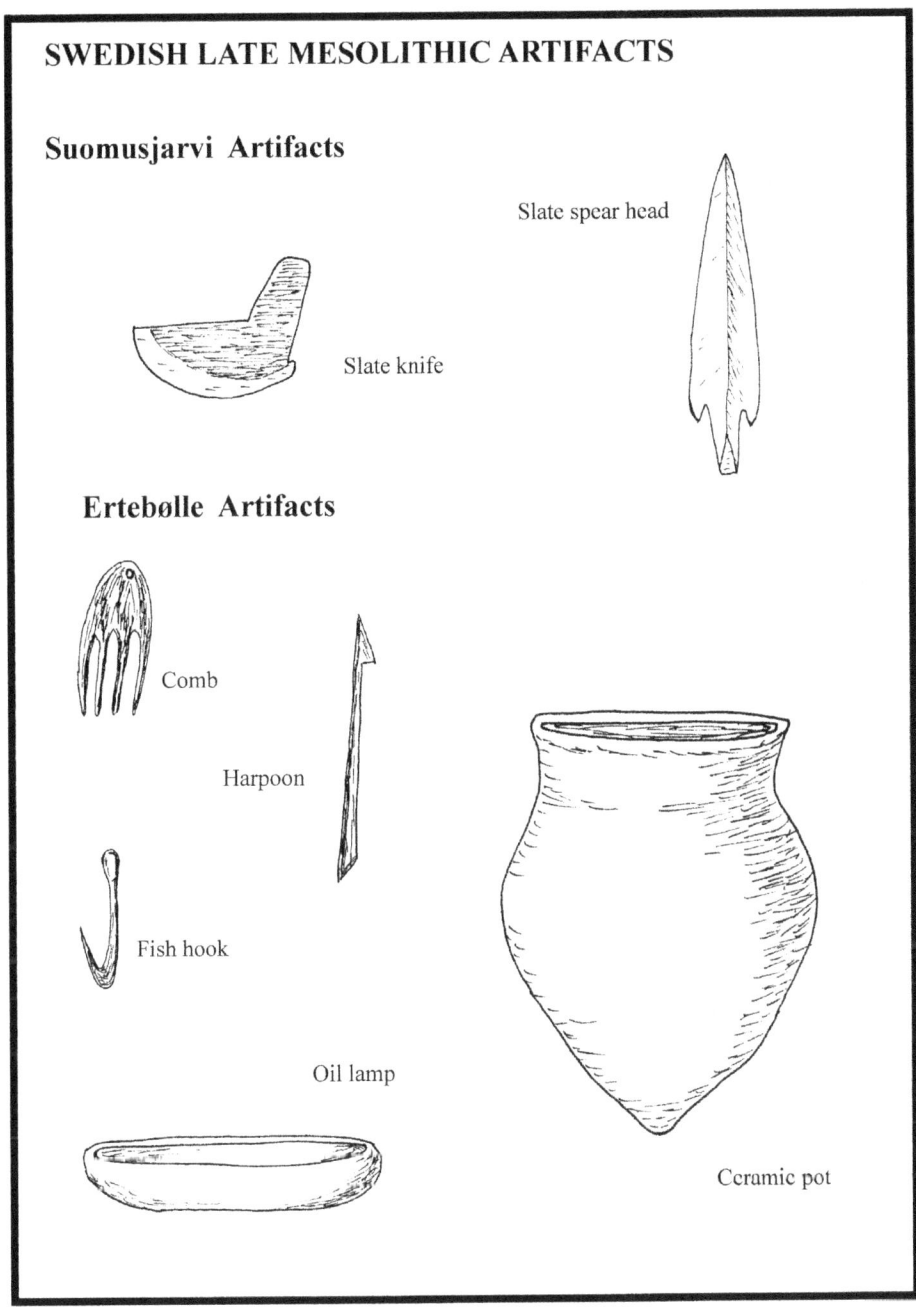

fired on open beds of hot coals reaching temperatures of 500–700°C. Two primary articles were produced by the Ertebølle people: beakers and lamps.[33]

Beakers were pot-bellied jars narrowing to a neck at the top with a flange. They were formed by laying coils in rings and ranged in size from 4 inches to 2 feet. The early culture decorated the entire surface of the beakers with horizontal bands and fingertip or fingernail impressions. The later culture decorated with chevrons, cord marks and punctures made with animal bones. Also in the later period, the walls of the vessels were made thinner, and sometimes handles were added and the rim was turned inward instead of flared out.[34]

The second type of pottery associated with the Ertebølle is a blubber lamp molded from a single piece of clay.[35] Such a device indicates that there were family or social activities taking place in the huts after dark. Though winters were milder than they are today, winter nights were just as long, a significant number of hours even at the latitudes of southern Sweden.

Dwellings were still huts of a framework covered with bark, usually constructed over a pit or depression. A trend has been noted by archaeologists, however. Early Maglemose huts were built to house a single family, but the late Maglemose houses were often multi-family dwellings of greater size and permanency. Logs may have been used in some cases for part of the construction. Ertebølle homes were inevitably multi-family dwellings, some as large as 15 by 18 feet, built according to an oval or rectangular floor plan, often with a central pole for roof support. Floors were of sand or clay, but many "bark floors" have been found; coverings of bark, twigs and/or leaves were laid down for insulation. Part of the floor space was often covered by a platform of wood, possibly a sleeping area.[36]

Settlements are of two types: coastal and inland. The inland sites seem to be temporary campsites, probably for seasonal hunting, whereas the coastal gathering places are more permanent, with large shell middens and cemeteries associated with them.[37]

The construction of the Ertebølle living quarters indicates that these settlements were not permanent. Yet these people did create cemeteries for their dead, so either they did stay at one location for a significant period or they roamed a set territory. Burials have also been found under dwellings and in isolated locations. Both cremation and interment were practiced. Some corpses were decorated with ochre.[38] Women were sometimes buried with jewelry (a red deer tooth pendant around the hips, for instance). Flint knives are found in the graves of both men and women. Men were sometimes buried with antler axes and bone spatulas. And some burials have no grave gifts, suggesting class or social distinctions were observed.[39]

There are two sites of special note. At Skateholm, Sweden, in addition to the human cemetery, there is a dog cemetery containing the same ochre and antlers left as grave gifts, an indication of the close relationship these people had with their canine companions. The second site is the Korsør Nor harbor settlement on the coast of Zealand, Denmark, where a body was buried in a dugout canoe. Some archaeologists have suggested this was a precursor to the Scandinavian ritual boat burials of the Viking period. Precursor or not, it does tell us the type of boat technology being used at the time by these people.[40] The dugout canoe had replaced the hide-covered wooden-frame boats.

A third site—that of Tybrind Vig, off the coast of Fyn Island, Denmark—provides additional information on the Ertebølle water craft. At this underwater site, archaeologists have found three dugouts of lime wood, the longest being some twenty-eight feet in length. In two of these, a slab of clay was laid in the stern of the boat to serve as a fireplace, suggesting long voyages, perhaps ocean-going travels. Paddles from this site have three-foot-long shafts attached to heart-shaped blades fifteen inches in diameter, some of which are decorated.[41]

Fish was a mainstay in the diet of these people. Three methods were employed in procuring this necessity. Wicker fish traps have been found at the Tybrind Vig site, as have fish hooks made from red deer bone used in angling. And finely made tines used in spear fishing have likewise been excavated.[42] Textiles made from spun plant fibers have also been recovered from the Tybrind Vig site.[43]

Though limited, some skeletal remains have been recovered, enough to give us an idea as to the physical appearance of these people. The average height of a man was 5 feet, 5 inches, and women averaged a little over 5 feet.[44] Both the Ertebølle and the preceding Kongemose populations were already a mix of heritages. For the most part, these remains differ little from the skeletons of modern Scandinavians. Of course, soft tissue features (eye color, skin color, etc.) are not preserved. Nonetheless, a number of skulls from this period show characteristics associated with those belonging to Paleolithic skeletons, generally referred to as Cro-Magnon man—that is, an elongated head, protruding jaw, flat nose and pronounced brow ridge.[45] This evidence reinforces the thesis that the cultural changes exhibited by the transformations in tool-making traditions were a process of absorption of ideas brought on, in most cases, through assimilating an immigrant population but seldom, if ever, up to this point, by the wholesale displacement of a population.

Graves also give us some clue as to the economy of the Ertebølle. As we've seen, dugout canoes were the mode of transportation along the water systems that were always associated with this culture. The bones of certain cetaceans have been found at settlement sites—killer whales, as well as white-beaked and bottlenose dolphins. The remains of seals have also been discovered. Though not found in the Baltic Sea today, the ringed, harp and gray seals were common in the Litorina Sea of the Atlantic Period. Sea fish bones have also been identified in village middens—cod, flatfish, sharks, haring, dogfish, mackerel, garfish and sea perch.[46] The evidence is substantial that the Ertebølle were accomplished seamen.

Besides food from the sea, the middens testify to the consumption of freshwater fish, such as pike, whitefish, ling, perch, bream, eel, catfish, roach, trout and salmon. As we've seen, these were acquired by means of wickerwork traps, tined spears and hooks made of red deer bone. And shells of oysters, cockle, clams and mussels make up the majority of refuse from the middens. Judging from settlement refuse, much of the food came from the water, either the sea or nearby lakes and streams.[47]

Still, these were hunter-gatherers, and they did hunt large forest mammals, such as red and roe deer, wild boar, elk and occasionally aurochs and wild horses, which were becoming rare at this point. Fur-bearing animals were also hunted—wolves, beavers, squirrels, badgers, foxes and lynxes. Water fowl and woodland game birds rounded out a varied meat diet, including divers, pelican, capercaille, grebe, cormorant, swan and duck.[48] As for gathering, these people harvested the raspberry, dewberry, wild strawberry, rowan berry and crab apple.[49]

With this wide range of food sources, the Ertebølle people had the time and sufficient security from hunger to engage in two enterprises once thought applicable only to later cultures. The first was art. In addition to decorative work on utilitarian items like pottery and boat paddles, these people made jewelry, as observed in the necklaces and belts of animal teeth and shells worn by women and found in the graves.

The second practice was warfare. The picture once envisioned of the Ertebølle villagers peacefully fishing and trapping alongside their placid lakeside settlements is called into question by an arrowhead found in a pelvis at the site of Skateholm in Sweden, as well as bone points discovered lodged in a throat at Vedbæck, Zealand, and in a skeletal chest at Stora Bjers, Sweden. Even more disturbing are cracked human bones found at Dyrholmen in Jutland and Møllegabet on Ærø Island in Denmark. Bones are broken open for one purpose, and that is to obtain the marrow inside. Since the Ertebølle had multiple sources of protein available, these sure signs of cannibalism were not diet driven. The bones were not interred, so this was not part of a funeral ceremony of ancestor worship. Certainly, this is evidence of ritualistic cannibalism to obtain the power of the enemy, a practice usually associated with warlike tribes. The Ertebølle thus may have been much more aggressive than earlier thought.[50]

The Ertebølle culture was successful and expanding, reaching north to the Lihult peoples in central Sweden and in the south spreading from Denmark along the Baltic coast to Rügen. Then it was suddenly displaced by the Funnel Beaker culture, though the two may have overlapped, existing side by side for a time.[51]

3

Sweden of the Neolithic Age

With the Funnel Beaker, or *Trichterrandbecher* (or simply *Trichterbecher*—TRB) in German, people, we find a giant leap in progress with the introduction of agriculture and some metal (copper) tools. Indeed, farming constitutes the dividing line between the Mesolithic (Middle Stone) Age and the Neolithic (New Stone) Age. The name "Funnel Beaker" comes from the funnel-shaped rims of this culture's characteristic ceramic beakers and amphorae.[1] The pottery was manufactured indigenously, using native clays tempered with sand, crushed stone and organic materials.

Beakers were pot-bellied or conical with a flanged top turning outward. The amphorae ranged in size from 3 to 20 inches in height with flat bottoms. Often the entire surface was decorated with bands or marks made with fingertips and fingernails. Later products had chevrons and designs made with grains, cords and animal bones.[2]

The most significant advancement of this culture, however, was in agriculture. It was the Funnel Beaker people who introduced Sweden to agriculture, activities long practiced in Southern Europe and the Middle East. Animal husbandry was the predominant form of agriculture for the Funnel Beaker people, including domesticated sheep, cattle, pigs and goats. Some farming was also practiced, though on a limited scale.

Cattle were used for milk, meat and draft animals. A pot dated to about 4,000 BC depicts a four-wheeled cart, and wagon tracks have been found under a megalithic long-mound at Flintbek in northern Germany. Oxen were used to pull these vehicles and plows. A pot handle from Krężnica Jara, Poland, and another from Poznan, Poland, show a pair of yoked oxen.[3] (There are also bones of wild and domesticated horses found in association with this culture, but even the tamed horses seem to have been used for meat and not as draft animals.[4])

Pigs appear to have been the preferred meat source of this culture in Sweden and Denmark, though goats and sheep were also important. Goats, of course, could also supply milk, and sheep provided wool. Fragments of textiles have been found, but these are of linen.[5]

Flax was an important crop, producing an edible seed that could also be used to make linseed oil, and the stem of the plant provided fibers to make linen. Emmer, einkorn, club wheat and barley were likewise cultivated, and wild fruits, apples and nuts were gathered.[6]

Garden plots were established using slash-and-burn methods. This approach to cultivation necessitated frequent moves to find new ground to farm. However, since the

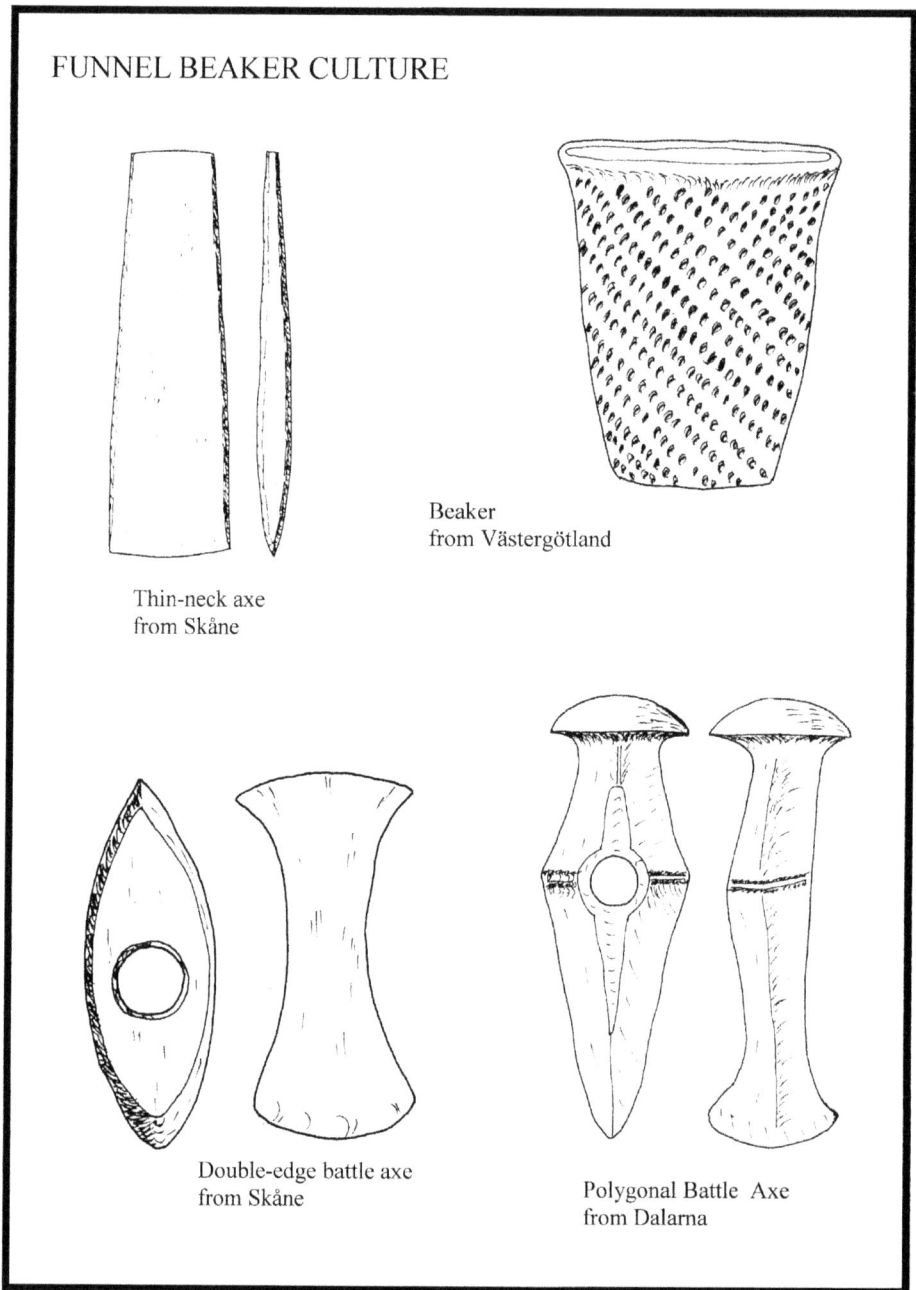

FUNNEL BEAKER CULTURE

Thin-neck axe from Skåne

Beaker from Västergötland

Double-edge battle axe from Skåne

Polygonal Battle Axe from Dalarna

plots were small, they could have been relocated many times before a family move was required, and that relocation need not have been far, allowing for a much more sedentary lifestyle than was possible with the former hunter-gatherer societies.[7]

The more settled condition permitted the use of more substantial dwellings. The hunter-gatherer multi-family hut was exchanged for a single-family daubed house of about 18 by 36 feet. Settlements were established by locating several houses around a grave monument devoted to an ancestor, chief or, perhaps, a god.[8]

Religion was apparently an integral part of this culture. Tools and ceramic vessels were deposited as sacrifices in streams and lakes near farmland. At Sarup, on the Danish island of Fyn, a cult center of some 85,000 square yards was built surrounded by earthworks and a moat. Another center at Stävie near Lund, Sweden, covers some 30,000 square yards.[9]

Sarup and Stävie are examples of massive projects, but this culture is noted for the many (and somewhat smaller) earthen structures scattered across Northern Europe, including Sweden. These mound constructions are of two types: utilitarian and funerary.

Archaeologists are uncertain as to the purpose of the non-funerary earthworks associated with the Funnel Beaker culture. These enclosures may have been defensive structures, trade centers, cattle corals, or used for ritual purposes. They consist of earthen walls, with palisades, fences and ditches encircling them.[10]

The funerary mound structures often include large stones as part of the construction. They consist of a mound, containing a burial chamber, surrounded by upright stones. The mounds vary in shape from circular to nearly square; trapezoidal, rectangular and kidney-shaped structures have also been found. In terms of materials, stones, clay, or sand were used—whatever was available locally. Entrances sometimes have doorframes and even sliding gates.[11] These are communal burial sites and one of the most distinctive features of this culture. In coastal areas these graves may be all stone "dolmens" (above-ground rock chambers).[12]

A site at Alvastra, located in Östergötland, Sweden, may be another example of a religious (and perhaps social) center. The site was occupied over a 40-year period around 3000 BC. Platforms built on stilts supporting the huts of seasonal visitors covered a 1,000-square-yard area. After the occupation, the platforms were used as a cemetery for the tribe's dead. Some 100 hearths were scattered more or less evenly across the platforms. Refuse around the hearths include the bones of domesticated stock, cattle, sheep and pigs. The remains of game are present—red deer, moose, wolf, bear, ducks, grouse and fish. Tools, weapons and pottery appear to have been brought to the site as items of sacrifice. An interesting complication of the tool-making tradition at the site is that while the weapons and tools are from the Funnel Beaker culture, the pottery is from the Pitted Ware culture.[13]

Funnel Beaker tool material was primarily flint, which was employed in making the culture's characteristic polygonal and double-edged, thin-necked battle axes. Another style of flint axe, the thick-necked axe, was common to both the Funnel Beaker and the Pitted Ware cultures.[14]

Whether the Funnel Beaker culture arrived in Sweden via an infusion of ideas only or via immigration has long been a subject of debate. Funnel Beaker settlements are located close to the old Ertebølle sites, always adjacent to open water. The cultural replacement seems to have been rapid and without any wholesale upheaval. It was previously believed that the changeover was the result of cultural diffusion, with no replacement of the indigenous population. However, modern scholarly opinion has shifted toward immigration.[15] One of the factors contributing to this change in opinion comes from the field of genetics. Certain genetic markers indicate an influx of people, particularly the gene that allows adults of Northern European descent to digest lactose. This gene is universally prevalent in areas the Funnel Beaker culture inhabited.[16]

The area where the Funnel Beaker culture prevailed stretched from Norway and Sweden to the Czech-Austrian border and from the Netherlands to Ukraine. This is the same geographic area where the highest levels of milk tolerance are found—that is, lactose tolerance among the adult population. Babies of all races are able to consume and digest milk, but this ability is often lost long before adolescence. Only among the descendants of Northern European populations is lactose tolerance prevalent.[17] Countries with the highest milk consumption today are Finland, Ireland, Sweden, Iceland

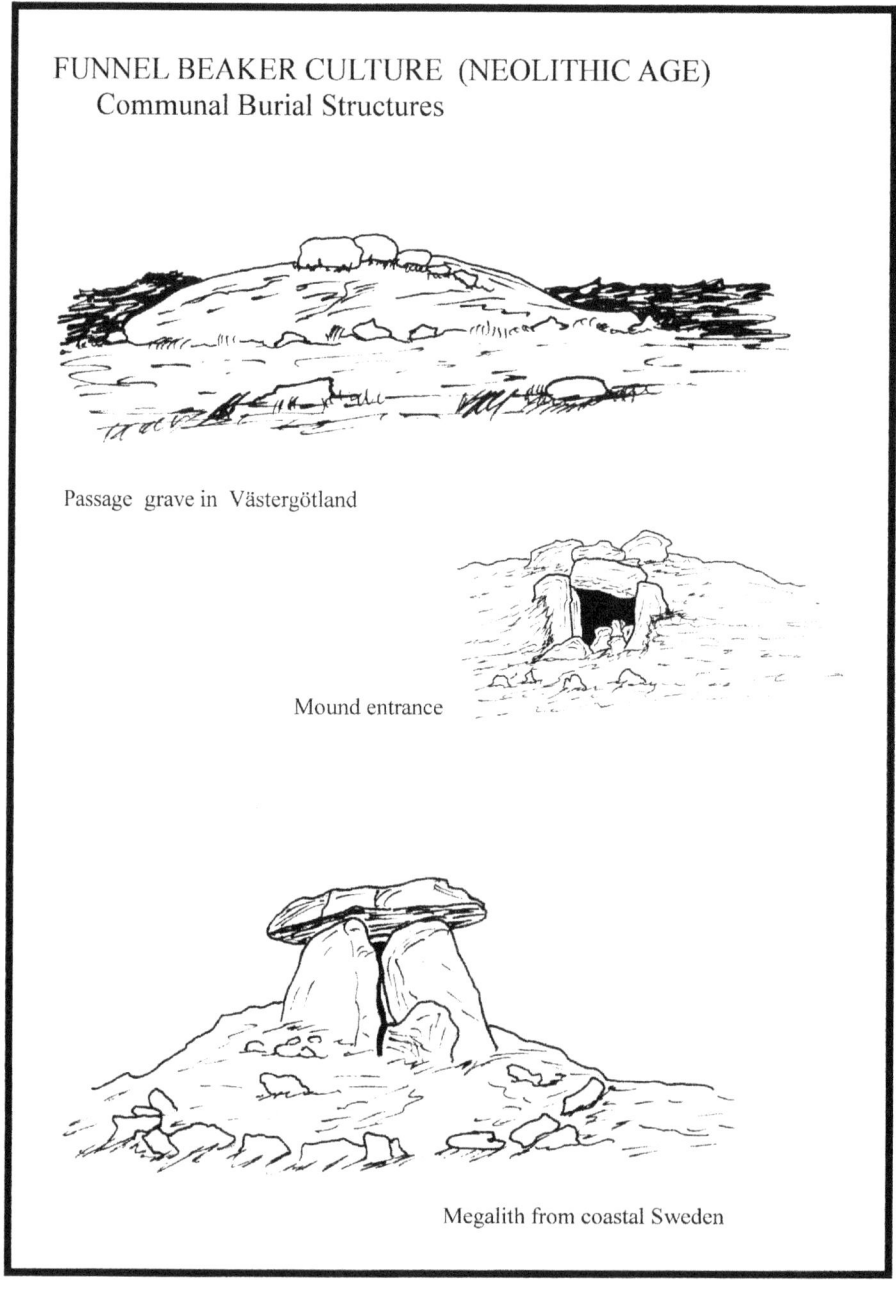

FUNNEL BEAKER CULTURE (NEOLITHIC AGE)
Communal Burial Structures

Passage grave in Västergötland

Mound entrance

Megalith from coastal Sweden

and the Netherlands—all areas inhabited by the Funnel Beaker culture, except for Iceland (which was later settled by Vikings who came from Northern Europe) and Ireland (also invaded by Vikings for a long period of time, perhaps enough to pass on the lactose-tolerant gene).[18] It has even been suggested that the flared rim characteristic of the Funnel Beaker culture was developed to facilitate milking cows, with the flat bottom and outward-turning top of the pots making it easier to catch the milk as it was wrung from the animal's teats.[19]

The Funnel Beaker culture was concentrated in Swedish Bohuslän, Västergötland and Skåne. As has been indicated, it extended south through Denmark into the Netherlands, northern Germany and beyond. As the culture advanced north to Uppland, it met the Lihult tribes, as had the Ertebølle, but this time there was a cultural exchange. The Nøstvet and Lihult peoples adopted many of the cultural items and practices of the Funnel Beaker tribes, but not agriculture or the communal burial practice. Though the more advanced tools and tool-making techniques were adopted, the Nøstvet/Lihult tribes remained hunter-gatherers. However, with the newly adopted practices, this culture has been identified by a new name: the Pitted Ware culture.[20]

The name "Pitted Ware" comes from the pottery produced by these people, made in a style similar to that of the Funnel Beaker culture, but with its own peculiarity. The Pitted Ware people decorated their pottery with distinctive small round pits and a cross-hatch line pattern imprinted on their beakers. Also unique to this culture were small ceramic figurines of wild animals, which is in keeping with the fact that these tribes retained their hunter-gatherer customs. They continued to use the tanged flint arrowheads but also had in common with the Funnel Beaker tribes the thick-butted axe and the thick-necked axe of flint. As noted, the site at Alvastra, Östergötland, seems to have been used by a tribe or clan that was a mix of the two cultures.[21]

Surprisingly, once the Nøstvet-Lihult culture was replaced by the Pitted Ware society, the new culture began to push south into formerly Funnel Beaker territory. Whether this was an invasion by the Pitted Ware tribes conquering territory from their southern neighbors, or simply the Funnel Beaker frontier tribes reverting back to a hunter-gatherer status is unknown. The cause of them losing their agricultural lifestyle is open to question.[22]

Trade was an important part of the economies of both cultures, facilitating the exchange of ideas and customs. Grains and copper items, especially daggers and axes from Central Europe, were imported into Funnel Beaker territory from the south, possibly in exchange for furs, flint and amber. Gotland Island has yielded tools of bone and antler, and many imported objects from mainland Sweden, Denmark and Germany date to this time.[23] Overseas commerce, as practiced by these Neolithic people, was sophisticated and argues for an already-existing maritime trade tradition.

As to language, the clues are meager. It is thought that the people of both cultures may have spoken languages related to the Finno-Ugric group or a tongue that some linguists call Old European. It has generally been assumed that up to this point in Sweden, the languages were pre–Indo-European, though this assumption has not been without its challengers. So far any conjectures regarding the identity of the languages of these early Stone Age peoples remain only speculation.[24]

The Funnel Beaker culture survived from about 4000 BC to around 2800 BC in

Sweden and was replaced by a cultural wave of enormous proportions, referred to by archaeologists as an archaeological horizon.[25]

This "horizon" was the expansion of the Battle Axe culture, which spread across Northern Europe to the Rhine River in the west and the Volga in the east. It brought with it new elements such as alcohol, the horse as a domesticated beast of burden, metallurgy, and woolen textiles, and it would ultimately usher in the Nordic Bronze Age. From about 2900 to 2450 BC, this wave swept through the continent, depositing its distinctive corded pottery everywhere. This cultural revolution has been called by several names: Corded Ware for its distinctively decorated ceramic pottery, Single Grave for its burial customs, and Battle Axe because of its trait of depositing a stone battle axe—a symbolic gesture, as the implement was by then outdated as a weapon of war—as a male grave offering.[26]

It was once thought that this cultural inundation was the result of a single massive impulse, an invasion originating in the northern German plains by a warlike, pastoral people that savagely expanded in all directions. Evidence now suggests, however, the process was much more complicated. The Corded Ware cultural horizon did indeed spread across Northern Europe, initiating a range of new elements (including the characteristic corded pottery), and certainly immigration was involved, but it was of a localized nature. There is little evidence of any full-scale overall migration. Also, even though some cultural traits were universal (the corded ware, livestock and battle axe as an authority symbol, for example), it was not totally homogeneous. Each region had its own peculiarities, and there were variations even in groups that were in close geographic proximity.[27]

Pottery of this culture included beakers and wide amphorae, usually brown to tan ocher in color. Cord impressions are common—thus one of the names for the tradition. Other impressions on the pottery are round and rectangular holes, barbed-wire designs and chevrons.[28]

The metallurgy introduced by this culture centered on copper. A variety of copper axes have been found; in some cases, just the head is metal, while some have projecting tubes for mounting to a shaft. There have also been finds of whole axes (head and shaft) made of copper. These axes are usually decorated, often with a chevron design. Along with the axes, spiral bracelets of copper are common.[29]

Besides the copper axes and jewelry, stone implements have been found, including the famous battle axes of various designs. In these axes, the shaft hole may be in the center or offset toward the butt or missing altogether. Also, stone was chipped to create triangular arrowheads, dagger blades, scrapers and knives.[30]

Adornment was not just of copper; jewelry was made from amber, shells, bone and perforated animal teeth.[31]

There is evidence from the Netherlands, Denmark and Switzerland that the people of this culture made use of wagons pulled by horses as well as oxen. Horses were thus used as draft animals (but probably not ridden).[32]

The remains of houses are rarely found. Based on an engraving found in Poland and excavations conducted in a marsh in southern Germany, longhouses seem to have been the preferred design. Walls were built by erecting double poles that held horizontal planks or logs. These structures were not built as permanent structures, since this cul-

3. Sweden of the Neolithic Age

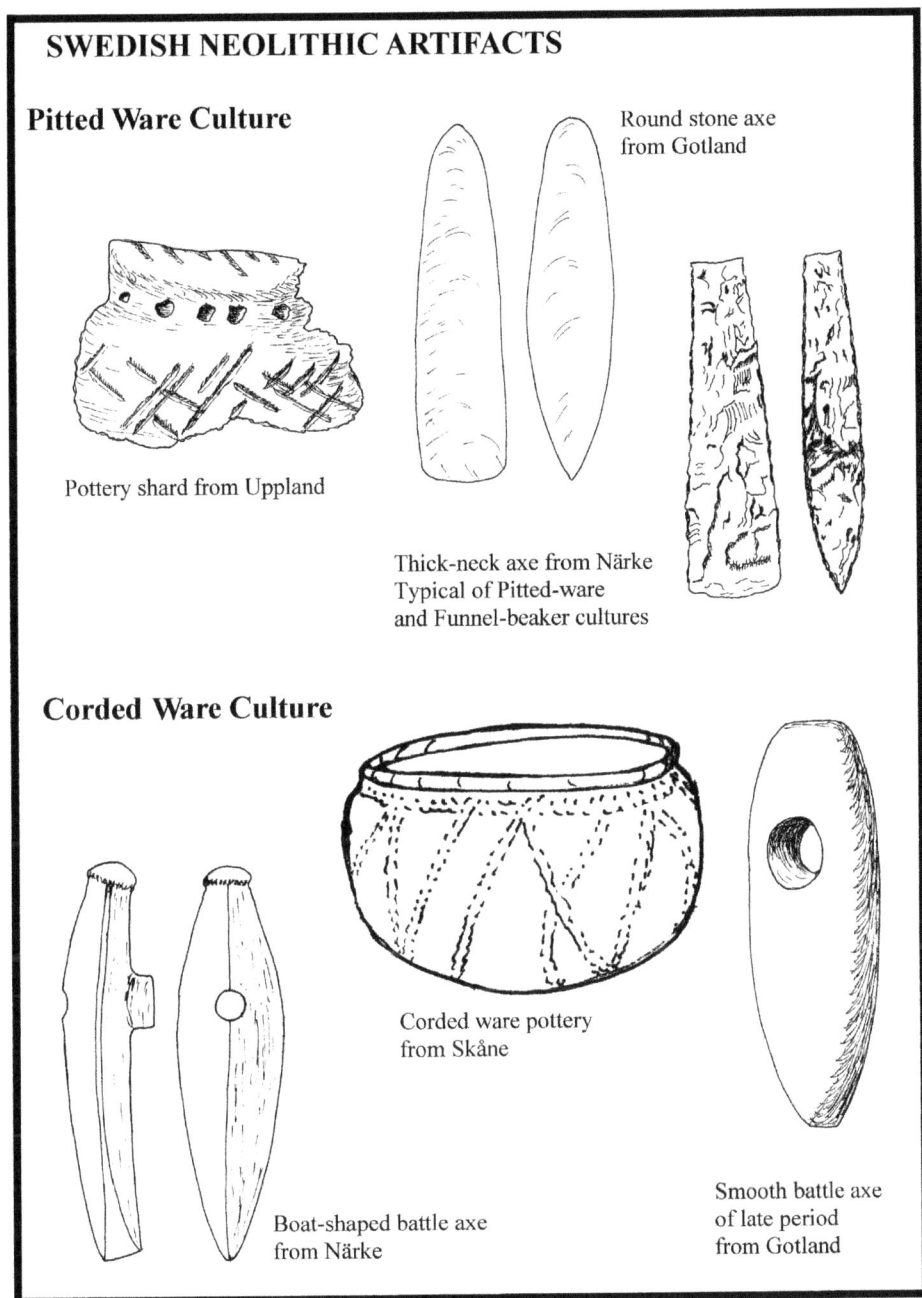

SWEDISH NEOLITHIC ARTIFACTS

Pitted Ware Culture

Pottery shard from Uppland

Round stone axe from Gotland

Thick-neck axe from Närke
Typical of Pitted-ware
and Funnel-beaker cultures

Corded Ware Culture

Corded ware pottery from Skåne

Boat-shaped battle axe from Närke

Smooth battle axe of late period from Gotland

ture was primarily pastoral, based on cattle. Again, there was much variation depending on locality. In some regions farming was an important part of the economy.[33]

Finally, it was once believed that this culture was the source of the proto–Indo-European languages. This thesis has been much debated. The most widely held opinion now is that the culture did promulgate the ancestral Satem dialects (Proto-Balto-Slavic) to the east and the Centum languages (Proto-Germanic, Proto-Celtic and Proto-Italic) in the west.[34]

In Sweden the new culture arrived in about 2800 BC, becoming established from Skåne to Uppland.[35] Again, there is no evidence of a population displacement, though some immigration is believed likely. Primarily, the cultural changeover seems to have been a peaceful one in which the Funnel Beaker people simply adopted the new technologies, textiles, metallurgy and associated practices, battle axe symbolism, single-grave funerary practices, corded pottery, and (very possibly) the Proto-Germanic language.[36]

However, the cultural shift was so encompassing and rapid that it seems hard to explain except by invasion and conquest. Yet there may be a clue to the speedy and pervasive exchange in the rock carvings of the Swedish Bronze Age. These petroglyphs show thousands of ships. We have already noted indications of Baltic commerce from the Funnel Beaker period in Gotland. Precursors of the Bronze Age boats must have been plying the Baltic Sea in this late Neolithic period. Seafarers of the Baltic and the North Sea would have been able to spread the new culture rapidly to a people already located along the waterways of southern Scandinavia. In fact, a subdivision of the Battle Axe culture—the faceted and boat-shaped axe subculture—seems to have reached Sweden by way of the Baltic without passing through Denmark. The peculiar band-pattern pottery of this Swedish subculture is most closely related to southeastern Middle Europe, not the culture of Danish Jutland.[37]

With the arrival of the Battle Axe culture, the large communal burial mounds of the Funnel Beaker culture disappeared, to be replaced by single graves. In Sweden these graves are not even marked by small mounds. The dead were simply interred facing east, generally in a crouching position.[38]

The Corded Ware, Single Grave or Battle Axe culture swept into Sweden, establishing itself from Skåne to Uppland with scattered settlements further north, even above the Arctic Circle. The culture flourished and dominated the region into the Early Bronze Age.

4

Bronze Age Sweden

The advent of the Bronze Age in Sweden settled, without equivocation, the question of the prominence of trade with the outside world. First identified as an important economic factor of the Funnel Beaker culture and suggested again as the means of importing and rapidly spreading the Battle Axe culture from overseas (the Baltic and North Sea), the reality of seaborne commerce was substantiated in the Bronze Age (about 1700–500 BC).[1]

Sweden lacks tin and its deposits of copper (the two ingredients of bronze) had not yet been discovered at this point in history. Bronze, therefore, had to be imported as finished goods, bronze alloy or raw material. Examples of items of foreign manufacture are twelve swords from Hallstatt, Austria, found in central Sweden and a circular bronze shield discovered in Halland.[2] Still, the majority of the bronze articles recovered from this period are of local manufacture.

There developed in Sweden at this time a vibrant bronze industry, aided (if not based on) an important and native raw material: soapstone. This dense but soft rock has no cleavage and can be easily sawed and carved.[3] Since it is also heat resistant, it makes an ideal material for bronze molds. During this period, nearly all bronze items were cast; only toward the end of the Bronze Age did some hammered work appear. Examples of these soapstone molds have been found along with an amazing variety of bronze artifacts. There are daggers, spear- and arrowheads, swords, massive battle axes with shaft holes, and what are thought to be war trumpets. Though most utilitarian tools of the period were still made of flint or other stone materials, there were items of bronze that fall into this category. The presence of these high-value items employed in common tasks indicates that there was a social hierarchy. Bronze sickles, saws, knives, bowls, axes, combs and buttons are common. Finally, of course, there are objects of adornment and decoration: necklaces, brooches, collars, bracelets of many different styles, and a decorative axe with plates of bronze covering a clay core. It might be noted that also falling under this category are items of gold from this period, including tweezers, bracelets and bowls.[4]

Based on the typology of these bronze items, Oscar Montelius, a Swedish archaeologist, divided the Nordic Bronze Age into the following subgroups[5]:

Period I: 1800–1500 BC
Period II: 1500–1300 BC
Period III: 1300–1100 BC
Period IV: 1100–900 BC

Period V: 900–700 BC
Period VI: 700–500 BC

Though Montelius proposed these periods in 1885, they have proven their worth even with the advent of carbon-14 dating and are still used today, although modern archaeologists place the beginning of the Nordic Bronze Age closer to 1500 BC. Periods

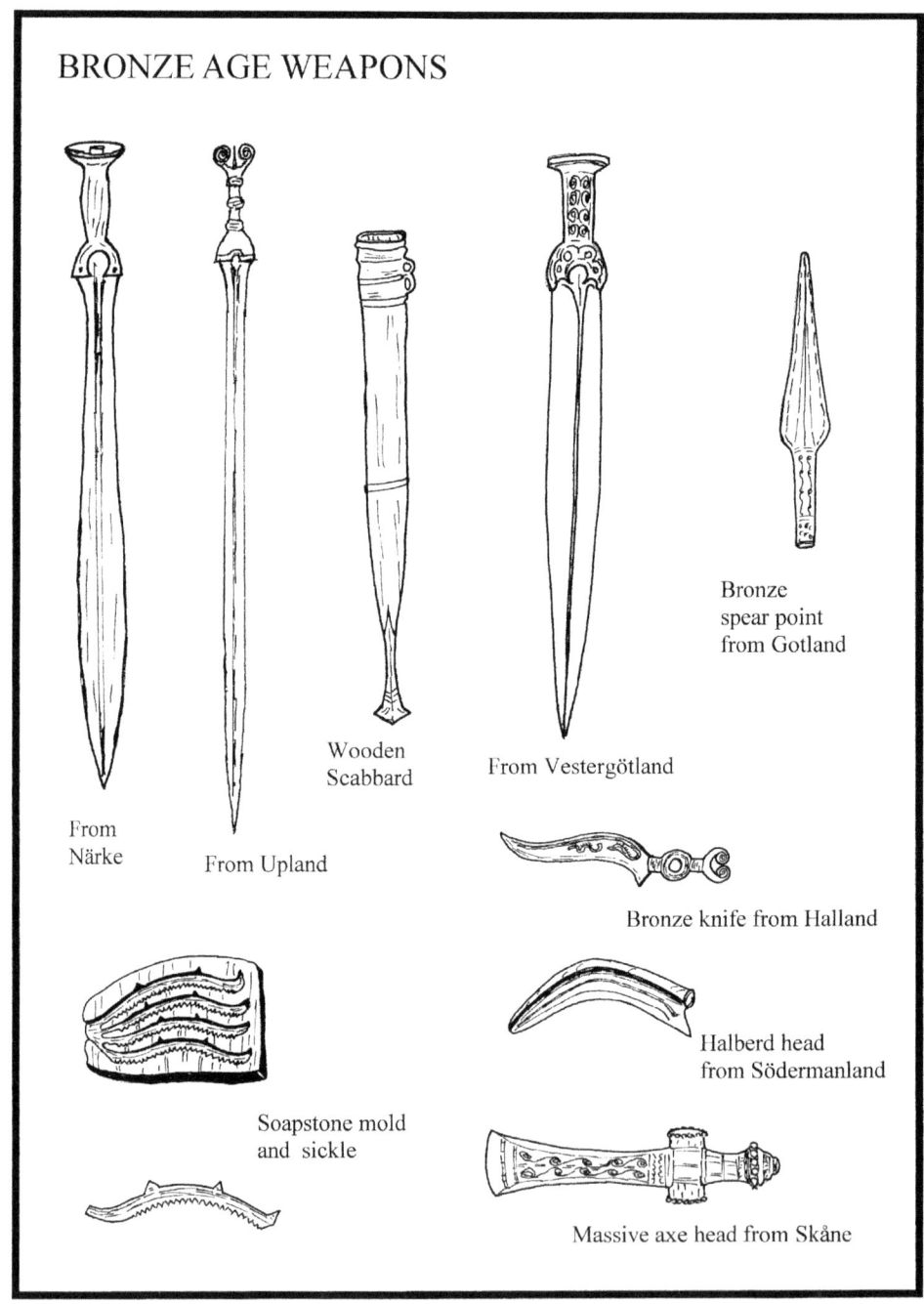

I–III above correspond with what is usually termed the early Bronze Age (1500–1100 BC), and periods IV–VI constitute the late Bronze Age, the references generally used in this book.

The importance of the sea trade is testified to by another source—rock carvings found along the west coast, Skåne and east-central Sweden. In the absence of a written language, these carvings are an important information source. The ubiquitous petro-

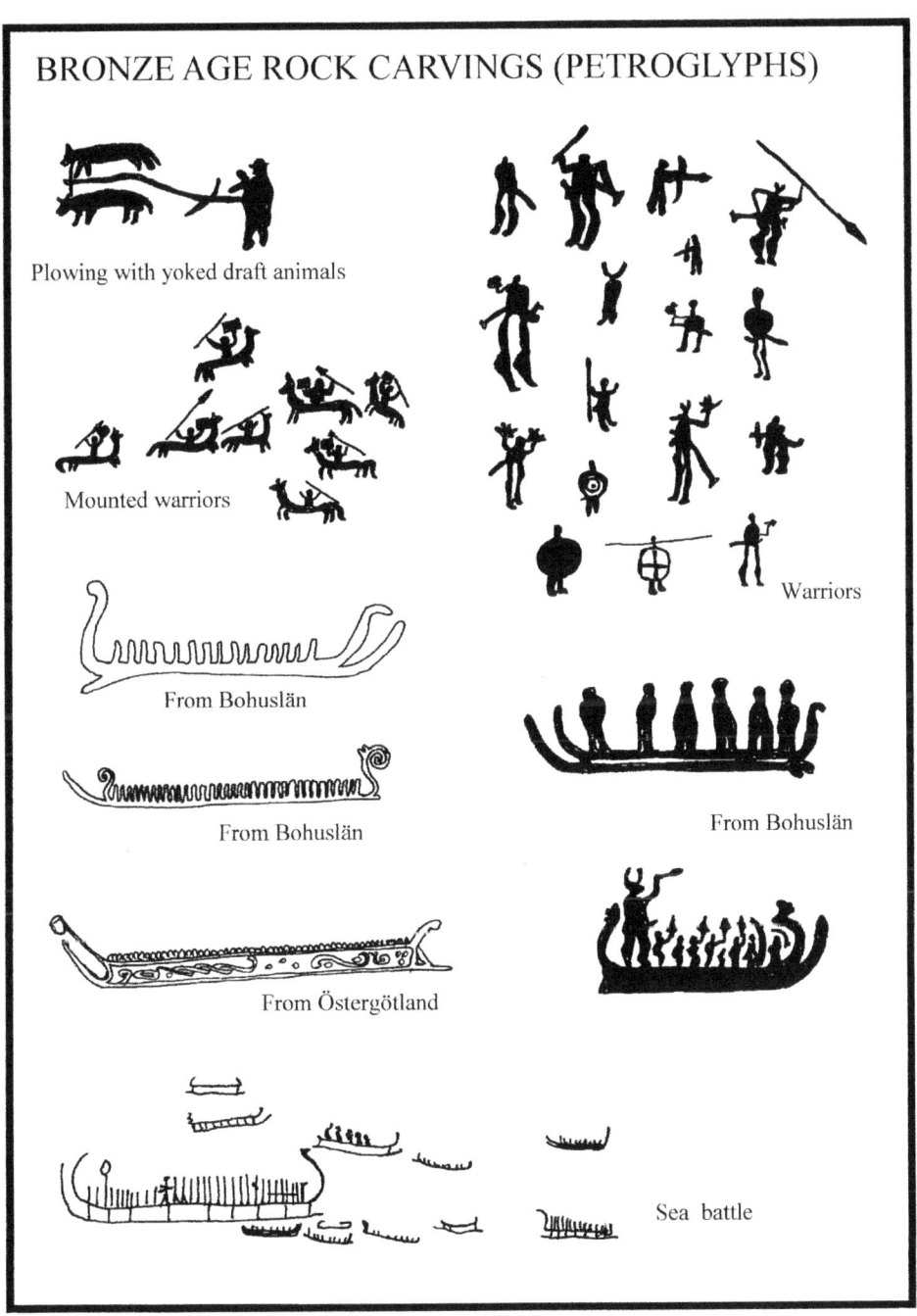

glyphs are etched into granite slopes facing fields and meadows. Though not deep, the carvings are in excellent condition and portray men (many with immense erect phalluses) and other items. There are warriors with swords and shields, chariots and wagons, battles and men dancing, horses, cows, dogs, snakes, deer, birds, and fish, and everywhere there are boats. The watercraft thus pictured range from large ships to small boats, all being rowed. There are no sails depicted anywhere.[6]

Some of the boats have identical upturned prows at both ends, reminiscent of the later Viking ships, but most have dissimilar ends. Some boats have only a few rowers, while others appear to be big ships with a great number of rowers. Some scenes are of ships in battle, while others would seem to represent ships engaged in trade.[7] The prevalence of boats in these rock carvings indicates an important role for sea trade in the economy of these people.

Sweden entered the Bronze Age somewhat later than Mediterranean Europe. By 3000 BC the Aegean region was importing tin to combine with local copper. In about 1600 BC the Danubian people learned the technology from the Mycenaean Greeks and passed it along to Northern Europe via trade routes.[8] Within a hundred years it reached Sweden. But the bronze alloy had to be imported to the northern regions. So how was it paid for; what was exchanged for the precious metal?

In all likelihood, the trade goods moving south in exchange for the bronze alloy and finished bronze items were the products readily available to the people of the region at that time—furs, wool and slaves. But the most valuable item for trade was undoubtedly the Baltic amber, so prized that some archaeologists have termed this trade route "the Amber Road." The trade routes were extensive and far reaching. Baltic amber has even turned up in Mycenaean graves dating from this period.[9]

Among the rock carvings we find a couple depicting a man handling two draft animals harnessed to a plow.[10] While trade and seafaring may have been an important part of Sweden's Bronze Age culture, the economy was basically agrarian. Cattle, sheep, goats and hogs, introduced at the time of the Funnel Beaker culture, were husbanded and grains were cultivated. At least two varieties of barley were grown, along with several species of wheat, including emmer (used for livestock feed) and rye. New cereals also emerged in Sweden during this period: millet and oats.[11] The diversity of crops produced in Bronze Age Sweden is truly amazing. Here we have crops requiring various soils, from sandy loams to heavy clays, suggesting an in-depth knowledge and sophisticated use of these crops.

It must be remembered that this late Sub-Boreal climate was one of relatively warm and dry conditions.[12] Crops could be grown that are not possible today in the same locations. "Grapes ripened and cattle could graze the year round."[13] It was only in the waning decades of the Nordic Bronze Age that temperatures began to moderate to conditions approximating our twenty-first-century climate. Then it continued to cool until reaching the cold temperatures of the early Iron Age.

As to dwellings of the Bronze Age, archaeology is very helpful. Recent finds have verified that even by the late Neolithic Period, clay-daubed houses had, for the most part, been replaced by much more substantial "longhouses," which survived with little change into the early Bronze Age. These structures featured local variations but in general had certain elements in common. A thatched roof was supported by a row of posts running lengthwise along the center line of the house, creating what is known as the two-isles longhouse. During the early Bronze Age this two-isles design gave way to the three-isles longhouse—that is, there were two rows of posts offset from the center line of the house, creating the three isles.[14] The change in construction is thought to have been made to facilitate building livestock stalls along the walls of the longhouses.[15] However, this is only one of many possible motives for the architectural shift.

These longhouses were rather grand, as big as ninety feet long by eighteen feet wide.[16] Longhouses became smaller on average as the Bronze Age progressed.[17] Houses were also "bigger, sturdier and more impressive the further north we go."[18]

The question of occupancy within these longhouses remains open. Were there multiple family units in one house? Were cattle and other livestock kept inside during the long winter nights? Given the size of the longhouses, one or both of these situations was probably the case. Longhouses have been excavated that have a clear interior division, with two sections that differ in internal structure. It is assumed that one section was a dwelling area and the other a byre for animals. Hearths have sometimes been discovered in what seem to be the living quarters of these houses.

As mentioned, there is a great deal of variation in the longhouses, besides size and the two versus three isles. Materials used to make the outside walls vary. Most walls are of wattle-and-daub construction, but many structures seem to have had solid timber walls and some had turf walls.

Wattle-and-daub was frequently used because the construction materials were readily available. Wooden strips or pliable twigs were woven into a lattice (the wattle). A plaster-like mud was then "daubed" onto the matting to create the solid wall. The mud used in this process was some combination of soil, clay, straw and animal dung. When dried, it made a very serviceable wall.

Longhouses appear to have been located in settlements, but the size and density of these "villages" is hard to ascertain. The Bronze Age practice of building a new dwelling close to the old, or even next to it, makes identifying what houses were in existence and occupied at any given time difficult. Population densities are still being investigated.[19]

Besides the longhouses, there was a second common style of dwelling. This was the sunken-floor hut. These structures appear to have been clay-daub huts with floors dug down below the terrain surface. It has been suggested that the longhouse tradition dates back to the Funnel Beaker culture, whereas the sunken-floor huts were introduced by the Battle Axe people.[20]

Another possibility proposed by archaeologists is that a farming population lived in the longhouses and a group of more mobile people with a mixed economy based on animal husbandry, short-term farming, hunting and fishing used the huts. Still, the fact that the two types of lodgings existed at the same time, but in different settlements, may mean they merely served different purposes within the same agrarian system, with the longhouses being the permanent central location, while the huts represented seasonal habitations for hunting, fishing, herding or gathering. The relationship between the two types of dwellings is yet to be determined.

Burial practices during the Bronze Age were varied and featured some truly bizarre aspects. However, there are certain trends that have been identified by archaeologists.

In southern Sweden, inhumation burial in an imposing barrow or natural hill early in the age gave way to cremation and burial in urns in cemeteries or in already-existing barrows, burial hills and stone ship monuments. As the monuments became less significant, so did the grave goods buried with the deceased.[21] These shifts in the Bronze Age people's methods of dealing with the deceased were gradual, spanning the thousand years of the age.

Though the trend went from inhumation to cremation, both methods of bodily disposition existed side by side throughout the Bronze Age, particularly in central Sweden.[22] Still, at the beginning of the age, cremation was relatively rare. The dead were often buried in monumental grave mounds of about 60 feet in diameter and 10 feet high. Construction of the largest of these barrows generally dates from the early Bronze Age, with the mounds becoming less impressive later in the age and disappearing altogether by the end of the period. The mound might be composed of sand, earth or loose stones.[23] The larger barrows were collective burials, with traces of several interments present (though it might be that the original intent was for a single burial grave monument, and extra burials were added later). Natural hills were also used and even modified to look like a monumental mound.[24]

A few of these barrows have yielded detailed information on clothing of the age. In excavating some mounds archaeologists have discovered tree-coffins. These are made from a section of an oak tree trunk cut in half lengthwise and hollowed out to receive the body. The acids from the oak have acted as a preservative for cloth buried with the body, preserving the deceased's clothing for some 3,000 years. In Ribe, Denmark, a tree-coffin was discovered in 1861 containing the remains of a Bronze Age warrior. The clothes, made of woven wool, consisted of a billess cap, a round cut mantle, a stout tunic, wool leggings and leather shoes. The tunic was held in place by a woolen belt that encircled the body twice and was knotted in front. The ends of the belt were decorated with fringes. By the left side of the body there lay a bronze sword in a wooden sheath lined with animal skin. At the foot of the coffin was a round wooden box containing another woolen cap, a horn comb and a bronze knife in the shape of a straight razor. The coffin was lined with cow hide. Though the clothing and articles were well preserved, the body (including the skeleton) had totally disintegrated, except for the hair and brain protected by the wool cap.[25]

In another grave near Arhus, Denmark, a tree-coffin was found in 1871 that contained the remains of a woman. In this case the skeleton was preserved, so gender was not in doubt. Her long hair was apparently fastened with a horn comb and covered by a well-knotted, worsted net. A second such net was also found in the coffin. The body was clothed in a full-length woolen dress consisting of a jacket with sleeves and a long robe. The jacket was sewn together under the arms and down the back with the front open, but probably fastened with a string or the little bronze *fibula* found in the coffin. The robe was held together by two woolen belts that ended in ornamental tassels. Also found in the coffin were a spiral finger ring, two bracelets, a torque and three round, beautifully decorated plates of different sizes with points projecting from the middle. These would have been parts of a belt.

Most interestingly, a bronze dagger lay by the side of the woman's body. Similar daggers have been found in other coffins and graves containing the remains of women.

In other coffins, fine linens have also been found, along with an array of decorative items, such as bronze buttons, brooches, torques and combs. Also recovered have been silver items and gold tools like tweezers.[26]

The woolen clothing found in these tree-coffins may represent the finest apparel available at the time and might be thought of as "Sunday best." There is ample archaeological evidence suggesting that everyday cloths included many items of animal skin,

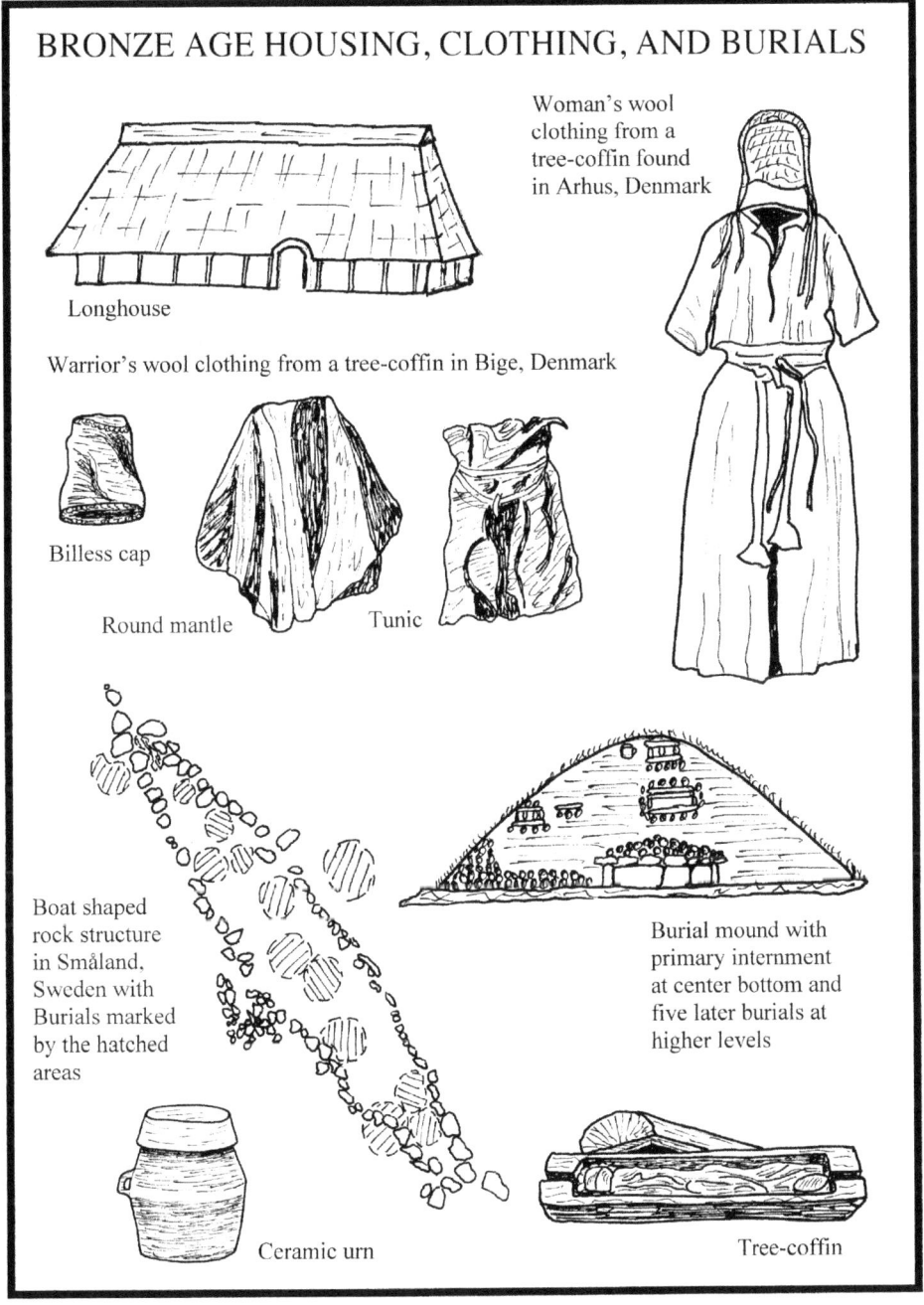

with perhaps an article or two of wool. Likewise, many of the commonly used tools were of flint or other stone rather than bronze, which would have been expensive and hard to get.

Contemporary with the barrows were "cists composed of flat stones placed edgewise and covered with similar stones."[27] Some graves were marked with boulders, and others were unmarked. In trying to make chronological sense of these variations in burial customs, archaeologists have concluded:

> that inhumation was prevalent during the early Bronze Age and that later, during periods III and IV, transition to cremation occurred. In accordance with this perception it is accepted that the dead, from the late Neolithic up to and including the earlier phases of the Bronze Age, were buried in gallery-grave (barrows) or gallery grave-like stone cists beneath stone-settings and cairns.[28]

Further, we can generalize that the early Bronze Age cists, cairns and barrows tended to be large, often containing multiple unburned skeletons. Later monuments were smaller, often containing only a single interment. Burned bones began to appear in the smaller cists and as later burials in existing barrows. As time passed, the cists became smaller and often contained, not burned bones, but an urn enclosing cremated remains. Still later, the cists and barrows were abandoned altogether and the burial urns were deposited in the ground, covered by just a flat stone. Finally, there are places of concentrated burials—cemeteries—with burned bones deposited in the ground and urn fields where a great number of the plain and simple burial urns were deposited in the ground. These last are devoid of tools and ornaments, whereas the large monuments of the early Bronze Age were rich in tools and weapons. The transition was not smooth, of course, and varied a great deal from location to location.[29]

On a field next to a ledge that drops 60 feet to the Baltic Sea, there is the outline of a boat constructed of stones. This ship-like burial monument is near Hellerö, Västra Ed Parish, Småland, Sweden. The rock structure is some 57 feet long by 10.5 feet wide, with a pointed prow and somewhat flattened stern. In and around this stone outline are thirteen burned bone concentrations (ten inside, one partly in and two just outside the rock perimeter). The remains are of adults and children, male and female. This stone boat outline in Småland is an example of the ship burial monuments found scattered around the coastal areas of the Baltic, especially the island of Gotland. These monuments date to the late Bronze Age, but variations, buried under barrows or boat-shaped cists, may have been constructed as early as the first part of the Bronze Age and as late as the conclusion of the Iron Age. There is also evidence that boat monuments of the late Bronze Age and early Iron Age had cremated bones scattered over the entire area of the structure.[30]

It is tempting to connect these ship burial monuments to later Viking boat graves or even the Viking funeral ship pyres. But the significance of the stone ships is not clear. Probably it was an attempt to provide the deceased with a means of transportation in the afterlife, or it may have been a way of commemorating the life of a particularly successful sailor—a monument used in hero worship, even the center of a hero cult.

Another Bronze Age burial practice that may have involved an ancestor worship aspect is the aristocratic death rituals involving longhouses and symbolic houses. In Linköping, Sweden, archaeologists have found a fire-cracked stone heap, the remnants of just such a ritual. Excavation indicates the spot was already a burial site prior to the beginning of the ritual, as evidenced by scattered cremated bones in the area.[31]

The ritual steps can be reconstructed from the archaeological evidence. First, a small (10 × 4.5 foot) structure, a "house model," was built. This house model stood for a short time and then was destroyed. It was replaced by a second, larger house structure, and in the second house the actual burial was carried out. Here there was a pit found to contain cremated bones, a bronze razor dating the site to period VI, a bronze ring and fragments of the burial urn. This second house was then burned and a mound of fire-cracked stones erected on the site.[32]

In some cases actual longhouses were constructed, used for a short period (probably for ceremonies, or perhaps to accommodate visitors and relatives), and then destroyed, usually burned. The actual interment was on top of these ruins, and then a mound was constructed on top of everything.[33]

Obviously these elaborate funerary rituals were carried out by a wealthy class of people. Only an aristocracy would have the means to build and rebuild houses solely for the purpose of honoring their dead. Perhaps this ostentatiousness was a way of maintaining their social status. It's possible the ship burial monuments and the aristocratic death rituals involving the destruction of houses were both attempts to elevate certain exceptional people or family members to heroic status, similar to the Homeric heroes of Bronze Age Greece.

The variety in burial practices raises the question: What part did religion play in all this?

> In prehistoric Scandinavia society, there were no priesthoods or institutions that continually reproduced a normative image of the world or provided a unified ritual praxis for people dwelling in a large region. This does not, however, imply that there were no religious, mythical or ritual ideas and themes spread throughout large regions that with time would become ideologically stable.[34]

A clue to Bronze Age mythology may be found in the Trundholm sun chariot discovered in Zealand, Denmark. The sculpture depicts a horse mounted on four wheels pulling the sun, mounted on two wheels. Since only one side of the sun is gilded, it is thought that this represents the idea that the sun is pulled across the sky, giving off its light, and then returns to the east at night. The importance of the sun in Bronze Age religion is also indicated by several rock carvings showing a man holding the sun.[35]

Another common figure in the petroglyphs is a male figure holding a hammer, a possible precursor to the Norse god Thor. All in all, though, the clues are limited. For the time being, Swedish Bronze Age religion will remain something of an enigma.

In terms of social structure, political systems and warfare, there is little more to go on. As we've seen, agriculture of this period probably produced a surplus due to the warm climactic conditions. The burial practices, particularly the use of longhouses and symbolic houses in funeral rituals, indicate class division, and perhaps the existence of an aristocracy or ruling class. Were these tribal chiefs, community leaders, settlement strong men, or something greater?

That there was warfare, there can be little doubt. The plethora of bronze weapons and depictions of combat in the rock carvings make this situation clear. Yet settlements do not seem to have had defensive walls, nor are there fortifications evident. So this area is not well understood.

The Bronze Age discussed here applies to the southern part of Sweden, extending as far north as Uppland. These people were agrarian, practicing both farming and animal husbandry. To the north, however, were mobile hunting societies, little affected by the Bronze Age. Other than acquiring a limited number of bronze items through trade, they continued to rely on stone, horn and wooden tools as implements for hunting, fishing and what little farming they did practice.

By the late Neolithic Age, the people of Norrland had transitioned from a mobile society of the Mesolithic period to a more sedentary life. They hunted mainly elk and beaver, gathered berries and fished for perch, pike and salmon in their forest home. Rock carvings from this time depict mostly elk, probably associated with hunting rituals.

But during the early Bronze Age these people began to invade the mountain foothills, adding reindeer to their diet. At the higher elevations they also found trout and char with which to vary their diets. As the Bronze Age progressed the northerners began to depend more and more on reindeer as their main source of food. This shift in diet and hunting practices demanded a more mobile lifestyle. By the Iron Age, the people of northern Norrland had become completely dependent on wild reindeer for their survival.[36]

Two other characteristics of the Bronze Age in the north are thin quartzite arrowheads made using a bifacial thinning technique and asbestos-tempered ceramics. Instead of bronze, Norrlanders began using the quartzite arrowheads in the beginning of the age and continued the practice into the Iron Age. The asbestos-tempered ceramics was a technique adopted from the east. This style of pottery was common in northern Russia and Finland.

Some archaeologists believe they can detect an ethnic difference between the Bronze Age people of southern Norrland and the inhabitants of the north. The northern Norrlanders, these scientists believe, were a Samish (Lappland) population, while the southerners were of northern Germanic stock. This differentiation, at least at the time of this writing, is still being debated.[37]

The Swedish Bronze Age closed out with a cooling of the climate and the introduction of a much harder metal, one available to Swedes as a native ore. Iron would become one of the country's major assets in the centuries to come.

5

The Iron Age Comes to Sweden

With the coming of the Iron Age to Sweden, around 500 BC, there is an abrupt disruption in the archaeological record. The treasure of artifacts from the Bronze Age disappears, and there is scant evidence to work with in reconstructing this period in Sweden's past. For 400 years, from 500 BC to the first century BC, archaeological evidence is scattered and finds are rare.[1] This period is sometimes called the "Findless Age" by archaeologists.

The early Iron Age in Scandinavia, from 500 BC to the end of the pre–Christian era, is named the Pre-Roman Iron Age, which is followed by the Roman Iron Age (AD 1–400). At the dawn of the Christian era, contact with the outside world seems to have been reestablished, though now the artifacts clearly reflect a Roman influence.

The Iron Age arrived in Scandinavia late as compared to the rest of Europe. The oldest wrought iron so far discovered is a group of knives from Gerar, Palestine. These weapons have been dated to 1350 BC. A hundred years later, iron appeared in Egypt at the time of Rameses II. A century later, it reached the Aegean. From there iron spread into Western Europe, first at Hallstatt, Austria, in about 900 BC, and later in Switzerland in 500 BC as the La Tène industry.[2] By 750 BC iron was in use in the Danube Basin, where trade carried the technology north to the Baltic.[3]

Iron first appeared in Sweden as the Bronze Age was closing. A small, fire-damaged fragment of iron has been found at a burial place in southeastern Scania dating to the late Bronze Age. The bit of iron was mixed in with items of bronze, flint, wood, potsherds and burned bones.[4] Other examples of iron from the late Bronze Age have been found in Denmark, usually as inlays on bronze.[5] These first traces of the advancing Iron Age were almost certainly imported or the work of immigrant (probably itinerant) metal workers rather than indigenously manufactured. However, once the technology reached Sweden it was rapidly adopted.

Iron is easier to work than bronze and more versatile in usage. What's more, iron ore was easy to extract and readily accessible in Sweden in the form of ore from peat bogs. Wood for smelting was close at hand in the ubiquitous forests of the country. Whereas bronze had to be imported, iron was available for the taking.

During this Pre-Roman Iron Age, bronze was still in use, but it was confined to mostly ornamental items, such as collars, bracelets and brooches. New alloys surfaced, including brass (an amalgamation of not just copper and tin but also lead and/or zinc).

SWEDISH TIMELINE

Geological Time	Holocene Epoch								
Climate Periods	Sub-Boreal			Sub-Atlantic					
Climate	Warm Period	Cold Period	Warm	Cooling	Cold	Uneven temperature moderation		Medieval Warm Period (Peak)	Little Ice Age / Warm
Archaeological Periods	Neolithic Age	Bronze Age Sweden (I, II, III, IV, V, VI, VII)			Pre-Roman Iron Age	Roman Iron Age	Ger. Iron Age / Migration Period / Vendel Period	Viking Age / Medieval Sweden	Kalmar Union / Swedish Empire / Modern Sweden
Historical Events				Pytheas' voyage to Scandinavia		Ostrogoths take Ravenna—493 / Ostrogoths take Scandinavia—325	Vikings reach N. America	Black Death—1350	Battle of Lützen—1632 / Hammarshkjöld: Sec. Gen. U.N.—1953-1961
Timeline	1,500 BC		1,000 BC	500 BC	0 AD	500	1000	1500	

Common in this early period are iron pins; less plentiful are iron knives and iron swords with iron scabbards.[6]

It was just at this time that a blanket of economic hardship seemed to settle over Scandinavia: "The wealth and liveliness of the Bronze Age dulled and contracted; there was little gold and as yet no silver; grave offerings become fewer and poorer, field and bog offerings came almost to an end. And whereas bronze and bronze artifacts had found their way as far north as latitude 68°, early iron fails at latitude 60°, approximately that of present-day Oslo and Uppsala. And everywhere artistic standards were in decline. Why should this be so? What impoverished the northern countries and for a time interrupted their lines of communication south?"[7]

At least three reasons may be given for this sudden austerity in Sweden during the early Iron Age. First, there was the shift from bronze to iron as the primary metal for making tools and weapons. The manufacture of bronze tools, first in the Mediterranean world and later in Scandinavia, fostered trade. Copper and tin are almost never found in the same region in commercial quantities. The Phoenicians, chief among the ancient Mediterranean merchants, were driven to Iberia and even to Britain to obtain tin, which they combined with copper from Cyprus and traded to the Etruscans, Greeks and Egyptians. Sweden, along with the rest of Scandinavia, was dependent on trade as a means of acquiring bronze; though Sweden did possess soapstone for molds, the tin and copper alloy had to be imported. Iron, however, was indigenous to Sweden and easy to obtain. Trade was no longer required to acquire the basis for tool and weapons manufacturing, though iron items from outside the country have been recovered, proving that all commerce did not cease.

A second factor may have been the deteriorating climate. We have seen some indication of a cooling trend during the late Bronze Age—the switch to the three-isles longhouse, possibly to accommodate the stabling of livestock in the winter, and the increasing austerity in graves and burial goods. But now the temperatures took a serious plunge. From 550 to 50 BC there was an abrupt and significant cooling event.[8]

The variety of grains grown during the Bronze Age was reduced to just three: hulled barley, oats and wheat, with barley being the dominant crop by far. Fields became more or less permanent, with manure used as fertilizer. Though lower in protein, barley responds more productively to this stabilized cropping and heavy soil preparation.[9]

Longhouses of this period show regional development; they differ in each region but are uniform in any given area. In some regions all the houses grew in size, while in others they shrank over time. About the only characteristic they all have in common is a narrowing of the center aisle. This longhouse structural modification began at about 500 BC, and the aisles continued to be reduced in width during the entire pre-Roman period.[10] This slight metamorphosis might have been to accommodate livestock stalls, or additional stalls along the longhouse walls, or to provide more room along the walls for other activities that were now done inside, such as threshing. In any case, the cold of the Pre-Roman Iron Age brought socioeconomic degradation and undoubtedly forced changes in customs and traditions of the people of Sweden—indeed, of all Scandinavia.

The third probable factor contributing to the dark period of the early Iron Age was the expansion of a militaristic people known as the Celts. The Celts originated in the upper Rhine and Danube basins.[11] They were already skilled metallurgists, using zinc, tin and mercury in their artwork. But, above all, they were expert iron workers and had developed a double-edged cutting sword that proved quite affective against their early enemies armed with bronze weapons. They also carried a large dagger for stabbing and used iron-tipped throwing javelins and spears.[12]

The Celts fought both on foot and on horseback. In some instances, two riders would enter battle on one horse; the back rider would launch his javelin and then dismount to fight as infantry. It is difficult to generalize about the Celts because they were not an organized nation, but rather an amalgamation of tribes that had in common a language, certain customs and iron technology.

The Celts seem to have come out of nowhere, bursting on the European scene and then driving to all corners of the continent. In terms of origin, they are associated with the Hallstatt culture (named for a site in Austria) and the La Tène culture (named for a site in Switzerland) of east-central Europe, which flourished from about 800 to 50 BC and, as already noted, were some of the earliest European iron workers.[13]

They stormed and plundered to the Black Sea, crossed the Bosporus and established an enclave in Asia Minor. To the west, other tribes of Celts migrated into Gaul, crossed the Pyrenees and invaded Iberia. Still others crossed the English Channel and occupied the British Isles, pushing all the way to the northern coast of Scotland and west coast of Ireland.

> They were a people of chariots and horsemen. They were less addicted to the hill-forts in which the existing inhabitants put their trust. They built new towns in the valleys, sometimes even below the hilltops on which the old fort had stood. They introduced the first coinage of silver and copper. They established themselves as a tribal aristocracy in Britain, subjugating the older stock. This active, alert, conquering, and ruling race established themselves wherever they went with ease and celerity.[14]

Even the Italian peninsula was not spared the inundation of these marauders: "around 400 BC, the as yet almost unknown [to the Etruscans, Italians and Greeks of the peninsula] Celtic people came down over the Alps and, attracted by the paradise of what is nowadays the South Tyrol and the lush fertility of the Po valley, decided to settle there. Neither courage, excellent weaponry nor technology could save the Etruscans."[15] The Celtic invasion broke the Etruscans and put them into decline.

The widespread chaos resulting from the Celtic migrations would certainly have disrupted the old commercial avenues of Bronze Age trade. A whole new cast of characters had been interjected into the system of markets and trade centers that had connected the Mediterranean world with Scandinavia.

These factors—the conversion from bronze to iron, the cold interval and the Celtic expansion—all worked to plunge Scandinavia, including Sweden, into the dark period of the early Iron Age.

Interestingly, this is exactly the time that we find our first reference and description of Scandinavia from an outside source. The geographer who provides this information is Pytheas, a member of an expedition that departed from the Greek colony of Massilia (today's Marseille) in about 325 BC to explore the coast of Northwestern Europe.[16] At the time Massilia was a rich and powerful city-state with trade routes penetrating deep into continental Europe via the Rhône valley. Fingers of this commercial network no doubt reached all the way to the Baltic, and it was these sources of goods that would

5. The Iron Age Comes to Sweden

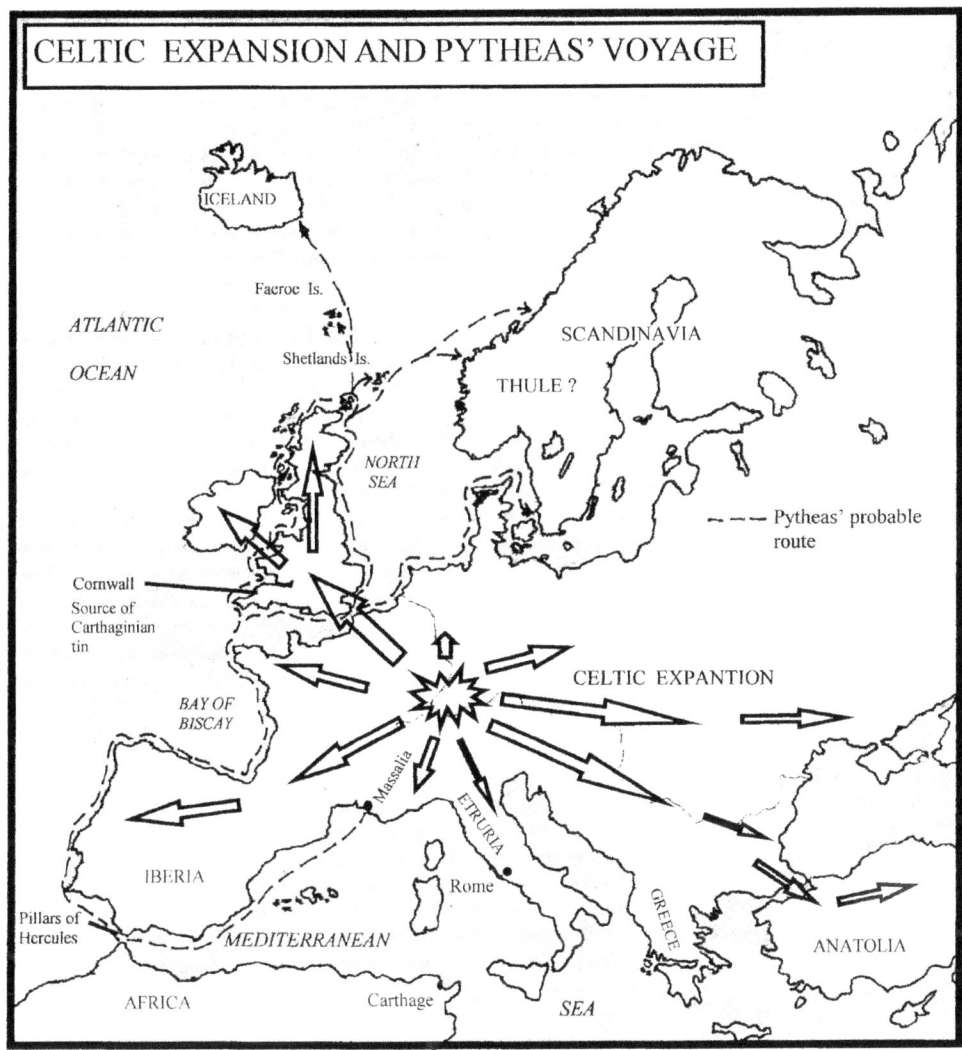

have been cut off by the encroaching Celts. Perhaps this expedition was an attempt to reestablish a trade route to the furs and amber of the far north by sea.

At the time Massilia was an ally of Rome and Etruria, and it had treaties with Carthage allowing the city a relatively free hand in trading and navigating in the western Mediterranean (at least along the north coast), a privilege denied the residents of Italy and Sicily by the Carthaginians.[17] This relationship with Carthage may have been why Pytheas' expedition was able to pass through the Pillars of Hercules (Strait of Gibraltar), a passage guarded jealously by the Carthaginians to protect their route to Cornwall, England, a prized source of their valuable tin.[18]

Passing the Strait of Gibraltar, Pytheas sailed north along the west coast of Iberia to Britain, where he investigated the tin industry of Cornwall. He also sailed along the coast of Britain, which he explored and apparently charted fairly extensively, perhaps even circumnavigating the island and touching on Ireland. All this was contained in his *Survey of the Earth*. Unfortunately, this entire book is now lost. We are completely dependent on other writers who had access to the work or edited versions of it. According to these second-hand or third-hand accounts, Pytheas sailed on from Britain and Scotland to a land he called Thule, "which Pytheas says is six days' sail north from Britain and near the Frozen Sea."[19]

There has been much speculation as to where exactly Pytheas reached landfall and just what he was referring to as Thule. Researchers have proposed several different areas over the centuries—Jutland, the west coast of Sweden, the Norwegian coast (particularly the area around Trondheim), the Faroe Islands, the Shetland Islands, Iceland, even Greenland. That Pytheas did reach some part of Scandinavia is attested to by references to Arctic conditions. Strabo, the Greek geographer, records, "It is true that Pytheas of Marseilles affirms that the furthest country north of the British islands is Thule; for which place he says the summer tropic and the Arctic Circle is all one."[20] Evidence that Thule was indeed some part of Scandinavia can also be found in Pliny the Elder's *Natural History*:

> The most remote of all that we find mentioned is Thule, in which, as we have previously stated, there is no night at the summer solstice, when the sun is passing through the sign of Cancer, while on the other hand at the winter solstice there is no day.... At one day's sail from Thule is the frozen ocean, which by some is called the Cronian Sea.[21]

It seems most likely Pytheas touched some part of the western Swedish coast, the southern tip of Norway or the Norwegian west coast. The Faroe and Shetland Islands are also possibilities, but Iceland seems unlikely, as this would have required a voyage over open ocean and stormy seas, a navigation feat beyond the capabilities of even Pytheas. He also provided some description of the living conditions of Thule, and Iceland would have been uninhabited at this time.

In terms of what light Pytheas can shed on the society of this far north country—customs, agriculture, houses, and so on—the information is frustratingly brief. We learn only that "people bordering on the frozen zone would be destitute of cultivated fruits, and almost deprived of the domestic animals; that their food would consist of millet, herbs, fruits, and roots; and that where there was corn (cereal grains) and honey they would drink of these (mead?). That having no bright sun, they would thresh their corn, and store it in vast granaries, threshing-floors being useless on account of the rain and want of sun."[22] (This last point is apparently a reference to threshing being done in a barn or inside the longhouse instead of outside, as would be the custom in Mediterranean areas.)

Lastly, we have an entry concerning a trade item of the north that would surely have arrested Pytheas' attention:

> Pytheas says that the Gutones, a people of Germany, inhabit the shores of an æstuary of the Ocean called Mentonomon, their territory extending a distance of six thousand stadia; that, at one day's sail from this territory, is the Isle of Abalus, upon the shores of which, amber is thrown up by the waves in spring, it being an excretion of the sea in a concrete form; as, also, that the inhabitants use this amber by way of fuel, and sell it to their neighbors, the Teutones.[23]

It is tempting to equate Gutones with the Goths of central Sweden, and this may not be too great a stretch. The Isle of Abalus could be the southern tip of Sweden, the island of Zealand or Jutland, and the trading of amber to the Teutones of Germany certainly rings true.

Reviewing the evidence thus assembled for the Pre-Roman Iron Age, it seems to be a period of change, particularly during what is termed the early Iron Age (400–100 BC). There was a dramatic shift, not just from bronze tools to iron, and all that it implies, but also in social organization. During the late Bronze Age there existed what might be termed a large-scale social system.

> Because of the total lack of evidence of a regulated land use, like enclosures or boundary-walls, the Late Bronze Age production system must have been very open and extensive. Cattle and sheep might have been allowed to move around in large herds ... with the clan or subtribe as the most important socioeconomic instanced of society, it is further likely that production and ownership were also related to these levers of social organization.[24]

The evidence points to the clan or subtribe being the basic socioeconomic unit, with the family subservient to this larger organization in terms of production and land ownership. But during the early Iron Age this socioeconomic system disappears. The patterns of settlement and burial are not specific. There seems to be a profound transformation taking place. "We can only observe what was before and what was after."[25]

The new pattern that emerged after this transformation might be called the small-scale socioeconomic structure versus the large-scale structure of the late Bronze Age: "The individual farmstead—an extended family—has now become the most important basic unit in production and social organization."[26] Not only do boundary walls appear to mark land areas between neighbors, but they also divide land owned by a given family into categories—pastures, hay meadows and farmland. By the end of the Pre-Roman Iron Age, land usage was well defined and production much more concentrated than in the Bronze Age.

During the last century of the pre–Christian era, the climate began to moderate. Average temperatures started a slow trend upward, although there would still be cold intervals until the Medieval Warm Period (MWP) that commenced around AD 950. The rising trajectory would crest at about AD 1000 with the peak of the MWP.[27]

At the beginning of the Christian era the dark shroud lifts, archaeologically speaking, and suddenly there is a wealth of material to illuminate the search for understanding. However, the artifacts from this period of recovery have a decidedly different cast.

During the 400 years of Scandinavian "material and cultural impoverishment,"[28] the Mediterranean world had changed dramatically. In 500 BC the eastern Mediterranean was dominated by the Persian Empire, which would try to extend its control over European Greece as it had done with the Greeks of Asia Minor. The Greek city-states were forced to take time away from fighting each other to defend themselves against the Persians.

In the western Mediterranean, the struggle for supremacy was between the Carthaginians, the Etruscans (just then reaching their zenith) and the various colonies in Sicily, Italy and the northwest Mediterranean coast. Rome was, at this point in history, a petty city-state trying to free itself from Etruscan domination.

While Sweden shifted from bronze to iron and from large- to small-scale socioeconomic patterns, the Mediterranean world experienced the Persian wars with Greece, the Peloponnesian War, the conquest of the Persian Empire by Alexander the Great, and the Punic Wars, which left Rome master of the western Mediterranean. By the beginning of the Christian era, Rome had conquered the eastern Mediterranean and was fighting the Parthian Empire along the Tigris and Euphrates rivers. The Romans had also pursued a push toward Northern Europe in the early years of their empire:

> Julius Caesar had incorporated the river Rhine into the empire by 31 BC but had refused to allow expansion further east; not only did he believe the dark forests were home to fearful beasts and magical creatures like unicorns, but he and other Romans considered the Germans to be too barbaric to be absorbed into the empire. It was Julius Caesar's adopted son Augustus who decided to capture the land east of the Rhine and to push the boundary of the empire up to the Elbe. In a campaign led by Augustus' stepsons Nero Drusus and Tiberius, Roman troops reached the mysterious river bank in 3 BC. The legate L. Domitius Ahenobarbus actually crossed the water to meet some of the tribesmen in order to conclude *amicitia* or treaties of peace.[29]

Had the Roman legions continued to advance, it was but a short distance from the Elbe to the Baltic, where the Romans would have come into contact with Swedish traders then plying the Baltic Sea as merchants. The meeting of Roman and Swede was not to be, however.

In AD 9 the Romans under Varus were ambushed in the Teutoberg Forest by a coalition of Germanic tribes led by Arminius, chief of the Cherusci tribe. It was a disaster for the Roman army. Three legions were wiped out, destroying the Roman occupational force between the Rhine and the Elbe. The empire pulled its borders back to the Rhine, and there they would stay. The German interior and Scandinavia were safe from Roman military domination. The Roman Empire would expand in other areas—in Britain, Dacia, the Middle East and Africa—but in Northern Europe its advance had been checked.

The stability of the Roman occupation of Gaul did, however, facilitate the return of an active commercial network reaching into Scandinavia. The Celtic intrusion had been mitigated by the Roman conquest of Gaul. Trade routes developed along the Elbe to Jutland and along the Vistula to the Baltic islands and Sweden. To the east there were commercial pathways from the Black Sea through Russia, and to the west merchants from Gaul made use of the Rhine to reach Scandinavia.[30] But these merchants were usually Germans or Gauls, for "only a handful of [Roman] traders dared brave the dangers of the 'Amber Road' which led up to the Baltic Sea. Those who returned continued to fascinate Rome with their tales of the strange religious rituals and the fierce tribesmen to be found in the land beyond the Elbe."[31]

6

Roman Iron Age in Sweden

Commercial intercourse with the Roman world was sufficient to influence the design and motif of the tools and ornaments produced in Sweden and the other northern countries, so much so that this period (AD 1–400) is known in Scandinavia as the Roman Iron Age.

A striking example of this influence may be found in the Roman coins found in Scandinavia. Most of these are silver coins known as *denarii*. For instance, there is a coin with the head of Antonius Pius on one side, struck shortly after the emperor's death in AD 161. To gauge the distribution of these coins, it is useful to cite an entry from a Swedish book originally written in 1888 that gives an account of the location of coins found up to that time:

> Out of about 4,760 Roman coins of this time at present known from Sweden, no less than 4,000 were found in the island of Gotland, 90 in Öland, 650 in Skåne, but only 23 on the mainland of Sweden, excluding Skåne. Besides these, about 250 were found in Bornholm, and 600 in other parts of Denmark, but only 3 in Norway.[1]

The distribution of these coins argues for an active commerce in the Baltic, with less trade passing through the North Sea. Gaul, via the Vistula and Oder, was likely the primary source of Roman manufactured goods, but there is little evidence of commerce with Britain.

Besides coinage, Roman artifacts found in Sweden include bronze vessels, glass beakers, clay vessels, glass beads, iron axes and an 11-inch bronze statue of Juno dated to the late second century AD. In Västmanland a large bronze vase was found full of cremated bones. An inscription on the vessel reads, "APOLLINI GRANNO DONVM AMMILLIVS CONSTANS PRÆF TEMPLI IPSIVS VSLLM," meaning the vase was dedicated to Apollo Grannus by Ammillius Constans, temple warden. Thus a precious temple vessel was transported to Sweden to serve as a burial urn. Just what surreptitious route the bronze vessel took to get to Västmanland is hard to fathom. Tools of war, originally from the empire, have also been discovered—iron swords with Roman trademarks, coats of mail, scabbards and helmets.[2]

Much more profuse than the articles of foreign manufacture, however, are items of native origin, though even these artifacts of Scandinavian manufacture show the unmistakable influence of the Roman world. There are anvils, tongs, gold rings, bracelets, ceramic vessels, sledges of iron, hammers, axes, awls, knives, scrapers, planes and files. And a new item, unknown until this period—scissors—likewise shows up.

Weapons, though made of iron, generally follow designs found in the Bronze Age. Spear and lance heads are common. Iron arrowheads were used on wooden shafts two or three feet long, with four rows of feathers attached with pitch and thread. We know of these arrows because examples have been recovered from the peat bogs of Denmark. Iron-tipped spears of this period were sometimes as long as eleven feet.[3]

Shields were round and flat, made by joining thin, planed strips of wood; diameters

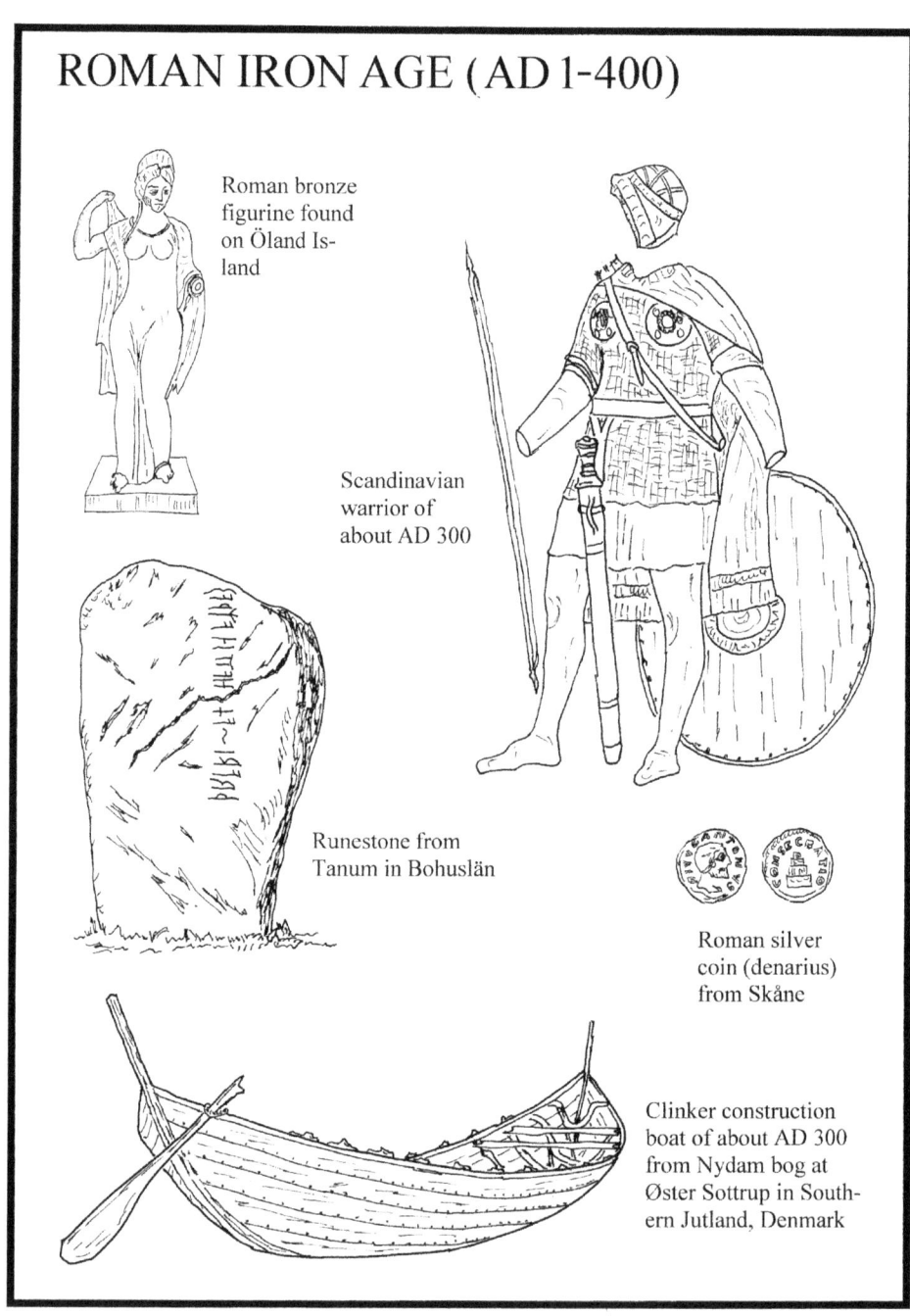

varied from two to four feet. The edges were sometimes encircled by a ring of bronze or silver. In the center was a hole for a handhold covered by a boss of iron, bronze, brass, silver or wood.

Iron swords differed from the old bronze weapons in that they were designed for cutting as well as thrusting with one or two sharp edges. They were also provided with a cross-guard to protect the hand. Hilts were made of wood or horn. Scabbards were made of wood trimmed with metal or ivory. Two new items of defense show up in this period: coats of mail and helmets.

Thanks to the peat bogs of Jutland, we have quite an accurate picture of what a Scandinavian warrior of the Roman Iron Age wore. He would have had a long jacket with sleeves reaching to the wrist. Breeches were held at the waist by a strap serving as a belt, and there were socks sewn to the breeches for the feet. All the clothes were made of wool, finely woven. The feet would also be covered by a light leather shoe or sandal. Over the jacket was a coat of mail, and thrown over the shoulders was a woolen cloak with a long fringe at the bottom edge. As to weapons, the warrior was armed with a sword carried in a scabbard attached to a belt at his waist, a bow with arrows in a wooden or leather quiver and, for defense, the large round shield and a close-fitting helmet.[4]

Transportation on land was on horseback, with pack horses in common use. Spurs, bridles and pack frames have been found, but not stirrups. These did not come into use until the late Iron Age.

As to sea travel, we have examples of boats from the peat bogs of Denmark and Västmanland. The design had changed from the Bronze Age seagoing vessels depicted in the rock art. Instead of something reminiscent of a Mediterranean ship, these boats were wide and open. They were still rowed—no sign of a mast—but were upturned at both bow and stern, a characteristic of the later Viking ships. They were made of both pine and oak. An especially well-preserved boat found in southern Jutland is 78 feet long by 10.75 feet wide at mid-ship. It was rowed by 14 pairs of oars and had a rudder fixed to one side of the boat near the stern.[5]

Longhouses continued to be the form of housing used in Sweden, and local diversity, begun in the early Iron Age, intensified. In some areas the longhouses became smaller and were assembled into villages. In other regions the longhouses were of a medium size, with outbuildings in the form of sunken-floor huts and post-constructed sheds with open sides. In general, regional differences were becoming more acute and well defined.[6]

As to agriculture, hulled barley continued to be the predominant crop, but two grains were introduced or reintroduced in this period—rye and flax. Both these plants fit well with a crop rotation system. Flax works best as a crop for newly broken land, whereas rye does well on land farmed for some time and was used as a last crop before retiring land from farming to lie fallow or else revert to pasture land.[7]

With the growth of villages (at least in some areas), cemeteries became the norm. Cremation persisted, but increasingly inhumation became more common, possibly a trait of the hierarchy. These burials were modeled after Roman interments, with bowls, dishes, wine, beakers and flagons accompanying the dead.[8] Even the cremation burials began to include tools, jewelry and weapons. This may have been a Roman influence or simply an indication of returning prosperity.

A curious finding is that in the course of many excavations carried out in Uppland, burial monuments of fire-cracked stone, stone fences and even rock carvings have been found without any sign of a body. In fact, "empty graves exist in most burial-grounds [and are] more of a rule than an exception in Scandinavian archaeological context."[9] The most prevalent theory, among several, holds that these are monuments to people who died somewhere else, though no one explanation has been generally accepted. Were these monuments to people who had immigrated across the Baltic and never returned, or were they raiders who died in a far-off land and whose remains could not be recovered? The mystery remains unsolved.

Another adaptation from the Romans, or at least from some part of the Mediterranean world, appears to be an alphabet and indigenous writing. For the first time we have written information to add to our understanding of ancient Sweden in the form of runes. These early runes are distinct from the much more common later runes of the Viking period found all over Scandinavia in great profusion. The letters of this early form of Northern European writing are as follows:

Early Runes.

The early runes were apparently designed to be used on wood—thus horizontal lines (marks that would blend with the grain of the wood) were avoided. Curved lines were also kept to minimum, as they would be hard to produce with a chisel. Though there must have been large numbers of runes made on wood, most of the inscriptions that have survived from this period are those made on stones.[10]

Rune characters first showed up around AD 150 among Germanic tribes, these being the Teutonic people with the closest contacts to the Mediterranean world. There is much debate as to what Mediterranean alphabet served as a basis for the runes. Latin, Greek and Etruscan have all been cited. Perhaps it was some combination of these.

By at least AD 300 rune usage had spread to Sweden. Inscriptions have been found on stones (some of these being burial monuments), buckles, amulets, pieces of bone, gold pendants, weapons and metal bosses of shields. The writing is used on monuments and many common items, suggesting that runes were understood by a large segment of the population, not just an elite class of scribes.

An example of an inscription is one found on a runic stone in Bohuslän, which reads, "THRAWINGAN HAITINAR WAS." This translates to "[The stone] was called Thrawinge's."[11] Not really informative, as is the case with nearly all the inscriptions. No historical person or event has been found recorded in these early runes. They do, however, verify that the language of these Swedes was Teutonic and provide some clues as to the things that were important to the people of that period.

Nor do the runes shed any light on the religion of the period. We can only surmise that Thor was, by this time, worshipped as the chief deity and the god of war. Place names from this era survive containing his name, "such as Thorsharg, Thorslunda, Thorsvi and others."[12]

The discussion in this chapter has so far applied to the peoples of central and southern Sweden, roughly from Uppland west and to the south. However, the peoples of the north (Norrland) were mostly unaffected by these changes and carried on in quite a different manner. In northern Norrland the nomadic hunters were becoming more and more dependent on the reindeer as their primary food source. They began to use "large pits filled with coal and fire-cracked stones."[13] It is thought that these "earthen ovens" were used to dry meat as a hedge against lean times, which were bound to occur when nearly total dependence for food was confined to one source. Gradually, during this period iron points and tools came to replace flint and slate implements, which would have improved hunting expectations.

Further south, in southern Norrland and Jämtland, elk remained an important source of meat. A clear distinction between the two peoples, those of Lappland and those further south, became well defined. These more southerly tribes were becoming increasingly involved in trade, which would continue to evolve into the Viking and medieval eras.[14]

In addition to archaeology, we begin to get a little more meaningful information from outside sources. In the early years of the Christian era Caesar Augustus commissioned a fleet to explore the north coast of Europe beyond the Rhine and Elbe. The ships rounded Jutland, sailing as far as the Kattegat (the sea between Jutland and the west coast of Sweden, north of Zealand), and therefore may have touched the west coast of Sweden. Augustus declares that the people of these lands—the Cimbri, Charades, Semnones and others—sent delegations of friendship to his court in Rome.[15]

Quite possibly as a result of this expedition, references to the Kattegat and the Baltic Sea began to show up in Roman literature. First in Pomponius Mela's *Description of the World*, written around AD 43, "On the other side of the Albis [Elbe], the huge Codanus Bay [Baltic Sea] is filled with big and small islands. On the Bay are the Cimbri and the Teutoni; further on, the farthest people of Germany, the Hermiones."[16] In this great bay notched in the north coast of Europe, Mela identifies a main island he calls Codanvia, which must be Zealand or the southern tip of Sweden.

During Nero's reign, in about AD 60, another Roman fleet may have penetrated the Baltic Sea itself.[17] Pliny the Elder works from Mela in terms of nomenclature, but he has additional information, very possibly from this latest expedition. He seems to have some sense that this is more than just a large bay when he describes the body of water, "which forms an immense gulf along the shore as far as the promontory of the

Cimbri. This gulf, which has the name of the 'Codanian,' is filled with islands; the most famous among which is Scandinavia, of a magnitude as yet uncertain: the only portion of it at all known is inhabited by the nation of the Hilleviones, who dwell in 500 villages."[18]

The Cimbri were already recognized as the inhabitants of Jutland, so this can be used as a reference point. This is certainly one of the earliest uses of the name "Scandinavia," and it seems likely that Pliny is indeed writing about the Scandinavian peninsula. As to the Hilleviones and their 500 villages, this may be confirmation that the people of Scania had collected themselves into many settlements by this time. It is also possible that the name Pliny uses for these people, "Hilleviones," has been preserved in the name of the province of Halland.

Late in the first century AD, Tacitus, the Roman historian and geographer (c. AD 55–117),[19] provides a little more information on the inhabitants of Sweden at that time. He writes, "Next occur the communities of the Suiones seated in the very Ocean, who besides their strength in men and arms, also possess a naval force."[20] These can be none other than the Sveár (Sviar, Svea or Swedes) of Uppland in central Sweden, already stronger and better organized than their neighbors.[21] Tacitus goes on to describe the Suiones' navy and government:

> The form of their vessels differs from ours in having a prow at each end, so that they are always ready to advance. They make no use of sails, nor have regular benches of oars at the sides; they row as is practiced in some rivers, without order, sometimes on one side, sometimes on the other, as occasion requires. These people honor wealth; for which reason they are subject to monarchical government, without any limitations or precarious conditions of allegiance.[22]

And he mentions another nation beyond the Suiones:

> The several communities of the Sitones succeed those of the Suiones; to whom they are similar in other respects, but differ in submitting to a female reign; so far have they degenerated, not only from liberty, but even from slavery.[23]

Perhaps these were the Kainulaists (Kvenir or Kvænir) of Kvenland on the western shore of the Gulf of Bothnia just north of Uppland.[24]

By the second century AD more knowledge of the north country was filtering into the empire, and this change is reflected in Ptolemy's (c. AD 100–178)[25] *Geography*. In describing areas outside the Roman domain (in this case, Northern Europe), he gives us an indication that a more accurate picture of Scandinavia was beginning to come into focus.

> §33–34. It is properly called Scandia itself; and its western region is inhabited by the Chaedini, its eastern region by the Favonae and the Firaesi, its northern region by the Finni, its southern region by the Gutae (Gautae) and the Dauciones and its central region by the Levoni.[26]

Ptolemy has almost certainly registered here what was known of the Scandinavian peninsula. His description suggests that there were many different nations or peoples. The only recognizable names are "Gautae" (quite possibly the Gautar [Gauts] of Västergötland and Östergötland, beginning to organize politically) and the "Finni" (a possible reference to the Finns to the east of the Gulf of Bothnia). The other names might represent any number of tribes or incipient states that would eventually coalesce into the small kingdoms of Viking Age Sweden.

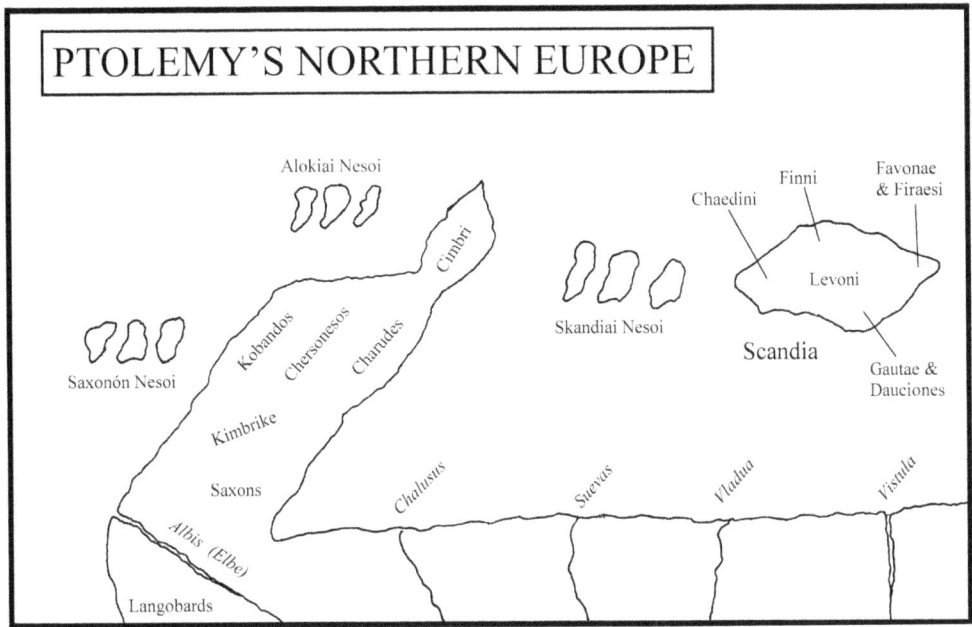

With Ptolemy's sketchy contribution to our knowledge of Scandinavia, there is an end to Roman literature describing the far northern part of Europe and its inhabitants. The empire seems to have been preoccupied by its own internal problems and threats from without, which would eventually bring down the great unifier of the western world.

7

Visigoths Defeat the Roman Empire

Theodoric, son of Thiudimir, known to history as Theodoric the Great, stood poised on the Italian frontier with his army ready to invade this rich and fabled land. Before him lay that fertile boot-shaped peninsula with its idyllic climate, protected from Arctic blasts by the Alps to the north and stretching south into the warm waters of the Mediterranean Sea. It had nurtured civilizations since the dawn of history—the Greek colonies in the south, the native Etruscans in the north and finally Rome, a city that had grown in power, eventually dominating the ancient western world.

Rome built an empire whose borders had once encompassed Central and Southern Europe, as well as North Africa and the Middle East to the Parthian frontier. The city was still a magnet drawing the "barbarian hordes" to its gates, though its days of supremacy and glory were long over. The city that became an empire had reached its zenith under the Caesars in the first two centuries of the Christian era; then it began its ponderous decline.

A state the size and complexity of the Roman Empire had a certain momentum and would not succumb overnight. But a series of incompetent emperors, usually placed in power by the army, and an inability to adapt militarily, socially and administratively to the changing times had decided its fate. The internal decay of the empire allowed the invasion of numerous Germanic tribes once held at bay along the empire's northeastern frontier by a powerful army. Overwhelmed, the latter-day emperors were reduced to hiring these same barbarians as confederates (*foederati*) to fight new invaders.[1] Finally, increasing the pressure, an Asian people, the Huns, began pressing in from the east, subjugating some Germanic tribes and driving others before them. The Huns built a Eurasian empire under their greatest leader, Attila (c. AD 404–453), though their dominance would quickly disintegrate upon his death, allowing several Germanic tribes to reassert their independence.[2]

As early as AD 285, Emperor Diocletian divided the administration of the empire between two capitals, Rome and Byzantium (later renamed Constantinople). In AD 395 the Roman Empire permanently split into the western (Latin-speaking) and eastern (Greek-speaking) empires.[3] Rome itself continued to decline in importance. The emperor of the Western Empire moved to Milan for safety, a city that had overtaken Rome as the Italian commercial center. As the barbarian encroachments increased, he relocated to Ravenna, which was more defensible and had access to the sea (the Adriatic).[4] Still,

Rome was the glittering prize sought by the nomadic Germanic hordes. It was the capital of Latin Christendom and home to the bishop of Rome, head of the western Christian Church.

In AD 410 Alaric and his Visigoths marched into Italy and captured Rome, after which they moved on, building a kingdom in Gaul and then Spain. In 455 the Vandals, another Germanic nation, sacked Rome, attacking via the sea from their base in North Africa, where they had taken Carthage, the culmination of a long migration from the Germanic region through Gaul and Spain.[5]

The sun was setting on the Western Roman Empire. Valentinian III, the last of the emperors of any importance, was murdered in 455.[6] He was followed by nine emperors in twenty years, the last being a youth named Romulus Augustus (or Augustulus), who is worthy of note only because he was the last ruler of the Western Empire.[7] Thus, the nation that was founded by the legendary Romulus and became an empire under Augustus ended under the namesake of both.

The final demise of the empire was brought about by a German who had at one time served the emperor. Odovacar (or Odoacer) was by birth a Scirian (another Germanic tribe that had been settled within the Roman Empire). This tribe had fought with Attila and then, after Attila's death, had been defeated and dispersed by the Ostrogoths.[8] Odovacar, whose father, Edecon, had been the leader of the Sciri, was left without a following. He wandered among the barbarians of Roman Noricum, eventually entering the service of the western emperor. He quickly rose in rank among the Italian garrison troops and eventually led a rebellion of these same soldiers against the empire. Inspired by the hope of better conditions and rewards, *foederati* from all parts of Italy flocked to the standard of this popular leader.[9]

Able to offer only limited resistance, the Roman government capitulated in AD 476.[10] Augustulus was exiled. The Roman Senate officially transferred the "seat of universal empire" from Rome to Constantinople, along with the "imperial ensigns" and "sacred armaments of the throne and palace."[11] The Roman Empire, which had had its beginnings over a thousand years earlier, ceased to exist except for the short-lived (457–461) rump kingdom of Soisson in Gaul. The glory of the great Roman Empire passed to the durable stepchild headquartered at Constantinople.

Odovacar wasted little time in consolidating his holdings. He was able to get Zeno, the eastern emperor, to confer on him the title of *patricius* and supreme commander in Italy, giving him legitimacy. He also made peace with the Visigoth king, Euric, conceding to him the alpine border. Odovacar then marched on the Rugian kingdom in Noricum, which was threatening to attack Italy, incited by the last of the Roman dissidents. He destroyed the kingdom and scattered the Rugian population, executing its king and queen. In Sicily, Odovacar arrived at a compromise with the Vandal king, thus securing his southern flank.[12]

Odovacar brought peace and a certain amount of security to Italy—even a triumph over a barbarian horde. This was the Italy that Theodoric and his Ostrogoths anticipated as they approached the Isonzo River, a land of plenty that might be theirs if they could but wrest it from its new Germanic overlord. For the Ostrogoths, this opportunity had been a long time coming.

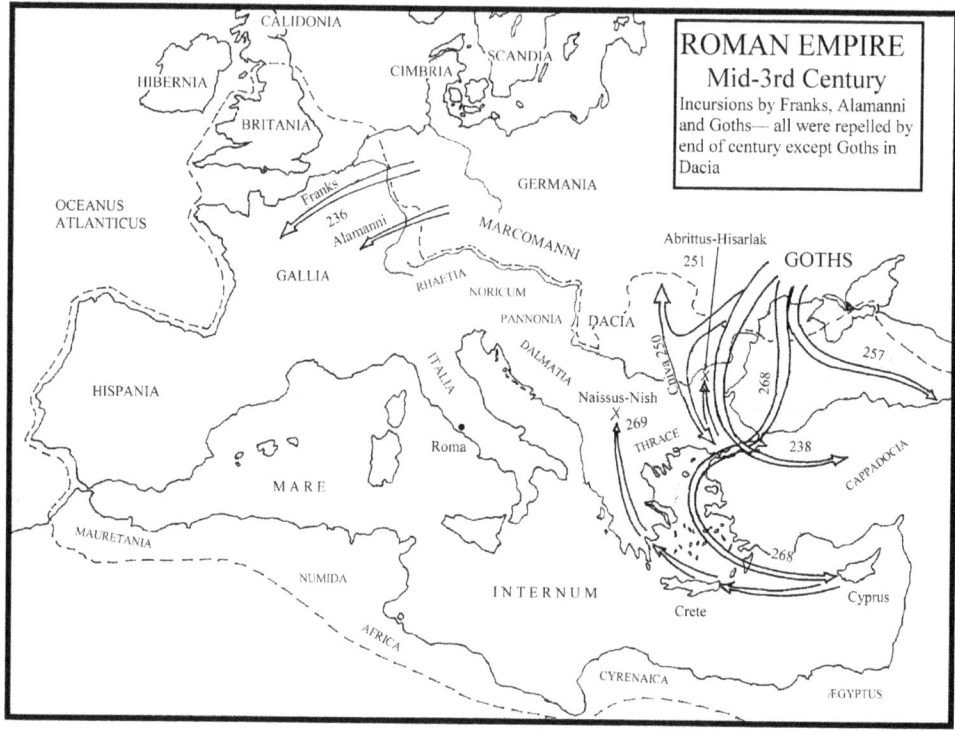

The Goths had become a factor in the Roman Empire's calculations as early as AD 238, when they launched a series of raids that ravaged the Balkan Peninsula and Asia Minor.[13] By this time the Gothic nation had established itself as the dominant force in an area bordering and to the north of the Black Sea in what is today Ukraine.[14]

The energies of the Goths and several other tribes of Germanic and Sarmatian origin were united under a great Gothic king, Cniva. In 250 this legendary monarch began a large-scale attack on the Roman provinces of Dacia, Moesia and Thrace.[15]

In response, the Roman emperor Decius led the Army of the Danube in a campaign to punish the Gothic invaders. Decius, along with his son, gained some victories over several roving Gothic bands, but he needed to bring the barbarians to heel in a great battle that would break their military might. In June 251 the two armies met in a decisive battle at Abrittus-Hisarlak near Razgard in today's Bulgaria.[16]

Cniva drew the Romans into a treacherous swampy area with which he was completely familiar. He then split his army into several tactical units, which he used to surround the Romans. The Army of the Danube was routed; the emperor and his son lay dead on the battlefield.

Failing to control the Goths militarily, the Romans tried bribery, agreeing to make an annual payment to the barbarians. This tactic also failed, as the Goths accepted the payoff but then attacked the empire by sea, ravaging the southern coast of the Black Sea in 257.[17] In truth, individual raids by tribes and bands of Goths were probably impossible to prevent, as no one king had anything like control over the Gothic nation except in times of war. In 268, the Goths sailed into the Aegean Sea with a large fleet bent on raiding and plundering.

The new emperor, Claudius II, reacted sending a force to intercept this new threat. The Romans won a great victory at Naissus-Nish, destroying the Gothic war party. The next emperor, Aurelian, crossed the Danube and defeated the Goths in their own territory in several battles. He then allowed the Goths to occupy part of Dacia, the only Roman province north of the Danube River.[18] This carrot-and-stick approach worked, and the Gothic problem seemed to be solved as far as the Romans were concerned.

For a century relations between the Goths and the Romans appeared to be relatively peaceful. In reality, the Goths were busy expanding their influence westward, taking territory and subjugating other tribes. They moved into Moldavia and occupied more of the formally Roman Dacia.[19] It was probably during this period that the Goths also consolidated their hold on Crimea.

During this time the Goths converted to Christianity. One Ulfilas, "Bishop of the Christians in the Getic lands,"[20] translated the Bible into the Gothic language, inventing his own alphabet incorporating elements of the Latin and runic characters imposed on a Greek base. The form of Christianity professed by Ulfilas and adopted by the Goths was Arian. In contrast to the Nicene Creed, the Arians believed Christ to be "not of identical essence (*homoousia*), but only of similar essence (*homoiousia*) to God the Father."[21] Ulfilas passed on his view that the three members of the Godhead were separate and individual—God the Father, Christ, and the Holy Spirit, the faithful servant of Christ. The Arian form of Christianity was adopted by many other Germanic nations as well, including the Vandals, Burgundians and Lombards.

It was also during this period that the Goths were divided into the Western Goths (Visigoths) and the Eastern Goths (Ostrogoths). The Gothic kings had always claimed kinship to the royal family of Amal, which was recognized as the monarchal lineage dating back to the origins of the Gothic people. As bands of Goths migrated westward into Moesia and Dacia, they ceased to acknowledge this Amal authority, developing monarchs of another lineage—the Balthic. Geographically, the dividing line between the Visigoths and the Ostrogoths was the upper Dniester and lower Prut rivers.[22] This split was reinforced by their trade relations with the empire. The Visigoths built a flourishing commerce with the Roman world to the west, while the Ostrogoths passed into obscurity as far as the Romans were concerned.

As has been noted, this was not necessarily a peaceful time for either the Visigoths or the Ostrogoths. Both were busy defending their territories and trying to extend their influence over neighboring tribes, such as the Vandals, Gepids, Sarmatians, and others. And there was the occasional spat with the Romans as well. However, the semi-placid situation was suddenly disrupted and thrown into turmoil by the entrance of an entirely new invader—the Huns.

The Huns were an Asiatic, nomadic people migrating west toward the European-Asian frontier, where they came into contact with the Alans. Most of the Alan nation was quickly subjugated, with a few bands escaping into Gothic territory. In AD 375 the Huns crossed the Don River and began attacking the Ostrogoths.[23] There followed a series of defeats of the Amal-led Goths, and they were forced to submit to the eastern invaders. However, a confederation of Ostrogoths, Alans and renegade Huns escaped the Hunnish onslaught and retreated into Roman territory. Within a few months the main body of Visigoths, marching under a military chief, Fritigern, crossed the Danube into Roman Moesia and upper Thracia, overrunning the Roman garrison stationed there.

The eastern Roman emperor, Valens, responded by leading his entire army from Asia Minor into Thrace; he then asked Gratian, the western Roman emperor, to join him with his army. Valens bivouacked at Adrianople to assemble his legions and await Gratian's arrival. However, discovering the close proximity of Fritigern and his Goths, Valens could not resist the temptation to attack what he thought was a relatively small force and hopefully annihilate the invading barbarians.

On August 9, 378, Valens left Adrianople, advancing on the Visigoth camp.[24] As was their custom, the Goths had entrenched themselves using their wagons as barricades. Then Valens received two surprises. First, the Gothic army was much larger than had been reported. Instead of ten thousand Visigoths, Valens was facing an army several times that size. Fritigern had with him not just his own Visigoths but also a confederation of Ostrogoths, Alans and disaffected Huns.

Second, the Goths and their allies employed a new tactic. They attacked with massed cavalry in what was called a "blitz attack." Using this strategy, Fritigern's army drove off the Roman cavalry, then surrounded the Roman infantry and cut it to pieces. Valens, his generals and most of his field officers, along with two thirds of his army, were slain on the spot. Following the crushing Roman defeat, the empire was forced to treat with the barbarians. The Ostrogoth–Alan–Hun confederation was given Dacia and northern Thracia to settle in as *foederati*.

As confederates, the Visigoths would be allotted land to settle on within the empire's boundaries, but they would be allowed to remain semi-autonomous—that is, have their own tribal leadership. The Visigoths, already in Dacia, were allowed territory on both sides of the Danube. They would receive an annual payment but would be expected to supply troops when called upon by the emperor. These troops would operate under a Gothic command that would be subordinate to Roman generals.[25] Thus, the Ostrogoth–Alan–Hun confederacy and the Visigoths became nominal subjects of the Roman Empire.

Now a new leader arose among the western Goths. This was Alaric, generally known to history as Alaric I. He was able to gain the leadership of the Moesian-Gothic confederates and some bands of Goths that had crossed from the north side of the Danube. With this force Alaric crossed the Balkan Mountains in AD 391 and invaded the interior of Thrace.[26] A year later the Romans managed to surround the invaders and defeat them at the Maritsa River. In 394, Alaric and his Goths were marching with the army of the Eastern Roman Empire in a holy war against the Western Empire, which was considered rife with pagan and Arian administrators. About the same time, the eastern Roman emperor elevated Alaric to outright king of the Visigoths, a kingdom within the Roman Empire.

At the Battle of Frigidus in September AD 394, the western army was vanquished, but at a fearful loss of life on the part of the Visigoths under Alaric. The eastern army generals had used the Goths as a vanguard and as shock troops.

During Alaric's absence from his kingdom, bands of Huns had crossed the Danube and raided the Visigoth settlements. Upon his return, Alaric gathered his people and once again invaded Thrace, threatening Constantinople and demanding a better area

7. Visigoths Defeat the Roman Empire

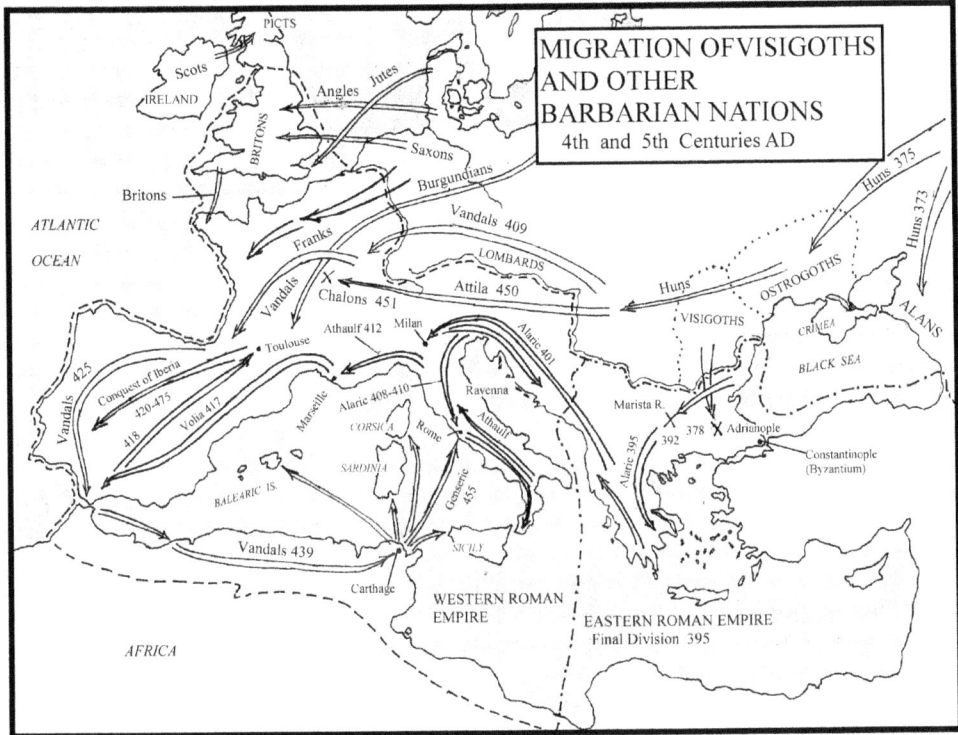

to colonize. The Visigoths were promised a sanctuary in Illyria, but due to squabbling between the eastern and western emperors, the deal was not consummated.

Once again frustrated, Alaric took his Visigoths on a march into Greece, first invading Boeotia, where they were paid off by the Athenians. Alaric then moved on to Peloponnesus, ravaging the countryside. After several battles with the western Roman field army, which had come to rescue the eastern emperor, the Visigoths moved on to Epirus, where they spread more devastation. The eastern emperor finally granted Alaric and his Visigoths settlement in Macedonia as confederates of the empire.

In AD 401, while the western emperor's attention was diverted by a new incursion of Vandals and Alans from Pannonia, Alaric led his Visigoths from Macedonia into Italy, laying siege to the imperial capital of Milan.[27] The western emperor acted decisively, sending an army from the south to break the siege and bringing in troops from the Rhine and Britannia to trap the Goths.

Alaric lifted the siege and met the Romans in a battle that resulted in a draw. Many women and children were captured by the Romans, but Alaric's powerful cavalry escaped intact. In a second battle near Verona, the Goths were decisively defeated and left Italy.

The Gothic invasion of Italy shocked the Romans into transferring the western imperial capital from Milan to the more defensible Ravenna. After leaving Italy, Alaric proceeded to ravage eastern Illyria until the eastern emperor granted him *foederati* status and permission to settle in Illyria.

Now more and more pressure was mounting along the Rhine by Germanic tribes trying to escape the Hunnish invasion until, in AD 407, the Roman defenses collapsed and a horde of Germanic tribes flooded the Western Roman Empire. Alans, Vandals and Suevi poured into Gaul, penetrating all the way to Italy. Alaric took this opportunity to once again march into Italy. He picked up reinforcements from among other Germanic invaders and was joined by slaves he freed along the way.

Twice, in 408 and 409, Alaric stood at the walls of Rome demanding concessions— a homeland, *foederati* status for his people and an annual payment. But the Western Roman Empire was now almost entirely impotent, trying to survive by playing the various Germanic and Hunnish tribes against each other, offering bribes of offices and territories.

Finally, in August AD 410, Alaric marched on Rome once more, and this time he attacked. The eternal city was taken and sacked. For three days the Visigoths pillaged, raped and plundered. It was a living nightmare for the citizens of this once greatest of all European cities.[28]

Leaving Rome, Alaric marched south, taking and plundering city after city until the Strait of Messina was reached. An attempt to cross over to Sicily failed, and the Visigothic army began a retreat northward. It was at this juncture that Alaric I, king of the Visigoths, the Arian Christian and conqueror of Rome, died.

Following the death of Alaric in 410, the Visigoths chose Athaulf as their new leader. Under Athaulf the Goths spread additional devastation along the Italian peninsula as they marched north, finally leaving Italy in 412. For the next two years the Visigoths ravaged southern Gaul, including the ancient Greek colony of Massilia (Marseille). The interplay between the "barbarians" and the Romans was manifested at this time by the marriage of Athaulf to Galla Placidia, the sister of the western Roman emperor, Honorius. There is a story that Placidia was captured by Athaulf during the plundering of Rome, which may or may not be true. In any case, the marriage took place in a Roman nobleman's home with Athaulf wearing a high-ranking Roman military uniform.[29] Unfortunately for Athaulf, he would die within a year, murdered by an unknown assassin.

The new king of the Visigoths was Valia, who made a treaty with the Romans. In return for grain to feed his people, Valia agreed to make war on the Vandals and Alans who had invaded and conquered most of Spain, much to the consternation of the Romanized Iberian population. After some successes, Ravenna called the Visigoths back to southern Gaul, where they were allowed to settle, and here Valia founded the Visigothic kingdom of Toulouse.[30] Finally the Visigoths seemed to have found a homeland.

The Visigoths were, by this time, the most Romanized nation of the Germanic barbarians then invading what was left of the once great empire. They answered to Ravenna and had become the only dependable army at the western Roman emperor's disposal.[31]

From their capital, Toulouse, in southern Gaul, the Visigoths expanded their domain across the Pyrenees into Spain. They responded to calls for assistance from Ravenna, but they were also often instrumental in determining successors to the imperial throne.

After subduing the Bretons, Alans and Bagaudae in Gaul, as well as the Bagaudae and Suebi in Spain, the Visigoths turned on the Roman provincials in those same areas. By AD 475 Iberia and southern Gaul were firmly under Visigoth control, and any pretense of accountability to Ravenna (the Roman capital) for stewardship of this territory was dropped. Likewise, the Franks had taken control of northern Gaul, discarding the pretention that they were serving the interests of Ravenna. The next year, 476, the last western Roman emperor was toppled. The Roman Empire in the west ceased to exist, replaced by Odovacar and his Italian kingdom.

8

The Ostrogoths Build an Empire

With the Visigoths established in southern Gaul and Iberia, let us return to the Ostrogoths, that eastern division of the Gothic nation north of the Black Sea, which was beginning, in AD 375, a defensive stand to repel a new invader from the east—the Huns. The Goths were unable to withstand the Hunnish blitz. While the Visigoths escaped to the west into Roman territory, the Amal-led Ostrogoths were defeated and subjugated by the Huns.

Though allowed to retain their own leadership, the Ostrogoths chafed under Hun domination. In 386 thousands of Ostrogoths attempted an escape, building rafts to cross the Danube into Roman territory. They were attacked by the Roman army in mid-stream and annihilated. The Ostrogoths would have to make the best of it under their Hunnish masters.[1]

In 444–445 a new chieftain arose among the Huns. This was Attila, who gained sole dominion by murdering his brother and then going on to subdue most of the Hunnish tribes, along with the Germanic tribes in the Hunnish realm, including the Gepids and Ostrogoths.[2] The empire of Attila would come to include Eastern Europe, except for the Balkans, and the western part of Asia north of the Black Sea, an expanse stretching from the Rhine into Central Asia.[3] For a decade he harassed the Western and Eastern Roman Empires, marching, at one point, to the very walls of Constantinople, which he spared after receiving an enormous ransom.

At the same time there arose among the Ostrogoths a leadership comprising three brothers of Amal descent: Valamir, Thiudimir and Vidimir. The brothers were able to not only establish rule over the Ostrogoths but also ingratiate themselves with Attila.

In 451 Attila turned his attention to Western Europe, having consolidated his rule over Eastern Europe and Western Asia. He amassed a huge army made up of warriors from Eastern European tribes. This included his own Huns, the Ostrogoths (under the three brothers), Gepids (under their king Ardaric), Rugians, Sciri, Heruli, Danubian Suebi and Sarmatians.[4] Attila crossed the Rhine and rolled into Gaul, taking city after city. Finally, he was met by an army from the Western Roman Empire. Besides Roman legionnaires, this army included so-called barbarians from Western Europe. There were Franks, Alans, Britons, Sarmatians, Burgundians, Saxons and Visigoths under their king, Theoderid.[5] In fact, Theoderid commanded the Roman right wing and his oldest son, Thorismund, commanded the left.

The battle was joined on the Catalaunian Fields with a sharp encounter between

Gepids and Franks in the evening before the main event. The next day, the two armies collided in an all-out engagement. The battle was technically a draw, though Attila was getting the worst of it when King Theoderid was killed, supposedly by an Amal Ostrogoth. Theoderid's son Thorismund broke off the battle at that point, or Attila might have suffered a monumental defeat. In any case, Attila's attempted conquest of Gaul was turned back. His army returned to their eastern steppes, defeated for all practical purposes.

But Attila's empire needed victories to survive, so the next year he invaded Italy. The Huns took Aquileia, Pavia and Milan, but then they were struck by a plague. Attila was forced to retreat once more. A year later he was dead, the victim of a massive hemorrhage—literally drowning in his own blood.[6]

At his death, Attila's empire fragmented into tribal territories, most of which were headed by his sons. The Huns tried to perpetuate their dominance over the non–Hunnish nations, but revolution was everywhere. A series of engagements culminated in the Battle of Nedao, in which the Hunnish forces were vanquished. Even the remnants of the once great empire of Attila were now destroyed. The Gepids took advantage of the situation to organize a kingdom in the very heartland of Attila's former realm on the north side of the Danube.

The Ostrogoths took this opportunity to escape Hunnish subjugation, migrating en masse westward into Roman territory, where they petitioned Constantinople for a homeland. The eastern Roman emperor permitted the Goths to settle in Pannonia in three districts, each headed by one of the Amal brothers, with Valamir recognized as the overall king. By the terms of the treaty, the Ostrogoths would receive a yearly payment in return for policing this territory as Roman confederates. The western-most subkingdom was ruled by Thiudimir, who had "married" Ereleuva, a Roman Catholic Christian. The marriage seems not to have been fully valid, as Thiudimir was, as most Ostrogoths were, an Arian Christian.[7] Nevertheless, the union produced a son who would rise to international prominence. This was Theodoric the Great.

In AD 457 the eastern emperor, Leo I, cut off the yearly payments to the Ostrogoths, whereupon Valamir led an army south into Epirus. The imperial government resumed payments as part of a new treaty, but it also received a hostage as a guarantee of Ostrogothic compliance. The hostage was Theodoric, son of Thiudimir, who would spend his childhood and youth up to the age of eighteen in the eastern Roman imperial capital of Constantinople.

In spite of Theodoric's hostage situation, there continued to be tension between the Ostrogoths and Eastern Romans. The new western emperor, Anthemius, considered the Goths the empire's number one enemy and believed they had to be eliminated. The Valamir Goths, for their part, raided Roman Noricum, threatening the capital of Teurnia. The Ostrogoths were also busy defending their own territory in Pannonia against Hunnish raiders from the east and other Germanic tribes. In a battle with one of the latter, the Sciri, Valamir was killed. Thiudimir succeeded his brother as overall king of the Pannonian Ostrogoths.

In 469 Anthemius launched a major campaign against the Visigoths and another aimed at eliminating the Pannonian Ostrogoths. The Visigoths were to be attacked by the combined forces of the Franks from northern Gaul and the Suevi and Romans from

Spain. To deal with the Ostrogoths, Anthemius assembled an army of Suevi, Sciri, Sarmatians, Gepids and Rugians. The eastern emperor, Leo, was to attack the rear with a regular Roman army from Constantinople.

The Visigoths under Euric preempted the attack in the west by opening a war in Iberia before Anthemius could assemble his proposed multi-national army. As a result, the Visigoths extended their holdings in Iberia, creating what would become their Spanish kingdom.

The Ostrogoths met Anthemius' army probably on the Pannonian border and defeated the Romans and their allies. Upon hearing of the Ostrogoth victory, Leo I recalled his army and sent Theodoric home laden with rich presents.[8] It was also this battle that broke the Sciri as a tribal force, leaving Odovacar without a royal inheritance. As previously detailed, after some wandering he would become a Roman soldier in Italy, eventually rising to the kingship of the peninsula and extinguishing the last embers of the Western Roman Empire.

Once at home with the Pannonian Ostrogoths, Theodoric assumed the kingship of the deceased Valamir's subkingdom. He almost immediately opened a war with the Sarmatians of Singidunum and defeated them. Two years later, in 473, the Ostrogoths abandoned Pannonia, moving deeper into Roman territory. Vidimir took his third of this kingdom on a campaign into Italy, where the Romans promptly defeated him, exiling the remnants of his tribe to the territory of the Toulouse Visigoths.

Thiudimir and his son Theodoric, however, migrated east into upper Moesia, probably with the full approval of Leo I. At the time Leo was being threatened by another

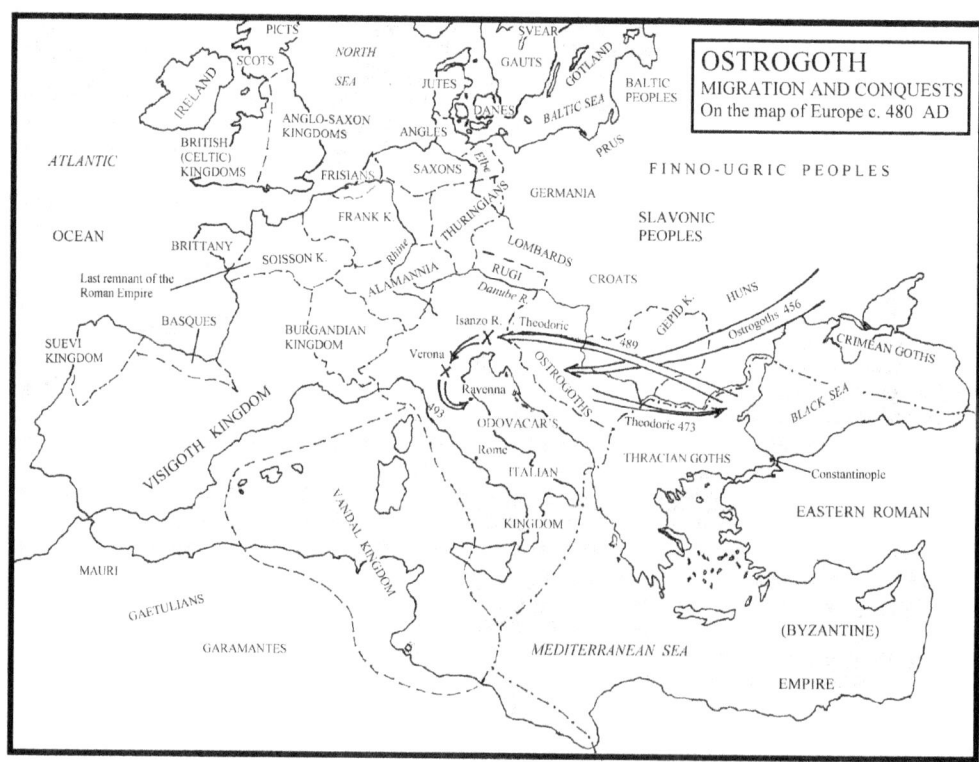

group of Goths, the Thracian Goths, who had coalesced under a new leader, Theodoric Strabo ("The Squinter"), threatening Thiudimir's position.

The year 474 saw the deaths of both Thiudimir, king of the Ostrogoths, and Leo I, eastern Roman emperor. Leo was succeeded by Zeno, who began a campaign to eliminate "The Squinter" and his Thracian Goths. Theodoric was raised to the kingship of the Ostrogoths and initiated a move of his people to lower Moesia. Zeno and Theodoric formed an alliance against "The Squinter," but the promised imperial forces to support a war on the Thracian Goths never materialized.

Theodoric then switched sides, forming an alliance with "The Squinter" in order to force concessions from the emperor. Such an alliance between competing Gothic monarchs could not last long, and a Gothic civil war was prevented only by the death of "The Squinter" in 481. Theodoric, son of Thiudimir, now became king of a united Thracian and Pannonian-Moesian Ostrogothic nation.

With his newfound might Theodoric attacked Constantinople directly, blockading the city, occupying portions of the suburbs and cutting off the water supply. Zeno responded with the usual buy-off and promises of annual payments. The assault having worked, Theodoric pulled back. But the incursion had exposed the weakness of Zeno's empire, which encouraged others to interfere.

Odovacar, having disposed of the last western emperor and replaced the decayed remnants of Roman Italy with his own kingdom, was busy meddling in Constantinople's politics on the side of an anti–Zeno faction. Zeno answered by calling upon one of his confederates, Feletheus-Feva, king of the Rugians in Noricum, to invade Italy and punish the upstart king.

But Odovacar was quicker, marching to the Danube with his Italian army, which included the last of the Roman legions. He destroyed the Rugian kingdom, capturing and executing King Feletheus and his Gothic wife, Giso. Their son, Frideric, escaped to lead the fragmented elements of the Rugian nation to the camp of Theodoric, who was already concluding a treaty with Emperor Zeno authorizing an invasion of Italy.

So Theodoric, son of Thiudimir, packed up his Ostrogoths one more time and began the march from the Balkans toward Italy. He was joined by Frideric's Rugians, a portion of the Thracian Goths and even some Romans, a total of about twenty thousand warriors followed by eighty thousand women and children in wagons with all their belongings.[9]

Theodoric had to force his way through Gepid territory, provoking a bloody battle that the Gepids lost. He also had to repel an attack by nomadic Sarmatians, but he finally reached the Isonzo River, where he found Odovacar and his entrenched army. Theodoric, son of Thiudimir, drew up his Ostrogoths and auxiliaries poised at the Italian frontier for a war that had been a long time coming. On August 28, 489, Theodoric attacked and drove the Italians from their defenses. Then he crossed the Isonzo and entered the fabled boot-shaped peninsula.[10]

Theodoric marched on, meeting the Italian king in a second battle near Verona, where the Ostrogoths were again victorious. Twice beaten, Odovacar retreated behind the defenses of Ravenna. Theodoric, meanwhile, was welcomed by much of Italy as the liberating representative of the eastern emperor. Even Tufa, Odovacar's supreme commander, submitted to Theodoric, bringing with him major elements of the defeated Italian army.

Believing he was now in control and that victory was within his grasp, Theodoric placed Tufa in command of his best troops and sent him to take Ravenna. However, once the Italian general had put some distance between himself and the invader, he switched sides again and engineered the destruction of the Gothic army assigned to him.

Theodoric's lapse in judgment cost him a swift conquest of Italy, for now he was put on the defensive, with Odovacar advancing from Ravenna to take the open field. The war in Italy turned into a free-for-all, with Burgundians seizing the opportunity to invade northwestern Italy and the Vandals landing in Sicily, attempting a takeover of the island. Both groups were beaten back, and Theodoric finally regained the initiative with the help of Alaric II, who sent a Visigoth army into Italy in a rare show of Gothic solidarity.

Odovacar was forced back into Ravenna, which had almost impregnable defenses and could be supplied by sea. By August 492, the Goths had rounded up enough ships to deploy an effective blockade. Six months later, the bishop of Ravenna brokered a treaty by which Theodoric and Odovacar would jointly rule Italy from Ravenna. In March 493, Theodoric entered Ravenna to claim his half of the throne.[11] Ten days later, Odovacar was dead, murdered by the hand of Theodoric himself, which made the Gothic king the uncontested monarch of Italy.

In 507, Alaric II, ruler of the Toulouse Visigoth kingdom, died in a battle with the Franks. Theodoric asserted his claim to the Visigoth throne as regent for the infant Visigoth king, son of Alaric II and Theodoric's daughter. After an inter–Gothic war, Theodoric secured the Visigoth crown in AD 511.[12] Theodoric the Great ruled an area stretching from the southern tip of Spain into Rhaetia, Noricum, Pannonia and Illyricum, including Italy and all Sicily (except for the very western tip, which was ceded to the Vandals).

Theodoric kept the peace in Italy by honoring the Roman nobility, allowing them to retain their Roman law and justice system, while ruling his Goths under traditional Gothic customs. He respected the Roman Catholic Church but let his Goths retain their Arian Christian religion.

At Theodoric's behest, Cassiodorus Senator (Senator was his surname, not a title) wrote a multi-volume history of the Goths. Cassiodorus was of noble Roman descent; his father was governor of southern Italy, and Theodoric had appointed Cassiodorus as one of his advisors. Unfortunately, this lengthy and detailed work has been lost to us, surviving only in a summary version written by a bureaucrat named Jordanes in AD 551 while in Constantinople. Besides being the only existing classical work providing a detailed account of early Gothic history, Cassiodorus' work clearly specifies the Amali as being the legitimate royal house of the Goths, a circumstance quite useful to Theodoric, who was trying to consolidate his hold on both the Ostrogoths and the Visigoths. Through diplomacy, a series of marriages of female family members to foreign nobility, and force of arms, Theodoric maintained his hold over the Ostrogoths and the Romans of Italy, as well as the Visigoths.

Upon his death in AD 526, Theodoric the Great was succeeded by his two grandsons. Amalaric, for whom Theodoric had served as regent, assumed his rightful position as king of the Visigoths.[13] As for the Ostrogoths, Theodoric had arranged for the succession of another grandson, Athalaric. However, Athalaric was only ten years old at the time of his grandfather's death, so his mother, Amalasuintha, served as regent, ruling the Ostrogothic kingdom on her son's behalf. Like her father, she successfully balanced the two parties, Romans and Goths, politically in order to remain in power. Even at the death of her son, Athalaric, she was able to take the crown as queen of the Ostrogoths.

Eventually, Amalasuintha was challenged by a cousin, and therefore an Amal, who was a leader of the Gothic hardliners, the anti–Roman, anti–Constantinople party. Backed by this powerful faction of Goths, Theodahad was made co-ruler in 534.[14] Within weeks Theodahad had Amalasuintha removed from Ravenna and exiled to an island in Lake Bolsena, where she was murdered a few months later.

Theodahad's politics and method of ascension to the throne provided Justinian, the eastern emperor, with the necessary motivation and pretext to attack the Ostrogoths. He sent his brilliant general, Belisarius, who had just conquered the Vandals in North Africa, into the Ostrogoth realm. Belisarius' first task was the subjugation of Sicily. This he managed quickly with only a small elite force. Defeating the Palermo garrison, the only major resistance, Belisarius marched triumphantly into Syracuse before the end of 535.[15] Belisarius then crossed over to Italy and moved north, taking Naples after a stiff fight.

Because of Theodahad's lack of response to the invading army, and his making no attempt to save Naples in particular, the Gothic army revolted. Theodahad was deposed and a general, Vitigis, was made king, though he had no affiliation with the Amal clan. The new "king of the army" left Ravenna with his troops and met Belisarius, now installed in Rome. The Ostrogoths laid siege to the great city for a year, but they could not take it. The Romans landed reinforcements in Italy, drove to the city, and broke the siege in aid of Belisarius.

Belisarius turned loose the imperial cavalry to ravage the Italian countryside. Additional Byzantine armies were landed at Genoa and in Picenum. By 539, Belisarius was at the gates of Ravenna, and in 540 he marched into the city, taking Vitigis captive.[16]

The war would rage for another fifteen years before the Ostrogoths were completely conquered, years in which the Italian peninsula was devastated by roving armies and marauding cavalry units. The Goths found a skilled leader and tactician in a new king, Totila, who, at one time, controlled nearly the entire Italian peninsula. But Justinian was relentless, sending generals and armies until the Goths were worn down. Finally, Totila was killed in battle, and his successor, Teja, likewise was killed just three months later. Scattered resistance lasted another three years, but by AD 555 the war was over and the Ostrogothic kingdom completely destroyed.[17]

The Visigothic kingdom would last a while longer, eventually terminated not by the Eastern Roman Empire but by an emerging power—Muslim Arabs. As we've seen, Theodoric the Great had taken control of the Visigothic kingdom as regent for his grandson Amalaric after defeating Alaric II's bastard son, Gesalec, in an inter–Gothic war. By this time, the kingdom of Toulouse had already lost Gualish Aquitaine to the Franks, who were pressing in from the north along with their sometime allies, the Burgundians. Aquitaine was forfeit, but Theodoric did hang on to Narbonensis (Mediterranean coastal Gaul), and the Visigoths had their territory across the Pyrenees, which included most of Iberia.

Upon Theodoric's demise, his grandson was installed as king of the Visigoths. Amalaric married the daughter of Clovis, king of the Franks, which should have ensured peace between the two nations. However, not even a marriage at the highest levels could prevent war between these two aggressive kingdoms. In a battle near Narbonne in AD 531, Childebert I, king of the Franks, defeated Amalaric, who fled to Barcelona and was there murdered.[18]

After Amalaric's three-year reign, the Visigoths turned to electing their kings. A series of these monarchs tried to deal with the many Visigoth enemies, but with only limited success. There were wars with tribes within Iberia itself, with the Suevi in the northwest, and with the Cantabrians and the Basques in the north (among others). At the same time, the Franks and Burgundians were crowding in from the north and the Byzantine Empire (the old Eastern Roman Empire) had carved out a province along the southern Spanish coast. The Visigothic kingdom was in decline and appeared to be on its way to extinction.

But just at this crucial moment, in AD 568, the Visigoths made an inspired selection for king: Liuva I. He was crowned in Narbonne, the old Visigoth homeland. Liuva had at least one particular gift—he recognized the talents of his younger brother, Leovigild. Liuva elevated his sibling to co-ruler and placed him in charge of their Spanish holdings. Four years later Leovigild became the sole ruler of the Visigoths.

In a series of campaigns in Iberia, Leovigild subdued multiple rebellions, including one waged by his own son in southern Spain. He waged war on the other kingdoms in the peninsula, the Suevi of Galatia, the Basques, the Cantabrians and others, until he had control of all Iberia, except for a strip along the southern Mediterranean coast that was claimed by the Byzantine Empire.

Leovigild tried to unify Spain religiously as well as politically by converting the Catholic majority to his Arian form of Christianity. He used political influence, reform of the Arian dogma and compromise while avoiding outright prosecution. In the end, however, he failed to win over the non-Gothic peoples to his religion.

Leovigild also reformed the body of laws, establishing a new code designed to equalize the status of Goths and Romans. The prohibition against intermarriage was abolished. With his new code, Leovigild strove for equality and unity for all his subjects.

At his death in 586, Leovigild was succeeded by his son, Reccared I. The new king successfully defended his realm against the Franks and reduced the size of the Byzantine enclave on the Mediterranean coast. Reccared was also successful in uniting Spain religiously; however, it was by inducing his Goths to accept the Catholic Church.[19]

There would be one more king in Leovigild's dynasty, and that was Liuva II, who succeeded Reccared I in 601, but he ruled for only two years, after which the Visigoths returned to electing their monarchs. The process was chaotic, producing seventeen kings in the seventh century.[20] In spite of the instability at the highest levels of government, the kingdom of Toledo thrived. Architecture and Latin literature flourished. The Visigothic kingdom became the real successor to the Roman Empire in the west.[21] In 625, Cartagena, the Byzantine provincial capital in Spain, was finally captured, giving the Visigoths control of all Iberia except for the Basque region, which was never completely conquered.

All this Visigoth supremacy was, however, about to come to an end. A new, vibrant enemy was approaching, an enemy energized by a new religion. The Muslim Arabs had erupted out of the Middle East in the seventh century. By late century Arab fleets were harassing the southern coast of Spain. By 710, the Muslims had reached Tangier and began raiding into southern Spain. A well-organized expedition was mounted in 711 under the leadership of Tarik, a Muslim Berber from western North Africa. At the battle of Guadalete River, he defeated the Visigoth king, Roderic, and went on to conquer southern Spain. The war continued for another fourteen years, until most of Iberia was ruled by the Spanish Caliphate. Even then, the struggle was carried on in the mountainous regions of Asturia and the Pyrenees. By AD 725, however, the last of the resistance was crushed. The kingdom of Toledo, the last of the Gothic nations, ceased to exist.[22]

9

Evidence of a Swedish Origin for the Goths

As we saw in the previous chapter, Theodoric the Great, once he had established the Ostrogothic kingdom in Italy and was extending his rule over the Visigoths, commissioned one of his advisors, Cassiodorus, to compile a history of the Goths.[1] Flavius Magnus Aurelius Cassiodorus Senator was born about AD 490 in southern Italy, where his father was a member of the Roman aristocracy and one-time governor of Sicily.[2] Cassiodorus obtained an education commensurate with his position as a member of the Roman nobility and served as a counselor to his father, gaining a reputation for having great knowledge of the law. He moved on to the Gothic court of Theodoric, eventually rising to the post of *magister officiorum*.[3] While serving at the Ravenna court, Cassiodorus wrote *Origo Gothica*, a history of the Goths contained in twelve volumes. Unfortunately, this entire work has since been lost. It survives only in an abbreviated form in *The Origins and Deeds of the Goths* (*Getica*) written in AD 551 by another bureaucrat, Jordanes, at the Byzantine court of the emperor Justinian.[4]

Unlike Cassiodorus, Jordanes was of Gothic descent, so he may have had a personal interest in this history. He says he was an unlearned man until his conversion and that he was not just any Goth—he also had royal Amal clan ancestry. (The "conversion" was probably from Arian Christianity to an Eastern Orthodox church espousing the Nicene Creed.) He also states that he was secretary to Gunthigis (or Baza), who was a general (master of soldiery) in the Ostrogoth army and another Amali.[5]

At some point, Jordanes became involved with the eastern Roman imperial court at Constantinople; there may be some tie to his conversion in this change. At the Byzantine court, Jordanes was laboring on a history of Rome titled *Romana* when he was persuaded by his brother, Castalius, to "leave the little work I have in hand"[6] and set to work on condensing into a small book the twelve volumes of Cassiodorus' *Origo Gothica*. Whether Castalius was a sibling or a brother in the church is not clear.

In his book, Jordanes admits he does not have direct access to Cassiodorus' work at the time of his writing, but he has read the volumes at least twice, one time over the span of three days. He says he does not recall the exact words but has a good recollection of deeds and stories. To this he will add some information found in Greek and Latin histories, as well as "things of his own authorship."[7]

However, when it came to the origin of the Goths, Greek and Roman historians would have had little to offer, as we've seen, and Jordanes would have had no special knowledge other than perhaps Gothic and family traditions. It is very likely that in the matter of Gothic ancient history he relied on Cassiodorus almost entirely.

After some discussion of the geography of the great "Ocean," Jordanes plunges right into the question of Gothic origin:

> The same mighty sea has also in its arctic region, that is in the north, a great island named Scandza, from which my tale (by God's grace) shall take its beginning. For the race whose origin you ask to know burst forth like a swarm of bees from the midst of this island and came into the land of Europe.[8]

Jordanes reiterates this genesis of the Goths again a little later in his text:

> Now from this island of Scandza, as from a hive of races or a womb of nations, the Goths are said to have come forth long ago under their king, Berig by name. As soon as they disembarked from their ships and set foot on the land, they straightway gave their name to the place. And even to-day it is said to be called Gothiscandza.

Jordanes goes on to describe the Goths' move along the coast until meeting the Ulmerugi, whom they battle and defeat. They then conquer the Vandals (according to Jordanes).

Five kings later, one Filimer, son of Gadaric, leads the Gothic soldiers and their families out of the coastal area to Scythia, or Oium, as it is called in the local tongue.[9] The Goths, under Filimer, enter Oium, where they meet the Spali, whom they defeat in battle. This victory allows the Goths to move on through Scythia (Oium) to an area near the sea of Pontus.[10]

Jordanes has covered the three stages of Gothic migration. First is the voyage by ship from Scandza to mainland Europe. Second, the Goths move, still along the shore, to the land of the Ulmerugi, whom they ultimately displace. Finally, five generations later, the Goths trek to Scythia (Ukraine), and at least some of the Goths settle "near the sea of Pontus." Pontica was the name the Romans applied to a large area on the southern coast of the Black Sea.[11] The "Sea of Pontus," then, can only mean the Black Sea itself. So this final migration is to the coast of the Black Sea.

The Gepids may have originally been part of the Gothic migration to the Black Sea area, breaking off and separating themselves once they arrived in the south. This could be the division referred to by Jordanes in *Getica*, where he describes the separation.[12]

The Goths went on to Oium (bordering the Black Sea), but apparently the Gepids were left behind to form their own nation.[13]

Since Jordanes' work was the only reference available on the early history of the Goths, it was accepted as fact (more or less) by historians for centuries. No less an authority than Edward Gibbon, writing about the time of the American Revolutionary War, asserts, "Many vestiges, which cannot be ascribed to the arts of popular vanity, attest the ancient residence of the Goths in the countries beyond the Baltic."[14] In modern times, however, Jordanes' story of the original home of the Goths being Sweden has been called into question, and a great deal has been written on the subject. So what is the evidence to support this origination of the Goths in Scandinavia and their journey to the Black Sea?

Even the casual investigator is struck by the name "Goth" in so many areas of Sweden. A quick scan of any modern map of Sweden turns up Göteborg, a major city on the western coast of Sweden, and Gotland, the large island off Sweden's east coast.[15] Historically, there were also the Swedish provinces of the late Middle Ages and Renaissance—Västergötland and Östergötland.[16] And there are continuous references in Swedish history. When he was crowned in AD 995, Olaf Eriksson, the first king of a united Sweden, took the title *Rex Sveorum Gothorumque*[17] (King of the Svear and Goths). Centuries later, in his speech before the Råd in 1630, King Gustav Adolf urged the nobility to remember their ancestors, the ancient Goths, and to follow their example in courage and steadfastness.[18] The use of the word "Goth" is ubiquitous in Swedish history and place names, but where does this name come from, and is it actually evidence of an ancestral connection?

The word "Goth" is derived from the root word "Gut" or "Gaut," meaning "one who pours out" or "men" (or possibly "stallions"), or it may be from "Gaut," the god of war.[19] The term "Gaut" is often used in early sources to indicate the people of Västergötland and Östergötland. The word first appears in about AD 16–18 in the form "Gutones" or "Gotones" in Latin and Greek literature and as "Guti" in Ptolemy's work of about AD 150. Jordanes refers to the Ostrogoths and Gauthigoths as being inhabitants of Scandza.[20]

Another reference is the name the Thracian Goths gave their homeland in the Balkans, *Gutthiuda*, meaning "land of the Gothic people."[21] Ancient Roman literature refers to the Getae, considered synonymous with Goth.[22] Thus, the name "Goth," in its many forms, argues strongly for a link between Sweden and the Goths of Roman and post–Roman history.

Earlier we reviewed Greek and Roman authors for information on Sweden and Scandinavia, but a closer examination of this literature might provide additional insight into the origin of the Goths. As early as 325 BC, we saw that, according to Pliny (chapter 5), Pytheas made contact with (or at least learned of) a people called the Gutones:

> Pytheas says that the Gutones, a people of Germany, inhabit the shores of an estuary of the Ocean called Mentonomon, their territory extending a distance of six thousand stadia; that, at one day's sail from this territory, is the Aisle of Abalus, upon the shores of which, amber is thrown up by the waves in spring, it being an excretion of the sea in a concrete form; as, also, that the inhabitants use this amber by way of fuel, and sell it to their neighbors, the Teutones.[23]

If Abalus is the southern tip of Sweden, then the Gutones would seem to indeed be in Germany on the shores of the Baltic Sea. This information is certainly not conclusive.

Another source is Tacitus, writing in AD 98:

> Passing the Lugii, we find the Gothones under the rule of kings. It is a slightly stricter rule than in the rest of the German peoples, but yet does not pass the bounds of freedom. Then, immediately bordering on the ocean, are the Rugii and Lemovii. All these people are distinguished by round shields, short swords and submission to regal authority.[24]
>
> The states of the Suiones that follow along the shore of Ocean are strong not only in arms and men but also in their fleets.[25]

Clearly Tacitus is placing the Gothones among the Germanic tribes. However, because of the lack of understanding regarding the geography of the Baltic, Swedes could have easily been confused with the Germans. The Suiones might be the Sviar, or Svear, Swedes of Uppland. In this case, the Gothones could be the Goths to the south on the Scandinavian peninsula.

One final report is that of Ptolemy, writing between AD 127 and 148. In his *Geography*, he makes a clear distinction between Germany and the Scandinavian peninsula:

East of the Cimbrian peninsula [Jutland] there are four islands called Scandian islands, three of them smaller ... but one of them very large and the most eastwards at the mouth of the river Vistula.... It is properly called Scandia itself; and its western region is inhabited by the Chaedini, its eastern region by the Favonae and the Firaesi, its northern region by the Finni, its southern region by the Gutae (Gautae) and the Dauciones, and its central region by the Levoni.[26]

In another chapter, Ptolemy places the Gutones "northwest of present-day Warsaw on the eastern, Sarmatian bank of the Vistula, in Greater Germany [today's Poland]."[27] Ptolemy understands that there is a Scandinavia (Scandia), and he locates the Goths (Gutae) there while locating the Gutones within inland Poland. These fragmented literary references suggest the Goths were in both places—that is, in south-central Sweden and in Poland at the same time. The Goths, Gaut, Gutones or Gothones were trading, raiding, conquering, even colonizing, south-central Sweden, the island of Gotland and coastal Germania.

The allegation that there were interchanges between southern Sweden and/or Gotland and the coast of Poland is bolstered by the findings covered at the end of chapter 3. The Corded Ware culture was carried into Sweden by seafarers. In fact, the faceted/boat-shaped axe subculture arrived via the Baltic without passing through Jutland and the intervening islands. By the time of the Gothic occupation of coastal Poland, seamen had been plying these routes for two thousand years. Commerce between Sweden and the Baltic coast of Poland was an established fact.

These bits and pieces of literature suggest the Goths had for some time, probably centuries, occupied territory in not just south-central Sweden and Gotland Island but also across the Baltic in Greater Germany. At some point they began expanding from this coastal base, along the coast and inland. This expansion is celebrated in Jordanes' *Getica* as the crossing of the Goths led by Berig from Scandza to Gothiscandza and the ensuing conquests.

Finally, there is archaeology as a source of information about the origin of the Goths. Archaeologists in Poland have discovered artifacts from a tradition they call the Przeworsk culture. This culture emerged at the beginning of the second century BC and grew to dominate southern and central Poland.[28] A subdivision or closely related culture, the Oksywie, occupied the lower Vistula region, extending into Pomerania. During the first decades of the Christian era, the Oksywie culture was replaced by an entirely new tradition—the Wielbark culture, which initially covered exactly the same geographical area as the old Oksywie culture. Characteristics of this new culture include burials of both cremation and inhumation, stone-covered burial mounds, stone circles, stelae, coffins of planking or hollowed-out tree trunks, and grave goods of ornaments and parts of clothing rather than weapons and tools, as was the case with Oksywie-Przeworsk graves. Bracelets, beaded necklaces, bronze buckles, and hairpins are commonly found. Two or three fibulae (a type of brooch for fastening robes) usually accompany female burials. Bronze spurs are the only warrior-related items found in these graves and are exclusive to male burials. The Wielbark culture left burials and artifacts very reminiscent of Sweden of the late Bronze Age (see chapter 4). In fact, this Wielbark culture is considered by archaeologists to be of Gothic (and possibly Gepid) origin.[29] Whether the conversion was due to a swift conquest, invasion/displacement, or adaptation from absorbing small groups of immigrating Goths over a period of time is debated.

In any case, the Wielbark culture, once established, expanded, replacing the whole

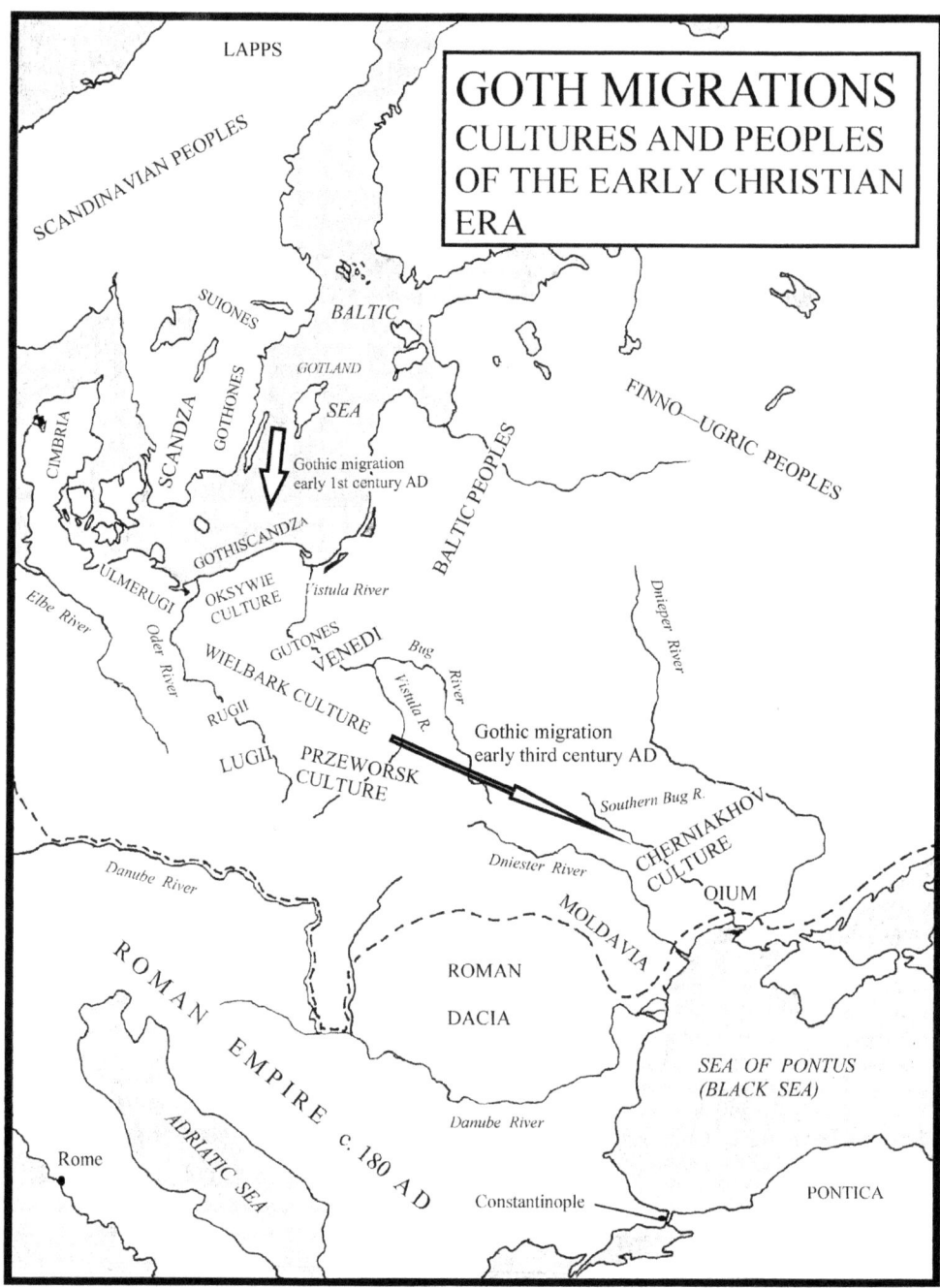

Przeworsk culture, absorbing the local Venedi and Rugii populations.[30] In the first half of the third century AD, the Wielbark culture removed itself from Pomerania and northern Poland, expanding to the south and east until it reached the Ukraine.[31] Modern scholars conclude:

> Such a picture helps explain the flourishing of the Pomeranian-Mazovian [Wielbark] culture in the middle of the second century and its decline in the fourth, when grave fields became widely scat-

tered, with poor grave furnishings. The leaders and with them the most vibrant forces had departed southward.[32]

In Ukraine, the Wielbark culture encountered another well-known archaeological tradition—the Cherniakhov culture, which occupied an area between Kiev and the Black Sea along the lower reaches of the Dnieper, Bug and Dniester rivers. The Cherniakhov civilization was an amalgamation of Roman traditions and native Ukrainian (Scythian) ones, combined with German from the "barbarians" descending the three rivers. To this mix the Goths added their legacy.

Archaeologists place the development of the Cherniakhov culture in the second to third centuries AD. Small agrarian villages located along the river systems and their tributaries were constantly being inundated by Eastern European agrarian-gathering-hunting tribes less sophisticated culturally but willing to adapt. Among these tribes were the Goths, arriving as small bands or perhaps all at one time as a major tribal unit. Once they had arrived and established themselves, the Goths came to dominate the many groups/tribes of the region.[33]

Archaeology has proved to be a big help in the search for the origin of the Goths. Findings indicate at least a connection between the Wielbark culture and Scandinavia (or Sweden, to be more precise). Whether the migration from Sweden to Poland was outright conquest, or the slow assimilation of small bands crossing the Baltic spread over an extended length of time, is still being argued.

Archaeology also provides us with locations both geographically and temporally. The first Goths arrived on the coast of what is now Poland around the Vistula estuary and moved eastward into Pomerania in the early first century AD. For a century and a half, the Goths expanded their domain in northern Poland, into central Poland and finally eastward toward Ukraine, actually giving up Pomerania. Finally, in the early third century, they left Poland altogether, migrating to the northern Black Sea area, where they emerged as the warrior Gothic nation that confronted the Romans.[34] Thus Gibbon writes:

> To cross the Baltic was an easy and natural attempt. The inhabitants of Sweden were masters of a sufficient number of large vessels, with oars, and the distance is little more than one hundred miles from Carlscrona to the nearest ports of Pomerania and Prussia. Here, at length, we land on firm and historic ground. At least as early as the Christian era, and as late as the age of Antonines, the Goths were established towards the mouth of the Vistula and in that fertile province where the commercial cities of Thorn, Elbing, Koningsberg, and Dantzic were long afterward founded. Westward of the Goths, the numerous tribes of the Vandals [Jordanes' Ulmerugi] were spread along the banks of the Oder, and the sea-coast of Pomerania and Mecklenburg. A striking resemblance of manners, complexion, religion and language, seemed to indicate that the Vandals and the Goths were originally one great people. The latter appear to have been subdivided into Ostrogoths, Visigoths and Gepidæ.[35]

Though not proven as yet, the evidence strongly favors a Swedish origination for the Gothic nation, which eventually became the Visigoths and Ostrogoths of Roman and post–Roman history. This wave of people bursting onto the continental European scene was the first of three invasions launched by the peoples of Sweden. The other two were the Vikings and the Swedish military conquests of the seventeenth and eighteenth centuries. The first of these two movements is the next subject for examination.

10

Sweden in the German Iron Age Migration Period (AD 400–575)

In chapter 6 we left Sweden at the end of the Roman Iron Age, around AD 400, with descriptions of Scandinavia provided by Roman authors. The Roman Iron Age was followed by the German Iron Age, so named because it was the Germanic peoples, including the Scandinavians, who initiated most of the significant cultural advances of the next 400 years.[1] The German Iron Age is divided by historians into two periods: the Migration Period (AD 400–575) and, in Sweden, the Vendel Period (AD 575–790).

The Migration Period is so named because this was the time of a mass movement of barbarian nations into the vacuum left by the collapse of the Western Roman Empire. By AD 575 these relocations were essentially complete. As Southern and Central Europe adjusted to this new state of affairs, one in which the "Pax Romana" no longer existed, Scandinavia advanced toward what would come to be known as the Viking Age. In Sweden, this intermediate step between the Migration Period and the Viking Age is understood through archaeological finds recovered in Uppland, mainly at Vendel (thus the name of the period).

To gain a picture of the situation in Sweden during the Migration Period, we again turn to literature from the Mediterranean world, this time Byzantine authors, one of whom we are already familiar with—Jordanes. In his *Getica*, Jordanes describes the original homeland of the Goths (Scandza) and the various nations living there:

> In the northern part of the island the race of the Adogit live, who are said to have continual light in midsummer for forty days and nights, and who likewise have no clear light in the winter season for the same number of days and nights.[2]

Clearly, Jordanes is describing a group of people living north of the Arctic Circle. He goes on to relate how these people suffer and have great joy alternately due to these extreme effects of the sun. Jordanes then describes another nation not far away:

> There are the Screrefennae, who do not seek grain for food but live on the flesh of wild beasts and birds' eggs; for there are such multitudes of young game in the swamps as to provide for the natural increase of their kind and to afford satisfaction to the needs of the people.[3]

One is tempted to equate the Adogit race with the Lapps and the Screrefennae with the hunter-gatherers in the forests north of Uppland—a reasonable conclusion.

Jordanes continues with his description of the northern peoples:

10. Sweden in the German Iron Age Migration Period (AD 400–575)

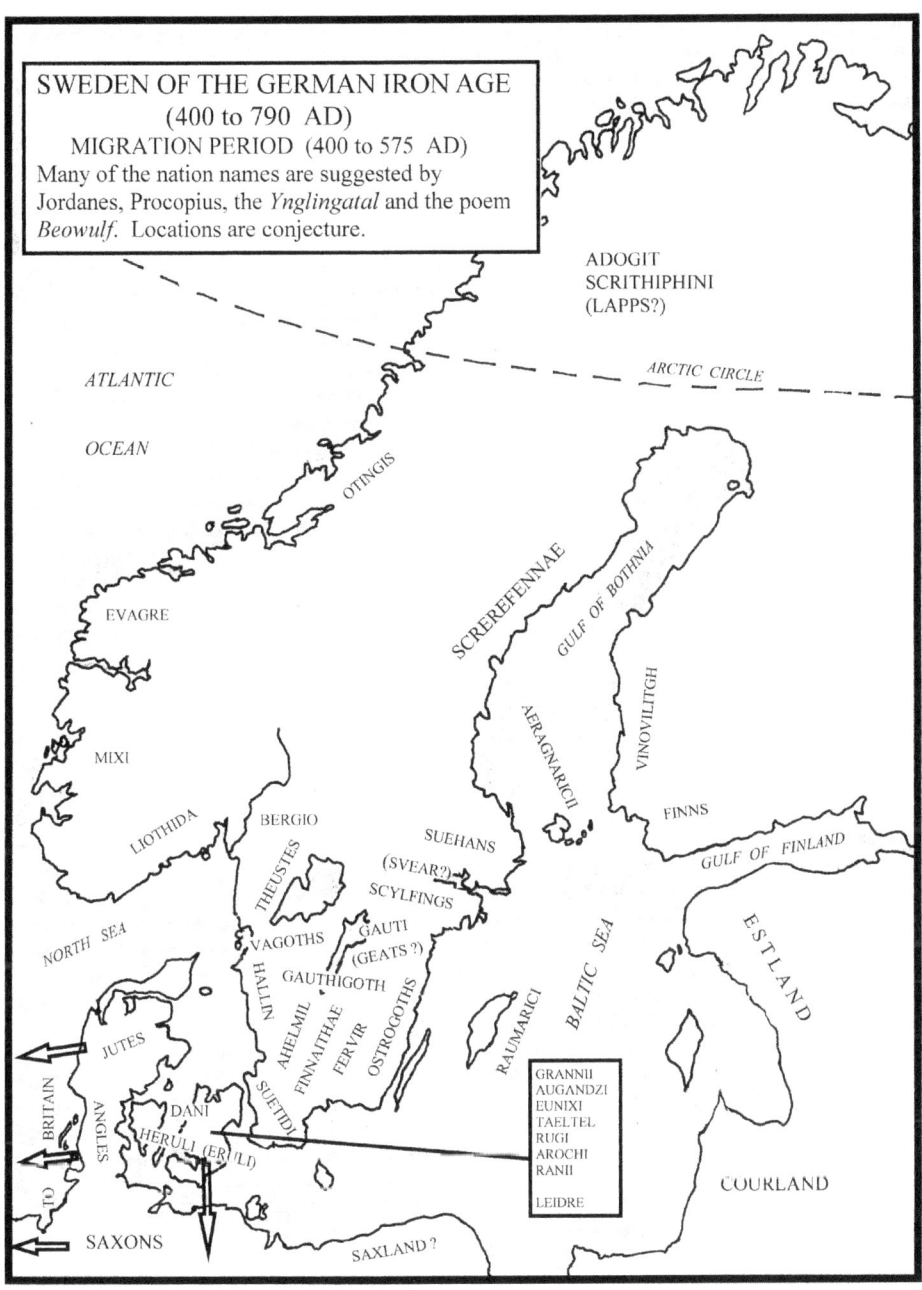

> But still another race dwells there, the Suehans, who, like the Thuringians, have splendid horses. Here also are those who send through innumerable other tribes the sappherine skins to trade for Roman use. They are a people famed for the dark beauty of their furs and, though living in poverty, are most richly clothed.[4]

Jordanes singles out the Suehans for comment, recognizing their fine horses and beautiful furs, which even reach the Roman (Mediterranean) world. This may be a reference to the Svear or Swedes of Uppland, already more organized as a commercial nation than other Scandinavian peoples.

Jordanes names some twenty-five additional tribes and/or kingdoms existing in Scandinavia. Some of these appear to have recognizable names. There are the Vagoths (possibly preserved in the name Västergötland) and the Hallin (represented in the provincial name Halland). Some names are obviously familiar: Gauthigoth, Ostrogoths, Finnaithae, Finns and Dani. And, finally, there are the Heruli or Eruli, which are referenced not just by Jordanes but also by a second Byzantine author named Procopius (more on Procopius below).

> The Suetidi are of this stock and excel the rest in stature. However, the Dani, who trace their origin to the same stock, drove from their homes the Heruli, who lay claim to preeminence among all the nations of Scandza for their tallness.[5]

From Jordanes we obtain a picture of sorts of Sweden—indeed, all of the Scandinavian peninsula, for he makes no distinction—made up of a large number of tribes and kingdoms, some fairly advanced like the Screrefennae (Svear?), who are horse breeders and fur traders, and others quite primitive, such as the Mixi, Evagre and Otingis, who "live like wild animals."[6] All in all, Jordanes does not provide a very clear picture of Sweden except to say all the Scandinavians are war-like and "surpass the Germans in size and spirit and fought with the cruelty of wild beasts."[7]

A contemporary of Jordanes, Procopius of Caesarea, provides some additional information on the residents of Scandinavia at this time. Procopius was a Byzantine historian who accompanied the general Belisarius on his expeditions in North Africa and Italy.[8] In about AD 550 he wrote a summary of these campaigns in his *History of the Wars*. As part of this treatise, Procopius traces the exploits of the previously cited Eruli, who were participants in the invasions of the Migration Period (AD 400–575).[9] Their ancestral lands were in southern Jutland, the Danish Islands or Skåne, Sweden.[10] Sometime during the third century, the Eruli left their homeland, apparently expelled by the Danes. They are mentioned as being on the Black Sea and are credited with invading Gaul in AD 289. They were defeated by Ermanaric and the Goths in about 350. Next the Eruli drove to the Spanish coast, where they engaged in some plundering and despoiling. Here they were defeated again, this time by Theodoric, king of the Goths, circa 490.[11] Finally, the roving nation was vanquished by the Lombards in about 505. The surviving Eruli then struck out for their ancient homeland.[12] On the way they passed through the territory of many Slavic tribes.

> After these, they passed the nations of the Dani, without suffering violence at the hands of the barbarians there. Coming thence to the ocean, they took to the sea, and putting in at Thule, remained there on the island. Now Thule is exceedingly large; for it is more than ten times greater than Britain. And it lies far distant from it toward the north. On this island the land is for the most part barren, but in the inhabited country thirteen very numerous nations are settled; and there are kings over each nation.[13]

Procopius goes on to describe the Scrithiphini (Jordanes' Screrefennae), almost certainly the Lapps. He dwells in some detail on the midnight sun and the strange customs of these people, which he apparently derives from hearsay, judging from his rather fantastic descriptions. He then details the other nations of Scandinavia:

> But all the other inhabitants of Thule, practically speaking, do not differ very much from the rest of men, but they reverence in great numbers gods and demons both of the heavens and of the air, of the earth and of the sea, and sundry other demons which are said to be in the waters of springs and

rivers. And they instantly offer all kinds of sacrifices and make oblations to the dead, but the noblest of the sacrifices, in their eyes, is the first human being whom they have taken captive in war; for they sacrifice him to Ares, whom they regard as the greatest god. Thus, then, do the inhabitants of Thule live. And one of the most numerous nations there are the Gauti (Gautoi), and it was next to them that the incoming Eruli settled at the time of question.[14]

The Gauti may be the Gauts (Goths), already numerous and beginning to organize into a recognizable nation.

From these Byzantine authors we may conclude that the Swedish people of the early German Iron Age (Migration Period) were divided into a dozen or more tribes and petty kingdoms.[15] Chief among these entities were the Gauti (Gauts or Goths) and the Suehans (Suetidi, Sviar, Svear or Swedes), who were already of commercial significance, breeding horses and trading in furs, as well as amassing some wealth (though Jordanes describes them as poor but richly attired).

In addition to the works from the Mediterranean world, now, for the first time, we can investigate Swedish history though literature actually from Northern Europe. Unfortunately, none of these sources are from Sweden, but they are from peoples who had close contact with or make references to Sweden. This literature ranges from Icelandic sagas to the earliest literature from England. Much of it is based on oral histories and legends, but it can be useful in painting a picture of Sweden in this time of relative historic darkness.

First, we may turn to an Old English (Anglo-Saxon) poem, *Widsith*, which is also the purported name of the author and central character. Historians generally agree the poem was written in the ninth century but is based on earlier oral traditions handed down among the Anglo-Saxons. The work comes to us as part of a manuscript of Old English poetry called the *Exeter Book*, compiled in the late tenth century.

In 144 lines of verse, Widsith (the name means "far journey") tells of traveling all over Europe and the Middle East, meeting kings and "being with" a very large number of nations, peoples and tribes. It is unlikely, however, that one person could have traveled so extensively and been introduced to so many different nations and heads of state at this time. Widsith is used simply as a vehicle in identifying (and in some cases describing) the rulers and peoples of his time. Of interest to us is a sentence in Old English dealing with Scandinavia: "*Ic wæs mid Hunum ond mid Hreðgotum, mid Sweom ond mid Geatum ond mid Supdenum*."[16] In the first phrase of the sentence, Widsith says he was with the Huns and "glorious Goths," which makes sense given that both groups were prominent during the Migration Period. In the second part of this sentence, he says he was with the Swedes first, then the Geats, and finally the South-Danes. The Swedes are the Svear of Uppland and the South-Danes are certainly the Danes of Zealand and perhaps Skåne.[17] But what of the Geats' location? If the sequence of the names means anything, the Geats are between the Svear and the Danes, the area occupied by the Gauts.

Keeping this in mind, we may consider a second Old English source—the epic poem *Beowulf*. This work was also written in England, this time by an unknown poet from Northumbria. The poem's setting is the Scandinavia of the sixth and early seventh centuries.[18] *Beowulf* is one of the most analyzed pieces of literature of all time. Volumes have been written about it, dissecting and interpreting the meaning of the words written early in the eighth century. The poem survives in only one manuscript copied around AD 1000.

The story contained in these verses is straightforward. The poem opens with a preamble that tells of Scyld, who arrives as a child on the shores of the "spear-armed" Danes. He becomes king and establishes the Scylding royal dynasty of Danish kings. After a long reign of conquest and glory, Scyld dies and is "buried" in a splendid funeral ship that is floated out to sea.

In a few lines, the story passes on to Scyld's great-grandson, Hrothgar (or Hoögar), who again is a great and successful warrior-king. To celebrate his victories, Hrothgar builds a magnificent mead-hall named Heorot, where he and his warriors (*thanes*) can feast and be entertained.

However, all this merrymaking arouses the indignation of a troll-like monster, Grendel, who invades the great hall one night and carries off thirty of the king's thanes, taking them back to his lair, where he and his mother (a creature even more evil and craven than Grendel) slaughter the warriors. The following night Grendel returns, committing further atrocities.

Hrothgar and his thanes try everything to rid themselves of this ogre. They attack him but are defeated. Sacrifices to the gods are no help. Finally, they abandon Heorot, leaving the great hall to their adversary during the dark hours.

Word of this great tragedy reaches the kingdom of Hygelac, king of the Geats. His greatest warrior, Beowulf, vows to come to the aid of the imperiled Danes, and he sets sail with fourteen companion thanes.

The Geatish warriors arrive in Denmark, landing on the coast near Heorot. They are challenged by Hrothgar's warriors, but after explaining why they have come, they are taken to the Danish king. In the audience with Hrothgar, Beowulf declares that he has come to fight Grendel without weapons, as the monster is armed only with brute strength.

Beowulf is called out by one of the king's men, Unferth, who says Beowulf is not such a great warrior, as he was once defeated in a swimming match by a companion named Breca. Beowulf rebukes Unferth, explaining that he and Breca had begun the contest each armored and armed with a sword. They swam in the sea for five days and nights until they were separated. Monstrous whales attacked Beowulf, but he was protected by his armor and succeeded in killing several of the demons, thus winning the contest.

Hrothgar accepts Beowulf's story and allows Beowulf and his warriors the honor of guarding the hall while Hrothgar and his thanes bed down elsewhere, as has become their custom. Exhausted, the Geats fall asleep. Grendel enters the hall and devours the first warrior he finds. Beowulf, who has been only feigning sleep, accosts Grendel, and a great struggle ensues. In the midst of the battle, Beowulf succeeds in tearing off one of Grendel's arms. The monster escapes to his lair, where he dies in the presence of his mother.

Enraged, Grendel's mother enters Heorot, where Hrothgar, Beowulf and their thanes are sleeping after celebrating the victory over their prodigious adversary. She kills Æschere, the greatest of the Danish warriors, and retrieves her son's arm, after which she escapes to her lair.

Hrothgar, Beowulf and their warriors follow Grendel's mother's trail to her lair, which is at the bottom of a lake. Beowulf enters the water after accepting from Unferth the famous sword Hrunting. He swims to the bottom, where he meets Grendel's mother, who drags him into her lair. There the two fight for some time. Beowulf discovers that his sword, Hrunting, will not bite into his adversary's hide. As the battle rages on, Beowulf finds another ancient sword hanging on the wall and uses this weapon to finally behead Grendel's mother. Beowulf returns to Heorot a hero and is given a reward by a grateful King Hrothgar.

Beowulf and his Geatish warriors then sail back to their homeland, where Beowulf gives his treasure to his king, Hygelac. Sometime later, Hygelac is killed during a Geatish raid on the Franks and Frisians. Hygelac's son, Heardred, is crowned king. But Heardred is soon killed in a battle between the Geats and the Svear. At this point, Beowulf becomes king and rules successfully for fifty years.

Beowulf, however, is called upon to face one more great menace. There was in the kingdom a dragon that guarded a fabulous treasure of gold. For three centuries this great beast had remained quiescent. However, a runaway slave had crept into the dragon's lair and stolen a golden cup to give to his master as a gift. The slave wanted to return to his master and was asking to be forgiven for having deserted such a good and kind overlord. When the dragon discovers the cup is missing, he goes on a rampage, burning farmsteads and crops as he devastates the countryside.

Beowulf and eleven warriors set out to give battle to the dragon. Beowulf once again insists on fighting the dragon alone, but, due to his advanced age and diminished strength, he is overcome by the dragon's flames. All the thanes flee except for one: Wiglaf, a prince of the Geats. Wiglaf comes to the aid of his lord, but he is too late to prevent the dragon from delivering a mortal wound to Beowulf's neck. Wiglaf and Beowulf dispatch the dragon, but Beowulf dies as a result of this final contest.

Beowulf receives a hero's burial, a funeral pyre, where his body is consumed by flames along with his armor, weapons and treasure. Then a great mound is erected over the site of the pyre to commemorate forever this warrior-king.

Though not written as a historical piece, this epic poem does give us a picture of the period and its people. There is the hero and main character of the poem, Beowulf himself. The consensus of historians is that Beowulf is strictly a fictional character.[19] Are the Geats, then, to be considered fictitious as well? One might argue this, except the Geats are also mentioned by Widsith and identified in the same phrase as the Swedes in his poem. If the Geats were a historical people, where were they located? In *Beowulf*, the warriors board a ship to sail to the land of the Danes, presumably Zealand or one of the other Danish islands. This representation, along with Widsith's suggestion that the Geats and Swedes are in close proximity, suggests the Geats were located on the Scandinavian peninsula close to the Svear (Swedes) of Uppland. The Gauts, or Goths, of Västergötland and Östergötland also fit this description, and, indeed, R.W. Chambers, the eminent *Beowulf* scholar, equates the Geats with the Gauts of history.[20] Since *Beowulf* was written in Old English, "Geats" would seem to be the Old English form of "Gauts." *Beowulf* and *Widsith* each use the term, and both are written in Old English.

The Gauts, Geats or Goths were a strong nation that, by this time, may have consolidated its hold over a large area in south-central Sweden including Västergötland,

Östergötland, Dalsland, Närke, Värmland and northern Småland.[21] The Geats' gathering strength meant they would inevitably be challenged by the Svear for supremacy of Sweden.

As to the dating of the events in *Beowulf*, we have solid evidence from literary sources. The poem describes the death of Hygelac during a raid on Frisia:

> Hygelac Geat, grandson of Swerting,
> on the last of his raids this ring bore with him … feuds with Frisians.
> … under shield he died.
> Fell the corpse of the king into keeping of Franks.[22]

The historical truth of this raid is corroborated by Bishop Gregory of Tours, who devotes a whole chapter (Book III, Chap. 3) to it in his *Historia Francorum* (written in about AD 594).[23]

Another contemporary Frankish work is *Liber Historiæ Francorum* (author unknown), and there is also an English manuscript called *Liber Monstrorum*. These sources tell of a Geatish (*Getis*) king, one Chochilaicus-Huiglancus-Hyglac, who is killed during an attempted raid on a Frisian population that is part of the Frankish Empire.[24]

Hygelac is described as a very large man (monstrous, in fact). In spite of his size, Hygelac is killed and his raiders defeated by an army led by Theudobert, the son of Theudoric, king of the Franks. King and son are both known historical figures. Using these references, the raid can be dated to AD 519 or 520.[25]

There is some question as to whether the raid in *Beowulf* is indeed the same expedition described in the histories, because the Frankish works name Hygelac as king of the Danes instead of king of the Geats. The explanation for the error may be that "Danes" was a generic term used by the Franks for any of the Scandinavian peoples. The Frisians and the Franks made no distinction between the raiders coming from Denmark, Norway or Sweden. They all came from the same direction, looked pretty much the same and spoke essentially the same language.

Using these rather meager sources, we can construct a partial list of Gaut (Geat) kings:

Hrethel
Hæthcyn, son of Hrethel
Hygelac, son of Hrethel (died in about 520)
Heardred, son of Hygelac
Beowulf (probably a fictional character)

Hrethel, the earliest king mentioned, had three sons: Herebeald, Hæthcyn and Hygelac.[26] Hæthcyn accidentally killed his brother Herebeald, which led to King Hrethel's death from grief. Thus, Hæthcyn became king as the next oldest.

Hæthcyn became entangled in the Svear-Geat feud, leading a raid into Svear territory that netted the elderly wife of Ongentheow, the Svear king. In spite of his advanced age, Ongentheow and his Svear pursued the Geat thanes, killed Hæthcyn and rescued the old lady. The Svear were about to dispatch the Geat warriors when Hygelac arrived just in time to intervene and save the Geats. The Geats then slew the Svear thanes and their king.[27] Eventually Hygelac died, leading to Beowulf's long reign.

> Now further if fell with the flight of years,
> with harrying horrid, that Hygelac perished
> and Hæthcyn, too, by hewing of swords
> under the Shield-wall slaughter lay....[28]

> Then Beowulf came asking this broad
> realm to wield; and he ruled it well
> fifty winters, a wise old prince.[29]

In the latter part of *Beowulf*, the author refers to wars and warfare on a national level. The poem speaks of the "warlike-Scylfings"[30] and the "fighting-Scylfings,"[31] referring to a Swedish (Svear) dynasty of Uppland. This war between the Geats and the Svear dominates the action in the final part of the poem:

> The bloody swath of Swedes and Geats
> and the storm of their strife, were seen afar,
> how folk against folk the fight had wakened.[32]

> Such is the feud, the foeman's rage,
> death-hate of men: so I deem it sure
> that the Swedish folk will seek us home
> for this fall of their friends, the Fighting-Scylfings.[33]

Buried in this story of Beowulf the hero and the struggle with the Svear is a subplot dealing with the Svear dynasty of Scylfing. The earliest king mentioned is Ongentheow, who rescues his aged wife from the Geats.[34] Ongentheow is succeeded by his son Ohthere, who is succeeded by his brother, Onela. Ohthere's two sons, Eanmund and Eadgils, flee for their lives to the Geats. Onela tracks the brothers down and kills Eanmund along with the Geat king Heardred, which leads to Beowulf gaining the Geat crown.[35] The Geats back the remaining son, Eadgils, who defeats Onela and becomes king of the Svear. The poem provides a limited list of Swedish (Svear) kings:

Ongentheow
Ohthere
Onela
Eadgils

Thus, from *Beowulf* we gain a few names of the kings of the Geats and Svear, as well as a sense of the war between the two nations. The poem does not tell us the outcome of the war, but there is a feeling of almost resignation by the Geats in the poem, hinting that ultimately the Svear are going to be victorious.

Other than *Beowulf*, literature provides little to use in reconstructing the line of kings of the Geats (Gauts), but for the Svear there is more information. Again, the sources come from outside Sweden. *Ynglinga Tal* (or *Ynglingtal*), which lists the kings of the house of Yngling, is a poem that was composed in the ninth century by Thjodolf the Learned of Hvin, who was court poet of King Rognvald the Glorious. Rognvald was the chief of a petty kingdom in Norway and a cousin of Harald Fairhair. The poem traces Rognvald's ancestry back to the Swedish (Svear) dynasty of kings (Scylfings?), apparently providing legitimacy and glory to this obscure Norwegian king.[36]

The poem survives in three versions: *Historia Norwegiæ*, *Íslendingabók* and the best-known, Snorri Sturluson's *Heimskringla*, in which the *Ynglinga Tal* is included as an introduction to his work. *Ynglinga Tal* begins with the original ancestor, who is Odin. Here the Scandinavian god is treated as a mortal but with superpowers.

> Odin could transform his shape: his body would
> lie as if dead, or asleep; but then he would
> be in the shape of a fish, or worm, or bird,
> or beast.[37]

Certainly the first three kings are mythical, and generally the first seventeen are considered unreliable in terms of being actual historical figures.[38] The following is a list of kings, along with their deaths and occasionally their deeds in an abbreviated form derived from the work[39]:

Odin—purely mythical.
Njord—continued the blood sacrifices to the gods at Uppsala.
Frey (or **Yngve**)—"built a great temple at Uppsala,"[40] began the Yngling dynasty, and was buried in a grand mound.
Fjolne—drowned in a vessel of mead while visiting Frode in Zealand (he tripped and fell into the vat while attempting to relieve himself after an evening of carousing).
Swegde—went on a quest seeking Godheim and Odin.
Vanlande—traveled to Finland, where he married Driva, daughter of Snæ the Old.
Visbur—died in a house fire; so sings Thjodolf:

> Have the fire-dogs' fierce tongues yelling
> Lapt Visbur's blood on his own hearth?
> Have flames consumed the dwelling
> Of the here's soul on earth?[41]

Domald—ruled in a time of famine. He sacrificed oxen the first autumn, and then men during the second, but the famine persisted, so the chiefs sacrificed Domald the third autumn.
Domar—died in his bed at Uppsala.
Dygve—first to be called king instead of *drottnar* (ruler).
Dag—so wise he understood the language of the birds. Dag led a raid on Gotland Island, where he was killed by a thrall throwing a hay fork.
Agne—led an expedition to Finland.
Alric and **Eric**—ruled as kings together and were great horsemen.
Yngve and **Alf**—stabbed one another and were buried under mounds in Fyrisvold.
Hugleik—killed in a battle at Fyrisvold by a celebrated sea-king, Hake, who subdued the country and became king of the Svear.
Hake—died from wounds received in a battle with Eric and Jorund, sons of King Yngve and famed marauders in Denmark. Hake was put to sea in a burning funeral ship.
Jorund—captured and hanged during a raid in Denmark.
On (or **Ane**, or **Aun**)—involved in wars with Halfdan and Fridleif of Denmark; lived to be very old by sacrificing his sons to Odin. On died of old age and was buried in a mound at Uppsala. Thjodolf tells:

> In Uppsala's town the cruel king
> Slaughtered his sons at Odin's shrine—
> Slaughtered his sons with cruel knife,
> To get from Odin length of life.[42]

Egil—put down a rebellion with the help of Frode the Bold of Denmark. He was buried in a mound at Uppsala.

Ottar—killed during a marauding expedition in Denmark that was in retaliation for a raid on Uppsala by the Danes.

Adils—a great lover and breeder of horses. He raided Saxland (Saxony?), where he captured a girl who would become his wife. He battled the king of Leidre (Lejre or Hleiðra in Zealand—thought by some historians to be the site of *Beowulf*'s Heorot).[43] Adil also fought with another king in Uppland whom he finally defeated in the storied battle on the ice of Lake Venner. He was buried in a mound in Uppsala. Section 34 contains this interesting statement:

> In those days many kings both Danes and Northmen, ravaged the Swedish domains; for there were many sea-kings who ruled over many people, but had no lands.[44]

This reference to sea-kings who exercise power but do not actually rule over any land area will surface again both in the pre–Viking era and during the Viking period.

Many historians maintain that Ongentheow of *Beowulf* is the same king as Egil cited in the *Ynglinga Saga*.[45] If true, the kings of the Svear of Uppland from the two sources would line up like this:

Beowulf	*Ynglinga Saga*
Ongentheow	Egil
Ohthere	Ottar
Onela (Ali)	Adils (Athils)
Eadgils	Eystein

From *Beowulf* we know Ongentheow to be a contemporary of King Hygelac of the Geats, who was killed in the Frisian raid of AD 519 or 520. This would place Egil, Ottar, Adils and Eystein in the early to mid-sixth century.

There are three large burial mounds located in the Mälar region of Sweden known as Gamla Uppsala. These mounds have long been thought to be the interment sites of three kings from the *Ynglinga Saga*: Aun, Egil and Adils.[46] A fourth mound a few miles away has been identified with Ottar.[47] Excavations at two of these mounds have produced cremated human bones contained in ceramic vessels. Other objects were burned in a funeral pyre, including domestic animal bones, gold, sword hilts and a helmet, glass beakers, gaming pieces and gold thread. There was sufficient material found to determine the mounds were created in the sixth century.[48]

The mounds were obviously the grave sites of rich kings who controlled a large enough population to provide the manpower required to build them. Were these indeed the final resting places of the kings Aun, Egil, Ottar and Adils? It is impossible to know. However, these mounds do tell us there were rich and powerful monarchs in the Uppland region of Sweden in the sixth century.

To continue with the kings according to the *Ynglinga Saga*:

Eystein—killed during an invasion by a sea-king, Solve, from Jutland.

Solve—made himself king of the Swedes but was eventually betrayed and killed by them.

Yngvar—made peace with the Danes but made war upon the east country (eastern Baltic coast). He was defeated by an Estland army, was killed and buried there in Estland.

Onund (**Anund**)—ruled during what was mostly a peaceful time for the Swedes. Onund did raid Estland successfully and returned with a great treasure. He had large areas of forest cleared for settlement, thus becoming known as the Road Maker.

Ingjald—married Gauthild, daughter of King Algaut, who was the son of Gautrek the Mild and grandson of Gaut. For this line Gotland (Gautland) was named.

There were many district kings in Sweden at the time of King Ingjald, each vying for control of more territory. Ingjald killed King Algaut of West Gotland (Västergötland?) and the kings of Fjädrundaland, Nerike (Närke?) and Aattundaland at a banquet he arranged. King Granmar of Södermanland did not attend and was therefore spared. Ingjald then proceeded to conquer the murdered kings' domains.

King Granmar, meanwhile, formed an alliance with King Hjorvard (Ylfing of Denmark?), sealed by the marriage of Hjorvard to Granmar's daughter. Ingjald then made war upon Granmar and Hjorvard, who were joined by Hogne, king of East Gotland (Östergötland?) and Granmar's father-in-law. Ingjald's new subjects soon deserted him, and he was forced to retreat to Uppland. Eventually, a peace was made between Granmar and Ingjald.

Sometime later, Ingjald killed Granmar and Hjorvard in a raid, after which he conquered their domains. King Hogne of East Gotland began plundering Ingjald's kingdom via cavalry raids.

Ingjald's daughter, Aasa, was married to Gudrod, king of Scania. She deceived Gudrod into killing his brother, Halfdan. Next Aasa conspired to bring about the death of her husband, after which she fled back to Uppsala.

The new king of Scania, Ivar Vidfavne, a nephew of Gudrod, raised an army and invaded Sweden, whereupon Ingjald set fire to his own hall and died in the flames. Ivar went on to conquer all of Sweden, Denmark, most of Saxland, all of the east country (Estonia) and a fifth of England (Northumbria). This ended the Yngling dynasty in Sweden and began the new dynasties of Sweden and Denmark.

King Ingjald's son, Olaf, escaped to Nerike (Närke?) with the Swedes who remained loyal to him, traveling on to Vermeland (Värmland?), where he cleared forests for settlement and thus became known as Olaf Tree-feller. He married Solva (or Slveig) of Soleyar (a district in Hedmark, a province in Norway), "and a Norwegian royal clan claimed him as its earliest ancestor."[49] Having thus arrived at the Norwegian line of kings, Thjodolf disregards the Swedish rulers in favor of the various kings in Norway for the remainder of his poem.

What can we conclude from this Nordic literature, which, though not written in Sweden, nonetheless deals extensively with Swedish history, or at least Swedish legends?

First, there is the political situation. Vilhelm Moberg, the Swedish historian, says of this time in Swedish history:

> Petty kings and kings of hundreds were in reality tribal chieftains, who had seized power and authority over the common people by the sword. In those days wars were not waged between whole peoples or nations. Petty kings and their warriors—individual magnates and earls who had raised themselves above the peasant class—fought over provinces and small districts. A great peasant rose to be a chieftain; and a chieftain could become king.[50]

This would seem to be a good description of the circumstances covered by these early literature sources. By far the majority of the kings named were not kings of nations, but rather tribal chiefs or kings of a subdivision of a nation. Thus the early rulers were not kings of the Gauts (Geats) or the Swedes (Svear) but kings of just a tribe or an area, a subdivision of those people. Only with the last few kings named in the *Ynglinga Saga* do we begin to see the formation of nations and kings of large areas. In the saga, Ingjald is credited with uniting the Svear and Gauts into a single nation. This is possible, though it is more likely that he united the Svear and annexed some of the Gaut lands.

The creation of the large empire by Ivar of Scania seems unlikely. However, he may have indeed ruled Scania, Gautland, Uppland and holdings in other lands, such as Saxland, Estonia and England. He might also have conquered Zealand, next to Scania, and much of the island territories of Denmark. All this is conjecture, however, and an attempt to rationalize how later writers may have derived their claims regarding his empire.

From this cited literature we can make some generalizations. During the fifth century, Scandinavia was divided into first tribal territories, and then, as the tribal entities broke down, into minor kingdoms. During the sixth century many of these mini-kingdoms or districts were consolidated into petty kingdoms up to the size of a province. This seems to have been particularly true in Jutland, Zealand, Scania, West Gotland, East Gotland, Uppland of the Swedes (Svear) and Gotland Island.

11

Sweden of the Vendel Period (AD 575–790)

In seventh-century Sweden, we see continued consolidation, but now the small states began to conduct wars of conquest against each other. For example, the king of Scania invaded Gautland and Uppland, and there was war between the Gauts and the Svear at the same time that the Gauts from Västergötland were strengthening their hold on Östergötland, Dalsland, Närke, Värmland and northern Småland. The Svear, meanwhile, were also consolidating their grip on Uppland and possibly Gotland Island.

By the seventh century the main struggle in Sweden was between the Gauts and the Svear (Swedes) for preeminent power in the country. Sometime between 600 and AD 1000, the Svear triumphed, subjugating the Gauts, who by this time controlled an extensive area in central Sweden.[1] Thus, by at least AD 1000, the Svear had become the dominant political power in Sweden.

This is an oversimplification, of course. The literature reviewed so far makes it clear that there was much give and take with wide-ranging interchanges between the Gaut and the Svear kingdoms. Betrayals, rebellions, and shifting loyalties, with Scanians, Danes, Norwegians and Saxons thrown into the mix—a long-running war like this is inevitably complicated. In the end, the Svear triumphed. Perhaps the place of sacrifice being in Svear territory and the king of the Svear being, in effect, the high priest of Uppsala was just enough to decide the issue in his favor.

The *Ynglinga Saga* makes several references to the sacrifices offered to the gods at Uppsala in Uppland by the king of the Svear or the king at Uppsala. This was his primary responsibility, and it helped sustain his position. As the saga points out, even kings of other states came to Uppsala to participate in the slaughter of animals (and sometimes humans) or to make their own sacrificial offerings. This recognition of the importance of Uppsala may have made the difference in the success of the Uppland Svear in their conquest of the Gauts.

The pantheon of gods worshipped by the Scandinavian peoples was quite extensive and varied depending on time and place. Icelandic gods of the tenth century were somewhat different from Danish or Swedish deities of the fifth. However, in general there were two races of gods—the Æsir, which included Thor, Odin and Tyr, and the Vanir, including Frey, Freyja, and Njord—not to mention the Valkyries, giants and a myriad of elves (mountain elves, woodland elves, field elves, hill elves, wild elves and sea elves).[2]

However, the most important gods and those deities remaining more or less unchanged over time were Odin (the All-Father); Odin's wife, Frigg; and Thor (the Thunder-Maker), with his hammer that produced lightning and thunder.[3]

Thor was often regarded as the god of the less fortunate, the poor and thralls (slaves). He was worshipped by the hunters and fishermen. Yet he was often given the place of honor in the great halls of chiefs.[4]

Frey, the fertility god, was associated with the agricultural people of the late Stone Age and Bronze Age.[5]

Odin was a late arrival, not appearing in Scandinavia until the Iron Age. He was the chief god and the god of war. It was Odin to whom the warriors prayed before entering battle.[6]

Frigg was the goddess of marriage and fertility. Warriors who died bravely in battle passed on to Odin's court (Valhalla) or to Frigg's (Fensalir), where they were waited on by handmaidens, the Valkyries, who satisfied their every desire.[7]

The gods themselves dwelled in the kingdom of Asgard, a land situated in the sky. The earth was Midgard, and there was also an underworld, Niflhel, where cowards, serpents, evil spirits and other undesirables abided.[8]

As to the temple and form of the effigies worshipped by the Swedes, we have a description provided by Adam of Bremen. Though written in AD 1075, at a time when Christian missionaries were working to convert the pagan Swedes, his account gives us a sense of the ancient customs and the form of the gods worshipped:

> Now we shall say a few words about the superstitions of the Swedes. That folk has a very famous temple called Uppsala, situated not far from the city of Sigtuna and Björkö. In this temple entirely decked out in gold, the people worship the statues of three gods in such wise that the mightiest of them, Thor, occupies a throne in the middle of the chamber; Wotan and Frikko have places on either side. The significance of these gods is as follows: Thor, they say, presides over the air, which governs the thunder and lightning, the winds and rains, fair weather and crops. The other, Wotan—that is, the Furious—carries on war and imparts to man strength against his enemies. The third is Frikko, who bestows peace and pleasure on mortals. His likeness, too, they fashioned with an immense phallus. But Wotan they chisel armed, as our people are wont to represent Mars. Thor with his scepter apparently resembles Jove.[9]

Bremen goes on to describe the sacrifices offered to these gods, a form of worship that must have been horrifyingly repugnant to the Christian missionaries:

> The sacrifice is of this nature: of every living thing that is male, they offer nine heads with the blood of which it is customary to placate gods of this sort. The bodies they hang in the sacred grove that adjoins the temple. Now this grove is so sacred in the eyes of the heathen that each and every tree in it is believed divine because of the death or putrefaction of the victims. Even dogs and horses hang there with men.[10]

These, then, were the sacrifices the kings of Uppsala made for the people, petitioning the gods for good crops, fertility, and success in both trade and battle. To not make the annual sacrifices was to invite disaster and would scandalize the people. The religious tradition was an instrument of coercion useful to the Svear of Uppland, a precursor to the "divine right of kings" authority. Here the king was ruler and priest.

Permeating all the literature are innumerable references to naval expeditions. Early in the German Iron Age these were mostly pirate-style raids to acquire booty and/or slaves, kidnap women, or rectify some perceived injury, usually involving the killing of a local king. The Baltic and eastern North Seas appear to have been highways transporting countless piratical expeditions. Svear, Gauts, Scanians, Danes and Norwegians conducted these attacks against each other and against the peoples of Finland, the eastern Baltic coast and Saxland and Wendland. There was the documented raid on Frisia related in *Beowulf* in about AD 520, but raids further west seem to have been restrained. The unleashing of the Viking onslaught that would terrorize Europe did not begin until the end of the eighth century.

Snorri Sturluson's *Ynglinga Saga* refers to "sea-kings,"[11] even "Viking expeditions,"[12] and, in one case, "sea-kings without lands."[13] As the German Iron Age (AD 400–790) matured and the Period of Migrations (AD 400–575) waned to become the Vendel Period (AD 575–790), the sea expeditions became more and more not just raids for plunder but also military campaigns of conquest. Norwegians, Jutland Danes, Zealand Danes, Gauts and Svear attacked each other and various overseas territories. Gotland Island, Finland and Estonia were perennial targets. And there are increasing references to land warfare, such as Scania's invasion of Gautland, the Gauts' war with the Svear and so it goes.

It does seem likely that by the end of the Vendel Period and German Iron Age (AD 790) the Svear were making progress in overcoming the Gauts and had conquered Gotland Island. The Danes had coalesced into a kingdom that, at least from time to time, included Zealand, the adjacent islands, parts of Jutland and Scania. Norway, meanwhile, was still struggling to unite its many petty kingdoms stretched across its mountains and along the fjords of its extensive coastline.

There may have been some attempts at uniting two or more of these nations. As we've seen, the *Ynglinga Saga* credits Ivar Vidfavne of Scania with the conquest of Sweden, Denmark, much of Saxony, Estonia and Northumbria in England. This is no doubt an exaggeration, as there is no corroborating evidence to confirm the existence of such a wide-ranging empire at this time. But Ivar may very well have conquered parts of Denmark, Sweden and coastal Germany, obtaining fealty from kings in these areas rather than ruling directly. Ivar is also credited with putting an end to the Yngling dynasty of the Svear and initiating the royal lines of both Sweden and Denmark. This, however, is hard to reconcile with other sources that identify Scylfing (or Skilfing/Scylfingas) as the ancient line of kings of the Swedes (Svear)—not to be confused with the Scylding (or Skjolding) Danish dynasty identified in *Beowulf*. Quite possibly the Yngling and Scylfing lines were two separate Svear royal families ruling discrete realms in Uppland, with the Scylfing line eventually winning out for leadership of the Svear.

Other sources, such as the *Chronicles of the Kings of Lejre* and the *Annals of Lund*, tell of Rakkæ, a little dog (perhaps a metaphor for a dwarfish man) that was crowned king of Denmark by conquering Swedes.[14] More believable is the story of Harald Hilditonn (Wartooth), grandson of Ivar, who united Jutland, Zealand and the islands in between into a Danish kingdom, and then went on to conquer Scania, Gautland and maybe Uppland. If factual, this empire would have been more of a confederacy of regional kings forced to swear allegiance to Harald. In the end, Harald was challenged by his nephew, Hring, king of Uppland, or East Gautland, or both. The two kings fought a great battle, recounted in various legends, in which Harald was killed.[15] This battle probably occurred in the early eighth century.[16] Thus another attempt to unite the various kingdoms of Denmark and Sweden fell apart.

11. Sweden of the Vendel Period (AD 575–790)

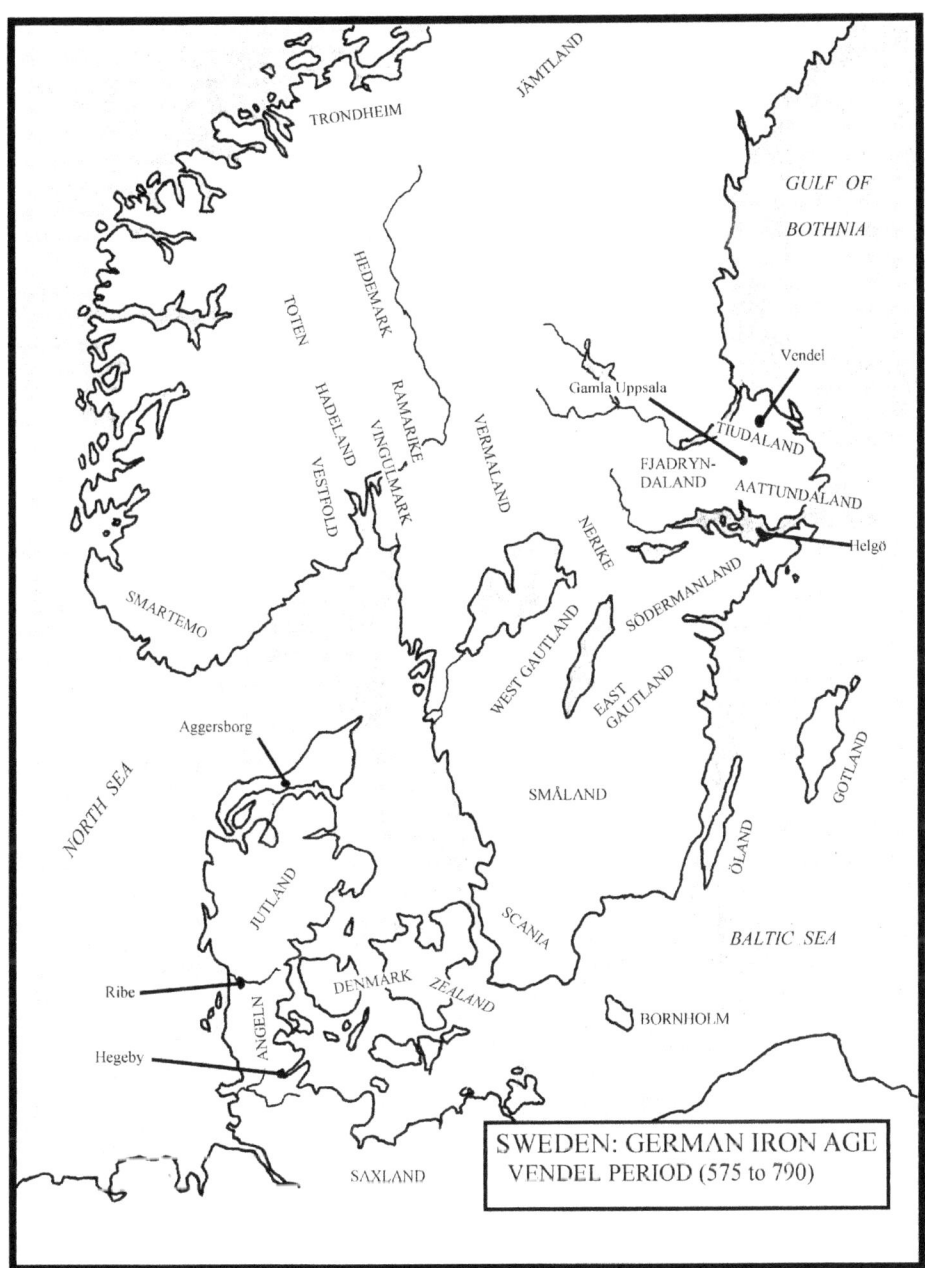

   There is certainly a grain of truth to these stories, though they are often confusing and contradictory. Still, they give us a sense of what was going on at the time, even if exact historical figures, dates and events are lacking, exaggerated and sometimes obviously false.
   To get a more complete picture and provide some order, we will once again turn to archaeology. Ancient literature has provided some human insight lacking previously, but it also leaves large gaps in the record that can only be filled in by pick and shovel work.

As already noted, the German Iron Age is subdivided into the Migration Period (AD 400–575) and, in Sweden, the Vendel Period (AD 575–790), leading into the Viking Age.[17] The Migration Period saw the Huns, Visigoths, Ostrogoths, Vandals, Lombards, Franks and other (mostly Germanic) nations invade and occupy formerly Roman territory. With the withdrawal of the Roman legions from Britain (AD 400–410), the native population, a mix of Celts and pre–Celtic peoples, was increasingly subjected to raids and harassment from Scots (Irish), Picts from Scotland, and Saxons from the mainland.[18] The Britons appealed to the Roman emperor Honorius for assistance in repelling these tormentors but were turned down with the admonition, "The cantons should take steps to defend themselves."[19] Left to their own devices, the Britons turned to the continent and the warlike Angles of Jutland for help, allotting them some land in Ebbesfleet in exchange for support against the Picts.[20]

The Angles came in three longboats, and with their support, the Picts were defeated. But the Angles had discovered a rich, weakly defended land. Additional and uninvited Angles soon arrived, followed by Saxons and Jutes.[21] A full-scale invasion ensued, driving the Britons back into Wales and Wessex-Cornwall. By 449, boatloads of Britons were escaping from Cornwall to the mainland, where they settled in what ultimately became the enclave of Brittany in northwestern France.[22]

Whereas the Migration Period was a time of tumult in Central and Southern Europe, it was a period of relative economic stability in Scandinavia.[23] To be sure, there were cross-border raids, expeditions by sea and even conquests (vouched for in *Beowulf* and the *Ynglinga Saga*), but there were no mass invasions by foreign tribes, as was the case to the south.

The basic economic unit in Sweden at this time was the family farm. We've traced the development of the longhouse in Sweden (see chapter 4), a structure usually built of fieldstone walls and a roof of sod or thatch. This roof was supported by two rows of posts running the length of the building, which could be as much as 115 feet long. About one third of the interior was used as a living space for the family, with a hearth in the middle surrounded by walled-off rooms.[24] Another third was used as a barn for large animals, cattle or oxen. And the last section was reserved for storage of grain and perhaps feed for the animals. Outbuildings were used for storage and workshops. All this was surrounded by a fence or stone wall.

In Sweden, these farmsteads were scattered as single, independent operations or sometimes located in a small group around a central location. This is the only move toward the development of villages.[25] Cities and towns were nonexistent, with one exception: the trade center of Helgö on Lake Mälar near today's Stockholm.

Besides cattle, farmers kept sheep, pigs and horses. Grains cultivated included oats, barley, rye and wheat.[26] Raising grain and livestock, each landholder strove to make his farm self-sufficient. The laborers were the family members, with the help of one or more thralls (slaves).[27]

Thralls, or bondsmen, were a common feature of Swedish society, and they constituted the majority of the labor force throughout pagan Sweden. They might be captives taken in war or on raids, the product of thralls already owned by the family, or voluntary bondsmen (those who sold themselves into slavery, usually due to indebtedness).[28] Bondsmen in Sweden were better off than those to the south, however. If a thrall committed a crime, it was his master who was held responsible. A child who resulted from the union of a bondswoman and her master was considered part of the master's family. And in Uppland, a freeman and a bondswoman could even marry.[29]

Grave sites at these farmsteads indicate that this was a time of prosperity. Gaming pieces and imported items such as beakers from the Black Sea area have been found buried with the wealthy landowners.[30]

During the Migration Period, farming expanded. New land was brought under cultivation in already settled areas, and colonies were established to the north and west of Uppland, opening up additional areas for farming. New trade routes were instituted from Trondheim on the Norwegian coast across the mountains to the Gulf of Bothnia in Sweden.[31]

Once the spring planting was accomplished, the farmer might turn to the sea, sailing off with neighbors and returning for the fall harvest. Or he might join a crew gathering under some local chieftain with a reputation for successful pirate raids (referred to in the *Ynglinga Saga* as sea-kings). He might even go adventuring with a leader whose career was that of the Viking, the "sea-king-without-land" cited in the saga.

During such absences, the farmer's wife, the mistress of the manor, would have to pick up the duties left by her absentee husband. In addition to running the household, she was now responsible for the entire farm. One Swedish landowner inscribed a runestone as a tribute to his wife for her diligence in maintaining the family estate during his absence: "No better mistress will come to Hassmyra, to look after the farm."[32]

These sojourns by the menfolk were not without remuneration. The excursions across the Baltic and sometimes the North Sea often brought gold and silver to the farms of Sweden. In fact, "No other period glitters in quite the same fashion."[33] Such booty has turned up in graves from that time, but more often caches were in the ground—a family's wealth hidden from robbers, or raiders, or invaders. Other valuables have been located in peat bogs, perhaps left as sacrifices to the gods. Gold has been found in the form of ingots or bars bent to form gold rings. Sometimes the gold and silver were fashioned into intricate jewelry or used to decorate swords, scabbards and shields. Often gold coins are found, particularly the Roman *solidi*.

Some of these hoards are quite substantial. In Södermanland, 32 pounds of gold was discovered in one cache, and at Timboholm in Västergötland, 90 pounds of gold was found dating from this period.[34] Two celebrated golden horns (probably drinking horns) were uncovered in the same field at Gallehus in southern Jutland, one in 1639 and the other in 1734. Together, the solid gold pieces weighed over 20 pounds. One horn had a runic inscription on it. Unfortunately, both horns were later stolen and melted down.[35]

The primary source of these riches was the collapsing Roman Empire.[36] Provinces were overrun; estates, government buildings and churches were looted; and Roman citizens and soldiers were held for ransom. The empire's gold and silver flowed into the coffers of the invading Germanic tribes. Through raiding and trading, a good deal of this treasure made its way to Scandinavia (and Sweden in particular).

Much of this wealth was no doubt acquired through the sea raids referred to in both *Beowulf* and the *Ynglinga Saga*. But a good deal of it was also obtained through trade.[37] The Svear of Uppland had long since gained a reputation for their furs and fine horses. Amber had likewise been a staple of trade for thousands of years, and Swedish iron was certainly a trade commodity by this time.

On the island of Helgö in Lake Mälar near Stockholm, archaeologists have discovered a most unusual type of settlement. Villages are rare enough in the Sweden of the Migration Period, but this community was not just a town—it was a market center. Trade was conducted here as well as manufacturing. Excavations have turned up evidence of large building complexes that contained workshops where gold, silver, bronze and iron articles were manufactured. Everything from weapons of war to jewelry was created here. Artifacts made from molds discovered at Helgö have been found in northern Sweden, Gotland and Finland. Caches of Roman gold coins have been discovered, along with items from Britain, Central Europe, the eastern Baltic and beyond.[38] At its height, from AD 400 to 700, Helgö was certainly the most important trade and manufacturing center in Sweden, and maybe in all Scandinavia.

By AD 575 the Migration Period had ended. The turmoil and chaos of the age subsided, with some semblance of stability returning to Central and Southern Europe. The Angles, Saxons and Jutes had organized kingdoms in England and were busy driving the Britons (Welsh or Celts) eastward and the Picts (Scots) back to the north. The Anglo-Saxon Chronicle records the following for the years AD 577 and 603:

> 577. Cuthwine and Ceawlin fought the Britons, and killed three kings, Conmail, Condidan and Farinmail, in the place called Dyrham. They took three cities: Gloucester, Cirencester and Bath.[39]
> 603. Aedan, king of the Scots fought the Daelreodi [an Irish people living in Britain[40]] and Aethelferth, king of Northumbria at Daegsanstan; almost all his troops were killed. Never since has any Scottish king dared to lead an army into this nation.[41]

In Central Europe, the Franks had overrun what is now Germany and the northern parts of the old Roman Gaul, the Burgundians having taken the southern portion. The Visigoths were ensconced in Spain and the Ostrogoths in Italy. Though there were wars aplenty, the collapse of the Western Roman Empire was complete and the vacuum filled.

As the Migration Period waned in Sweden, there was a decided decline in the cultivated area. Many villages and farms were abandoned, especially those on marginally productive land and in newly opened areas. But even many of the old established farms were deserted. This same contraction is evident in other parts of Northwestern Europe at this time.[42] The cause might have been a change in climate, new agricultural practices, shifting trade patterns, increased warfare, a move toward urbanization or some combination of these factors.

There clearly were changes going on, and there are indications that warfare was involved. Archaeologists have recovered weapons and other equipment related to warfare from peat bogs dating to this period, some of Frankish origin. It was a common practice in Scandinavia to submerge the war equipment taken from a defeated enemy in a sacred lake or bog as a sacrifice to the gods. As time went on, only the sword hilts, scabbard mounts, buckles and shield décor were offered, as giving up the entire sword or shield was considered impractical and a little too much of a sacrifice.[43]

The remains of forts have also been found, often some distance from a village or farm, an indication that a safe refuge was needed from time to time—a sanctuary from a marauding army or piratical raiders.

The island of Öland, off the coast of Småland, Sweden, held a very exposed position, subject to raiders and invaders coming from both the north (Svear Uppland) and the south (Skåne and the Danish kingdoms). Even its proximity to Småland across a narrow channel made it a tempting target from that side. The use of forts on this island began earlier than in other regions, probably as early as the fifth century. However, the majority of the sixteen forts so far discovered on the island were in use during the end of the Migration Period. The largest of these, Gråborg, is 360 feet in diameter.[44]

Another fort on Öland, near Eketorp, was originally built in the fourth century as a temporary refuge in times of danger. In the fifth century it was enlarged to a diameter of 240 feet, enclosing not just houses but also barns. For over two hundred years this was a fortified village, a testament to the threats of this unsettled time.[45]

Further out in the Baltic is the Swedish island of Gotland. Here, during the Migration Period, there developed a unique innovation repeated nowhere else in Northern Europe. Only on Gotland are found large limestone picture monuments at grave sites and along ancient roadways. Some 375 such picture stones have been discovered, dating from the fifth century into the eleventh. The monuments from the Migration Period were up to ten feet tall, shaped like a single-bladed ax standing on its butt with the convex top.[46] In these stones, one side has been smoothed and decorated with a relief of circles, whorls and spirals. Beneath these abstract designs, in the lower part of the monument, there is sometimes a rowed boat of the Baltic style. Traces of paint have been found on these designs. The effect of the monuments when brightly colored must have been remarkable.

By the eighth century, the form of these picture stones had changed. They became mushroom shaped and as much as twelve feet in height, with an abstract swirl motif forming a border around a series of scenes. As many as six horizontal strip pictures are present, showing warriors, horses and even women, but there is always a sailing vessel in the bottom panel.[47] The scenes seem to depict battles, warriors being welcomed by the Valkyrie of Valhalla and, at the bottom, the hero being carried in a ship to the land of the dead. These monuments reached their artistic peak after the Migration Period, during Vendel Period.

As noted earlier, the Vendel Period (AD 575–790) takes its name from the rich graves excavated at Vendel in Uppland, Sweden. Here, fourteen closely grouped graves have been found in one "cemetery." Twelve of the men in this cemetery were buried in boats up to 30 feet in length, and two were interred in coffins. A second important graveyard of this period was found at Valsgärde in Uppland. Between the two, twenty-five boat burials have been excavated.[48] Similar graves have been found in other parts of Uppland and in the Mälar region. These were the funeral grounds of wealthy agricultural families and, in some cases, families from which the kings were chosen.

Grave goods include cooking utensils, the bones of slaughtered animals, swords with gold or silver hilts, shields with abstract and stylistic animal designs, iron helmets complete with nose guards, and face protection made of sheet metal or chainmail. Many items are embossed with bronze, gold or silver and decorated with stylistic motifs or panels showing warriors in battle; all appear to be of Swedish manufacture.[49]

The Vendel Period boat graves in Sweden have a parallel in Britain in the well-known Sutton Hoo cemetery located in what was then the kingdom of East Anglia. Here similar ship burials have been excavated. Shield parts and decorations, and par-

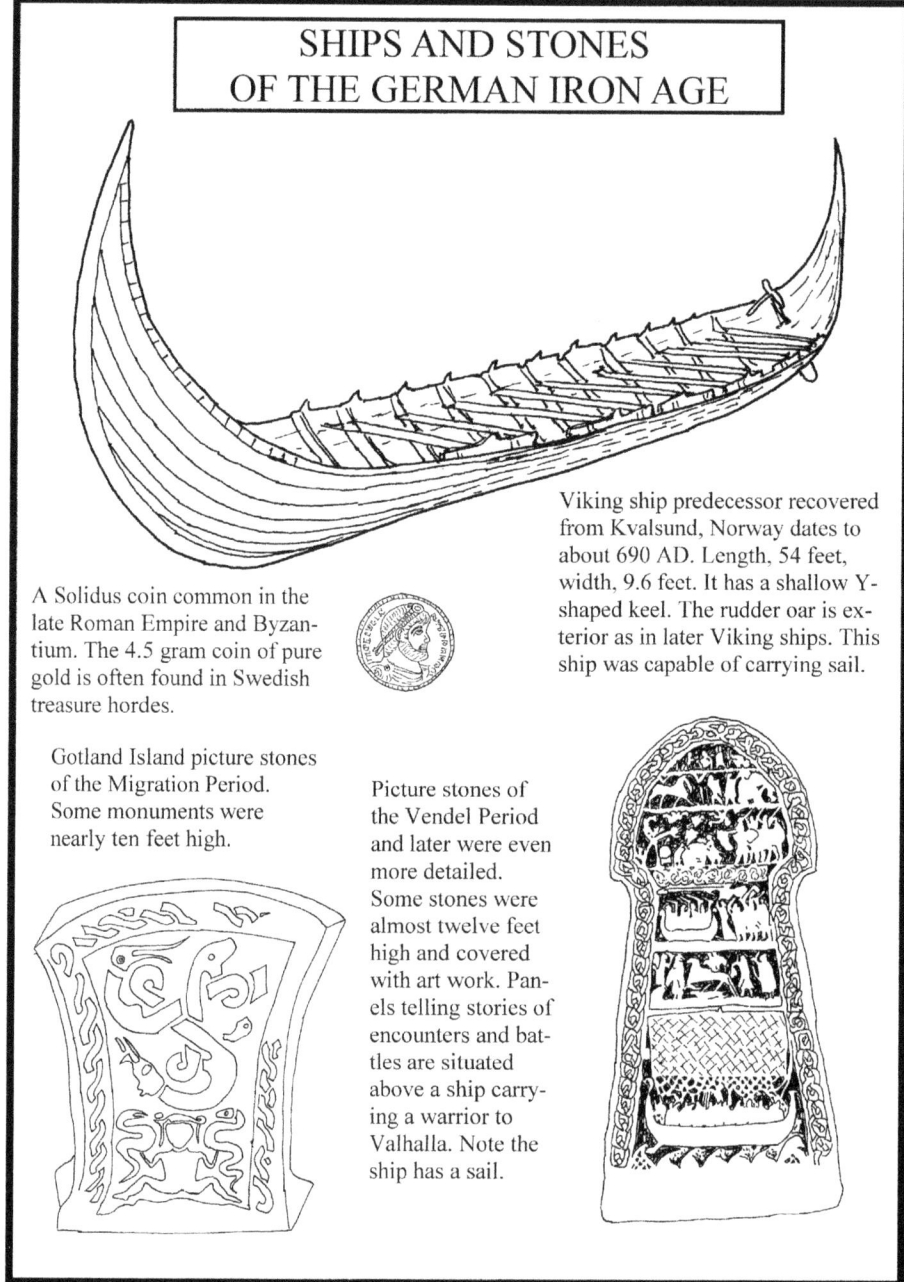

ticularly helmets, quite similar to those found in Sweden have been recovered.[50] More recently, a hoard of some 3,500 pieces was discovered in 2009 in Staffordshire in what was once the kingdom of Mercia. Among the items recovered were 11 pounds of gold in sword hilts, sword pommel caps, scabbard pendants and parts of a warrior's helmet.[51] This seeming close connection between Sweden and the Anglo-Saxons of England brings to mind *Beowulf*, the poem composed in Britain but set in Denmark/Sweden. In particular, there is the description of a ship burial in the poem:

11. Sweden of the Vendel Period (AD 575–790)

WEAPONS AND ARMOR OF GERMAN IRON AGE (400 to 790 AD)

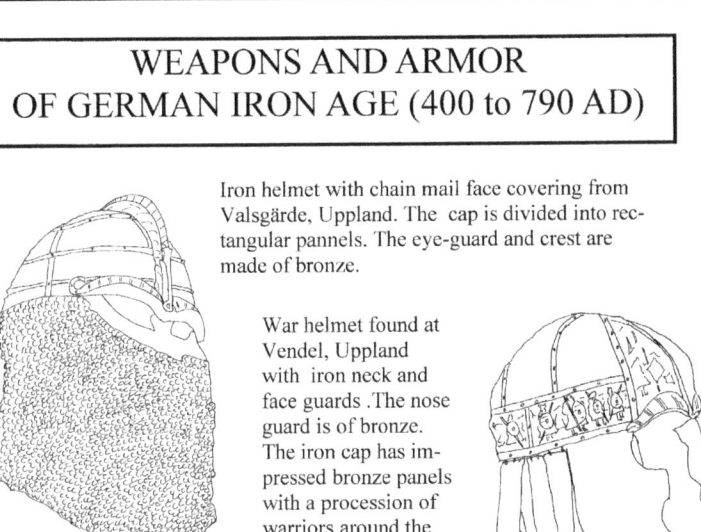

Iron helmet with chain mail face covering from Valsgärde, Uppland. The cap is divided into rectangular pannels. The eye-guard and crest are made of bronze.

War helmet found at Vendel, Uppland with iron neck and face guards. The nose guard is of bronze. The iron cap has impressed bronze panels with a procession of warriors around the rim and a battle scene in the front.

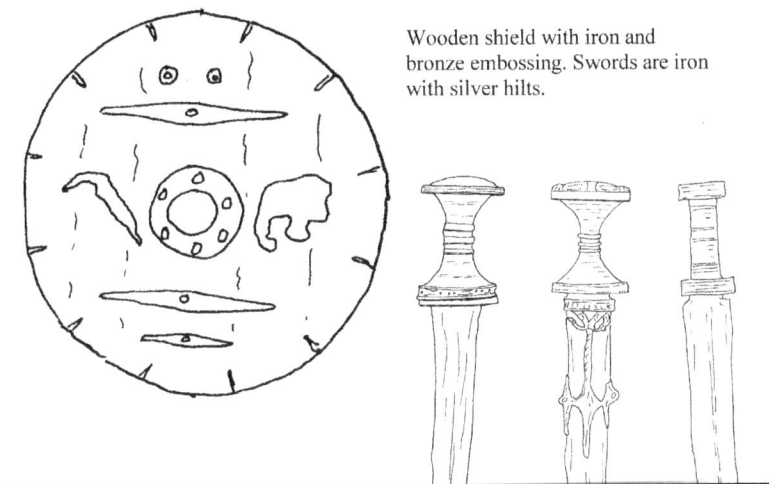

Wooden shield with iron and bronze embossing. Swords are iron with silver hilts.

> Then they bore him over to ocean's billow,
> loving clansmen, as late he charged them.
> While wielded words the winsome Scyld,
> the leader beloved who long had ruled....
> In the roadstead rocked a ring-dight vessel,
> ice-flecked, outbound, atheling's barge:
> there laid they down their darling lord
> on the breast of the boat, the breaker-of-rings,
> by the mast the mighty one.[52]

Weapons and armor are loaded on the ship with the body. Treasure and gifts are added, along with a banner of woven gold waving high overhead. The ship is then shoved off to "let billows take him, g[i]ve him to ocean."[53]

The poem indicates that the ship was simply floated out to sea to drift aimlessly until it eventually sank. No mention is made of firing the ship. Though this was a burial at sea and no doubt represents many such actual funerals conducted in both England and Scandinavia, burial in a boat on land was probably very similar.

Though the grave-boats of Uppland and Mälar have left only an impression in the soil, providing few details as to their construction, a complete ship dating to about AD 690 has been recovered from a peat bog at Kvalsund in Norway. The pre–Viking ship is 54 feet long and almost 10 feet wide.[54] Whereas Scandinavian boats of earlier periods were propelled by oar only, this width of this ship suggests that it was built to handle sails. The use of sails is further attested to by the Gotland picture-stones showing vessels under sail. An oar-propelled boat was adequate for coastal travel and navigation among the Scandinavian islands, but to travel the far reaches of the Baltic, conquer the North Sea and venture out into the Atlantic, sails were necessary.

The Kvalsund craft has another feature new to Norse ships: a rudimentary keel. By the Vendel Period, Scandinavian longboats were being built with keels to provide stability and allow the effective use of sails. The Vendel Period boat was one step removed from the Viking Age longboat. It was a rather marvelous and versatile instrument for voyaging, the finest ship in the world at that time. The Scandinavian longboat was sturdy, stable and seaworthy enough to take on the storms of the North Atlantic. Propelled by either sail or oar, it could travel long distances; yet its shallow draft allowed it to navigate relatively shallow rivers. The North Sea, the Atlantic, the Mediterranean, the Black Sea and the vast river systems of Western and Eastern Europe were all arteries for raiding and trading open to the Scandinavian Norsemen because of the Viking longboat.

By the end of the Vendel Period, Scandinavians had the ability to reach nearly all parts of Eastern and Western Europe, and even North America, but what was it that propelled the Viking invasion, with their longboats suddenly appearing everywhere in Europe? As we've seen, the Norse had a long tradition of raiding and trading among themselves and harassing the coastal areas of the Baltic and eastern North Sea, but the abrupt expansion into all parts of Europe may have been triggered by a sudden expansion in population. "Just proceeding the Viking age, we find evidence of a marked population explosion. The number of burials multiplies and place names increase."[55] Thus the manpower was available for adventures abroad—indeed, such exploits may have been necessary to drain off the excess population.

While the reason for this sudden overflow in inhabitants has not been determined, there may have been more than one cause. Perhaps the initial Scandinavian wars had subsided, releasing warriors for foreign adventures. Maybe the effects of the approaching Medieval Warm Period (MWP) that would peak in about AD 1000 were being felt, providing greater food production. Whatever the cause, the result was a surplus of people available and well prepared to explore new territories, settle where possible, establish new trade enterprises and plunder where there was an accumulation of wealth.

By the end of the Vendel Period, new trade centers were being established in Jutland that would rival and surpass Swedish Helgö. Ribe on the Ribe River in Jutland had easy access to the North Sea. Here were iron and bronze smithies, cobblers, comb makers, and bead makers who cut and polished locally found amber and glass imported from the south. Like Helgö, this was both a trade center and a manufacturing center. To trade for imported glass and metals, the merchants of Ribe had the much-valued amber of Jutland and various agricultural products, such as beeswax, honey and particularly cattle, valued for meat and leather.[56]

Similar settlements were founded in Denmark, such as Aggersborg at a crossing of the Limfjord. (Later one of the largest fortresses of the Viking Age would be built there.) Another town was Hedeby, established on a branch of the Schleifjord, which cuts deep into the Jutland peninsula. It is a short portage to reach the Treene and Ejder rivers draining to the west, providing a natural crossing point connecting the North Sea and the Baltic. It is also on the north-south road between the Jutland interior and Germany to the south. Hedeby would become one of the most important trade centers of the Viking world and the object of conquest for several Scandinavian kings.

All the factors were in place. The great Viking onslaught was about to erupt upon the European stage. Scandinavia, almost unknown to contemporary Europe, was on the verge of unleashing its fury on an unsuspecting world. The people of Sweden would thus, for a second time, become significant players in European history.

12

Norwegian Vikings Assault the British Isles

On a wintery January morning in AD 793, a Norwegian Viking fleet appeared off the English east coast of Northumbria in the vicinity of Lindisfarne, a wealthy and prestigious monastery, the repository of the relics of St. Cuthbert.[1] Its location on an island, a feature meant to preserve its isolation from the outside world, made it an attractive target for what is considered the first Norse raid of the Viking Age.[2] According to the Anglo-Saxon Chronicle, "On January 8th, the ravaging of heathen men destroyed God's church at Lindisfarne through brutal robbery and slaughter."[3] The monastery was savagely attacked. In addition to making off with the gold, jewels and sacred emblems housed in the buildings, the raiders slaughtered the livestock and the monks (or at least those unlikely to fetch a good price at the slave market).

A loud hue and cry echoed across not just England but all of Western Europe. Alcuin, a Northumbrian scholar and teacher ensconced at the court of Charlemagne, lamented:

> Lo, it is almost three hundred and fifty years that we [Anglo-Saxons] and our forefathers have dwelt in this fair land, and never has such a horror before appeared in Britain, such as we have just suffered from the heathen. It was not thought possible that they [the Norse] could have made such a voyage.[4]

But this was merely the opening salvo of what was to be more than 250 years of pillaging, rape, murder, conquest and trade perpetrated by the warriors from Scandinavia.

The next year, 794, a Norwegian fleet returned to the Northumbrian coast on another raid, no doubt expecting an equally easy time of pilferage and slaughter. The Chronicle records:

> The heathens in Northumbria ravaged and robbed Ecgfrith's monastery at Jarrow. There some of their war-leaders were killed; also some of their ships were broken up in bad weather, and many drowned. Some came alive to shore and were quickly killed at the river's mouth.[5]

The Norwegian warriors got their noses bloodied this time and would look for easier pickings elsewhere. At about the same time, there was a raid along the southern coast of England in Wessex by either Danes or Norwegians, but this proved to be an isolated attack, and the English coast would remain free of the Viking intruders for another forty years. When the invaders did return, it would be Danes, not Norwegians, who would exact tribute in gold and blood.

Norwegian Vikings started earlier than the other Scandinavians in this overseas adventurism. With very limited farmland along the fjords and mountain meadows of

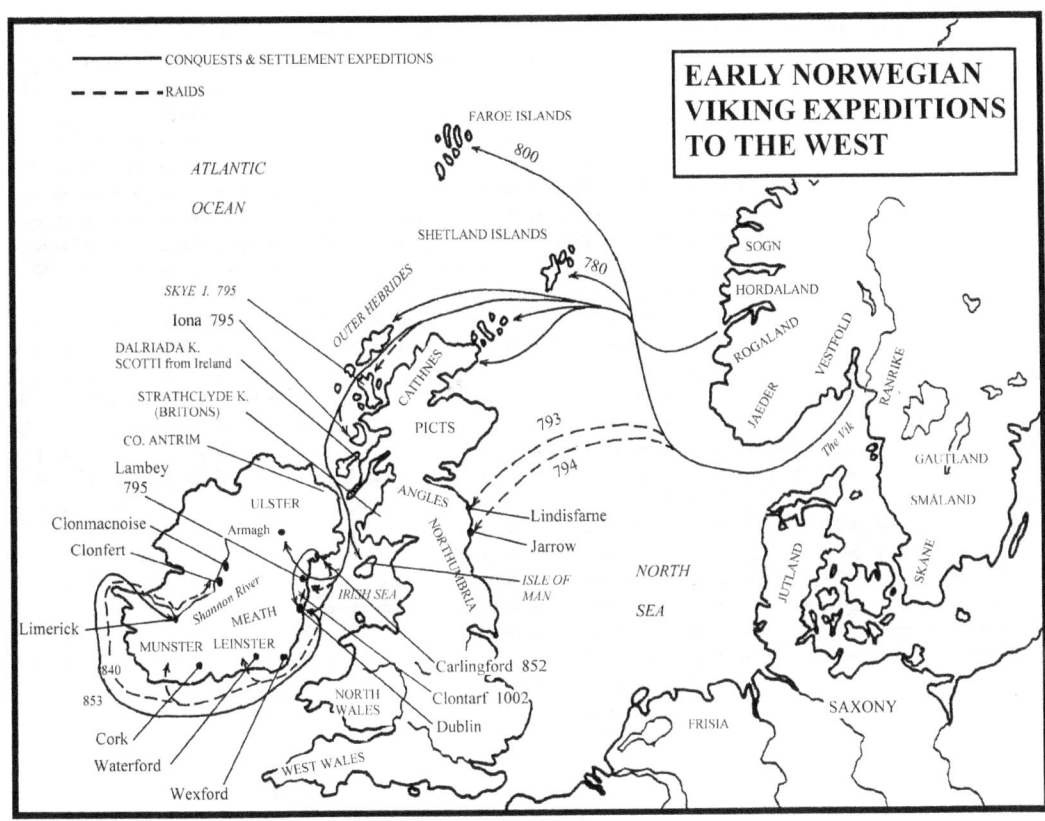

their native land, they put out to the open sea in search of land and booty perhaps half a century before their Danish and Swedish cousins.[6] By AD 780, the Norwegians had crossed the 180 nautical miles between their coast and the Shetland Islands, a two-day sail with fair winds.[7] Here they found new lands to farm that were sparsely inhabited by immigrant Picts from Scotland.[8] From the Shetlands, it was a short hop to the Orkney Islands, which were conquered, colonized and then incorporated into an earldom founded in the late ninth century that would grow in power to dominate the Shetlands, northern Scotland and the Scottish western islands.

In reaching Scotland, the Norwegians found a land more thickly settled and better organized politically than the archipelagos to the north. The north and east of this most northerly part of the British Isles was populated by Picts. To the south and west the invaders encountered the Scottish kingdom of Dalriada, founded by Irish immigrants of the Scotti clan from County Antrim, Ireland. Still further south was the old Celtic (Welsh, Briton) kingdom of Strathclyde, and in the southeast they discovered Anglia, the northern extremity of the kingdom of Northumbria.[9]

The first recorded raid in Scotland was the sacking of the monastery of Iona, the center of Christianity in Scotland, in AD 795. Sites on the island of Skye, also on the west coast of Scotland, were hit the same year.[10] Certainly there must have been earlier raids on remote islands and isolated farmsteads prior to these recorded raids, but such incidents are missing from the historical record.

In spite of the resistance found in Scotland, the Norse were able to make inroads.

The northern end of Scotland (Caithness) was subdued, colonies and trading stations were established along the west coast and the Hebrides were occupied. The mainland core of Scotland remained the purview of the Picts, Scots, Britons and Angles, but the northern and western extremities became Norse territory.

Next in the path of the Norwegian Viking advance were Ireland and the Isle of Man. In the middle of the Irish Sea, the Isle of Man was a natural way station for Viking voyages coming south and for traffic between England and Ireland. It was occupied by the Norse, who established an overlordship that would last for the next 200 years. Eventually, after becoming Christianized, the island was linked to the Hebrides as part of a bishopric to balance the power of the Orkney earldom.[11]

The first recorded raid on Ireland was at Lambey in AD 795, just a year after the attack on Jarrow, Northumbria, and the same year as the sacking of Iona in Scotland.[12] Ireland presented an attractive target for the men of the north. Here was a fertile land, thoroughly Christianized, which meant a great number of monasteries, churches and abbeys to pillage. The population was divided into numerous quarreling clans and petty kingdoms that could be played against one another, but they made conquest problematic, as there were no large political states to take over.[13] Subjugation would mean occupation, and the Norsemen did not have the manpower for this kind of campaign. Yet local victories were likely, as the war arts were not as advanced in Ireland as they were in Scotland or England. Ireland was, however, fairly densely populated, and the Norsemen did not establish the dominant colonies they did in the Shetlands, Orkneys or Hebrides. After the initial raiding and plundering, activities tended more toward tribute, conquest and the establishment of trade centers.

Following the Lambey raid, the depredations continued sporadically, reaching far inland thanks to the extensive river systems of the country, to the point that the keeper of the *Annals of Ulster* complained, "The sea spewed forth floods of foreigners over Erin, so that no haven, no landing-place, no stronghold, no fort, no castle might be found, but it was submerged by waves of vikings and pirates."[14]

Though burdensome, the brutal and savage early raids did not change the political face of Ireland. That circumstance ended, however, with the arrival of a Norwegian fleet commander by the name of Turgeis sometime prior to 840.

Turgeis quickly established his overlordship of all Norse in Ireland; then he fell upon Ulster, taking Armagh, the most important town in the north and the ecclesiastic center of Ireland.[15] He involved himself in a civil war in Munster, sailed up the River Shannon and sacked the monasteries of Clonmacnois and Clonfert, dispersing their resident monks.[16] As if to make a final point, his wife, Ota, defiled the great religious shrine at Clonmacnois by offering pagan ritual sacrifices at the center's high alter.[17]

Turgeis even drew a following among some Irish who renounced Christianity and adopted a form of religion incorporating various features of Viking and Celtic paganism. These were known as the Gall-Gaedhil (Foreign Gaels or Foreign Irish), who originally joined the Norse but soon developed their own armies and leaders. They became another faction in Ireland during the mid–800s, fighting on whichever side seemed most advantageous. When otherwise unoccupied, they contributed to the general misery of the island by engaging in their own pillaging.[18]

While Turgeis and his ilk terrorized the Christian centers, they did contribute something in return. This was the opening of Ireland to the outside world through trade. Early Norse trade stations were established at Dublin, Annagassan in County Louth, Lough Ree on the River Shannon and Strangford Lough. By the early tenth century the Norse had developed harbor-strongholds, true centers of commerce, at Dublin, Waterford, Wexford, Cork and Limerick. Of these, Dublin was the most important, a wealthy manufacturing and merchant community that traded with Scandinavia, England, Scotland and France; it was at Dublin that the first coins struck in Ireland were minted in the 990s.[19]

Turgeis' reign of terror and conquest was, thankfully, cut short. In 845 he was captured by Mael Seachlainn, king of Meath, and killed by drowning in Lough Owel, Westmeath. There was little respite for the Irish, however, for in 850 a Danish fleet landed warriors at Carlingford Lough in County Down. The next year they captured the Norwegian port of Dublin along with a great deal of booty in gold, silver and women.[20]

The Norwegians were not about to give up this rich land so easily. In 852 they attacked the Danes at Carlingford. The Irish sided with the Danes, and the Norwegians were slaughtered in a battle lasting three days.[21] The next year a fleet from Norway arrived led by Olaf and Ivar, two sons of a Norwegian king (which Norwegian king has not been determined). The newcomers gained the fealty of the resident Norwegians immediately, as well as the loyal service of many Irish. Some Danes submitted, while others shoved off for parts east—namely, England and France.[22] Olaf settled in Dublin, while Ivar moved on to Limerick on the River Shannon.

But the high point of Viking Ireland had been reached. Reinforcements were being drawn off to new lands discovered to the west—the Faroe Islands, Iceland and Greenland. Also, the Norse intervention at Erin had forced the Irish to unite into larger political states that eventually became effective in dealing with the invaders. In 902, Cearbhall, king of Leinster, seized Dublin, forcing the Norse ruler to submit to him.[23] By 1002, Brian Boru, king of Munster, was (in fact as well as in name) high king of Ireland. He defeated the Norse in the pivotal Battle of Clontarf, where Viking dominance of Ireland was destroyed.[24] Scandinavians would remain a factor in Irish history, in terms of both raiding and trading, for another couple of generations, but their hold on the Emerald Isle was forever broken.

13

Danish Vikings Invade England

In the previous chapter we discussed the first Norse raids on Northumbrian monasteries in AD 793 and 794, which were followed by a cessation of Viking activity along the English coast for almost 40 years. England was a tougher proposition than Ireland in many ways. For example, it was better organized politically. The dozen or so original Angle, Saxon and Jute kingdoms had, by the eighth century, been consolidated into four entities: Northumbria in the north, Mercia in central England, the remnants of East Anglia on the east coast, and Wessex, which had overrun the old kingdoms of Essex, Kent and Sussex. Three areas of Celtic Britons still remained unconquered—West Wales (Dumnonia), west of Wessex; North Wales (Gwynedd, Powys and Dyfed); and Strathclyde in southwestern Scotland.[1] Militarily, the English were more akin to the Vikings in weapons, armor and tactics then were the Irish. However, the country was rich in prizes:

> On all sides were abbeys and monasteries, churches, and even cathedrals, possessed in that starveling age of treasures of gold and silver, of jewels, and also large stores of food, wine, and such luxuries as were known. The pious English had accepted far too literally the idea of the absolution of sins as the consequence of monetary payments to the Church. Their sins were many, their repentance frequent, and the Church had thrived. Here were easy prizes for sharp swords to win.[2]

And there was also land, women and able bodies for the slave markets, though these would be a bit harder to obtain.

The first verified Danish assault occurred in AD 835, as the Anglo-Saxon Chronicle notes: "Heathen men ravaged Sheppey."[3] This short notice of the attack on an island off Kent was followed almost annually by reports of raids up and down the English shoreline, testing the defenses of Cornwall and the southern coast (836–842), then moving back to Kent and East Anglia.[4] In 850 a new and alarming phase began with the Danes spending the winter in Kent. Still more disconcerting was the large force, known as the "Danish army," that landed in 866, apparently intending to permanently occupy territory.[5] The "army" adopted the strategy of fortifying its camps much as the Romans had done.[6] Having left their ships, the Scandinavians were very good at securing horses, and they became a mobile cavalry force fighting mounted or as dismounted infantry, whichever was to their advantage. They operated in companies, each company made up of a ship's crew, so there was a natural military organization built around this basic division of a group of warriors intimately familiar with one another—brothers in arms and at sea.[7] The Chronicle notes that in 866, "a great heathen force came into

England, and they took winter-quarters in East Anglia; there they were horsed, and they made peace with them."[8] In this early phase, the entire army would not have numbered more than 1,000 men.[9]

Scandinavian legend holds that the invasion was prompted by an incident involving one Ragnar Hairy-breeches, who was Norwegian by birth but related to a Danish royal family. After being defeated at the gates of Paris and enduring a plague while in France, Ragnar took his Viking fleet to England, where he was again defeated; this time he was

also captured. In the end, King Ælle (Aelle or Ella) of Northumbria threw Ragnar into a snake pit. According to the legend, as Ragnar was dying among the vipers, he prophesied "that the little pigs will grunt when they hear how the old boar died." By "little pigs," Ragnar meant his four sons: Ubbi (Bjorn Ironside), Halfdan (Hvitserk), Sigurd Snake-eye and Ivar the Boneless. They would be committed to carrying out a particular act of vengeance on Ælle—namely, the "Blood-red Eagle."[10] In this rite, the victim's ribs are cut away from the spine and the lungs pulled though the opening thus created and spread out on his back like wings.[11]

Ivar the Boneless turned out to be a very competent military commander. It was he who planned and led the "Danish army" in the campaigns that conquered central England.[12] He is sometimes equated with Ivar of the Irish-Norse wars, but the evidence for this is sketchy and contradictory.

After wintering in East Anglia, Ivar marched on York and took the stronghold. Ælle brought his army south to meet the Danes but was soundly defeated, and legend says the brothers exacted the prescribed retribution, subjecting Ælle to the Blood-red Eagle rite. The old kingdom of Deira, the southern half of Northumbria, passed into Danish hands.

Mercia was next, but here the king paid off the invaders after a stout (though short) resistance. In 869, Ivar and Ubbi led the Danes back into East Anglia, where they defeated King Edmund, who earned sainthood for his stand. He was cruelly executed and his kingdom joined Deira as part of Danish England. In 870 Halfdan led an attack on Wessex and its king, Ethelred. After several battles, most of which were won by the Danes, a truce was called and the Danish fighters moved back into Mercia, where English defenses had collapsed by 874.[13]

The Danish army, which had grown over time, was now divided. Halfdan took a portion into Deira, where he employed his warriors against the Welsh of Strathclyde and the Picts to secure his northwestern border. Another leader, Guthrum, moved back into East Anglia with the other half of the army. A section of the conquered area called the Five Boroughs (Yorkshire, Nottingham, Lincoln, Derby, and Leicester) was divided and settled by Danish farmers prepared to make their living in this foreign land. Some of these settlers were the thanes involved in the invasion, and some were new immigrants from Denmark.[14]

Guthrum, meanwhile, conducted a series of attacks on Wessex that were effectively countered by the new king, Alfred. When Ethelred had died, he had had a son in line as heir to the throne, but, interestingly, the crown instead went to his brother, Alfred, perhaps fourth in line. It was an unusual but fortunate selection for England.

Alfred successfully parried the Danish thrusts through defensive actions and truces until, in the dead of winter 878, Guthrum made a surprise attack:

> Down swept the ravaging foe. The whole army of Wessex, sole guarantee of England south of the Thames, was dashed into confusion. A strong contingent fled overseas. Refugees arrived with futile appeals at the Court of France. Only a handful of officers and personal attendants hid themselves with Alfred in the marshes and forests of Somerset and the Isle of Athelney [an island in the swamps of Somerset] which rose from the quags. This was the darkest hour of Alfred's fortunes.[15]

The subjugation of all England by the Danish Vikings seemed inevitable. "But if Alfred despaired we do not hear of it."[16] Slowly, he gathered men from Somerset, Wiltshire, and Hampshire to his cause. Alfred first turned on West Wales and smashed a threat from that direction, thus securing his rear. Then he attacked the Danes to the east, defeating them at Eddington and pursuing them to Chippenham, where he laid siege to Guthrum's forces. The struggle was settled by the treaty of Wedmore, by which Guthrum agreed to withdraw from Wessex and be baptized, an important first step in the Christianization of the Danes in England.

By 879 Guthrum was back in East Anglia, distributing lands to his occupational forces. Northampton, Huntingdon, Cambridge, Bedford, Norfolk, Suffolk, Essex and London were settled as part of the Danelaw, a region of England distinguished from Anglo-Saxon or Welsh territory by its laws, language and social customs—a Danish country on foreign soil.

Having saved at least part of Saxon England, Alfred turned to consolidating his gains and building defenses. The Danes had installed a puppet monarch in western Mercia who answered to them, but his successor went over to Alfred's side, pledging allegiance to the Wessex king. Alfred also regained control of London, becoming king of all Saxon England not occupied by the Danes. Meanwhile, the Welsh princes and the Angles of northern Northumbria (the old Kingdom of Bernicia) were doing some fence sitting, staying out of the fighting to the south.

Militarily, Alfred divided his peasant militia, the strength of his army, into two sections, one to be in the field while the other was at home, thus solving the problem of his soldiers only serving for 40 days and then escaping to their farms. He built a series of fortresses and strong points throughout his realm for defense. Finally, he constructed a navy, featuring ships of his own design, not like the Viking longboats or the Frisian model, but very large ships of up to sixty rowers. Thus Alfred was able to prevent the Danelaw from expanding further.[17]

Alfred, dubbed "The Great" by many historians for his successful defense of England, died in 899. He was succeeded by his son Edward (the Elder). This led to a quarrel with a cousin named Ethelwald, who fled to the Danelaw and was able to rouse the Northumbrian and East Anglican Danes into attacking the new Wessex king. In the ensuing conflict, Ethelwald and the Danish king were killed. The new king of the southern Danelaw, Guthrum II, signed a peace treaty with Edward.[18]

War was renewed in 910 by the Danes, but Edward of Wessex and Ethelred of English Mercia pressed the attack, building forts and fortifying the towns they captured, ever reducing Danish territory. The two were also in-laws, as Ethelred had married Edward's sister. In 911, Ethelred died, only to be replaced by his wife, Ethelfleda (known as "The Lady of the Mercians"), who was at least as diligent in prosecuting the war against the Danelaw as her husband had been. Brother and sister worked in concert in conducting the war, something the Danes failed to do, which in the end left them at a serious disadvantage.[19]

Edward and Ethelfleda invaded East Anglia and then southern Mercia, fortifying towns and hilltops as they advanced. They were ready to deliver the final bow to Danish Mercia when Ethelfleda died. Edward assumed the crown of Mercia in addition to his own Wessex and turned toward the attenuated Danelaw. The now Christian Danes capitulated, and Edward exacted no revenge. He wanted the Danes as allies, for there was a new threat from the northwest.

Since the beginning of the ninth century, Norse from Ireland had been migrating to the west coast of England north of Wales. A leader arose from among these Vikings, Rognvald, who, with encouragement and maybe even support from the Angles of Bernicia, united these Norsemen and invaded York, making himself king in 919. (York had long been one of the great trade centers of the Viking world.) Two years later Rognvald died, leaving the York kingdom to his kinsman, Sigtrygg. The Anglo-Saxon Chronicle entry of 920 reads:

> He [Edward] was chosen as father and lord by the king of the Scots and all the Scottish people; by Raegnald [Rognvald], and Eadulf's sons, and all who dwell in Northumbria, English, Danes, Norse and others, and the king of the Strathclyde Welsh, and the Strathclyde Welsh themselves.[20]

Edward the Elder would thus seem to have gained at least nominal overlordship of all England and Scotland. He would die four years later, leaving his country once again in the hands of the English.

Edward's successor was his son Athelstan, who inherited all of Anglo-Saxon England, including the Danelaw, except for Northumbria, which saw itself as a traditionally independent kingdom and had selected Olaf, son of Sigtrygg, as its youthful king at York, with Guthfrith of Dublin as guardian. Athelstan invaded and drove the two Norwegians out, setting the stage for the pivotal battle of Brunanburh in 937.

In this battle Athelstan and his brother led the forces of Wessex and Mercia against the Norsemen of Ireland under Olaf, the Scots led by Constantine and the Strathclyde Welsh under Eugenius. Though the Icelandic *Egil's Saga* claims that the Welsh of Wales were also involved, there is no corroboration of this story.[21] The saga reports the outcome of the battle:

> When King Athelstan realized that Olaf's column was breaking up he shouted encouragement to his troops and had his banner carried forward in the fierce onslaught, routing Olaf's men and cutting them down in large numbers. King Olaf was killed along with most of his army, for everyone caught running away was put to death. So King Athelstan won a great victory there.[22]

Athelstan would rule Northumbria as part of his kingdom, but his successor, his brother Edmond, would be challenged and the throne at York bounced between Irish Norsemen, Danelaw Danes, and the king of England. Finally, in 954, the issue was settled with the expulsion of Eric Bloodaxe, the last Norse king of York, and England was finally united, though there would always be that section of England that carried the Scandinavian stamp in terms of race, place names, language and customs.[23]

14

Viking Raids and Conquests in Continental Europe

At the same time that the British Isles were being pillaged by the Vikings, the continent was also suffering from raids launched by men from the north. We have already noted an early raid (about AD 520) on Frisia by the Geats of Sweden recorded in *Beowulf* (chapter 10). According to the poem and other sources, the Geatish leader, Hygelac, was killed by Theudobert, the son of Theudoric, a king of the Franks. Stories in the *Ynglinga Saga* tell of raids and even conquests on the western continent, Frisia and Saxland (northern Germany), before the Viking Age proper. The old Roman Gaul and parts of Germany to the east were ruled by the Franks before and during the Viking Age. Many small Frankish kingdoms were first united by Clovis I in AD 509. Per Frankish custom, his empire was divided among his sons, one of those being Theudoric I. Upon his death, Theudobert, the military leader who defeated the Geatish raid on Frisia, became king of Austrasia, a part of the Frankish domain. The Franks were again united under Chlothar II in AD 613, only to be redivided among his heirs and then united again under Charlemagne (Charles the Great) in 768.

Charlemagne stretched the Frankish territory into a true empire, conquering from Zaragoza and Barcelona in Spain to the Oder in Germany, south into the Balkans to Dalmatia and even into Italy.[1] He maintained an empire well organized politically and militarily, providing few opportunities for the Vikings to raid and plunder without heavy risk.

That's not to say they didn't try. In AD 799 Viking raiders began their first attacks in Aquitaine. Further intrusions forced Charlemagne to build fortifications along his northwestern frontier to defend against the intruders.[2] For the most part his defenses worked, and the pirates from the north were held at bay.

There was also direct contact between the Danes and Franks on land. With Charlemagne's conquest of Saxony in AD 772–808, Denmark and the Frankish Empire had a common border at the base of the Jutland peninsula. Continuing warfare along this frontier motivated the Danish king Godfred to begin constructing an earthen wall, the Danevirke, across the neck of Jutland to defend his territory in 808. Resent archaeological finds suggest the series of walls and fortifications may have been started as early as 737 and were added to and modified throughout the Viking Age.[3]

In AD 814 Charlemagne died and, as per tradition, his empire was divided between

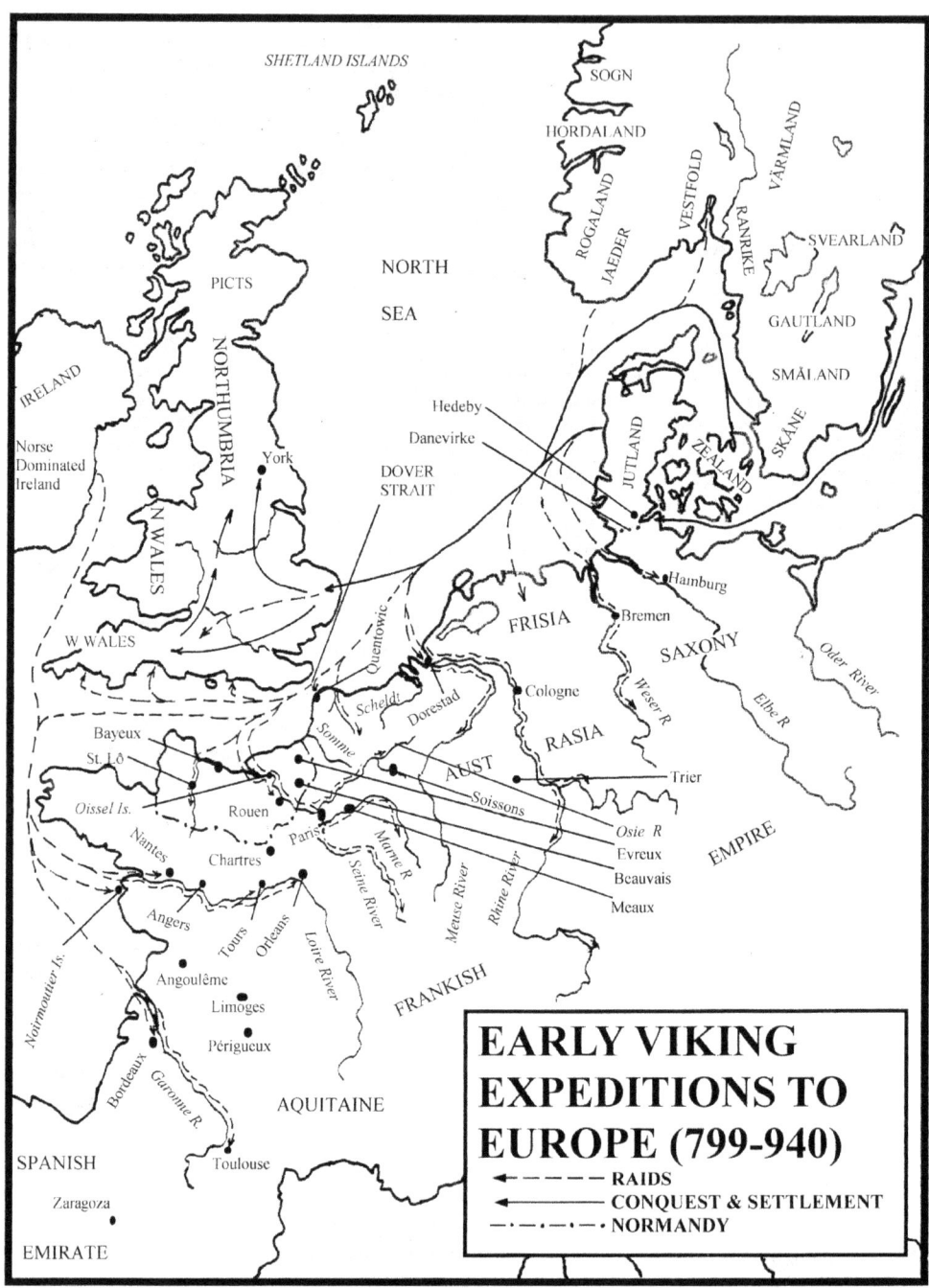

his sons. The western third went to Charles the Bald, the eastern third to Louis the German, and the area in between to Lothair.[4] The three brothers (particularly Louis and Charles) set about attacking each other, which left their lands open to the Vikings, ever on the prowl for new opportunities.

Beginning in AD 820, Frisia was the target for repeated (albeit isolated) raids. By 834 Danish fleets were operating on both sides of the English Channel; sometimes a fleet would attack the Anglo-Saxons and then cross over and hit the Franks as well. In 834 the Danes plundered Dorestad on the Lek, an arm of the Rhine. Dorestad was one of the great trade centers of the Viking Age, minting a silver penny much prized on the continent and in Scandinavia. Though the town was protected by water, palisades and a fortress, the Danes made short work of the defenses and laid waste to Dorestad. They would revisit this trade center many times until its destruction in 864 due to a change in course of the Rhine.[5]

Noirmoutier, a monastic site and trade center specializing in wine and salt, was also attacked. In 841 Asgeir sailed up the Seine and raided Rouen, escaping before defensive forces could gather. The next year it was Quentowic, across the channel from the Straits of Dover. This was another trade center, similar to Dorestad and York, with close trade ties to Anglo-Saxon England. It, too, had its own mint, an inviting target for the Danes.

That same year, 842, a Norwegian fleet of some sixty-seven ships appeared off Loire, Aquitaine. This force was ostensibly from Vestfold, Norway, but probably a good share of the men and ships hailed from Norse Ireland.[6] There is some evidence that the Vikings had been invited by a rebel, Count Lambert, who was attempting to liberate Nantes from the Western Frank kingdom of Charles the Bald. His pilots and scouts were said to have guided the Norwegians up the river, past sandbars and shallows that were thought to provide absolute protection from the northern pirates. The assault was timed for St. John's Day so that the town would be filled with celebrants. The attack was brutal in the extreme. Priests, bishops and congregations were murdered in their churches. Streets, houses and merchant shops ran red with blood from the onslaught. Rape, pillaging and kidnapping were the order of the day. After it was all over, the fleet sailed away downriver laden with plunder and captives for the slave markets and for ransom.

The Norsemen likewise hove to at Noirmoutier. The monks had abandoned the monastery due to previous raids, but the merchants were still there, dealing in wine and salt. Since the town was on an island, it made a good defensible position for the raiders. In fact, for the first time in Frankish territory, they stayed the winter—an ominous development.

Hamburg was sacked in 845 by a fleet of six hundred ships (or so it was said).[7] That same year a Danish chief named Ragnar led a fleet up the Seine. Given some warning, Charles the Bald collected an army and made ready to trap the intruders. He split his forces, placing a division on either side of the river. Ragnar merely attacked the smaller of the two elements and defeated it, taking 111 prisoners, whom he promptly hanged in full view of the other division. He then sailed on up the river and ravaged Paris on Easter Sunday. The effect was much as it had been at Nantes. The Danes killed and plundered at will, massacring citizens and clergy, sparing the most fit for the slave trade. Charles paid 7,000 pounds in silver to be rid of the menace, beginning an evil precedent that would eventually lead to the infamous "Danegeld" in England.[8]

The depredations continued in Bordeaux, Périgueux, Limoges, Angoulême, Toulouse, Angers, Tours and Orleans. The Seine was invaded again and again. Rouen, Beauvais, Meaux, Chartres, Evreux and Bayeux were taken and looted. On one occasion the Franks were able to turn one group against another. Charles the Bald paid the Viking Weland 5,000 pounds of silver to besiege a band of Danes under Bjorn Ironside, who had occupied the island of Oissel in the Seine. Bjorn had to buy his way out, paying Weland another 6,000 pounds of silver to be allowed to escape.[9]

Charles the Bald died in 877 and was succeeded by his son, Louis the Stammerer, who died within 18 months. By 884 Louis' two sons and successors had died, and the Franks were once more united under Charles the Fat. His empire encompassed most of the old domain of Charlemagne, but he proved to be a weak king. The atrocities continued along the Scheldt, Meuse, Somme, Marne, Seine, Loire, Rhine, and Oise, river roads leading to Cologne, Trier, Rouen, Soissons, Bayeux and St. Lô. Of particular note was the siege of Paris, begun in 885 by the Danish king Sigfred, which lasted a year. The city was successfully defended by Odo, Count of Paris, and Charles the Fat finally bought off the Danes for a measly 700 pounds of silver. It was a bargain, but the deal got Charles deposed, and the Franks were once more divided, making them easy pickings for the opportunistic Vikings.[10]

Another ploy the Franks tried in their attempts to neutralize the Vikings was giving them land instead of silver as a payoff or, in some cases, attempting to give them a sense of responsibility for defending an area against other Viking raiders. The Frankish emperor Louis I gave lands in Frisia, including Dorestad, to Rorik (or Roerik), a ruler in Jutland, in an attempt to mollify Rorik's greed for land. Unfortunately, the buyoff didn't work. Rorik plundered adjacent lands, sacking Bremen in 859.[11] Louis was incensed by the betrayal and stripped Rorik of all lands in 860. But in 882 Charles the Bald restored the Friesland domains to Rorik, who was supposed to have converted to Christianity as part of the deal.

The most consequential land giveaway, however, was the dispensation of Normandy in northwestern France to the Viking leader Rollo or Hrolf. It is certain that Rollo had been operating along the French coast for some time, pillaging in the usual Viking manner (he besieged and looted Chartres in 911), when the offer of land was made by Charles the Simple. It is uncertain whether Rollo was Danish or Norwegian (Icelandic sagas identify him as Norwegian, but Norman traditions list him as Danish). His army seems to have been predominantly Danish with elements from Norse Ireland and Scotland. Rollo and his band were ceded territory around the lower Seine valley and the city of Rouen, according to the treaty of Saint-Clair-sur-Epte. The land was granted in exchange for Rollo's fealty to Charles and his baptism. Further grants were allotted in 924 to Rollo by Charles' successor, Rudolf, and again in 933 by Rudolf to Rollo's successor, Count William Longsword. Thus the duchy of Normandy was created.[12]

Rollo divided up the land among his senior officers, who in turn allotted land to their subordinates and so on down the line. From the beginning this was a feudal autocratic political system. The old traditions of Scandinavian democracy never played a role in Normandy; no democratic assemblies (Things or "hundreds") are mentioned. There were apparently few Norse or Danish women involved in the settling of the army, so intermarriage with the local population accelerated the development of a unique Normandy society and people.[13] This was a nation that would affect the history of the continent from Sicily to Scotland.

By the late ninth century, the Franks had developed tactics to block the Viking incursions. Like the Saxons, they built strategically located fortified strong points (the beginning of the medieval castles) and developed mobile, heavy cavalry that could catch and defeat the Viking foot soldiers.[14] Like the castles, heavy cavalry (the knights and armored nobility) would become a signature of medieval France. Defenses were organized on a local level around the fort, which could be used to defend against a Viking attack and then serve as the place to organize a counterattack. All this increased the power of the local lord, promoting development of the feudal system. These tactics, along with other events (the successful defense of Paris by Count Odo, the settling of Normandy and the defeat of the Swedish ruler of Hedeby by the German king Henry Fowler in 934), signaled the end of the Viking rampage in continental Europe. For the next few decades there would still be occasional raids and cross-border clashes, but the Viking open season on France and Germany had been curtailed.[15]

Before leaving the heyday of the Viking Age in Central and Western Europe, it is necessary to examine a couple of rather remarkable voyages to the southern part of Europe. The first was that of a fleet said to be 150 ships strong.[16] This flotilla, which set out in 845, first entered the Garonne and sailed almost to Toulouse, raiding and plundering as it went. Next the fleet appeared off the coast of Asturias in northern Spain, where it met stiff resistance in attempting some piracy and was mauled both on land and at sea. Licking their wounds, the Vikings moved down the coast to Lisbon, where they were more successful in their plundering. They sail on to the Guadalquivir River, now down to 80 vessels, according to Moorish records.[17] Entering the river, they sailed upstream to the city of Seville, which they occupied for a week, slaughtering the men and rounding up the women and children (considered especially sacrilegious was the killing of a group of old men who had taken refuge in a mosque). The Moorish emir in Córdoba sent a flying column of light cavalry and infantry to head off the invaders from the north. In the ensuing battle or battles, more than a thousand Vikings were killed, and 400 were captured. Over thirty of their ships were destroyed, some by flaming naphtha, a new experience for the Northmen. The captives were promptly hanged. This first encounter between Viking and Moor must have been a little sobering for both sides. The surviving Vikings made a deal for enough food and clothing to get home in exchange for a peaceful retreat and the release of the captives they had taken.[18]

The second expedition was nothing if not spectacular. This venture was led by Hasteinn and Bjørn, two well-known and highly respected Viking war chiefs. They were examples of the "sea-kings" referenced in the *Ynglinga Saga*. Perhaps their intention was a voyage into the Mediterranean from the very beginning, a feat that would enshrine their names in Viking lore. With 62 ships they left France in AD 859, sailing south and plundering the Iberian coast in a leisurely fashion. They passed through the Strait of Gibraltar, taking time to raid the nearby Moorish Algeciras and burning the town's grand mosque. This was probably the first time Viking longboats had sailed the blue waters of the Mediterranean Sea.[19]

There seems to have been no Moorish ships in the region to oppose the Northmen, for next they crossed over to the African side and pillaged the area of Cabo Tres Forcas, where they captured a large number of prisoners, including some Negroes whom they called the "blue men."[20]

Crossing back to the European coast, the marauders sacked the ports and towns of eastern Spain, the Balearics and southern France. By this time winter was approaching, so the fleet put in at an island in Camargue on the Rhône delta. Rather than while away the winter months in inactivity, the Northmen proceeded to despoil all the countryside within range, up to a hundred miles inland, including Arles and Nîmes. But here they were challenged by Frankish forces, and they decided to sail on.

After sacking Pisa, they hit a storm and were blown to another city along the coast. The Vikings were dazzled by the grandeur of this city—all the marble, white stone, and so many other splendid things convinced them that they had found Rome itself. The defensive walls were too much for the Northmen, so they came up with a ruse. They sent a message to the city saying they were poor Christian souls, storm-tossed to this shore, in need of food. What's more, their captain was sick and about to die. They pleaded for him to be given a Christian burial and last rites by a priest.

The city fathers complied with their request and allowed the long procession of "mourners" carrying the coffin of their chief into the city to the grave site. At the point of interment, the body of Hasteinn came to life, driving his sword through the belly of the attending bishop, and the mourners threw off their sackcloth and began butchering the city's inhabitants. In the midst of plundering and looting, the despoilers discovered that the city was not Rome at all but Luna—a great disappointment.[21] They burned the city and massacred the citizens except for the young women, whom they took with them.[22]

From Italy the fleet sailed on east, possibly to Alexandria (the records are sketchy and inconclusive on this point). Eventually the fleet had to head west to get home, which would require passing through the Strait of Gibraltar. The Moors, also knowing this, gathered a great fleet to deliver a punishing blow of retribution to the unwelcome Mediterranean invaders. The Northmen had no choice but to run the gauntlet, and the Moors inflicted a crushing defeat on their antagonists, destroying ships and killing crewmen. Those who did escape sailed north with enough fight left in them to stop at Navarre and capture Pamplona, extracting a huge sum for the ransom of its prince.

Finally, in 862, the remaining 20 ships pulled into the mouth of the Loire in France.[23] Hasteinn, Bjørn and the surviving Vikings were home with plunder and honor and stories that would become sagas. Some part of the fleet must have been from Norse Ireland, as the "blue men" from Africa reportedly ended up as great curiosities in that land.[24]

15

Viking Ships and Navigation

Viking raids, invasions and finally outright conquests in Western Europe were remarkable, but even more incredible were the voyages to the west, beyond the horizon, out of sight of land for days and weeks. Only in the Pacific were such feats of navigation duplicated, as the Polynesians worked their way across the vast ocean, populating its islands one at a time. But in Europe–Asia–Africa such bold exploits were unheard of. Sailing was done along coastlines or in enclosed (or nearly enclosed) bodies of water like the Mediterranean and Black seas, the Persian Gulf or the Red Sea. The jump from India to the Arabian peninsula and then on to Africa was daring for that time. To venture out of sight of land into an ocean was simply beyond the capability of medieval mariners. Yet this is exactly what the Vikings did in the North Atlantic, braving not only the open sea but also the severe storms and icebergs of these treacherous waters, navigating to islands such as the Faroes, Iceland, Greenland and, eventually, North America. What made these feats possible was the seamanship of these sailors and the watercraft they had at their disposal.

Scandinavians of the Viking Age had several types of boats and ships to choose from for any particular purpose. There was a variety of rowboats, from the small two-oar skiffs to craft carrying four or more oars (*bátr*). For the shallow waters of the Scandinavian coasts, islands and rivers, there was the *karfi*, which could be used as a warship, or a merchant boat, a good all-purpose craft. But the true warship, the sight of which struck terror in the hearts of Saxon, Irish and Frank alike, was the longship (*langskip*). For large cargos, the Vikings used a ship broader in beam that rode deeper in the water with a higher freeboard, the *hafskip* or *knörr*, also called a merchant ship, or *kaupskip*.[1]

Fortunately, we have several examples of these ships recovered from various parts of Scandinavia. A prime example is a ship from a grave site in southern Norway at Gokstad, now on display at in the Viking Ship Museum in Oslo. This beautiful product of Viking shipbuilding craftsmanship is 76.5 feet long, with a beam of 17.5 feet. It is just over 6 feet, 4 inches from the bottom of the keel to the top of the gunwale at mid-ship.[2] The T-cross section keel is made from a single oak timber and measures 57 feet, 9 inches long.[3]

The hull is clinker-built (*lapstrake*), made of 16 strakes (a row of planks joined end to end) of different thicknesses. The thickest strake is at the waterline (1.75 inches). Strakes above this and below are 1 inch, except the oar strake, which is 1.25, and the top two strakes (7/8th inches).[4] "Clinker-built" means that the strakes are overlapped rather than placed side to side as in the carvel-built construction used in Southern Europe. The smooth surface of the carvel-built hull would seem to be more efficient and aqua-dynamic, but in fact the clinker construction allows for a lighter ship for a given cargo capacity. In addition, this design allows the boat to flex in heavy seas, a must in the storms of the north seas. Since the exposed edges of the planks run parallel with the direction of travel, they provide no impediment to sliding through the water; in fact, the design adds to the stability of the boat.

In the Viking Age, the planks or strakes were held together by round-headed iron rivets driven from the outside and clinched inside over square iron plates. Tarred animal hair or wool was used to caulk the hull. Nineteen ribs and cross beams formed the frame of the ship. Strakes below the waterline were lashed to this frame, with pliable roots of spruce providing the ship's elasticity. Most of the ship was made of oak, except the 30-foot mast, which was pine. This supported a 37-foot yard, which carried the 23-by-36-foot rectangular sail. This sail was made of white woolen cloth with sewn-on red stripes. The other method of propelling the craft was the 16 pairs of pine oars mounted in closeable holes in the fourteenth strake. Steering was provided by a side-rudder fastened to the starboard quarter. Fully loaded, the ship's draft would not have exceeded 3.5 feet.[5] This was a remarkably seaworthy craft; yet it could also navigate the shallow rivers and coasts of Europe and sail away with speed if needed. In 1893, a replica of this ship was sailed across the Atlantic from Bergen, Norway, to Newfoundland in 28 days. Even though the rigging was not up to Viking standards, the amateur crew reported achieving speeds of up to 11 knots.[6]

The Gokstad ship would be classified as a *langskip* (longship), but it had some of the seagoing qualities of a *hafskip*. This was a good all-purpose ship combining the best design features of its day for the specific task for which it was intended. Given the 16 pairs of oars, this ship presumably carried a crew of 32–35 men. Most raiding ships were of this size or smaller, though larger longships of up to 87 feet have been found that could carry 50–60 men.[7] A seagoing cargo ship (or *knörr*)[8] that traveled the Iceland–Greenland–Vinland routes and supported trade in Western Europe was in the range of 50 feet long by 14 feet abeam. These cargo ships carried a small crew of 15–20 men and depended almost entirely on sails for their propulsion.[9] With a hold midship, half decks fore and aft, and higher freeboards, a *knörr* could carry 15–20 tons of cargo.

Despite their excellent seagoing transportation devices, the Scandinavians still had to have the navigation skills to find their destinations with some certainty. Critical to Viking navigation would have been the ability to determine latitude. If you are leaving Norway to find Iceland, for instance, you merely sail north along the coast until you reach the latitude of Iceland, and then you sail west until you hit the island. But you must be able to maintain your course on the proper latitude, and this was well understood by the Norsemen. At night the North Star is available, and since it is stationary, it makes an excellent guidepost. You simply measure the angle of the star against the horizon to find your latitude.

Using the sun in daytime (or at night during the Arctic summers) is a little trickier, as it is not fixed but migrates across the sky throughout the year. However, experience would have taught the mariners how to account for this change in the altitude of the

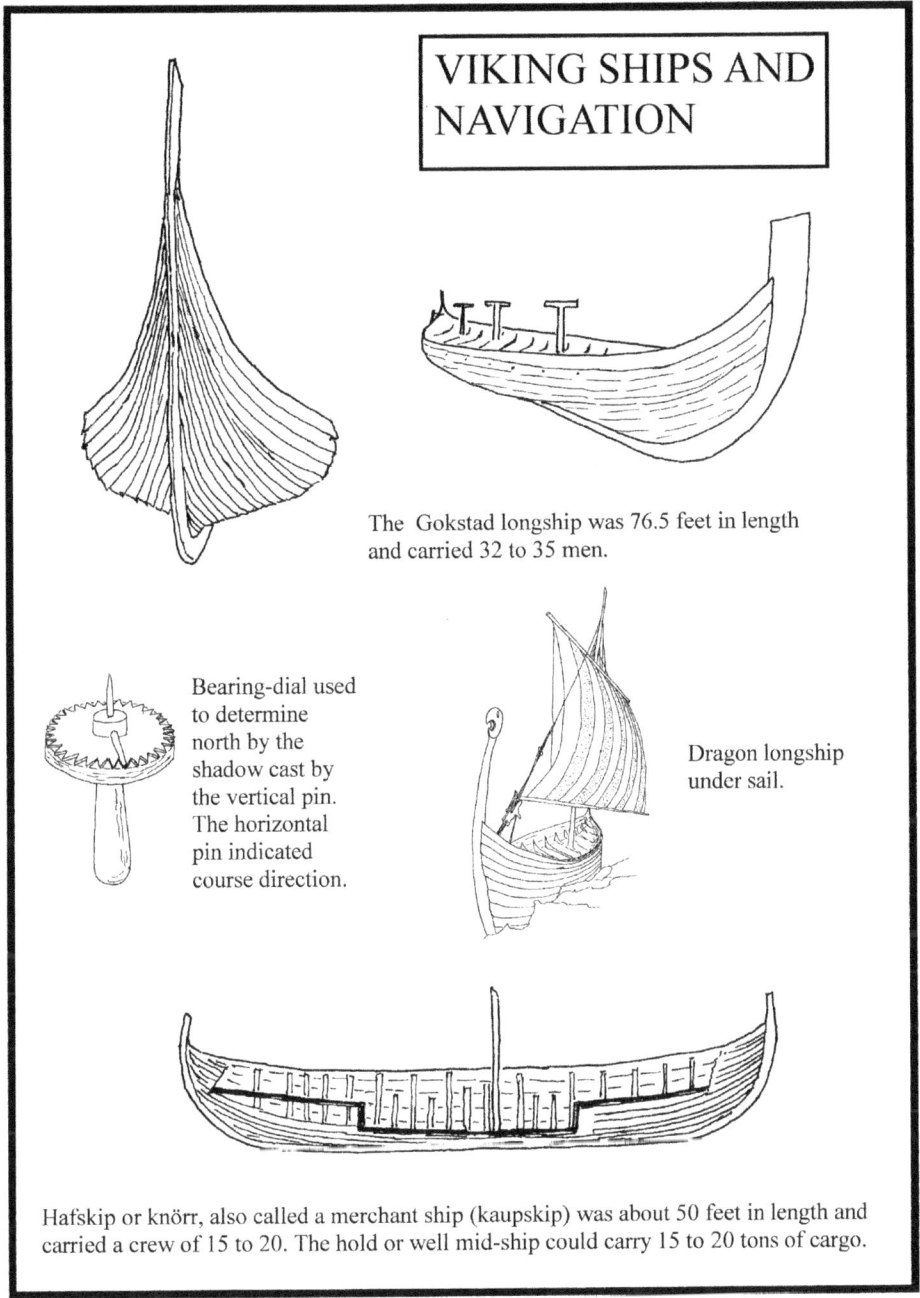

The Gokstad longship was 76.5 feet in length and carried 32 to 35 men.

Bearing-dial used to determine north by the shadow cast by the vertical pin. The horizontal pin indicated course direction.

Dragon longship under sail.

Hafskip or knörr, also called a merchant ship (kaupskip) was about 50 feet in length and carried a crew of 15 to 20. The hold or well mid-ship could carry 15 to 20 tons of cargo.

sun, particularly regarding where the sun rises and sets on the horizon for any given day of the year. We know the Vikings knew this because a table of such readings compiled by an Icelander named Stjerne-Oddi (Star-Oddi) in the late tenth century has come down to us. Angles in this table were measured in "half-wheels" (roughly half the diameter of the sun, or about sixteen degrees of arc).[10]

Various Scandinavian writings refer to a *solbrädt* (sun-board), apparently an instrument used to measure the angle of the sun, though an example has yet to be found.[11]

What has been found, however, is half of a wooden disc with a hole in the center and evenly spaced notches along the outside edge. If the disc were complete, there would be 32 notches dividing the horizon. This piece appears to be part of a device called a bearing dial, used to determine a ship's course via the shadow cast by the sun onto the dial.[12]

Another device mentioned in Scandinavian sagas is a "sun-stone." Some believe that this was some kind of primitive compass, possibly a magnetized piece of iron mounted on wood floating in water or oil. However, this seems unlikely, as the first known use of a compass was not until 1300 and magnetic compasses become notoriously inaccurate as you approach the North Pole anyway.[13] It is more likely that the sun-stone was Icelandic spar or calcite, a mineral that will polarize the sun's rays and allow an observer to locate the sun on an overcast day.[14] According to one saga, Holy King Olaf of Norway checked the sun's location during a foggy and snowy day of voyaging by observing how the stone was radiating.[15]

Determining latitude was no doubt mastered by the Viking sailors, but longitude was an entirely different matter, since accurately gauging longitude was not accomplished until the invention of the chronometer in the eighteenth century. Once on the right latitude, the sea-chief would have to use rough estimates to determine how close he was to landfall. Such decisions would be influenced by bow wave and the direction and strength of the wind, determined in part by how full the sail was and its orientation. On long or open sea voyages the crew might include a pilot or *kendtmand* (man who knows).[16] Even for short cruises a knowledge of the flight of birds, weeds found floating in the sea, the color of the water and other clues as to location and where landfall might be found was essential.

The sagas treat voyages, even long cruises to distant lands like Iceland, with offhanded casualness. As an example, there is *Egil's Saga*, which tells of a "black-haired and ugly"[17] warrior and poet, Egil Skallagrimsson, who was born and raised in Norway but travels from place to place almost on a whim. As a young man, he goes off on a longship to sail the Baltic for plunder, winding up in Courland (eastern Baltic) trading with the local population. Next comes an attack on Denmark (Lund, to be specific), and then it's back to Norway. Egil subsequently heads up a Viking expedition to plunder Jutland and Friesland; then he lands in England, where he fights alongside Athelstan against Olaf of Ireland (referred to earlier). Leaving on good terms with the English king, Egil takes a longship back to Norway. He then takes command of a merchant ship heading to Iceland. Back in Norway once again, he takes another trip to Iceland after having a tiff with King Eirik of Norway. Then it's back to Norway, on to York in England, Norway, Iceland, Norway again, a raiding expedition to Friesland, Iceland and so forth.[18]

King Alfred of Wessex was visited by a Viking trader named Ohthere, who hailed from Hålgoland, where he farmed and traded with the Lapps. Every year he made the 3,200-mile voyage from his northern home to Hedeby and back to exchange goods.[19]

In all this traveling the actual sea voyages are treated very matter-of-factly, as if they are just jaunts and not some dangerous undertaking to be approached with caution or trepidation. A trip to Iceland, the other end of the Baltic, or to Ireland are mere cruises. For this to be the case, the Scandinavian seamen had to be masters of navigation and possess an intimate knowledge of the sea.

And so the farmers and fishermen of the forests, fjords and coastal plains, those northern peoples, joined together as ship companies to seek adventure and fortune across the seas, or, as Edward Gibbon puts it:

> The vast, and, as it is said, populous, regions of Denmark, Sweden, and Norway were crowded with independent chieftains and desperate adventurers, who sighed in the laziness of peace, and smiled in the agonies of death. Piracy was the exercise, the trade, the glory, and the virtue of the Scandinavian youth. Impatient of a bleak climate and narrow limits, they started from the banquet, grasped their arms, sounded their horn, ascended the vessels, and explored every coast that promised either spoil or settlement.[20]

Thus the Vikings descended on Western Europe, wreaking havoc and mayhem, but they would go much further afield than just France, the British Isles and the Mediterranean; they would also strike out to the west into the open sea, and there the objective would be the search for new lands to settle instead of raiding and plundering.

16

The Viking Search for New Lands

We have seen the Norwegian advance through the North Sea and the North Atlantic islands, reaching the Shetlands in roughly AD 780 and Scotland and Ireland by 795. Sometime around 800 they reached the Faroe Islands, west and a little north of the Shetlands. There was no native population in the Faroes, but the Northmen did find a few Irish monks who had preceded them by about 100 years.[1] It is possible that the discovery of the islands by the Vikings was due to information obtained in Ireland during those early raids. Led by one Grim Kamban, according to the *Färoeinga Saga* (*Faroe Saga*), the Vikings took over the twenty-one islands, dispensing with the monks in one way or another. The Faroe Islands are divided by treacherous currents; they are windswept, bleak and treeless, but the Norse found them well suited for raising sheep. However, the total land area is only 540 square miles, so the perennial wanderers were soon looking for the next landfall.[2] This would prove to be Iceland.

The discoverer of Iceland in about AD 860 was either Naddod the Viking or Gardar Svavarsson from Sweden, depending on the source one believes. According to historical record, Naddod sailed from the Faroes, probably for the Hebrides, and was blown off course, accidentally reaching Iceland. He landed in Reydarfjord in the Eastfirths and climbed Reydarfjall in the hope of finding a village or some indication of human habitation. His search was in vain and he sailed away, giving the island the name *Snæland* (Snowland).[3]

By contrast, Gardar Svavarsson left Sweden on a trip to the Hebrides to claim an inheritance his wife had received from her father. A severe storm drove his ship to the coast of Iceland, just east of the Eastern Horn. He sailed on around the island, wintering at Husavik in Skjalfandi. The next summer, he circumnavigated the island. Returning home, he praised the land, naming it *Gardarsholm* (after himself).[4]

A third Viking sometimes offered as the discoverer is Floki Vilgerdason, who sailed from Norway with livestock in what appears to have been an attempt at settlement. The effort failed, but not so much from poor planning as from bad execution. Floki spent the summer fishing for the bountiful trout and exploring without preparing for the winter. Winter did come, of course, starving the would-be settler's livestock for lack of hay. Floki sailed away from the island, giving it the name *Ísland* (Iceland), the name that has stuck.[5]

Iceland had no native human population, but, as in the Faroes, the Norsemen found that they had been preceded by a few Irish monks they called *papar* (priests). These

16. The Viking Search for New Lands   123

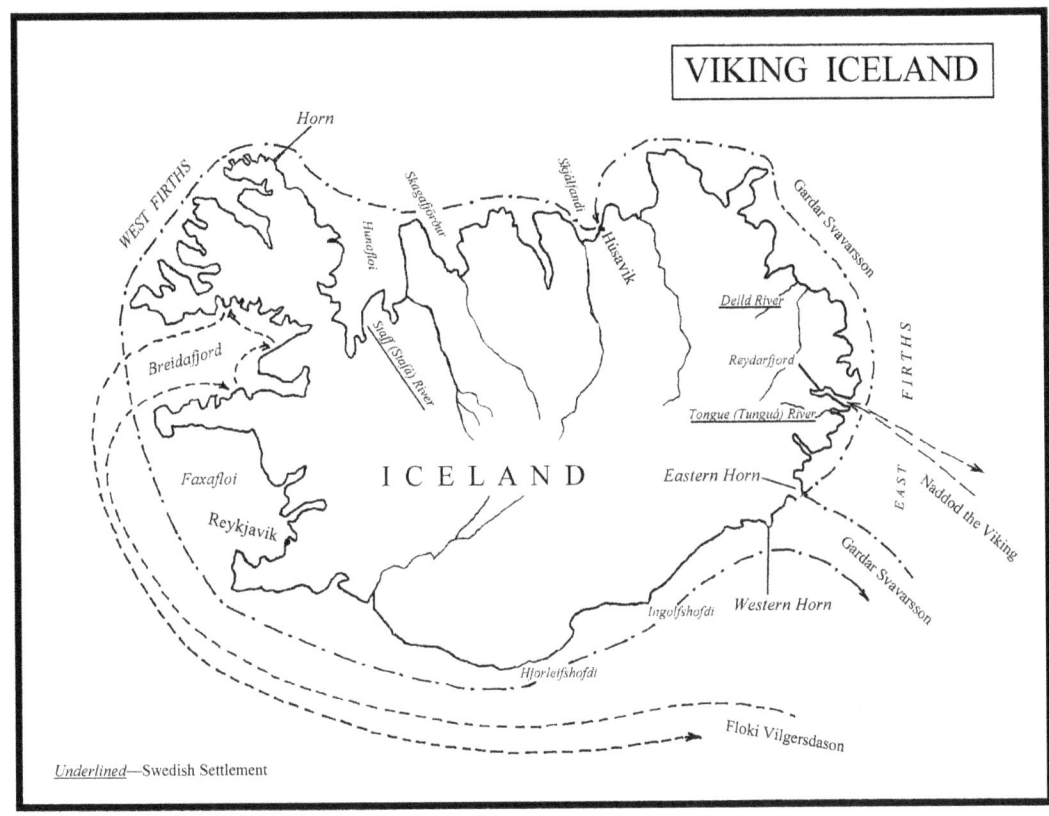

hermits had apparently made their way from Ireland, or perhaps the Faroes, in *currachs* (small oar-propelled boats of skins stretched over wicker frames). These true discoverers of the island fled in the face of the oncoming heathens, whom they could not abide.[6]

Regardless of whom the original discoverer was, within a decade settlers were flocking to Iceland to be part of the "land-taking." Norwegians came from Norway, the Shetlands, the Faroes, the Hebrides and Ireland. Those immigrating from Ireland brought with them Celtic slaves and Irish wives. The land rush attracted Vikings from Denmark and Sweden as well, but the predominant culture would remain Norwegian.[7]

Though far to the north—the northern tip of the island touches the Arctic Circle—Iceland is habitable because of the warm currents of the Gulf Stream. Fish abound in the lakes and streams and in the waters of the surrounding seas, where whales are also plentiful. There were birch woods to provide kindling and to make charcoal for iron smelting, utilizing the bog iron of the island. Sheep grazed the pastures, and barley could be grown on the coastal plains.[8]

It is estimated that by AD 930, some 30,000 people inhabited the island. As was customary among the Scandinavians, a Thing (Þing) was formed among each of the island's communities as a means of self-government. In 930, a national assembly (Althing) was established with representatives from the local Things. It is interesting to contrast the feudal, autocratic form of government instituted by the Normans in France with the democratic government founded by the Icelanders. As Adam of Bremen would write in 1076, "They [the Icelanders] have no king; only law."[9]

Once again, the new lands discovered by the Vikings were quickly settled, and the search for additional territories continued. To the west lay Greenland, first encountered by one Gunnbjörn Ulf-Krakason, who was blown off course on a trip to Iceland. The prospect of this land was not taken advantage of for some 50 years while the Vikings settled Iceland. But in AD 982 a Norwegian who was ill tempered even by Viking standards was exiled from Norway for murder and then banished from Iceland for three years for manslaughter. Without a lot of options open to him, Erik the Red formed a ship's company and sailed west to look for the land sighted by Gunnbjörn. He found Greenland and spent the next three years exploring this largest island in the world.[10]

Erik and his companions discovered a land rich in fish, birds, fox, bears, caribou and seals, with green pastures and birch trees, particularly along the southern west coast. And there were no inhabitants to contend with—not even the Irish hermit monks had traveled this far west. Over the centuries Greenland had been peopled by waves of Paleo-Eskimo cultures from North America. The last of these, the Late Dorset, if they had not died out altogether by this time, were confined to the northwest corner of the island. The Thule-Inuit people would not arrive for another 300 years, so here was land for the taking, and that is what Erik and his men did. They marked the sites of their future farms and homes, taking the best land. Then, at the end of his three-year exile, Erik sailed back to Iceland with glowing reports of the new land to the west.

Pent-up demand and Erik's propaganda had the desired effect, and a fleet of 25 ships weighed anchor in Iceland in AD 986. Fourteen of the ships made it to Greenland—some turned back and others were lost at sea—landing the first European settlers, perhaps 450 souls, on this far west corner of the European world. This colony, known as the east settlement, was centered around Brattahlid. It would grow to include 190 farms, 12 parish churches, a cathedral, an Augustinian monastery and a Benedictine nunnery.[11] Within a decade a second colony was established 300 miles to the north, the western settlement, which would eventually encompass 90 farms and 4 churches. The Viking Greenland population had climbed to about 3,000 people by the year 1300, with a constitution modeled on that of Iceland, a code of laws and an assembly. Trade was vital to maintain the colony, which lacked iron, wood for ships and other structures, grain, and European-style clothes and luxuries. In return, the Greenlanders offered sea ivory, woolens, rope, hides, furs, falcons and the much-prized white bear skins and narwhale tusks (actually a specialized tooth). And so the colony thrived, though it must have been a marginal existence. An unusually harsh winter, an early frost or a late freeze could have been devastating. Still, trade and contacts with Europe made life possible on this most remote of the Viking colonies.[12]

As close to the world's end as Greenland presumably was, the Vikings would push still further afield in their search for new lands. As seems to be the rule, the western extremity of the Viking territories would be discovered by a ship blown off course. In this case, it was a merchant, Bjarni Herjolfsson, who plied the trade route between Iceland and Norway. Bjarni left Norway for Iceland to spend the winter with his father, as was his practice. He must have been surprised to find upon his arrival that his father, Herjolf, had sold his lands in Iceland and joined Erik the Red on his venture to colonize Greenland. Bjarni was able to order or convince his crew to follow the expedition to the new settlement, and so they departed Iceland with what must have been very sketchy directions.[13]

With limited information and the added problems of fog and contrary winds, Bjarni missed Greenland altogether and eventually found himself cruising along a coast of rolling hills covered with forests. From descriptions of Greenland he had heard before he left Iceland, Bjarni know this could not be the land he was looking for. He sailed north, passing a flat wooded area and then glacier-covered mountains. Nowhere along this strange coast did Bjarni put ashore; instead, he pointed his prow into the sea, heading north and then east until he hit the southern tip of Greenland and the settlement he was searching for.[14]

For fifteen years Bjarni's discovery was not followed up; the Greenlanders had all the new land they needed for the time being and were busy building their colony. But in AD 1001 Erik the Red's son, Leif Eriksson, bought Bjarni's ship, assembled a crew of 35 men, and set sail for North America. He traveled Bjarni's route in reverse, striking the coast where Bjarni had seen the mountains and glaciers. This was no doubt Baffin Island, just north of the Hudson Strait. Leif named it Helluland (Flat-stone Land). Pushing on to the south along the coast, the crew next encountered the forested flat land Bjarni had described, which Leif called Markland (Woodland). This was surely Labrador. Sailing further south, the explorers found Bjarni's forested hilly coast, which they called Vinland or Wineland (today's Newfoundland), and here they decided to winter.[15]

There has been much discussion as to the naming of this area. The translation from the sagas has traditionally been "wild grapes," but it could also be "wineberry."[16] Due to this translation, the actual location has been disputed, as no wild grapes grow in Newfoundland today and therefore (or so the argument goes) the campsite must have been further south where wild grapes do grow—say, in Nova Scotia or even Maine. However, one must take into account that this exploration occurred at the height of the Medieval Warm Period, and it is quite possible that wild grapes did grow in Newfoundland during this warm spell. Another possibility is that the "wineberry" translation is correct, meaning red currents, gooseberries or mountain cranberries, which do grow that far north. In any case, the question of where Leif camped that first winter would seem to have been settled by the archaeological discovery of the ruins of a Viking community at L'Anse aux Meadows on the northern tip of Newfoundland in 1960.[17] Here Leif and his crew built huts, and then a longhouse, where they stayed for the winter. The following summer they sailed back to Greenland with tales of a land rich in those things absent in Greenland, such as unlimited timber, vast pastures, winters with no frost and the sun shining well above the horizon even in mid-winter—indeed, a land full of promise.[18]

Before Leif could mount another expedition, his father died, leaving family responsibilities to his son. Leif, now landbound, lent his ship to his brother, Thorvald, who sailed with a crew of thirty men back to North America. They found Leif's old encampment and spent the summer exploring the coast to the north and south, wintering at *Leifsbudir* (Leif's hut). Continuing their explorations the next summer, the Vikings encountered a band of Indians whom they called *Skraelings* (the Norsemen applied this term to Indians, Dorset Paleo-Eskimos and Thule-Inuits alike). A scuffle ensued in which eight Skraelings were killed and Thorvald received a mortal wound from an Indian arrow. The crew wintered at Leifsbudir once more; then they sailed for Greenland the following spring.[19]

Up to this point there had been no attempt to establish a colony in North America,

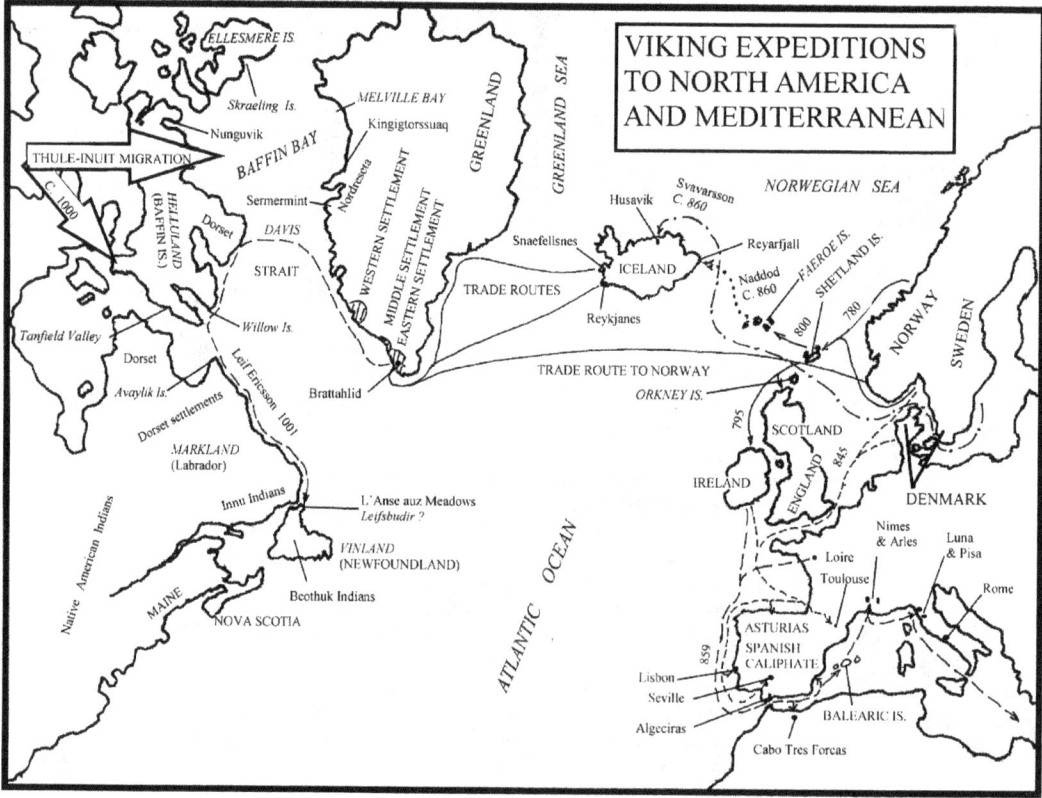

but that changed with the next expedition. Thorfinn Karlsefni was an Icelander who came to Greenland to trade, commanding a cargo ship. He wintered at Brattahlid, staying with Leif Eriksson. During that winter Thorfinn became enamored of Gudrid, the widow of Leif's brother, and married her before spring. At his new wife's urging, Thorfinn assembled an expedition for the new land. The two sagas that tell of this venture, *Grænlendinga* and *Eiríks*, differ as to the details, but both agree that this was to be an attempt to make a permanent settlement.[20] Three ships were fitted out, carrying 150 men and women along with their livestock.[21]

The expedition sailed to North America, camping not far from Leif's old campsite. The winter was mild, and the cattle grazed without the need of hay. In spring the company came into contact with the Skraelings, who offered furs for trade. They initially wanted the Vikings' weapons, but Thorfinn would not allow any of these to be turned over to the Indians. Finally, the Skraelings settled for milk from the cows, which they desired enough to give over all their pelts. Later trades were made for red cloth in exchange for more pelts.[22]

One morning the camp was attacked by a multitude of warriors in skin boats. The whole company might have been massacred except for the courage of Freydis, Leif Eriksson's sister. The sagas relate how she was forced to stand and fight because she could not run due to her advanced pregnancy. She grabbed a sword off a fallen Viking and faced the Skraelings head on, baring her breasts and slapping them with the sword. The astonished Indians took fright, fled to their canoes and rowed away.

Along with the Indian problems, jealousies and fights over the women began to develop. Finally, after a three-year stay, the would-be settlers abandoned the colony and sailed back to Greenland.[23] One last legacy left by this group of colonists was that Thorfinn's wife Gudrid gave birth to a son, Snorri, the first European born on North American soil.[24]

A fourth and the last voyage recorded in the *Grænlendinga Saga* was initiated by Freydis, who persuaded her husband and two brothers, Helgi and Finnbogi, to make the voyage to the west. Two ships left Greenland for Vinland, each with 60 men and their women; one was commanded by the two brothers and the other by Freydis and her husband.[25] Freydis' ship arrived late, only to find Helgi and Finnbogi occupying Leif's house. No slight was intended by the first crew, and they seem to have been perfectly willing to share the abode with the late arrivals. But Freydis and her crew took up lodging in another building. She appears to have had her father's ill temper, for she badgered her husband into punishing the "offenders" (as she saw them). The saga records:

> He could not endure this baiting of hers. He ordered his men to turn out immediately and take their weapons, which they did, and crossed straightway to the brothers' house and marched in on the sleeping men, seized them and bound them, and led them outside, each man as he was bound. And Freydis had each man killed as he came out.
> Now all the men were killed, but the women were left, and no one would kill them.
> "Hand me an axe," said Freydis.
> Which was done, and she turned upon the five women they had there, and left them dead.[26]

This bloody and dramatic reduction in the number of settlers left the would-be colony too small to remain in North America's exotic environment, and the expedition pulled up stakes, heading back to Greenland. Leif Eriksson eventually found out the truth of what his sister had done, but he refused to punish her aside from placing a hex on her.

That there were other visits to the North American continent by the Greenlanders is not in doubt. First, there is the Indian arrowhead found by Aage Roussell in 1930 in the northwest corner of the churchyard at Sandnes in the western settlement of Greenland. The quartzite arrowhead matches the type of arrowhead found by Jørgen Meldgaard in an ancient Indian settlement by the Northwest River at Lake Melville, Labrador, in 1956. Second, there is the "Maine penny" found under reputable archaeological circumstances. This coin has been determined to be of genuine Norwegian vintage, minted between 1065 and AD 1080. It is possible the coin was left in that northern state by the Viking visitors, or it may have arrived from the north through trade from Labrador or Newfoundland.[27]

And, finally, we have the archaeological findings at L'Anse aux Meadows on the northern tip of Newfoundland, discovered in 1960 by Helge Ingstad, a journalist, and his wife, Anne Stine Ingstad, an archaeologist. It is the only confirmed Viking site in North America outside of Greenland. Excavated were a charcoal kiln, a forge, boat sheds along the old shoreline, cooking pits, a sauna, a work shed, a large house and four smaller houses along with a natural bog iron-ore source. Carbon-14 dating indicates the site was active around AD 1000. This could very well have been Leifsbudir or the site of a later settlement.[28]

Certainly there were later expeditions to the continent, if for no other reason than for timber of a size suitable for home and ship construction, which was plentiful in North America but completely lacking in Greenland. And crossing the Davis Strait would have been a lot easier than sailing all the way back to Norway. We know the Greenlanders ranged far afield in their pursuit of game and trade items. In 1824 an Inuit named Pelimut discovered a runestone on the island of Kingigtorssuaq, near Upernavik, Greenland, just short of 73°N. The inscription tells of three Greenlanders who wintered there in 1333.[29]

Historia Norvegiae, written in the thirteenth century, relates the story of an expedition that reached Melville Bay, Greenland, at 76°N in 1267 and made contact with Skraelings who "possessed no iron whatsoever."[30] These may have been the remnants of the Dorset peoples who had once occupied much of northwestern Greenland or the newly arrived Thule-Inuit, who would eventually compete with the Viking Greenlanders for the island's resources.

Archaeological findings on Ellesmere Island suggest that the Greenlanders crossed over in their hunting expeditions to this far northern section of North America. Boat rivets of the type used in Viking boat construction, box sections made of oak, parts of barrel bottoms, Viking-style knife blades and spear points, and a piece of woolen cloth have been discovered on Skraeling Island, off the coast of Ellesmere Island. Other findings show that Dorset as well as Thule peoples lived in the area at one time or another.[31] Perhaps this was the site of an intersection of all three cultures—Viking, Dorset and Thule-Inuit. If so, the Thule prevailed. There was little here to attract the Greenland Vikings in terms of a permanent settlement—no timber or grasslands, only furs, walrus ivory and other trade items. This was pretty inhospitable country to the European culture of the Vikings, even during the comparatively mild climate of the Medieval Warm Period.

Further to the south, additional evidence of a Viking presence (and perhaps occupation) has been found. At three sites on Baffin Island (Nunguvik, Willow Island and Tanfield Valley) and one off northern Labrador (Avayalik Island), yarn has been discovered among the ruins of Dorset village sites.[32] The yarn was made from the hair of the Arctic hare, but neither Dorset nor Thule people spun yarn or wove cloth; they relied on skins and furs for clothing and bedding. The yarn must have been traded to the Dorset villagers by the Vikings.

Archaeological excavation at the Tanfield Valley site has turned up additional evidence of at least a Viking outpost. Here, the ancient Native Americans had built a settlement long before any Vikings arrived, known today as Nanook. The site has a natural harbor and an abundance of turf to build sod shelters. Excavations have brought to light wooden sticks marked with notches, of a type used by Vikings as tally sticks, as well as a piece of whale bone with two holes drilled in it (the Dorset did not have drills, but Vikings did). Another piece of whale bone was carved into the form of a shovel, exactly like spades found on Greenland and used to cut sod for buildings. A building has been excavated some 40 feet in length, far larger than the bedroom-size huts constructed by the Dorset. Among the ruins are the remnants of turf blocks and a foundation of rock, building materials used by Vikings but completely foreign to Native Americans of this time and area.[33]

Both the Dorset and the Thule-Inuit thrived in the environment of northeastern North America, but in a contest for resources, the Thule would ultimately win. The Dorset did not use the bow and arrow or the kayak, leaving them ill prepared to compete with the more advanced newcomers. Where the Dorset lived in small groups—two or three families at most—because of their limited ability to acquire significant quantities of food, the Thule often hunted in large groups, as in their whaling expeditions in skin boats on the open seas.[34]

The Norse, however, would have searched out coasts further south, where there were forests for timber and grasslands for livestock, yet far enough north so they would not have to contend with Indians. The Dorset of Labrador they could handle in relative safety. Evidence of later expeditions to North America is provided by the Icelandic Annals of 1347, which recorded that a ship containing seventeen or eighteen Greenlanders arrived after being blown off course on a trip from Markland to Greenland.[35]

Perhaps there were even settlements in North America that survived for a period of time. We do know that Bishop Erik Gnupsson of Greenland came to Vinland in 1121, possibly to look after some of his flock who had taken up residence there.[36] However, the exact purpose of his visit is not recorded.

In any event, the northern coast of North America—possibly as far north as Ellesmere Island, certainly Labrador and Newfoundland, and perhaps further south into Nova Scotia or Maine—was the westward fringe of Viking exploration. This was the high-water mark of this western adventure.

17

Danish Unification During the Viking Age

While plundering, trading and settling expeditions were being launched against Central Europe and the North Atlantic islands, the instigating nations—namely, Denmark and Norway—were struggling toward unity and nationhood (a process that would ultimately involve England as well). Denmark progressed rapidly because of the ease of communication between its land areas. Jutland, the major land mass, was accessible not only by sea but also by road networks that were relatively easy to build compared to the rest of Scandinavia, where high mountains and deep forests divided the land. The islands of Denmark and the southern tip of Sweden (Scania) were easy to reach by water, a medium of transportation the Vikings had completely mastered. Norway, however, was divided by high mountains and deep fjords, with a long and treacherous coastline.

Even in Denmark, where nation building proceeded apace, trying to trace this progress is difficult. Royal lineage must be pieced together from legends and sagas. Kings and heroes are mixed together in stories meant to entertain and not necessarily preserve history. We have already noted Scyld, the Danish king in *Beowulf* who, according to the epic poem, founded the royal Scylding dynasty of the Danes (see chapter 10). There is also his grandson Hrothgar, described in the same poem. But these rulers, if they existed at all, were lords of some of the petty kingdoms that ruled Denmark around AD 500.

That is not to say there were never occasional monarchs who rose to prominence and united a larger part of Denmark for a time. We have already mentioned Rakkæ, backed by the Swedes; Rakkæ was succeeded by Snio, who was eaten alive by lice at a Thing in Jutland in about AD 550. And there is also the legendary Amblothæ (Amleth or Amlethus) of Jutland, the inspiration for Shakespeare's *Hamlet, Prince of Denmark*. Amblothæ, in the guise of the bard's Prince Hamlet, intones the following lines:

> Now might I do it pat, now he is praying;
> And now I'll do't. And so he goes to heaven;
> And so am I revenged. That would be scann'd.
> A villain kills my father; and for that,
> I, his sole son, do this same villain send
> To heaven.[1]

Here he is speaking about his uncle King Feng (Shakespeare's Claudius), who killed Amblothæ's father, the king; seized the throne; and married his brother's wife, Amblothæ's mother.[2] Amblothæ ultimately killed his uncle, but unlike Hamlet in Shakespeare's tragedy, he lived to become a legendary king and conqueror. However, Feng and Amblothæ were kings *in* Denmark, not kings *of* Denmark (though Amblothæ may have eventually united Jutland).[3]

Still later, there was the blind Wermund and his son Offa, discussed by Widsith, and Ivar Vidfadmi (Far-reacher), who was king of Skåne in the seventh century, according to the *Skjöldunga Saga*.[4] We have discussed Harald Hilditonn (Wartooth), who laid claim to being king of not just Denmark but also much of Sweden. He was defeated by his nephew Sigurd Hring of Sweden at the great battle of Bravellir, at Bråviken near Norrköping in East Gautland, early in the eighth century.[5]

So, the Danish monarchs are traceable only through legends and sagas until the late eighth century, when Charlemagne, as king of the Franks, launched his campaign against the Saxons in order to secure his northern flank. We learn of Sigfred, king of the Danes, who sheltered Widukind, a Saxon chieftain, in AD 777.[6] In 800 Sigfred was succeed by Godfred, who extended Danish control over the Slavic Abodrits and built (or at least improved) the Danevirke, an earthwork series of fortifications constructed across the neck of Jutland to deter invaders.[7] He also fostered the growth of Hedeby as a merchant center by protecting the nearby north-south "Army Road" and the east-west eight-mile portage connecting the North and Baltic seas. He also destroyed Hedeby's chief rival, the Abodrit trade center Reric in Wendland. A military confrontation between Godfred and Charlemagne would surely have occurred but for the Danish monarch's death in AD 810 at the hands of one of his retainers. Godfred's successor, Hemming, wisely signed a peace treaty with Charlemagne in 811.[8]

Whether Godfred was ruler of a united Denmark is an open question. His dealings with the powerful king of the Franks indicate that he had significant resources. Certainly he ruled Jutland, probably Zealand and possibly Skåne, along with the islands in between, though his kingdom was likely held together by his personal power, for no sense of nation would have existed at that time.

Hemming's rule lasted only one year; after that, the kingdom seems to have dissolved into civil war once again as the sons of Godfred, returning from exile in Sweden, contested their rights to the crown against those of the descendants of the earlier king Harald. Two names emerge from this period: Horik, son of Godfred, and Harald Klak, son of Harald. Each obtained the title of king, ruling some portion of Godfred's former domain. Harald, who converted to Christianity, was driven from his throne, leaving Horik the sole ruler (or at least the major ruler) in Denmark.[9]

Though not a Christian, Horik did allow a church to be built in Hedeby in AD 850. Soon after, Horik was killed in battle, the victim of a rebellion led by his own kinsmen. His successor, Horik the Younger, assumed the throne in 853–854.[10] Following this king, there are only glimpses into the political situation in Denmark.

At the time that Danish Vikings were raiding and plundering Europe to the south, we have little to go on in terms of the Danish kingdom (or kingdoms). We hear of a Viking leader named Rorik in the 850s, and in 873 there were two kings, brothers, Sigfred and Halfdan. Adam of Bremen also reports that there were other kings in Denmark at this time.[11]

It would appear that Denmark, during the height of the Viking incursions into Europe, was a land divided. Therefore, these raids were not sponsored by a Danish monarch

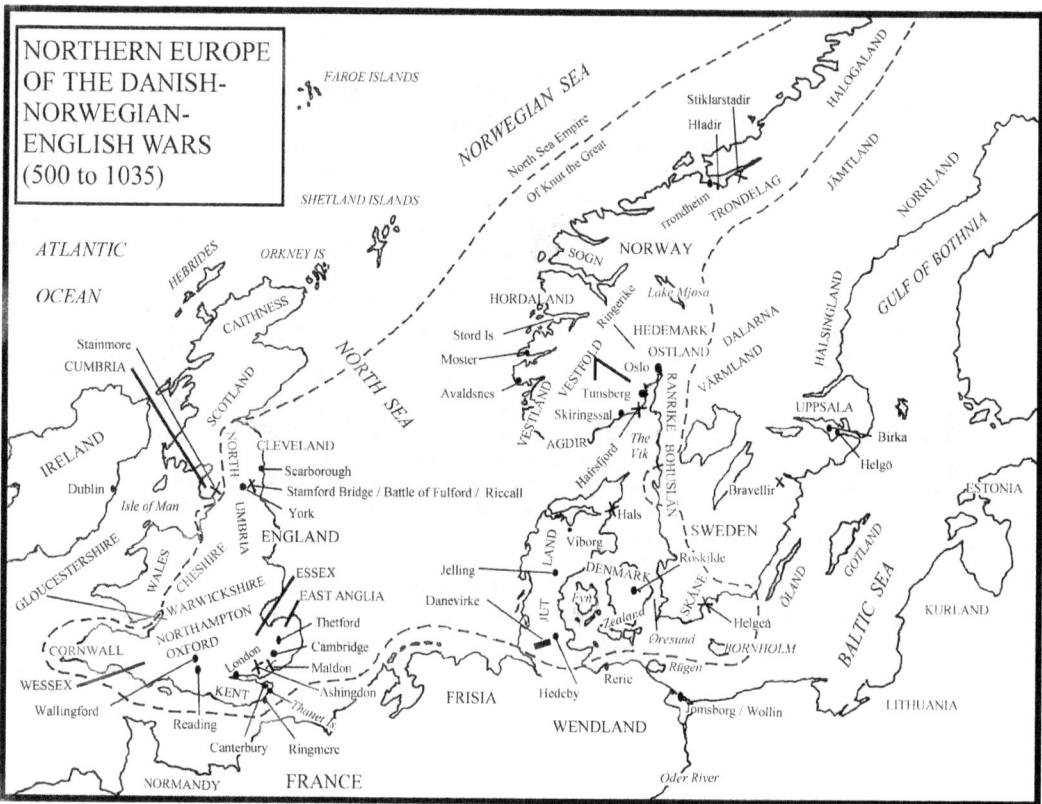

with some grand design; rather, the expeditions were instigated by petty kings, as some of the large fleets must have had the backing of a lord or king of some substance. Smaller ventures may have been the handiwork of lesser states or local leaders who were recognized as effective sea captains. There were even leaders who had no land holdings at all but thrived on the sea ventures alone, the "sea-kings without lands." Of course, many of these adventurers did pick up holdings in the foreign lands they plundered, such as England, French Normandy, and others.

Adam of Bremen does mention a king Helgi (Heiligo), ruler of southern Jutland (c. AD 900), who was succeeded by a Swede named Olaf. Olaf took the kingdom by force of arms and passed it on to his two sons, Chnob and Grud, who were succeeded by a king named Sigerich. But here the Swedish line ended. Sigerich was deposed by a Danish king, Hardegon Sveinsson.[12] It appears the Swedes had inserted themselves into a weakened and divided Denmark to secure for themselves the vital and flourishing trade routes of southern Jutland, including the rich merchant center of Hedeby.

The above-mentioned Hardegon (Hardaknut) Sveinsson, a king in northern Jutland with holdings in Norway inherited from his family, seems to represent the beginning of a resurgent Danish line of kings. Though documentation is incomplete and often contradictory, Hardegon apparently conquered all northern Jutland and then drove the Swedes from the south, establishing his court at Jelling in central Jutland. This work was accomplished in about 935–950 and was completed by Hardegon's son and successor, Gorm the Old, who may have also subjugated part of Wendland.[13]

Gorm and his wife Thyri (or Thyra), to whom he raised a runic stone, strengthened the Danevirke and pushed further the conquest of Danish territory. Their son, Harald Bluetooth, completed the unification of Denmark, including Skåne in what is now southern Sweden.[14]

But Harald's accomplishments went even further. He is also credited with converting Denmark to Christianity, probably influenced by his mother, Thyri, who seems to have been a Christian of English royal ancestry. Gorm, however, was decidedly of the Old Norse religious persuasion.[15]

According to some sources, Harald, who succeeded his father in about AD 950, conquered all of Norway, but this is an exaggeration, as we know that he was attacked by Hakon the Good of Norway in 954 in raids that plundered the coasts of Jutland, Zealand and Skåne.[16] The evidence strongly suggests that Denmark was a united nation by about 950.

18

The Norwegian Struggle for Independence

To gain some insight regarding the situation in Norway, it is necessary to return to the early days of the Norwegian Vikings, when the first expeditions ventured to the west in search of new lands and found and settled the Shetland Islands. Norway of this early Viking period was divided into four main regions. The eastern and central provinces, Värmland, Hedemark, and the area around Lake Mjøsa, were heavily influenced by the Swedes with their thriving commercial marts of Helgö and later Birka.

A second region, Østland (or the eastern region), was the area around the Oslofjord and the Vik. This was a particularly rich farming area that produced important market towns like Kaupang-Skiringssal, Tunsberg and Oslo.[1]

There was also the Vestland region on the southwest coast, with its deep fjords, where good farmland was scarce. The Viking tradition came early to the people of Vestland. They raided the Scandinavian and Frisian coasts, even adopting the Frankish scramasax, a short, one-edged sword, over the traditional Viking two-edged long sword and the heavy broad-bladed lance over the light spear preferred in the rest of Scandinavia.[2]

A fourth region was Trondelag, where there was an abundance (for Norway, that is) of good farmland. This area had for centuries maintained thriving commerce with the Frisians. The combination of rich farms and productive foreign trade had, by Viking times, produced a class of well-to-do landowners whose interest was in maintaining a stable and peaceful situation.[3]

To the north of Trondelag lay Halogaland and still further north Finnmark, sources of sea ivory, hides and furs. Halogalanders were particularly active in sea commerce, trading with their southern Norwegian neighbors, Frisia and Hedeby in Denmark.

All the main regions were divided into numerous chiefdoms and republics each with their assembly or Thing (*Þing*), as well as petty kingdoms, which might be subdivided into jarldoms (i.e., earldoms). The history of any of these many mini-states is obscure, with only an occasional glimpse of historical light shining on individual leaders, mostly through legends and sagas.

There was Olaf the Woodcutter from Sweden, as well as Halfdan the Generous.[4] Finally, we come to Gudrod the Hunting King, who ruled all Østland and died in about AD 840. He was succeeded by his son Olaf, who was subject to several setbacks that reduced his kingdom to just Vestfold. It was his son, Rognvald the Glorious, for whom Thjodolf the Learned composed the *Ynglinga Tal* (see chapter 10).

Gudrod's other son, Halfdan, was by Asa, his second wife, whom he abducted after killing her father, the king of Agdir, in southwestern Norway. At age 18 Halfdan the Black inherited the kingdom of Agdir. Later he received the eastern half of Vestfold from Olaf, his half-brother.[5] Through marriage, he acquired Ringerike and the remainder of Østland, or at least he established nominal control through the fealty of the local jarls. He was succeeded by his son, Harald Fairhair, who extended his rule around the Vik.

To the west, meanwhile, there had long been a move to protect the trade routes from Halogaland to the trade centers of Skiringssal in Vestfold and Hedeby in Jutland, establishing the "way north" (or Norway). Such security was also to the advantage of the agriculturists of Trondelag, so a unification process had been going on for some time along the west coast. The beneficiary of this activity was Hakon Grjotgardsson, jarl of Hladir, who was able to establish nominal control over Trondelag and Halogaland.[6]

Hakon and Harald come to an agreement dividing Norway between them except for the completely unruly Vestland. Officially, Hakon pledged fealty to Harald, but in reality he had free rein to rule in Trondelag. Harald married Hakon's daughter to secure the arrangement, and then he went after the Vikings of Vestland. This culminated in the great sea battle of Hafrsfjord.

At Hafrsfjord, Harald was up against not just the sea-going pirates of Vestland but also other disaffected jarls and chiefs of lands supposedly under his control. The battle was hard fought, but in the end Harald's fleet carried the day.[7] The date of the battle has been hard to establish. Present consensus is that it occurred between AD 885 and 900.[8]

In any case, his victory at Hafrsfjord left Harald as the dominant ruler in Norway, though he did not control all regions. The north paid little attention to who was ruling in the south, and the eastern inland mountains had little respect for the coastal kings. What's more, Harald's style of monarchy seems to have been somewhat tyrannical, even for Viking Scandinavia. *Egil's Saga* reports the following:

> Once he had established possession of these territories which were newly come into his power, King Harald paid close attention to the landed men and leading farmers, and all those from whom he suspected some rebellion might be looked for. He made everybody do one thing or the other: either become his retainers or quit the country, or, for a third choice, suffer hardship or forfeit their lives; while some were maimed hand or foot. King Harald seized possession in every district of all odal rights (absolute ownership) and whole land, settled and unsettled, and equally the sea and the waters, and all husbandmen should become his tenants, and those too who worked in the forests, and saltmen, and all hunters by the sea and land—all these were now made subject to him. But many a man fled the land from this servitude, and it was now that many desert places were settled far and wide, both east in Jamtaland and Helsingjaland and in the Western lands, Hebrides and the Dublin district, Ireland, and Normandy in France, Caithness in Scotland, the Orkneys and Shetland, and the Faeroes. And it was now that Iceland was discovered.[9]

The suggestion that all of the western movement by the Vikings of Norway occurred because of Harald and during his reign is an exaggeration. The colonization of the Shetlands and Orkney was certainly prior to Harald's rule, and probably that of the Hebrides as well, but the idea that Harald's tyranny drove the Norwegians to foreign lands is undoubtedly correct. And the Vikings from these western colonies would return to raid Norway just as quickly as they would plunder Frisia or Ireland.

To remedy the assaults on his homeland, Harald sent sea expeditions to conquer the Shetlands, Orkney and the Hebrides. Further, he created a standing coastal defense fleet. Every three families of free farmers were obliged to provide a warrior along with supplies to sustain him. These recruits became the crewmen for the ships maintained by each district.[10]

Harald recognized the need to gain the approval of local governments, which he did by working through the three *lagthings* (supra-Things) that existed at the time. One governed the small states in the eastern uplands around Lake Mjøsa; the Trondelag gathered at the Eyrathing, whereas the Fjords, Sogn and Hordaland congregated at the Gulathing. Harald also moved his capital from Vestfold to Avaldsnes on Karmøy Island in Vestland, the better to keep a tight rein on the notoriously unruly southwest Vikings.

Harald died in about AD 945, having lived into his eighties.[11] The two primary contenders for his throne were two sons—Eirik Bloodaxe, already in Norway, and Hakon the Good, who had been stashed safely away at the English court of Athelstan by enemies of Harald. Though only 15 years old, Hakon set out immediately for Norway, probably backed by his English protectors. Without so much as a single battle Eirik forfeited his right to the throne and left Norway to become king of York. Thus, Hakon acquired his father's title as king of all Norway.[12] (This was the Hakon who raided the coasts of Jutland, Zealand and Skåne in the time of the Danish king Harald Bluetooth.)

Hakon the Good proved to be a pragmatic and effective ruler. Although raised a Christian in England, he converted to the religion of Thor and Odin upon finding his subjects completely opposed to the faith in one god.[13] He accommodated the jarls where he had to and installed relatives as earls where he could. Hakon also promoted reliance on laws and strengthened the power of the lagthings. Together they established the rule of a united Norway. He further developed the system of ship levies (*skipreiður*) begun by his father.[14]

Hakon seems to have had his kingdom firmly in hand, but that was about to change. Eirik Bloodaxe, Hakon's dispossessed half-brother who had twice made himself king of York, was finally killed in battle at Stainmore in Northumberland in 954. Eirik's wife, Gunnhild, fled England with her five sons to the court of her brother Harald Bluetooth in Jutland.[15]

Gunnhild then began a campaign to recover Norway for her sons, a project Harald was only too happy to support. Harald opened the conflict with an attempt to dominate the Vik and gain access to Østland. Hakon not only defeated him but also carried the war to the shores of Denmark—this was the season of plundering the coasts of Jutland, Zealand and Skåne referred to previously.

But the sons of Eirik Bloodaxe were nothing if not tenacious, and they attacked the Norwegian fleets again and again. Finally, in their third campaign, Hakon was killed in battle at Stord at the mouth of the Hardangerfjord in about AD 960.[16] The five sons, led by Harald Greycloak, returned to Norway as rulers. This Harald proved to be an unpopular monarch. This may have been due partly to his insistence on remaining Christian and opposing the traditional Norse gods, and partly because he ran into the ambition of his uncle and the jarls of Hladir, Trondelag and Halogaland. He was killed in a battle off Hals in northeastern Jutland. His fleet was overwhelmed by a large force assembled by the jarls united against him.[17]

Jarl Hakon of Hladir assumed control of western Norway, pledging fealty to King Harald Bluetooth of Denmark, who assumed rule over eastern Norway directly. Norway was effectively divided politically as well as religiously, for Jarl Hakon promoted the old gods of Æsir while Harald, who had converted in 960, pushed Christianity. On top of this, Harald was busy attempting to extend his territories in both the Slavic Wends and Sweden.

Harald was beaten back on both fronts. An expedition led by Styrbjorn Starki (the nephew of the Swedish king Eirik Sigrsæll and husband of Thyri, Harald's daughter) consisted of Danes and Jomsvikings from the legendary Viking fortress of Jomsborg in Wendland. The army was crushed in Uppsala by Eirik and his Swedes, earning for Eirik the title of "The Victorious."[18]

To the south, Harald's forces, though supported by Jarl Hakon's Norwegians, were pushed back beyond the Danevirke well into Jutland by Otto II, the German emperor. Harald was rescued by his son, Svein Forkbeard, who, in 983, led the army that drove the Germans back south out of Jutland, restoring Harald's kingdom.[19]

For Harald, however, the victory was short lived, for within two years Svein turned against his father, driving him from the throne. Harald fled to Wendland, the homeland of his second wife, where he died a short time later.[20]

Svein Forkbeard was king of Denmark with claims to both Norway and England. Though ambitious and capable, he would meet fierce resistance on both fronts. Norway, Denmark and England were now intertwined in a complex political triumvirate. To fully appreciate this situation, it is necessary to catch up on English history, covered in the next chapter.

19

The Empire of Knut the Great

England had advanced significantly since the time of Alfred the Great, when he barely saved the island nation from being overrun by the Danes. The war to hold and unite the country had been carried on by Alfred's descendants, Edward the Elder and Æthelstan, who defeated Alfred's old foes—the Scots, Irish Norse, Northumbrians, Icelanders and Danes—at the pitched battle of Brunanburh. (The location of this battle has not been determined.)

Æthelstan was succeeded by Edmund the Magnificent, who held onto his brother's hard-won gains. And finally, Edward the Elder's youngest son, Edred, maintained the kingdom after the death of Edmund, again mainly by force of arms. It was under Edred that Eirik Bloodaxe was expelled from York for the second and final time, thus uniting England under one king.[1]

For 25 years under three kings, England advanced in relative peace, in terms of political organization, religion, literature and agriculture. But in AD 980 the Vikings returned, beginning a new wave of raids. This time the pillaging was for booty only; there was no attempt to occupy territory. The goal was not land or colonization; it was to loot a country grown rich and prosperous.[2]

The unfortunate king at the time was Ethelred, who gained the label "The Unready." The strongholds and castles that had worked so successfully against the Danish invasion years earlier were ineffective against a mobile force bent on spoils only. The raiders merely bypassed the strong points or avoided them altogether, striking booty-rich targets ill prepared to defend themselves. The Anglo-Saxon Chronicle records:

> 980 ... and in the same year was Southampton plundered by a pirate-army, and most of the population slain or imprisoned. And the same year was the isle of Thanet overrun, and the county of Chester was plundered by the pirate-army of the North.[3]

The pillaging continued, affecting Oxford, Cornwall, Thetford, Cambridge and Northampton.[4] Finally, in 991, the Vikings were drawn into a pitch battle to decide the issue. The Battle of Maldon was fought in Essex and is commemorated in a great Anglo-Saxon poem.[5] Leading the Viking army was the legendary sea-king, Olaf Tryggvason of Norway, who taunted the English with these words: "Send quickly rings [of gold] for your safety; it is better for you to buy off with tribute this storm of spears then that we should share the bitter war."[6]

The English army was led by Byrhtnoth, earl of Essex, who replied, "They will give you in tribute spears, and deadly darts, and old swords. Here stands an earl not mean, with his company, who will defend this land, Æthelred's home, my prince's folk and field."[7]

Unfortunately for the English, the earl was decisively defeated and killed in the battle. Ethelred then turned to another means of dealing with the marauders: the payment of tribute, which became known as the Danegeld. Eight hundred years later, Rudyard Kipling would recall this period in English history by saying, "If once you have paid the Dane-geld, you never get rid of the Dane."[8] He went on to warn:

> We never pay any-one Dane-geld,
> No matter how trifling the cost,
> For the end of the game is oppression and shame,
> And the nation that plays it is lost![9]

In 991, Ethelred paid a bribe of ten thousand pounds of silver and provisions to the Viking army in order to rid himself of the invaders.[10] In 994, the tribute was sixteen thousand pounds of silver, but Olaf of Norway did agree to be baptized by a Roman Catholic priest. In 1002 the price was twenty-four thousand pounds of silver. The Danegeld was becoming intolerable, and Ethelred searched for another answer. But in doing so, he managed to bungle even further and set the stage for his own demise.

Ethelred's new tactic was to hire Danish mercenaries to build an effective defense force he could use to defy the blackmailers. But he grew distrustful of his new deliverers and decided to massacre them, along with all other Danes in southern England, even those who were peaceful citizens of his country.

The slaughter began on St. Brice's Day AD 1002. Among those executed were a Viking chief named Pallig and his wife Gunnhild. Unfortunately for Ethelred the Unready, Gunnhild turned out to be the sister of Svein Forkbeard, king of Denmark.

Svein was quick to extract retribution. He dispatched an army that savaged Exeter, Wilton, Norwich and Thetford. The bloodletting was stanched only when a famine interceded in 1005. So severe was the drought that the Danish army had to be withdrawn for lack of forage.[11]

But Svein was back in 1006, pillaging and massacring in Reading, Kent and Wallingford. In the end, Ethelred was able to buy off the ravagers with thirty-six thousand pounds of silver. This was three or four years of the total English national income.[12]

The English tried to build a fleet to defend themselves, but even this attempt became an expensive fiasco that accomplished nothing. A last a Danegeld of forty eight thousand pounds of silver was paid in 1012, accompanied by a final indignity recorded in the Anglo-Saxon Chronicle:

> 1012 ... On the Saturday, the army [of Vikings] was much stirred up against the bishop [Ælfheah, archbishop of Canterbury]; because he would [not] promise them any fee, and forbad that any man should give any thing for him. They were also much drunken; for there was wine brought them from the south. Then took they the bishop, and led him to their hustings, on the eve of the thirteenth before the calends of May; and there they shamefully killed him. They overwhelmed him with bones and horns of oxen; and one of them smote him with an axe-iron on the head; so that he sunk downwards with the blow; and his holy blood fell on the earth, whilst his sacred soul was sent to the realm of God.[13]

England lay defenseless and on the brink of destitution thanks to the Viking sea-kings, one of the most prominent, successful and enriched being Olaf Tryggvason of Norway.

Olaf was the great-grandson of Harald Fairhair and the son of Tryggvi Olafsson, a king in Østland in the days of Hakon the Good. Tryggvi was killed by the sons of Eirik Bloodaxe, forcing Olaf's mother to flee with her infant son (born in 968–969) to eastern Norway and on into Sweden. According to legend, Olaf's mother was taking him to the court of Vladimir (Valdimar), duke of Novgorod, where her brother, Sigurd, was a government official. But her ship was captured by Esthonian pirates on the Baltic and the refugees were sold into slavery.[14]

Six years later, the story goes, Olaf was discovered in Esthonia by Sigurd, who purchased the youth and took him to Novgorod, where he grew to manhood, learning the war arts of the Rus. At 18, Olaf began his Viking career in the Baltic, but during a particularly severe storm he was driven onto the shores of Wendland. He was rescued by the daughter of King Boleslav of Wendland. As in any good legend, the two were married, but Boleslav's daughter died of some sickness and Olaf returned to his Viking ways.[15]

Legends aside, Olaf is credited with raids on Northumbria, Scotland, the Hebrides, the Isle of Man, Ireland, Wales, Cumbria and France. Some of these were in concert with Svein Forkbeard, but most were carried out as an independent Viking captain. He was truly one of the great "sea-kings without land." Olaf shared in some of the huge Danegeld payouts and was baptized in 994, as noted earlier.

Now rich and captain of a powerful fleet manned by battle-hardened Viking warriors, Olaf began his journey to take possession of his native Norway. He sailed by way of Orkney, landing at Moster, at the entrance of Hardangerfjord. From there he moved north aggressively, taking Jarl Hakon by surprise. The jarl's initial favorability with his subjects had deteriorated over the years. This situation, combined with the surprise assault, resulted in only a slight resistance that was easily brushed aside by Olaf. Hakon fled and, according to tradition, was killed by his own thrall, who cut his throat.[16]

Local landowners and chiefs came forward to pledge their fealty to Olaf. He was proclaimed king at the Thing in Trondheim, just as his great-grandfather Harald Fairhair had been. Next the southern and eastern regions changed sides, renouncing their allegiance to Svein Forkbeard and joining Olaf. Olaf was now king of all Norway and would become one of the most famous Viking heroes, regaled in legend and saga.[17]

The celebration of Olaf was not just in Norwegian legends and Icelandic sagas but also in American literature. Henry Wadsworth Longfellow devoted a series of twenty-two poems in his *Tales of a Wayside Inn* to the Norwegian king (a favorite, by the way, of President Theodore Roosevelt). Longfellow's epic poem covers Olaf's entire life, including his miraculous discovery and rescue from Esthonian slavery:

> How a stranger watched his face
> In the Estonian market-place,
> Scanned his features one by one,
> Saying, "We should know each other;
> I am Sigurd, Astrid's brother,
> Thou art Olaf, Astrid's son!"[18]

Though much acclaimed, Olaf's rule would be rocky and abbreviated. In large measure, his difficulties stemmed from his loss in popularity due to his imposition of Catholicism on the country. Early writers credited Olaf with Christianizing Norway, but this is an overstatement, though he did his best. His efforts were most rewarded in

Østland and lands around the Vik, regions where Harald Bluetooth and Svein Forkbeard of Denmark had done some preparation. The high country of the eastern region received little attention from Olaf and kept not only its old gods but also its local jarls and chiefs.[19]

Trondelag was another matter. Here the old religion was still well embedded, and Olaf spent much time and effort in converting this region. In the process, he founded a new town on the river Nid, which eventually grew into the important city of Trondheim. Olaf also strove to implant Christianity in Halogaland, where Thor and Odin were even more solidly ensconced.[20]

Around the year AD 1000, while Olaf was still consolidating his hold on Norway and fostering Christianity, his enemies were gathering: Svein Forkbeard of Denmark; Olaf (Olof) Skötkonung, the first Svear king to rule over the Gauts in Sweden; and Eirik, son of the dispossessed Jarl Hakon. Olaf knew this alliance was forming against him and that he needed allies of his own.

In the summer of AD 1000, Olaf set sail from Trondheim with a powerful armada of some sixty ships, including the Long Serpent, the greatest warship in the north. He passed through the Øresund into the Baltic, passed Rügen and continued on to the mouth of the Oder, where he met with Boleslav the Pole, king of Wendland. Boleslav was the father of Olaf's first wife and ex-husband of his present wife, Thyri. Ostensibly, Olaf had come to settle his wife's estate, property she had given up when she fled Wendland as well as her marriage to Boleslav. The real reason for the journey was more likely that Olaf was attempting to establish an alliance with a monarch unfriendly to Svein and the Danes. The meeting was cordial and may have led to an advantageous arrangement for both monarchs, but the relationship would not be allowed to mature.[21]

Accounts vary, but we do know that in that same year, AD 1000, Olaf met his opponents in a decisive sea battle. Either he was ambushed by the alliance during his return to Norway or he assembled a new fleet and attacked his adversaries later. The battle was either in the Øresund or off Rügen. Olaf may have been supported by Boleslav and his fleet of sixty ships, or not. Olaf's own fleet may have been the original sixty ships he left Trondheim with or as few as eleven ships. All these variations stem from inconsistencies in the accounts presented in *Óláfs Saga, Tryggvasonar*, Adam of Bremen's report and the story written by Snorri Sturluson. The outcome of the battle, however, is not in doubt. The Danish–Swedish–Eirik confederation soundly defeated Olaf's armada, and the legendary warrior forfeited his kingdom and his life. Longfellow describes the battle's conclusion in verse:

> The decks with blood are red,
> The arrows of death are sped,
> The ships are filled with the dead,
> And the spears the champions hurl.
> Over the slippery wreck
> Of the Long Serpent's deck
> Sweeps Eric with hardly a check,
> His lips with anger are pale;
>
> Seeking King Olaf then,
> He rushes aft with his men,
> As a hunter into the den
> Of the bear, when he stands at bay.

> But the young grew old and gray,
> And never, by night or by day,
> In his kingdom of Norroway
> Was King Olaf seen again![22]

As a result of the battle, Norway was once again a divided country. Olaf Skötkonung of Sweden received the eastern Norwegian provinces, and Svein regained his overlordship of the Vik and Østland region, while Jarl Eirik enjoyed sovereignty over western Norway. However, Svein's position in Norway was stronger than it would at first appear. He directly controlled the rich Østland and the area around the Vik. Jarl Eirik of Hladir, who ruled the west coast to a point beyond the Arctic Circle, pledged fealty to Svein just as his father had done. Even the eastern highlands and Ranrike-Bohuslän area, formerly Gaut territory now under Swedish control, was subject to Svein's influence, for King Olaf of Sweden appointed Jarl Eirik's brother as lord of much of this region. Thus, Svein's influence, if not direct control, was extensive in Norway. His northern flank was thus protected, and he could turn his attention to England.[23]

In AD 1013 Svein Forkbeard sailed for England with his youngest son Knut, a Danish fleet and an army. The Yorkshire Danes and the five boroughs of Danelaw were quickly subdued. Northumbria and Danish Mercia capitulated with little resistance. London alone thwarted the Danish invasion. But Sven's conquests were enough; he was proclaimed king of England, and Ethelred fled to Normandy, having previously married the duke's sister.[24] Svein was now ruler of an empire stretching from the Arctic Circle to the south of England, but not for long.

Early in 1014, Svein Forkbeard died and the English turned once more to Ethelred, inviting him to return from Normandy as king. Faced with a resurgent English resistance, the 18-year-old Knut pulled the Danish army out of England and sailed for Denmark, where his older brother, Harald, now ruled.[25]

Backed by Harald, Knut assembled a new invasion force. He was joined by Jarl Eirik of Hladir, an experienced warrior and sea captain, and by Thorkell the Tall, a mercenary who had fought on both sides in England and now commanded his own fleet.[26]

In the summer of 1015, Knut sailed for England on a quest for the island's crown. He arrived to find England divided at a time when unity was essential for its survival as an independent nation. Knut first attacked Wessex and Warwickshire. The earls of this region joined the Danes to save themselves. Northumbria was next, and it readily succumbed. Knut then turned on London, that last bastion of resistance that had so often defied Viking incursions.

At this point in the war Ethelred the Unready died. The English lords of "free" England chose his son Edmund, who came to be called Ironside, as their king and champion against the Danes. Edmund had escaped the siege of London, raised an army and liberated Wessex. He then attacked the London besiegers and temporarily drove them off. The siege was renewed, but London could not be broken.[27]

Knut lifted the siege and gathered his forces in Essex. A large Danish army was attacked by Edmund in Kent, and he delivered a crushing defeat to the Danes at Otford, just southeast of London. The decisive battle, however, was at Ashingdon in Essex, and here Knut routed his English opponent. Edmund escaped once again, finding refuge in Gloucestershire.

To bring the war to a conclusion, Knut made a deal with Edmund: Edmund would rule Wessex, and Knut the rest of England. The matter would not have rested there and further bloodshed was assured, but in 1016, at the age of 22, Edmund died. Knut was subsequently proclaimed king of all England.[28]

In about 1017 Knut divided England for administrative purposes. Jarl Eirik received Northumbria and Thorkell the Tall was given East Anglia. Knut retained direct control of the remainder of England.

In 1018–1019, Knut's brother Harald, king of Denmark, died, leaving the crown to Knut, who then ruled the empire his father had ruled, extending from the south of England to the Arctic Circle.[29] While Knut was preoccupied with consolidating his hold on England, however, parts of this empire began to slip from his grasp.

First, a new Olaf appeared in Norway. This was Olaf Haraldsson, born around 995, the son of a minor jarl in eastern Norway. He could lay claim to the Yngling royal lineage and certainly had the ambition to go with his ancestry.

At age 12, he shipped out as crewman, participating in Viking raids all over the Baltic. He served under Thorkell the Tall, fighting at London, Ringmere and Canterbury. But when Thorkell joined Ethelred, Olaf moved on to the continent, participating in raids in France and Spain. While serving Richard II of Normandy in about 1013, he was baptized a Roman Catholic. By 1015, he was back in Norway.[30]

Olaf established himself in Trondheim. With Jarl Eirik away in England fighting with Knut, Olaf was able to take control of the Trondelag by 1016. From there Olaf spread his rule over southwestern Norway and eventually Østland and the Vik. He pushed back the Swedes in eastern Norway and acquired the fealty of the Faroes, Orkney and the Shetlands.[31]

Olaf's main contribution to Norway was his modernization of the country, bringing it out of European isolation. This was done by furthering the written law and local assemblies, the Things, and by bringing the nation into the Roman Catholic sphere. This last task was achieved with uncompromising brutality where necessary. Østland and the Vik were already on their way to conversion, but the western coastal provinces were resistant, and they felt Olaf's heavy hand. The eastern inland area took even longer to convert, a process not completed until after Olaf's passing.[32]

In international politics, Olaf made a pact with Onund Jacob of Sweden, son and successor to Olaf Skötkonung, against Denmark. Olaf began raiding Zealand with his sixty-ship fleet, and Onund attacked Skåne with an even larger armada.[33]

Knut's problems were not confined to Norway. In Denmark, Jarl Ulf, Knut's brother-in-law and regent of the country, was moving precipitously toward independence. All this had to be dealt with, and in 1026 Knut sailed for Denmark with a force to settle scores.

Knut's combined English-Danish fleet met the Norwegian-Swedish fleet in the mouth of the river Helgeå, on the Baltic coast of Skåne. It is not clear who won the battle or if there was a decisive victory, but the result of the encounter was a nullification of the Norwegian-Swedish alliance. Onund headed back to Sweden, while Olaf, trapped on the wrong side of the Øresund, abandoned his fleet and traveled overland back to Norway. Knut retired to Denmark, where he had Jarl Ulf murdered in the Roskilde church.[34]

Knut then began a campaign of threats and bribery in Norway to undermine Olaf's control of the jarls, lords and chiefs. By the time Knut arrived off Norway with a powerful fleet in 1028, he was unopposed. All Norway proclaimed him king, and Olaf fled east to Sweden and then on to the land of the Rus and the court of Yaroslav, his kinsman.

From the frozen rivers of Novgorod Olaf made a last bid for reinstatement. Collecting warriors as he went, Olaf sailed to Gotland, then on to Sweden, and then he crossed to Dalarna, where he met his young half-brother Harald Hardradi and a band of Norwegian recruits. Olaf and Harald pushed on into Norway, where they met a Norwegian army at Stiklarstadir in 1030. Badly outnumbered, Olaf's band was routed and Olaf himself was killed. Knut the Great was once again the sovereign of an empire that included England, Denmark, Norway and Skåne, with nominal control of the Faroes, Shetlands and Orkney. He would rule his realm from his capital in England, where he died in 1035.[35] Upon his death, the Anglo–Danish–Norse Empire, the North Sea Empire of Knut the Great, would dissolve.

20

William the Conqueror Invades England

Upon Knut's death, the English made Harald Harefoot, Knut's son by his mistress Ælgifu, first regent and then king of England. Denmark was ruled by Hordaknut, Knut's son with his wife Emma, widow of the ill-fated king Ethelred and sister of Robert of Normandy.[1]

Norway, meanwhile, took Knut's demise as an opportunity to regain independence. When Olaf left Russia for his final attempt to retrieve the Norwegian crown, he left behind a son at the court of Yaroslav of Novgorod. The Norwegian lords sent a delegation to the Rus to retrieve this son, Magnus Olafsson, and though only a boy of eleven, the lords made him king of Norway.[2]

Harald Harefoot died prematurely of an unidentified sickness in AD 1040, at which time Hordaknut made his move to recover England. He sailed for England with a fleet and an army and successfully established his rule over the country, only to die in 1042. The English then turned to their own lineage for a king and selected Edward, Hordaknut's half-brother and the son of Emma and Ethelred.[3]

Harald's death also left the Danish throne vacant. Magnus moved quickly to fill the void. He crossed to Jutland and was elected king by the Viborg Thing. He then attacked the Slavic Wends, who had taken advantage of the disarray in Danish leadership to invade southern Jutland. Landing in Wendland in 1043, Magnus destroyed Wollin and, it is thought, put an end to the old Viking stronghold of Jomsborg in 1043. Magnus then brought his fleet to Hedeby, trapping the Wendish army and cutting off their supply lines. In concert with Ordulf and his Saxons, Magnus defeated and annihilated the Slavic army.[4]

Magnus was now ruler of two parts of the Anglo–Danish–Norse triad. He must have looked longingly to the west and the rich prize of England. But Edward was firmly established on the island and prepared with a fleet ready to meet any attempted invasion. Also, Magnus had other would-be usurpers to worry about.

At the Swedish court of Onund Jacob lurked two of these ambitious Viking princes during the winter of 1045–1046. One was Svein (referred to as Ulfsson, after his father, Jarl Ulf, or Estridsson, after his mother, Knut's sister). The other was the legendary Viking warrior Harald Hardradi. We met him earlier at the age of 15, fighting alongside his half-brother, Olaf, at the battle of Stiklarstadir.

Harald recovered from his battle wounds in a local, simple farmhouse attended to by a peasant family. Once recovered, he crossed the mountains into Sweden and sailed to the land of the Rus. In the service of King Yaroslav, he took part in the Polish campaign of 1031. Three years later, leading 500 Rus warriors, he entered the service of the Byzantine emperor. He is credited with fighting in the Achaean Islands, Greece, Asia Minor, the Caucasus, Palestine, Sicily and Bulgaria, becoming commander of the emperor's Varangian Guard. Eventually, he made his way back to Scandinavia via Kiev, Novgorod and Aldeigjuborg (just off Lake Ladoga), arriving at the Swedish court of Onund.[5]

At the Swedish court, Svein Estridsson and Harald Hardradi made a pact to attack and take over Magnus' dual kingdom. They even decided how they were going to divide up the territory after their victory. They began their war with some raids on Zealand and Fyn, but before they could do anything of significance, Magnus died in 1047.[6]

Svein was in Skåne at the time and immediately left for Denmark proper. He was acclaimed king at the Isøre Thing on Zealand and again at the Viborg Thing in Jutland. He would rule Denmark until his death in 1074.[7]

Harald attained the rule of all Norway by 1047, but he was then obliged to defend Norwegian interests vis-à-vis the Swedes. In a series of battles Harald secured the Norwegian border with Sweden. Thereafter, he carried on a running war with his former partner Svein that gained neither king any advantage. Crops were destroyed, homes and barns burned, and a host of people, mostly innocent farmers, killed. Finally, in 1064, a truce was agreed to by the two warring kings: Harald would have Norway and Svein retained Denmark.[8] The Viking Age was nearing its conclusion; only a few years remained and just a few actions, though these would be of great importance.

On January 5, 1066, Edward, king of England, died. The next day the English installed Harold Godwinson, son of Godwin of Danelaw (the real power behind Edward's throne) and brother to Tostig, former earl of Northumbria, as king in order to forestall any foreign intervention. This tactic did not work.

In the fall of AD 1066 Harald Hardradi, king of Norway, sailed for England with a fleet and an army. On the English coast, he was joined by Tostig (deposed earl of Northumbria) with his troops and the jarl of Orkney. Their combined force was said to have reached 300 ships and 9,000 men.[9]

The combined fleet moved along the English coast, raiding Cleveland, Scarborough and Holderness, perhaps attempting to intimidate both Harold Godwinson and William, duke of Normandy, whom Harald knew to be a fellow competitor for the throne of England. If that was the intent, it worked in neither case.

Harald sailed up the Humber and the Ouse to Riccall, where he disembarked his army. Any hope of taking Northumbria without a fight was shattered as Harald marched toward York. His path was blocked by an army led by Edwin, earl of Mercia, and Morcar, earl of Northumbria. The battle of Gate Fulford on September 20 was closely fought and inflicted heavy casualties on both sides, which would affect the later battles of Stamford Bridge and Hastings.

By day's end, the English force had been broken and was in retreat. The way to York and York itself lay open to Harald. He could have taken York, but instead he retired to his ships at Riccall to recuperate. Harald then negotiated with the citizens of York, attempting to persuade them to become allies. He marched his army to Stamford Bridge, possibly to take hostages or to intimidate the citizens of York.[10]

20. William the Conqueror Invades England

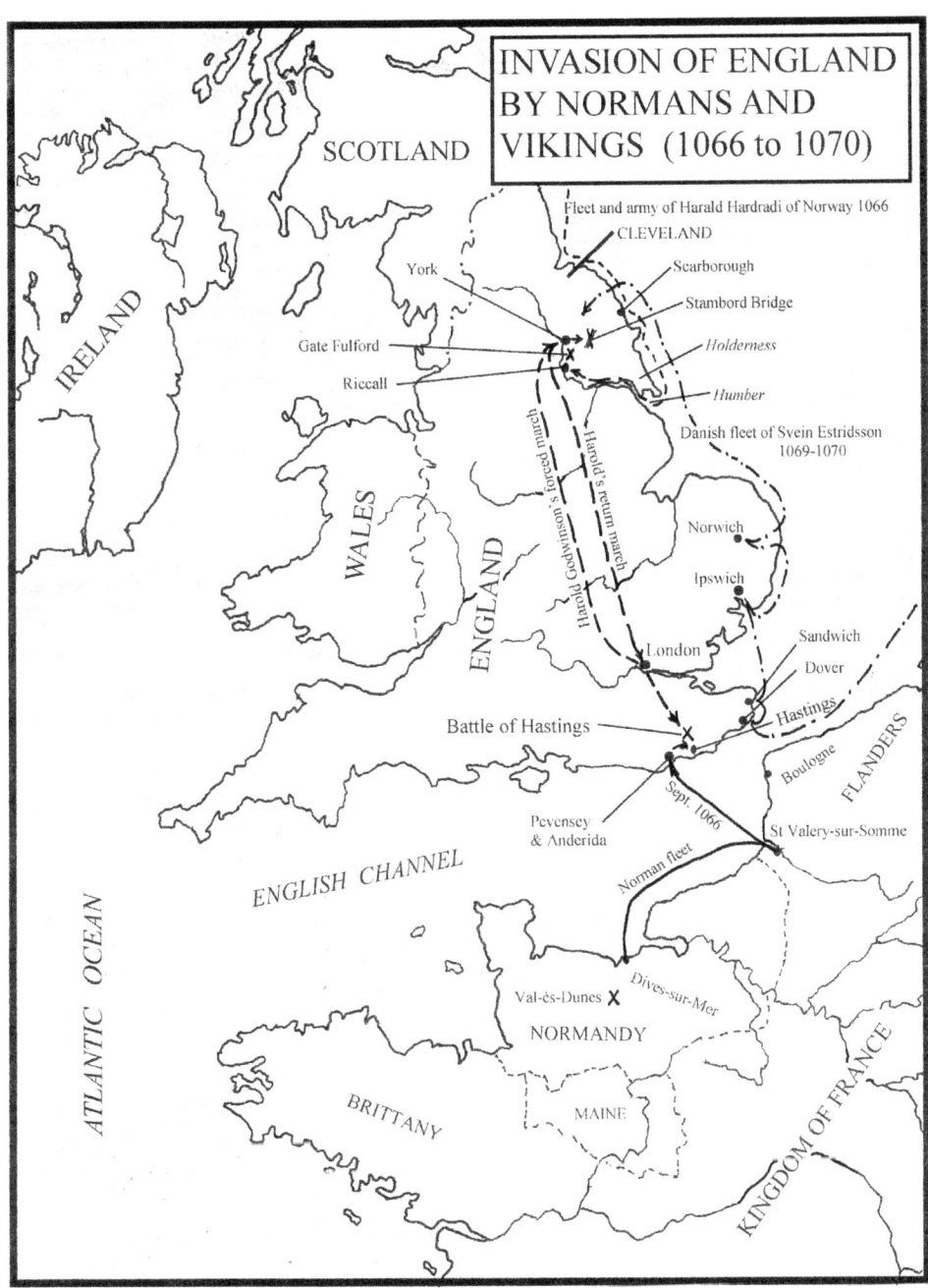

Unbeknownst to Harald, Harold Godwinson was moving north with his army with all possible speed. On September 25 Harold force-marched seventeen miles through an undefended York to take the Norwegians completely by surprise at Stamford Bridge. Though unprepared and lacking time to don their armor, the Norsemen were still able to form up and give battle.[11] The Anglo-Saxon Chronicle records:

> Then came our king Harold on the Norwegians unawares, and met them beyond York at Stamford with a great host of English folk; there was that day a very fierce battle fought on both sides. Harald

> Hardrada [Hardradi] was killed, and Tostig; the Norwegians that were left were put to flight, and the English fiercely struck them from behind, until some of them came to ship. Some drowned, some were burnt, some perished in various ways, so that there were few left, and the English had had the power of the battlefield. The king made terms with Olaf, the Norwegian king's son, their bishop and the earl of Orkney, and all left on the ships.[12]

Harald's son and successor, Olaf Kyrre (the Gentle or Peaceful), sailed home via Orkney to rule Norway in peace until his death in 1093.[13]

Harold Godwinson had achieved a remarkable victory over a fierce and formidable foe, but there would be no rest or victory celebration, for no sooner had the battle been won than Harold received news that his other nemesis, William the Bastard, with his Norman army, had landed at Pevensey in the south of England.[14]

We have already noted the founding of the duchy of Normandy by the Viking Rollo according to the treaty of Saint-Clair-sur-Epte in AD 911 and its expansion, first by Rollo and then by his successor William Longsword (927–943). Territorial enlargement continued through the rule of Duke Richard I (943–996), William Longsword's son and successor, as a new infusion of Vikings joined the colony in the 960s.[15]

At the same time, these Normans were shedding their Viking ways, becoming less and less Scandinavian in culture as they increasingly adopted the manners and habits of the French. Those not already Christian were baptized. The democratic institutions of the hundreds, assemblies and Things were discarded in favor of a strict feudal system. Only the duke could build castles. Knights and nobles held lands at the discretion of the duke in exchange for military service. They, in turn, parceled out fiefs to lesser lords under the same conditions. Even the bishops and abbots of the church were ducal appointments.[16] These conditions produced the most vigorous and powerful military state in Europe.[17]

So Normandy expanded while power was consolidated under successive rulers: Richard II (996–1026), Richard III (1026–1027) and Robert I (1027–1035).[18] By the 1030s, Robert of Normandy had designs on the English crown, to which he was connected through his sister Emma, that most remarkable woman, who had two husbands and two sons who were kings of England. Some move toward a takeover would certainly have occurred but for the demise of the duke. Robert also complicated matters by leaving no legitimate heir to carry on the project, a void that would be remedied in an unusual manner.

Legend has it that Duke Robert was out riding one morning when he chanced upon Arlette, the daughter of a tanner, who was washing clothes in a stream. He was so taken with her that he had her brought to his castle. Robert lived with Arlette for the rest of his life in spite of the fact he was already married to a lady of rank.

Born to this union in 1027 was a son whose life was in jeopardy immediately upon Robert's death. Just seven years old, the child, William, survived only because King Henry of France recognized him as the legitimate heir to the office of duke of Normandy.[19]

When William was 20, a new conspiracy was hatched by rebellious Norman lords who planned to kill him and split the duchy. William was forced to flee and again appealed to King Henry for aid. An army of loyal nobles and the king's men took to the field and vanquished the rebels at the battle of Val-ès-Dunes, fought entirely by cavalry, securing William's position as duke of Normandy.[20]

Duke William went on to expand his base in France through marriages, conquests and treaties. Count Eustace of Boulogne was at least an ally, if not a vassal, who supported William with troops at the Battle of Hastings. Count William of Flanders, William's father-in-law, was another ally. William conquered Maine, France, in 1063, adding it to his domains and its troops to his invasion force. Brittany, a target of repeated Norman incursions, had been sufficiently subdued that this remnant of Celtic peoples supplied a large contingent for the English project.

The Norman invasion of England was not a bolt out of the blue. There had been notable penetration prior to 1066. The first was associated with Queen Emma. Not only did she supply the foundation for William's claim to the English crown, but she also brought the first Normans with her to England as part of her household when she married Ethelred. Her son Edward brought more Normans to England when he returned from exile in Normandy (where he had fled after Ethelred's death) and ascended the throne in 1042. There developed in England a party favorably disposed to the duchy of Normandy and its rulers. This Norman faction was subdued during Knut's reign but saw an opportunity following his death.[21]

So, backed by a solid base on the continent and confederates in England, William prepared for the invasion. Having given up their Viking ways in favor of a landed domain, the Normans had to build a fleet to ferry the army across the channel. Some 696 ships are said to have been assembled for the task at Dives-sur-Mer, then moved to Saint-Valery-sur-Somme, where the armada lay at anchor for six weeks awaiting favorable winds for the crossing.

The delay, though frustrating for William and his allies, proved providential. A defense force assembled by Harold Godwinson during the summer of 1066 had been stationed in the southeast of England, ready to repel any attempted invasion from France. But this army was disbanded on September 8 due to the exhaustion of food supplies needed to sustain it. Most of the elements of this army traveled north with Harold to meet Harald Hardradi coming from Norway. And there were, of course, the battles of Gate Fulford and Stamford Bridge (September 25), which weakened the English militarily.

William finally received the favorable winds he needed and sailed from Saint-Valery-sur-Somme across the English Channel to land unopposed at Pevensey on the night of September 27–28. He brought with him an estimated 7,000 men (4,000–5,000 foot soldiers and 2,000–3,000 knights and mounted squires).[22] This was a prodigious army by the standards of its day. The Normans took the old Roman fortified town of Anderida, guarding the area, and then moved on to seize the castle at Hastings.[23]

Harold received news of the landing on October 1 while still at York. He left immediately, retracing his steps back to London, covering the 190 miles in thirteen days. He brought with him his victorious army from the north, stopping long enough in London to gather additional troops. Then Harold marched for Sussex with an army roughly equal to William's in size. His intention was to again surprise his enemy, but this time it was Harold who would be surprised.

Harold approached Hastings late in the day of October 13 and was spotted by Norman cavalry scouting the area. The Norman army formed up that night and advanced on Harold the next morning, catching the English off guard. Nevertheless, Harold had the advantage in holding the high ground. He assembled his army, all on foot, into the classic close-packed Saxon-Viking "shield-wall," anchored by his elite troops armed with the dreaded two-handed battle axe.[24]

William, by contrast, arranged his forces into three divisions—Bretons on the left, Normans in the center, and French allies on the right. Each division was subdivided into lines, with light infantry (archers and cross-bowmen) first, then heavy infantry, followed by light cavalry and then the heavy cavalry—that is, the knights.[25] The Norman knights, as illustrated in the magnificent Bayeux Tapestry, were in full-body armor with kite-shaped shields and conical helmets. The armor, made of chain mail, was heavy enough to be an effective deterrent to spear and sword but light enough to allow the knights to fight on foot.[26] While the Saxons had the advantage of the high ground, the Normans had the edge in mobility.

The battle raged all day. The Normans hurled all they had at the shield-wall, but the densely packed Saxon infantry held. Not even the Norman knights could penetrate the Saxon ranks and were thrown back time after time. But the repeated attacks were taking their toll on Harold's army, as more and more men lay inert on the field of battle. Finally, at dusk, a last charge by Norman heavy cavalry and heavy infantry broke through. As recorded by the Anglo-Saxon Chronicle, "There king Harold was killed, eorl Leofwine his brother and eorl Gyrth his brother, and many good men. The French held the field of the dead as God granted them because of the people's sins."[27] The flower and youth of warrior Saxon England now lay dead on the battlefield.

Though the Battle of Hastings broke the back of Saxon resistance and William the Conqueror was crowned king of England at Westminster on Christmas Day 1066, it took another five years for him to consolidate his hold on the island nation.[28]

There would be one final act in the Viking Age drama. This last deed, fittingly, was instigated by Svein Estridsson, king of Denmark. Svein had watched his old competitor, Harald Hardradi of Norway, assail the rich prize of England and come up short. He must have been perplexed to see a duke from France, a bastard with no real claim to the throne, successfully invade the Saxon bastion. Before William could get thoroughly entrenched in his new realm, Svein would intercede and attempt to take what he felt was rightfully his.

Svein assembled a fleet, which he sent to England in 1069. The Danes raided Dover, Sandwich, Ipswich and Norwich before joining Edgar Aething, Earl Waltheof, and Cospatric, the earl of Northumbria, in an attempt to overthrow William.[29] The rebels and the Danes gained some early successes, but by the time Svein arrived from Denmark in 1070, William had regained the initiative, and the situation for the insurgents had deteriorated to the point that Svein made peace with William and returned home with his army and fleet.[30] Thus ended the last significant Viking adventure in the west. The chapters of the Viking Age were now closed.

21

Norman Kingdom of Italy and Sicily

There is one last product of the Viking Age in the west that must be mentioned before moving on. That is the Norman conquest of Sicily and southern Italy, creating a Norman kingdom on the blue waters of the Mediterranean.

As we've seen, the Italian peninsula was conquered by the Ostrogoths, who were in turn expelled by the eastern Byzantine Empire, the stepchild of the once great Roman Empire. The Byzantine emperor then lost most of Italy to a new invader from the north, the Germanic Lombards, who by AD 572 had driven the Greeks out of the country except for the southern extremity. Meanwhile, Arab Muslims had invaded Sicily and removed the island from Byzantine control. At the same time, the western German empire claimed all of Italy but only occasionally made any move to enforce its authority over the peninsula. And lastly, the popes in Rome had established their own territory, the Papal States, as a defense against the Lombards.

By the end of the tenth century, Italy south of Rome and the Papal States comprised a patchwork of small principalities, counties, city-states and even monasteries, each controlling a bit of land subject to other feudal lords and dukes, Lombards in the north and Byzantines in the south. These tiny states operated, for the most part, independently. The heel of the peninsula (Apulia) and the toe (Calabria) were nominally under the control of Constantinople through its Byzantine, Italian capital of Bari. Even more independent were the Lombard states to the north, theoretically under the jurisdiction of the Holy Roman Emperor. Sicily, though technically under Saracen domination, was also fragmented politically. This was a situation ripe for intervention and conquest. As Gibbon notes:

> The broken provinces of the Greeks, Lombards and Saracens were exposed to every invader, and every sea and land were invaded by the adventurous spirit of the Scandinavian pirates. After a long indulgence of rapine and slaughter, a fair and ample territory was accepted, occupied and named by the Normans of France: they renounced their gods for the God of the Christians; and the dukes of Normandy acknowledged themselves the vassals of the successors of Charlemagne and Capet. The savage fierceness which they had brought from the snowy mountains of Norway was refined, without being corrupted, in the warmer climate; the companions of Rollo insensibly mingled with the natives; they imbibed the manners, language, and gallantry of the French nation; and, in a martial age, the Normans might claim the palm of valor and glorious achievements. Of the fashionable superstitions, they embraced with ardor the pilgrimages of Rome, Italy, and the Holy Land.[1]

The first recorded incident involving Normans in southern Italy was the result of 40 Normans passing through Salerno on their return from a pilgrimage to Jerusalem.

The city was attacked by a Saracen raiding party, probably from Sicily. The Normans were baffled and shocked by the lack of response from the citizens. Acquiring horses from Gaimer IV, prince of Salerno, the Normans attacked and drove the Muslims from the city.[2]

The military ability of the Normans was duly noted, and soon they were in demand as mercenaries by all factions in the extremely divided south of Italy. Individual knights, small groups of knights, and men-at-arms began to arrive to offer their service to cities and principalities. No kings or dukes from Normandy were involved—only lower-level

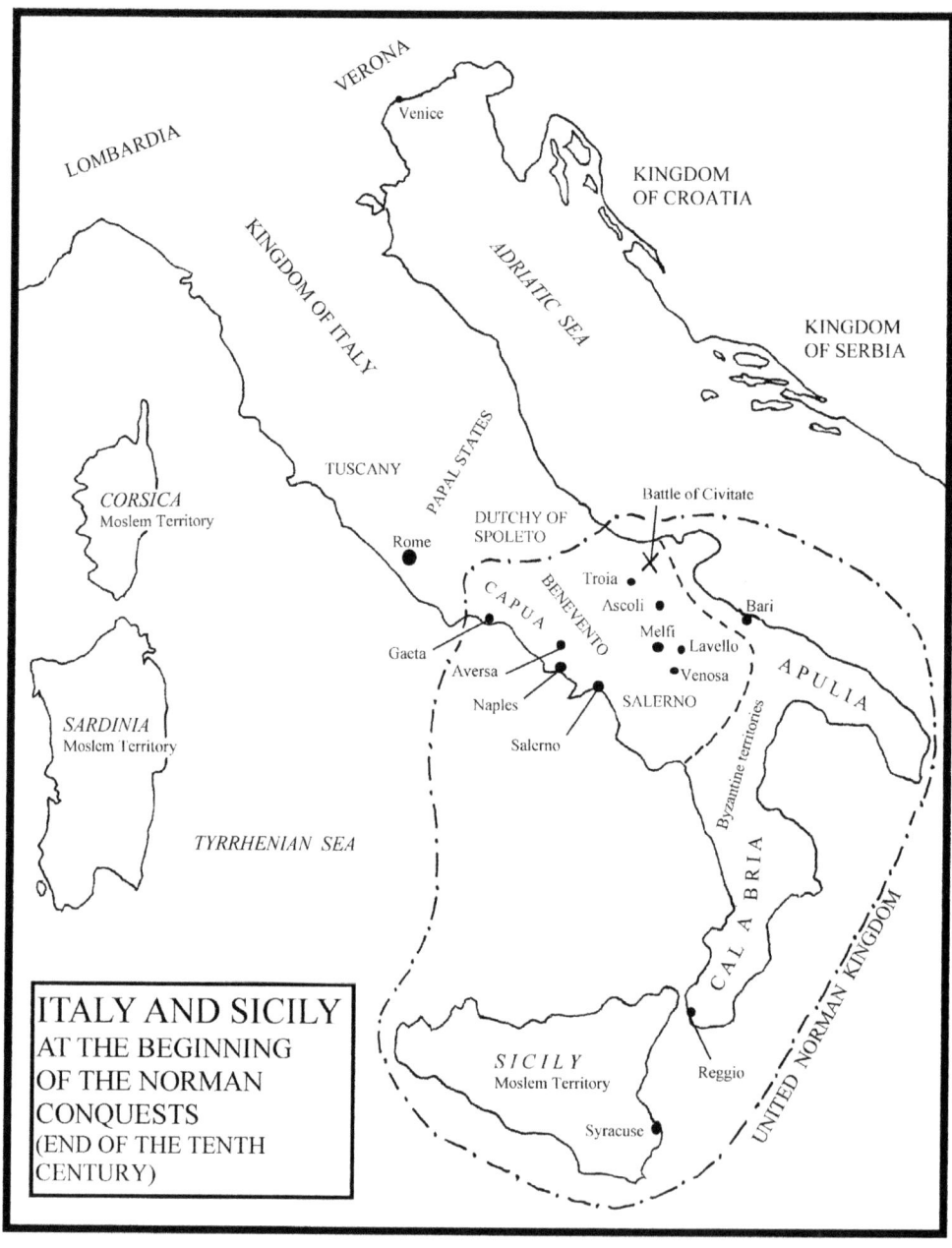

warriors, knights, squires and, occasionally, a company captain. At this time, Normandy had a surplus of third, fourth and fifth sons of nobles who would inherit no land. Undertaking a journey to find employment and wealth was their only option, and Italy provided such opportunities.

Of course, it was only a matter of time before the Normans were going to realize, being the dominant military force in the region, that they could be fighting for their own territory and not just selling their services to the highest bidder.[3]

In AD 1030, Rainulf "Drengot" took over the town and associated land of Aversa just north of Naples. This was the first Norman overlordship in Italy, and it began a trend. Before he died in 1045, Rainulf would acquire Gaeta. His successor, Richard I, began as count of Aversa and duke of Gaeta, but by 1058 he was prince of all Capua (Campania).

In 1035 there arrived the first of the Hauteville brothers: William, Drogo and Humphrey. In a family of twelve sons, there was insufficient patrimony for all, so eight of the brothers ultimately immigrated to Italy. These first three siblings reached Aversa just in time to become part of a 300-man contingent sent by the Lombard prince of Capua and Salerno to the army being gathered by Michael IV, the Byzantine emperor, to invade Muslim Sicily.

The expedition was a failure and returned to Italy. The only significant event of this foray into Muslim territory was a duel between William of Hauteville and the emir of Syracuse. William of the Iron Arm (Bras-de-Fer) unhorsed the emir in single combat and killed him.[4]

In 1041, a Lombard chief, one Arduin, led a revolt against the Byzantines in Apulia. Three hundred Norman knights from Aversa were offered to the rebel chief, including the Hauteville brothers. The Normans were stationed at the fortified town of Melfi and within days they had seized Venosa, Lavello and Ascoli. But in 1042, Argyrus, the current Lombard chief, defected to the Greeks, leaving the Normans at Melfi not only unemployed but also vulnerable to Byzantine retribution.[5]

The Normans in southern Italy were now congregated in three main groups— those at Aversa, Melfi and a garrison at Troia serving the Byzantines of Apulia. Representatives from the three groups met at Melfi in 1042 to decide on a course of action. They resolved to conquer southern Italy for themselves, even deciding who would receive which lands after the conquest. William Bras-de-Fer was proclaimed count of all Apulia, including Melfi and Troia, and all lands acquired from the Greeks. Venosa went to Drogo Hauteville and so forth until all the lands were assigned. With this division of territories, the Norman conquest of southern Italy began in earnest. At the same time, another Hauteville brother arrived. This was Robert, who was sent to Calabria to begin his own conquests.[6]

Once the Normans turned territorial, the old rulers of Italy became alarmed. They complained of the invaders' greed, high-handed tactics and cruelties. All of southern Italy rose up against them. Pope Leo IX called for the formation of an army from northern and central Italy to be joined by a Byzantine force from the south. The combined army would be enough to wipe out the mercenaries from the far north.

But the Normans were not just superior soldiers; they were also agile. They pulled together and attacked the pope's army before it could rendezvous with the Byzantines.

Battle was joined at Civitate. The mostly Lombard army fought using the German massed-infantry, shield-wall formation. The pope's army was routed by the Norman heavy cavalry. Upon hearing of the outcome of the Battle of Civitate, the Byzantine army aborted its move northward. The campaign to drive the newcomers from the peninsula collapsed, and Leo was forced to acknowledge the Norman lords as legitimate rulers and protectors of the church.[7]

After Civitate, the Norman conquest proceeded apace. By 1057, Richard, nephew and successor to Count Rainulf of Aversa, had taken all of Capua. In 1076 Robert Guiscard took Salerno, the last of the Lombard principalities in southern Italy. Reggio fell in 1060, marking the end of Byzantine rule in Calabria. With the fall of Bari in 1071, all Byzantine presence in Italy ended.[8]

In 1056, Roger, the eighth and last of the Hauteville brothers to come south, had begun his own conquest—that of Sicily. The war against the Muslim emirs began in 1061 and was completed thirty years later.[9]

All these Norman principalities were finally consolidated into one Norman kingdom that included Sicily and southern Italy in 1130. The first ruler of this united Norman state in Southern Europe was Roger II, son of Roger I, count of Sicily.[10] By then the Viking Age had long since ended and lived only in legend and the sagas.

22

Swedish Participation in the Western Expeditions

Having surveyed the expeditions to the west, which were primarily the purview of the Danes and Norwegians, the question arises: To what extent did Swedes take part in these adventures? It has long been a maxim that Norwegian Vikings went west, the Danes south and the Swedes east. In general this is true, though, as we have seen, there was much mixing of nationalities, especially between Danes and Norwegians, in those expeditions to the south and west.

When we speak of *nations*, we are using the term in the modern sense, for it was during the Viking Age that Denmark, Sweden, Norway and Iceland congealed into states that might fairly be called nations, though the final borders would not be established until much later. Also, it must be remembered that in the Viking Age loyalty or fealty was to a person—a lord, noble, or monarch—not to the state. Nationalism, a sense of loyalty to one's nation, was not part of the medieval culture. Thus boundaries and territories, even leaders, could be changed quickly and easily; a country, or county, or dukedom was a fluid thing in terms of land area and loyalties. So the Sweden we are using as a reference here is the Sweden with today's geographic boundaries.

In this chapter, we will examine to what extent Swedes participated in the adventures so far described—that is, the Viking movement to Western Europe and the North Atlantic. Wilhelm Moberg, the Swedish novelist and historian, writes:

> During the latter half of the Viking age (according to latest research) the Swedish Vikings also went west to a greater extent than has earlier been supposed. This means they must have participated in the huge and devastating raids on the British and Frankish kingdoms, the two Christian countries hardest hit by the heathen invasions.[1]

The same might be also said for the expeditions to Scotland, Ireland, Iceland and points west. We have already noted, for instance, that one of the probable discoverers of Iceland was Swedish. In fact, his voyage is illustrative of this Swedish involvement in the westward movement.

Gardar Svavarsson discovered Iceland by accident in about AD 860, having been blown off course on a trip from Sweden to the Hebrides to claim an inheritance his wife had received from her father.[2] As we've seen, Norwegian Vikings had reached the Shetland Islands by AD 780; then they went on to Orkney and Scotland. Soon after 800, they were in the Hebrides, and it appears that some Swedes were involved. At the very least Gardar's family had land in the Hebrides. Unless his wife was Norwegian, her father must have been a Swedish Viking participating in the settlement of these Scottish islands.

Among the most important records available on Viking history is the *Landnámabók* (The Book of Settlement), which recounts the early settlement of Iceland, listing the names of the settlers, often genealogies and sometimes biographies. One of these family histories is that of a Swede named Bjorn, who left Sweden for Norway after killing Solver, king of the Gauts, by burning down his house with Solver and thirty men inside. Apparently Bjorn had riches with him, as he had to flee one rest stop because the head of the household tried to kill him for his money. Later he was joined by Eyvind, his son, also from Gautland, who fitted out a fleet and sailed for Ireland.

In Ireland Eyvind (called the Eastman for his Swedish origins) no doubt participated in some raiding, plundering and conquering. Eventually, he settled down and married Rafarta, the daughter of an Irish chief. This union produced a son, Helgi, who, interestingly, was sent to the Hebrides to be raised, suggesting a Swedish connection there, probably kinsmen.

Helgi was either mistreated or in the care of an impoverished family, for the *Landnámabók* tells us that on a visit to the Hebrides, Eyvind and Rafarta found their son so malnourished that he gained the name "Helgi the Lean." They brought Helgi back to Ireland, where he eventually recovered, married and had several children. It was Helgi who then immigrated to Iceland with his family and thus was listed in the *Landnámabók*.[3]

So from the *Landnámabók* we have evidence that at least some Swedes participated in the taking of the Hebrides and in the Viking raids and conquests of Ireland. There were undoubtedly many more Swedes who joined in the Viking expeditions to Scotland and Ireland of whom we have no record. However, some of the other Swedes who migrated to Iceland are recorded in the *Landnámabók*:

> There was a renowned lord in Sweden called Gorm, he had for wife Thora, the daughter of King Eirek at Upsala; their son was named Thorgils, he had to wife Elin, the daughter of King Burislaf of Novgorod in the east.... Their sons were Hergrim and Herfinn, who had to wife Halla.... The daughter of Herfinn and Halla was named Goa, she was the wife of Hroar, and their son was Slettu-Bjorn, who settled the land first between the Grjot river the Deild-river, before Hjalti and Kolbein came out; he dwelt at Slettubjornstead.[4]

A second example is a "Swede" of mixed ancestry:

> There was a man called Fridleif, a Gotlander by his father's side, but with a Flemish mother called Bryngerd. Fridleif took possession of the whole of Slettahlid and Fridleifsdale between Fridleifsdale and Staf [Stafá] Rivers, and lived at Holt. His son was Thjodar, the father of Ari and Bryngerd, mother of Tongu-Stein.[5]

And then there is Thord:

> There was a man, a Swede by kindred, named Thord Knapp the son of Bjorn at Hang. Thord settled land up from Stifla to the Tongue [Tunguá] river and dwelt at Knappstead.[6]

In all, the *Landnámabók* identifies the origins of 1,003 of the 3,000-plus first settlers of Iceland. Of these 1,003 thus identified, 30 came from Sweden.[7] If we extrapolate these numbers, we can estimate that, out of the 3,000 early Iceland immigrants, 3 percent were of Swedish origin (which comes out to roughly 90 Swedes). As we've seen, by AD 930 there were 30,000 inhabitants of Iceland (see chapter 16). With the mixing of peoples in succeeding generations, perhaps two to three thousand of these would have been Swedes or descendants of Swedes.

After AD 986 the Vikings moved on to Greenland. Since the 450 early colonists who settled Greenland were from Iceland, there would have been a sprinkling of Swedes among them. Eventually the Greenland population would grow to about 3,000 souls, with a representation of Swedes mixed in with the other Vikings.

Finally, there were the expeditions to North America around AD 1000. The explorers and would-be settlers of Vinland were from Greenland. Thus, descendants of Swedish stock were certainly among those hardy individuals who set foot on this immense and unknown world at the very edge of the European experience.

From the Norwegian Viking movement, let us turn to the Danish expeditions against England and France to see how Swedes were involved. This long period of pillaging, plundering, invasion and outright conquest began in AD 835 with the raid on English Sheppey and ended with Svein Estridsson's attempt to overthrow William the Conqueror of England in 1070, an interval of some 235 years.[8] During this period we saw the seasonal Viking raids on both England and France become wintering-over occupations, which led eventually to the establishment of the Danelaw in England and Normandy in France. Finally, there was the return of the Vikings to England after a brief hiatus and the extraction of the Danegeld, ending in the takeover of all England by Svein Forkbeard and his son Knut. In all this action Danes were the dominant players, but Norwegians played a role from time to time and there were also Swedes who were actively involved.

First, it must be remembered that Scania (Skåne), Halland and Blekinge, provinces in what is present-day southern Sweden, were during this period generally tied to Denmark. At the beginning of the Viking Age, Skåne was an independent kingdom, but as Denmark developed into a united kingdom, Scania became included within these boundaries.[9] Blekinge was, from time to time, lost to Sweden, and Halland to either Sweden or Norway, but both were Danish for most of this period. The three major land areas of Viking Age Denmark, then, were the peninsula of Jutland, the island of Zealand (where today's Danish capital of Copenhagen is located) and Scania, which is today Swedish. True, Falster, Lolland, Møen, Fyn and other islands were no doubt important, but Jutland, Zealand and Scania contained the populations needed for the Viking expeditions launched by the Danes. Thus, Swedes from Scania were recruited and served in these ventures, and some number would have ultimately ended up in Danelaw and Normandy.

Confirmation of Scania's participation is found in a runestone discovered at Valleberga in Lund, Scania. The inscription reads:

> Sveinn and Þorgautr/Þorgunn made this monument in memory of Manni and Sveini. May god well help their souls. And they lie in London.[10]

Swedes from Scania would have been recruited (probably drafted at times) as crewmen and warriors for the Danish operations in England and France. Some perhaps went unwillingly, but, by all indications, most were perfectly happy to enter the world of pillaging and plunder where riches, land and women were available for the taking. The

Scandinavian culture of that time produced warriors who needed little encouragement to go adventuring for gold and glory.

As to the rest of Sweden, runestones provide a rich documentation of travelers to the west, though they are a little short on details. From Södermanland we find stones inscribed as follows:

> Ólafr raised this stone in memory of Sylfa/Solfa, his son. He died in the west.[11]
> Gunni raised this stone in memory of Ragni, his good son; [he] died on the western route.[12]

Some provide a little more information, like the Kålsta stone from Uppland:

> Styrkárr and Hjörvarðr had this stone raised in memory of their father Geiri, who sat in the Assembly's retinue in the West. May God help [his] soul.[13]

The Kålsta stone was raised in the mid-eleventh century to a member of an elite corps of personal guards of the Danish-English kings that existed between 1016 and 1066, late in the Viking Age.

Other stones may be dated to an earlier time, such as a stone from Orkesta, Uppland:

> And Ulfr has taken three payments in England. That was the first that Tosti paid. Then Þorketill paid. Then Knútr paid.[14]

These payments would have been when Ulfr was with Skagul Tosti in 991, with Thorkel the Tall in 1012 and, lastly, with Knut the Great in 1018. This Swedish Viking was not only successful, managing to live through several campaigns, but also undoubtedly very rich.

Another successful warrior is commemorated on the famous Kjula Runestone from Södermanland:

> Alríka, Sigríðr's son, raised the stone in memory of his father Spjót, who had been in the west, broke down and fought in townships. He knew all the journey's fortresses.[15]

("Spjót" means spear and may be a warrior's nickname earned through feats of valor.)

Some stones hint at emotion and maybe a forlorn hope for the return of a long-absent father:

> Ingjaldr and Ölvir raised this stone in memory of Þorbjörn, their father. He has been long in the west.[16]

Other stones tell us where the warrior died:

> Guðbjörn [and] Oddi raised this stone in memory of Guðmarr, their father. He who died stood valiantly in the staff of the ship; [now] lies inhumed in the west.[17]

And some stones are a testimony to a warrior's character, as in this one from Västergötland:

> Tóla placed this stone in memory of Geirr, her son, a very good [and] valiant man. He died on a Viking raid on the western route.[18]

The "western route" could refer to any of a number of territories—France, Ireland, Scotland, even Iceland.

However, most of the memorials were raised to travelers or warriors engaged in the raids, wars and conquests in England and, to a lesser extent, France. This is borne out in the number of runestones that specifically mention England. There are some 30 stones found in Sweden that refer to England by name. That is on a par with the number of runestones referencing Greece, where the Swedish Vikings were the acknowledged leaders in the quantity of expeditions. An example is a stone from Tång in Uppland:

> ... had the monument erected in memory of his father Bósi [Bausi?] and his brother Kuru. May God help them who fell abroad in England.[19]

Or a stone from Hjälsta, Uppland:

> ... his father. He died in England.[20]

Or this stone raised by someone who actually made it home:

> ... had [this stone] cut ... [in memory of] himself, traveler to England, grandfather of....[21]

Again, a person's character may be vouched for, as in this memorial from a stone located in Transjö, Småland:

> Gautr placed this stone in memory of Ketill his son. He was the most unvillainous of men, who forfeited his life in England.[22]

Only rarely, however, are the stones explicit as to the location of the warrior's grave, as in the Nävelsjö stone from Småland:

> Gunnkell placed this stone in memory of Gunnarr, his father, Hróði's son. Helgi, his brother, laid him in a stone coffin in Bath in England.[23]

There were also those who fought in both England and the continent, as shown by a stone in Grinda, Södermanland:

> Grjótgarðr [and] Einriði, the sons, made [this stone] in memory of [their] able father. Guðvér was in the west; divided [up] payment in England; manfully attacked townships in Saxony.[24]

The "payment in England" probably refers to the Danegeld. Other inscriptions reference such payments that warriors participated in and gained part of the distribution of wealth. A stone from Väsby, Uppland, reads in part, in Old English, "Hann tok Knuts giald a Ænglandi."[25]

Some stones name the leaders of the expeditions that the warriors were with, as in the Gåsinge stone from Södermanland, which reads:

> Ragna raised this stone in memory of Sveinn, her husbandman, and Sæfa and Ragnbjörg in memory of their father. May God help his spirit. I know that Sveinn was in the west with Gautr/Knútr.[26]

"Knútr" refers to Knut the Great, one of the more frequently cited leaders, as in this stone from Landcryd, Östergötland:

> Væringr raised this stone in memory of Þjalfi, his brother the valiant man who was with Knútr.[27]

However, other well-known leaders are also named, as in this stone from Uppland:

> Gunni and Kári raised the stone in memory of.... He was the best husbandman in Hákon's dominion.[28]

Here was a Swede who was a member of Jarl Hakon Eriksson's army in England. And there is also this stone from Småland:

> Tófa raised this stone in memory of Vrái, his father, Earl Hákon's marshal.[29]

This was evidently a man of some importance to the earl. Another stone from Småland speaks to those who fought on the side of England:

Tumi/Tummi/Dómi raised this stone in memory of Ôzurr, his brother, he who was King Harald's seaman.[30]

(King Harald is identified as the English king Harold Harefoot.)

The activities of such Swedish mercenaries are further attested to by the quantity of English and French coins from this period found in Sweden. Silver pennies (deniers) from Frankish Dorestad have been found in large numbers.[31] In all, 154,776 Frankish and German coins have been discovered in Sweden.[32] Nearly 34,000 Anglo-Saxon silver coins have likewise been recovered in Sweden, an indication of the wealth extracted from England in the Danegeld.[33] The great hordes of coins found in Sweden far surpass anything found in either Denmark or Norway.[34]

Except for the conquest of Frisia by Rurik in 850 and the subjugation of Hedeby and southern Jutland by Olaf, his sons and Sigerich in about 900, Sweden as a nation (peopled by the Svéar and Gauts) did not mount the great expeditions to the west generated by Norway and Denmark. Nevertheless, significant numbers of individual Swedes and even whole ship's crews did participate in the movement to the west and south.

We have noted the four-way conflict in southern Italy and Sicily between Saracens, Byzantines, Lombards and Normans, in which the Normans ultimately prevailed, creating a Norman kingdom in the Mediterranean. Swedes were also players in this multifaceted struggle, though on the other side. A runestone found in Uppland reads:

Guðlaug had the stone raised in memory of Holmi, her son. He died in Lombardia [the Old Norse name for Italy].[35]

This grieving mother actually raised two stones to her lost son. Two other monument fragments likewise refer to Swedes who died in Italy:

He met his end on the eastern route abroad in Lombardia.[36]
Inga raised this stone in memory of Óleifa, her.... He ploughed his stern to the east, and met his end in the land of the Lombards.[37]

These three warriors were almost certainly members of the Varangian Guard, the elite troops of the Byzantine emperor. They died defending the emperor's Italian territories from the Muslims, Lombards, or, very possibly, the Normans.

Thus, Swedes were involved in all areas of the Viking western operations in one way or another, as settlers, conquerors and occupiers. Their contributions to the Viking movement to the west and south were as individuals, small groups, ship's crews, draftees (in some cases in Scania) and mercenaries. But while the Swedish involvement in the Viking wave that inundated Western Europe and the North Atlantic was significant, it was the movement to the east where Swedish influence was personified.

23

Swedish Unification

With the development of Norway and Denmark as nations and a summary of the westward Viking movement as background, we are ready to delve into Sweden's Viking Age. In chapter 11, we left Sweden still a divided country at the end of the Vendel Period (AD 575–790), a subdivision of the German Iron Age (AD 400–790) and the immediate precursor to the Viking Age.

In the far north were the reindeer-herding, nomadic Lapps identified by the writers of the Mediterranean world, Jordanes and Procopius. These same authors recognized various tribes of semi-nomads living in north-central Sweden between the high ridge of the Scandinavian (Scandes) mountain range and the Gulf of Bothnia in the forests of northern Sweden. This region may be referred to as Norrland, an area populated by hunter-gatherers.

We find hints of a kingdom among these northern tribes in the Icelandic sagas. In *Egil's Saga*, Thorolf meets the king of Kvenland somewhere north of Uppland along the west coast of the Gulf of Bothnia[1]:

> He'd penetrated well to the east when some people of the Kven tribe came and told him they'd been sent by King Faravid of Kvenland. They said the Karelians were attacking Faravid's kingdom and he wanted Thorolf to go there and help him.[2]

According to the saga, Thorolf arrived at Kvenland by traveling south from Finnmark, where he was trading with the Lapps. There is some question as to which side of the Gulf of Bothnia Thorolf was actually on. The Karelians referred to in the quote above were in eastern Finland, so Thorolf may have been on the east side of the gulf, not the west. (An odd side story was created by this section of the saga because the word "Kven" is so similar to the Old Norse word for woman—*Kván* or *Kvæn*—that Kvenland became mistakenly known as the land of the Amazons.)[3]

South of Norrland is Uppland, the land of the Svear. Better organized than their northern neighbors, the Svear had, by the beginning of the Viking Age, developed a system of kingdoms that warred with each other and their neighbors. They were noted, as we've seen, for being traders and breeders of fine horses. And we have noted several references in the sagas of trade and raiding expeditions mounted from this region.

South of Uppland was the domain of the Gauts, which by the beginning of the Viking Age probably included Västergötland, Östergötland, Närke, Södermanland, northern Småland and perhaps Värmland, though this last shifted between Norwegian, Gaut and Svear control. The opening of the Viking Age found the Gauts and the Svear locked in a struggle for supremacy and domination of Sweden. This war or series of wars cannot be characterized as a conflict between a united Svear state and a Gaut nation, though at times that may have been the case. The situation was generally much more complicated, with individual Gaut kings forming alliances with kings in Uppland, and there was substantial interference from foreign rulers—Danish, Norwegian, even Saxon and Wendish. This war would rage on for most of the early Viking Period.

Wedged between these two powers, interestingly, there grew into existence possibly the greatest merchant center of the Viking world, rivaling Danish Hedeby. This was the trading town of Birka, with its commercial tentacles reaching to England, the Arctic, the Byzantine Empire, Persia, even the Silk Road to China. Located on the island of Björkö in Lake Mälar, Birka only came into existence at the beginning of the Viking Age, competing with Helgö, an established trade center located in the same lake. Birka would come to eclipse Helgö, replacing it as Sweden's dominant commercial center. Helgö had always, it seems, been under Svear jurisdiction. Birka, however, may have been self-governing from time to time. But such a rich prize would not long stay independent; becoming a grand addition to either the Gaut or the Svear realm was inevitable.

On the southern border of the Gauts was the plateau region of Småland. This rocky, less fertile area of mostly small farms may have formed its own kingdom at one time, at least according to an Icelandic Viking romance saga:

> There was a king called Hring who ruled over the Smalands. He was married to Ingibjorg, daughter of Earl Bjarkmar of Gotaland. They had two children, a son called Egil, and a daughter called Æsa.[4]

To the south of Småland was Scania, an independent kingdom at various times, comprising Skåne, Halland and Blekinge, though the last was often part of Sweden during the Viking Age. As we've seen, Scania had conquered Sweden prior to the Viking Age, in the mid-seventh century, according to the *Ynglinga Saga* (see chapter 10).

In order to gain some perspective on the political situation in Sweden during this period, it is necessary to return to the *Ynglinga Saga*. We pick up the story with Yngvar, son of Eystein, being king of the Swedes (the Svear). The saga describes Yngvar as a great warrior defending Sweden (Svearland) with warships against Danish and East-country pirates who are raiding his domain. He makes peace with the Danes, and then he leads an expedition against Estland (probably Estonia, Latvia or Courland) and is killed in battle. His demise is celebrated in verse in the saga:

> Certain it is the Estland foe
> The fair-haired Swedish king laid low.
> On Estland's strand, o'er Swedish graves,
> The East Sea sings her song of waves;
> King Yngvar's dirge is ocean's roar
> Resounding on the rock-ribbed shore.[5]

There is a certain ring of truth to this story of Yngvar. Raids by Danish Vikings along the coast of Sweden were certainly common, and battles in the eastern Baltic are recorded in various sagas. But dating Yngvar's reign is difficult. He is generally placed in the mid-sixth century, based on chronology.

Yngvar was succeeded by his son Onund, who was blessed with a time of peace and prosperity in his domain. He fostered the clearing of lands for cultivation and the

23. Swedish Unification

LEGENDARY KINGS OF SWEDEN

FROM SWEDISH KINGS LIST OF JOHANNES MAGNUS		MAGNUS	SAXO	MAGNUS
Magog (Grandson of Noah)		Sigurd I	Gotar	Thord III
Suevus (Ancester of Svear)		Charles III	Heroldd	Algod II
Gothar I (Ancester of Gauts)		Erik IV	Sorke	Godstagus
Ubbo (Eponym of Uppland)		Halfdan II	Ragnar	Arthus
Siggo I		Yngvin	Hwitserk	Hakon II
Erik I		Ragnvald I		Charles IV (Karl IV)
Uddo		Amund I (Hamund I)		Charles V (Karl V)
Ale		Hakon Hamundarson (Haki)		Borgar
Osten I		Sigurd II	**FROM HEIMSKRINGLA**	Erik V
Charles I (Karl I)		Ingi I	**THE YNGLINGA SAGA**	Thord IV
Bjorn I		Njord	Odin	Bjorn III
Gothar II		Froda	Njord	Alrek III
Siggo II		Yrban	Frey	Bjorn IV (met Ansgar at Birka-820)
Berich (Berig:Goths to Poland-Jordanes)		Osten II	Fjolne	Bratemunder (Braut-Onund)
Humble (Humli)		Fjolner	Swegde	Sigrud III
Gothilas		Sverker I	Vanlande	Heroth (Herraud)
Sigtrygg	**GESTA DANORUM**	Vanlandi	Visbur	Charles VI (Karl VI)
Svarin	**BY SAXO**	Visbur	Domald	Bjorn V
Svipdag	**GRAMMATICUS**	Domaldi	Domar	Ingjald
Asmund	Sigtryg	Domar	Dygve	Olaf I Tractelja - 850s
Uffo	Swipdag of Denmark	Adils III	Dag the Wise	Ingi II
Hunding	Hunding under Denmark	Dyggvi	Agne	Erik VI Wederhatt
Ragnar	Ragnar	Dag	Alric and Eric	Erik VII Arsaell
Hodbrodd	Hothbrodd	Alrek II	Yngve and Alf	Eirik (Erik) VIII Sigrsaell
Adils I	Helge of Denmark	Ingemar I	Hugleik	"The Victorious" (970-995)
Hodr	Rolf of Denmark	Ingjald	Hake	Olaf (Olof) Skötkonung Eriksson
Rorik	Athisl	Jorund	Jorund	(Ruler of Svear and Gauts - 995-1022)
Adils II	Hiartuar under Rolf of Den	Hakon I	On (Ane)	**FROM BEOWULF**
Botvild	Hother also ruled Denmark	Egil	Egil --------- Ongentheow - 520s	
Charles II	Athisl	Gothar IV	Ottar ------- Ohthere	
Gram	Homod and Hogrim	Fasti	Adils -------- Onela	
Thord I	Hugleik	Gumund	Eystein ----- Eadgils	**ADAM OF BREMEN**
Gothar III	Alrik	Adils IV	Solve the sea-king	Anund	Late 700s
Adolph	Eric I of Denmark	Osten III	Yngvar	Björn	Late 700s
Algod I	Halfdan	Ingemar II	Onund	Erik (V?)	
Erik II	Siward	Halsten I	Ingjald	Björn (IV?)	Mid 800s
Lindorn	Eric II	Bjorn II	Ivar Vidfavne of Scania	Olof	
Alrek I	Halfdan of Denmark	Ragnvald II			
Erik III	Alver	Svartmann		Ring	Mid 900s
Godric	Olaf	Thord II		Erik Emundsson	
Halfdan I	Ing	Rodulf		Erik Sigrsaell 970-995	
Filmer	Ingild	Hatin		Olof Skötkonung	
Nordian	Ring (Hring-Bravic War)	Adils V (Attila IV)			995-1020

building of roads to new settlement areas, so much so that he was known as Onund Roadmaker.

The next section of the saga deals with the upbringing of Ingjald the Bad and is most revealing:

> Onund had a son called Ingjald, and at that time Yngvar was king of the district of Fjadryndaland. When Ingjald was grown, Onund applied for him to King Algaut for his daughter Gauthild. Algaut was a son of Gautrek the Mild, and grandson of Gaut; and from them Gotland (Gautland) took its name. King Algaut thought his daughter would be well married if she got King Onund's son, and if he had his father's disposition; so the girl was sent to Sweden [Svearland] and King Ingjald celebrated his wedding with her in due time.[6]

It is clear from this passage that Gotland (Gautland) is not part of the Sweden (Svearland) referred to in this section of the saga. The girl from Gotland is sent to Sweden of the Svear. Svearland and Gotland are separate and distinct nations, though the Svear would seem to be a consolidated monarchy ruling district kingdoms, one of those being Fjadryndaland, whereas the Gauts are divided into several kingdoms.

The division between the Gauts and the Svear is further attested to by the Icelandic sagas. In a Viking romance saga, *King Gautrek*, we find that "King Gauti ruled over West Gotaland which lies east of the Kjolen [Scandes] Mountains between Norway and Sweden and is separated from the Uplands by the Göta River."[7] Uplands as used here was the region in Norway west of the Göta River. Here again we have Gauti, king of West Gotaland (West Gautland, Västergötland), distinct from Sweden of the Svear. And there is King Gautrek, the hero of the saga, who is recognized by his father, Gauti:

> "I've decided to hand over my authority to my son Gautrek, and with it the title of king." His friends were all in favor of this, and after King Gauti's death, Gautrek was made king over Gotaland. He's mentioned in many of the old sagas.[8]

Later in the story, another king is identified:

> There was a king called Olaf the Keen-eyed ruling over Næriki in Sweden, a powerful ruler and great warrior.[9]

"Næriki" is likely Närke, which may have been considerably larger in territory than the later province. Sweden here is used as a general term to indicate the region east of Norway and does not imply that Olaf was subject to the Svear.

Thus, as Ingjald comes to the throne of the Svear, he rules some number of district kings in Uppland and faces the Gauts divided into several kingdoms—East Gautland, West Gautland, Närke and Södermanland. Through deception and murder, Ingjald consolidates his hold on the Svear and acquires some of the Gaut kingdoms as well. According to the *Ynglinga Saga*, as quoted earlier, he invites the kings and their nobles to a feast. Then, when everyone is drunk, he burns down the hall, killing all within, earning the title "The Evil-adviser."[10] He completes his dastardly plan by conquering the now leaderless kingdoms.

There are, however, two holdouts: King Granmar of Södermanland and King Hogne of East Gautland. Granmar did not attend the murder feast, and he fights Ingjald successfully until he, too, is burned in a mead-hall fire by Ingjald in a sneak attack.[11] King Hogne carries on the fight, pillaging Ingjald's territories with cavalry raids and holding out until his dying day.[12]

Ingjald, then, may have been the first king to rule both the Svear and the Gauts, or at least most of the realm. An estimate of the time of his reign is around the end of the sixth century, working backward from future generations.

Ingjald's mischief was not confined to incinerating his fellow Swedish kings, however, for next he contracted a marriage between his daughter, Aasa, and Gudrod, king of Scania. Aasa, once in Scania, arranged the murder of her new husband and then fled back to Uppland.[13]

Gudrod was succeeded by his nephew, Ivar Vidfavne, as king of Scania (c. AD 650–700).[14] Ivar assembled an army and invaded Sweden. Upon hearing of Ivar's approach, Ingjald fired his own great-hall with himself and Aasa inside, a pyromaniac to the end.

According to the saga, Ivar went on to conquer all of Sweden, Denmark, much of Saxland (Saxony), the East Country (Estonia, Latvia and Courland), and a fifth of England.[15] This is an exaggeration, of course. A "fifth of England" generally refers to Northumbria, and there is no mention of Ivar in the Anglo-Saxon Chronicle, where the lineage of the kings of Northumbria is listed.[16] He may have subjugated kings in the other countries, but it is doubtful that he could have ruled directly. Rather, this was an empire of lords who pledged fealty to Ivar, a loose confederacy of kingdoms.

According to the sagas, Ivar's empire was replicated by his grandson, Harald Hilditonn (Wartooth), albeit without some of the inflated claims. Harald seems to have reconquered Jutland and Zealand, acquired Scania by inheritance, and then subjugated Gautland and the Svear. Again, sub-kings were left in place who could cause trouble if an opportunity arose.

And a challenger did surface. This was Sigurd Hring, Harald's own nephew and king of the Svear or East Gautland (or both). The rivalry resulted in the Bravic War, culminating in the famous Battle of Bravellir, which is thought to have occurred near Bråviken, north of today's Norrköping, on what was then the northeastern border of East Gautland.

According to Saxo Grammaticus' *Danish History*, Harald moved in from the south with an army studded with heroes and legendary warriors. The list reads like the heroes of the Trojan War. Included were Hakon Cut-cheek and Wisna, a woman warrior with her maidens covered with "little shields."[17] Also with Harald were Ubbe the Frisian, Geir the Livonian, Brat the Jute, Orm of England, Ari the One-eyed and Har from Aland, along with many others named by Saxo. Aside from these noted warriors, the army was made up of Danes, Scanians, Livonians, Saxons, Slavs and, presumably, West Gautlanders.

Harald brought a fleet so numerous it filled the sound between Zealand and Scania so that one could cross the Øresund without getting wet. The fleet arrived at Kalmar and prepared for battle.

Arrayed against this mighty force was Hring's army, with its own heroes of legend. Egil the One-eyed, Styr the Stout, Saxo the Splitter, Sali the Goth, Thord the Stumbler, Throndar Big-nose, Thorolf the Thick, Thengel the Tall, Birwil the Pale, Krok the Peasant, Odd the Englishman, Regnald the Russian and Mar the Red from Iceland (which had not yet been discovered). Hring also brought two navies, one fleet from Sweden (Svearland) and another from Gotland, for a total of 2,500 ships. His army comprised Svear, East Gautlanders, Norwegians, Kurlanders, Esthonians and warriors from assorted other nations.

When both sides were ready and the battle lines drawn, the trumpets sounded and the clash of arms began. According to legend, the hail of spears was so thick the sun was blotted out. A river of blood flowed from the many wounds. Spears, arrows, bolts and the slinger's missiles were expended, and then the warriors moved in for the fight at close quarters.

The battle ended with Harald's death, which precipitated the disintegration of his Danish-Swedish empire. It is thought that this battle celebrated in legend and saga occurred in the eighth century.[18]

With the death of Harald, we have only the Icelandic sagas to go on for information regarding the Swedish kings for a time. Presumably, Hring became ruler in Sweden of both the Gauts and the Svear. Scania was likely lost to Denmark.

In the sagas we find references to the Swedish king lineage of this time. From the Viking romance saga, *Bosi and Herraud*:

> Hring was married to a fine-looking, even-tempered woman called Sylgja, the daughter of Earl Seafarer of the Smalands.
> Hring and his queen had a son called Herraud.[19]

The saga ends with the words "Herraud became king of all the territories his father had once ruled."[20]

Added to the mix, we have the Sparlösa runestone inscription dating to about AD 800 that memorializes a king named Alrik, the son of Uppsala king Eirik, who ruled Västergötland. Again, this suggests a Svear dominance over at least part of Gautland at this time.[21]

Finally, for the early ninth century we gain some dependable insight. This information comes from the writings of Bishop Rimbert, author of *The Life of Anskar*. Rimbert was the companion and successor to St. Anskar, missionary to the northern peoples.

After serving for a short time as the young monk of Corbey, Father Anskar departed for Sweden in 829. Rimbert describes his harrowing sea voyage, during which Anskar's ship was attacked by Viking raiders. He arrived at Birka on foot, minus his holy books and most of his belongings, which were lost to the pirates. At Birka, Anskar was welcomed by Björn (IV?), a son of Eric (V?).[22]

Anskar was not able to convert King Björn, but he did baptize Herigar, prefect of the town and a counselor to the king. Herigar later built a church on his own property and remained a faithful Roman Catholic for the rest of his life.[23]

Anskar then returned to France, where he was consecrated archbishop of the diocese of Hamburg. In Rome he was named papal legate, jointly with Ebo of Rheims, to all the northern peoples—Swedes, Danes, Slavs and others—by Pope Gregory IV.[24]

Ebo sent a relative of his, Bishop Gautbert, and a companion, Nithard, to continue the missionary work in Sweden. The pair was again received warmly by King Björn, and they found support among some of the Birka residents.[25] Undoubtedly there were some Christians among the tradesmen and merchants in this commercial center that attracted traders from as far away as England and Constantinople. Gautbert and his companions preached the gospel according to Roman Catholic precepts and began building a church in Birka.

Perhaps their success was their undoing, for there seems to have been a general uprising among the Swedes of Birka against the missionaries. Nithard was killed, Gautbert's residence was burned, and Gautbert himself was driven out of the town along with some of his disciples.[26]

Meanwhile, Anskar was having his own problems in France. Emperor Louis, Anskar's friend and patron, died in AD 840. The Frankish empire dissolved into three kingdoms, led by Lothar, Charles the Bald and Louis the German. The three kings then proceeded to make war on one other.[27]

The Danes took advantage of the ensuing chaos to recover some of their lands lost to the Franks in southern Jutland. During this turmoil, Hamburg was sacked in 845 by the Danes. Anskar escaped with some books and sacred relics, but his church, school and library were burned.

Louis the German responded by combining the sees of Hamburg and Bremen, over which Anskar was made archbishop. Anskar traveled to Denmark in 849, where King Horik allowed him to build a church in Hedeby.[28]

In 850 Anskar sent the hermit Ardgar to Birka to contact the faithful Herigar. Rimbert reports:

> On his arrival he was courteously received by Herigar and his presence brought great joy to the Christians who were there.
> On the suggestion of Herigar, and with the counsel and permission of the king who was then reigning, he began to celebrate the divine mysteries in public.[29]

The reference to "the king who was then reigning" implies that it was someone other than Björn, whom Rimbert was familiar with. Later in the same chapter, Rimbert provides some additional information on the Swedish king, recounting an event that occurred before Ardgar's arrival, when there was no one with priestly authority in Birka.

The story is about Birka and a Swedish king or sub-king named Anoundus. Anoundus had been driven from his throne and escaped to the Danes for protection. Once safely in exile, he began agitating for a return to his kingdom. He convinced the Danes to support him by offering to give them Birka and all its treasures.

The Danes were enticed and put at his disposal a fleet of 21 ships with warriors ready for battle. Anoundus combined these with his own 11 ships and set sail for Sweden. Anoundus and his fleet surprised Birka while the king was absent. Herigar, the prefect, was the chief authority left in charge.[30]

Faced with the threat of annihilation, the people fled to the nearby city of Sigtuna, where they made vows and sacrifices to their pagan gods. Herigar reprimanded the people for this action, telling them their only hope was to pray to the one and only true god. Desperate, the people complied.[31]

Anoundus seems to have had a change in heart after receiving 100 pounds in silver from the people of Birka, for he tried to convince the Danes to not destroy Birka and Sigtuna. He suggested they cast lots to determine the will of the gods. The war party concluded that the gods wanted them to spare the Swedes and attack a Slavonian town instead.

The raiders thus cast off and sailed south. They attacked and plundered a town in Wendland, appeasing their appetite for treasure. (The town they savaged may have been Bineta on the island of Wollin, a town destroyed by Viking raiders in the ninth century.)[32]

The Anoundus referred to in this story is thought to have been Anoumd (or Emund), a brother of Björn (IV?), who ruled for a short time and was driven from the throne.[33]

Herigar died in 851, at which point Ardgar left Sweden to return to France and his preferred life of solitude. Sweden was left once again bereft of any representative of the Catholic Church.[34]

Anskar again became an active missionary among the Danes, finding favor with the Danish king Horik (the Elder), who came to regard him as a friend and counselor. Rimbert says Anskar was allowed to build a church at Hedeby, though there should have been a church there since the time of Harald.[35] Maybe this was a larger church, or perhaps the old one had been destroyed.

With the assistance of King Horik, Anskar returned to Birka to find King Olaf (Olof) on the throne.[36] After overcoming a strong opposition from the worshippers of the old pagan religion, Anskar was able to get the king and the assembly (Thing) to agree "that churches might be built among the people, and that priests might come to them and that whoever so desired might become Christian without let or hindrance."[37]

Having furthered the work of the church in Sweden, Anskar returned to Denmark, only to find that his old friend and patron, King Horik the Elder, had died, leaving the crown to his son, Horik the Younger. Anskar was obliged to reestablish a favorable situation for the preaching of the gospel under this new king.[38]

Rimbert relates an interesting incident that occurred after Anskar's departure, which sheds some light on Swedish relations with the people of the eastern Baltic. He tells of "a certain people named Cori [Courlanders]" that had been subject to the Swedes. Eventually, these people rebelled and threw off the yoke of servitude.

The Danes, aware of the Courlanders' rejection of the Swedes, mounted a campaign against this country, sending a large number of ships to seize goods and property. Their ultimate aim was to subjugate the Courlanders themselves. But the Danes were defeated by the Courlanders, who massacred half their number and plundered their ships.[39]

After Anskar's departure from Sweden, Olaf assembled an army and sailed for Courland. He attacked a town identified as Seeburg (thought to be Seleburg on the Duna River). The army overwhelmed the defenders and ravaged, plundered and burned the town.[40]

The army then marched five days inland to a second town, Aputra (thought to be Pilten on the Windawa River), home to some 15,000 fighting men who were barricaded in the town. The two armies battled for eight days, fighting to a stalemate.

The Swedes were in a desperate situation. If they tried to flee, the Courlanders would pursue them and cut them to pieces. Yet they did not seem to be able to take the town. After casting lots to determine which of the pagan gods might come to their aid and finding none, Christians in the party persuaded the leaders to turn to Christ in prayer and supplication. This they did and were rewarded with an offer from the townsmen to pay them an indemnity and to once again place themselves under Swedish subjugation.

This story demonstrates that the Swedes or Svear had in the past not just raided and plundered the eastern Baltic coast but actually conquered parts of it, extracting scat or taxes. And now, in the mid-ninth century, they were again in control of at least some of Courland.

In leaving Sweden, Anskar left behind the missionary Erimbert.[41] He was joined by another priest called Ansfrid, who was of Danish descent and had been trained by

Ebo. The two missionaries were well received and administered to the Christians in Birka.[42]

Following their departure, two more Catholic missionaries were commissioned to go among the Swedes, but both died before reaching Birka. Finally, a missionary named Rimbert (it is not clear whether this is the same Rimbert who is the author of *The Life of Anskar*), arrived in Birka. He was welcomed and labored among the Swedes for some time. Unfortunately, no mention is made of the king or kings in power at that time.[43]

Having exhausted Rimbert as a source of information, we turn to an English (or Norwegian) traveler named Wulfstan, who reports on a journey he took from Hedeby to Truso on the Vistula. The report was given to King Alfred (r. AD 870–899) on Wulfstan's return to England. Wulfstan claims he made the trip in seven days. He notes the lands he passed and their nationalities. To the starboard lay Wendland for the entire trip. On the port side he passed the islands of Langeland, Lolland and Falster, and Skåne on the Scandinavian peninsula. All of these lands belong to Denmark, he says. To port was Bornholm, which was a kingdom unto itself. After Bornholm he passed on the port side Blekinge, Öland and Gotland, all of which belonged at this time to the Swedes.[44]

Snorri Sturluson, in his *Heimskringla*, written in the early thirteenth century, mentions a King Eirik at Uppsala shortly after 850 and a later Bjorn who ruled for 50 years.[45]

Wulfstan, in his report to King Alfred, confirms that Skåne was then under Danish control. He speaks of Swedish lands, making no mention of the Gauts. It appears that by the late ninth century, at least, the Swedes (Sveur) were masters of the country, including Gautland and Blekinge.

There is a tradition that commemorates a Danish expedition during King Harald's reign. According to this legend, Styrbjorn Starki, a nephew of the Swedish king Eirik Sigrsæll (the Victorious) and the husband of Harald's daughter, Thyri, led this expedition against the Swedes. With an army comprising Jomsborg-Wollin Vikings and Danes, Styrbjorn attempted to seize his uncle's kingdom. He marched north until he encountered Eirik in Uppland, and there Styrbjorn's forces were annihilated. It was from this victory that Eirik gained the title "The Victorious."[46]

Aside from the recognition Eirik received, there is further evidence that this attempted conquest did occur. Among runestones found in Skåne, there are several inscriptions thought to memorialize some brave Scanians who stood their ground and lost their lives in that battle in Uppland.[47]

And finally we come to the great sea battle between the kings of Norway, Denmark and Sweden, which occurred in about AD 1000. On one side was Olaf Tryggvason (king of Norway and legendary sea-king) and perhaps his ally Boleslav the Pole (king of Wendland). On the other side was the coalition of Svein Forkbeard (king of Denmark), Olaf Skötkonung (king of Sweden), Jarl Hakon and Jarl Eirik of Trondelag. Olaf was the first Swedish king to take the title of king of the Svear and Gauts at his coronation. He was a stepson of Svein and pushed further to Svein's corner when Olaf Tryggvason's sister married Rognvald, the earl of Västergötland, a potential enemy.[48]

As we've seen, the site of the battle is unconfirmed, but the results are not. Olaf Tryggvason was defeated and paid with his life. Olaf Skötkonung ruled a unified Sweden—that is, both the Svear and the Gauts.

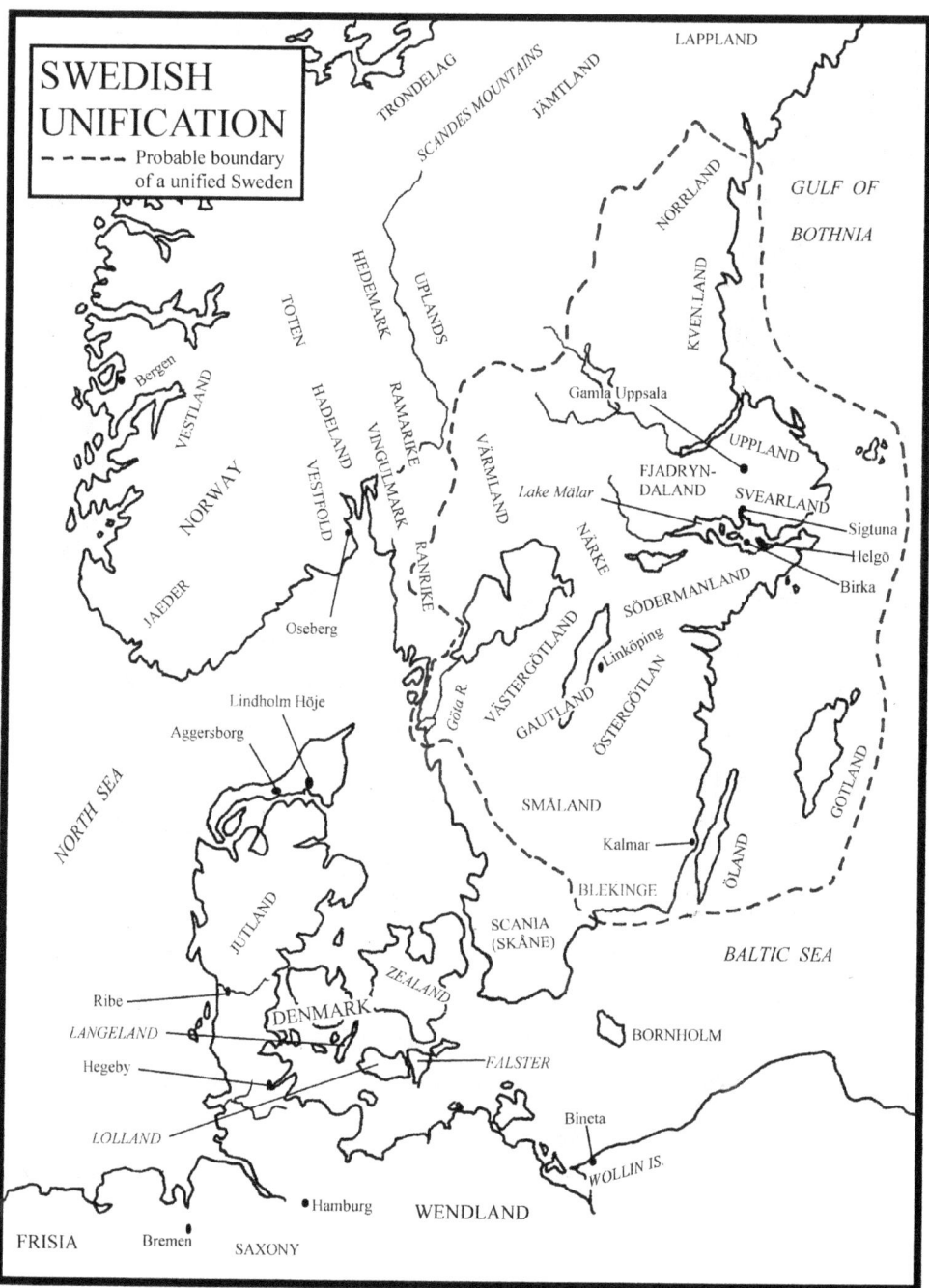

The line of Swedish monarchs following Erik Sigrsæll and Olaf Skötkonung, kings of a united Sweden, is a matter of record. Prior to Erik and Olaf, however, the picture is much less clear, though a very compete list was assembled by a sixteenth-century Swedish archbishop.

Johannes Magnus was born in Linköping, Sweden, in 1488. He was chosen by Swedish King Gustav I Vasa to fill the office of archbishop in 1523. Unfortunately for Johannes, this appointment occurred at the time of the Swedish Reformation. By the time Johannes had traveled to Rome for the ordination, the Swedish Lutheran Church had separated from the Catholic Church of Rome, leaving Johannes without a diocese in which to officiate. He lived the rest of his life in Rome, with plenty of time to read, study and write.

Among the works Johannes produced was *Historia de omnibus gothorum sueonumque regibus* (*History of All Kings of Goths and Swedes*). It was published in 1554 by Johannes' brother after his death. The first 16 volumes of this behemoth delved into the early kings of Sweden up to AD 1000. Johannes developed a list of 111 kings, beginning with Magog, the son of Noah. Johannes' list of kings was accepted by Swedes for several hundred years as "true and definitive."[49] In fact, it was because of Johannes' list of Swedish kings that Gustav I's sons were able to claim the titles of Erik XIV and Karl IX. This numbering sequence has been carried on to the present day, with the present king of Sweden being Karl XVI Gustav.

However, in the eighteenth century the validity of Johannes' list began to be questioned, and his kings, "with few exceptions[,] have been deported from the world of reality to the realm of myth."[50]

Perhaps this modern assessment of Johannes' kings is a little too harsh. If we lay the list of Swedish kings derived from the *Ynglinga Saga* alongside Johannes' list, it is readily apparent that he used many of these names in his catalog of Swedish kings. A second source Johannes used for names was Saxo Grammaticus' *Gesta Danorum*.

Saxo Grammaticus, also known as Saxo the Learned, was a Danish historian who published a nine-volume work on Danish history in the early thirteenth century. Because of the intercourse between Denmark and Sweden, Grammaticus recognizes a series of Swedish kings. The list provided on the "Legendary Kings of Sweden" chart is extracted from this work.[51]

Johannes incorporated names from these lists, kings from Jordanes' *Getica* and kings he claimed to have obtained from ancient runic records. These last are the ones that modern scholars are inclined to regard as names derived from Johannes' imagination.

In fact, Grammaticus' list and the *Ynglinga Saga* list overlap in time rather than being sequential, as shown on the chart. (The four Svear kings and their relationship to the *Ynglinga Saga* have already been discussed.)

Another author who needs to be considered is Adam of Bremen, who was scribe-historian for Adalbert, archbishop of Hamburg-Bremen, in the late eleventh century. He produced a four-volume history of the archdiocese from 780 to 1073, when Adalbert died. In Book VI, *Description of the Nordic Islands*, Adam provides a partial list of Swedish kings.[52] This list is shown on the chart "Legendary Kings of Sweden."

Comparing the three lists of kings—Grammaticus', the *Ynglinga Saga* and Adam of Bremen's—there seems to be very little agreement on the names of the Swedish kings prior to Eirik Sigrsæll. There are a couple of reasons for these inconsistencies. First, each author represented a different point of view. Grammaticus was writing to promote Danish interests, slanting his history to favor Danish supremacy. The *Ynglinga Saga* was written to glorify a Norwegian line of kings, while Adam of Bremen was mainly interested in the history of the Hamburg-Bremen archdiocese (the German perspective). We thus have three points of view with conflicting interests.

The second reason for the disparity is that each author was dealing with a different kingdom in Sweden. Adam's information came from the missionaries sent to Sweden, who inevitably stayed and worked in Birka. By contrast, the *Ynglinga Saga* seems to concentrate on a Svear kingdom in Uppsala, a line of royalty that produced a king who moved to Norway. Grammaticus, at least, does recognize other kingdoms existing in Sweden at that time. He names kings of Gotland Island and kings of the Goths (Gauts?) in addition to the kings of the Swedes (Svear).

Additional names can be gleaned from various Icelandic sagas, but they only increase the confusion. Reconciling information provided by the various authors is a hopeless task. Given the discrepancies in the various lists of kings of Sweden prior to Eirik Sigrsæll, it seems impossible to arrive at a consensus on a list of Swedish royalty prior to about 970.

With no internal historical sources, scholars must rely on external literature, which has proved inconsistent and contradictory. The history of the Swedish unification process will likely remain obscure and something of a mystery.

24

The Swedish People of the Viking Age

We have traced the lineage of the kings of the Svear, Gauts and other peoples who eventually became the nation of Sweden as best we could. We've seen the chiefs of tribes develop into kings of minor states and minor states evolve into major kingdoms; these kingdoms, in turn, struggled for dominance. But what of the people, the farmers, fishermen and tradesmen who became the merchants, marauders and conquerors of the Viking Age? Who were these people, how did they live, and what propelled them to leave their native Sweden and embark on journeys fraught with peril?

Ethnically, Swedes are Teutonic.[1] The Swedish language is Germanic, but in the Viking Age Swedes spoke Old Norse, a language more or less common to all the Scandinavian peoples except the Finns and Lapps. Sometimes referred to as the "Danish tongue," it was distinct from other Germanic languages to the south and certainly the Slavic languages of the Wends.[2] Judging from the sagas, the various Viking traders and raiders did not seem to have any problem communicating with one another, whether they were from Uppland, Jutland, Trondelag or Iceland. The spoken Old Norse seems to have varied more in dialect and accent from community to community than from country to country.

Racially, the peoples who would become Swedes were a mixture, as we've seen in earlier chapters. It has long been recognized that there are two main physical types of Scandinavians. This dichotomy was recognized in the Viking Age and is emphasized in the sagas. Egil of *Egil's Saga* is described as "just as black-haired and ugly as his father."[3] Yet Egil had a son characterized quite differently:

> Thorstein Egilsson grew up to be an exceptionally handsome man. He was fair-haired and fair-complexioned, and tall and strong though not quite in his father's way.[4]

The epic Norse poem *Rigsthula*, written in the first half of the tenth century, makes the same differentiation: "A son bore Edda, with water they sprinkled him, with a cloth his hair so black they covered."[5] Another in the poem is described as follows: "Her brows were bright, her breast was shining, Whiter her neck than new-fallen snow."[6] And her son was of the same ilk: "Blond was his hair, and bright his cheeks."[7]

While the two physical types were recognized—the one tall, fair or of a ruddy complexion, blond and blue-eyed, with a long skull, and the other short, stocky, dark-skinned, and brown- or green-eyed, with a broad face and round skull—there doesn't seem to have been any prejudice associated with these racial characteristics. Though the darker, stockier people are generally described as ugly and the tall blonds characterized as handsome, both are represented as achievers and recognized as rulers. After all, it is the dark and "ugly" Egil who is the great poet and hero of *Egil's Saga*. Among rulers there was Harald Fairhair of Norway, whose father was Halfdan the Black. Though the two physical types exist everywhere in Scandinavia, the tall blonds are more prevalent, particularly in Sweden, where the percentage of blond, blue-eyed, tall, long-skulled peoples is higher than in other Scandinavian countries.[8]

The Eddic poem *Rigsthula* (*Rígsþula*), cited above, contains a mythical story of the creation of the social classes of Viking Scandinavia. This poem was included in the *Codex Wormanius*, a manuscript of Snorri Sturluson's *Prose Edda*. Along with the sagas, the poetic *Edda* was a most remarkable achievement of Viking literature. In Viking Scandinavia, poems were "sung" by scalds. These were wandering minstrels who had to memorize the verses, as the Scandinavian runes were not used to record poems and stories. With the coming of Christianity and the Latin alphabet, these poems were written down. Our most important source for this literature is a manuscript known as the *Codex Regius*, written in Iceland at the end of the thirteenth century.[9]

Rigsthula is unlike anything else in the *Edda* or the sagas in that it deals with the culture of Viking Scandinavia. This may be due to the Celtic influence evident in the poem, though it is certainly Norse in style.[10] The poem tells of the old god Heimdall, calling himself Rig, who "did go striding"[11]:

> Forward he went on the midmost way,
> He came to a dwelling, a door on its post;
> In did he fare, on the floor was a fire,
> Two hoary ones by the hearth there sat,
> Ai and Edda, in olden dress.[12]

Rig gains entrance to the abode because he "knew well wise words to speak."[13] Edda serves bread, "heavy and thick and swollen with husks,"[14] and boiled calf's flesh. Rig beds down with the couple, one on either side. After three nights, Rig leaves; nine months later a son is born to Edda, and the couple name him Thræll. He is described in the poem as follows:

> The skin was wrinkled and rough on his hands,
> Knotted his knuckles....
> Thick his fingers, and ugly his face,
> Twisted his back, and big his heels.[15]

Thræll grows strong, able to carry loads all the day long. Then one day there comes to this home one with crooked legs, stained feet and sunburnt arms. She is called Thir.[16] Thræll and Thir live together, have children and are happy. (According to the poem, this was the origin of the thralls.) Their work is to take care of the house, dung the fields and feed and guard the swine and goats.[17]

Rig next visits a couple of less humble circumstances. This is Afi and Amma, who own a house described in the poem as a "hall." When Rig arrives, the couple is engaged in their tasks:

> The home-folk sat there hard a-working;
> by them stood on the floor a box;
> hewed the husband wood for a warp-beam;
> trim his beard and the locks o'er his brow,
> [his clothes close fitting,] but mean and scanty the shirt he wore.

> The wife sat by him plying her distaff,
> swaying her arms to weave the cloth,
> with snood on her head and smock on her breast,
> studs on her shoulders, and scarf on her neck.[18]

These tasks are more skilled than those of the thralls. Afi's clothes are close fitting, a reference to tight-fitting trousers as opposed to the more slovenly baggy pants of a slave. Amma wears a snood (a cloth or net holding her hair) and a smock, a rectangular cloth worn front and back over a pleated petticoat. The kerchief fastened with a clasp is a shawl, the fashion of the day.

Again Rig's visit produces a son they name Karl. He rules over oxen, which he uses to plow his fields. He builds a house and barn, carts and a plow. Karl is a landowner who works his land and has not just a home but also barns and other buildings and implements, including a cart or wagon.

Then Karl takes a wife who wears goatskin clothing. He marries Snör in a formal wedding with an exchange of rings, as opposed to the thralls, who just live together. And Snör wears the set of keys that is the symbol of the mistress of the house.[19] This union, according to the poem, produces the yeoman race—that is, the peasant or freeman (*karls*).

Rig takes to the road once more, finding a hall that is the abode of "Fathir and Mothir."[20] As before, Rig beds down with the couple, and nine months later Jarl is born. He brandishes shields and fashions shafts to fit his bow. He wields the lance and sword. He rides horses and unleashes the hounds. In short, Jarl is a warrior.[21] And so begins the noble class of jarls (earls), great chiefs and kings.[22]

In Sweden, as in the rest of Scandinavia, this class of rulers was very small and unstable in the sense that earls and even kings could be easily replaced if they were unjust or ineffective. They held their positions at the will of the people, as expressed in the Thing or other assembly.[23] Allegiances shifted easily. A chief today might become an earl or even a king tomorrow, or he might just as easily slide back into the peasant class with no authority and even less respect, if he was unlucky. All too often, a ruler's loss of office occurred in battle or an execution. This was particularly true in the Sweden of the early Viking Age, when there were many small states. The ruling class, though not necessarily the individual rulers, became more solidified by the late Viking period with the consolidation of states into more permanent and larger kingdoms.

The large and broad peasant class, or, more properly, the middle class of freemen, was the core of Swedish society and the economy. These were the landowners who might control a few acres or hundreds of acres. Technically and legally, it made no difference; all had the right to bear arms and vote at the Thing.

In theory there was no rank distinction among freemen. However, large landowners wielded more power than the small landholders. And it was from the families of the largest landowners that the leaders, the earls and kings, would usually arise. As we've seen, leaders and even kings could gain power through wealth derived from Viking expeditions and/or trade.

The family farm was the economic base of Viking Sweden. And here the landowner was lord and master over his family and his thralls. His land was his domain, where he could expect to raise his crops and livestock unmolested by legal intruders.

It was the freemen, the peasants, the landholders, who could bear witness in a court case and vote in the elections for local leaders and kings. They worked the land, carved the wood, and made many of their own tools and weapons. They were the warriors in times of trouble and manned the ships on foreign expeditions.[24]

The farmer's wife, the mistress of the manor, held nearly as high a position as her husband. She was ruler in the home and often the whole farm when her husband was away on a Viking or business expedition. It is significant that the symbol of the housewife was a ring of keys she habitually carried at her belt or wore suspended on a chain around her neck. Grave goods show no marked difference in terms of the value of those items interred with the farmer and his wife.[25]

Thralls, or slaves, were the third and lowest class in Viking Sweden, as had been the case in previous periods. The thrall belonged to the landowner, as did his livestock. He had no legal rights and could not carry weapons. Thralls were assigned the hard work on the farm requiring the least skill.

A freewoman who had a child by a bondsman risked having both her child and herself reduced to slavery. However, a child produced by a master and a bondswoman was at least considered a useful addition to the farmer's workforce and might be brought up as a member of the farmer's family.[26]

The pride and wealth of a farm family was its children. They were necessary as part of the farm workforce and to carry on into the future. In times of famine or sickness or war, the young would be preserved at the expense of the old and, if need be, even the young adults.[27]

Farms of the Viking Age were nearly self-sufficient. At times, however, a particular farm might be without the services of a needed craftsman—a blacksmith, cooper or wheel-wright, say. At such times a professional tradesman would be engaged. These craftsmen constituted a fourth class, though they would likely also be landowners.[28]

Finally, there were luxury items—jewelry, fine linens and fabrics, some weapons and armor—that would be purchased from merchants who formed another class. Again, these merchants might very well possess their own farms, though some craftsmen and merchants traveled from farm to farm practicing their trades or selling their wares. Whether landowners or itinerant, the tradesmen and merchants were scattered about the country, except for those residing in Helgö and later Birka. At these trade centers there was a concentration of truly professional craftsmen and merchants. And here, in Sweden's commercial centers, they mixed with merchants from many nations, trading goods as exotic as Arab silver, Chinese silk, Arctic pelts and North Sea ivory.

Helgö and Birka were the exceptions in Sweden of the Viking Age; the country, not yet a nation, was made up almost entirely of farms that had to be wrested from the wooded lands. And, as noted, these farms were almost totally self-sufficient.

The ever-present forests supplied an abundance of wood for buildings and tools. The woodlands also provided food and hides, small game caught with traps and large game (deer, boars and bears) killed with bow and arrow or spear. Birds were sought after for not just their meat but also for feathers and the much-prized soft down.

Streams, rivers, lakes and the sea produced fish, which was eaten fresh, dried or salted for preservation. Scania in particular was noted for its professional fishermen, who harvested the Baltic as well as the North Sea. But even these seafarers generally had at least a bit of land on which to grow crops and raise livestock.[29]

In the end, the farm was the mainstay of Sweden's economy. Staple crops were raised, such as oats, barley, rye, flax and wheat.[30] From the Bayeux Tapestry, Anglo-Saxon manuscripts and an archaeology site at Lindholm Höje, Denmark, we know the moldboard plow was in use in Scandinavia by the beginning of the eleventh century. This is a plow-shear fitted with a curved iron plate designed to cut, lift, turn over and pulverize the soil. The plowed field would then be harrowed in preparation for seeding.[31]

The introduction of the moldboard plow increased the land area a farmer could maintain under cultivation. Plowing was faster and soil preparation more effective than turning the soil over with a shovel or oxen-drawn straight stick plow. This also encouraged a three-field crop rotation instead of the old system of two fields. Under the old system, one field lay fallow while a second field was cultivated. Under the three-field system, one field lay fallow to build up nutrients. A second field was planted with fall crops, winter wheat or rye, and a third field was used for spring crops, including oats, beans and barley.[32]

At the same time, horses were replacing oxen as the preferred farm draft animal. This was made possible by the introduction of the horse collar and horseshoes. The horse moved faster and could work longer hours.The horse, the moldboard plow and the three-field crop rotation increased the farmer's food production and may have been an important factor in the population increase that fueled the Viking outburst of activity.

In addition to work animals, the farm raised dual-purpose (milking and beef) cattle, goats, pigs, sheep and poultry.[33] Combined with the wild game available, the inhabitants of a typical farm could indulge in a widely varied diet.

From the Edda poem, *Rigsthula*, we gain a glimpse of what a meal on the farm might be like. In the poem, we saw the thrall serving a loaf of bread, "heavy and thick and swollen with husks," and boiled calf's flesh.[34] At the jarl's house, the setting and fare were quite different:

> Then took Mother a figured cloth,
> white, of linen, and covered the board;
> thereafter took she a fine-baked loaf
> white of wheat and covered the cloth:
> next she brought forth plenteous dishes,
> set with silver, and spread the board
> with brown-fried bacon and roasted birds.
> There was wine in a vessel and rich-wrought goblets;
> they drank and reveled while day went by.[35]

Meals were cooked and served in the main house of the farm, a longhouse that had remained essentially unchanged since the Migration Period. Often 40 or more yards long, construction was of timber with walls made of wood, turf, or wattle-and-daub. The roof of turf or thatch was supported by the same two rows of posts used in prior periods. The primary difference in the design of the Viking Age longhouse was that the long side-walls were often curved and the roof arched.[36]

A hearth was located at one end of the house for cooking, warmth and light during

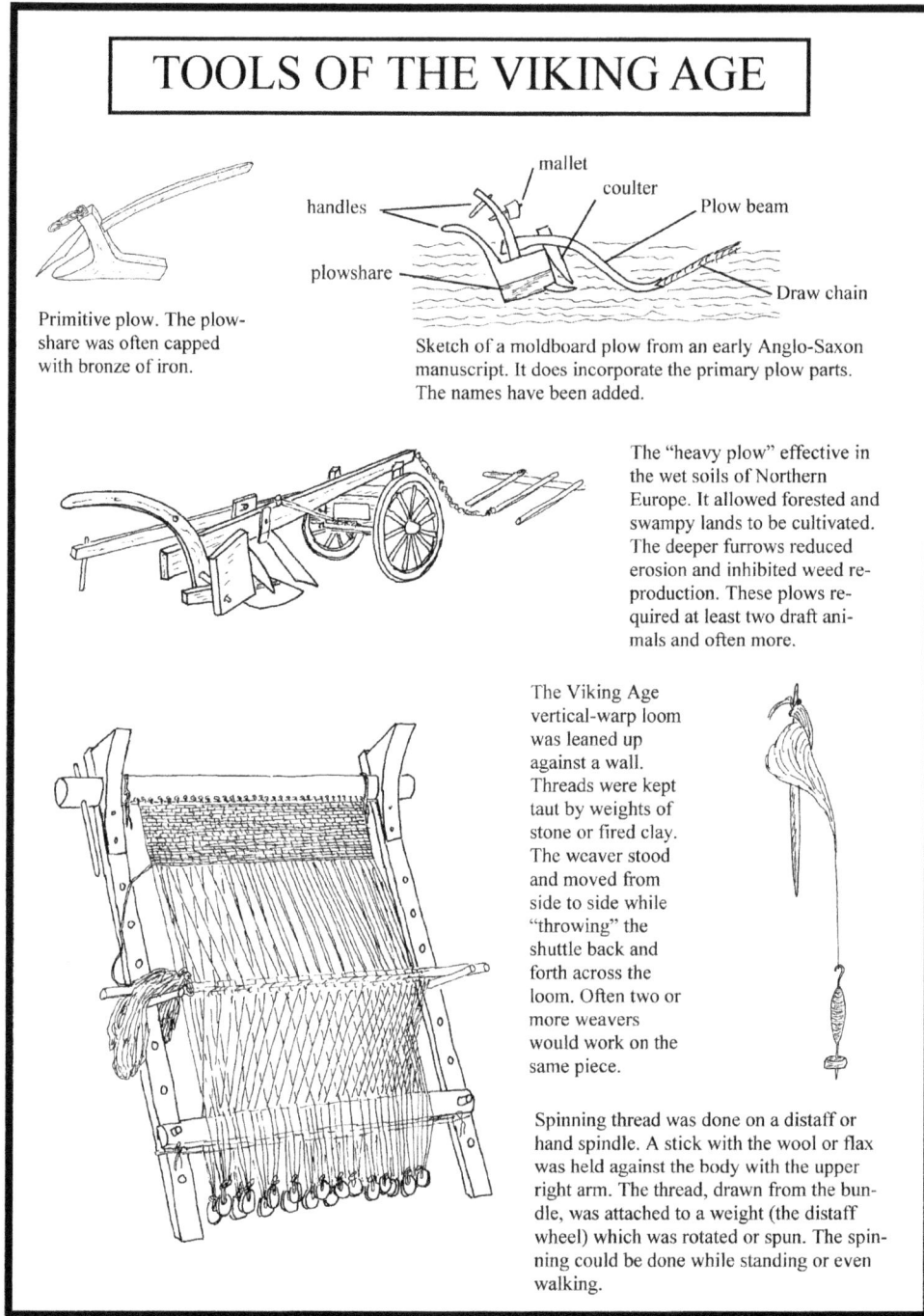

TOOLS OF THE VIKING AGE

Primitive plow. The plowshare was often capped with bronze of iron.

Sketch of a moldboard plow from an early Anglo-Saxon manuscript. It does incorporate the primary plow parts. The names have been added.

The "heavy plow" effective in the wet soils of Northern Europe. It allowed forested and swampy lands to be cultivated. The deeper furrows reduced erosion and inhibited weed reproduction. These plows required at least two draft animals and often more.

The Viking Age vertical-warp loom was leaned up against a wall. Threads were kept taut by weights of stone or fired clay. The weaver stood and moved from side to side while "throwing" the shuttle back and forth across the loom. Often two or more weavers would work on the same piece.

Spinning thread was done on a distaff or hand spindle. A stick with the wool or flax was held against the body with the upper right arm. The thread, drawn from the bundle, was attached to a weight (the distaff wheel) which was rotated or spun. The spinning could be done while standing or even walking.

the long winter nights. The other end of the building was reserved for house animals and storing goods for the winter months.[37] Near the long-hall were outbuildings, granaries, summer workshops, and possibly a blacksmith forge and furnace. All this would be enclosed by a fence, usually made of stone gathered from the fields and pastures.

The Viking Age saw an increase in the use of locks. Outbuildings, sheds and shops

VIKING LONGHOUSE

The longhouse shown has walls of wattle-and-daub, though most walls in Sweden would have been wood or turf. The roof shown is thatch, but turf was often used.

The roof was supported by two rows of posts with cross beams. Benches along the walls were often constructed as work spaces or to sleep on. Stalls might be constructed at one end of the longhouse to hold livestock.

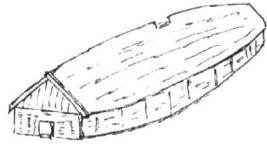

The one innovation of the Viking Age was the curved walls and arched roof sometimes used.

often had door locks. Chests and cabinets in the main house had locks or were secured with padlocks. These locking devices were similar to the old Roman designs, but they had been improved and made simpler to facilitate manufacture by local blacksmiths.

Traditionally, it was the wife of the farmer, the mistress of the house, who carried the keys to all these locks, a symbol of her station in life. In fact, the Old Norse law granted the wife the right of divorce if she was deprived of the household keys by her husband.[38]

Scales were common during this period, used to measure payment, usually in silver. Many were quite compact and portable, particularly those used by traveling merchants.[39]

Flour made from the rye, barley and wheat grown on the farm was ground using hand-mills, a tedious and time-consuming process usually relegated to thralls. Ground cereal grains were used for porridge and for the flour for bread, which was baked in small round pans that had a central rivet, allowing the pan to be rotated so as to prevent burning the bread.[40]

Most of the cooking, however, was done in a kettle hung above the open hearth by chains. Kettles held between seven and eleven pints and were made of riveted iron, copper sheets or soapstone. Soapstone, in fact, was a common material for making cooking utensils, bowls, plates and pots. This is the same soapstone that was used for making molds in the Bronze Age. It is found in much of Sweden, is soft and easy to carve, has no cleavage and holds heat well.

For eating, each family member, including children, had his or her own knife and spoon made of wood or horn. The spoon was for soup and other liquids and the knife to cut up meat, bread and vegetables, which were eaten with the fingers.[41]

Meat was boiled in the kettle or grilled over the open fire. Grilling forks and spits of iron have been found in graves, suggesting this was a common form of cooking.[42]

Items made of wood included ladles (to stir the soup or stew in the kettle), troughs (for kneading bread dough and for serving), buckets and barrels made of staves with brass or iron hoops. Wood was also used in the construction of beds, chairs, chests and trunks.

In making these items, a carpenter would rough out a piece with a hand axe. In Sweden, even today "to *yxa till*" (to make with an ax) still means to rough something out quickly. The finishing touches would then be applied with a knife, rasp, adze, scraper or file. Decorations were often added in the form of carvings, nails or some type of wood or metal inlay.[43]

The carpenter's tools, as well as kettles, locks, farm tools, weapons and armor, were manufactured by the blacksmith. If a farm did not have a skilled carpenter or smithy in its household, this lack was filled by traveling craftsmen. Itinerant tradesmen, wood carpenters, boat builders, and coopers roamed the trails and roadways to find work, staying at a farm as long as their services were needed.

Most of the cloth used to make clothes, blankets, tapestries and other items was a product of the farm itself. The farm's sheep produced wool, and flax was grown to make linen. After shearing or harvesting, the wool was combed and cut, the flax prepared, and then they were spun into thread. Spinning was an art all girls had to master. The tedious and time-consuming chore was done using a distaff or hand spindle. The flax or wool thread was wound into skeins or balls of yarn for storage until used.[44]

Weaving was also done on the farm using a vertical-warp loom of the type called a warp-weighted loom. Such a loom is described in an Icelandic saga, *The Story of Burnt Njal*. In the saga, a man named Daurrud is out riding on Good Friday morning in Caithness. He sees twelve people riding in a group toward a rustic cottage. He loses sight of the riders but is able to look through a window of the cottage and sees women inside working on a loom. They are singing a song, which Daurrud memorizes.

> See! Warp is stretched
> For warriors' fall,
> 'Tis wet with blood;
> This woof is y-woven
> With entrails of men,
> This warp is hardweighted
> With heads of the slain,
> Spears blood-besprinkled
> For spindles we use,
> And arrows our reels;
> With swords for our shuttles
> This war-woof we work;
> So weave we, weird sister,
> Our warwinning woof.[45]

This grisly section of the saga seems to be using the weaving as a metaphor for battle; nevertheless, it does describe the weaving process used during Viking times.

The loom frame is erected vertically. The warp (vertical threads) are kept taut by hanging weights on them at the bottom of the loom. The weft (horizontal threads) are woven into the warp by the weaver walking back and forth in front of the loom. The weft is beaten upward. Patterns were achieved by using different colored yarns, and elegant tapestries could be produced by inserting colored threads by hand. One, two or three weavers might work on a single loom at one time.[46]

Besides home-spun cloth, imported goods have been discovered in archaeological finds from this age. Graves have produced silk and examples of the famous "Frisian cloth," fine woolens with thread counts of 125 or more per inch.[47] Some of the finest cloth was used in clothing, particularly women's clothing.

Women's fashions changed dramatically in the Viking Age. Prior to this period, Swedish women had worn coarse woolen clothing, as had all Scandinavians, Germans and other northern people. But at the beginning of the Viking Age Scandinavian women began wearing a linen undergarment (a petticoat, shift or chemise), a fashion adopted from the Gallic Romans, who had picked it up from the Celts. This petticoat was pleated and full, and it would be draped around the arms to form sleeves. It was designed to fit close around the neck and in some instances was drawn closer by a ribbon or drawstring. Women's clothing at the time did not incorporate buttons, hooks or lacing. Belts, drawstrings and pins were used to hold clothing in place.[48]

Worn over the petticoat was an outer garment of two large rectangular sheets, one in front and one in back, held up by shoulder straps connected by a pair of brooches in front of the shoulders. The rectangular sheets were often of the finest fabric, demonstrating the wealth of the owner. The pins of the brooches were completely hidden under the hollow shell of the clasp. Brooches were elegant, another opportunity to show off one's status.

During the Viking Age another piece of clothing became fashionable. This was the shawl, inspired by the clothing of Constantinople and Frisia. The shawl was a rectangular cloth draped around the shoulders that hung down to the knees and was open in the front. Or it could be folded into a triangle, in which case it covered more of the chest area but hung to only the waist. In either case, the shawl was fastened by a brooch close to the neck. Since the shawl hid the shoulder brooches securing the outer garment sheets, they became less decorative, the affectation being transferred to the shawl brooch.[49]

Little is known about women's choices of headdress. We do know that generally married women were required to have their hair covered.

Sewing tools were suspended by fine chains from a pin attached to the outer garments or hung around the neck. Beads might be worn around the neck and bracelets on wrists.[50]

Men's fashions remained essentially unchanged from the Vendel Period through the Viking Age. The same tunic reaching to just below the hip was worn. A bead acting as a button was often used to close the collar around the neck. Trousers were slim fitting and often combined with stockings to make a single garment from toe to waist. A second style was the loose, full-length trouser open at the bottom.

The only fashion innovation in menswear during the Viking Age was the addition of a cloak, which may have been inspired by Byzantine custom. The nobility of medieval Europe adopted the wearing of a large cloak carried over both shoulders. The Scandinavian Vikings, however, wore the cloak draped over the left shoulder and fastened at the right shoulder or hip, leaving the right arm free to work or wield a sword. The fastening device was a brooch or *penannular* (a semi-circular brooch). Like most things of the Viking world, men's clothes were simple and functional.[51]

This simplicity and functionality carried over to weapons and armor of the Viking Age. Vikings were nothing if not practical. The Hollywood and cartoon characterization of a Viking warrior as a big man dressed in skins and toting a big, round wooden shield, wielding an oversized sword and sporting a helmet sprouting horns or wings, is pure fiction.

As we've seen, weapons and armor in the centuries prior to the Viking Age were ornate and costly, substituting fashion and ostentatiousness for practicality and serviceability. Swords of the German Iron Age (fifth century) were decorated with gold hilts and inlaid blades; although golden decorations were beautiful, this made for a weak weapon. As gold became scarce, the hilts were made of bronze or were gilded. But at the commencement of the Viking Age all these decorated swords disappear from the grave sites. In their place are new swords with iron hilts and blades made using a technique called *damascening*. This manufacturing method was used by the Franks to make sword blades and spear heads. Vikings no doubt acquired some of these blades through raids and by trading. Discovering the blade's superior strength, they learned how to make such weapons for themselves.[52]

Damascening was a process in which strands of iron and steel wire were twisted together, welded and then hammered into shape.[53] This technique is similar to today's drop forging, which produces strong, durable tools.

Helmets also evolved. As noted, helmets of the pre-Viking periods tended to be ornate. An iron helmet would be inlaid with silver, bronze or even gold. Early examples found in boat graves dating to before AD 500 were of the late Roman style. Later, in the Vendel Period graves of Uppland, rich warrior's or chief's helmets have been found with nose and cheek guards, neck protection or shielding around the eyes and chainmail face covering. Bronze panels showing battle scenes were often impressed on the helmets (see chapter 11).

VIKING CLOTHING AND WEAPONS

The undergarment of the Viking woman was a pleated linen petticoat. Over this was worn two rectangular sheets of fine cloth, one in front and one in back held in place by straps connected by right and left brooches at the shoulder. Fashionable in Viking times was a shawl hanging full length or folded in a triangle held at the front by a shawl brooch. The head of a married women would be covered by a headscarf and there was always the sewing tools hanging at the ready.

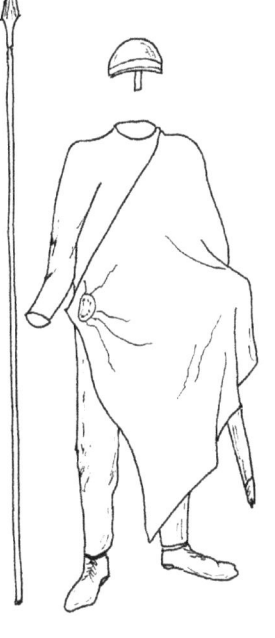

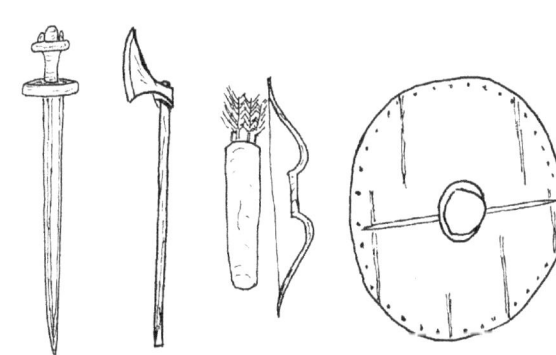

The Viking warrior wore close fitting pants or loose trousers open at the bottom, a short tunic and a cloak fastened at right shoulder or hip leaving the right arm free. The long part of the cloak was to the front so that he did not sit on it while in the saddle. The helmet was a simple skull cap with maybe a nose guard or eye protection. He would be armed with sword and shield and one or more additional weapons, battle-axe, bows and arrows, spear or javelin.

With the coming of the Viking Age, all this finery in helmet style disappears. Judging from an example found in Norway and fragments found in other parts of Scandinavia and Russia, the Viking helmets were simple and utilitarian. The helmets were plain iron of a conical shape, sometimes having a nose guard and/or eye protection. These are the helmets depicted in the Gotland picture-stones and the Bayeux Tapestry.[54]

The Bayeux Tapestry, which commemorates and illustrates the events of the Norman Conquest, shows warriors on both sides—the cavalry of the Normans and the infantry of the Saxons—wearing chainmail armor from head to knees. Such armor was used by some rich Vikings, but it was fairly rare.[55]

The one item usually associated with the Viking warrior that is accurate is the large wooden shield. This was round and might be reinforced with iron, leather or bronze.

The Vikings also made extensive use of bows and arrows, as well as javelins for throwing and spears for thrusting. Iron arrowheads, spear points and the lighter javelin tips have been found by archaeologists at Viking Age sites.[56]

Another weapon associated with the Vikings was the dreaded battle axe. Capable of killing a horse with one blow, this long-handled, triangular-bladed broad axe was much feared by Viking opponents. Its disadvantage was that both hands were required to wield it properly, and it was therefore exclusively an infantry weapon.[57]

A company of Viking warriors disembarking from a longboat and charging ashore toward some medieval village, castle or monastery, well armed with battle axes, swords, javelins, spears, and bows and arrows, must have been a fearsome sight indeed.

The ubiquitous forests of Sweden provided its Viking Age population with an almost inexhaustible supply of timber. Wood was used in the construction of the longhouses and other farm buildings. Furniture, tools and containers were carved or hewn from trees of the forests.

Four-wheeled wagons were made from forest wood, as were sleds used in the long winter months on snow and on the frozen surfaces of the lakes, creeks and rivers of Sweden. Frozen waterways were smoother and easier to travel than the wintery roads of the Viking era.

A curious aspect of the wagons of this period was discovered in a wagon found at Oseberg, Norway, the only complete wheeled vehicle so far located from the Viking Age. What is odd is that the wagon tongue, to which the horses would be attached, is not connected securely to the front axle in a way that would allow the tongue to turn the front wheels and thus guide the wagon. Instead, steering traces would be attached to the horse's harness, one on each side, by iron mounts called *rangels*, and then attached to the hubs of the front wheels of the wagon. Thus, the horse or horses would steer the wagon via the traces instead of the wagon tongue.[58]

The availability of lumber in Sweden also facilitated the building of ships, the hallmark of the Viking Age. The Viking longboat was unique and superior to any ship of its day in versatility and strength. It could glide up narrow rivers and anchor in shallow ports or beach on shores with no landing at all. Yet longships could also cover great distances in the stormy seas of the North Atlantic.

As the Viking Age progressed, the design of the longships diverged into two classes: warship and cargo ship. The cargo ships were wider and deeper than the standard longboat and were meant to operate under sail only. Therefore, the crews were few in number, maximizing cargo size and profits. Such a ship was discovered in Kalmar, Sweden, providing further evidence of the Baltic trade network benefiting not just Birka but also other parts of coastal Sweden (in this case, the port city of Kalmar).[59]

Much of what we know of everyday life in the Sweden of the Viking Age is derived from archaeology and fleshed out by the literature of the times. This literature comes down to us in the poems of the *Poetic Edda* and verses "sung" by the scalds or bards of

Scandinavia. (We have already been introduced to an example of one of these in the *Rigsthula* from the *Poetic Edda*.) Somewhat later, but still part of the Viking era, are the sagas, which were stories told in prose. Neither the poems nor the sagas were written down until the twelfth century, when the Latin alphabet arrived in Scandinavia (along with Christianity). Strangely, it was the remote island of Iceland where the poems and sagas flourished and where they came to be written down. While the sagas and poems preserved the lore of the Viking Age orally, the only contemporary literature remaining from this period are the runes. Recalling again the *Rigsthula*, we find:

> But Kon the Younger learned runes to use,
> Runes everlasting, the runes of life;
>
> With Rig-Jarl soon the runes he shared,
> More crafty he was, and greater his wisdom;
> The right he sought, and soon he won it,
> Rig to be called, and runes to know.[60]

Runes were cited not just in the Eddic poetry but also in the sagas. In *Egil's Saga*, there is a story concerning Egil and his men coming to a friend named Thorfinn to ask for help in their current venture.

While the troop is eating, Egil notices a young woman lying on a dais, obviously in severe distress. The woman is Thorfinn's daughter. She has been weak and in great pain for some time. Thorfinn says he had a farmer's son try to treat her by carving runes, but she became even worse. She cannot sleep at night and is wasting away. Egil asks if he might see if he can help the girl.

After the meal, Egil goes to Thorfinn's daughter and speaks to her. He has her lifted from her bed and has clean sheets put on the bed. Among the sheets removed Egil finds a whale bone with runes inscribed on it. After reading the runes, Egil scrapes the figures from the bone and burns it in the fire. He then recites a verse:

> None should write runes
> Who can't read what he carves:
> A mystery mistaken
> Can bring men to misery.
> I saw cut on the carved bone
> Ten secret characters,
> Those gave the young girl
> Her grinding pain.[61]

Egil carves new runes and places them under the girl's pillow. Instantly, she is better. She says she is cured but still a little weak. Thorfinn is overjoyed and offers Egil and his men any help they might need.

This story from *Egil's Saga* is an example of using runes for curses, lifting curses and curing diseases. Runes were at times, and under certain circumstances, credited with magical qualities. They were also used in the construction of monuments commemorating warriors and traders who had died or been absent for some time. Examples of these runestones have been discussed in connection with the western journeys of Swedish Vikings.

Runes, then, are a third form of literature available to historians attempting to develop a picture of Sweden in the Viking Age. They have the advantage of being contemporary with the Viking period. Unfortunately, they were not used to write down stories or poems

VIKING RUNESTONES

Möjbro Runestone from Uppland, Sweden is an example of Elder Futhark runes. Like other early runic inscriptions this is written left to right, thus the letters are reversed. Later runes were written left to right.

Designated Sm 46 in the Rundata database, this runestone from Småland, Sweden has a Younger Futhark inscription. The stone is 6 feet, 9 inches in height. The inscription reads: "-vé made these monuments in memory of Sveinn, her son, who met his end in the east in Greece."

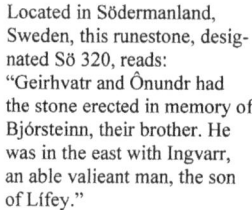

Located in Södermanland, Sweden, this runestone, designated Sö 320, reads: "Geirhvatr and Ônundr had the stone erected in memory of Bjórsteinn, their brother. He was in the east with Ingvarr, an able valieant man, the son of Lífey."

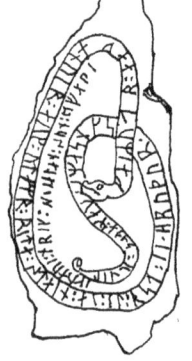

This runestone of grey granite from Uppland, Sweden is designated U 792. It is 5 feet, 5 inches in height. The inscription in Younger Futhark reads, "Kárr had this stone raised in memory of Haursi, his father; and Kabbi [or Kampi] in memory of his kinsman-by-marriage. [He] traveled competently; earned wealth abroad in Greece for his heir."

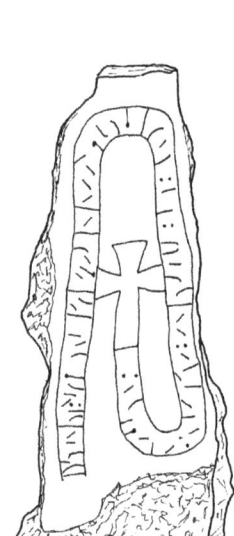

Runestone Hs 12 from Hälsingland is an example of an inscription written in staveless runes.

or any kind of narrative, and all that has survived the passage of time are short phrases carved into stone.

The rune alphabet—known as the futhark, named for the first six letters (like ABCs)—appeared at the beginning of the Christian era. That first futhark, which we discussed in chapter 6, consisted of 24 phonetic symbols. It is known as the Elder Futhark and was used throughout Scandinavia prior to the Viking Age.

24. The Swedish People of the Viking Age

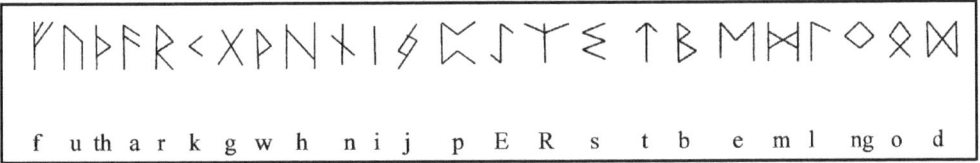

Elder Futhark.

These letters were used to write down words in the Old Norse language that was common to all Scandinavian peoples.[62]

By the Viking Age (AD 700–1050), the futhark had been simplified to just sixteen letters, an alphabet referred to as the Younger Futhark.

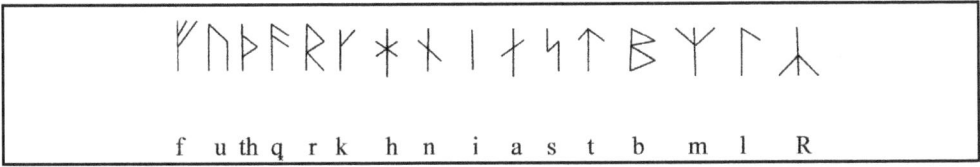

Younger Furthark.

However, this proved unsatisfactory, since some letters had to serve as two phonetic sounds. Thus, three letters were added during the eleventh century.[63]

Local variations of futhark proliferated during the Viking Age—Anglo-Frisian runes, the "Marcomannic runes" and others.[64] The move toward simplification culminated in the staveless or so-called Hälsinge runes.[65]

These runes have been found in Hälsinge, Medelpad and Södermanland, Sweden, as well as Bergen, Norway.

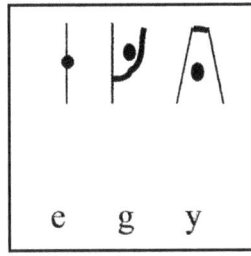

Added Letters.

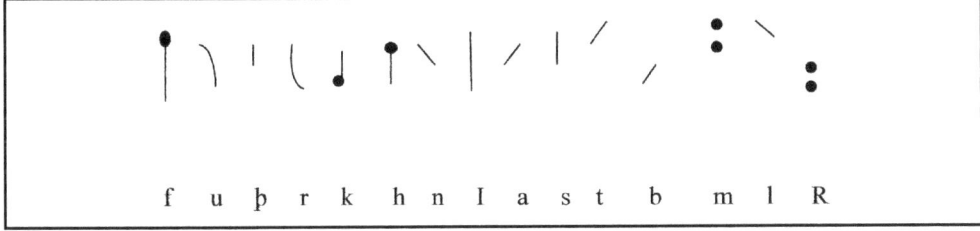

Staveless.

Rune inscriptions traveled with the Scandinavians to almost every corner of the Viking world. Though none have been found in North America as yet, they have turned up in Greenland as far north as latitude 72°45'N.[66] They have also been found in the British Isles, especially the Isle of Man and in the Orkneys.[67] They are likewise found in Istanbul, carved in the Hagia Sophia, and on a marble lion at the port of Athens.[68]

It was once thought that runes were used only for monuments and for magic, curses, spells and healing. It was assumed that the letters were carved by rune masters, a class of scribes who alone knew the art. From the sagas, however, it is clear that at least the leaders and upper classes generally were conversant in reading and inscribing the futhark. Moreover, excavations in Bergen, Norway, have brought to light over 500 inscriptions indicating that runes were common to all levels of society. These runes are engraved on small sticks called *runakefli*. They carry the messages of common people about common things. Examples are "Kiss me, my darling," "Ingedjørg loved me in Stavanger," and the order from an irate wife to her husband dallying in a local tavern, "Gyda says that you are to go home."[69]

Thus, runes were widely used geographically and socially for memorials, magic and everyday messages—but always for relatively short communications. Lengthy poems and stories are not found in futhark engravings. These had to await the coming of the Latin alphabet.

Scandinavian people were primarily farmers engaged in an agrarian lifestyle. Yet from these seemingly domestic folk came the warriors who wreaked havoc throughout much of Europe. Swedish peasants and nobility certainly had the means to go "Viking." But what incentive drove these farmers to leave their comfortable estates and farmsteads? Why would they trade a relatively secure home life for braving the icy seas and facing possible, even probable, death on a foreign shore or atop some hill surrounded by a strange people speaking an unknown tongue?

Overpopulation is always given as one important factor in the Viking drive to explore, trade, raid, settle and conquer.[70] This explanation is undoubtedly more applicable to the Norwegian and Danish seafarers than the Swedish. Both Denmark and Norway had limited farming lands that could be exploited, and these areas were occupied quickly and early. Sweden, however, had an abundance of arable land, limited only in the north by the coldness of those latitudes. And just across the Gulf of Bothnia was more land in Finland. Yet any new farmland had to be wrested from the pervasive forests of Sweden, an arduous endeavor requiring commitment and a propensity for hard work. To many, the adventurous life of a Viking must have had its attractions.

Rather than carve out a new farm from the forest, an easier and surer route was to inherit the family farm, already developed into a successful economic enterprise. But here, too, there were limitations that left some without this recourse.

There were, no doubt, many disinherited sons whose future did not lie with the family farm. The general rule in Viking Age Sweden was that all sons inherited equally, but this varied from region to region, and even from family to family. In cases where the oldest sons inherited the whole estate, the other sons were left to their own devices, and raiding and trading was certainly an alternative to the hard work of grubbing out a new farm in the forest.

There were instances of inheritances being divided equally between all offspring of the family, including daughters, in which case a good-sized farm would become many small farms in just a couple of generations.[71] An ambitious son, not content with having a garden plot for a farm, might well look longingly at the sea to make his fortune.

As to numbers, there seemed to be an ample supply of manpower for the Viking Age requirements. Scandinavians proved to be a "vigorous and fast breeding race,"[72] providing a considerable increase in population from the seventh through the tenth centuries.

But overpopulation and the availability of landless sons are not the whole answer. We've seen in both the Icelandic sagas and the Swedish runestones that many Vikings were fathers and landholders with families and estates. What is more, recent archaeological evidence testifies to a peasant society in Viking times that was prosperous, not in the impoverished state that would drive men to risk so much on sea voyages.[73] Greed no doubt played a role. To enrich oneself by raiding and plundering would have had its allure, especially when the victims were no match for the warriors from the north.

In the end, however, a prime factor in the evolution of peasant to Viking was the motivation provided by the quest for glory and honor (*ära'*), which could only be obtained by the sword. Dying in one's bed of old age (the "straw death") was considered a disgrace. The honorable death was to die in battle, thus making one eligible for a place in Valhalla.[74]

Thus, once this population of Scandinavia had the means (and that was supplied by their magnificent dragon ships), they were ready, willing, and able to spread terror and trade to every corner of Europe and reach into the far crevices of Western Asia. As Gwyn Jones, a Viking scholar, put it:

> Take self-confidence and professional skill, add resource, cunning, no nonsense about fair play, a strong disregard for human life and suffering, especially the other man's, and you have a good soldier. Give a ship's crew or a mounted commando of such men a leader in whose intelligence, tactics, valor, profitability, and record of success they can trust, and you have a good unit. Multiply the units, find them a general ... [and] ... it is not surprising the vikings prospered overseas as much as they did.[75]

These were the men who spread out across the Baltic and invaded the rivers to the east. Though most were Swedes, there were elements from Denmark and Norway, even Iceland, as well. This is the story we shall examine next.

25

Sweden's Early Viking Expeditions to the East

Sweden, as well as the other Viking countries, had for some time explored, raided and traded along the eastern Baltic coast. Expeditions involving both trading and plundering would seem to be a strange combination, enterprises that would be mutually exclusive due to the crews required (merchants versus warriors) and differing cargoes (trade goods versus weapons). Yet such ventures seem to have been common in the Baltic, especially in the pre–Viking and early Viking periods. We have an example of such an exploit described in *Egil's Saga*:

> But in the spring they started getting a big long ship ready. Once it was manned they went plundering that summer in the Baltic, won a great deal of loot and fought a good number of battles. They sailed all the way to Courland and lay there at anchor for two weeks of peaceful trading. Then they started plundering again and made attacks on several places.[1]

At one point further on in the saga, the invaders pull into a particularly large estuary but find no inhabitants. They decide to split up into groups of 12 and go hunting for settlements. Deep in the forest Egil and his party find a large farmstead partly enclosed by a deserted stockade. The Vikings are not slow in taking advantage of the situation, looting the many buildings of the settlement and leaving with all they can carry.

But as they leave the buildings to head back into the forest, the Vikings find that their way is blocked by a large force of Courlanders. Egil and his men are thus trapped between the fierce defenders of the farm and the stockade. During the ensuing battle Egil and his warriors are captured.

> The owner of the estate was a wealthy man with a grown-up son, and on the question of what was to be done with the prisoners, the farmer recommended killing them one by one. His son said that since night had fallen, it was too dark to get much fun out of torturing them, and it would be best to wait till morning. So [the] people threw them into a building and bound them firmly, Egil with his hands and feet attached to a pole. After that the place was securely locked, and the Courlanders went into the hall to eat, drink and enjoy themselves.[2]

After a time, Egil is able to free himself and his men from their bonds, but they can't find a way out of the well-constructed log building.

> Then they heard voices from beneath their feet and after looking around they discovered a trap door in the floor. They opened it to find a deep pit, from which the voices they heard were coming. Egil

asked who was there and a man answered, saying that his name was Aki. Egil asked if he wanted to come up out of pit and Aki answered that he would like nothing better. Egil lowered the rope they had been tied with into the pit, and pulled out three men. Aki said the other two were his sons, and that they were Danes who had been captured the previous summer.[3]

Aki leads Egil and his men out of the building and shows them where the farmer stores his weapons, gold, silver and jewels. Egil, his men and the Danes arm themselves, and then, taking all the loot that they can carry, they make their escape into the forest. But once safely away, Egil has a change of heart.

> They were inside the wood when Egil stopped in his tracks. "This is a poor sort of expedition," he said, "it's not warrior like. We've stolen the farmer's property and he doesn't know it. We mustn't let a shameful thing like this happen. We'll go back to the farmstead and tell people what's been going on."[4]

True to his word, Egil goes back to the farmstead, where the Courlanders are drinking and feasting in the main hall, and he sets it on fire. "In no time at all the hall was burned to the ground, and of all those inside not one survived."[5] Satisfied that the encounter with the Courlanders has been properly concluded, Egil, his men and the three Danes make their way to the ship and set sail.

Such incursions by Norwegian and Danish Norsemen were not uncommon, but it was the Swedish Vikings who dominated this region even prior to the Viking period. As we've seen, the *Ynglinga Saga* tells of King Yngvar of Sweden battling the Estlanders—how he led a great army, landing at a place called Stein, and was there overpowered by even stronger force of Estlanders.[6] Later in the *Ynglinga Saga*, another reference to the East country is made. Ivar Vidfavne, another king of Sweden (AD 630–647), whom we've already discussed, is credited in the saga with conquering Denmark, Sweden, much of Saxland, a fifth part of England, and all of the East country.[7] The East country is certainly a reference to the eastern Baltic region and implies that there was an area being contested between the native Courlanders and the Swedes.

Additionally, there is Rimbert's *Life of Anskar*, written in about 870, which says that "a certain people named Cori [inhabitants of Courland] had in former times been in subjugation to the Swedes, but had a long time since rebelled and refused to be in subjection."[8] Rimbert goes on to describe expeditions by both Danes and Swedes to reconquer this region and identifies two towns therein—Seeburg (Grobin) and Aputra (Apulia or Apuolé). These towns are located in modern Latvia and Lithuania.[9]

We also have archaeological evidence indicating a Swedish presence on the eastern and southern coasts of the Baltic and even further inland. Excavations at the Latvian town of Grobin and further east at Staraja Ladoga in Russia verify a Swedish presence before AD 800.[10]

From this evidence we may conclude that Swedes, primarily from Uppland and Gotland Island, had, since well before the Viking period, been engaged in the eastern Baltic lands and had penetrated into Russia itself. Here they raided and traded, even conquering and taxing certain towns of wealth.

This intrusion into Eastern Europe is referred to in another saga, *Arrow-Odd*. In this romance saga, Odd, the hero, with his fifty ships, meets his blood-brother Sirnir (as well as the forty ships belonging to Sirnir) east of Wendland in the Baltic. They sail to Novgorod in Russia, which is described as

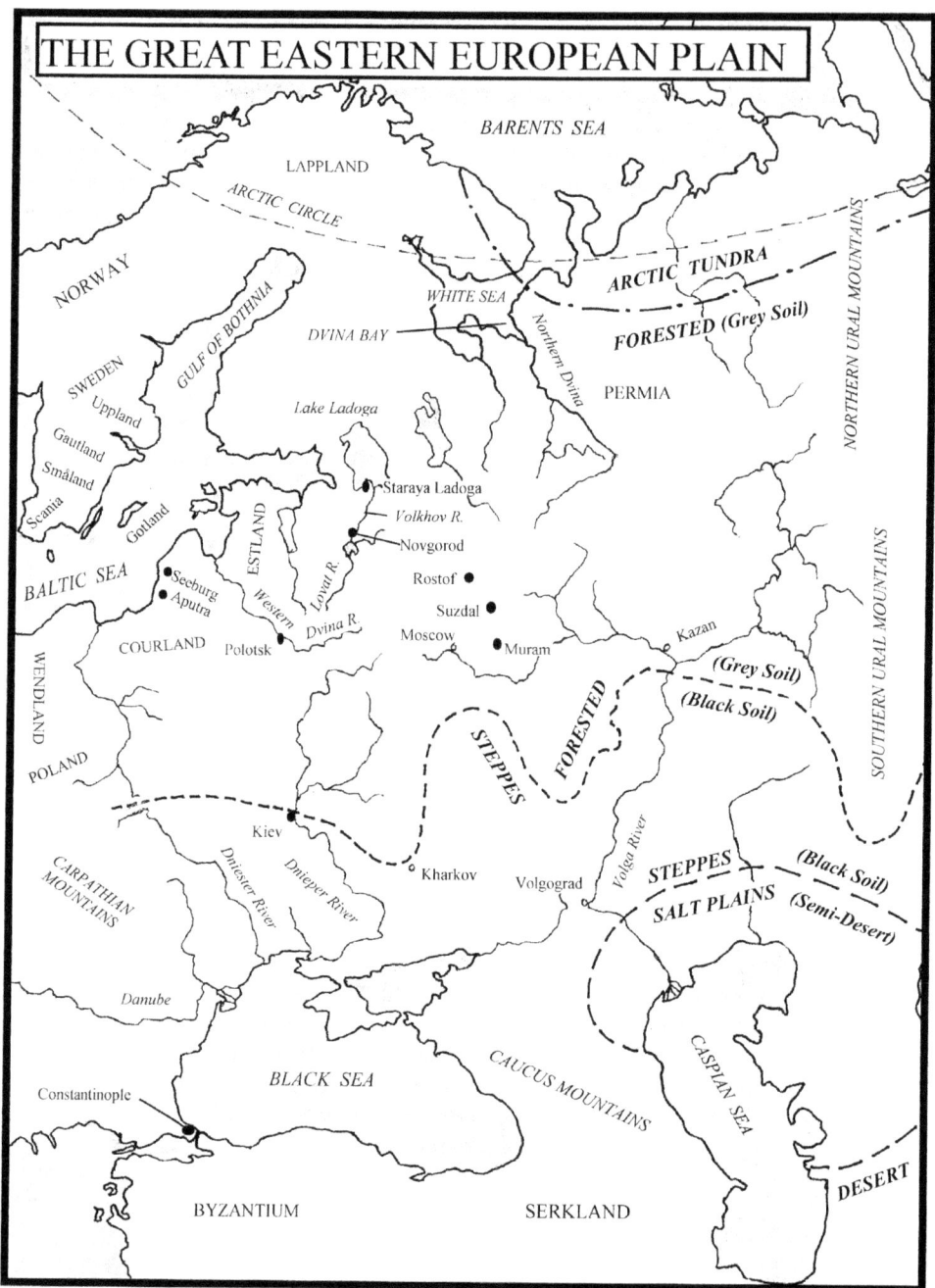

a vast country, with a number of different kingdoms. There was a king called Marro who ruled over Muram, which is a part of Russia. A king called Rodstaff ruled over a land called Rostof, and another king, Eddval, ruled a kingdom called Suzdal. The king who ruled over Novgorod before Quillanus was called Holmgeir. There was a king called Paltes who ruled over Polotsk; and one called Kænmar ruled over Kiev.[11]

In another adventure, Odd sails "north of Lappland"[12] to Permia, a land identified as being east of Russia. He sails up the Northern Dvina and encounters the strange inhabitants of this region. The story certainly indicates that early Viking voyages were undertaken around the northern tip of Norway to the White Sea and Dvina Bay and up the Northern Dvina River. These early expeditions to the far north would probably have been to trade for furs.

So what of this land to the east, a region of mountains, plains and river systems? Here was an immense geographical area where the eastern Baltic was merely the entry point. Like the open seas, islands and continents to the west and south of Scandinavia, it was a vast territory ripe for Viking exploitation. What, then, constituted this massive land area, and who were the peoples that inhabited it? What were the tribes, kingdoms and nations that were about to meet the Norse merchant and feel the Viking spear?

26

The Geography and People of Eastern Europe

The eastern Baltic was the doorway to Eastern Europe. This immense area comprises today's Baltic States (Estonia, Latvia, and Lithuania), eastern Poland, Belarus, Russia, Ukraine and western Kazakhstan. Geographically, this is the Great Eastern European Plain. There are no significant mountain ranges in this region. Instead, the mountains are on the periphery and help define the plain. The Ural range is to the east, the Carpathians to the west and the Caucasus to the south between the Black and Caspian seas.

Vegetation varies greatly from north to south on this expansive plain (or, rather, series of low plateaus). To the north of a line roughly marked by Kiev, Kharkov, and Kazan, the country is forested. As far north as Moscow, there are deciduous trees—oak, elm, birch, and so forth. Further north, however, there are only the trees of Scandinavia—pine, fir, larch and silver birch.[1]

The soil in the forest area is what the Russians call grey soil, which is a poor clay mixture, unproductive for farming. South of the forest region the soil is rich and black and easily cultivated. At the time of the Viking Age, it was covered with grasses of various kinds and was part of the great steppe migration highway connecting Eastern Europe with Asia.

A third area is the treeless and sterile salt plain around the northern end of the Caspian Sea. Still part of the steppes, it resists cultivation and urban human settlement.

Through all of this territory meander the great river systems of the eastern plains. Flowing west and north are the Western Dvina, Lovat, and Volkhov rivers, emptying into the Baltic Sea and Lake Ladoga. Flowing southward are the great river systems of the Dnieper, emptying into the Black Sea, and the Volga, emptying into the Caspian Sea. The headwaters of the south-flowing rivers and the Baltic tributaries are in close proximity with no intervening mountains, so establishing portages was easy and accomplished early. Thus, a system of waterways connected the Baltic Sea with the riches of not just Russia but also Constantinople, the Fertile Crescent, Persia and beyond. Norsemen, already poking around at the northern end of this inviting watery highway, would quickly discover its advantages and would not be slow to exploit its possibilities.

To capitalize on the potential riches of this vast region, the Vikings would have to deal with a variety of people, many of whom would seem strange and mysterious to the

26. The Geography and People of Eastern Europe

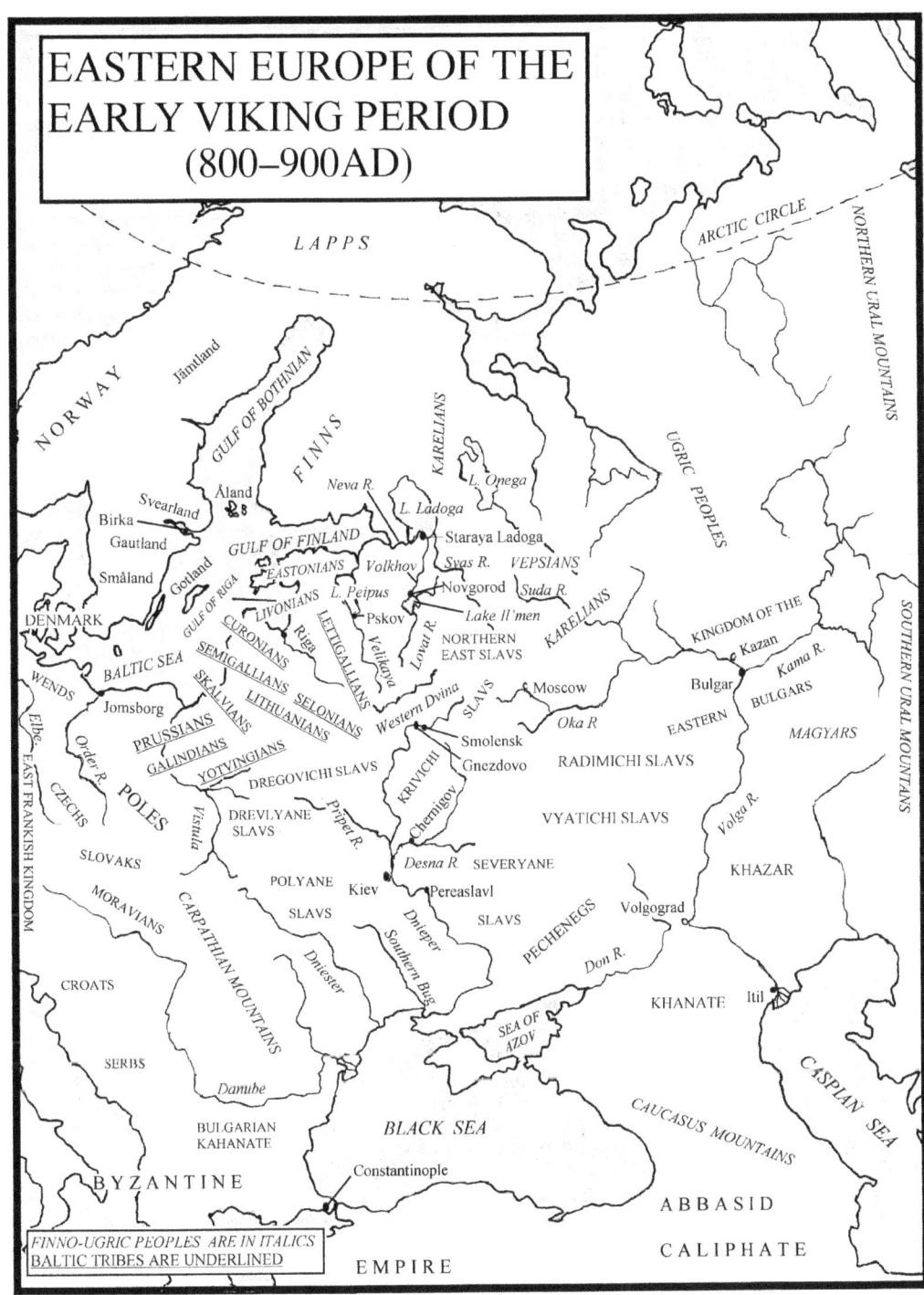

Scandinavians. After all, this immense area was easily accessible from the east, west and south, and it had been influenced by cultures from all three directions. We have seen that the pre–Viking Norsemen had dealings with people of the eastern and southern Baltic coast. They found three groups with distinct languages and origins.

Along the southern Baltic, east of Jutland, lived the Slavic Wends, so named by their German neighbors. The Wends were an extension of the Poles, who occupied an area along the Baltic at the beginning of the Viking era roughly from the Oder to the Vistula, but, unlike the Wendish lands, which were cut off to the south by the Franks, Polish territory extended south, well away from the coast.[2]

We have already encountered the Wends in our earlier discussions of Viking history. It was the Wendish king Boleslav who lost his wife to Olaf Tryggvason of Norway but still may have aided him in the great sea battle in which Olaf died around AD 1000. It was in Wendish territory that the stronghold of Jomsborg was located, headquarters of the legendary Jomsborg Vikings. Eventually, this most westerly point in the distribution of the Slavic-speaking peoples was absorbed by the Franks and became part of the Holy Roman Empire.[3]

The Poles, the northern branch of the Western Slavs, began occupying an area around the mouth of the Vistula as early as the fifth and sixth centuries, fanning out from the sea and cutting off earlier settlers who occupied the eastern Baltic coast. Here they would consolidate and eventually form the Polish state. In the process, the Poles displaced or absorbed a portion of another Indo-European-speaking people—the Balts.

By the Viking Age, the Baltic tribes were confined to an area along the Baltic coast from the Vistula to the Gulf of Riga. The Baltic people spoke an Indo-European language distinct from the German and Slavic tongues, and they were thought to have been part of the Corded Ware culture that migrated into the region in about 3500–2500 BC. There is evidence, in terms of river names, suggesting that the Balts at one time were spread across a large area from the Oder to Moscow. Their territory shrank as other migrants—first the Germans, and then the Slavs—crowded the Baltic tribes into the region occupied during and immediately preceding the Viking Age.[4]

Thus, the Vikings and pre–Vikings met and dealt with the Baltic tribes located along the southeastern Baltic Sea coast from roughly the Vistula to Lake Peipus. The tribes were the Prussians, Galindians, Yotvingians (Sudovians), Skalvians, Lithuanians, Curonians, Smigallians, Selonians and Lettigallians (Latvians). These major divisions were further divided into sub-tribes.[5]

To the north, the Balts were constrained by a non–Indo-European-speaking people: the Finno-Ugrics. These people were scattered across Northwestern Asia, Eastern Europe (particularly in the vicinity of the Ural Mountains), and Northern Europe. Peoples speaking this family of languages included the Saami (Lapps) in northern Scandinavia, the Finns of Finland, the Karelians to the east of the Finns, and another group of Karelians in central Russia. The Vepsians, also part of this language group, were located in between the two Karelian groups, and there were also the Livonians and the Estonians on the Baltic coast. The Hungarians or Magyars, another member of this language group, were in the area of the Urals at the beginning of the Viking Age, but they would clash with the Varangians as they migrated from the Urals to the Carpathian basin in about AD 895.[6]

There is some genetic evidence that the Finno-Ugric peoples originated in northern China, spreading north and then west some 12,000–14,000 years ago.[7] After congregating in the area of the Urals, some tribes split off during the fourth millennium BC, migrating to the west and northwest, settling in Northern Europe and along the

Baltic.[8] The Finno-Ugric peoples have always been a bit of a mystery, a people using a non–Indo-European language surrounded by Germans, Scandinavians and Slavs, all speaking Indo-European languages.

So these were the nations the pre–Viking Scandinavian marauders had contact with: the Western Slavs, Wends and Poles; the Baltic Prussians, Skalvians, Lithuanians, Lettigallians and Curonians; and the Finno-Ugric Livonians, Estonians, Finns and Lapps. If the Scandinavians had penetrated the Gulf of Finland to Lake Ladoga (and there is evidence, as we have seen, that the Swedes did), they would have made contact with the Eastern Slavs and Finno-Ugric peoples of the Great Eastern Plain.

By the beginning of the Viking Age, Slavic peoples were spread over a large area of Eastern and Central Europe. Their original homeland may have been located between the Vistula and the Dnieper rivers,[9] although some historians argue for a site further south (say, on the eastern slopes of the Carpathian Mountains).[10] From whichever point of origin, the Slavs spread out to occupy the river basins of the Vistula, Pripet, Dnieper, Western Dvina, Southern Bug and Dniester.[11]

The movement of the Slavic tribes was not, for the most part, militaristic. The Slavs were, above all, cultivators. As farmers, they were always on the lookout for more and better lands to develop. Thus the Slavs migrated into promising regions, ever expanding and occupying. This was an agrarian migration. While the Germanic tribes stormed across Europe, pillaging and conquering, the Slavs quietly pushed their frontiers of occupation outward in all directions, assimilating some peoples and displacing others.

The collapse of the Roman Empire and the tumult caused by the rampaging Germanic and Asiatic tribes opened up new areas for the Slavs to inhabit. They split into three groups identifiable by linguistics. The Western Slavs pushed into Central Europe to become the Wends, Poles, Czechs, Slovaks and Moravians. The Southern Slavs migrated toward the Balkans, producing the Serbs, Croats and Bulgarians. And the Eastern Slavs pressed east and north, the ancestors of the Russians, Belarusians and Ukrainians.[12] These Eastern Slavs did not reach the Gulf of Finland until the eighth and ninth centuries, just in time to experience the early probing of the Viking expeditions penetrating inland from the Baltic.[13]

The land of the Eastern Slavs was known to the Scandinavians as the land of forts (*Gardarike*).[14] Such stockades were necessary for the protection of the tribal goods and for food storage, but they were also the focal points for settlement and the tribe's economic, social, religious and cultural life. If located in a good site, a fort might become a trading post and even (if the site was particularly favorable) a major trade center.

An example of such a trade center was the joint Finno-Ugric/Slavic settlement of Staraya Ladoga, situated on Lake Ladoga, a natural commercial station on the trade routes leading to the upper Volga and thus to Central Asia and Asia Minor.[15] Another commercial center located at an especially favorable site was Novgorod on the Volkhov River, in addition to Pskov to the west on Lake Peipus.[16]

Further east and to the south, the Severyane Slavs founded Chernigov on the Desna River and Pereaslavl on the Dnieper. A little to the west, the Polyane Slavs established one of the earliest trade centers at Kiev, built on the right bank of the Dnieper. To the north, the often belligerent Krivichi Slavs formed a trading post at Smolensk on the upper reaches of the Dnieper.[17] Surrounding these isolated outposts of commerce and settlement were Slavic tribes of a primitive and disorganized nature—the Dregovichi and Drevlyne Slavs west of the Dnieper, and the Radimichi and Vyatichi Slavs to the east. Interspersed among these were Finno-Ugric tribes that were even less advanced. This was particularly true in the north. In fact, it was said that a Finnish-speaking merchant could travel among his own people from the Gulf of Finland to Bulgar, a trading post near the confluence of the Volga and the Kama rivers. From there it was an easy journey downriver to the second major trading center on the Volga: Itil.[18] Bulgar, however, was under the control of the Bulgars, and Itil was capital of the Khazar nation.[19]

The Bulgars were a Turkish-speaking people, probably a nomadic steppe nation originating in the Sea of Azov area. During the seventh and eighth centuries they migrated north to the Volga Bend at the confluence of the Volga and Kama rivers, where they came to dominate the local Slavic and Finno-Ugric tribes, creating, by the ninth century, the kingdom of the Eastern Bulgars.[20]

Still restless, a number of bands split off from the Eastern Bulgars and moved west, eventually reaching the Balkan peninsula south of the Danube. In the seventh century they conquered the native Romanized Thracians and recently arrived Slavs. By the Viking Age, the Turkish-Slavic Bulgarians had established the Bulgarian khanate as a military power able to contend with the Byzantines and other nations of the region.

Another late migrating nation was the Magyars, a Finno-Ugric tribe that had crossed the Ural Mountains in the fourth and fifth centuries; by the beginning of the Viking Age, they ranged between the southern Urals and the Volga River. During their sojourn in this region, the Magyars were initially under the control of the Khazar khanate.[21]

The Khazar state dominated a large area from the Caucasus on north, including the region north of the Black and Caspian seas. It controlled trade on the lower Don and Volga rivers as well as the caravan routes running east and west between China and Constantinople. The Khazar capital was Itil, at the mouth of the Volga River on the Caspian Sea. The Khazars, as stated earlier, were of Turkish origin, although they built their state on the ruins of various peoples in this region, including the Goths, the Huns, and, more recently, the Magyars and the Slavs who pushed into the area between the Dnieper and Sea of Azov. It was the Volga Bulgars and Khazars who held in check the local Asian Turkish peoples and those to the east.[22] When Turkish tribes did break through, they could wreak havoc with the trade routes, like the savage Petchenegs, who were the scourge of the lower Dnieper.

Though they were strong enough to dominate the Magyars and other tribes along the Volga, and to hold off the Arab caliphate at the Caucasus, the Khazars were not so much militaristic as commercial, charging a reasonable 10% toll on goods passing through their country. In keeping with their mercantile orientation, the Khazars were tolerant of all religions. The khakan (prince) adopted the Jewish faith, as did much of the nation, but persecution of any religious group was not tolerated.[23]

South of the Caucasus was the dominion of the Arab caliphate headquartered in Bagdad. The Muslim empire that had exploded out of the Middle East in the seventh century reached its zenith by the beginning of the Viking Age. The old Omayyad caliphs had conquered an immense empire stretching from the Pyrenees to the Indus. In the east, the armies of Islam turned north, conquering the legendary Samarkand and crossing the Jaxartes River (Syr Darya River) into Central Asia. But with the revolt and takeover of the Islamic empire by the Abbasid caliphs, the west was lost. Independent Muslim states in North Africa and Spain split off from the larger empire. At the Caucasus the forces of the Abbasid caliphate were held at bay by the Khazars, and to the west the Byzantine Empire blocked the entrance to Europe.[24]

The Byzantine Empire, with its capital Constantinople (*Miklagård* to the Vikings), still glittered in the eyes of Asians and Europeans alike. However, this last relic of the once great Roman Empire was now reduced to an area that included Asia Minor and Greece, though, as we've seen, the Byzantines still had a toehold in Italy.[25]

Though not the territorial giant it once was under Emperor Justinian and his brilliant general Belisarius in the sixth century, the Byzantine Empire had managed to stave off the Arab Muslim juggernaut that consumed southwest Asia, northern Africa and Iberia in the seventh, eighth and ninth centuries. The sudden resurgence of Byzantine vigor and power was due to the reforms made by Leo III the Isaurian (AD 717–741), which strengthened the empire's administration, finances and legal machinery.[26]

By the ninth century, Constantinople was a cosmopolitan city. The old Roman aristocracy had died out. Even the Greek hold on politics had faded in favor of Asians. And most recently Slavs had come to dominate the empire's European population. The founder of the dynasty that ruled the empire of the ninth and tenth centuries was a Slav, Basil I, known as the Macedonian (r. 867–886).[27]

This was the Eastern Europe about to be visited by the Vikings. The Finns and Balts would get a taste of Swedish steel first, but the Slavs, Turks and Greeks would not be far behind.

27

Swedes of the Rus Khaganate

Unlike the expeditions to Iceland and Greenland, the eastward Viking movement would not be for land as much as for goods. Wealth would be acquired by raiding, trading, conquering and even hiring out as mercenaries. While the Norsemen pillaged and plundered Western Europe, Eastern Europe was not to be spared. As Edward Gibbon put it:

> Piracy was the exercise, the trade, the glory, and the virtue of the Scandinavian youth. Impatient of a bleak climate and narrow limits, they started from the banquet, grasped their arms, sounded their horn, ascended the vessels, and explored every coast that promised either spoil or settlement. The Baltic was the first scene of their naval achievement; they visited the eastern shores, the silent residents of Fennic and Sclavonian tribes; and the primitive Russians of Lake Ladoga paid a tribute, the skins of white squirrels, to these strangers, whom they saluted with the title of Varangians or Corsairs. Their superiority in arms, discipline, and renown commanded the fear and reverence of the natives. In their wars against the more inland savages the Varangians condescended to serve as friends and auxiliaries, and gradually by choice or conquest, obtain the dominion of a people whom they qualified to protect.[1]

In describing the Varangian invasion of northern Russia, Gibbon was perhaps drawing on two chronicles that provide some information on the earliest incursions into Slavic Eastern Europe. These are the *Chronicles of Novgorod* and the Kievan Chronicles, known as *The Russian Primary Chronicles* or *Tales of Times Gone By*. The nursery of the Russian chronicles was the Monastery of the Caves, located on the right bank of the Dnieper River. Here, in the plethora of subterranean passages deep inside the cliffs overhanging the river, monks first systematized these chronicles at the beginning of the twelfth century. Each individual district developed its own style and psychology in recording the historical events of its region. The work was considered a holy task, so accuracy was paramount.[2]

Thus, we have *The Chronicle of Novgorod*, which contains in its introduction a section on Novgorod and the Scandinavians:

> The history of Novgorod and of Russia begin with the Scandinavian settlement which civilized, and in the high sense, created both. And during the earlier centuries the Scandinavian connection is naturally close [c. 862–1060].
>
> Novgorod is often mentioned in early Scandinavian records as Holmgarih—"because it stood on a holm," or low flat river-bank, near where the Volkhov issues from Lake Ilmen."
>
> According to Nestor, Rurik settles first in Novgorod, when he enters Russia to rule the tribes that had invited the Rtis.[3]

Not much information is provided prior to the establishment of the Rurik dynasty, but this source does give an indication of the Swedish role in the founding of Russia. The Kievan chronicle is a little more helpful:

> 860–862 [The four tribes who had been forced to pay tribute to the Varangians—Chuds, Slavs, Merians, and Krivichians] drove the Varangians back beyond the sea, refused to pay them further tribute, and set out to govern themselves. But there was no law among them ... and they began to war one against the other. They said to themselves, "Let us seek a prince who may rule over us, and judge us according to custom [*po nravu*]."[4]

Here at least we have an acknowledgment that Vikings (Varangians) were in what is now Russia before the Rurik "invitation." These Varangians were numerous enough and strong enough to require several tribes in the area—the Chuds, Slavs, Merians and Krivichians—to pay tribute to them.

The term "Chuds" was used in the chronicles to identify Estonians and other Finnish-speaking tribes of the eastern Baltic area.[5] "Slavs" is used to cover the Slavic-speaking peoples in general. In this context, these would be the northern branch of the eastern Slavs. "Merians" is used to define Finnish-speaking tribes of northern Russia (i.e., the Volga Finns located among the headwaters of that river).[6] The Krivichi was a tribe of eastern Slavs that had moved into the Lake Peipus region and established a settlement at Pskov.[7] Clearly, the chronicles are describing a territory of Finnish- and Slavic-speaking peoples stretching from the Baltic to the headwaters of the Volga River.

Vikings had for some time raided, traded and even subjugated the tribes of the Baltic coast. But here is evidence that for a time the Viking presence was felt much further east, to Lake Il'men and beyond.

We have, then, some information on the time that might be called the "Rus Khaganate" period of Viking-Rus history. The name comes from one of the very few outside sources for this period, which stretched from the beginning of the Viking Age to the beginning of the Rurik period (roughly AD 790–862).

In AD 839 an embassy from the Byzantine emperor, Theophilus, arrived at the court of the Frankish emperor, Louis the Pious, at Ingelheim near Mainz. According to the *Annales Bertiniani* reporting for that year, the delegation included certain men who called themselves Rhos (*qui se, id est gentem suam, Rhos vocari dicebant*). They said they had been sent by their king, Chacanus, as ambassadors to Theophilus. Theophilus could not allow these emissaries to return home the way they had come (presumably via the Dnieper), as they would be subjected to great danger from the wild and savage peoples along the river (the Petchenegs, among others).[8] Voyagers were especially vulnerable at the rapids of the lower Dnieper, where portage was often required. Theophilus requested that Louis arrange for their safe conduct through his empire en route to their home.[9]

However, Louis' curiosity was aroused, and he interrogated the Rhos delegation at length, only to discover that they were of Swedish nationality (*comperit eos gentis esse Sueonum*) and therefore associated with the Viking raids and plundering of his western and northern coastal and river territories. He suspected they were spies and decided to detain them until he could determine their true purpose. Louis sent word back to Theophilus to that effect.[10]

These Rhos were of Swedish origin, but they were not from Sweden itself. They were

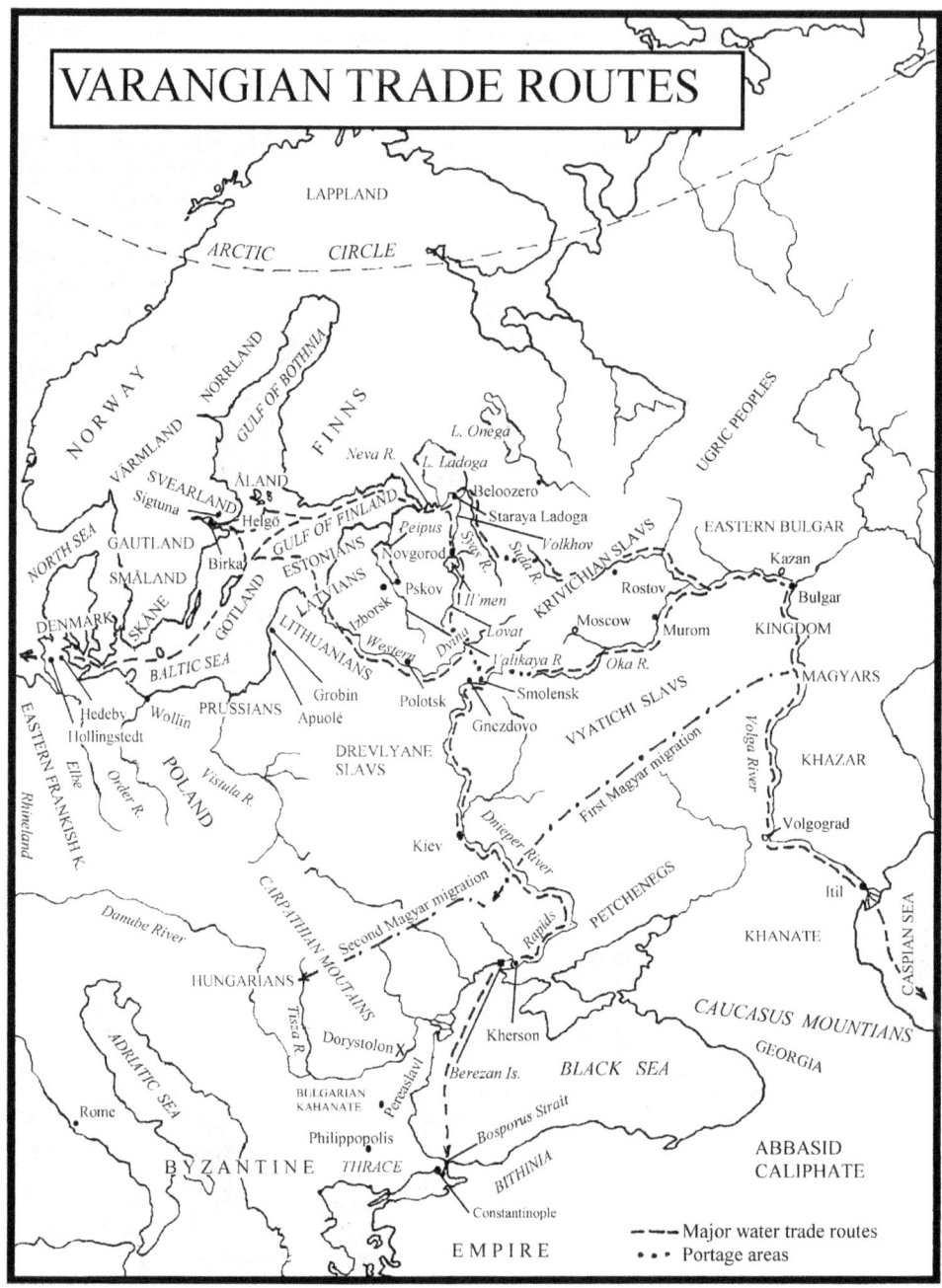

in fact Rus from a kingdom, settlement, colony, or city-state located in the region of the headwaters of the south-flowing Dnieper and Volga rivers and the north-flowing Lovat and Western Dvina. Here was situated a ruler strong enough to claim independence from Sweden and assume the title of *chacanus* or *khagan*, a Turkish label used by the Khazar and Bulgar kings and the chiefs of other Turkish tribes to the east, and one that was evidently recognized by the Byzantine emperor. How large a territory this Rus khagan ruled is undetermined.[11]

One other contribution to our knowledge is provided by a Persian geographer named Ibn Khordadbeh, who wrote in about AD 840. In his *Book of Itineraries and Kingdoms* he describes the Rus as coming from Saqālibāh (a term used to indicate the region of Northeastern Europe). According to Khordadbeh, Rus merchants sailed down the Volga, passing through the land of the Khazars, who extracted the customary fee but allowed the Norsemen to travel on to the Caspian Sea. The Rus landed at Jurjān (Gorgān) on the southeastern shore of the Caspian, where they would transfer their merchandise to camels for the overland trip to Bagdad.[12]

This information seems to confirm that as early as the Rus Khaganate period, Varangian merchants were reaching the Muslim Arab capital via the Volga River and Caspian Sea. This certainly implies trade with the Volga Bulgars and the Khazars along the way. The embassy delegation that the Rus Khaganate state sent to the Byzantine capital almost certainly traveled the Dnieper River route to get to Constantinople. Can there be any doubt that the Varangians were traveling this route, trading and raiding along that Dnieper river system and into the Black Sea during this early period?

The exact site of the Rus Khaganate has not been determined, but it could have been any one of a number of towns located in Northeastern Europe or, more likely, a group of these towns and trading centers brought under the control of one ruler for a time. These towns were located along the trade route between the Baltic and the main trade arteries, the Dnieper and the Volga.

The starting point for the northern route was Lake Ladoga, connected to the Baltic through the Gulf of Finland by the Neva River. Aldeigjuborg (today's Staraya Ladoga) was located a few miles up the Volkhov River, just off Lake Ladoga. Here, in the oldest layers of the settlement, square log houses have been excavated, typical of Swedish colonies. Among the ruins, a piece of wood has been discovered bearing a runic inscription in Skaldic verse referring to an obscure mythology characteristic of ninth-century Scandinavia.[13]

South along the Volkhov River near Lake Il'men was located Holmgård (Novgorod), which would later come to dominate the region. This was on the route to the south-flowing rivers. The course ran from the Baltic to Lake Ladoga, then south along the Volkhov, across Lake Il'men to the Lovat River and down to the Gnezdovo-Smolensk area and portage to either the Dnieper or the Oka, which would lead to the Volga. A more northerly route was along the Syas River, with a portage to the Suda leading directly to the Volga.[14] In the Ladoga-Onega area many burial mounds have been found. The 400 or so that have been excavated indicate the presence of Finnish and Swedish traders and colonists.[15]

To the west other trade routes came from the Baltic. One stretched from Lake Peipus to the trading town of Pskov, which served the Velikiye River area. More popular was the route through the Gulf of Riga and the town of the same name, located at the mouth of the Western Dvina, up the river to the trading town of Polotsk, then on to the Gnezdovo-Smolensk portage area.[16]

Except for the northern route, via Lake Onega or the Suda River, all routes passed through the Gnezdovo-Smolensk portage area, making this region a major commercial center. Here, cargos had to be unloaded and hauled to the next river, and ships had to be carried overland to the next stream. Passage was north to south, east to west, and vice versa. The voyages of these merchants were slowed to a crawl, and trading thus became inevitable. There would also be opportunities to supply tools, repair materials, food and clothing to travelers caught short. It is in this region, around Gnezdovo, that over 3,000 grave-mounds have been discovered. Many of these are obviously Scandinavian, for they contain the remains of burned ships. Swords and armor resembling war equipment from known Viking graves are likewise present.[17]

Throughout this Northeastern European area, Arab silver and Western European coin hoards have been found, but there is a concentration of these burials in the Gnezdovo-Smolensk area. Clearly this whole region was thriving commercially with trade from the east and the west.[18]

One of these towns or trade centers apparently produced a ruler stable and strong enough to send that embassy to Constantinople. This may have been a powerful city-state, such as might have grown at Gnezdovo-Smolensk, or one of the trade towns may have conquered several other towns, creating a more extensive kingdom. A more definitive answer to the question of the Rus Khaganate state will require further investigation.

Whatever the Rus Khaganate amounted to, this first attempt at Varangian dominance of Russia came to an end sometime before 862, the date of the rise of the Rurik dynasty. After penetrating and exploring the river systems of Eastern Europe, Swedish Vikings were ready to enforce their rule over this vast commercial empire that spread across the great plain and connected to the trade routes of Baghdad, China and India.

28

Sweden the Great

The Varangians, those eastern Vikings involved in the invasion of Northeastern Europe, appear to have been initially the Svear of Uppland, Gotlanders and Ålanders. But as commerce and conquest expanded in Russia, other Swedes became involved: Gautlanders, Smålanders, and adventurers from Södermanland and other provinces. To these Scandinavians, this vast land beyond the Baltic was *Garðaríki* (the kingdom of fortified towns) or simply *Svíþjóð hinn mikla* (Sweden the Great).[1]

There can be little doubt that the Svear were involved, as testified to by the *kufic* (an early Arabic calligraphic script) coins found in Birka graves. The Gotlanders were likewise a factor, as indicated by the fact that half of the silver coins from the Viking Age discovered in Scandinavia have been found on that island. Åland also seems to have been part of the Svear kingdom throughout the Viking Age and thus became a participant in the penetration of the Russian river systems.[2]

Gotland was subject to the Uppland kings during this period. According to the *Guta Saga*, a legendary king named Awair Strabain made peace with the Svear and, in return for an annual tribute, gained protection and access to the Uppland markets.[3] When Alfred the Great's Wulfstan sailed past Gotland in the late ninth century, he reported that it was already part of the Uppland kingdom.[4]

The Gotlanders and Svear appear to have worked together in the commercialization of the eastern Baltic and Russia. Two sites in Kurland (modern Latvia) provide evidence of this symbiotic relationship. At Grobin and Apuolé (the two sites already discussed in chapter 25) there is evidence of Scandinavian interest as early as the mid-eighth century. At these two sites cemeteries reveal the presence of both peoples, but with a distinction. Svear burials are generally of warriors interred with their weapons; the militaristic overtones are unmistakable. But burials associated with the Gotlanders are of both men and women, and they lack armaments. This suggests that while the Svear were there as warriors and conquerors, the Gotlanders were more interested in colonization and trade.[5] There is no reason to believe these differences in approach did not carry over to the invasion of Russia.

The Åland archipelago at the juncture of the Gulf of Bothnia and the Baltic Sea was a natural way station for voyagers on their way to the Gulf of Finland and beyond. But archaeological evidence indicates that the islanders were not just passive hosts to passing convoys; instead, they took an active part in the mercantile and colonization efforts of the Swedish Vikings in Eastern Europe.[6]

Even more strategically located was the island of Gotland. Positioned well out in the Baltic, it has a long history of commerce extending back to the days of imperial Rome (as demonstrated by the discovery of objects from this time period at sites on the island). Throughout the Viking Age, Gotland was a trade center, as evidenced by the 40,000 Arabic, 38,000 German and 21,000 Anglo-Saxon coins found on the island.[7]

However, no town-like settlements of this period have been discovered on Gotland. Apparently the island farmers doubled as merchants and seamen, as indicated by the richly furnished burials of the Viking period.[8]

The island has few deep harbors, but beaches are common, which would have provided adequate anchorage, or beaching, for the shallow-draft Viking ships.[9]

Gotland's prosperity grew continually during the Viking Age, rivaling Birka by the middle of the tenth century. The island went on to outlast Birka as a prosperous trade center, continuing until the middle of the fourteenth century.[10]

The third group of participants in the Viking incursion into Eastern Europe were the Svear of Uppland, with their great trade center of Birka, which at its height was perhaps the greatest trading center in Scandinavia. Unlike Gotland, which seems to have had no town-like settlements to act as a focal point for trade, the Svear developed a commercial center through which trade routes from the north, west and east were brought together.

By the beginning of the Viking Age, Birka had surpassed Helgö as the main Swedish trade center. The town was ideally located on the small island of Björkö in Lake Mälar, about 18 miles east of present-day Stockholm. To reach the site, ships had to navigate 30 miles of a labyrinth of islands and skerries east of today's Stockholm, and then complete the last 18 miles through the islands of Lake Mälar, where the character and purpose of any incoming ship could be determined well before its arrival.[11]

In this time of raiding and plundering, precautions were necessary. The town itself was protected by a fortification about 100 feet from what is known as the Black Earth — that is, the town site where the ground is discolored due to the long human occupation. This Black Earth area covers 22 acres to a depth of 8 feet.[12] An abundance of weapons found between the fort and the town and inside the fort, along with an absence of women's goods, suggests that there was a permanent garrison guarding the town.

Though originally unprotected by a defensive wall, such a structure was built shortly after AD 925. (A coin dating to that time period was found under a section of the earthen rampart.) Today the earthwork is still visible, some 6 feet high and 20–40 feet wide, encircling the Black Earth, guarding the landward approaches to the town and adjoining the fort. No doubt there was a wooden palisade with towers at the entrances surmounting the earthwork.[13] Safety from invaders was a paramount concern.

As important as physical protection was, legal protection was also imperative. Situated as it was near the frontiers of two of the Svear kingdom's provinces, determining jurisdiction over a town on the island of Björkö was difficult.

Under the old Swedish system of laws, each province had its own code of laws, which were designed to provide some protection for the citizens of that province. Persons guilty of murder or manslaughter were subject to a fine or indemnity paid to the relatives of the deceased. But if the murdered man was from another province, the assessed compensation was much less, and if he was from abroad, there was no protection for him at all.¹⁴ Such a legal situation was intolerable in a town that depended on foreign traders for its existence. Frisian, Danish, German, English, Finn, Balt, Greek, Arabic and Swedish merchants had to have an assurance of protection, safety and fair play under the law.

As Björkö was near the border between Uppland and Södermanland, there was a question as to which provincial law had jurisdiction. So Birka came up with its own code of laws (preserved in the Bjarkeyjarréttr [the law of Bjarkey or Björkö]) designed to foster a commercial atmosphere with protection for all residents and visitors.¹⁵ The Svear king would be inclined to observe and support such laws, which allowed merchants to ply their trade with a reasonable expectation of safety, because he profited from this vital commerce in his realm. The wealth he thus gained may have been the determining factor in the ultimate Svear triumph over the Gauts.¹⁶

The law, of course, had to be administered by a government, and here again Birka's location had its advantages. Björkö on Lake Mälar was at the juncture of three hundreds (roughly equivalent to our counties), each with its own Thing. With jurisdiction in doubt, the town had the opportunity to create its own assembly. From Rimbert's *Life of Anskar* we have confirmation of exactly that: "These included the perfect of this town named Herigar, who was a counselor to the king and much beloved by him."¹⁷ And, in a later chapter, "On one occasion the King himself was sitting in an assembly of the people, a stage having been arranged for a Council on an open plain."¹⁸ This Thing is mentioned again in subsequent chapters: "When the day for the assembly[,] which was held in the town of Birka[,] drew near."¹⁹

Birka, then, had its own town council, or Thing, under the leadership of a prefect (*præfectus regis*), though the king seems to have maintained a good deal of authority over the trade center, which produced so much wealth for him.²⁰

Birka was the hub of a commercial wheel with spokes extending west, north, south and especially east. It was connected with England and Frisia in the west and Hedeby and Wollin (a trading market at the mouth of the Oder River), Norway and the fur traders of the far north. The town itself, as indicated by the so-called Black Earth, bordered a shelf-beach ideal for the beaching of the shallow-draft Viking ships. Outside the wall surrounding the town, there were additional mooring sites. Two of these have names that have been preserved: Korshamn and Kugghamn. The last was possibly named after the Frisian cogs, merchant ships that had greater draft and needed a deep-water harbor.²¹

Houses of the town were mostly wattle and daub, with some built of timber. There are no ruins suggesting large-scale manufacturing. There is some evidence that bone and glass were carved to make beads, and metal worked to produce ornaments. Coins, including the rare Birka coins modeled after the Carolingian currency of the Franks, have been discovered. Birka was, first and foremost, a trade center.²²

Excavations of the Black Earth area have turned up Rhineland pottery and glassware, a book mount from England, scraps of high-quality woolen cloth from Frisia and coins from Western Europe. There are also traces of pelts—bear, fox, martin, squirrel, beaver, and others—along with reindeer horn and walrus ivory.²³

As varied as these items from the west and north are, it was the eastern trade that made Birka such a great commercial success. The Dnieper, and particularly the Volga connection, drove the town's economy. Muslim coins are seven times more abundant than currency from the west. Arab silver and Chinese silk followed the river road of Eastern Europe to the trading market of Birka. Glass rings and necklaces traveled the same route. A single necklace from a Birka grave brought together a silver coin with the impression of the Byzantine emperor Theophilus (AD 829–842), two pendants from the Khazars of the lower Volga, an Arab silver bowl fragment and a miniature silver chair.[24] The accessibility of the faraway eastern markets is one of the remarkable attributes of this western Baltic trading center. This access was inaugurated by the Svear–Gotland–Åland invasion of the river systems of Eastern Europe and the resulting Rus Khaganate.

Much of our knowledge of Birka comes from the more than 2,000 graves surrounding the town. The ninth-century graves indicate that there was extensive trade with Western Europe (in the form of Rhineland pottery, Frankish jewelry and Anglo-Irish bronze), but tenth-century graves are notable for their lack of Western European items in favor of furnishings from the east—the Volga, the Arabs and the Byzantines.[25]

The wealth of this town is especially evident among the dead of Birka. There are graves of warriors complete with shields, battle axes, swords, daggers, knives, arrows, spears, stirrups, horses, bowls and combs. There are also graves of merchants buried with their high-quality balances and fine weights.[26]

Women were no less cared for in death. One particular grave is that of a merchant's wife interred in a chamber-grave (a wooden chamber built in a large pit) fully clothed. The clothing is silk; around her neck are beads of silver and gilded bronze. Buried with her are a Frisian-style jug, a glass beaker from the Rhineland and a bronze cauldron of Anglo-Irish origin. Of more utilitarian use were the two wooden buckets and a small box containing a comb of bone left in the chamber.[27]

The Rus Khaganate period ended some time before the establishment of the Rurik dynasty in Russia in 862, and here we may turn again to the Kievan chronicle, detailing the early history of Russia.[28]

> 860–862 [The four tribes who had been forced to pay tribute to the Varangians—Chuds, Slavs, Merians and Krivichians] drove the Varangians back beyond the sea, refused to pay them further tribute, and set out to govern themselves.[29]

It is tempting to equate this reference to the rule and demise of the Rus Khaganate, and this may have been the case, but there is little evidence to support such an assumption except chronology. In any case, according to the chronicle, Russia was free of foreign (i.e., Viking) overlordship by AD 862.

A complete departure of the Vikings is unlikely and more the stuff of legend than reality. There were, almost surely, many towns and trading stations continuously visited by (if not under the control of) the Varangians throughout this time.

Still, there may be a grain of truth embedded in this record. The Kievan chronicle entry could be a reference to the collapse of the Rus Khaganate state or a Slavic uprising that drove the Svear–Gotland–Åland Vikings out of many of the trade towns. The chronicle continues:

> But there was no law among them, and tribe rose against tribe. Discord thus ensued among them, and they began to war one against the other. They said to themselves, "Let us seek a prince who may

rule over us, and judge us according to custom [*po nravu*]." Thus they went overseas to the Varangians, to the Rus. [And they] said to the Rus, "Our land is great and rich, but there is no order in it. Come reign as princes, rule over us."[30]

According to the chronicle, three brothers were selected to reign: Rurik ruled in Novgorod, Sineus at Beloozero and Truvor in Izborsk. Within two years, however, Sineus and Truvor were dead, and Rurik became sole ruler. "Rurik gathered sole authority into his own hands, parceling out cities to his own men, Polotsk to one, Rostov to another, and to another Beloozero."[31] Thus the Varangians came to rule northern Russia.

The Novgorod chronicle supports this narrative of Rurik's rule over the Rus, dominating the Slavic and Finno-Ugric native population:

> According to Nestor, Rurik settles first in Novgorod, when he enters Russia to rule the tribes that had invited the Rtis [Rus]. "And the Russian land, Novgorod, was called (i.e. Rus) after these Varangians."[32]

Though Rurik and his kin may be semi-legendary (or even purely legendary) figures, the association of the early rulers of Novgorod with Sweden is inescapable.[33] Clearly the city-state of Novgorod came to be governed at this early time (mid- to late ninth century) by Swedish, almost certainly Svear, Vikings. From there, their influence, if not outright authority, spread across the river systems and trading towns of northern Russia, as is indicated by the reference in the Kievan chronicle to Sineus being located at Beloozero on the headwaters of the Volga River.

Some historians have attempted to equate Rurik with Rorik the Viking, active in Frisia and southern Jutland in the 850s. Although this is certainly a possibility, there is little evidence to substantiate such a claim.[34]

Under the early Rurik dynasty, trade continued to flourish. Chinese silk, Arabian silver, Persian glass, narrow-necked bronze bottles from east of the Caspian Sea and spices from India moved along the river road back to Novgorod, Gotland and eventually the homes and graves of Swedish Uppland. In exchange, honey, amber, walrus ivory, weapons, wax, furs and slaves flowed east and south.[35] Trade boomed and Novgorod blossomed, or, as Gibbon puts it:

> Rurik, a Scandinavian chief, became the father of a dynasty which reigned above seven hundred years. His brothers extended his influence; the example service and usurpation was imitated by his companions in the southern provinces of Russia; and their establishments, by the usual methods of war and assassination, were cemented into the fabric of a powerful monarchy.[36]

With Novgorod firmly under the control of Swedish Vikings, the Kievan chronicle next deals with the conquest of Kiev. According to the chronicle, two of Rurik's men (Askold and Dir) led a force down the Dnieper with the intention of attacking Constantinople. On the way, they passed a town on a hill along the river and inquired as to the ruler of the town. The townspeople informed the Rus that the town was subject to the Khazars, to whom they paid tributeo. Askold and Dir gathered an army of Varangians and established dominion over the area.[37]

After establishing themselves in Kiev, Askold and Dir departed to carry out their original plan of attacking Constantinople:

> 863–866 Askold and Dir deployed their armed forces against the Greeks, appeared there in the fourteenth year of the reign of the [Byzantine] Emperor Michael.[38]

The emperor was away at this time, heading a campaign against the Arab Saracens. Upon learning of the attack by the Varangians, he rushed back to the city, but not before the Rus had slaughtered many Christians and laid siege to Constantinople with two hundred boats.[39] The emperor entered the city and prayed all night with the patriarch Photius. The sacred vestments of the Virgin were carried to the sea and dipped into the water.

Although the weather had been clear and the sea calm up until now, a sudden windstorm arose. Waves scattered the boats of the Rus. The fleet was dashed against the shore and the boats smashed. Few of the Rus escaped to make it back to Kiev.[40] Thus the Rus made themselves known to the "civilized world."

The attack on Constantinople in AD 865 was recorded by the Byzantine patriarch Photius.[41] This first assault was not exactly an auspicious introduction of the Varangians to the eastern world. Even though they spread fear in the Byzantine capital, they were, in the end, destroyed.

The disastrous foray against the Greeks may have weakened the Rus forces at Kiev substantially, for next we hear of an attack by the Novgorod Rus and their new prince:

> But the great northern town (Novgorod) soon ceases to be their capital. After some twenty years, Rurik's successor, Oleg, takes Kiev and makes it his capital, and even the name of Rus vanishes from Novgorod, and is usually, for centuries, connected with Kiev.[42]

Other sources provide some details on how this takeover was accomplished. These records tell us that Oleg arrived outside Kiev in 882 and invited the Kievan leaders aboard his ship, where he murdered them, opening the city to his rule.[43] This may be an oversimplification, but perhaps there is some truth to the tale.

In spite of no longer being the capital of northern Varangian Russia, Novgorod continued to thrive as a great trade center. The Novgorod chronicle explains:

> Yet, though abandoned by the sovereign clan of the Rus, Novgorod maintains its superior, of Kiev among the early Russian states (880–1220). In Novgorod the Scandinavian element is stronger even then in Kiev—so strong indeed that Nestor considers it a Varangian town. Elsewhere we hear of the Varangian's church, of the Guildhall of the Gotlanders in twelfth century Novgorod, and of other matters which prove the early prominence of Scandinavians, and especially of Swedes, in Novgorod traffic.[44]

Oleg, having cemented his position as Grand Prince of all Varangian Russia, began a campaign to reestablish the interrupted trade routes to Constantinople.[45] The disturbance may have been due to the increased activity of marauding Slavic tribes along the lower Dnieper or the savage, Turkish Petchenegs, always a threat in the region south and east of Kiev. Particularly dangerous were the seven rock-strewn rapids of the lower Dnieper. Even during times of high water, some of these cataracts required portage, an invitation to pirates and plunderers.[46]

The interruption may also have been due to the migration of the Magyars from their abode west of the southern Urals to the Carpathian basin. This Finno-Ugric people had been subjugated by the Khazars from the seventh to the ninth centuries, but they finally managed to throw off the yoke of Khazar servitude. The Khazars attempted to reconquer the Magyars, first by themselves, and later enlisting the help of the Petchenegs. But instead of conquering their adversary, the Petchenegs merely drove the Magyars west to lands between the Dnieper and lower Danube rivers in 889.[47]

Seeking some kind of protection, the Magyars joined the Byzantine armies of Leo VI in his war against the western Bulgars. But the Bulgars emerged victorious, exposing a still weaker Magyar nation to Petcheneg atrocities. In desperation, the Magyars migrated westward once more, crossing the Carpathian Mountains and finally settling in the drainage basin of the Danube and Tisza rivers.[48]

All this movement of peoples and the associated warfare no doubt had a disruptive effect on the Varangian trade with Constantinople and could very well have been the reason for Oleg's foray downriver. Once he had cleared the waterway of troublemakers and reopened the trade routes, Oleg was left with a substantial fighting force (though the 2,000 ships claimed is probably an exaggeration) at the gates of the imperial city, a temptation too strong for any Viking to resist. The attack on Constantinople proved to be another disaster, but it did lead to the Treaty of 911 and to a second, later treaty that produced relatively peaceful trade relations for the rest of Oleg's reign and well into that of his successor Igor (Ingvar).[49]

With the reign of Igor (912–945) the Swedish mercantile empire reached its zenith. The first half of the tenth century saw an open trade route from Kiev down the lower Dnieper across the Black Sea to Constantinople. The Grand Prince of Kiev controlled the waterways of Eastern Europe feeding the Dnieper and Volga rivers, and, except for the lower Western Dvina, he ruled the area of the connecting rivers flowing into the Baltic and the portage areas between them. The middle Volga was under the jurisdiction of the Volga Bulgars, and the lower Volga was controlled by the Khazar khanate. But both of these nations brought in trade from the east at their trade centers of Bulgar and Itil and allowed the Varangian Vikings to use the river to reach the Caspian Sea, where camel trains carried their goods to Saracen Bagdad, Persia and, ultimately, India and China.[50]

From the Gulf of Riga and the Gulf of Finland, Viking merchant ships sailed to Gotland Island and to Birka, making it the greatest trading center of the Viking world. Beyond Birka was the recently conquered commercial town of Hedeby on the Jutland peninsula, now ruled by a Swedish dynasty.

Hedeby was ideally located to facilitate the transportation of trade goods from the Baltic to the North Sea. The town came into being early in the eighth century, growing rapidly in the ninth at the natural passageway on the Jutland peninsula between these two seas.[51] Trade goods from the Baltic traveled easily up the long Schlei Fjord to Hedeby, where cargoes were unloaded and portaged the short ten miles to Hollingstedt on the North Sea.[52] Hedeby was also on the north-south landside trade route from Jutland to Central Europe, controlling the trade between Scandinavia and the Frankish kingdom.

The town was protected by a forty-foot-high earthwork enclosing an area of 68 acres. Stretching west from the Hedeby wall across the Jutland peninsula to Hollingstedt was a series of defensive earthworks called the Danevirke. Hedeby had to defend itself from not just Viking raids but also the Franks, Slavs and Germans coming from the south.[53]

The Swedish takeover of Hedeby occurred as a result of Danish weakness. Danish armies had suffered many defeats with heavy losses during the 890s. These military setbacks placed the Danish king Helgi (Heiligo), referred to earlier, in a vulnerable position. Adam of Bremen informs us, "To him succeeded Olaf who came from Sweden and seized royal power in Denmark by force of arms." It seems quite likely that a Svear leader, flush with wealth from the eastern Baltic and Russian trade, was able to mount an attack in about AD 900 that conquered at least Hedeby and possibly much of southern Jutland.[54]

Olaf was succeeded by two of his sons, Chnob and Gurd, who were in turn succeeded by one Sigerich.[55] Adam himself seems a little confused as to these rulers and their domains: "It is very uncertain whether some of these kings (or rather tyrants) ruled the Danes at one and the same time, or whether one survived another for a short time."[56] Corroboration of these kings' existence at Hedeby can be gleaned from a runestones found between Selker Noor and Haddeby Noor. It is cataloged as DR 2 in the Rundata system and reads,[57] "Ásfriðr made this monument in memory of Sigtryggr, her son and Gnupa."[58] Gnupa would be the Norse form of Chnob, and Sigtryggr Norse for Sigerich.[59] Thus, the Sigerich who succeeded Chnob was his son.

A second Hedeby runestone, DR 4, found among the ramparts of Gottorp Slot, memorializes the same figures: "Ástriðr, Oðinkárr's daughter, made this monument in memory of king Sigtryggr, her son and Gnupa's. Gorm made the runes."[60] There are also references to a member of this Swedish dynasty of Hedeby kings in several German chronicles, including Widukind's late tenth-century *Res gestæ Saxonicæ*. According to these sources, Henry the Fowler, king of the eastern Frankish kingdom (Germany), invaded Jutland in AD 934 to punish the "Danes" for raids on Frisia. Chnob was forced to pay tribute and submit to baptism in the Roman Catholic Church.[61] The evidence is clear that for a time in the early to mid-tenth century, a Swedish line of kings ruled Hedeby at least, and maybe much of Jutland as well. That is not to say that Chnob in Hedeby was under any obligation to Ring in Birka or Oleg in Kiev; each would have pursued his own interests. Still, since all were of Swedish origin, cooperation was likely, especially given the interrelationships of marriages and family at the royal level. The Swedish commercial empire was at its height, stretching from Hedeby to the Black and Caspian seas.

As to life at this westernmost outpost of Swedish trade towns, we have the testimony of an Arab traveler, Ibrahim al-Tartushi, who visited Hedeby in about AD 950. He reports that the townspeople

> worship Sirius, except for a few who are Christians and have a church there. They hold a feast where all meet to honor their deity and to eat and drink. Each man who slaughters a sacrificial animal—an ox, ram, goat, or pig—fastens it upon poles outside the door of his house to show that he has made his sacrifice in honor of the god. The town is poorly provided with property or treasure. The inhabitant's principal food is fish, which is plentiful. The people often throw a newborn child into the sea rather than maintain it. Furthermore women have the right to claim a divorce; they do this themselves whenever they wish. There is also an artificial makeup for the eyes: when they use it beauty never fades; on the contrary, increases in men and women as well.[62]

Clearly this Arab traveler is none too impressed by the Viking communities he comes in contact with. The mud and log structures of Hedeby would certainly pale in comparison to the grand structures of Bagdad and Cordoba. Still, this was a thriving market town with goods from as far away as Persia, Ireland and the Arctic flowing through it.

Thus, Hedeby, for a time, was the westernmost extension of a commercial network dominated by kings of Swedish origin. From Hedeby, the tentacles of trade stretched to England, Ireland, Norway, Iceland and even Greenland.

At the other end of this Swedish mercantile empire were the Rus, who plied the Volga to Bulgar, Itil, the Caspian Sea and beyond. Again we have the observations written by an Arab traveler describing what he encountered in meeting Varangian merchants at Bulgar.

Ibn Fadlan accompanied an embassy from the caliph of Bagdad to the Volga Bulgar khanate, headquartered at Bulgar on the Volga, in 921. In his *Risala*, Ibn Fadlan relates his impressions of the Varangians:

> I saw the Rus as they came on their trade mission and taken up quarters on the river Atil [Volga]. I have never seen more physically perfect specimens being tall as date palms, blond and ruddy and wearing neither tunics or caftans. The man among them wears a garment with which he wraps up one side of the body and it is through this opening that he lets one of his hands out. Every one of them has an ax, a sword and a knife, and he is never without these items mentioned.[63]

Fadlan's description of the cloak-like garment agrees with the evidence derived from graves in Sweden itself (see chapter 24). Further, he describes the warriors as carrying weapons with them at all times. All the warriors are tattooed from head to foot with dark green, green or blue-black figures, trees and animals.

Fadlan also relates his impression of the Rus women:

> Each woman wears on either breast a box of iron, silver, copper or gold; the value of the box indicates the wealth of the husband. Each box has a ring from which suspends a knife. The women wear neck rings of gold and silver, one for each 10,000 dirhems which her husband is worth; some women have many. Their most prized ornaments are beads of green glass of the same make as ceramic objects one finds on their ships. They trade beads among themselves and they pay an exaggerated price for them: for they buy them for a dirhem apiece. They string them as necklaces for their women.[64]

Following these fairly objective observations, Fadlan, as a Muslim Arab, seems to let his prejudices cloud his description:

> They are the filthiest of God's creatures. They have no modesty in defecation and urination, nor do they wash after pollution from orgasm, nor do they wash their hands after eating. Thus they are like wild asses. They build big houses of wood on the shore, each holding 10 to 20 persons more or less.[65]

He then launches into a description of the Varangians' sexual customs concerning slave girls and their complete lack of modesty.

Fadlan's sensibilities are further tested by what he discovers in terms of the Varangian morning cleansing customs. As a Muslim, required to bath and wash only in running water, he seems truly horrified by the Rus practice of washing, combing out one's hair, blowing one's nose and spitting in a basin of water furnished by a slave girl. He claims the basin is carried from household to household without being emptied—a little hard to believe.[66]

A sick man, Fadlan says, is set apart in a tent and given some bread and water. He is then left there, receiving no visitors until he dies or recovers. If he recovers, he returns to the general population. If he dies, he is cremated (unless he is a poor man or a slave, in which case he is left to be eaten by the dogs and birds). A thief or robber caught by the Rus is hanged in a tree and left until his body falls to pieces.[67]

Ibn Fadlan also witnessed the funeral of a Varangian chief:

> On the day when he and the slave-girl were to be burned I arrived at the river where his ship was. To my surprise I discovered that it had been beached and that four planks of birch and other types of wood had been erected for it. Around them wood had been placed in such a way as to top of this

wood. They advanced, going to and fro around the boat uttering words which I did not understand, while he was still in his grave and had not been exhumed.

Then they produced a couch and placed it on the ship, covering it with quilts made of Byzantine silk brocade and cushions made of Byzantine silk brocade. Then a crone arrived whom they called the "Angel of Death" and she spread on the couch the coverings we have mentioned. She is responsible for having his garments sewn up and putting him in order and it is she who kills the slave-girls. I myself saw her: a gloomy, corpulent woman, neither young nor old.[68]

The Rus warrior had been buried for ten days, but Fadlan observes that he didn't smell bad. Though his skin had turned black, there were no other signs of decomposition.

The dead man's clothes were then removed, and he was dressed in trousers, stockings, boots, a tunic and a caftan of brocade with gold buttons. A hat of brocade and fur was placed on his head, and he was carried to his ship and placed beneath the pavilion.

Beside him were placed intoxicating drinks, fruits, fragrant plants, bread, meat, onions and a dog that had been cut in two. The man's weapons were also brought to the pavilion, along with two horses that had been cut to pieces. Finally, the slave girl was strangled and stabbed to death, then placed alongside her master in the pavilion on the ship. Wood was piled around the ship and set ablaze.[69]

And actually an hour had not passed before the ship, the wood, the girl, and her master were nothing but cinders and ashes. Then they constructed in the place where had been the ship which they had drawn up out of the water something like a small round hill, in the middle of which they erected a great post of birch wood, on which they wrote the name of the man and the name of the Rus king and they departed.[70]

In contrast to Ibn Fadlan's rather critical description of the Rus, we have the writings of Ahmad ibn Rustah, an early tenth-century Persian explorer and geographer who may have actually visited Novgorod. He relates:

As for the Rus, they live on an island that takes three days to walk around and is covered with thick undergrowth and forests; it is most unhealthy.... They harry the Slavs, using ships to reach them; they carry them off as slaves and ... sell them. They have no fields, but simply live on what they get from the Slav's lands.... When a son is born, the father will go up to the newborn baby, sword in hand; throw it down, he says "I shall not leave you with any property: you have only what you can provide with this weapon."[71]

Ibn Rustah is favorably impressed, for the most part, with Rus customs and traditions, noting that the Rus are hospitable and protective of their guests but quarrel among themselves to the point that they often have to settle disputes in single combat. However, when they are faced with an enemy, they come together and close ranks, fighting as one man.

They have priests of their religion who make sacrifices of men, women and cattle. When a chieftain dies, they make a grave like a big house and put the dead man inside with his weapons, food, drink, clothes, gold and jewels. Lastly, the warrior's favorite wife, slave girl or concubine is placed with him and the doors of the grave are closed so that she dies.[72]

It is assumed by many historians that Ibn Rustah is writing about Novgorod, especially given his opening statement about the city being on an island and the Norse name for the city (Holmgård or Hólmgarðr, meaning "Island-garth" or "Island-town").[73] Yet Ibn

Rustah's description could apply to any one of a number of Varangian trading towns spread across northern Russia from the Baltic to Kiev. At the height of the Swedish commercial trading empire, all these were under the control of Igor, Grand Prince of Kiev. The Baltic and Birka were the realm of the Svear, ruled by Eric Edmondson or the later Ring, or even the still later Eric who ruled around AD 950. Hedeby was dominated by Chnob or Sigerich. Extending beyond this Swedish core were branches reaching Greenland in the west and China and India in the east. This was truly an intercontinental trading system.

Trade relations seem to have gone well for Igor, Grand Prince of Kiev, for most of his reign, but toward the end there were indications of some problems. Igor conducted two military expeditions against Constantinople. The first, in 940, caused great consternation in the imperial city. Igor's fleet passed down the Dnieper into the Black Sea and landed forces on the coast of Thrace and Bithynia. The Vikings plundered the coastal towns and treated the inhabitants with particular cruelty, crucifying, burying alive and driving nails into the heads of priests.[74]

The main Byzantine battle fleet was away from Constantinople at this time. It was left to a patrician, Theophanes, to assemble a small flotilla of 15 ships and attack the Varangians. The Rus attempted to board and overwhelm the attackers, but they were repelled by the Byzantines' use of Greek fire. The Varangians suffered huge losses. Their landing parties were cut to pieces, and all prisoners taken were beheaded. Finally, the Rus just tried to escape and save themselves, but they were overtaken by Theophanes and destroyed; very few lived to return to Kiev.[75] Igor's expedition was an abject failure militarily, but it did result in another treaty (943) with the Byzantine emperor.

In 944 Igor again advanced downriver with an invasion force, this time supported by the Petchenegs. Deputy Emperor Romanus I was warned of their coming and sent envoys who met the allies at the mouth of the Danube. A peaceful resolution was worked out, and the Varangian-Petcheneg force retired.[76]

A year after Igor's second foray against Constantinople, the Grand Prince was killed while trying to forcibly extract an extravagant tribute from the Slavic Drevlyanes. Igor's son was still a minor at the time of his father's death, so the reins of government were turned over to his mother, Olga (Helga), Igor's widow. Olga was from a Swedish family that had settled in Pskov. She proved to be an energetic and astute ruler.[77]

Olga's first order of business upon taking control of the government was to exact retribution upon the Drevlyanes who had killed her husband. According to the Russian Kievan chronicle, upon learning of Olga's rise to power, the Drevlyanes (or Derevlians in some translations) sent a delegation of 20 of their most prominent leaders to Kiev by boat to offer a proposal of marriage between Olga and their own ruler, Prince Mal.

Olga received the Drevlyanes envoys with feigned respect and was cordial long enough to entice them to enter her prearranged trap. The Drevlyanes emissaries were then either buried alive or burned to death in a bathhouse, depending on which version of the chronicle you credit.[78]

Olga then set out for the Drevlyanes' lands, where she asked that a feast be prepared in honor of her late husband. The Drevlyanes were curious as to the whereabouts of their delegation but were assured they would soon arrive.[79]

At the great feast Olga and her retinue encouraged the Drevlyanes to imbibe heavily until the lot of them were staggering drunk. She then ordered her entourage to slaughter the inebriated revelers. The chronicle reports that 5,000 Drevlyanes were killed.[80]

The next year, 946, Olga and her young son, Sviatolsav (Svyatolsav), rode at the head of an army invading Drevlyane territory. After a year-long siege, the Drevlyane fortress city was taken and burned to the ground.[81]

Having dealt with the Drevlyanes, Olga next tackled the nation's finances, regulating tribute and establishing depots called *pogosty* for its collection. Many of these pogosty would survive and prosper into Christian times as trade centers where churches would be located, ultimately becoming parish centers. Olga was the first of the Rurik family to accept Christianity, being baptized into the Greek Orthodox faith at Constantinople in 957.[82] By then, Sviatoslav was old enough to take his position as Grand Prince of the Rus in fact as well as in name.

It might be noted that Sviatoslav is not a Swedish name. The new prince was the first of the Rurik dynasty to have a Slavic appellation. He refused baptism, afraid his *druzhina* (military company) would not take him seriously, although there were certainly Christians among its members by this time. In fact, this imperial company was no longer purely Varangian, having become quite cosmopolitan, with adventurers joining from Lithuania, Hungary and Poland, along with nomads from the Russian steppes. The Rus Empire was becoming more and more Slavic in makeup.[83]

As for Sviatolsav himself, we have a description recorded by Leo Diaconus in 971, when the young prince signed a treaty with the Byzantine emperor Johannes Tzimiskes on the Danube:

> He had bushy brows, blue eyes, and was snub-nosed; he shaved his beard but wore a long and bushy mustache. His head was shaven except for a lock of hair on one side as a sign of the nobility of his clan. His neck was thick, his shoulders broad, and his whole stature pretty fine. He seemed gloomy and savage. On one of his ears hung a gold earring adorned with two pearls and a ruby set between them. His white garments were not distinguishable from those of his band except for cleanliness.[84]

Along with his name, Sviatoslav abandoned Viking tradition in other ways. He traveled without baggage—no tent or couch, no cauldron or kitchen. His saddle sufficed for his pillow. He was the consummate campaigner, and campaign he did.[85]

Where Olga's energies were spent securing the realm's economic empire, her son was more pugnacious. He warred against the Khazars, Vyatichi Slavs, and Volga Bulgars.[86] In fact, it may very well have been Sviatoslav's campaign against the Volga Bulgars that interrupted the flow of Arab silver to Scandinavia. This conclusion is based on the sudden decline of kufic silver coins found in the graves at Birka:

Date of Coins	Number Found in Birka Graves[87]
700–750	12
750–800	14
800–850	17
850–890	4
890–950	42
950 and after	1

Other contributing factors may have been the increasing number of Christians found among the warrior-merchant class of the Rus, the gradual adoption of the Slavic language (replacing Old Norse) by the same people and a contraction of the silver supply from Arab sources, which led to a silver crisis among the Muslims.[88]

In any case, the loss of the silver from the east was devastating to Birka. Rapid decline set in, and by 970 the town had ceased to be of importance. By 980 (certainly by the end of the tenth century), it disappeared as a significant trading center.[89] Trade moved north to Sigtuna and the indefatigable Gotlanders.[90] Scandinavia's addiction to silver was now fed by sources in England and Germany.[91]

Likewise, Hedeby had passed from Swedish control. Sometime between 935 and 950 Danish rule of Jutland was reestablished and Hedeby was recaptured, removing the Swedish dynasty. The trade center itself would last another hundred years, being burned in 1050 by Norwegian King Harald during a battle with Danish King Svein Estridsson. It was finally attacked and destroyed by Slavs in 1066, and its role was taken over by Schleswig on the northern shore of the Schlei.[92]

Having punished the Khazars and Volga Bulgars, Sviatoslav turned his attention from the east to the west, establishing himself on the Danube in Bulgaria. This intrusion attracted the attention of the Byzantine emperor Nicephorus II, who sent an envoy carrying 1,500 pounds of gold to Sviatoslav with an invitation to join him in a war against the western Bulgarians.[93]

Sviatoslav promptly invaded Bulgaria, and in 968 he defeated the Bulgarians, taking their capital Pereaslavl (Preslava). However, the Rus grand prince was forced to leave Bulgaria to rescue his own capital, Kiev, which was being attacked by those pesky Petchenegs.[94]

Having made peace with the Petchenegs, Sviatolsav formed an alliance with the Hungarian Magyars, building a 60,000-man army with which he conquered all of Bulgaria. He went on to Thrace, taking its capital of Philippopolis, where he massacred 20,000 of its citizens.[95]

Sviatolsav next advanced on Constantinople with the intention of extracting tribute, but the defeat of one of his units left in Bulgaria caused him to retrace his steps across the Balkans. The threat to Constantinople, however, alarmed the Byzantines enough to move against this Varangian threat.

Deputy Emperor John Zimisces, one of the truly great Byzantine generals, left the capital in the spring of 971 with an army to pursue the Rus grand prince. He sent 300 ships up the Danube to cut communications and supply the army. Zimisces met the Varangians in the pitched battle of Arcadiopolis, where he was the victor, inflicting 8,500 casualties on Sviatoslav's troops. Zimisces then took Pereaslavl, which was defended by 7,000 Rus and Bulgarians. Zimisces brought Sviatoslav to heel at Dorystolon (Silistria), where the Rus fought a desperate last stand. The Byzantines invaded the town, building trenchworks in preparation for a long siege. Sviatoslav tried to break out several times but was repulsed by the Byzantine heavy armored cavalry and archers. After a two-month siege and an army reduced to 22,000 men, Sviatoslav offered to come to terms.[96]

Zimisces granted generous conditions: The Rus were not to invade Kherson (an important Greek city) or Bulgaria again, and the old commercial treaties were reaffirmed. Sviatolsav was allowed to retire with the remainder of his forces.

The Varangian army marched to the Black Sea, where it suffered more reverses before moving up the Dnieper for home. At the rapids, Sviatolsav and the remnants of his once mighty army found the way blocked by Petchenegs. In the attempt to break through, Sviatolsav was killed (972). His skull became the drinking cup of his vanquishers.[97]

At the time of his death, Sviatoslav left three sons, each claiming a slice of the Rus empire. The eldest, Yaropolk, went after the second son, Oleg, and defeated him in battle. Oleg died in the retreat, leaving Yaropolk to rule from Kiev.

The third son, Vladimir, chose to escape and left immediately for Sweden. Either in Sweden or in Novgorod (perhaps both) Vladimir recruited an army, with which he started for Kiev. His successful campaign brought him to the gates of the capital city, where he discovered that Yaropolk had been murdered by his own counselor, leaving his only remaining brother to rule as Vladimir I (980).[98] As Gibbon put it:

> But when the Scandinavian chiefs had struck a deep and permanent root into the soil, they mingled with the Russians in blood, religion, and language, and the first Waladimir [Vladimir I] had the merit of delivering his country from these foreign mercenaries.[99]

Changes were taking place. Vladimir began his reign as a typical Viking despot. He had a large number of wives and was brutal in his suppression of Slavic tribes. He attacked Rogvolod (a Viking prince who ruled the kingdom of Polotsk), defeated him, and took his lands. He also drove to the Baltic, campaigning against the Estonians and Latvians (Lettigallians). Nor were the Poles spared. He defeated them once and, reversing course, defeated the Volga Bulgars twice. He likewise crushed the menacing Petchenegs. His tactics in war and in winning the peace were ruthless and brutal.

However, rather than the Swedish gods of Thor and Odin, Vladimir erected effigies of the Slavic gods in front of his palace: Svarog (the father of the pantheon), Dazhd-Bog (the sun god's son), Veles (the patron of cattle), Stribog (the god of wind) and Perun (the thunder god and chief of the Slavic deities). Another idol of Perun was placed conspicuously at Novgorod by Dobrynya, a favorite boyar of Vladimir's. To celebrate his triumphs over his adversaries, Vladimir sacrificed something like 1,000 souls to these pagan gods.[100]

However, this excessive outburst of barbarism seems to have had an effect on Vladimir, for next he showed an interest in effecting a complete change in the empire's religious constitution. According to the Russian Primary Chronicle,

> 987: Vladimir summoned together his boyars and city elders, and said to them: "Behold, the (Volga) Bulgars came before me urging me to accept their religion. Then came the Germans and praised their own faith (Catholicism); and after them came the Jews (most likely rabbis from the receding Khazar Khaganate). Finally the (Eastern Orthodox) Greeks appeared, criticizing all other faiths but commending their own, and they spoke at length, telling the history of the whole world from its beginning."[101]

Vladimir then asked his own councilors, "What is your opinion on this subject?" Vladimir's vassals and elders observed that men do not condemn their own institutions but in fact praise them. To know the truth, they advised sending servants to investigate each of these religions. Emissaries were thus dispatched to the three nations (the Jewish Khazars seem to have been forgotten).

> The envoys reported: "When we journeyed among the Bulgars, we beheld how they worshiped in their temple, called a mosque, while they stand ungirt. The Bulgar bows, sits down, looks hither and thither like one possessed, and there is no happiness among them, but instead only sorrow and a dreadful stench. Their religion is not good. Then we went among the Germans, and saw them perform many ceremonies in their temples; but we beheld no glory there. Then we went on to Greece,

and the Greeks led us to the edifices where they worship their God, and we knew not whether we were in heaven or on earth. For on earth there is no such splendor or such beauty, and we are at a loss how to describe it. We know only that God dwells among men, and their service is fairer than the ceremonies of other nations."[102]

Besides the Greek Orthodox religious services, "fairer than the ceremonies of other nations," there were also commercial interests at stake. More and more the Varangians were becoming Slavic in culture, traditions, language and race. Ties with Sweden and Scandinavia in general were weakening in favor of relations with the Byzantines (even in preference to the Muslim empire).

Having apparently settled on the Greek Orthodox form of Christianity as the religion for his people, Vladimir moved to acquire this religion in a typical Viking way. In 988 he marched on Kherson, an important city on the Black Sea coast near the mouth of the Dnieper. He besieged the city and eventually captured it.[103]

> Vladimir and his retinue entered the city (Kherson), and he sent messages to the emperors Basil and Constantine, saying: "behold, I have captured your glorious city. I've also heard that you have an unwed sister. Unless you give her to me to wife, I shall deal with your own city as I have with Kherson."[104]

Anna, the sister in question, was sent to Kherson, where upon Vladimir was baptized a member of the Greek Orthodox Church and miraculously cured of an eye disease that had blinded him. With this confirmation of the true religion, he married the Byzantine princess and left Kherson for Kiev, returning the Greek city to the emperors as a wedding present.[105]

Upon his return to Kiev, Vladimir destroyed the pagan idols and sponsored a mass baptism of his citizens. Dobrynya in Novgorod forced Christianity on the northern Rus with fire and sword. But in general acceptance of the new religion seems to have gone relatively smoothly, for there were already a great number of Christians among the merchants and even the warriors of the Varangians. Only a few of the more remote areas resisted in an attempt to preserve their pagan ways.[106]

The first priests came from Constantinople, but Vladimir built schools to train the sons of good families as clergy. One of his most pivotal decisions was making the language of the new church Slavic, as opposed to Greek or Scandinavian.[107] He used the clergy as counselors in his government and sponsored the building of churches throughout his realm. So, Russia was converted during the rule of just one man, an act that strengthened commercial ties with the Byzantine Empire and further weakened trade relations with pagan Sweden.

Upon his death Vladimir left twelve sons (born of various mothers) to fight it out for supremacy. Svyatopolk, based at Kiev, had several of these siblings murdered, which alarmed Yaroslav, a son who ruled at Novgorod. Once again the clash was between the northern Novgorod and the southern Kiev. And, as before, the northern capital proved the stronger. Svyatopolk was driven from Kiev. But he appealed to his father-in-law, Boleslaw the Brave, king of Poland, who backed him with a Polish army.[108]

Svyatopolk retook Kiev, but his Polish soldiers were killed one by one while quartered among the population. Svyatopolk was expelled from Kiev once again by an army from Novgorod. Desperate for an ally, Svyatopolk turned to the Petchenegs for help. But these troublemakers betrayed and killed him, ending the threat to Yaroslav's reign.[109]

Once secure, Yaroslav moved his residence from Novgorod to the nominal capital of Varangian Russia—Kiev. With a few exceptions, his long reign (1019–1054) was generally peaceful. He did crush the Petchenegs in one final victory in 1036, and they subsequently disappeared from history. He also warred with Poland, pushing back that frontier and retaking Galicia.[110]

At one point, Yaroslav sent his son with a fleet to intimidate the Byzantine emperor in retaliation for the murder of a Rus merchant in Constantinople. The ill-advised expedition ended in disaster with the loss of the Varangian fleet.[111] Yaroslav was more successful in reestablishing control over Estonia, and he made the Dnieper river route to Constantinople absolutely secure.[112]

While Vladimir had built strong bonds with the Byzantines, his son seems to have made a concerted effort to reestablish the Rus-Scandinavian connection. He married the daughter of Olaf Skötkonung, king of a united Sweden (995–1022). He also provided aid and comfort to Olaf Haraldsson after Olaf lost his Norwegian kingdom to Knut of Denmark. It was from Vladimir's court that Olaf launched his attempt to recover his kingdom, which ended in his death at the battle of Stiklarstadir (see chapter 18).

When Olaf departed from Yaroslav's court on his death journey, he left behind a son, Magnus Olafsson, a child whom the Varangian grand prince succored until he could return to Norway as king.

Yaroslav likewise took in Harold Hardradi, half-brother and ally of Olaf, after he was wounded at Stiklarstadir. The Rus ruler provided employment in his army and gave his daughter, Elizabeth, to the future king of Norway in marriage.[113]

Diplomacy through marriage was an integral part of Yaroslav's foreign policy. He married his sister Mary to Kazimir I, king of Poland. His daughter Anastasia married Andrew I of Hungary, and his daughter Anne was married to Henry I of France. Yaroslav's favorite son Vsevolod married the daughter of the Byzantine emperor, Constantine Monomachus.[114]

Yaroslav died in 1054, leaving his Novgorod-Kiev empire to several sons. He left each son a section of his domain, divided in such a way that they would have to depend on each other to survive. Yaroslav's hope was that his sons would work together to preserve the empire, and for a generation this worked reasonably well, but soon interfamily feuding prevailed and civil war broke out once more.

But that story delves into Russian history and is no longer germane to the narrative of the Vikings. "Increasingly the Rus looked first to themselves and next to Byzantium, and the gap between Svíþjóð and Svíþjóð hinn mikla, Sweden and Sweden the Great, grew wider."[115] With the death of Yaroslav, the account of the Varangian water-road passes from Viking to Russian history. The assimilation of the warrior-merchants from Svear, Gotland, Åland and other parts of Sweden was complete, and the empire they had founded was no longer their domain.

29

Words Written in Stone

In terms of historical literature, up until now we have had to rely, for the most part, on sources from outside Sweden. Beginning in the ninth century, however, we have an indigenous source for information. This Swedish contemporary literature is of some help to researchers, though it is often cryptic and always too brief. This body of literature is preserved for us in stone and written in the rune script. These carvings deal with the voyages, campaigns, raids, mercenaries and merchants traveling the water-road to the east. Most of the memorials discovered in Sweden were inscribed in the eleventh century, during the Christianizing of the country, when the making of runestones was in fashion. A few mentioning the east date back into the tenth and even ninth centuries.

The earliest runestone inscription concerning an expedition to the east dates from the ninth century at the time that the Svear, Gotlanders and Ålanders were raiding and exploring the eastern Baltic, the Gulf of Finland and the rivers of Northeastern Europe. Interestingly, this Kälvesten runestone is not from Uppland, Södermanland or Gotland, but rather from Östergötland. Apparently the Gauts were active in raiding and trading at this time (or at least were members of expeditions to the east). The inscription reads:

> Stigr/Styggr made this monument in memory of Eyvindr, his son. He fell in the east with Eivísl. Víkingr coloured and Grímulfr.[1]

It appears this Gaut Viking died somewhere on the Baltic coast or in the interior of Eastern Europe, along with the expedition leader, Eivísl.

As we've already noted, Scandinavian Vikings, particularly the Svear and Gotlanders, had long been plundering and trading with Baltic and Finno-Ugric peoples of the eastern Baltic coast, including Finland. This contact continued throughout the Viking Age, as is substantiated by runestones found in Sweden identifying places of death. For example:

> Bjôrn and Ígulfriðr raised the stone in memory of Otryggr, their son. He was killed in Finland.[2]

And from Västergötland we have Ólafr, who was killed in Estonia.[3] Likewise, there is Bjôrn from Uppland, who fell in Virland.[4] Virland was, during this period, an independent state in what is now eastern Estonia. This must have been a hotspot for a time, as others gave their lives there as well:

> Sigþrúðr had the stone raised in memory of Ônundr, her son. He was killed in Virland.[5]

Livonia (Lífland, Livland) was another Baltic region that had been subjected to the spears and swords of the Swedish Vikings for some time, as we've noted in reviewing early literature from outside Sweden, including the sagas. Now we have a record from Sweden itself:

> ... had the stone raised in memory of Ásgeirr, his son. He fell in Lífland, abroad in Freygeirr's retinue.[6]

Finland exacted a heavy toll, as not just plundering and trading were in play but also outright territorial conquest.

> Sigtryggr's heirs had the stone made over Auðvaldr, their brother, who died in Finland.[7]

Another stone, this one from Gästrikland, Sweden, tells of Egill, who died in Tafeistaland while bearing the battle standard for Freygeirr, the expedition commander. The standard was then picked up by his brother, Brúsi, who lived to return home and raise a monument to his fallen sibling.[8] (Tafeistaland [Tavastia] is a province in Finland that was part of Sweden during the Viking Age.)

Not all runestones commemorated those killed in battle:

> Hermóðr had [the rock] cut in memory of Bergviðr/Barkviðr, his brother. He drowned in Lífland.[9]

And some were erected on behalf of merchants:

> Sigríðr had this stone raised in memory of Sveinn, her husbandman. He often sailed a valued cargo-ship to Seimgalir and Dómisnes.[10]

Seimgalir (Zemgale) was a historical area in what is now Latvia and Lithuania; Dómisnes was the Old Norse name for Cape Kolka at the northwestern edge of the Gulf of Riga. Sigríðr wanted people to know her husband had managed a valuable *knarr* (cargo ship) that passed this treacherous cape many times. He was, she is saying, a skilled pilot.

One merchant voyage thus memorialized in these stones ended in disaster:

> and Ingibjörg in memory of her husbandman. He drowned in Holmr's sea—his cargo-ship drifted to the sea-bottom—only three came out [alive].[11]

"Holmr's sea" refers to a sea related to Holmgård (Novgorod). This could be the Gulf of Finland or Lake Il'men adjacent to Novgorod.

From the eastern Baltic coast, let us turn to monuments commemorating the warriors and merchants who invaded the great river systems of Eastern Europe and the empire of the Rus. Most are simple and direct, like one from Södermanland that reads, "Óttar and ... met his end in the east,"[12] or the following messages from Uppland: "...had raised ... in memory of Geirbjôrn, [their] brothers.... They died in the east"[13]; "Sveinn and Ulfr had the stone raised in memory of Halfdan and in memory of Gunnarr, their brothers. They met their end in the east"[14]; and simply "...died on the eastern route."[15]

Some inscriptions actually name Russia or its Viking equivalent:

> Ölvé had this stone raised in memory of Arnfast, his son. He travelled to the east to Garðar.[16]

"Garðar" (meaning "land of fortresses") was the Old Norse name for the region that is now Russia, Belarus and Ukraine. The term covers a large area.

Some memorials are more explicit: "Oddgeirr/Bótgeirr. He died in Holmgarðir"[17]

(Holmgarðir [or Holmgarðr] being the Old Norse name for Novgorod, a term well understood in Viking Sweden). Another example would be the following:

> Ingifastr had the stone cut in memory of Sigviðr, his father. He fell in Holmgarðr, the ship's leader with the seamen.[18]

It would seem from this message that Sigviðr was the captain of a ship and that he and his crew died in Holmgarðr (Novgorod). Were they involved in some kind of uprising while they were in the city and away from their ship? Or is this a reference to a fight somewhere in the neighborhood of Novgorod? Again, the runes are frustratingly abbreviated.

Occasionally, a monument has some length to it, as in this one from Uppland:

> Rúna had the landmark made in memory of Spjallboði and in memory of Sveinn and in memory of Andvéttr and in memory of Rognarr, sons of her and Helgi/Egli/Engli; and Sigríðr in memory of Spjallboði, her husbandman. He died in Holmgarðr in Ólafr's Church. Œpir carved the runes.[19]

Spjallboði may have died in a church fire, or, since churches of that time in Russia were often defensive structures, he could have died defending the church, which was named after a Scandinavian saint.[20] This inscription provides further evidence of the establishment of the Swedish Vikings in this northern Russian city.

Some runestones do provide more information, and, though often cryptic, you can get a feel for the adventure that the traveler was experiencing:

> Side A: Ketill and Bjǫrn, they raised the stone in memory of Þorsteinn, their father; Ônundr in memory of his brother and the housecarls in memory of the just (?) [and] Ketiley in memory of her husbandman. These brothers were the best of men in the land and abroad in the retinue, held their housecarls well.
> Side B: He fell in battle in the east in Garðar, commander of the retinue, the best of landholders.[21]

Housecarls (or *húskarlar* in Old Norse) were bodyguards or household troops.[22] Combined with the reference to "commander of the retinue," it appears that these brothers were members of the Rus grand prince's personal troop, the druzhina. The stone has been dated to the mid-eleventh century, which would make the grand prince Yaroslav I.[23]

Another stone of particular interest is a monument from Gotland Island:

> Hróðvísl and Hróðelfr, they had the stones raised in memory of [their] three sons. This [one] in memory of Hróðfúss. Black men betrayed him on a voyage. May God help Hróðfúss' soul. May God betray those who betrayed him.[24]

A little unchristian-like vindictiveness here. The "black men" (*blökumen* in Old Norse) have been variously interpreted as Walachians from Romania or Polovcians from Central Asia.[25]

Of even more interest is this stone from Pilgårds, Gotland:

> Hǫgbjǫrn raised this stone glaring [and his] brothers Hróðvísl, Eysteinn, Edundr, who have had stones raised in memory of Hrafn south of Rofstein. They came far and wide in Eifor. Vífill bade....[26]

Some interpretation is needed to fully understand this monument. Instead of "glaring," another translation is "colored or painted." Eifor (Aífor) is one of the most dangerous of the notorious cataracts on the lower Dnieper River. The inscription thus pertains to a voyage down the Dnieper, with the four brothers as members of the company led by Vífill. Hrafn lost his life in the rock-strewn rapids, and his brothers raised a monument to him south of Rofstein (Fufstein).[27] The stone on the Dnieper has not been found.

The three surviving brothers traveled on into the Black Sea and, crossing this body of water, came to Constantinople. Since they were from Gotland, it is likely that they were merchants coming to the great city on the Bosporus to trade. Apparently, the three brothers made it back across the Black Sea and up the Dnieper, crossing to the Western Dvina or Lovat rivers, and then sailing the Baltic back to Gotland. On their home island, they raised this stone in memory of the brother lost at the cataracts of the lower Dnieper, a continent away.

The Viking Age was the period of Swedish Christianization. Most of the monuments exhibit an expression of Christianity in the runes, as in a stone from Uppland: "Steinhildr had this stone erected in memory of Viðôrn, her husband, Grikkfara (a traveler in Greece). May God and God's mother help his soul. Ásmundr Kári' son marked."[28] Or the Christian symbolism might be part of the decor carved in the stone, as in the case of another runestone from Småland. The translation is:

> Guðfastr placed the stone ... his father. May God betray the one who betrayed him and to life.[29]

Most monuments indicate that those so honored (or at least the monument sponsors) were Christian. However, there are a few that are judged to be pagan, as with a runestone from Södermanland: "Vésteinn ... in memory of Freysteinn, his brother, [who] died in Greece. Þuli/Þulr cut."[30] Here we have the pagan god Frey as part of a personal name. Another stone was considered heathen by its discoverers and therefore consigned to oblivion as part of the foundation of the Uppsala Cathedral. The inscription of the now-buried monument reads:

> Ingimundr and Þórðr [and] Jarl and Vígbjôrn had the stone raised in memory of Ingifastr, their father, a captain who travelled abroad to Greece, Ióni's son; and in memory of Ígulbjôn. And Œpir carved.[31]

It is not clear whether his riches came from selling his sword or from trading in merchandise. Another runestone tells us directly the subject was a merchant:

> Ljótr the captain erected this stone in memory of his sons. He who perished abroad was called Áki. [He] steered a cargo-ship; he came to Greece. Hefnir died at home.[32]

This sounds like a family of traders: the father, the ship's captain; one son, the man at the helm; and another son, a new member. Two out of the three made it home. Merchants were probably much more likely to survive an expedition to Constantinople than were warriors.

Not all runestones deal exclusively with lost loved ones. Some include documentation about inheritance.

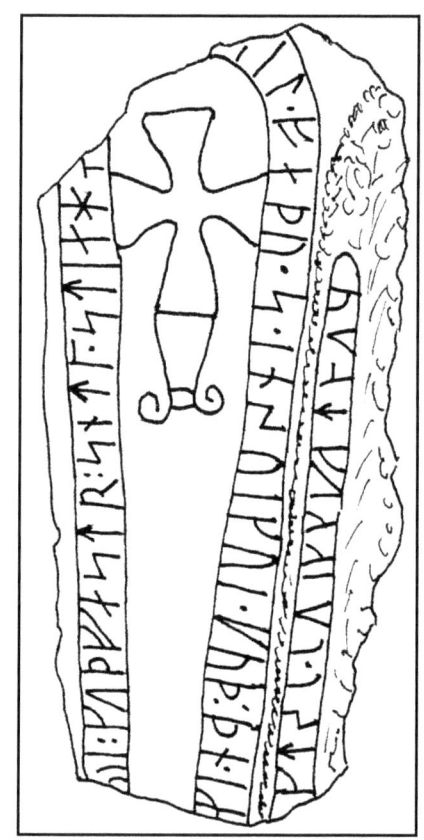

Sm 46.

> These landmarks are made in memory of Inga's sons. She came to inherit from them, but these brothers—Gerðarr and his brothers—came to inherit from her. They died in Greece.[33]

If it was Inga's sons who "died in Greece," then it seems clear that Inga inherited some kind of wealth from her sons, who died without offspring. This property, whatever it may have been, was then passed to Inga's brothers. There are, of course, other explanations for these words, but there can be little doubt that the inscription involves an inheritance.

Finally, we have the only runestone found in Gotland that mentions the Byzantine Empire. This six-proper-noun message reads, "Ormilka, Ulfhvatr, Greece, Jerusalem, Iceland, Serkland."[34] This stone was apparently inscribed to honor two Gotlanders, Ormilka and Ulfhvatr, who traveled and traded in the Byzantine Empire, Iceland and the land of the Muslim caliphate (Serkland). The trip to Jerusalem might have been commercial or a pilgrimage (or both). The passage demonstrates the wide range of travels undertaken by a Viking merchant or warrior from Arctic Iceland to the deserts of the Tigris-Euphrates valley. This is simply amazing considering that the average person of the Middle Ages never traveled more than a few miles from his home in his whole lifetime.

Not all the Vikings who sailed down the Dnieper and crossed the Black Sea came as merchants. Many were warriors who entered the service of the emperor as members of the Varangian Guard. Some thirty runestones have been found relating to voyages to or service in Grikkland (Greece). As usual, many of these are very simple. For example, these four inscriptions from Uppland: "Jarlabank.... He met his end in Grikkium [Greece]"[35]; "Ingiþóra ... and in memory of Ketell- ... her father, [a] Grikkfara [traveler to Greece]"[36]; "...had this stone erected in memory of.... He fell in Grikklandi [Greece]. May God help [his] soul"[37]; and "He died in Grikkium [Greece]."[38] (I have included the Old Norse script for the various Viking names for the Byzantine Empire, or, as they called it, Greece.)

Gold was the lure for these extraordinary journeys, as testified to by several monuments. From Södermanland we read, "Þryðríkr [raised] the stone in memory of his sons, able valiant men. Óleifr/Gulleifr travelled to Greece, divided up gold."[39] Another monument from Södermanland reads, "Guðrún raised the stone in memory of Heðinnj [he] was Sveinn's nephew. He was in Greece, divided [up] gold. May Christ help Christians' spirits."[40] The phrase "divided [up] gold" may mean that these warriors distributed the pay or plunder among the Varangian Guard, or that they received payment as members of the Guard.

Not all the warriors traveling to the land of the Byzantines died there. A few made it back to Sweden and could boast of their accomplishments. An example is the famous Ed Stone, named after the place where it was found in Uppsala. This rock, or rather boulder, measures 59 feet in circumference and has rune inscriptions on two sides:

> Side A: Ragnvaldr had the runes carved in memory of Fastvé, his mother, Ónæmr's daughter, [who] died in Eið. May God help her spirit.
> Side B: Ragnvaldr had the runes carved; [he] was in Greece, was commander of the retinue.[41]

Ragnvaldr had reason to proclaim his achievements for he apparently served as a member of the Varangian Guard, rising to the position of commander. He no doubt returned to Sweden a rich man.

Another monument leaves no question as to the prosperity of the one returning from the Byzantine Empire:

> Kárr had this stone raised in memory of Haursi, his father; and Kabbi/Kampi/Kappi/Gapi in memory of his kinsman-by-marriage. [He] traveled competently; earned wealth abroad in Greece for his heir.[42]

The Varangian Guard was one element that outlasted the Rus in terms of a direct connection with Scandinavia. It served the will of the Byzantine emperor. The sword arm of the northern warrior was a valuable commodity, and what better place to serve than at the glittering city on the Bosporus? Individuals, contingents, even small armies of Rus—some from Varangian Eastern Europe, others coming directly from Scandinavia—joined this elite fighting force.[43]

We have already noted these warriors' service on behalf of the emperor in Italy, but their participation was wide ranging. From tenth-century documents we know they fought in Crete, Mesopotamia, Dalmatia, and the lands around the Caspian Sea. Their ships sailed the waters of the Mediterranean, the Caspian and the Black seas, not to mention the rivers and straits adjoining these bodies of water.[44]

By AD 1000 the Varangian Guard was organized as the emperor's personal troop. We've noted Harald Hardradi's exploits in this corps between 1034 and 1042, suggesting it was still dominated by Swedish Vikings at that time. But after the Norman conquest of England, many Saxons and Danes left the conquered island nation for military employment with the emperor. They were joined by disaffected Normans and Frenchmen. Although the Guard would remain in service at Constantinople until the early thirteenth century, it would lose its axe-wielding Viking flavor after 1066. The last bonds between Sweden and the Varangian East were thus dissolved.

30

The Last Great Expedition to the East

One final class of runestone monuments must be considered. These are carvings commemorating the warriors who died on an expedition to the mysterious lands between the Black and Caspian seas—the fabled Colchis of ancient legend. Some 25 of these stones have been found in eastern Sweden dating to the early and mid-eleventh century.[1] They are outnumbered only by runes mentioning Greece and England. This must have been a great expedition involving a large host of men. It would also have been one of the last, if not *the* last, sizable foray mounted in Sweden that passed through Russia and went all the way to the Caucasus Mountains on the far side of the Black Sea. In the late tenth and early eleventh centuries, such voyages were not uncommon, but by the mid-eleventh century expeditions reaching the caliphate's territories commenced in the lands of the Rus rather than starting from the far side of the Baltic.

Most of the inscriptions commemorating this campaign, as usual, are simple and direct:

> Geirvé and Gulla raised this stone in memory of Ônundr, their father, who died in the east with Ingvarr. May God help Ônundr's spirit.[2]
>
> Gunnarr and Björn and Þorgrímr raised this stone in memory of Þorsteinn, their brother, who was dead in the east with Ingvarr.[3]
>
> Bergviðr/Barkviðr and Helga, they raised this stone in memory of Ulfr, their son. He met his end with Ingvarr. May god help Ulfr's soul.[4]

Ingvarr is Yngvarr Víðförla (Far Traveled), the leader of this expedition. For some of his company we have a bit more information:

> Herleif and Þorgeðr had this stone raised in memory of Sæbjôrn, their father, who steered a ship east with Ingvarr to Estonia/Serkland.[5]

Here we have a skilled seaman, perhaps the pilot. And another man was a sailor of some importance:

> Andvéttr and Kárr and [?] and Blesi and Djarfr raised this stone in memory of Gunnleifr, their father, who was killed in the east with Ingvarr. May God help their spirits. Alríkr, I carved the runes. He could steer a cargo-ship well.[6]

Gunnleifr was a pilot or helmsman, and he left quite a list of progeny behind.

One set of grieving parents chose to memorialize their son with several monuments, one of which reads:

> Þjalfi and Holmlang had all these stones raised in memory of Banki/Baggi, their son, who alone owned a ship and steered to the east in Ingvarr's retinue. May God help Banki's/Baggi's spirit. Áskell carved.[7]

Here was a man so successful that he owned his own ship, which he took to the east as part of Yngvarr's fleet.

There were also warriors who served in the west—some in England, others in France—before joining this campaign to the Muslim east. For example:

> Side A: Myskja and Manni/Máni had these monuments raised in memory of their brother Hróðgeirr and their father Holmsteinn.
> Side B: He had long been in the west: died in the east with Ingvar.[8]

It seems the father, Holms, had served in the western regions before taking his son on this great adventure to the Black Sea and beyond.

There are monuments that leave no doubt as to the ultimate destination of the expedition, at least in general terms:

> Spjóti [and] Halfdan, they raised this stone in memory of Skarði, their brother. From here [he] traveled to the east with Ingvarr; in Serkland lies Eyvirdr's son.[9]

Clearly, the campaign left from Sweden and ended in Serkland, the Old Norse name for the land of the Saracens, the realm of the Muslim caliphate, including the countries of the Caucasus.

Some monuments are fairly graphic:

> Tóla had this stone raised in memory of her son Haraldr, Ingvarr's brother. They traveled valiantly far for gold, and in the east gave [food] to the eagles. [They] died in the south in Serkland.[10]

Was this Tóla the mother of Yngvarr Far Traveled? Probably not. Haraldr and Yngvarr might have been half-brothers, with Tóla being the mother of only Haraldr. The phrase "gave food to the eagles" meant to be killed by an enemy.

A couple of other incomplete stones—"Ei ... the stone cut ... Eimundr's son ... in the south in Serkland,"[11] and "-ve had this monument made in memory of ... Ulf's brother. They in/to the east ... with Ingvarr in Serkland"[12]—make clear the ultimate destination of the expedition.

Yngvarr's campaign was so well known that it inspired an Icelandic saga. This saga was not written down until the twelfth century, by which time the actual story had been transformed into legend, with many imaginary details added. Still, there may be some information to glean from the tale. The saga begins:

> A king called Eirik ruled over Sweden: He was called Eirik the Conqueror [Victorious]. He married Sigrid the Haughty, but since she was a hard woman to live with, overbearing in everything she did, he divorced her—though he let her have Gotaland. Their son was Olaf the Swede.[13]

"Olaf the Swede" would be Olaf Skötkonung (AD 995–1022), whose son was Onund Jacob (1022–1050), king of a united Sweden at the time of Yngvarr's expedition.

Yngvarr is described in the saga as follows:

> Yngvarr was a man great in stature, handsome and strong and fair-faced, wise and well spoken, kind and generous with his friends, but grim with his enemies, courteous and quick and alert, so that wise men have likened him in accomplishments to his kinsman Styrbjorn, or to King Olaf Tryggvason, who was the most renowned man there ever was or will be in the northlands, forever and aye, both before God and man.[14]

30. The Last Great Expedition to the East

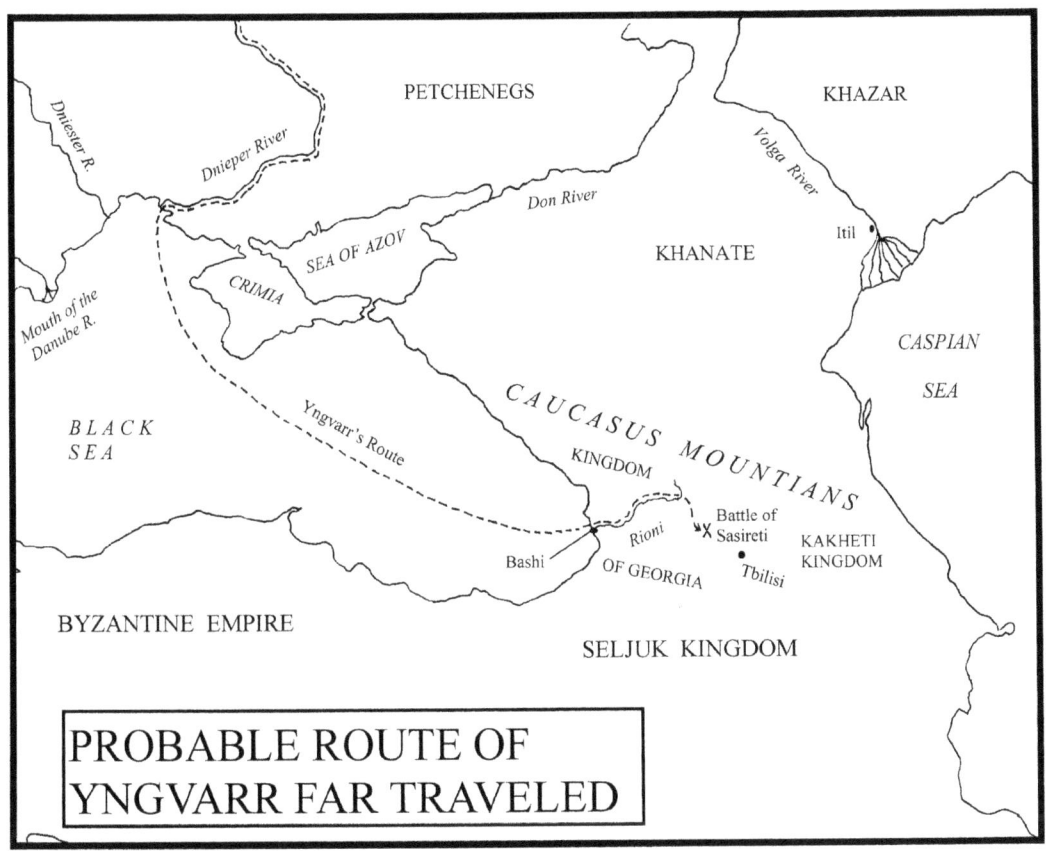

PROBABLE ROUTE OF YNGVARR FAR TRAVELED

An accurate portrait or merely legend? The saga goes on to say that Yngvarr is related to the Swedish royal family. This may have been true, and at the very least he must have been accomplished to have assembled a fleet and men for such a large undertaking. The saga says that Yngvarr was equipping an expedition to seek a kingdom abroad. He selected men from his country and built a fleet of 30 ships.

Yngvarr sailed with his fleet from Sweden to Russia and King Jarizleif (the Russian grand prince Yaroslav [AD 1019–1054]).[15] After his stay with the Rus—the saga says three years—Yngvarr made ready to depart from the border of the prince's domain into foreign territory.

> Then Yngvarr got ready to leave Russia and he meant to try and explore the length of this river. He had a bishop bless his flint and fire ax. Four men are named among Ingvar's companions on the journey: Hjalmvigi and Soti, Ketil, who was called Garda-Ketil—he was an Icelander—and Valdimar. Anyway, after that, they set out onto the river with thirty ships, and Yngvarr turned the prows to the east and made a rule that no one should go ashore without his leave.[16]

The river referred to here is lost in the legend, but we may have a clue from another source. The old chronicle of Georgia, the *Kartlis Tskhovreba*, tells of Varangians landing at Bashi on the Rioni (Phasis) River in western Georgia on the coast of the Black Sea.[17] If this connection is correct, Yngvarr would have sailed down the Dnieper and then across the Black Sea to Georgia, a land fabled for riches since the days of Jason and the Argonauts and their search for the Golden Fleece in ancient Colchis.

The saga goes on to describe how the expedition sailed for many days and through many regions until the colors and animals changed, so that they knew they were in a distant country. Yngvarr and his men then sailed up a river until they came to a city.

> Then towns and big buildings rose in view, and then they s[aw] a magnificent citadel. It was built of white marble. As they neared the citadel, they saw great crowds of men and women. They marveled then at the beauty which they saw there, and the grace of the women, many were strikingly beautiful. But one among them stood out both for dress and beauty.[18]

The one who "stood out" was, of course, the queen of the city, who welcomed the travelers into her domain.

After staying the winter at the queen's city, Yngvarr continued up the river, presumably deeper into Georgia, where he met Jolf, king of this region. Many historians equate Jolf with King Bagrat IV of Georgia. At the time, Bagrat was at war with the Muslim Arabs who had taken Tbilisi and occupied it for over one hundred years.[19]

The *Kartlis Tskhovreba* describes a civil war between King Bagrat and his former general, Liparit Baghvashi, who supported Bagrat's half-brother, Demetre (or Bjolf), in a bid to replace Bagrat as king of Georgia. Liparit and Demetre had an army with soldiers from the breakaway province of Kakheti in eastern Georgia, as well as Byzantine troops. Bagrat turned to the Vikings, whom he had aided with supplies and housing:

> Now you must give me help against my brother Bjolf, who is also called Solmund, because he and his eight sons want to steal my kingdom from me.
>
> Now both kings gather their forces and come to the place they decided on between them. And even when Yngvarr had formed up his troops, Bjolf had by far the most men. King Jolf drew up his forces against his brother. And when both sides are ready they roared the battle cry.[20]

According to the chronicle, Bagrat and the Varangians were defeated at the Battle of Sasireti. As a result, it would take Bagrat another 30 years to establish his suzerainty over Georgia. After the battle, the Varangians beat an undeniable retreat.

> Well, after this, Yngvarr made ready with all haste and left with all his men, and they go on their way now, and travel night and day now, as fast as they can. But such a sickness begins to spread in their crew that all their best people died, and more died than lived. Ingvar took sick too.... And when Yngvarr breathed his last, 1041 years had passed since the birth of Jesus Christ. He was twenty-five when he died.[21]

Thus, Yngvarr's expedition came to an end.

Of the Swedish casualties, many undoubtedly died in the battle, but most succumbed to disease afterward, including their leader. According to the saga, Keril led several ships and crews back to Russia while Valdimar took one ship to Miklagård (Constantinople). Vikings from one or both parties made it back to Sweden to tell the tale and inspire the creation of so many monuments. A fitting epitaph comes from a runestone found in Uppland:

> Klettr and Bleikr raised this stone in memory of Gunnviðr their father. He traveled away with Yngvarr. May Lord God help the spirits of all Christians. Þórir carved the runes/Þórir the Crane carved.[22]

"May Lord God help the spirits of all Christians," as opposed to heathen pagans and Saracens, the carver might have added.

Some 3,000 runestones have been found in Sweden; yet in Swedish Eastern Europe only four have been discovered.[23] Two of these, the inscriptions on wood found at

Staraja Ladoga, we have already discussed. Perhaps these two monuments are typical of those carved in Eastern Europe, where wood was plentiful and stone relatively rare. It is possible that many runes were indeed inscribed, but since they were carved on this perishable material, they ultimately did not survive.

A third inscription has been found chiseled in stone on an island in the Black Sea. Berezan Island (Island of St. Etherius to the Byzantines) is about half a mile long and two-tenths of a mile wide.[24] It is situated in the Black Sea near the mouth of the Dnieper River. It was a natural way station for Viking ships coming and going.

A traveler from the north found refuge here after passing through the treacherous cataracts, sandbanks and hazarders shoals of the lower Dnieper. Here, in the shelter of the island's bays, ships were repaired and fitted with sails for the sea voyage to Constantinople. Later, on the return trip, the island served as a last resting place before facing the rapids, portages and backbreaking oar work of fighting the river's currents.[25]

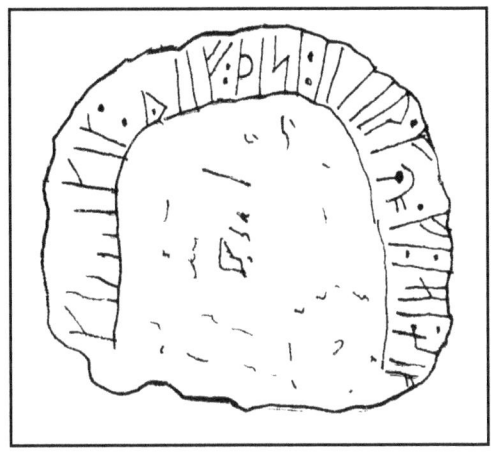

Berezan Stone.

There can be little doubt that this island was used by Varangians, for here was found a runestone with an inscription that reads, "Grani made this vault in memory of Karl, his partner."[26] The shape of the stone and the inscription suggest these partners were from Gotland. The two merchants would have left Gotland for the purpose of trade in Constantinople.[27] Either coming or going Karl died, and Grani raised this monument to honor him.

The fourth rune inscription is on the shoulder and side of a large stone lion that stands outside the gate of the Venice Arsenal. The marble lion originally stood in Piraeus, the port of Athens. Here at the ancient Greek harbor some Swedish Viking carved an inscription on this statue—graffiti is apparently common to all ages. The rune is too worn to read, but the design is similar to eleventh-century Swedish runestones.[28] Was the carver a member of the Varangian Guard with too much time on his hands, or was he some passing merchant wishing to leave evidence of his presence at this remote (from Sweden) outpost? Who he was, we cannot know, except that he was a Swedish Viking far from home.

31

End of the Viking Age

By AD 1070 the Viking Age had ended. A year earlier, Svein Estridsson, king of Denmark, had mounted the last Viking campaign, an attempt to conquer England. He was successfully repelled by William of Normandy, who had conquered the island nation four years earlier, defeating Harold, king of Saxon England, who had just defeated King Harald of Norway that same year. Three great expeditions mounted within four years—a fitting conclusion to the Viking Age.

In Ireland the tide of Viking conquest was receding. In AD 1014, High King Brian Boru was able to organize the forces from several kingdoms, plus the southern O'Neills and Ospak of Man, into an army that met the Vikings at Clontarf, now part of Dublin. The Northmen were commanded by Dubhgall, brother of Sigtrygg Silk-beard. With him were the Dublin Vikings—Jarl Sigurd the Stout of Orkney, Brodir of Man and Maelmordha with his Leinstermen. The slaughter was great. Some 4,000 Irishmen died, but the Viking losses were even worse, with more than 7,000 killed. The Viking domination of Ireland was broken. However, the Norsemen would continue to play a part in the island's politics and commerce until the 1160s, when the English arrived.[1]

In the west, Iceland settled in as an independent nation, establishing its own republic with the administrative acts of 930 and 965.[2] The island nation entered a golden age of literature during the 1100s and 1200s. It was during this time that the Icelandic sagas (referred to extensively in this history) and Eddas (stories about the Viking gods) were written down. Of particular importance were the works of Snorri Sturluson (1179–1241), a historian and poet.[3]

In the far west at the close of the Viking Age, Greenland seemed to be thriving, but colonies in North America, if established at all, did not survive for long. Interestingly, we know that in 1121 the bishop of Greenland, Bishop Erik, did travel to North America.[4] Was this a trip to visit settlers in Vinland, as has been speculated, or just a voyage of curiosity for the bishop who went along with Greenlanders on a lumber-gathering expedition? There were indeed such trips to collect this scarce commodity, and they lasted for at least a couple of hundred years. The Icelandic Annals of 1347 record that a ship manned by Greenlanders arrived after being blown off course on a return trip from Markland.[5] There were no doubt trips to Labrador for timber and to Baffin Island and even Ellesmere Island, as we've seen, for the walrus ivory and hides and other furs essential to Greenland's trade with Europe. But these expeditions persisted only as long as the Greenlanders had their own ships.

Gradually, the trips to North America dwindled as the large cargo ships (*knarrs*) became more and more scarce in Greenland. This was apparently due to a lack of iron available on the island. As early as 1189 a Greenland ship reached Iceland that was held together with wooden pegs instead of iron nails.[6] Not that iron ore was unavailable—Greenland, like Iceland and the rest of Scandinavia, had adequate quantities of bog iron—but the refinement required large quantities of wood to make the charcoal necessary for the smelting process. Greenland had only willow, birch and juniper trees, which did not produce the large timber that was also needed for constructing large buildings and ships. This lumber had to come from Continental Europe, primarily Norway, or from North America. This double and interrelated problem of lacking two essential items put a strain on the colony.

However, despite these challenges, the resilient Viking population in Greenland seems to have coped. The colony of some 5,000 people (1,000 in the western colony and 4,000 residing in the eastern)[7] converted to Roman Catholicism around AD 1000. In 1118 Greenland received its first bishop, and he was followed by nine other bishops over the centuries. Greenland would come to have a cathedral (St. Nicholas' Cathedral at Gardar), thirteen large parish churches, many small churches, a monastery and a nunnery.[8]

After the Viking Age, however, fortunes turned against the colony. The Medieval Warm Period, which peaked in about AD 1000, began to wane precipitously after 1200, and by the mid-fifteenth century the climate had become frigid; this was the beginning of the Little Ice Age (1350–1850). The growing season shortened, pastures and hay crops were reduced and starvation haunted the people of Greenland.[9]

Two other factors put even more strain on the colony. The Dorset people, whom the Vikings had encountered in Labrador and on hunting trips to the far northwest of Greenland, were replaced by the much more aggressive and capable Thule-Inuit. These people had domesticated dogs and therefore had dog sleds for travel and hauling payloads. They used bows and arrows for hunting, tools not known to the Dorset people. The new arrivals also had kayaks, useful for solitary travel and fishing. And they had large ocean-going boats called *umiaqs* for hunting the bowhead whale, a resource not available to the European colonists.[10]

The Viking descendants might have adopted some of the practices of the Inuit culture and thus survived, but they stuck doggedly to their European institutions. Greenlanders followed European customs, from the manner of burying their dead to the latest style in combs, linear measurements (as Norwegians switched from the Roman foot to the shorter Greek foot, so did the Greenlanders), and clothing for both men and women.[11] The Greenlanders thought of themselves as Europeans, and they would steadfastly remain European Christians to the end.

The second factor was the decline in value of walrus ivory, the chief export of Greenland in terms of a cash commodity. The Crusades, which began in AD 1095, opened European access to Asian and African elephant ivory, a source that had been cut off by the Arabian Muslim conquests. Ivory from the far north was replaced by this new source. To make matters worse, furs and hides from Russia were flooding the European markets, and Dutch and English cloth was competing favorably against the Greenland woolens.[12]

Without their own ships, the Greenlanders were completely dependent on ships from Iceland and Norway, but because of the lack of commercial incentive and the colder weather causing the ice floes to push further south, making the voyage more dangerous, shipping between Greenland and Europe slowed to a crawl. The king of Norway promised an annual royal trading ship (the Greenlands Knorr), but it sank in 1368 and was not replaced. After that only four ships are recorded as having landed in Greenland, in 1381, 1382, 1385 and 1406. The last ship stayed in Greenland for four years before returning to Norway in 1410. After that there is only silence.[13]

The Inuit pushed south from their entry point in northwestern Greenland. They established a large community called Sermermiut at Nordrseta, prime hunting grounds for the Norsemen, further hampering the Vikings' ability to obtain trade goods.[14] By 1340 the Inuit had driven to the western settlement, and shortly thereafter Ivar Bardarson, who had been sent by the Swedish king Magnus IV (then king of Norway as well) to help drive the encroachers away, reported, "The Skraelings hold the entire Western Settlement."[15] A settlement around Ivigtut (called the "middle settlement") succumbed by 1380.[16]

The final bastion of Greenlander resistance was the eastern settlement, but it would not be spared for long. An entry in the Icelandic Annal of 1379 reads, "The Skraelings assaulted the Greenlanders, killing 18 men, and capturing two boys and one bondswoman and made them slaves."[17] Lacking iron to make armor, shields and weapons, the Norsemen had no inherent advantage over the Inuit in combat, and they certainly lacked the environmental adaptations that the invaders from the north possessed.

Thorstein Olafsson, captain of the last ship to leave Greenland in 1410, brought back to Norway three bits of information: A man named Kolgrim was burned at the stake for practicing witchcraft in seducing a woman named Steinunn, who later went mad. Lastly, Olafsson, the captain of that last ship, married a Greenland girl named Sigrid Bjornsdotter on September 14, 1408, in the Hvalsey church. These events—an execution, a case of insanity and a marriage—are the last news we have from Norsemen of Greenland. Within the next few decades, the Greenland Norse became extinct.[18] Descendants of those Swedish adventurers who had help settle Iceland and then moved on to Greenland were lost.

The Viking Age came to an end with the aforementioned expedition of Svein Estridsson that attempted to overthrow William the Conqueror in 1070. In the far west, the frontier of Viking realm had reached North America but had now receded. First the contacts with North America were lost and then, eventually, communication with Greenland, leaving Iceland as the westernmost outpost of the former Viking domain.

In the east, the great water road to Constantinople and Arabian Bagdad was sliding from the Swedish orbit. Yaroslav had tried to maintain the connections with the northern realm, but with his death in 1054, the empire of the Rus was more Slavic than Swede, and its ties were to the south and the Byzantine Empire. The divide between Svíþjóð (Sweden) and Svíþjóð hinn mikla (Sweden the Great) widened to the point that it could no longer be bridged. Yaroslav's successors took Russia on its own path into the late Middle Ages, and Sweden would have to learn to get along without its eastern river road to riches.

32

Medieval Sweden (AD 1070–1350)

By the end of the Viking Age in AD 1070, Sweden, Denmark, Norway, Iceland and even Greenland had settled into a less rancorous and chaotic state. The freewheeling trading and plundering expeditions conducted by individual leaders who could inspire crews of kinfolk and neighbors to follow them on dangerous, but potentially enriching, ventures were over. Such expeditions were now the purview of monarchs and intended for the purpose of conquest, not just pirate raids. Note the enterprises of William the Conqueror against England, Danish king Svein Estridsson's attempt to retake England from Duke William, and the Norwegian king Harald Hardradi's expedition to take England before William's conquest. There was also the aborted plan to invade England again by Canute IV of Denmark in 1085, and Norwegian king Magnus III (Barefoot or Bare Legs), who attacked Orkney, the Hebrides and the Isle of Man, and then Ireland, where he did manage to take Dublin before being killed in 1103.[1] These excursions provided an outlet for the hot-blooded young Scandinavian men seeking glory and gold. But they were now part of the king's herd, not adventurers sailing in a single ship toward some unsuspecting town or monastery.

The subsiding of the Viking voyages of trade and plunder was due in large measure to the consolidation of political power in Western Europe. England was now united, first under the Saxons, then under Norman rule, providing a strong defense against petty marauders. After a series of weak French kings of the Capetian Dynasty, Philip II came to the throne in 1180.[2] He tightened the reins of the monarchy over the feudal lords and established a permanent capital at Paris. Having already learned to deal with the Viking raiders using mobile, heavy cavalry, the nation was now nearly impregnable to the roving sea raiders.

Even Ireland, long a target of Norse pillaging, had become more proficient in the art of war. The island had reduced the number of rulers to a few with real power who would pull together when necessary to repel the Viking assaults, as was done in 1114 when High King Boru commanded an army gathered from several kingdoms to defeat the Vikings at the battle of Clontarf.[3] Norsemen were still active in Ireland as merchants and sometimes ruled a port town or small enclave. But the days of the uncontrolled Viking marauding and conquests in the Emerald Isle were over.

The Hebrides were ruled by the king of the Isle of Man.[4] Caithness and Orkney were firmly controlled by the Earl of Orkney, and to the south Scotland was under the rule of Malcolm III.[5] The people of these areas were descendants of Scots, Picts and Vikings, all warlike and able to defend their homelands.

Out in the North Atlantic, the Shetland and Faroe Islands, Iceland and the habitable parts of Greenland had long since been colonized. Only North America lay open to penetration by explorers and settlers, but repeated attempts to establish a European foothold there had proven too great a stretch.

In the east, Slavic Eastern Europe had cut its ties with Sweden in favor of Constantinople, and even the southern and eastern Baltic coast had become less inviting with strengthening France in the west and the encroaching Germans in the east replacing the Slavic Wends.

Thus the former recipients of Viking raids and expeditions of conquest were no longer the easy prey they once were. Vacant lands previously open to settlement were now occupied. Trade routes that once extended from Greenland and Iceland to Bagdad and Constantinople had been taken over (particularly in the east) by local merchants. The Viking *knörr* still plied the Baltic, North Sea and North Atlantic, but its range and frequency of travel had been curtailed.

The other consolidation of power that was a factor in ending the Viking Age was the development of the Viking nations themselves. This period witnessed the growth and effectiveness of the Danish, Norwegian and Swedish monarchies, while Iceland went its own way, establishing a republic. But in all cases laws evolved and controls, including taxation, were placed on citizens by central governments. Monarchs were concerned with the stability and peaceful development of their kingdoms. Only the king's army would be tolerated; all other private armies were banned. "Monarchs had taken over the business of war."[6] All of these developments tended to restrain the kind of independent and uninhibited expeditions typical of the Viking Age.

It is interesting to note that after two and a half centuries of overseas expansion, conquest and rule, the Viking peoples ended up occupying the same lands that were part of their domain at the beginning of the Viking Age (with the exception of the North Atlantic islands they had colonized). The Norsemen simply had no staying power. There were four primary reasons for this lack of permanency.

First, the Vikings warred against each other as much as against their adversaries. Second, they seem not to have been able to induce other peoples to adopt their political, social and religious systems. Instead, the Vikings tended to assimilate into the societies they conquered. Third, the peoples and nations they encountered were in the main stronger, richer and more self-sustaining than they themselves were. (Examples are the Franks, the English, the Byzantines, the caliphate and, in the end, even the Slavs.) Finally, and most important, the Vikings lacked manpower. They were just too few compared to the populations they were contending with. When conditions changed and they lost their initial advantage, the Scandinavian peoples found themselves about where they were two and half centuries earlier (geographically speaking).[7]

To the common man, of course, there was no sense that an era had come to an end. The farmers, fishermen, carpenters, coopers and merchants went on with their lives unaware of any shift in historical periods. True, Hedeby and Birka were gone. But they had been replaced by Sigtuna in Sweden, Nidaros (Trondheim) in Norway and Schleswig in Denmark. A keen observer might have detected a change in clothing. Among men there was the adaptation of the rather ridiculous full, baggy trousers copied from Serkland costumes, and among women linen petticoats had replaced the old standby woolens.[8]

The effect of the end of the Viking Age on families and society was less subtle, and certainly unmistakable. Sons could no longer look forward to leaving home for a life of adventure and fortune in some foreign land. There were no new islands to be settled or rich territories to conquer. Second and third sons had to settle for a share of the family property or else find another calling. Many hired themselves out as laborers, a possibility made available by the enfeeblement of the thrall class. Viking raids had been the main source of slaves in Scandinavia. With the cessation of these pirate expeditions, the supply of human merchandise slowed and then ended all together. As a result, slavery and the thrall class disappeared.

Housing was also changing in the Middle Ages. The characteristic longhouse of the Viking and pre–Viking periods was giving way to less massive structures. Some of these were smaller versions of the longhouse, but without the posts in the middle of the building supporting the roof. The weight of the roof was born entirely by posts that were part of the walls of the building. Other buildings were of the sunken-floor type that had been around since before the Viking Age and might be a variety of shapes, from rectangular to round. Where the longhouse was often the centerpiece of a farmstead, more and more buildings were now gathered into villages. In many cases the village was dominated by a more substantial manorhouse, indicating a hierarchical social structure.[9]

Sweden was more fortunate than the other Scandinavian countries in that it still had lands to conquer and settle. There were the northern territories north of Uppland along the Gulf of Bothnia, forested areas where land-hungry farmers could find new tracts to clear and cultivate. There was also Finland, a whole new country open to settlement, conquest and trade. In fact, Finland provided the opportunity for crusades blessed by Rome that could be parlayed into campaigns of conquest.

As we've seen, the Viking Age produced the consolidation of power in Scandinavia that led to the formation of four nations: Norway, Denmark, Sweden, and Iceland. It was also the period in which these states became Christianized. As noted, the first attempt to penetrate Sweden's paganism was launched by the Benedictine monk Anskar in 829, who had some success with the ruling class of Birka. While Anskar came from the Franks, other missionaries arrived from England, approaching from the North Sea side and proselytizing in Västergötland. Progress was sporadic for the next 300 years, as the Swedes demanded of their gods demonstrable benefits in terms of good crops, freedom from disease, fertility and success in warfare. Less important were the promises of a paradise-like afterlife, but this, too, was promised by the Asa gods (at least for warriors).

For 300 years the battle for the souls of Sweden seesawed back and forth. Usually the two religions existed side by side in a peaceful coexistence, if not in harmony.[10] To the pagans, the Christian God (whether Roman Catholic or Orthodox) was just another deity to be worshipped by those who were so inclined. They had no objection as long as the devotees to the new god did not interfere with their pagan rituals and sacrifices.[11]

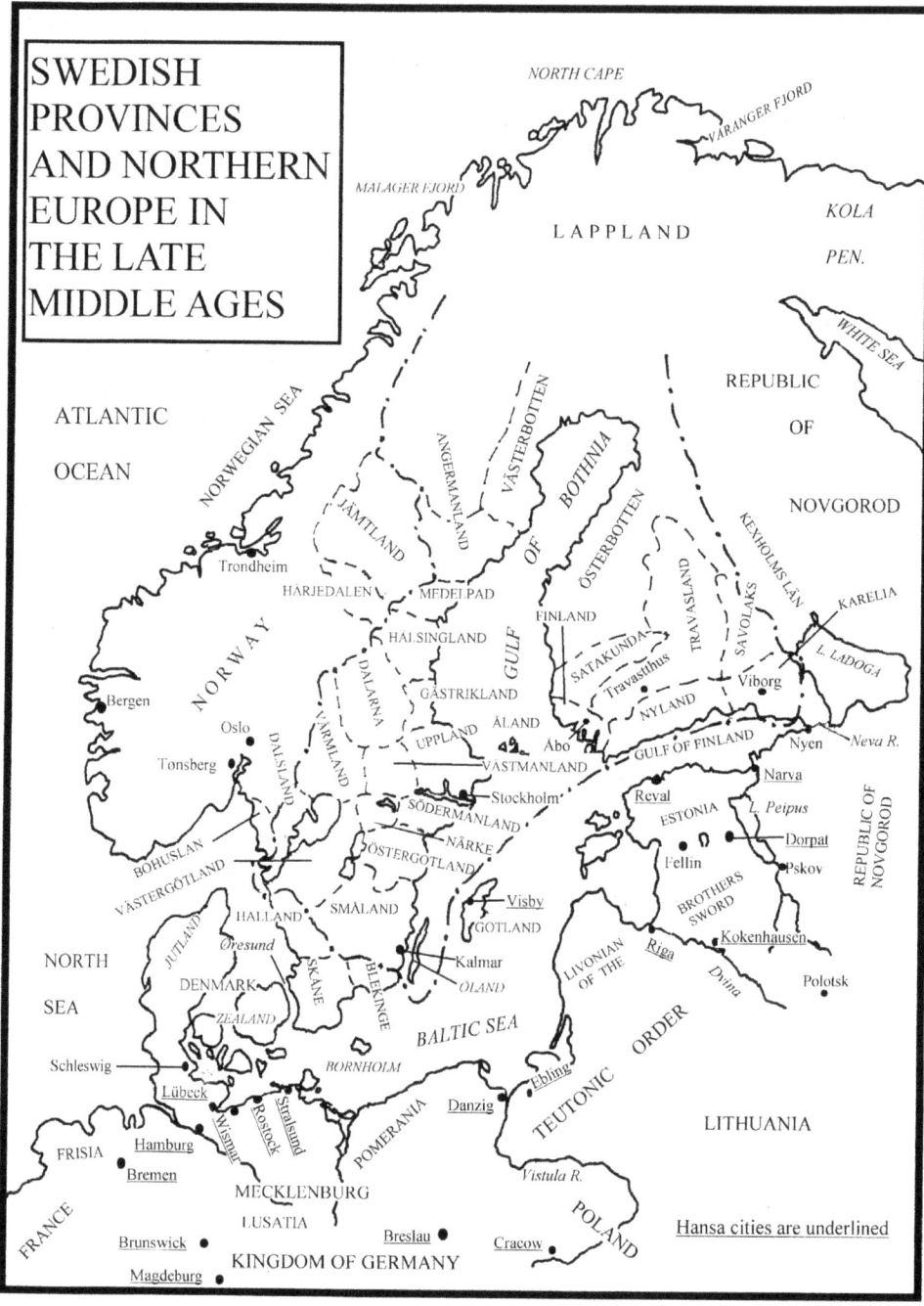

Christians were less tolerant, abhorring the sacrifices of animals and especially human oblation. However, as long as the Christians were outnumbered, they kept their peace, observing their religious practices as best they could. Thus, the two religions were practiced by the citizens of Birka without armed clashes of any sort.

Eventually, the Christians gained in numbers to the point that they could take control and dominate. The struggle came to a head at the end of the eleventh century, when

King Inge the Elder was driven from the Council of the Svear by rock-throwing disciples of the Asa gods for refusing to conduct the pagan sacrifices. The king's Christian backers then rose up, tore down the heathen temples and burned the wooden images of the pagan gods. The long struggle for the souls of the Swedish people had been decided, at least in the stronghold and shrine of the Asa gods. But there were pockets of resistance that would not succumb for a while yet.

In the forests of Småland the old gods retained their following—the last significant resistance to Christianization in the last Scandinavian country to be converted. Finally, King Sigurd Jordalafar of Norway launched a crusade to stamp out the remaining embers of heathenism. This campaign took place in 1122, the year before the great darkness of August 11, 1123 (a reference to a total eclipse of the sun).[12]

The crusade is known as the "Kalmar *Ledung*" (Kalmar Raid), as that trading town was the campaign objective. Kalmar was reduced to ashes and Småland was ravaged. The Smålanders were forced to accept Christianity at the point of the sword and had to pay a tribute of 1,500 animals to their Christian benefactors. Sigurd, an experienced crusader— he had taken part in an 1107 expedition in Jerusalem—knew how to conduct a successful crusade. He returned to Norway having Christianized Småland, and he carried back wagonloads of loot. The last significant pagan holdout in Sweden had been converted.[13]

The Christianizing of Sweden, as was the case for all Scandinavian countries, did have an effect on the lives of its citizens. An individual human life now had value. Human and even animal sacrifices were no longer required. The new "White Christ" had paid the price by sacrificing Himself.[14]

Infanticide was banned. Babies with blemishes or abnormalities were allowed to live. The practice of depositing newborns out in the forest, especially girl babies in times of famine, was no longer acceptable.

Private revenge killings were curtailed, though the practice was a long time in being completely abolished. Injustices were now to be taken to the courts, where a judge and tribunal would decide the issue based on written laws. Thus, laws were required, and legislatures were needed to construct those laws.

Christianity opened up new possibilities where Finland was concerned. Not just trading posts and coastal settlements were in order, but wholesale crusades of conversion and conquest were also blessed by the Holy See in Rome. The first of these crusades was led by King Eric the Holy, who became Sweden's patron saint after his martyrdom in 1160. By then the Viking Age was long past, and Sweden was united and Christian.

Let's step back for a moment to look at the kings of a united Sweden and the process of Christianizing the new nation. This dynasty of kings that first ruled a united Sweden was of the house of Yngling (dates are approximate).

AD 983–994	Erik (Eirik) the Victorious (Sigrsæll)
995–1022	Olaf of Sweden (Skötkonung)
1022–1050	Onund Jacob
1050–1060	Emund the Old
1060–1066	Stenkil of Sweden (Ragnvaldsson)
1066–1080	Inge the Elder (Stenkilsson) with Halsten Stenkilsson (died 1070)
1080–1083	Blot-Sweyn
1083–1105	Inge I (the Elder)
1105–1130	Inge II (the Younger) with Philip Halstensson (died 1110)[15]

Erik the Victorious we've already discussed (see chapter 23). It is Erik who is generally credited with uniting Sweden (the Svear and Gauts) into a single nation. His son Olaf Skötkonung was the first to be named king of the Gauts and the Svear at his coronation, and it is with Olaf that the line of Swedish kings traditionally begins. He was also the first baptized Christian Swedish king, though his subjects were by no means completely converted at the time of his coronation.[16] In fact, under Olaf pagans and Christians lived side by side in peace.[17] In addition, it was this Olaf who participated in the sea battle defeating Olaf Tryggvason of Norway.

Olaf's son Onund Jacob was the first Swedish king to have a Christian name.[18] Although Onund promoted Christianity during his reign, Sweden remained a divided nation in terms of religion.

Onund was succeeded by Edmund the Old, who saw the last trade connections with Russia slip away with the death of Yaroslav in 1054.[19]

Inge I (the Elder) was driven from the throne because he would not conduct the sacrifices to Thor, Odin and Frey at Uppsala. He was replaced by his half-brother Blot-Sweyn, who oversaw the ritual sacrifices satisfying the pagan population. Yet three years later Inge was able to retake the throne, a clear indication that a shift in the dominant religion had occurred.

Though the religious question may have been settled, the political power of the king was very limited. He served at the behest of the Uppland nobility. In AD 1105, two brothers occupied the throne: Inge II (the Younger) and Philip Halstensson. Apparently this was a deliberate attempt to keep the monarchy weak and subject to the will of ruling nobles.

This weakness of the Yngling kings was exemplified by the condition of the monarchy in terms of a capital—there was none. The king and his court had to move from place to place (usually the king's own estates) in order to not burden any one possession beyond its capacity to support the monarch and his retainers.

With the death of Inge the Younger, the Yngling line of kings ended, to be replaced by a series of monarchs from two noble Swedish families, the Sverker and the Erik:

1130–1156	Sverker I (the Elder)—House of Sverker
1156–1160	Erik the Holy—House of Erik (led the first Finnish crusade)
1160–1167	Karl VII of Sweden (Sverkersson)—House of Sverker
1167–1196	Knut I of Sweden (Eriksson)—House of Erik
1196–1208	Sverker II of Sweden (the Younger)—House of Sverker
1208–1216	Erik X (Knutsson)—House of Erik
1216–1222	Johan I (Sverkersson)—House of Sverker
1222–1229	Erik XI (Eriksson—the Lame or Lisper)—House of Erik
1229–1234	Knut II of Sweden (Holmgersson)—House of Sverker
1234–1250	Erik XI (Eriksson)—was returned to throne—House of Erik[20]

During the reigns of the early Yngling kings, Sweden lost the last of its trade routes along the water roads of Russia. But Swedish mercantile interests became even more restricted during the latter part of the dynasty as German colonists moved into the plains and coasts of the southern Baltic, absorbing and conquering the Slavic Wends as their migration progressed. Much of this was done in the guise of crusades. The Crusades began in AD 1096 as a war against Muslims in an attempt to recover the Holy Land for Christians, but they were soon diverted into campaigns against any pagan people, particularly those of Northern Europe.[21] Thus we have the Wendish Crusades (1147–1185), in which Saxons, Danes and Poles conquered and converted the tribes of Mecklenburg and Lusatia with full approval from Rome (papal bull, *Divina dispensatione*).[22]

Further east, a Polish prince, Konrad Mazowiecki (Conrad of Mazovia), made the mistake of hiring an unemployed military order to even the score with Prussian tribes that had been raiding his domains. This order, the Teutonic Knights, was originally created for work in the Holy Land. Once the knights were no longer engaged there, they turned to this new assignment with enthusiasm. The contract became a crusade in 1230, with charters from both the pope and the Holy Roman Emperor. The Teutonic Knights not only conquered and converted the Prussians but also occupied and ruled a large territory around the southeastern and eastern Baltic coast.[23]

The eastern Baltic coast north of Teutonic Knights' domain was conquered and converted by a kindred order, the Livonian Brothers of the Sword, founded by the bishop of Riga. The order, headquartered at Fellin (Viljandi), tended to go its own way in conquests and conversions. The remaining area, Estonia, was converted by a Danish crusade. Thus, Sweden was left with only Finland out of all its once extensive eastern possessions.[24]

Only in Finland could the Swedes continue their Viking-style raiding, trading and conquering, even though the plundering was now conducted as a crusade with approval from Rome. The first of these crusades was led by King Erik the Holy, as noted earlier, who was also the first of the line of kings from the house of Erik. His crusade was successful in extending the conquered portion of Finland and thus converting more of the Finnish tribes.[25]

After one battle, according to legend, Erik wept over the bodies of the fallen enemy, moved in sorrow that so many souls were lost that should have had a chance at eternal life. Eventually, Erik was martyred and became Sweden's patron saint.[26]

Though the campaigns in Finland were carried out by the king of Sweden as crusades to convert the heathen tribes, the conquest of Finland soon became the purview of the jarl of Mälaren. This position, which may have grown out of the office of prefect of Birka, was one of the legs of the triumvirate of medieval Swedish power centers. The nation was controlled not by a single person or group, but rather by three factions: the jarl, the king and the Swedish nobility, primarily the Lords of the Svear.

After subjugating the Gauts, the Svear of Uppland had retained the right to select the king, whose primary responsibilities were to conduct the sacrifices to the Asa gods and lead the country in the time of war. Thus, during the reigns of the Yngling kings and the Sverker-Erik monarchs there was a constant struggle between these three power centers, with one component gaining dominance only to be eclipsed by another claimant when there was a change in personnel. The nobles kept the monarchy weak as part of their policy. The king's influence was further eroded by the Swedish conversion to Christianity, for he was no longer required as the intermediary in conducting the pagan sacrifices at Uppsala.[27]

Meanwhile, the jarl of Mälaren grew in strength as he led the campaigns to subjugate western Finland, which was becoming his personal fief. Not only was the land being conquered, but the coastal areas were also open to settlement by colonizers from Sweden.[28]

Outside Finland, however, Swedish interests continued to decline. As German domination spread along the Baltic coast, former Viking merchant towns were taken over and converted to German commercial centers. Such was the case of a former Norse town on the Trave River, which was occupied by Germans in AD 1143. A new town was founded, Lübeck, which quickly grew into a vibrant merchant city dominating the trade in the vicinity. Other commercial centers were established at Hamburg, Wismar, Rostock, Danzig and Ebling. Even Visby on Gotland Island was appropriated by German merchants, displacing the long-standing Swedish control. In the eastern Baltic they built Riga, Narva and Reval into thriving port cities spreading into Novgorod and Polotsk. In Finland they became established in Åbo and Viborg. In the west, German merchants entrenched themselves in Bergen, Norway, and appropriated the Skånian fisheries from the Danes.[29] Inland trade centers were established at Brunswick, Magdeburg, Breslau and Cracow.[30]

These German commercial cities early on determined that it was to their mutual benefit to band together for protection and to facilitate trade. The first association was initiated at Visby in AD 1161 under the name "United Gotland Travelers of the Holy Roman Empire." The organization spread until it encompassed German cities from the Atlantic to the Gulf of Finland.[31]

When the Germans could not gain outright control of a city, they established merchant colonies in the city limits, as in Kalmar and Söderköping in eastern Sweden and Lödöse on the west coast. They also founded offices in London, York, Oslo and Copenhagen.[32]

The *Bund van der dudeschen hanse*, or "Hanseatic League" (Hansa for short), rose to prominence in Northern Europe, peaking in the fourteenth century, with some 200 cities as members. The Hansa had no formal constitution or central government, but a body of laws and customs accumulated that guided the organization. There was a court of appeals established in Lübeck to hear grievances among the members. A general assembly met, usually in Lübeck, to further the interests of the organization.[33]

The league's success in displacing the old Viking system of trade was based on a new approach to sea commerce. Instead of the longboat, the Hanseatic cog was the cargo carrier of choice. The short stubby ship, 60 or more feet in length, carried two or more masts. It had more draft than the Viking longboat, but the advent of ports with docks at trading cities eliminated the need for ships that could be beached in order to unload cargoes. Cogs were not a particularly new invention, as demonstrated by the special docking area at Birka in the ninth and tenth centuries for Frisian cogs, but the Hansa perfected the use of the cog in a new commercial system.

With its larger, deeper hold, the cog carried more cargo than the longboat. Whereas the Viking longboat's captain and crew were the ship's owners and traders, the cog might be owned by its captain or a company, or even by a Hansa city. It was a ship hired by merchants to carry a cargo, merchants who might never set foot on the vessel. This new and more efficient cargo-carrying system came to dominate Baltic and North Sea trade. In 1368 over 700 cogs sailed from Lübeck in that year alone.[34] Except in Russia, where even the Hansa was held at bay, Sweden's once vast trade network was superseded and replaced by the Hanseatic League.

The original purpose of the Hansa was to protect the rights and privileges of its members—the rights of anchorage, storage, and protection from local laws and harassment. These privileges were basic to the Hansa members' ability to trade and conduct business, and they were obtained by the use of the *Verhansung* (commercial boycott). But as the power of the league grew, it began to use a more direct means of coercion. A naval force was built using the money from a levy on Hansa cities. This navy was first used to suppress pirates who were plying their trade along the commercial routes of the Hansa merchants. But the league found such a force was useful in dictating terms with even monarchs of the region.[35]

In 1361, Danish forces sacked Visby, a Hansa port city, which led to the first Danish war. In this war the Danes prevailed against an alliance of Norway, Sweden and the Hansa. But in the second Danish war (1368–1369), league troops captured Helsingborg, destroyed Copenhagen and took over the Sound. By the terms of the Treaty of Stralsund (1370), Denmark agreed that the selection of future Danish kings had to be approved by the Hanseatic League. Further, Hansa ships would not be subject to the Sound Toll (that is, the tax levied on ships passing through the Øresund strait).[36]

The Hanseatic League was at its height in power, but thereafter the league would see a slow decline in its strength as the formerly weak kingdoms began to consolidate their authority and control. England, the Netherlands, Denmark, Norway, Prussia, Russia and finally Sweden gradually usurped the league's dominance of the northern waters.[37] By the beginning of the Thirty Years' War (1618), the league's once far-flung commercial empire included only three cities—Lübeck, Hamburg and Bremen. Sliding into obscurity, the league's last general assembly was held in 1669.[38]

But the Hansa's decline was in the future. During late twelfth century, the league was in ascendance, competing with a divided and impotent Sweden. During the reigns of Knut Eriksson (1167–1196), Sverker the Younger (1196–1208) and Erik Knutsson (1208–1216) the Uppland nobles schemed to keep the monarchy weak.

Johan Sverkersson died at age 21, having been king since he was 15 (1216–1222). The next king came to the throne at an even younger age: Erik Erikson was made monarch at six years old. He was removed seven years later, before he had even come of age. His replacement, Knut Holmgersson, died five years later, whereupon Erik was reinstalled as king (Erik XI).[39] Thus, the monarchy remained impotent thanks to the Uppland nobility.

As the Sverker and Erik clans clashed over dominance of the monarchy, a new faction grew in strength to the point of becoming a major factor in the country's politics. This was the Roman Catholic Church. As early as the reign of Sverker the Younger (1196–1208), special privileges were granted the Church and clergy. Erik Knutsson (1208–1216) was the first king to be anointed with holy oil at his coronation, thereby accepting the church's protection for his throne and kingdom. His authority was confirmed by Rome as proceeding from the will of God. In return the crown granted the church exemption from all taxes and duties. The monarchy thus established an alliance with the church, providing political advantages to both.[40]

It was not as if the church and crown were one, however. At the Skänninge Assembly of 1248, a papal legate decreed that all bishops, priests, monks and clerics owed their allegiance to the pope alone. They were exempt from swearing any oath of fealty to the Swedish king. The church, therefore, maintained its separation from the crown and a certain independence.[41] This fractured governmental situation was an open invitation for meddling by Sweden's neighbors: Norway, Denmark and the German states.

The jarl of Mälaren, meanwhile, gathered to his office more and more power. He ruled the Lake Mälaren district, the key trade center for all of central Sweden. The jarl's campaigns in Finland likewise proceeded apace. In 1238 Satakunda and Tavastland were conquered, and the fortress of Tavasthus was built to maintain the subjugation of these Finns.[42] Finland was treated as the jarl's personal fief.

Under King Erik Eriksson (Erik XI, the Lame or Lisper) the jarl of Mälaren was an especially capable individual. Birger Jarl was a descendent of the house of Sverker who was also married the king's sister. Thus he was tied to both the ruling families. And, as was the practice, he was free to make war in Finland where and when he pleased. Having subdued most of the Finnish tribes, the Swedes had worked their way to the border of Novgorod. In 1236 Birger Jarl led a crusade incited by the pope against the Orthodox Russians of Novgorod.[43] The campaign was repelled at the Battle of the Neva and came to naught. In 1250 Birger Jarl was again campaigning in southwestern Finland when he received word that King Erik had died and his own son, Vlademar, had been elected as the new monarch.[44]

Vlademar I initiated a new line of Swedish kings: the Folkung dynasty. The Folkung clan, interestingly, was not from Uppland, but rather from Västergötland and Östergötland.[45] Apparently the merger of the Svear and Gauts was by this time complete. The Folkung kings were as follows:

1250–1275	Vlademar I (Birgersson)
1275–1290	Magnus III of Sweden (Birgersson), Ladulås (Barn-Locker)
1290–1318	Birger of Sweden (Magnusson)
1319–1364	Magnus IV (Eriksson, Smek)
1364–1395	Albrecht of Mecklenburg (ended the Folkung dynasty)[46]

The newly elected king, Vlademar I, was only an infant, a ploy likely instigated by the nobility to maintain a hold on the government. If that was their intention, however, it failed miserably. The child king's father, Birger Jarl, arrived in Stockholm from the year-long campaign in Finland to secure the throne for his son and act as regent until they boy reached maturity. As regent and jarl, Birger suddenly found himself in control of two of the reins of the government, a position of power not seen in Sweden since the days of the early Yngling kings.[47]

The nobility and the Germans recognized that this concentration of power could be a problem and began to assemble an army to deal with the situation. They were backed by a faction of the Folkung clan that regarded Birger Jarl as an illegitimate clan leader. However, Birger already had a core fighting force in the battle-hardened troops he had led in his Finnish campaign. To this he added levees raised from Swedish supporters who saw in the new king and his father an opportunity to best the Uppland nobles and the German foreigners.

The two armies met at Herrevad Bridge in 1251 in Västmanland, where the Kolbäck River flows into Lake Mälaren. According to tradition, this was the first use of Swedish cavalry in a pitched battle.[48] Birger Jarl's troops crushed the rebel army, and the leaders (Filip Knutsson, Knut Magnusson and Filip Pettersson) were beheaded after being captured.[49] The jarl then proceeded to put to the sword all the opposing nobility and any pretenders to the throne who might threaten his son's claim to the Swedish crown.[50]

With the nobility under control, Birger moved to counter the German threat by negotiating alliances with Norway (1254) and Denmark (1257). To cement these ties, he married his daughter, Rikissa, to the Norwegian heir, Häkon Häkonsson, and his son, Vlademar, to the Danish princess, Sofia. After the death of his own wife, he married Mechtild, the widow of the Danish king, Abel.[51]

To curb German commercial influence over Sweden, Birger established trade agreements with Henry III of England, and he made treaties with Lübeck and Hamburg defining trade relations between Sweden and these Hansa cities.[52]

With foreign and domestic adversaries thus checked, Birger Jarl turned to reforming Swedish government and society. During the late Viking period, each region of the country was obliged to provide a certain number of men to serve aboard the king's ships, similar to the Norwegian conscript system developed by Harald Fairhair in the early tenth century. Birger converted this service obligation to a tax paid to the crown, giving the monarchy a means of supporting itself.[53]

With the support of the church, Birger instituted legal reforms that banned the practice of private revenge killings, a tradition dating back to well before the Viking Age.[54] He doubled the penalties for crimes against women, the church, homes and the meeting of the Things.[55] He also abolished the ordeal by fire used in administering justice.[56] All this was part of the transformation of Swedish society that had been going on since the Viking Age.[57]

Though most of Birger Jarl's actions involved Sweden as a whole, as jarl of the Lake Mälaren district, he took a special interest in this area. And very early, perhaps even before becoming regent, he recognized the strategic importance of a rocky island located between two streams that flowed from Lake Mälaren into the Baltic. In 1250, shortly after gaining power, Birger began constructing a fort on the island. This stronghold would control access to the lake from the sea and thus dominate commerce between central Sweden and the outside world.

But Birger wanted more; he envisioned a city to rival the Hansa commercial centers in trade and shipping. To do this, he would have to give concessions to merchants to entice them to come to the outpost but without losing his own control—a fine line, to be sure. In the treaty of 1252 with Lübeck, Birger granted German merchants the right to trade at the site without paying custom fees. They were also given tax-free status. The outpost was, for all practical purposes, an open free-port.

In addition, traveling German merchants would be subject to German law. But any permanent residents would be considered Swedish subjects and would fall under Swedish jurisdiction. The community would be governed by a council, half to be Swedish and the other half German.

Germans from Lübeck flocked to the new city, and Stockholm flourished from its inception. Although 35–40 percent of the city's population was German and they dominated trade, Birger Jarl maintained control; Stockholm never became a member of the Hanseatic League. The Lübeck Germans thus gained a commercial advantage in central and northern Swedish trade, and Birger built his city.[58]

Upon Birger Jarl's death in 1266, Vlademar I became king in fact as well as in name. He seems to have accomplished nothing of note and is remembered mostly for his sexual liaison with his sister-in-law, Princess Jutta of Denmark. The princess had previously been confined to the nunnery at Roskilde in Denmark, a circumstance not entirely to her liking. She escaped and fled to her sister and brother-in-law at the Swedish court. Jutta is reputed to have been a beauty and quickly attracted the attention of Vlademar, who apparently had an eye for the ladies, though none of his other dalliances reached the same level of scandal. Vlademar's liaisons with the runaway nun produced a child, perhaps two, which was the great royal scandal of thirteenth-century Sweden.[59]

To make amends for his misdeed, Vlademar traveled to Rome, where he pledged fealty to the pope, Clement IV. His penance was to levy a tax on the Swedish people to be paid directly to Rome. Attempts to collect the tax met with adamant resistance among the Swedes and were used by Vlademar's enemies as an excuse to revolt. Vlademar's three brothers saw this as an opportunity to dispose of their sibling and, with Danish backing, led a rebellion. Vlademar was defeated in the ensuing battle and fled to Norway. Later he tried to make a comeback, supported by Danish factions loyal to his wife. He managed to seize some Swedish territory but was eventually routed, captured and imprisoned at Nyköpingshus fortress, where he died in 1302.[60]

The crown devolved to the next brother in line, Magnus. Another brother, Erik, died a short time later, and Bengt, the third brother, was given Finland as his fief. The rule of Finland was available because, following Birger Jarl's death, the office of jarl of the Mälaren district had been abolished by the nobles to prevent another such concentration of power from occurring. Thus Bengt was given the office of duke of Finland.

The nobility's attempt to keep any one person from gaining a majority of the political power in Sweden was a forlorn undertaking. The changing social structure of the country had already established a natural concentration of power in the king's hands, ready to be exploited by a strong personality. Magnus Birgersson would prove to be such a man.

Since the end of the Viking Age, Swedish society had been shifting. In Viking times there had been only two classes: slaves (thralls) and freemen. As we've seen, slavery disappeared due to the influence of the church and the lack of a reliable slave market. At the same time a few families in Sweden grew rich in land and resources far above that of the common freeman. These magnet families were called upon by the king to provide the heavy cavalry he needed for his medieval army, thus creating a warrior class. The status of this class was confirmed by King Magnus when he introduced the order of knighthood.[61]

In the new class structure, the king was at the pinnacle, and just beneath him was the new privileged class of nobility, the magnet families who supplied the knights in exchange for being exempt from paying taxes and duties. Also exempt were the church and clergy. Beneath this layer of society came the town burgers, still few in number and possessing little power.[62]

Lowest of all, supporting the entire social structure, was the mass of peasantry, the common folk (the *folket*), some 95 percent of the population.[63] Among the peasants were the small landowners and the landless peasants who worked for the largest estates or as "servants" for the small landowners. But even these landless peasants were not serfs in the sense that peasants were in Southern and Central Europe. They were still freemen able to move about at will, and they had the rights of freemen under the law. It was they who settled Ångermanland in northern Sweden and Österbotten and Nyland in Finland.

Magnus Birgersson had himself crowned in the Uppsala cathedral, securing the support of the Church of Rome and confirming that his rule was by divine right. He suppressed a revolt led by the Old Folkung clan, beheading the leaders (including two brothers, Johan and Birger Filipsson). Magnus invoked the old Roman law of treason (*lése majesté*) in this case, used for the first time in Sweden. Magnus then took for his wife the countess Hedvig of Holstein and had her crowned as the first queen of Sweden. The coronation took place at Söderköping in 1281 with such pomp and feasting that the fires got out of hand and burned down the town.[64] Though the king was still technically an elected office, Magnus did everything he could to secure the throne for his progeny.

Magnus' governmental reforms were many and had a lasting effect on the country. Besides creating the order of knighthood, he officially recognized the nobility in establishing a council of state called the *Riksens Råd*, made up of chosen leaders from the magnet families. The institution of the Råd would become an important, and at times dominant, faction in the Swedish government.[65]

Magnus held several feudal assemblies during his reign. These were supposed to represent the people of the realm, but in reality only members of the nobility were invited. This was the embryo, however, from which the later general assemblies would grow, which included the estates of the church, burgers and peasants in addition to the nobility.

King Magnus is remembered not just for governmental reforms but also for his protection of the common people, the peasants of Sweden. Most notable was his *Alsö Decree*, which instituted the "barn-lock." Since pre–Viking times it had been the tradition that peasants were obliged to feed and house any traveling lords, bishops, troops or men-at-arms and their retinues that stopped by, without recompense. This included feeding and stabling the horses and providing food and drink for the traveler and his train. But this practice of supplying hospitality was being abused to the point of becoming outright banditry. The accommodating peasant was often deprived of all his goods, stock and winter food storage. A single "visit" could leave a commoner or even a petty noble destitute and facing starvation.[66]

Magnus' decree was supposed to "put a lock on the barn door,"[67] protecting the peasants from such travesties. It was a noble attempt and gained him the title *Ladulås* (Barn-Locker), but longstanding traditions are hard to change with a single decree. It would take the activism of several kings before this type of outright robbery was finally curbed in Sweden.

To ensure that the throne would stay in his family, Magnus arranged to have his oldest son elected king (actually second king) when the lad was only four years of age. He also appointed a guardian who would rule until the young King Birger Magnusson came of age. When Magnus Ladulås died in 1290, Birger was only 10 years old, and Lord High Constable Torgils Knutsson ruled as regent to the end of the thirteenth century.[68]

Torgils seems to have been a capable and well-meaning leader, though Sweden suffered a couple of misfortunes in these last decades of the century. Crops failed due to adverse weather conditions. Plague also spread across the countryside, and there is evidence of starvation and misery among the general population.[69] But these were conditions outside the control of the Lord High Constable.

Torgils expanded Swedish territory in Finland, conquering the heathen Karelians and bringing them into the Christian fold. The Karelians were portrayed as an especially cruel and barbaric people who flayed their captured enemies alive and extracted their entrails to be eaten raw—certainly a people in need of salvation.[70] To secure this new section of the Swedish empire, Torgils built the strong fortress of Viborg, which would be of great strategic importance in Sweden's future.

With King Birger's coming of age, a power struggle ensued between the three sons of Magnus Ladulås. But before they could vie against one another, they had to rid themselves of the Lord High Constable, who still wielded much of the governmental power. King Birger seems to have had no qualms about intriguing against his former guardian and protector. Likewise, his brother Valdemar was a willing conspirator even though he was married to Torgils' daughter Kristina. The third son, Erik, certainly had no compunctions about joining in the plot and may have been the organizer.

On December 6, 1305, a company that included the three royal brothers attacked Torgils' estate at Lena outside Stockholm. The Lord High Constable was taken alive and transported, hanging upside-down under the belly of a horse, from Lena to Stockholm, where he was thrown into prison. On February 10, 1306, without the benefit of a trial or even formal accusations, Torgils Knutsson was beheaded and his body buried in a cemetery for common criminals.[71] Later, his corpse was exhumed by the Gray Monks of Stockholm and reinterred in their monastery graveyard with a headstone that read, "He who rests here was condemned innocent."[72]

With the Lord High Constable out of the way, the three brothers turned to dividing up the spoils. Birger, of course, was king, but Duke Erik proceeded to carve out his own kingdom along the Göta River in western Sweden. Valdemar appropriated various other sections of the country until Sweden seemed to be ruled by three monarchs, each with his own realm.

Given the greed of the three brothers, this triumvirate would not last long. The two dukes soon entered into a scheme to eliminate their rival for the throne of all Sweden. On September 29, 1306, only six months after Torgils' demise, they acted.[73] King Birger was celebrating St. Michael's Day with his wife, Queen Märta, and their children at the royal estate of Håtuna when his two brothers arrived, accompanied by their men-at-arms. The newcomers were at first welcomed to the feast, but very quickly the visit turned ugly. The dukes seized the king and his party, which included the bishop of Västerås, Nils Kettilson (a future archbishop). The king, queen, bishop and their servants were abducted and thrown into the dungeons of Nyköping Castle. The only member of the royal family to escape was Birger's oldest son, young Lord Magnus, who was hustled away by an alert servant and taken to Denmark to the court of King Erik, his mother's father.

Traditionally, crimes committed on Sunday and holy days were considered especially heinous, particularly if the victims were in the midst of a celebratory feast. Thus, this crime committed by the dukes was condemned as especially egregious and became known as the *Håtunaleken* (Håtuna Games).[74]

The Håtuna Games ushered in a period of war and deprivation for the Swedish peasant population. King Erik Menved of Denmark attempted to free his son-in-law by force of arms, but he succeeded only in ravaging southern Västergötland. The next year

Erik Menved again invaded Sweden, and there was actually a battle at which dukes Erik and Valdemar took flight, though no rescue was effected for King Birger.

The following year, 1309, both Denmark and Norway invaded Sweden. Håkan of Norway plundered Dalsland while Danish armies ravaged Östergötland and Södermanland. Duke Erik retaliated by pillaging parts of Norway.[75]

It is reported that while the dukes ruled, they staged lavish jousting tournaments, held elaborate courts and sponsored splendid feasts in an attempt to emulate the monarchies of their Southern European neighbors. Such extravagance was expensive and again was borne by the peasants through a new tax, the *Markgäld* (land tax).

Finally, in 1310, with the Swedish kingdom in near ruin, King Birger came to an agreement with his captors. Sweden would be split three ways, between the brothers, each having his own share of the country. This compromise seems to have at least quelled the repeated invasions by Sweden's neighbors. But even more taxes were levied to keep the government solvent. When Gotland refused to pay the added assessment, Duke Erik sent an army to the island to enforce collections, resulting in the usual plundering.

In the midst of this misery inflicted on the general population, the dukes decided to celebrate a double wedding complete with all the lavish pomp they could extract from medieval Sweden. Erik would marry Princess Ingeborg, daughter of King Håkon of Norway, age 11. Duke Valdemar, having put aside his former wife, Torgils' daughter, would marry Håkon's niece, also named Ingeborg, age 15. The double wedding took place in the Norwegian capital of Oslo on September 29, 1312, the sixth anniversary of the Håtuna Games.[76]

Four years later, both duchesses bore their husbands sons. Duke Erik named his son Magnus, and it was this child who would ultimately come to rule the largest kingdom in Europe. Now the dukes both had heirs capable of challenging Birger's own son, Magnus, for the crown. Birger had to act quickly if he were ever to recover sole authority over Sweden, and with these three brothers, intrigues and deceptions were the order of the day.

King Birger and Queen Märta were holding court at Nyköping Castle during the fall of 1317, where they intended to stay through Christmas. They invited the two dukes and their families to a banquet in honor of the holy season. So the three brothers gathered at Nyköping for a celebratory feast on December 10, 1317, a festival that would become known as the Nyköping Banquet. The party lasted well into the night, with a good deal of drinking and dancing.[77]

As the evening wore on and the participants grew weary, Birger arranged for the dukes' entourages to be quartered in the town on the pretext that there was insufficient room for all of them at the castle. The dukes then retired to their own rooms in the castle, inebriated, exhausted and completely defenseless.

In the middle of the night, a company of the king's men, led by Johan von Brunkow, rousted the two dukes from their beds, beat them and threw them into the Nyköping dungeon, where they were shackled in neck and leg irons. The king, in his moment of triumph, is said to have shouted to von Brunkow:

> Marshal mine, the Spirit be blessed;
> Now of all Sweden I'm possessed.[78]

This poetic pronouncement sounds almost Shakespearean.

Birger's elation was to be short lived, however, for all over Sweden his brothers' supporters rebelled against him. Armies gathered in Västergötland, Småland and Uppland.

King Birger, meanwhile, had left Nyköping Castle with his two brothers chained to the dungeon wall and left to die. Birger then moved his court to Stegeborg. The rebel forces converged on Stegeborg only to find the fortress commanded by the king's son, Lord Magnus, who had returned from Denmark to aid his father. The king was on his way to Gotland. The dukes' men eventually took Stegeborg, capturing Lord Magnus. On October 28, 1320, the king's son died under the headsman's axe. He was but 20 years of age.[79]

King Birger Magnusson, perpetrator of the infamous Nyköping Banquet, eventually made his way to Denmark, where he engaged in intrigues at the royal court, scheming for a return to his Swedish throne.[80]

Finally, in August 1318, the dukes' supporters stormed Nyköping Castle only to find the corpses of the two brothers still chained to the dungeon wall. The royal guests of the Nyköping Banquet had starved to death.[81]

As if the commoners of Sweden had not suffered enough, the outcome of the Nyköping Banquet was a brutal and devastating civil war pitting the king's supporters against the dukes' followers. The king of Denmark, Erik Menved, sent an army in support of King Birger, whereas King Håkon of Norway sent troops to support his son-in-law's side. And the Swedish peasantry were robbed, burned out and left with added burdens to bear.

The bloodletting and devastation was ended, finally, with the death of King Birger in Denmark in 1321 and the settling of the question of who would claim the crown. Norway's King Håkon had died in 1319, leaving his kingdom to his three-year-old grandson, Magnus Eriksson, son of Duke Erik.[82] On July 8 of that same year, the infant king of Norway was elected king of Sweden at Mara Mead outside Uppsala by an assembly that included not just the nobility but also the estate of the commoners. This is been called by many historians Sweden's first parliament.[83]

Magnus Eriksson (Magnus IV of Sweden and Magnus the VII of Norway) was now, technically, the sovereign of both Norway and Sweden, which included Finland. He would rule for 46 years (1319–1365), Sweden's longest-reigning monarch, besting Gustav V (1907–1950) by three years.[84]

For the first thirteen years of his reign, control was in the hands of a regency of nobles headed by Matts Kettilmundsson, chief advisor to Magnus' father, Duke Erik. At last peace settled over the land, and the regency seems to have done an adequate job of governing, albeit with one exception: the national treasury was drained. When Magnus, at age 16, took the reins of the government, he was head of a country quite destitute. Financial problems would be a constant source of trouble during his reign.

To maintain his government and his throne, King Magnus borrowed a large sum from the Hansa city of Lübeck. To pay back this loan, he arranged an even larger advance from the papal treasury. When this sum could not be repaid, Magnus was excommunicated.[85] In spite of these financial woes, however, King Magnus did not hesitate to expand his dominions when the opportunity arose.

For a time Denmark was ruled by the counts of Holstein, who mismanaged the country's finances to the point of insolvency. Their solution was to offer up Scania (including Blekinge and Halland) for sale. The transfer would solve two problems for the counts—one financial, the other political. The Scanians had been restive for some time, agitating for independence. In 1332 Magnus acquired Scania for 34,000 marks of silver—probably an exorbitant price, and certainly a lot of money for an impoverished government to pay.[86] Magnus Eriksson now ruled an empire stretching from Norway to Karelia, from North Cape to the Øresund, an immense empire, the largest in Europe at the time.

Since Magnus' empire included Norway, it also included Iceland and, by extension, Greenland. Here, at the extreme edge of medieval Europe, the islanders struggled to survive. Magnus seems to have taken a special interest in this remote outpost of the old Viking world and did what he could to maintain a connection. It was he who sent the ship (or ships) under Ivar Bardarson to investigate the status of the Greenland colony. Upon his arrival, Bardarson found that the western settlement had been overrun by the Skraelings. Under Magnus' stewardship the Greenland carrier (*Grænlands knörr*) made its annual trading run to the island, but in 1368, three years after he was deposed, the royal trading ship sank, cutting off the last regular contact with the Greenlanders.[87]

Iceland, however, not only survived but also flourished, establishing a republic in the tenth century and producing its golden age of literature in the eleventh and twelfth centuries. However, in the early thirteenth century conflict developed between the five magnet families of the island. Civil war ensued, causing many deaths and the devastation of farmlands. To put an end to the burnings and killings, the Icelanders invited the Norwegian king to rule over them, and in 1262 Iceland became a subject of the Norwegian crown. Thus, when Magnus became king of Norway, he also inherited Iceland and gained responsibility for the Greenland colony.

The first two decades of King Magnus' reign were a time of peace and prosperity for the Swedish people. The king married a beautiful woman, Countess Blanche (Blanka) of Namur (in today's Belgium). The court held by the royal couple was more cultured than earlier Swedish courts, an imitation of some of the European courts to the south. The marriage produced two sons, Erik and Häkan, a necessity for Magnus to continue the Folkung line.

The Swedish people—indeed, the population of the whole empire—enjoyed a period of relative peace, a chance to regain some prosperity.

Sweden's administrative justice system was reformed. A code of laws applying uniformly to the whole country was established, the foundation of Sweden's first constitution. Slavery was also legally abolished. Among the provisions was the important Magnus Eriksson Land Law, which dealt with land ownership, and there was a royal oath outlining the king's duties to his people.[88]

Once again the practice of traveling nobility extorting hospitality from peasants was addressed. Clearly, Magnus Ladulås' decree to "lock the barn door" had not been sufficient. Magnus IV issued two decrees on this subject, one in 1335 and a second in 1344. By these decrees, no one was permitted to travel with "great flocks." A bishop was allowed a retinue of 30 horses. Knights and squires were permitted twelve, and anyone below these ranks could only have six. Royal officials were allowed 45 unless accompanied by the king. Some form of entourage was necessary as protection from the highwaymen, thieves and robbers who infested the forested roads and trails, but commoners who were obliged to accommodate visitors were to have some protection of their lives and property as well. Noble travelers who resorted to violence in obtaining peasant hospitality were to be severely punished.[89]

King Magnus even had his own prophet, or, in this case, prophetess, in the person of Birgitta Birgersdotter, better known to the outside world as St. Birgitta, or Bridget of Sweden. She was a distant relative of Magnus' and for a time served as mistress of the king's household. Her relationship to Magnus was that of the Old Testament prophets to the kings of Israel: able to give advice from a spiritual perspective and quick to condemn if the king strayed from the straight and narrow.

Magnus Eriksson's reign began with much promise, and it was generally a time of prosperity for the people. However, his empire soon began to come apart. Early on, Magnus had problems wresting authority from the regency that had ruled during his minority, the members of which were loath to concede such power. A struggle ensued, with Magnus pushing to reassert the authority of the monarchy.[90]

At the same time, Magnus had problems with his mother, Duchess Ingeborg, who was a power-hungry woman trying to gain a position of influence in the government. It was she who arranged a marriage between the king's sister, Eufemia, and Albrecht of Mecklenburg. This alliance with a powerful German state seemed to be an advantageous move, but it would prove to be a problem for Sweden and a disaster for Magnus.[91]

King Magnus' purchase of Scania, with its fertile coastal lowlands, thriving fisheries, the prosperous city of Malmö and at least partial control of the Øresund Strait, was at first glance a judicious move. However, paying the 34,000-mark debt placed additional financial strain on a country already in severe economic straits.

Magnus also began to lose the respect of the general populace. This was partly due to rumors concerning his personal life. After the birth of his two sons, it was reported that Magnus had abandoned the royal conjugal bed. Whether this platonic marital arrangement was at the request of the queen or Magnus, or even whether it was true at all, is not known with certainty.

Additionally, the king was rumored to have had a homosexual relationship with a handsome young knight, Duke Bengt Algotsson. It is true that the duke was favored and promoted above others by Magnus, but there is no proof of an affair. Still, the king's enemies, principally the nobles, perpetuated and spread these slanderous rumors. It was enough to excite St. Birgitta's condemnation. She turned on the queen for not producing more heirs—the reason, in Birgitta's view, she had come to Sweden. Blanche's sinful French education and habit of wasting time in vain self-indulgences, jewelry, makeup and frivolous conversation did nothing to endear her to the prophetess.

In her *Revelations*, St. Birgitta attacked the king for engaging in the most unnatural vices, warning of his impending doom for such wrongdoing. The whole episode was sufficient to earn the king the nickname of "Magnus Smek" (Magnus the Fondler), which has stuck as a blot on his legacy.[92]

As the 1340s waned and Magnus' reign became encumbered with these internal problems, national debt, high taxes and the damage to the monarchy's credibility, the specter of war rose along Sweden's eastern borders. To understand this conflict, we must catch up on happenings in Eastern Europe during the High Middle Ages (1000–1299).

33

Eastern Europe in the Middle Ages

As we have already noted, by the mid-fourteenth century the Teutonic Knights, the Brothers of the Sword and Denmark had conquered the southeastern and eastern coast of the Baltic, sealing off Swedish access to the Eastern European trade routes they formerly dominated. The Swedish mercantile network was commandeered by the Hanseatic League, which now controlled Baltic and North Sea commerce.

For a time the two crusading orders (the Teutonic Knights and Brothers of the Sword) were united under one grandmaster, absorbing Estonia so that the eastern Baltic from Prussia to the Gulf of Finland was under one rule. The order also took Dorpat, the important commercial city in Estonia founded by Yaroslav of Kiev.[1]

To the south of the Teutonic order's Prussia lay the kingdom of Poland, which had developed a strong centralized government as early as the middle of the tenth century under its first king, Mieszko I.[2] Poland became Christian in AD 966, accepting the Roman pontiff as its spiritual leader. After a period of fragmentation and domination by outside governments, Poland reasserted itself in 1320 under King Wladyslaw Lokietek (the Dwarf), who again establish a strong monarchy. By 1340 Poland was ruled by his son, Kazimir the Great, also known as Kazimir III (1333–1370). His reign was a period of relative peace and prosperity for the country. The rule of law was established, roads were improved, and inns along the byways were built. Cracow (Kraków) was beautified and fortified, and Cracow University was founded in 1364.[3] Poland had taken its place as one of the major kingdoms of Eastern Europe.

Poland was in constant state of conflict with the Teutonic order, which had, by 1370, taken control of the Baltics and Prussia, having consolidated its hold over the Estonians, the Letts (Latvians), the Semigalls, and the Prussians. The knights promoted the German trade center of Riga until it became one of the major commercial cities of the Hanseatic League. The one group that escaped the knights' dominance was the Lithuanians, who were able to melt into their native forest, thus evading conquest.

Another reason the Lithuanians were able to maintain their independence was their very lack of unity. Generally located around the town of Vilna, they were divided into tribes, each with its own chief. There was no central authority to conquer and take over. The adaptable Lithuanian tribes could move, reform and stay away from the knights and their crusades with relative ease.

To the east were the Russian principalities. We last discussed the empire of the Rus at the death of Yaroslav in 1054, the last ruler of the water road with direct connections to Sweden. Yaroslav tried to bequeath his lands to his sons in such a way that they would have to depend on each other to survive. He called upon his progeny to preserve family unity. This division of the empire work reasonably well for the first generation of princes, primarily because of the threat from a new Asiatic people, the Kipchak Turks, also called the Polovtsy or Cumans, who replaced the Petchenegs as the primary menace to the Russian princes.[4] They dominated the areas between the Urals and the Volga and to the south along the Black Sea, north of the Caucasus and Caspian Sea. An eastern branch of the Cumans ranged to the east of the Urals into Central Asia.

After a period of division and squabbling between the Russian princes, one Vladimir Monomakh rose to power as Grand Prince of Kiev. He led a series of crusades against the heathen Cumans. In 1101, 1103 and again in 1111, Monomakh challenged the Cumans on their own ground and won.[5] The Cumans, if not conquered, were at least controlled, and their destructive raids were kept to a minimum.

Monomakh was followed by his son, Mstislav I (1125–1132), who abided by his father's admonition and attacked the Cumans but otherwise promoted peace among the Russian princes. There followed, however, a series of weak rulers in Kiev, with the result that the citizens of Kiev often chose their own prince. Outlying principalities gained in strength, challenging Kiev for the right of leadership. Vladimir in the northeast, Galicia in the southwest and the commercial city of Novgorod in the north all grew to be political centers. Beside these strong points, there were over a hundred princes, each with his own principality and fighting companies, or druzhiny, which had to be supported by the peasants. These princes were all interrelated and did, on occasion, display family loyalty and mutual support, but there was also sufficient feuding to keep the Empire of the Rus in constant turmoil. This instability, combined with the annual raids of the Cumans, led to the inevitable destruction of vital trade routes. Gradually, the Russian princes turned more and more to agriculture as a source of riches. Land was wealth, to be jealously guarded and preserved, a penchant of long standing among the Slavic peoples. Only in Novgorod did trade remain the basis for prosperity.[6]

This new emphasis on agriculture elevated the Slavic peasant in importance. He spread into the forests of northern and central Russia, combining with the Finno-Ugric people scattered across the area in small groups. Together they cleared the forests and brought the Russian lands under cultivation.

Of the three new power centers—Vladimir, Galicia, and Novgorod—Vladimir in the northeast on the Volga tributaries came to dominate, replacing Kiev as the location of the grand prince. Its newfound importance, however, was to be short lived. Far away in the Gobi Desert of Mongolia, events were unfolding that would have a cataclysmic impact on Russian history in particular and Eastern Europe in general.

Temüchin was the son of the chief of a minor Tartar tribe roaming the steppes north of China. His birth date is uncertain, perhaps 1155 or 1167. In spite of the death of his father while he was still a boy, Temüchin managed to collect about him a troop of young warriors and adventurers, with whose aid he began to take control of the tribes of the steppes. By 1206 Temüchin had made himself master of the Turko-Mongolian tribes of Mongolia, assuming the title of Genghis Khan.[7]

After consolidating his control of the eastern steppe people and developing his military machine, Genghis Khan turned his attention to China, the real prize and perennial objective of the northern barbarians. China of the early thirteenth century was divided into three empires: the Hsi Hsia in the northwest; the Chin in the northeast, which included Yen-Ching (Peking); and the Southern Sung Empire, the richest and most populous of the three. Genghis Khan conquered the Hsi Hsia kingdom between 1205 and 1209, but he left the local rulers in place. In 1211 he attacked the Chin Empire, which included Manchuria and Korea. He destroyed their capital Yen-Ching, acquiring the services of many learned men schooled in Chinese skills, such as mining, commerce, raising revenues through taxation and the art of conducting sieges.[8]

The conquest of the Chin Empire was a slow process. It would not be accomplished until 1234, after the great Khan's death. However, at the same time that he launched his campaign against the Chin, Genghis began operations westward into Central Asia and beyond into Eastern Europe.[9]

In 1218 Genghis Khan sent his general Jebe Noyan against the Buddhist Qara-Khitai Empire of Central Asia. This once powerful empire was already in decline. In 1210 it had lost the lands of Transoxiana, which included the rich trading cities of Bukhārā and Samarkand, to the rising power of the Khwarazm-shah (Khwarizmian) Empire to the south. Jebe, leading the efficient Mongol armies, quickly dispatched all Qara-Khitai resistance, adding the empire's territories to Genghis Khan's domains.[10]

Having conquered the Qara-Khitai Empire, the next target to be eliminated was

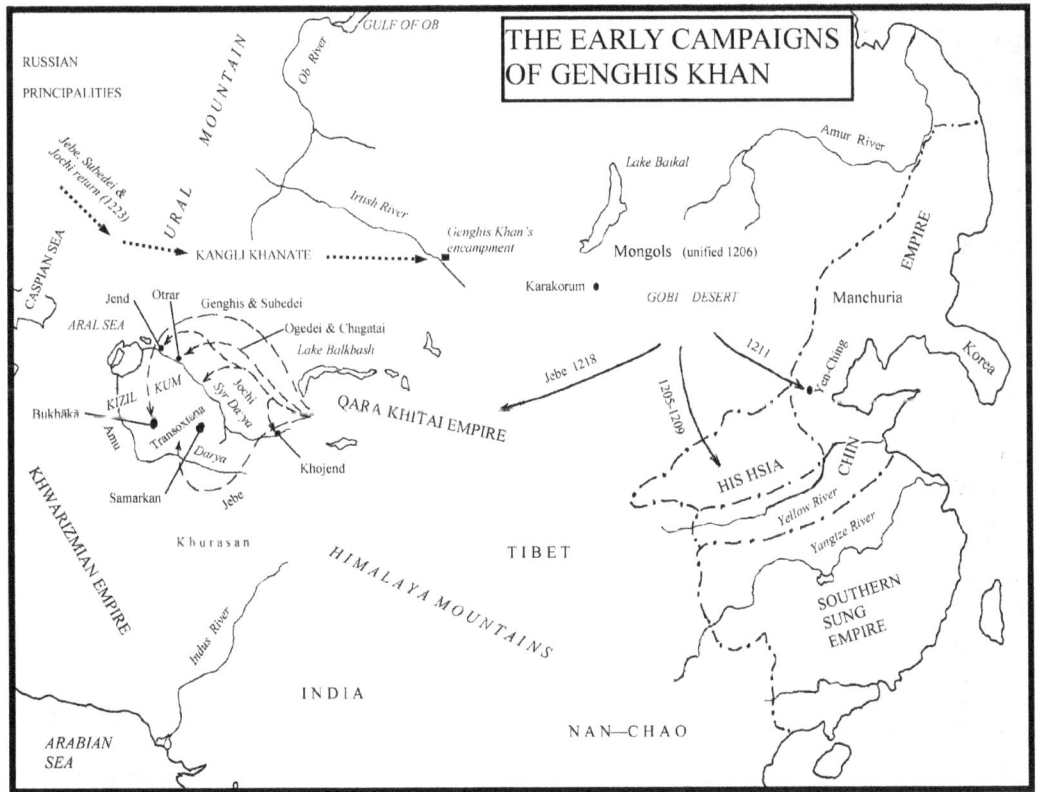

the empire of Ali ad-Din, Muhammad II of Khwarizm. Muhammad had amassed a huge empire stretching from the Persian Gulf and the Caspian Sea to the Indus River. His recent acquisition of Transoxiana gave him control of the east-west trade routes and the rich city of Samarkand, with its population of over 500,000.[11]

Through totally inept diplomacy, or maybe he was spoiling for a fight, Muhammad managed to provide the Mongols with excuse enough to attack. A Mongol caravan was ambushed, the merchants slain and the cargo looted. Muhammad seems to have been confident of his ability to take on the eastern power with his four-hundred-thousand-man Khwarizmian army supported by Turkish and Persian auxiliaries. In addition, he commanded thousands of armed slaves. This host was drawn up along the Syr Darya as a defensive line supplied by caravans of camels and elephants. Muhammad's cavalry was mounted on splendid thoroughbred horses, and his infantry was armed with forged steel weapons and burnished shields.[12] Muhammad must have thought such an army was invincible.

The Mongol invasion plan was devised by the khan's brilliant general, Subedei Bahadur. The two-hundred-thousand-man Mongol army would be split into four corps, each with its own artillery, Chinese engineers and siege equipment. The first corps, led by the khan's two sons, Ogedei and Chagatai, attacked the fortress city of Otrar, the site of the massacre of the Mongol caravan that had led to the conflict. Its governor, the perpetrator of the murders and theft of gold and silver, would receive no mercy. Ogedei and Chagatai laid siege to the city, with its eighty thousand defenders, taking it in five months. Another two months were required to conquer the citadel, where the governor was taken alive to be tortured until dead.[13]

Jochi, another son of Genghis Khan, led the second corps on a campaign to tie down the main Khwarizmian army by making hit-and-run attacks all along its five-hundred-mile front (roughly the Syr Darya). At the same time he invaded the two cities of Khojend and Jend, anchoring both ends of the line, taking them in short order.

Jebe Noyan, with the third corps of 20,000 men, swung south below the Amu Darya, entering Khurasan and outflanking Muhammad's main army, which was pinned down by Jochi. He then turned north, advancing into Transoxiana from the south through lightly defended territory. Muhammad assembled his last reserves of some 50,000 men and sent them against this new threat from the south. The Khwarizmian reserve force was annihilated.

Muhammad's defenses were now in tatters. But the worst was yet to come, for now he received the astonishing report that Genghis Khan and Subedei Bahadur, at the head of the fourth corps, were at the gates of Bukhārā, some four hundred miles behind Muhammad's defensive line. The wily khan had surreptitiously crossed the Kizil Kum Desert, thought to be impenetrable, and landed right in the middle of Transoxiana.[14]

Bukhārā was taken, looted, and burned. Then all four corps converged on Samarkand, the Khwarizmian capital. It, too, fell, and Genghis Khan entered the city as conqueror on March 12, 1220. Muhammad escaped, only to die a few months later, hunted, bereft of a military and impoverished. His son, Jalal ad-Din, fled to India, but he later returned to lead the resistance against the Mongol conquest. His erratic campaigns would only further devastate his country and others in southwest Asia.[15]

Having conquered the last empire in the west that Genghis Khan considered a threat to his realm, the great khan turned his attention back to China in 1223, where there were still two empires to reduce.[16] Before departing, he ordered his generals Subedei and Jebe to take part of the army and reconnoiter the area beyond the Caspian Sea, the western steppes that led into Eastern Europe. They were to take no more than two years for this expedition and then join Jochi for the conquest of the Volga Bulgars.[17] In the meantime, Jochi would be sent to reconnoiter the northern Ural area.

Subedei and Jebe set out with 20,000 men for the Caucasus Mountains, the first obstacle in their path to Eastern Europe. They bypassed Azerbaijan, which they had raided earlier during the last stages of the conquest of Khwarizm, extracting on enormous tribute in silver and horses.[18]

Their next contact was with the kingdom of Georgia. Since Yngvarr's Swedish Viking expedition of the early eleventh century, Georgia had become a respected power in the region. The embattled King Bagrat of the Yngvarr tale had managed to maintain the incipient kingdom long enough to give it a chance to grow. Rule had been consolidated and centralized under a series of stronger monarchs, and during the reign of Queen Tamara in the late twelfth century, Georgia had gained control of much of the Transcaucasia region.[19]

In 1221, as the Mongol reconnaissance force approached the Caucasus, Queen Tamara's son ruled as George IV (Giorgi Lasha—Light of the World). He had 30,000 Cuman cavalry under arms and was preparing his renowned Knights of Georgia for participation in the Sixth Crusade called for by Pope Honorius III.[20]

As Subedei and Jebe advanced up the Kura River toward Tiflis (Tbilisi), the Georgian capital, King George led his army into the field to intercept the invaders. During the subsequent battle, the Mongols employed their classic fallback tactic, stretching the Georgian army over a great distance until they were scattered and tired from the chase. Then, mounting fresh horses (every soldier had two or three extra ponies), the Mongols turned on the Georgians, delivering a shower of arrows. The vaunted Georgian army was cut to pieces. George IV and the remnants of his forces escaped to the capital to await the expected siege.[21]

But the attack never came. The Mongols had retired back to Persia to rest and resupply. Their objective was not the conquest of Georgia but merely to cross the Caucasus in order to reach the steppes north of the Caspian Sea. Pitched battles only served to slow them down and expend precious resources.

So, after sacking Hamadan and Maragha in Persia for horses and treasure, Subedei and Jebe again headed north. This time they hugged the Caspian seacoast in the direction of Derbend instead of Tiflis. However, this was still Georgian territory, and the king felt obliged to stop the foreign incursion. He raised another army, the last of his troops, and started off in pursuit of the Mongols.

This time, when Subedei employed the usual fadeaway tactics, the Georgians maintained order, following at a discreet distance, out of range of the Mongol archers' arrows. But Subedei was leading them into a trap engineered by Jebe. The Mongol general and 5,000 horsemen had maneuvered to the rear of the Georgian army. When George turned to face the ambush from behind, Subedei reversed direction and attacked the army's flank, rolling up the Georgian line. George's army was annihilated. He and some of his guard escaped to once again hole up in Tiflis. The Mongols moved on, descending on Derbend, where they were paid off by Rashid, the shah of Shirvan, with food supplies, treasure and guides to get them through the mountains.[22]

Georgia was left defenseless. The young George IV died a short time later, leaving the kingdom in the hands of his twenty-nine-year-old sister, who was proclaimed "Maiden King" of Georgia. She had to withdraw Georgia from participation in the Sixth Crusade, explaining to the pope that the country was destitute of military resources. In fact, the defenseless mountain kingdom would be ravaged for the next six years by raids conducted by Jalal ad-Din as he led an army of brigands that was ostensibly organized to drive out the Mongols but in fact just plundered Khwarizm and its neighbors.

Having dealt with Georgia and extracted tribute from Derbend, Subedei and Jebe proceeded through the mountain passes of the Caucasus. The winter journey proved to be a test of endurance. All of their artillery and much of their supplies were lost in the mountain snowdrifts. The Mongols finally descended onto the plains, only to find that they faced an army of Cumans, Bulgars, Khazars and Alans. Subedei and Jebe were pinned at the edge of the steppes by a numerically superior army with no room to maneuver.

The Mongols offered the Cumans treasure, horses and an alliance. The Cumans accepted the gifts, broke camp and left their erstwhile allies to face the Mongols alone. Subedei and Jebe made short work of the army left behind; then they tracked down the Cumans and defeated them, recovering their treasure and horses. They subsequently sacked Astrakhan on the Volga and slaughtered the refugee Cumans they caught along the Sea of Azov. The way to the west now lay open to the Mongol reconnaissance force.[23]

During the winter of 1222 Jebe and Subedei sent patrols up and down the Dniester, ravaging the populations and spreading terror throughout the country. Scouting patrols were dispatched into Hungary to capture prisoners for interrogation. The Mongols' Chinese scholars drew up maps of Russia, Hungary, Poland, Silesia and Bohemia, conducted censuses, and surveyed crops and climate conditions. The Mongols probably knew more about Eastern Europe than the Europeans themselves did at this time.

Having gathered the information they came for, Jebe and Subedei withdrew from the Dniester in order to rendezvous with Jochi for the attack on the Volga Bulgars that was part of their mission. But the horde from the east was not to get away so easily.

After the defeat of the Cuman army by the Mongols, Kotian, overall chief of the western Cumans, led his tribes north to Kiev and Chernigov in search of allies. He was joined by Mstislav the Daring, prince of Galicia, who was married to one of Kotian's daughters. Sufficiently alarmed by the terror spread by the Mongols, other Russian princes joined Kotian—Prince Oleg of Kursk, Prince Mstislav of Kiev and Prince Mstislav of Chernigov. Grand Duke Yuri of Suzdalia would send his nephew, the prince of Rostov, with an additional army. All told, some 80,000 men were available to defeat the scourge from the east.[24]

But the Mongols were now in their element—the broad sweeping steppes where they could maneuver, taking advantage of their speed and mobility. Still, they were far outnumbered, better than four to one. To slow the pursuit, Jebe and Subedei left behind a rearguard of a thousand men under Hamabek.

The Russian and Cuman troops rendezvoused at a point on the Dnieper where Hamabek had stationed himself to watch and oppose a crossing. Before all of the contingents had arrived, Mstislav the Daring crossed the river with 10,000 of his own Galicians and his father-in-law's Cumans and attacked the Mongol rearguard. Though the Mongol archers were deadly, inflicting heavy casualties, the odds of 10–1 were too great to overcome. The Mongols, ordered to stand their ground, died to a man.

Encouraged by this early victory, the Russian-Cuman army set out in pursuit of the retreating main body of the Mongol troops. Only Prince Mstislav of Kiev was cautious enough to stop and construct a fortified camp on the east bank of the Dnieper before advancing.[25]

The Mongols slowed their retreat enough to allow their pursuers to catch up. Their archers then rode back and forth in front of and to the sides of the Russian-Cuman army, delivering a hail of arrows until gaps began to open in the enemy ranks. Into these openings Jebe and Subedei sent their heavy cavalry armed with lances.

The Cumans broke first, fleeing headlong into the Russians behind them, causing chaos. The retreat became a rout, with all organization dissolving. Prince Mstislav of Kiev, bringing up the rear, did his best to cover the retreat and probably saved countless lives as the fleeing troops boarded their galleys and rowed across the Dnieper to safety. Only the prince of Kiev stayed on the east side, taking refuge in his fortified camp. It took three days for the Mongols to reduce the fortification, slaughtering the 10,000 men inside.[26]

The Battle of Kalka left the way into Russia open, but Jebe and Subedei had received a message from Genghis Khan ordering them to find Jochi, who was somewhere near the Volga, and return to the great khan's headquarters on the Irtish River.

Jebe and Subedei moved north and found and joined Jochi and his 10,000 reinforcements. Together, they attacked the Bulgars of the Volga, the same kingdom encountered by the Varangians in Viking times. These eastern Bulgars had grown rich from trade and had come to dominate a large area in the region of the Volga and Kama rivers, suppressing and enslaving the native Finnish and Slavic populations.

The Mongols routed the eastern Bulgars of the upper Volga but did not occupy their territory. Instead, they moved east, invading the domain of the Kangli, the eastern Cumans. This last threat to the khan's empire had to be dealt with. The Kangli Khan was ultimately killed in battle, and his army was destroyed; those of his people who were not slaughtered were scattered and forced to pay a crippling indemnity.[27] The two Mongol generals and the great khan's oldest son then rode home to meet with Genghis Khan at his headquarters.[28]

As quickly as the Mongols had appeared at the doorstep of Eastern Europe, they disappeared, leaving in their wake a path of destruction, defeated armies, slaughtered inhabitants and razed cities. To the Europeans, what had seemed like imminent disaster now suddenly vanished.

The campaign to reconnoiter and test the western end of the steppes had been completed successfully, but on the way back tragedy struck: the khan's great general Jebe Noyan died of a fever.[29] Only Subedei and Jochi would ride into Genghis Khan's headquarters at the head of their victorious army.

Shortly after this, while leading a campaign against the Tanguts (Hsi-Hsia kingdom), the great khan was injured in a fall from his horse. At about the same time he received news of the death of his oldest son Jochi. Genghis Khan died in 1227, having

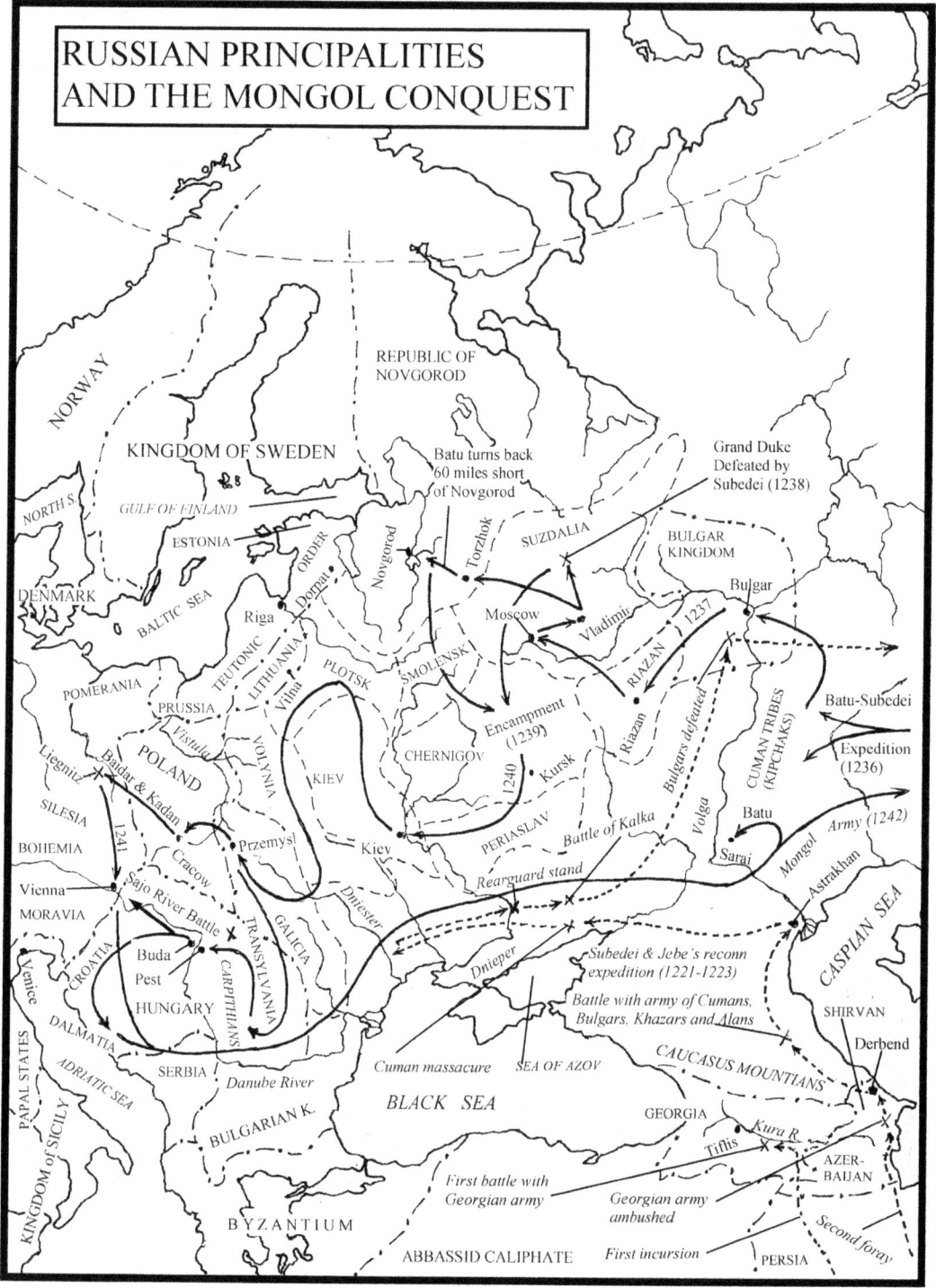

conquered Mongolia, Korea, a third of China, all of Central Asia and much of Southwestern Asia.[30]

With the death of the great khan, the Mongol Empire was parceled out among his male offspring in accordance with his will. His third son Ogedei was designated as ruler of the eastern portion of the empire and would be the overall khan. The eastern steppes, the Mongol homeland, were bequeathed to Tolui, the khan's youngest son. Chagatai, the oldest surviving son, received the southwest lands, including the territories previously part of the Khwarizm Empire. Orda and Batu, as the sons of the deceased Jochi, inherited the western steppes. Each of these progeny of the great khan would follow a program of expansion for his realm, but first there was the still-incomplete conquest of the Chin Empire to conclude. Ogedei, Tolui and the Mongol general Subedei resumed the war with the Chin. Before the final conquest in 1234, Tolui would die, a victim of his weakness for wine.[31]

In 1235 Ogedei Khan convened a council (*quriltai*) at Karakorum, the Mongol capital. Ogedei's two sons Koten and Kochu would begin operations against the Sung Empire, the last of the Chinese states left unconquered. Chagatai was already advancing into the territories of the old Khwarizm Empire with the purpose of subjugating this land, already destroyed by the Mongols. And a new campaign was agreed upon: the invasion of the western steppes, the plains of Eastern Europe.[32]

This was to be Batu's domain and his inheritance. But of all the realms left by Genghis Khan to his heirs, Batu's was the poorest. He commanded less than 20,000 warriors, and the lands that were his were not even conquered. Ogedei declared that the empire must assist Batu in a campaign to subjugate his realm. Royal *tumens* (divisions) would be provided, and the other princes would contribute troops from their provinces. This would be the empire's crusade, to vanquish territories allotted to Batu and secure the western steppes, a weak link in the Mongol defenses. Europe was finally about to feel the savagery of the Mongol fire and arrow.

Batu would be the nominal leader of the expedition, but the military genius behind the operation was the great Mongol general Subedei. He would command a fighting force of 50,000 Mongol cavalry, experienced and battle-tested troops. There were an additional 20,000 conscripts from other steppe tribes and several corps of Chinese and Persian engineers and siege experts. And there would be the usual Chinese administrators, scientists and logisticians. This formidable army formed up and moved out the spring of 1236.[33]

Advance units cleared the way by subjugating or exterminating the tribes of the Cuman Kipchaks between the Volga River and the Ural Mountains. On the middle Volga, the Mongols again met the eastern Bulgars, whom they had already defeated once. Now this Volga kingdom, which had flourished for five hundred years, faced annihilation.

The beautiful capital of the Bulgars, Bulgar, was leveled and its 50,000 inhabitants either massacred or dispersed; in the end, the kingdom was annexed as a vassal state within the Mongol Empire. By the winter of 1237, the Mongol army, 120,000 strong, stood poised on the banks of the Volga, ready to cross into Russia.

The first principality the Mongols encountered was Riazan. An army sent against them was defeated. The capital was subsequently bombarded, stormed and taken in five days. The women were systematically raped before the total population was massacred and the city burned to the ground. The other cities of Riazan received the same treatment. Terror for the Mongols was a military weapon.[34]

Next the Mongol army turned north and entered the principality of Suzdalia, taking Moscow and then attacking the real prize, the rising city of Vladimir. The assault was launched on February 7, 1238. The city fell the next day. During the resulting destruction, the royal family (except for the grand duke, who was assembling a rescue army) was burned alive in the city's cathedral.

Following the destruction of Vladimir, the Mongols split their army. Subedei marched north, surrounding and massacring the grand duke's army. Batu moved northwest to invade Novgorod. He took Torzhok after two weeks, but the delay put him into the spring thaw. Rivers flooded and the farmlands turned into marshes. The Mongol cavalry, so effective on the grassy plains of the steppes, had lost its advantage of mobility in the quagmire of the northern swamps. Just 60 miles short of Novgorod, Batu turned back; the high watermark of the Mongol northern advance had been reached. Novgorod was spared.

United again, Batu and Subedei turned south into Chernigov, where they rested on the plains, receiving horses and supplies from Mongolia. Rejuvenated, the Mongol invaders roused themselves the summer of 1240 to continue the conquest of Russia. The principalities of Chernigov and Pereiaslav were laid to waste as Riazan and Suzdalia had been—their cities destroyed, their populations massacred, the countryside burned and left desolate. By November the Mongols were at the gates of Kiev. The city was stormed and taken, plundered and destroyed. Among the ruins, only the magnificent Cathedral of St. Sophia survived. For some reason, the Mongols left it untouched, along with the tomb of Yaroslav the Wise located within its walls.

The Mongol army rampaged through Volynia and Galicia with fire and sword, leaving complete devastation in its wake until it reached the border of Hungary. Here, at Przemysl, the Mongols paused to make plans before resuming the invasion of Europe. Subedei applied his genius to the task of organizing the campaign. He would have about 100,000 men with the additions from the conquered steppe tribes that had been conscripted, trained in Mongol tactics and inducted into the army. It was decided that Baidar, the son of Chagatai, and Kadan, son of Ogedei, would lead two tumens (20,000 men) into Poland and Lithuania to distract and pin down forces on the northern flank, while the main army would advance across the Carpathian Mountains directly into Hungary.[35]

Unbelievably, in the face of this massive onslaught from the east, the European states carried on with their internal squabbling. Among other things, the Crusades to retake the Holy Land and subdue the pagans of Northeastern Europe were still ongoing. Besides the usual territorial feuds, there was also a major conflict between the pope (Gregory IX) and Frederick II, the Holy Roman Emperor. The Mongols knew the fractious nature of European politics and intended to take full advantage of it.

Bela IV of Hungary, however, was fully aware of the impending threat to his domain and did his best to prepare. He fortified the mountain passes of the Carpathian Mountains and garrisoned the emplacements with his standing army. He also had a second army of cavalry comprising Cuman warriors he had allowed to settle in Hungary after they arrived from the east, having been displaced by the Mongols. Bela's third recourse was his unruly barons, who would have to join the fight if the invasion entered Hungary proper. By the end of 1240 Bela received word that the Mongol army was on the move.

In January and February 1241, Moldavia and Wallachia were plundered and ravaged with the usual Mongol brutality. By mid–March, the Carpathian passes had been taken and Batu's main army was advancing on Pest on the Danube. Transylvania and southeastern Hungary were raped, pillaged and burned.[36]

To the north, Baidar and Kadan had invaded Poland, crushing a Polish army outside Cracow and killing Vladimir, palatine of Sandomir and Cracow. Cracow was subsequently burned to the ground. On April 9, 1241, the invaders encountered an army under Henry of Silesia at Liegnitz. This army included Poles, Teutonic Knights, Silesians, Moravians, Templars and Hospitallers. Regardless, the allied forces were routed and Henry beheaded. The Poles and Silesians were stunned into inactivity, and the Mongol northern flank was secure.[37]

By the end of March, Batu and Subedei had swept through eastern Hungary to the Danube and stood at the gates of Pest. Meanwhile, Bela was collecting his forces to counter the Mongol blitz. Then, suddenly, the Mongol horde was gone. Bela, believing the Mongols had decided that his forces were too great to defeat, and were in full retreat, ordered his army of nearly 100,000 men to pursue the "beaten foe."

The Mongols, of course, were merely withdrawing to a suitable site to engage the large Hungarian army. The inevitable battle took place at a stone bridge crossing the Sajo River. Bela built a fortified camp west of the bridge and sent patrols across the river, but they did not locate the Mongol army.

On the morning of April 11, 1241, Batu, with the main body of the Mongol army, backed by catapults used as field artillery, charged across the stone bridge to meet the Hungarians. Subedei, meanwhile, with 30,000 men, circled around the battlefield, building a wooden bridge over the Sajo. He was approaching the Hungarians from the rear. But this maneuver would take time, during which Batu had to defend himself against massed charges of, perhaps, the finest cavalry in Europe.[38]

Batu's numbers were being severely depleted when at last Subedei arrived at the Hungarian rear. Bela was trapped and in danger of being annihilated. But the Hungarians were experienced warriors and did not panic. Instead, they formed a column and fought their way back to their fortified camp.

The Mongols brought up their catapults and firebombed the camp, burning the tents and killing men and horses until many of the Hungarian barons had had enough and were ready to abandon their king. As the Mongols massed for a final assault on the camp, these renegade barons and their troops attempted a breakout. The Mongols let them pass through their lines to what seemed like freedom. But it was a ruse. Once clear of the camp and strung out in full retreat, the Mongols' light cavalry closed in and massacred the fleeing Hungarians with a shower of arrows.

The Hungarian camp was overrun in one final charge and the occupants killed. The contingent of Templars stood their ground and died to a man. In all, some 60,000 Hungarians and allies died. Bela and a few troops managed to escape to Buda on the west bank of the Danube.[39]

After their victory, the Mongols advanced on Pest, burning it to the ground. Then they pillaged the east bank of the Danube to the north and south, spreading their usual terror. Reconnaissance patrols crossed the Danube, sacked Buda, penetrated Austria to the outskirts of Vienna and advanced into Croatia and Dalmatia. The conquest of Central Europe appeared to be almost a certainty.

Then, just as the ultimate doom of Europe seemed imminent, the Mongol hordes pulled back from Austria and Croatia and disappeared from their Danube front. Hungary and Transylvania were abandoned. But as the hordes retreated, they once again delivered a blow with fire and sword, leaving an already desolate land a wilderness.[40]

Europe had been granted a reprieve due to events occurring at the other end of Asia. On December 11, 1241, Ogedei Khan had died. According to Mongol tradition, the princes were required to congregate in Karakorum for the selection of the new khan.[41]

Subedei and the princes of the Mongol Empire galloped east across the steppes, taking with them the imperial tumens, the core of the army that had invaded Eastern Europe. Batu was left with his Turkoman conscripts to hold a realm that extended from the Carpathians to the Urals. He broke with tradition and did not immediately return to Karakorum, delaying the coronation of the next great khan, Güyük, until 1246. Batu remained in the west, establishing his headquarters on the lower Volga at Sarai.[42] He had a newly conquered empire to secure.

Batu deployed his forces along the river systems of his empire. Four tumens, the main army, were kept at or near Sarai, which Batu used to cover the Volga. Two tumens were stationed beyond the Dnieper. Three tumens ranged between the Dnieper and the Don, and two more tumens were placed east of the Don. Interestingly, two tumens patrolled the banks of the Ural River, an indication of Batu's distrust of his neighboring khanate to the east, the White Khanate of Orda, and the ambitions of the great khan Güyük himself.[43]

Batu quickly grew rich and powerful through his control of the western steppes and the associated trade routes. He extracted taxes from the commerce and people in his realm, including Russia. His empire came to be known as the Kipchak Khanate, or Golden Horde. The "Tartar Yoke" was firmly established over the western steppes, including most of Russia. Of all the Russian principalities, only Novgorod had escaped the systematic destructive wave of the Mongols (or Tartars, as they were also known).[44]

To preempt any such invasion of his domain, Yaroslav II, prince of Novgorod, traveled to Sarai in 1242 to swear fealty to the khan. Batu appointed Yaroslav his vassal, ruler of all of the Russian northern principalities. In return, Yaroslav sent his son Constantine to Karakorum to pledge allegiance to the great khan, Güyük, who had finally taken the throne in 1246. Batu had conspired with other Mongol leaders to derail the coronation, but in the end Güyük's supporters won, led by his mother, who was utterly ruthless in defense of her son's throne. Yaroslav, for his part, was grand duke of not just Novgorod but also Vladimir and Suzdal.

One by one the princes of Russia made their way to Sarai or sent ambassadors on their behalf. Daniel of Galicia was well received by Batu Khan, but Andrew of Chernigov was executed because he would not kneel before an effigy of Genghis Khan.[45] (Actually, the slight incurred by not showing proper respect to the late khan was just an excuse to eliminate a Russian prince whom Batu didn't trust.) Between these two extremes, the treatment of the princes and envoys was perfunctory and unexceptional.

As a favorite of Batu, however, Yaroslav opened himself up to the animosity of the Karakorum court. He traveled to the Mongol capital as a representative of Batu. While there, Yaroslav received a special invitation to dine with the khan's mother, Toregene. She even served him herself, a great honor in Mongol circles. A week later the grand duke was dead, a victim of poisoning.[46]

After the murder of Yaroslav, his two sons, Alexander Nevsky and Andrew, were summoned to Karakorum. Güyük appointed Andrew the new grand duke of Vladimir and Suzdal, and Alexander became prince of Kiev. When Andrew proved to be less than cooperative with the Mongols, a punitive expedition from Sarai destroyed his army and forced him into exile. He took refuge in Sweden. Alexander Nevsky, a more amenable Mongol subject, was given Andrew's territories.[47] Alexander was now the most powerful of the Russian princes and thoroughly in the Mongol camp.

For all the intrigues and plots engaged in to secure the throne for Güyük, his reign was sadly abbreviated, as he died from complications related to excessive drinking. On July 1, 1251, Mangku was elected supreme khan, mainly through the efforts of Batu. In return, Mangku granted Batu essential independence.[48] The Golden Horde of the Tartars was now an empire unto itself.

While trying to placate the Mongols on his southern and eastern frontiers, Alexander had to defend his northern and western borders. In 1236, before he was ruler, he successfully stopped the Swedish invasion led by Birger Jarl, who landed an army at the mouth of the Neva River.

In 1241 the Teutonic knights invaded Pskov, blocking one of the main east-west trade routes. Alexander forced the knights to lift the siege and routed them at the Battle of Lake Peipus (the Battle on the Ice). In 1245 Alexander drove off Lithuanian raiders from Torzhok, and then he pursued and destroyed them.[49]

To keep the Tartars from invading and ravaging his lands, Alexander made four journeys to Sarai, pledging allegiance and offering tribute to the Mongols, following his father's example. The tactic worked, and Novgorod was saved from the Mongols' fiery sword. In fact and in practice, Novgorod became the bulwark protecting Swedish territory, the lands of the German knights and northern Lithuania from the Tartar terror.[50]

34

Novgorod the Great, Lithuania and the Rise of Moscow

After being crushed and brutalized by the invaders from the east, the Russian principalities were incorporated into the Kipchak Empire of Batu Khan, also known as the Khanate of the Golden Horde. From his headquarters at Sarai, Batu ruled a domain stretching from the Carpathian Mountains across the Urals to the Ob River and Aral Sea in Central Asia. Of all the Russian principalities, only Novgorod had escaped the devastation of the khan's armies.

The scourge from the east was bad enough, but now the Russian princes faced a new pagan menace, this time from the west. The heathen Lithuanians were first united and subjugated by a devious and thoroughly ruthless tribal chief named Mindovg. His son, Voishelk, was recognized as prince of Lithuania.[1] For the first time Lithuania was a unified nation.

The next expansionist ruler was Gedimin (1315–1339), who could not prevail against the Teutonic Knights in the west, so he began a campaign of conquest to the south and east. He took the towns of Pinsk, Brest and Polotsk, making himself master of White Russia (Polotsk and northern Kiev principalities). In 1320 he captured Vladimir-Volynsk, and a year later he took Kiev.[2]

Gedimin's son, Olgerd (1339–1377), continued the empire's expansion, capturing Vitebsk on the Dvina, Mogilev on the Dnieper, Bryansk on the Desna and Kamenets just off the lower Dniester. He drove to the Black Sea, where he controlled the coastal area from the mouth of the Dnieper to the Dniester.[3]

This immense Lithuanian state was not a kingdom but an empire. In the main, local Russian princes were left to reign as long as they professed allegiance and paid taxes to the Lithuanian grand prince. There was religious tolerance. Much of the population was or became Orthodox Christian, though large areas were baptized into the Roman Catholic faith.

The stunning growth of the Lithuanian Empire owed much of its success in expansion to the deteriorating condition of the once grand Russian Empire. First there was the fragmentation of Russia into principalities and the erosion of the previously lucrative trade along the country's river systems. Kiev was especially hard hit by the constant warfare with the Cuman tribes that continually raided and invaded the southern and eastern principalities. And finally, the Tartar invasion had left the Russian princes weak

34. Novgorod the Great Lithuania and the Rise of Moscow

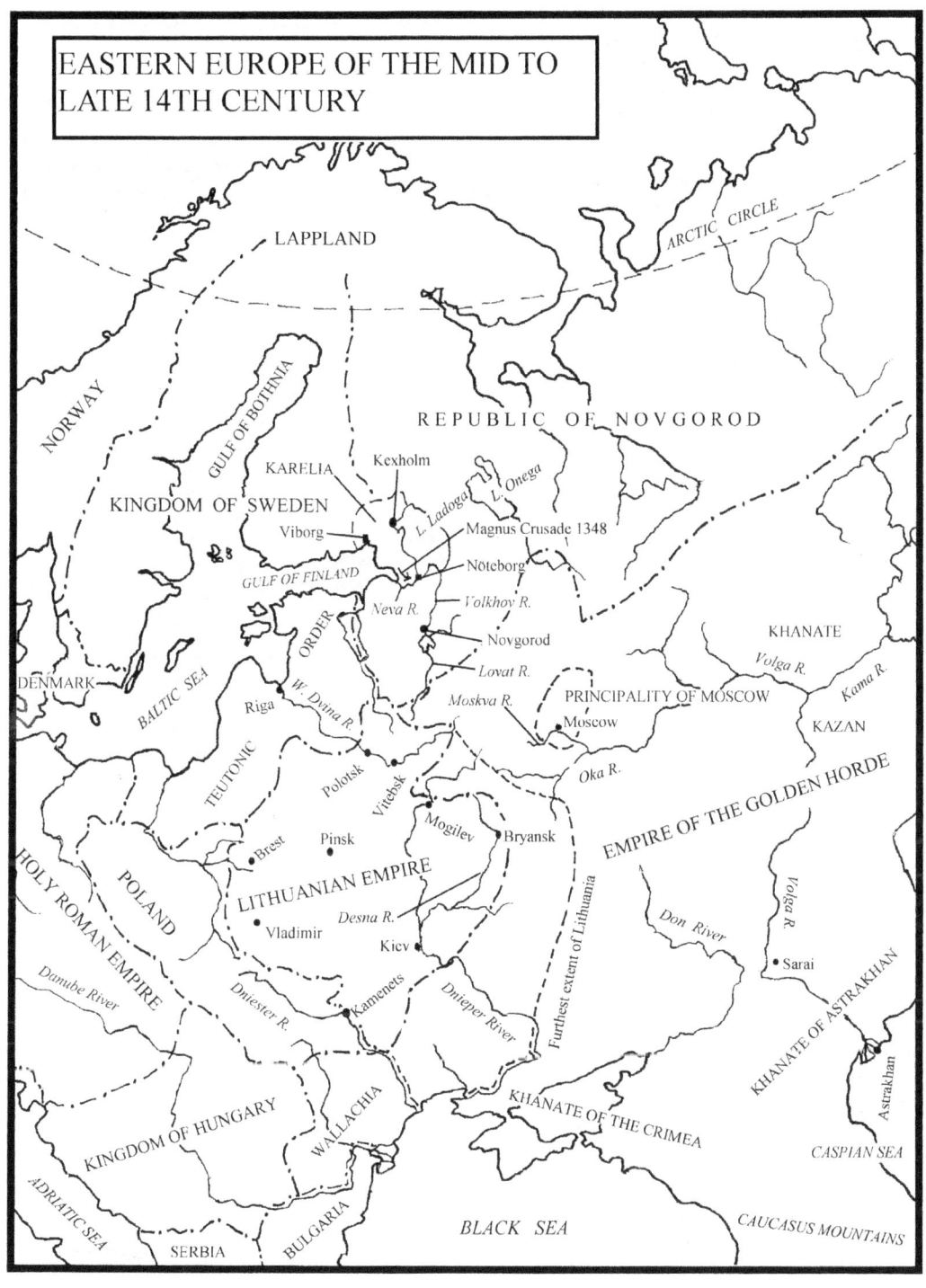

and vulnerable, forced to rely on their overlords from the east for protection. But the Golden Horde had lost some of its aggressive nature, especially in the far western region.

The Tartars and Lithuania divided up Russia between them, except for Novgorod, which stood as the bulwark protecting Northern Europe from the Tartar menace, especially the lands of the Teutonic order and Swedish Finland. The two developing political centers of Russia—Vladimir in the northeast and Galicia in the southwest—had been crushed. Russia south of Novgorod lay hoping for a spark to kindle an insurgence to challenge the oppressors from the east and west. Such an ignition was in the making.

Moscow in 1146 was a small town of little significance surrounded by a wooden wall. Its location, however, had advantages considering the country's vulnerability to invasion. Moscow is situated on the Moskva River, from which it gets its name. The Moskva flows into the Oka, which is a tributary of the Volga to the east. To the west, at the headwaters of the Oka, it is an easy portage to the Dnieper, the Lovat and the Western Dvina. Thus, the town had access to the Volga and, through that great river, the Caspian Sea. To the west, Novgorod, Riga and Kiev were accessible. Yet Moscow's location away from the Volga protected it from the Tartar incursions to which settlements along the river were subject. And the town was far enough east to avoid the Lithuanian conquests.[4]

Settlers from the Volga moved upriver and eventually found safety inside Moscow's wooden walls, which had to be rebuilt several times as the town grew. Immigrants from Kiev arrived, driven by Cuman atrocities and the expansion of Lithuania. The town on the Moskva began to grow and expand territorially, not unlike the ancient Latin-Etruscan town on the Tiber that transformed from a city-state into the Roman Empire.

The city gained further status when the Russian Orthodox Metropolitan Cyril left Kiev and moved first to Vladimir, and then to Moscow, establishing the city as the permanent home of the leaders of the church, a stabilizing influence. Whenever the political situation in Moscow became chaotic, the church provided authority and continuity.[5]

Early on, Moscow was ruled by minor princes or assigned to a major prince of a nearby principality. Thus we have the city under the jurisdiction of Yury, prince of Moscow (1303–1325) and grand prince of Vladimir (1318–1325). But with territorial expansion came recognition, and eventually the position of ruler of Moscow was elevated to grand prince, an office recognized and bestowed by the Khan of the Golden Horde. The Moscow princes were careful to ingratiate themselves with the Tartar khans to such an extent that John I of Moscow (1328–1340) was appointed collector of the khan's tribute from the Russian princes. If a prince was slow in providing the required assessment, the khan would put a Tartar army at the Muscovite ruler's disposal to enforce collection. The grand prince of Moscow thus had military power over other Russian princes. Simeon (1340–1353), John's son, was confirmed as grand prince by the khan, "putting all other princes in his hands."[6]

Through the fourteenth and fifteenth centuries Moscow continued to grow in territory and independence. Whereas the Russians had been defeated by the Tartars because of their lack of unity, now the situation was reversed. The Golden Horde, having broken away from the rest of the Mongol Empire, was essentially an independent state. Then the Golden Horde itself began to break up into independent khanates. The

Khanate of Kazan, the Khanate of Astrakhan and the Khanate of the Crimea were the Tartar states the Russians had to deal with on their borders. These independent states could be played against each other. Indeed, treaties were often made between a Russian principality and one khanate against another. The city on the Moskva River thus expanded in power and territory, becoming more and more dominant.[7]

Meanwhile, Novgorod was able to maintain more independence from the Golden Horde than any other principality. We have noted the growth of Novgorod over the years from a trading town connecting the heartland of northern Russia to the Baltic world in pre–Viking times. During the Viking Age, Novgorod grew into a city dominating the northern end of the great Varangian water road. Several times during the Viking Age, Novgorod challenged Kiev for leadership of the Empire of the Rus. With the end of the Viking Age, Novgorod gained more independence, as did all of the principalities, with the fragmentation of the Empire of the Rus into quasi-independent princely states.

The divided condition of the Russian people left them easy prey for the fast-moving cavalry of the warriors from the eastern steppes. Advancing across the plains of Eastern Europe, the Mongols, with their conscripted Turkish hordes and Chinese axillaries, swept into Russia, spreading terror and destruction. Only Novgorod evaded the Mongol host.

Novgorod is usually portrayed as a republic, and, at least in theory, this is correct. The city was divided by the Volkhov River, with the western portion containing the market of Yaroslav, while the Cathedral of St. Sophia stood on the eastern bank. The city itself was divided into *ends* (wards), each with its own assembly and officials. The ends were divided into hundreds, which were, in turn, divided into streets.[8]

For the most part, the city as a whole chose its own archbishop, though at times this chief cleric was appointed from Kiev, where church leaders resided until the move to Moscow. The city also selected its own *posadnik* (deputy or mayor) and second city official, the *tysyatsky* (thousandth man), who led the city troops and also served as police commander. The governing body of the city was the *Veche*, or city assembly. Every free citizen could attend the Veche, which had no regular sessions but could be called at any time by any citizen by ringing the town bell in Yaroslav.

As the town grew in size, this form of government proved impractical. A Council of Masters (*Sovet gospod*) developed, with a permanent office and government archives. Made up of over fifty past posadniks and members of the boyar class, the council prepared proposals to be considered by the Veche.[9]

A court system evolved, with the posadnik and prince being the court of last resort. There was also the archbishop's court and a court that was part of the Guild of St. John, which handled commercial and trade matters.[10]

Novgorod's social structure had its well-defined classes. Boyars were at the top. These were families with great estates, the large landholders. Next were the *zhityi*, or gentry. Like the boyars, they owned country estates, but they also engaged in trade to help support their families. Next were the *zemtsy*, or country folk who lived in the city but had small estates outside it. At the bottom of the social scale in the city were the merchants, artisans and working class. Outside the city the social ladder extended still lower. There were the *smerdy*, or independent peasants who owned their own land; the *polovniki*, who were sharecroppers; and, at the very bottom, the slaves.[11]

The prince of Novgorod was the military leader and conducted foreign affairs, but otherwise his powers were strictly limited. He lived outside the city in the fortress (*gorodishche*), and all judgments concerning the city were issued jointly with the posadnik. His revenues were derived from the estates defined as his and could not be increased. Ultimately the Veche decided issues important to the city, though the prince could raise issues for consideration.[12]

Novgorod had always been a commercial center. In pre–Viking times it was the port for trade between the Baltic and the Russian interior. During the Viking Age it was the northern terminus of the great river road. With the closure of the north-south trade route, the city became the center for east-west trade—that is, trade between the Baltic and the vast Novgorod hinterlands. Novgorod was dependent on this trade, without which it could not feed its population through its own resources (not even in a favorable agricultural year). An early frost or late winter left the citizens almost entirely dependent on trade for their survival. A blockade of the Volga would quickly bring the city to its knees, its one great vulnerability. This was the Novgorod the Great that Magnus IV of Sweden had to deal with—a vast empire encompassing the lands of northern Russia, mostly sparse in population. To the south, Novgorod held the Mongols in check, appeasing them as much as possible. To the west the principality contended with the German knights, and on its northern border were the Swedes.

We have already noted a crusade raised by Birger Jarl against the Orthodox citizens of Novgorod in 1236. Magnus IV attempted to keep this border peaceful by signing the Peace of Nöteborg between Sweden and Novgorod, represented by Prince Yury of Moscow, in 1323. But the peace was hard to keep, and in 1337 confrontations between the Roman Catholic Swedes and the Orthodox Karelians flared once more. The Swedes attacked Kexholm, Viborg and the fortress at Nöteborg. Among those killed in the conflict were Novgorod merchants. A full-scale war seemed about to erupt, but negotiations were opened between Fedor (the posadnik of Novgorod) and Sweden. However, before a treaty could be signed, additional attacks were carried out by Swedes on Karelians around Lake Ladoga and Lake Onega, stirring up additional problems for the negotiators. Finally, in 1339, the treaty was signed and the violence subsided.[13]

In 1348 Magnus again led a crusade against the Karelians and Novgorod. He marched up the Neva River, converting local tribes at the point of the sword, even taking Nöteborg once more. But here his campaign stalled. Novgorod retook the fortress after a seven-month siege, and Magnus was forced to fall back.[14]

St. Birgitta had come to the king while he was preparing to leave for the Neva with a plan for the campaign that she said was divinely inspired. Ignoring her advice, she proclaimed, would lead to disaster. Magnus dismissed her plan as "idle female chatter."[15] However, Birgitta Birgersdotter was proved right, and the king's crusade ended in a humiliating defeat. Magnus showed himself to be an inadequate military leader, a serious flaw for one whose position is that of warrior king.

Many of Magnus' problems stemmed from his own shortcomings. However, the worst disaster to befall Sweden during his reign originated outside the country. The devastating consequences of the Black Death would have stretched the abilities of any monarch to handle, let alone a king already in trouble.

35

Sweden and the Black Death

In addition to his political and military disasters, Magnus had to deal with the worst scourge to hit medieval Europe, perhaps the deadliest plague of all time. This was the Black Death, a pestilence that spread terror and ruin across the European continent, and the people of Sweden were especially vulnerable.

Historians estimate the total population of mid-fourteenth century Europe at about 100 million people. Plague historians calculate that the disease took some 25 million lives in Europe during the years 1347–1352, reducing the continent's population by a quarter. Any such drastic reduction in a populace is bound to affect social, economic and political developments. Italy, one of the earliest European victims of the pandemic, was especially hard hit; Florence is said to have lost 100,000 people to the disease. By August 1348, the scourge had reached England by way of the port of Melcombe Regis in Dorset. British historians estimate the dreaded plague carried off upward of 2 million souls in England.[1]

In August 1349, laborers at the harbor of Bergen, Norway, sighted a Hansa cog drifting out at sea. Bergen was Norway's second oldest city, and, together with Visby on Gotland Island, it was the most important trading city in Magnus Eriksson's entire realm. Upon bringing the vessel into the harbor, the men found a ship of corpses. No one was left alive. But the cargo of cloth and woolens was very much intact. The practical men of Bergen unloaded the cargo, and then they took the cog out to sea and scuttled it. That same day, some of those who had unloaded the ship fell ill. Within hours, they were dead. Two months later 40,000 citizens of Bergen had died out of an estimated population of 100,000.[2]

By October 1349, the plague had reached Halland. King Magnus called a council of his advisers to meet in Lödöse to determine how to deal with the fast-moving epidemic. The conclusion of the council was that the plague was God's punishment for humanity's sins. Magnus instructed his subjects to offer up one Swedish penny for every man, woman and child in honor of God and the Blessed Virgin Mary. They were to fast and pray, especially on Fridays. By the end of the year, however, the plague had spread to the neighboring provinces of Västergötland and Småland. The year 1350 would be the year of the Black Death (or, as it was called in Sweden, the Great Death) in the king's homeland. Fully a third of the Swedish population would succumb.[3]

The great minds of the medieval world were completely helpless in stemming the tide of death. The king of France called upon the eminently reputable University of

Paris for an explanation and cause of the pandemic ravaging his people. The medical faculty concluded that the plague originated in a struggle between the celestial bodies and the Indian Ocean. A lethal poison was being spread by the ocean winds. Even the air was contaminated. To survive, people should not drink water, but only liquids cleansed by fire—that is, distilled spirits. They should eat little and sleep only at certain times.[4]

To some in the church, this disease was Death itself as described in the book of Revelation: "And I looked, and beheld a pale horse: and his name that sat on him was Death, and Hell followed with him."[5] To many there was a sense of the world coming to an end.

Another faction held the Jews responsible for the spiraling death count. According to this theory, God had become disgusted with the division and outright war between the pope and the Holy Roman Emperor, so he gave the Jews the assignment of extracting retribution. They were to do this by poisoning the drinking water in Europe. As early as 1348 there were riots in Norbonne and Carcassonne in southern France in which the entire Jewish populations of these cities were wiped out. As many as 50,000 Jews were killed in Bourgogne. Mob rule spread to Central Europe, where 6,000 Jews were burned at the stake in Strasbourg. By 1349 human bonfires erupted in Frankfurt, Nuremburg, Wismar, Rostock, Griefswald and Stralsund.[6] But the mob psychosis dissolved at the shores of the Baltic, as there had been no known Jewish immigration into Sweden in the fourteenth century.[7]

Symptoms of the disease were unusually grisly. First the victim would be seized with spasms of uncontrolled shivering even in the heat of the day. He would have shortness of breath and complain of dizziness, headaches and an unquenchable thirst. Great boils developed under his armpits and on his neck and groin. Black spots would break out on the skin of the diseased, and the face would turn scarlet. Fits of uncontrolled vomiting would reduce the victim to a helpless state. The tongue would turn black, and he would cough up blood. Within three days he would be dead. A person developing these symptoms almost never recovered.[8]

The origin of the scourge is thought to have been Asia. Indian annals record the outbreak of a great plague in the subcontinent in the decades after 1325. China is also cited as a possible source. If this was the case, the path to Europe would have been along the old Silk Road, opened once again thanks to the conquest of the steppes by the Mongols.

In 1344 the Mongols were gobbling up territories around the Black Sea. They invaded the Genoese city of Kaffa on the Crimean peninsula. As part of the siege operation, the Mongols catapulted corpses of plague victims into the city, a crude form of biological warfare. The Genoese successfully defended their trade center from the Mongol expeditionary force, but many in the city succumbed to the disease. When the Italian merchants and soldiers sailed home to Genoa, they took the deadly infection with them. From Genoa as an entry point in the spring of 1347, the Black Death quickly spread across the face of Europe.[9]

The agent of death in transporting the pandemic so quickly and easily was the common wharf or skin-tailed rat, though mice, guinea pigs and trade rats were also potential carriers. They all were ready hosts of the species of fleas that carried the disease (*Pasteurella pestis*), and these fleas were equally at home on rats and on humans.[10]

Rats were ubiquitous in medieval Europe. They inhabited every corner of the land, from the lowly peasant's quarters to the lord's castle. Every city shop, house and stable had its share of the rodents. They traveled on ships from port to port and migrated along roads and through fields, an almost perfect carrier of this devastating pestilence.

Likewise, fleas were a common annoyance in Europe Middle Ages. They were shared between family members, soldiers and travelers, who often slept in beds in taverns with two or three other wayfarers. The flea merely bit its host, human or rodent, picking up the disease, and then later punctured the skin of a new host, releasing the microbe into the bloodstream. One can hardly imagine a more efficient agent of death than the rat-flea combination.

Reaction to the pandemic varied widely. Some, particularly the rich, tried to isolate themselves from the infection. Note Boccaccio's *Decameron*, which relates the stories told by a company of men and women to pass the time while they are sequestered in a castle until the disease has run its course in their area.[11]

Some abandoned all restraint in terms of morals and inhibitions, engaging in sexual orgies and giving themselves over to lust. Others turned to self-torment as a means of penance. Great societies were formed that moved from town to town while engaging in self-scourging. Mobs of men, women and children clad only in loincloths lashed their bodies until they were covered with blood. Such flagellant trains were most common in Germany, but they never reached Scandinavia. The bishop of Lübeck turned back a flock of scourgers, denying them access to the city, and the border into Denmark was sealed by royal ordinance from a wave of flagellants trying to gain access to the country.[12] For the most part, Scandinavia was spared the most gruesome social excesses of the plague, with the exception of human sacrifice.

In Sweden, there are records of young maidens and, more often, small children being buried alive in an attempt to appease the gods worshipped in the not-too-distant past. Most of these reports come from Västergötland and Småland, where devotion to the pagan gods had survived longer than in other parts of the country.[13]

The devastation wrought by the Black Death in Sweden was primarily the staggering number of deaths in so short a time. As stated previously, a third of the Swedish population was swept away.[14] Västergötland, Småland, Värmland and Uppland were the provinces suffering the highest mortality rates.[15]

Among the nobility, few died. They could move from an estate in a disease-plagued area to one in a healthier region. It was the peasants, who could not move away because they had no place to move to, that suffered the most, except for the local indigents, who were often completely exterminated.[16] Whole parishes were devastated, and even hundreds were left desolate. Fields went uncultivated, and farm animals left unattended roamed the pastures and forests, becoming wild beasts. Parish churches were filled with dead bodies and then abandoned or burned down.[17]

Many legends originated during this time period in Sweden that have a common theme. They relate a beautiful story of a young man or woman left as a lone survivor on a farm in an area devastated by the plague.[18] In Torsås Parish, on the boundary between Småland and Blekinge, such a legend survives. Here a young woman was left alone in the fields and forests of her ancestral estate, the last member of an ancient family that had cleared the trees and farmed the land for centuries. Central to the family's well-being had always been the Blue Spring, which supplied water for the family home. Each day the young woman carried water from the spring to supply her needs until she noticed that the spring was beginning to dry up. She took this as an omen that her ancient line was about to die out. Panicked, she took a birchbark whistle and fled into the forest, blowing the whistle to try and attract the attention of another living soul.

At this time a young man by the name of Bonde Gul was traveling southeast in the same forest in search of survivors. He was also the last of his family, which had possessed lands in Långasjö in Värend. He heard the whistle and found the young woman. He stayed with her at her estate near the Blue Spring. They married, and Bonde named their new "gård" Öjebomåla in honor of his family's ancestral estate. Öjebomåla would be owned and passed on in direct line of descent from then to the present day. The birchbark whistle that Bonde's wife used is preserved today in the Kalmar Museum.[19]

The Black Death was the last in a long list of calamities that beset Magnus in the mid-fourteenth century. St. Birgitta saw the Great Death in Sweden as God's punishment for their king's sinful life. Before leaving on a pilgrimage to Rome in 1349, she prophesied:

> Like a plow shall God's wrath pass over Sweden ... for corpses shall be upon corpses.... Where formally a thousand dwelt, scantily a hundred be left alive; and houses shall stand deserted.[20]

Her prophetic pronouncements were realized to the letter.

The Black Death was perhaps the final blow in the destroying Magnus Eriksson's already enfeebled Scandinavian empire. In the 1350s his realm began to come apart. Erik, the king's oldest son, took over much of Sweden, which he ruled independently, satisfying to some extent Sweden's anti–Magnus party and the nobles who were trying to reestablish their old authority. Håkan, Magnus' second son, became king of Norway (possibly with his father's consent).[21]

Denmark, meanwhile, had recovered some of its strength under a new king, Valdemar Atterdag. The Danes now regretted the loss of their Scanian domains and were looking for a chance to regain control of these rich and productive lands. The turmoil in Magnus' empire provided just such an opportunity. Valdemar invaded Skåne, whereupon the inhabitants rose up in support of the Danish king, having more loyalty to him than to a Swedish monarch who had ruled them for only a short time.[22]

Not satisfied with just the recovery of Skåne, Valdemar went on to invade Gotland Island. He was able to defeat the militias raised by the farmers and fishermen of the island, and he did so with great slaughter. The Danes then proceeded to plunder and ravage Gotland. The Hanseatic port city of Visby was sacked and pillaged, crippling the wealthiest trading city in all of Sweden. The devastation was so complete that Gotland never recovered. The rich farming, fishing and trading industries for which the island had been noted since before the Viking Age were ended. The once prosperous island sank into anonymity as a result of the destruction.[23]

Magnus, left with a much diminished empire, was fighting for his monarchical survival. His son Erik, who, backed by the Swedish nobility, had taken over part of the realm, became a casualty of the plague in 1359. As a result, Magnus recovered control of most of Sweden and moved to strengthen ties with his son Håkan, king of Norway. There thus seemed to be a glimmer of light for the besieged monarch.[24]

35. Sweden and the Black Death

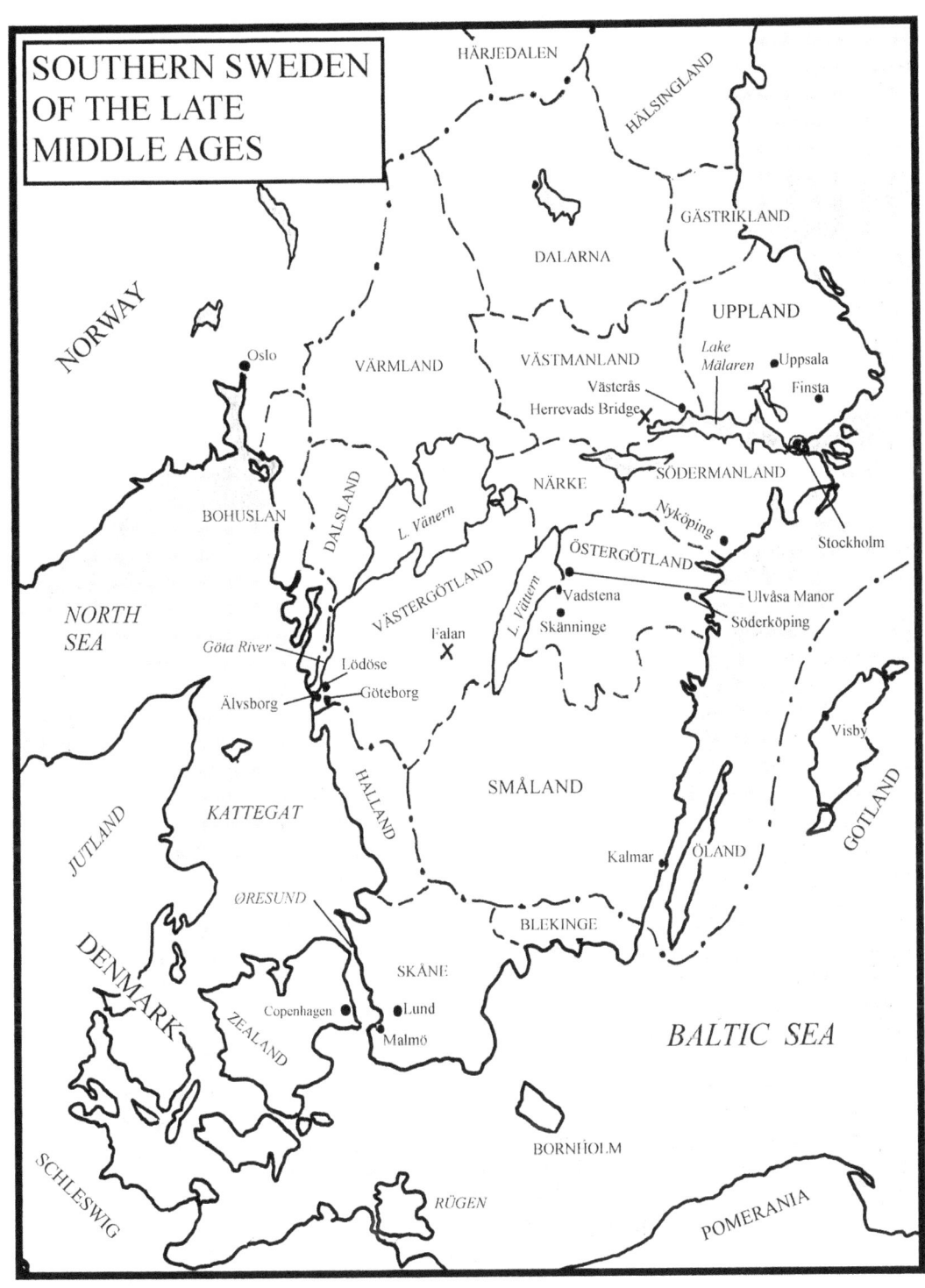

The nobility and the anti–Magnus party had lost Erik as a champion and were in research of a replacement, a relative willing to take on the Swedish monarch. Only too happy to oblige was Magnus' nephew, 20-year-old Albrecht, the son of Magnus' sister Eufemia. In Albrecht, the traitorous Swedes felt they had a winning combination—a relative with a claim to the throne and the resources to challenge the Swedish king.

Albrecht and his father, Duke Albrecht of Mecklenburg, appeared off the Swedish coast with an army of Germans borne by a Hanseatic fleet. They were joined by forces supplied by the anti–Magnus party in Sweden and the rebellious nobles. Against this alliance Magnus could muster only a small army of supporters and a contingent of Norwegians sent by King Håkan.[25]

It was not enough. Magnus was defeated, deposed as monarch and incarcerated in Stockholm Castle in 1365. For six years he languished in prison, sometimes apparently in chains. Finally, in 1371, he was released in exchange for a ransom of 12,000 silver marks. He spent the last years of his life in Norway under the protection of his son, Håkan. On December 1, 1374, the 58-year-old Magnus Eriksson was aboard a ship struck by a severe storm in Bömmel Fjord near Haugesund. Of all those on board, only Magnus was able to reach shore. But before gaining safety he was overcome by exhaustion or cramps, and he perished. However, his body was found, and he was given a burial in hallowed ground. Recovery of the body was considered a miracle by his apologists, one more extraordinary event in an extraordinary life.[26]

Having been instrumental in determining the new king of Sweden, the Hanseatic League next turned on the Danish king, Valdemar Atterdag, who had squandered his military resources in recovering Scania and invading Gotland. After a two-year war, Copenhagen was forced to surrender. The Hansa extracted favorable concessions from the Danes, concessions affecting the league's trade and commercial empire. The Hansa seized the rich Skånian fisheries and was granted free transit of the Sound. To ensure compliance with the last condition, Hansa garrisons occupied the fortified positions along the strait. The Hanseatic League was at the height of its power, able to dominate Baltic and North Sea trade and even have a hand in determining the monarchs of neighboring kingdoms.[27]

Sweden had exchanged a native monarch for rule by a German prince. The aristocrats had helped engineer this coup in the hopes of regaining more control of the country. It was a forlorn hope and a conspiracy they would soon regret. Once in power, the Mecklenburgers would reveal themselves to be much more despotic than King Magnus ever was.

36

St. Birgitta of Sweden

Before leaving the Magnus Eriksson era in Sweden, it is necessary to take note of a personality more enduring than the monarch himself. This is St. Birgitta (Bridget) of Sweden. We have already noted her presence at the court of King Magnus and her interjection into governmental affairs. She was the equivalent of the Old Testament Samuel, prophet to the occasionally recidivistic Saul. Birgitta proclaimed Magnus' sins and called him to repentance while prophesying that terrible retribution would follow if he did not comply.

St. Birgitta's legacy has been lasting and far reaching in the form of the order she founded and the abbeys created for the order. In 1346 she established an abbey in Vadstena, Sweden, with land and funds supplied by Magnus IV and his queen, Blanche. The abbey was further expanded by Birgitta's daughter St. Katherine (canonized in 1484). The abbey was unusual in that it contained both nuns and monks, though housed in separate facilities. The brothers supplied the heavy manual labor needed to maintain the abbey. The nuns and the monks each had their own leaders; however, the abbey as a whole was governed by an abbess. As a result of the Reformation, the Vadstena community was harassed by officials of Lutheran Sweden and finally closed in 1594 when the last nuns fled to Danzig.[1] The Vadstena Abbey was refounded in 1963, now called the Mary's Peace monastery, and thrives to this day.[2]

The Birgittine order and the founding of the Vadstena Abbey led to the creation of abbeys of this order being established in other countries. Monasteries sprang up in many countries throughout Europe during the Middle Ages. Most of these institutions closed during the Reformation, and others dissolved during the French Revolution. The Birgittine communities remaining today may be divided into four groups: the old or medieval group (those descended directly from the communities founded in the Middle Ages and retaining the original statutes), the Spanish group, the Swedish group and a new offshoot—the community of brothers.[3]

Included in the medieval group is the Birgittine Abbey of Syon, England, which can was the only English religious community to maintain an unbroken line from medieval times to the twenty-first century. The abbey was established by Henry V in 1415 at the instigation of a Yorkshireman, Third Lord Fitzhugh of Ravenworth. Fitzhugh had accompanied Philippa, daughter of Henry IV, who had traveled to Sweden to marry Eric of Pomerania. During this stay in Sweden, Fitzhugh visited the Vadstena monastery and became interested in the order. He enlisted the help of two Vadstena monks, John Peterson and Katillus Thorberni, who came to England in 1408 to guide the building of an abbey and direct the foundation of the branch in England. During the Reformation, the Syon Abbey community was forced out of England and resided in the Netherlands, and then in Lisbon, Portugal, before returning to England in 1861.[4] In spite of surviving for almost six centuries, Syon Abbey was dissolved in 2011 due to declining membership.[5] Three other monasteries in operation today that fall into the medieval classification are Mary's Refuge Abbey in Uden, The Netherlands (from which the Vadstena monastery was reestablished); Altomünster in Germany; and Mary's Heart in Weert, The Netherlands.[6]

In about 1630 a new branch of the order was founded in Spain. This "Spanish branch" operates under rules modified to accommodate Spanish circumstances. Breaking with tradition, the rules require all members to be female. Nevertheless, this branch has prospered. There are now four independent monasteries in Spain, four in Mexico and one in Venezuela.[7]

In 1911, a Swedish woman, Elizabeth Hesselblad, acquired the house in Rome that Birgitta had stayed in while she was in the Eternal City. Blessed Elizabeth (she was beatified in 2000) established a branch of the Birgittine order in this residence, which has propagated many communities around the world, including several in India. This branch operates under rules quite different from those of the older groups. All the communities are governed by one elected council and a general abbess located in Rome.[8]

The latest branch to emerge is that of the Brigittine Monks, founded in the United States. This community of brothers was started in 1976 in Amity, Oregon, and earns its keep by manufacturing and marketing gourmet confections.[9]

Besides the abbeys, other places of worship have been named after this Swedish saint. Churches named in her honor include St. Bridget's of Sweden Catholic Church in Lindsborg, Kansas[10]; St. Bridget of Sweden Catholic Church in Lindstrom, Minnesota, created in the late 1940s[11]; and St. Bridget of Sweden Catholic Church in Lake Balboa, California, a church built in 1955 that features Latin and Filipino Masses.[12]

This is quite an extraordinary list of convents and monasteries organized according to St. Birgitta's precepts, as well as churches named in her honor. Her fame and influence have indeed been extensive and of long standing.

Birgitta Birgersdotter was born on a farm in Finsta, Uppland, in 1303.[13] She is described as being "small of limb and slight of stature."[14] She was the daughter of Birger Persson, a Swedish knight, governor and lawspeaker of Uppland, one of the richest landowners in Sweden. Upon his death, his estate was divided between his three children. Birgitta became one of the wealthiest women in Sweden, and she received the best education available to a noblewoman of her day.[15]

At thirteen, Birgitta was married to Ulv Gudmarsson of Ulvåsa, who was five years her senior. For the first two years of their marriage, their relationship seems to have been platonic. Sex was considered, by the couple, a distasteful, even sinful, necessity to be indulged in for procreation only. Birgitta had her first child at sixteen and would eventually bear eight children, six of whom lived to maturity, an usually high number for medieval times.[16]

She was mistress of Ulvåsa for 20 years. During this time in her life Birgitta not only took care of her family and her husband's household but also found time to attend to the poor and afflicted. She would take her children with her on visits to the hospitals and slums, tending to the destitute and suffering, and teaching her children by example to serve others.[17] Birgitta gave generously to the poor and needy, and she fought unceasingly against promiscuity and immorality. She vocally condemned the practice of priests keeping concubines or engaging prostitutes, and she conducted a campaign to rescue fallen women from their degraded situation. In all this she was hard working and tireless.[18]

Though Birgitta persevered in her work to better the conditions of the less fortunate, her fame, widespread recognition and following were primarily the result of her prophecies. Birgitta's first vision is reported to have occurred when she was just 12 years old. Over seven hundred apparitions would follow. As part of her denunciation of King Magnus' alleged homosexual affair with a young nobleman, Birgitta prophesied his undoing. If the king persisted, she warned, great calamities would befall the monarch and the country. These predictions certainly came true.

She instructed the king on how he should live, especially how and when he should fast, and admonished him to give food and money to the poor by his own hand. Following Christ's example, he should wash the feet of the poor; specifically, he should cleanse the feet of thirteen indigents every Friday.[19]

As explained earlier, St. Birgitta's vision of how to conduct the war with Novgorod was ignored by Magnus, and the dire outcome she predicted occurred. In 1349, Birgitta prophesied the coming of the Black Death to Sweden: "Like a plow shall God's wrath pass over Sweden."[20] She named thirty-three monks at the Alvastra Monastery who would be carried off by the plague, and all thirty-three did in fact die of the pestilence. In all, Birgitta relayed some 700 revelations. They were written down in Latin and Old Swedish, although only two are said to have been written in her own hand. Generally, when a visionary state came upon her, she dictated her impressions to a scribe. Her most famous work, *Revelations*, was published in eight volumes.[21]

Upon the death of her husband Ulv, Birgitta moved into the king's home. She had formerly served as mistress of Ulvåsa; now she would serve as mistress of King Magnus' household. It was at this time that she founded her Birgittine order, which was established at Vadstena, on the shores of Lake Vättern, on land given to her by the king. Her monastery eventually assembled the largest library in Scandinavia, some 1,500 volumes.[22] But the Vadstena monastery was more than a center of learning, for it was also noted for its social work, caring for the poor, the sick and the wretched.[23]

Birgitta left Sweden in 1349 and moved to Rome. In 1372, a year before her death, she made a pilgrimage to the Holy Sepulcher in Jerusalem. Her canonization process proceeded for 13 years, pursued by her daughter Katherine and even supported by the new Swedish king, Albrecht. Birgitta Birgersdotter became St. Birgitta in 1391.[24]

37

Margareta and the Kalmar Union

The German regime of King Albrecht had not fulfilled the high expectations of the traitorous Swedish nobility. The peasants had never favored the Mecklenburg monarchy and now found their fears fully justified. The Germans levied tax upon tax; tallage and hospitalities left the common man impoverished. While Magnus was still in Stockholm Castle, the peasants of Uppland sent a letter to their brethren in Östergötland and Västergötland denouncing Albrecht and his father as tyrants and traitors and calling for the release and reinstatement of good King Magnus. In Småland, the peasants and minor lords rose in revolt, but they were quickly crushed.[1]

Even the nobles discovered their situation was deteriorating. Once in control of the central government, the Mecklenburgers began a systematic seizure of the provincial governments. Then the Germans initiated a program of confiscation of the largest state. Too late, the Swedish nobles realized the mistake they had made in inviting the Mecklenburg prince to assume the throne. The Germans now held all the power.[2]

The nobility cast about for help and received a response from Håkan, king of Norway. Håkon invaded Sweden with a Norwegian army. As he crossed the Swedish countryside, the army grew, adding contingents from both the Swedish peasantry and the aristocracy. By the time the army reached Stockholm, it had grown to the point that the Mecklenburgers could not stand against it.

But instead of a conclusive battle, a compromise was negotiated between the Swedish nobility and the Germans. Albrecht would retain his crown, but the estates would be returned to their Swedish owners and the provincial governments would be handed back to local officials. The Swedish nobles were the winners here, with very little help obtained for the commoners. But even these terms were never carried out, as all stipulations were voided upon the death of Håkan in 1380.[3]

With their champion removed, the Swedes began looking around for another savior to lead their cause. Following Håkan's death, the obvious choice was his son and heir, Olof. However, the new Norwegian king was only 17 years old, leaving the government in the hands of his mother, the widow Margareta. Olof would serve as a figurehead for the Swedish rebel movement, but any real success would depend on Margareta's capabilities. Fortunately for the Swedes, the widow of King Håkan would prove to be one of the most remarkable women in European history.

Margareta, daughter of King Valdemar Atterdag of Denmark, was born in 1353. At 10 years of age she was given in marriage to King Håkan of Norway, clearly a political union. Margareta spent the first six years of her marriage not at her husband's court in Norway but in Sweden at the home of Mareta Ulfsdotter, a daughter of St. Birgitta. (Birgitta had, by this time, left Sweden for Rome.)[4] Here Margareta was brought up under a regime of strict discipline and extensive religious instruction, which was not lost on her, for she remained a devout Christian all of her life. Her direct link to St. Birgitta was to also have a lasting effect. Once in power, Margareta took the Vadstena monastery under her wing, protecting it and supporting the facility and the order with lavish gifts.[5]

At the age of sixteen Margareta was sent to Norway to reside with her 30-year-old husband Håkan at Akerhus Castle in Oslo. A year later she bore her only child, Olof Håkansson, heir apparent to both the Norwegian and the Danish thrones.

With her husband traveling extensively, Margareta was left in charge of Akerhus Castle and the accompanying estate. She had, in effect, her own little kingdom to run, giving her experience in management, finances and even, in a limited way, foreign affairs.

In 1375 Margareta's father, Valdemar, king of Denmark, died. Margareta, with some astute political maneuvering, arranged to have her son, Olof, recognized as king. The other main contender for the throne was Albrecht, already king of Sweden. Margareta received the backing of the Danish nobles, who were worried about the rising power of the Germans now on their northern and southern borders. The Hanseatic League joined the coalition, wary of the Mecklenburgers' potential threat to Baltic and North Sea trade routes. Olof was thus named future king of Denmark.[6]

Then, in 1380, Margareta's husband died, leaving the Norwegian throne vacant. Here again Margareta was able to get the Norwegian nobility to back Olof and name him their future king.

Next Margareta began contacting the Swedish nobles who now saw Olof as their best chance of removing the Mecklenburg yoke from their necks. Intrigues were just beginning to become serious when Olof, age 17, died in 1387. The thrones of Denmark and Norway were once again vacant. The scramble for power began all over again.

This time, however, Margareta had the advantage. She already had contacts in place in Denmark and Norway, and both governments had had a taste of her wisdom and capabilities when she served as regent for her son. Furthermore, she was seen as far preferable to the Mecklenburgers. Therefore, Margareta was able to secure the responsibility of selecting the next king of both Norway and Denmark. Her choice fell upon her niece's son, Eric of Pomerania, age seven. The designee's youth would open the way for Margareta to become the head of state in both countries. On August 10, 1387, Margareta was selected regent of Denmark at Lund Cathedral. The following year she was elected "puissant lady and rightful master of the whole realm"[7] at a general assembly in Oslo.

Margareta was *de facto* ruler of Norway and Denmark. She now cast her eyes on Sweden, the land of her youth and a country chafing under foreign rule. What was needed was an excuse to make an entrance into the country. It would be only a matter of time before such an opportunity would arise.

The leader of the nobility and the richest man in Sweden was one Bo Johnsson Grip. In August 1386, Johnsson died. As a means of extending his wealth and hold on Sweden, Albrecht attempted to claim Johnsson's considerable estate. The Swedish aristocracy contested this move and put forward Margareta to represent their claim. In March 1388 the executor of Bo Johnsson Grip's will used the situation to declare Margareta "Sweden's all-powerful lady and rightful master."[8] This declaration gave Margareta a claim to the Swedish throne. But the matter would have to be settled by force of arms.

Albrecht already had his German mercenaries and Swedish traitors at his disposal. He imported additional troops from Mecklenburg until he had a sizable army with which to defend his throne. Margareta, for her part, had the general backing of both the Swedish aristocracy and the peasants. To these forces, she added levies from Norway and Denmark.[9]

On February 24, 1389, the two armies met on the plain of Falan near Falköping in Västergötland. Legend has it that the heavily armored German knights with their great steeds became mired down and immobile in the soft earth of the marshy flats. The lighter Scandinavian cavalry on their smaller horses were able to maneuver on the swampy ground, inflicting a decisive defeat on the Germans. As a result, King Albrecht and the crown prince were captured. Albrecht, who had derisively referred to Margareta as *Kung Bracklös* (King Trouserless), was now completely at her mercy. The Germans still held Stockholm and many of the castles in Sweden, but with the Mecklenburg king and prince in Margareta's power, the process of repatriation was only a matter of time. Still, it would be September 1398 before Margareta could ride triumphantly into the Swedish capital as the ruler of three countries.[10]

Even before this final triumph, Margareta pushed for a formal union of all three Scandinavian monarchies. This unification was presented at a conference at Kalmar in July 1397. The "Letter of Union" proposed a monarchy in common that would provide for a united defense and foreign policy. In all internal matters, however, each country would be governed by its own people according to local laws.

The Kalmar Union led to many positive consequences. Scandinavia would have 40 years of peace, which was particularly important to the peasants. At least for a time they would be spared the continual destruction of property and crops caused by the passage of troops and the associated plundering and hospitality levies. The German encroachment into Scandinavia, particularly Denmark and Sweden, was halted, and any further incursions would meet with a united front. The Hanseatic League and the rising German states would have to look elsewhere for territories to conquer and rule.[11]

The aristocracy had some room for complaint, as Queen Margareta did introduce a campaign of "reduction" in Sweden. Lands that the nobility had acquired during King Albrecht's reign were returned to their rightful owners, breaking up the huge landholdings of some of the magnet families.[12]

The Kalmar Union engineered and enforced by Queen Margareta was a grand idea and worked as long as there was an individual devoted to its success and strong enough to guarantee equality and sustain each country's rights. But imbalances were bound to occur. Dominance of one country in the union was only a matter of time. Denmark, as the oldest of the three cultures and the most highly developed, held the advantage. In terms of sheer numbers, the Danes dominated. It is estimated that in the year 1400 Denmark had a population of about 750,000, while Sweden had 500,000 and Norway 250,000. This imbalance would become apparent among Margareta's successors. But for the time being the union worked, and Scandinavia prospered in the late Middle Ages.[13]

Epilogue

As head of the Kalmar Union, Margareta ruled an empire that stretched from Lake Ladoga bordering Novgorod in the east to the west coast of Greenland. She regained Gotland Island for Sweden, purchasing it from the Teutonic order in 1407. Margareta maintained a delicate balance of power between the Scandinavian countries, not allowing one country to dominate or infringe on the rights of the other two. She excluded foreign intervention and kept the peace. Sweden and all Scandinavia prospered.

Margareta proved to be a blessing to the countries of the north, and she tried to arrange for a perpetuation of this circumstance after her death. She elevated Eric of Pomerania to king of the union once he reached his majority, though she retained true power until her passing. To further stymie any intrusion by the German states, Margareta formed alliances with other European countries, even arranging the marriage of Eric to Philippa, the daughter of Henry IV, king of England.

When Margareta died in 1412, Eric assumed control of the Kalmar Union. Unlike Margareta, however, Eric made no attempt to sustain peace either within the union or with its neighbors. His first move was to tighten his grip on Sweden by appointing Danes and Germans as judges, bailiffs and provincial officials. By Swedish law, these positions were reserved for Swedes so as to provide employment for the sons of the nobility and petty nobility.

Eric raised taxes to finance an army with which he attacked Schleswig in northern Germany. Eric's intention was to gain control of the entire Baltic coastline. He already held the Danish, Swedish and Pomeranian coasts, so why not all of it? Unfortunately for Eric, he was defeated by the count of Holstein, ruler of Schleswig-Holstein, and his campaign collapsed.

Eric also imposed a tax on non–Scandinavian shipping passing through the Øre sund. The Hanseatic League retaliated by blockading several Scandinavian ports, disrupting commerce. Sweden was especially affected by this action.

Resentment began to build against the Kalmar Union until open rebellion erupted in Sweden. Engelberkt Engelberktsson, a minor nobleman from Dalarna, led the Dalesmen against Eric's Danes in Sweden. Engelberkt was eventually murdered, creating a martyr for the cause. An ongoing civil war ensued, with Denmark as the oppressor of Swedish freedom and independence. The Kalmar Union had evolved into a Danish empire, and Sweden and Norway were essentially occupied countries.

Rebellion in Sweden was carried on at all levels. At times Sweden was able to operate independently with its own government, and at other times the Danish heel would squash resistance and the Danish king would rule unchallenged. This continual state of war culminated in the Stockholm Bloodbath of 1520, in which 94 dissidents and innocents were executed in the Stockholm public square.

This final atrocity committed by the king of Denmark provoked a rebellion that engulfed all Sweden. The leader of the rebellion was Gustav Vasa, a former hostage of the Danish king. He engineered the war that would free Sweden and earn him the crown as Gustav I of Sweden. From this starting point, Sweden would rise to become one of the great military powers of Europe, dominating the Baltic Sea and building an empire during the sixteenth and seventeenth centuries that encompassed lands previously ruled by Goths and Vikings.

Chapter Notes

Chapter 1

1. Adam, Jonathan. "Europe during the Last 150,000 Years." *Environmental Sciences Division, Oak Ridge National Laboratory*. n.d. 3. Web. Jan. 2014.

2. Yokoyama, Yusuke, Kurt Lambeck, Patrick DeDeckker, Paul Johnston and L. Keith Fifield. "Timing of the Last Glacial Maximum from Observed Sealevel Minima." *Letters to Nature* 406 (16 June 2000): 713–16. Web. Jan. 2014. http://www.nature.com/nature/journal/v406/n6797/full/406713a0.html.

3. Larsson, Lars. "The Late Palaeolithic in Southern Sweden: Investigations in a Marginal Region." *Archaeology Data Services* (ADS.UK). n.d. n.p. Web. April 2010.

4. Roberts, N. *The Holocene: An Environmental History* (second edition). Oxford: Blackwell, 1998. 70. Print; Wefer, Gerold, Wolfgang H. Berger, Karl-Ernst Behre and Eystein Jansen. *Climate Development and History of the North Atlantic Realm*. Berlin: Springer, 2002. 178. Print.

5. Wefer et al., 179.

6. Ibid.

7. Roberts, 70.

8. Dansgaard, W., J. W. C. White and S. J. Johnsen. "The Abrupt Termination of the Younger Dryas Climate Event." *Nature* (1989) 339: 532–34. doi: 10.1038/33952a0. Web. April 2010; Kobashi, Takuro. "4 + 1.5°C Abrupt Warming 11,270 Years Ago Identified from Trapped Air in Greenland Ice." *Earth and Planetary Science Letters* (2008) 268 (3–4): 397–407. doi:10.1016/j.epsl.foo8.01.032. Web. April 2010.

9. Aber, James S. "Paleoclimate Reconstruction." *ES 331/767 Lecture 11*. n.d. n.p. Web. Jan. 2014.

10. Johnsen, Sigfús J. "Warm Times/Cold Times: Holocene Climate Variability in the North Atlantic Region." Paper # 48–1, presented at the XVI INQUA Congress, Reno, Nevada, 2003. Web. May 2010.

11. Aber.

12. Scott, Franklin D. *Sweden: The Nation's History*. Carbondale: Southern Illinois University Press, 1988. 4. Print.

13. Smith, D.E., and A.G. Dawson. *Shorelines and Isostasy*. London: Academic Press, 1983. 189. Print.

14. Wefer et al., 209.

15. Ibid.

16. Donner, Joakim. *The Quaternary History of Scandinavia.*. New York: Cambridge University Press, 1995. 146. Print.

17. Smith and Dawson.

18. Roberts.

19. Wefer et al.

Chapter 2

1. Larsson, Lars. "12 The Late Palaeolithic in Southern Sweden: Investigations in a Marginal Region." *Archaeology Data Services* (ADS.UK). n.d. n.p. Web. April 2010.

2. Aber, James S. "Paleoclimate Reconstruction." *ES 331/767 Lecture 11*. n.d. n.p. Web. Jan. 2014.

3. Donner, Joakim. *The Quaternary History of Scandinavia*. New York: Cambridge University Press, 1995. 109. Print.

4. Ibid., 170.

5. Larsson.

6. Donner, 169.

7. Eriksen, Berit Valentin. "Reconsidering the Geochronological Framework of Lateglacial Hunter-Gatherer Colonization of Southern Scandinavia." *Proceedings of a U.I.S.P.P. Symposium, Stockholm, 14–17 October 1999*. Jutland Archaeological Society Publications, Vol. 39. Højbjerg. 25–41. Web. Jan. 2014.

8. Grimm, Sonja, and Mara-Julia Weber. "Dating the Hamburgian in the Context of Lateglacial Chronology." *Academia.edu*. Chapter 1. n.d. Web. Feb. 2014.

9. Eriksen.

10. Ibid.

11. Ibid.

12. Larsson.

13. Ibid.

14. Passarino, Giuseppe, Gianpiero Cavalleri, Alice Lin, Luigi Luca Cavalli-Sforza, Anne-lise Børresen-Dale and Peter Underhill. "Different Genetic Components in the Norwegian Population Revealed by the Analysis of mtDNA and Y Chromosome Polymorphism." *European Journal of Homan Genetics* (Sep. 2002) 10 (9): 521–29. Web. Jan. 2014.

15. Eriksen.

16. Larsson.

17. Karlsson, Andreas, Thomas Wallerström, Anders Götherström and Gunella Holmlaund. "Y-Chromosome Diversity in Sweden: A Long-time Perspective." *European Journal of Human Genetics* (May 2006) 14. National Publishing Group. 969. Web. Jan. 2014.

18. Eriksen.

19. Schmitt, Lou, Stephan Larsson, Corinna Schrum, Irina Alekseeva, Matthias Tomczak and Krister Svedhage. "Why They Came: The Colonization of the Coast of Western Sweden and Its Environmental Context at the End of the Last Glaciation." *Oxford Journal of Archaeology* (Feb. 2006) 25 (1): 1–28. Wiley Social Sciences and Humanities, 2006. Web. Feb. 2014.

20. Olofsson, Anders. "Pioneering Settlements in the Mesolithic of Northern Sweden." Diss., Umeå University, 2003. Print.

21. Hernek, Robert. "New Light on the Sandarna Culture: A Mesolithic Dwelling-site from the Province of Bohuslän." Diss., Göteborg University, 2005. Print.

22. Olofsson.

23. Ibid.

24. Ibid.
25. Bailey, Geoff, and Penny Spileins, eds. *Mesolithic Europe*. New York: Cambridge University Press, 2008. 107–23. Print.
26. Olofsson.
27. Ibid.
28. Ibid.
29. "The Stone Age." *SNPA.nordish.net/CNIITheStoneAge*. Society of Nordish Physical Anthropology. n.d. Web. May 2008.
30. Olofsson.
31. Bailey and Spileins.
32. "The Stone Age."
33. Jennbert, Kristina. "Ertebølle Pottery in Southern Sweden: A Question of Handicraft, Networks and Creolisation in a Period of Neolithisation." Lund University Publications, 2011. Web. Feb. 2014.
34. Ibid.
35. Ibid.
36. Gron, Ole. "Mesolithic Dwelling Places in South Scandinavia: Their Definition and Social Interpretation." *The Free Library by Farlex*. Antiquity Publications. 2003. Web. Feb. 2014.
37. Fowler, Chris. *The Archaeology of Personhood: An Anthropological Approach*. New York: Routledge, 2004. 71–84. Print.
38. Ibid.
39. Bailey and Spileins.
40. Thorpe, I.J.N. "Anthropology, Archaeology, and the Origin of Warfare." *World Archaeology* (2005) 35 (1): 155. Web. Jan. 2014.
41. Malm, Torben. "Excavating Submerged Stone Age Sites in Denmark: The Tybrind Vig Example." *Abc.se*, 2012. Web. Feb. 2014.
42. Ibid.
43. Ibid.
44. Bailey and Spileins.
45. "The Stone Age."
46. Bailey and Spileins.
47. Ibid.
48. Ibid.
49. Fowler.
50. Thorpe, 145–65.
51. Jennbert.

Chapter 3

1. Baldia, Maximilian. "The Funnel Beaker Culture (TRB)." *Comp-archaeology*, Version 4.15. 2009. Web. March 2010.
2. Müller, Johannes. "Megaliths and Funnel Beakers: Societies in Change 4100–2700 BC." *Gejouden Voor de Stichting Nederlands Museum*. Academia.edu, 8 April 2011. Web. March 2014.
3. Baldia, "The Funnel Beaker Culture."
4. Ibid.
5. Ibid.
6. Ibid.
7. Mallory, J.P., and D.Q. Adams, eds. "TRB Culture." *Encyclopedia of Indo-European Culture*. London: Fitzroy Dearborn, 1997. Print.
8. Ibid.
9. Ibid.
10. Baldia, "The Funnel Beaker Culture."
11. Ibid.
12. Montelius, Oscar. *The Civilization of Sweden in Heathen Times*. New York: Haskell House, 1969. 30–31. Print.
13. Burenhult, Hans, and Anders Carlsson, eds. "The Alvastra Pile Dwelling." *Theoretical Approaches to Artifacts, Settlement and Society*. Oxford: British Archaeology Reports, 1987. Print.
14. Montelius.
15. Mallory and Adams.
16. Holloway, Robert. "The Ancient Roots of Milk Consumption and Its Genetic Dependence." Nevada Technical Associates, Inc. n.d. Web. March 2014.
17. Ibid.
18. Ibid.
19. Ibid.
20. Ohlberger, Annesophie. "Distinguished by Culture." MS thesis, Stockholm University. n.d. Web. March 2014.
21. Burenhult and Carlsson.
22. Mallory and Adams.
23. Ibid.
24. Ibid.
25. Baldia, "The Funnel Beaker Culture."
26. Baldia, Maximilian. "The Corded Ware/Single Grave Culture." *Comp-archaeology*, Version 1.04. January 2006. Web. March 2010.
27. Skak-Neilsen, N.V. "The Genesis of the Battle Axe Culture: On Klaus Ebbesen's Doctoral Thesis. A Critique and Alternative Conclusion." Trans. Martin Rundkvist. *Fornvännen* (2006) 101 (4,s): [274]–77. Web. March 2014.
28. Baldia, "The Corded Ware/Single Grave Culture."
29. Ibid.
30. Ibid.
31. Ibid.
32. Ibid.
33. Ibid.
34. Kristiansen, Kristian. "What Language Did Neolithic Pots Speak?" *Kristian Kristiansen*, 930 view. Academia.edu (shared research). n.d. Web. March 2014.
35. Skak-Neilsen.
36. "The Stone Age." *SNPA.nordish.net/CNIITheStoneAge*. Society of Nordish Physical Anthropology. n.d. Web. May 2008.
37. Ibid.
38. Skak-Neilsen.

Chapter 4

1. Jones, Gwyn. *A History of the Vikings*. Oxford: Oxford University Press, 1984. 18–19. Print.
2. Scott, Franklin. *Sweden: The Nation's History*. Carbondale: Southern Illinois Press, 1988. 9. Print; Montelius, Oscar. *The Civilisation of Sweden in Heathen Times*. Trans. Francis Henry Woods. New York: Haskell House, 1969. 66. Print.
3. Fenton, Carroll, and Mildred Fenton. *Giants of Geology*. Garden City, NY: Doubleday, 1952. 303. Print.
4. Montelius, *The Civilisation of Sweden in Heathen Times*, 47–58.
5. Sørensen, Marie Louise Stig. "Scandinavia in the Bronze Age." *Jrank.org*. n.d. Web. June 2010. From a paper by Oscar Montelius, "Om tidsbestämning inom bronsåldern med särskilt avseende på Skandinavien," 1885.
6. Jones, 18.
7. Larsson, Thomas, and Hans Lundmark. *Approaches to Swedish Prehistory*. Oxford: B.A.R., 1989. 287–318. Print.
8. Franklin, 8.
9. Harding, Anthony. "Amber in the Mycenaean World." British School of Athens, 25 Jan. 2013. From "The Annual of British School of Athens." Vol. 69 (1979). 145–72. Web. March 2014.
10. Montelius, *The Civilisation of Sweden in Heathen Times*, 71; Larsson and Lundmark, *Approaches to the Swedish Prehistory*, 303.
11. Larsson, Lars, Johan Callmer and Berta Stjernquist, eds. *The Archaeology of the Cultural Landscape*. Stockholm: Almqvist & Wiksell International, 1992. 371–72. Print.
12. Roberts, Neil. *The Holocene: An Environmental History*. Oxford: Blackwell, 1989. 118. Print.
13. Moberg, Vilhelm. *A History of the Swedish People*. Vol. I. Trans. Paul Britten Austin. New York: Dorset Press, 1989. 36. Print.
14. Larsson, Callmer and Stjernquist, 289.
15. Ibid., 290.
16. Ibid., 296.
17. Ibid., 291.
18. Ibid.
19. Ibid.
20. Ibid., 295.
21. Ibid., 264.
22. Artelius, Tore, and Fredrik Svanberg. *Dealing with the Dead*. Ödenshög, Sweden: National Heritage Board, 2005. 253. Print.

23. Montelius, *The Civilisation of Sweden in Heathen Times*, 85.
24. Artelius and Svanberg, 202.
25. Montelius, *The Civilisation of Sweden in Heathen Times*, 58–65.
26. Ibid., 60–62.
27. Ibid., 84.
28. Artelius and Svanberg, 237.
29. Ibid.
30. Ibid., 159–71.
31. Ibid., 73–98.
32. Ibid.
33. Ibid.
34. Ibid., 214.
35. "Trundholm Sun Chariot." Archeurope.com. n.d. Web. April 2014.
36. Larsson, Callmer and Stjernquist, 66–67.
37. Ibid., 71.

Chapter 5

1. Scott, Franklin. *Sweden: The Nation's History*. Carbondale: Southern University Press, 1988. 9–10. Print.
2. Durant, Will. *The History of Civilization*. Vol. 1. New York: Simon & Schuster, 1935. 104. Print.
3. Davies, Norman. *Europe: A History*. Oxford: Oxford University Press, 1996. 83. Print.
4. Stjernquist, Berta. *Acta Archaeologica Lundensia*. Lund: Berlingska Boktryckeriet, 1961. 11. Print.
5. Ibid., 145.
6. Montelius, Oscar. *The Civilisation of Sweden in Heathen Times*. New York: Haskell House, 1969. 91–96. Print.
7. Jones, Gwyn. *A History of the Vikings*. Oxford: Oxford University Press, 1984. 19–20. Print.
8. Wefer, Gerold, Wolfgang H. Berger, Karl-Ernst Behre and Eystein Jansen. *Climate Development and History of the North Atlantic Realm*. Berlin: Springer, 2002. 285. Print.
9. Larsson, Lars, Johan Callmer and Berta Stjernquist, eds. *The Archaeology of the Cultural Landscape*. Stockholm: Almquvist & Wiksell International, 1992. 372–73. Print.
10. Ibid., 310–11.
11. Jones, 20.
12. Herm, Gerhard. *The Celts*. New York: St. Martin's Press, 1976. 126–27. Print.
13. Ibid., 118–28.
14. Churchill, Winston. *A History of the English-speaking Peoples*. Vol. I. New York: Barnes & Noble, 1993. 12. Print.
15. Herm, 6.
16. Barker, Felix, and Anthea Barker. *Encyclopedia of Discovery and Exploration*. Vol. 1. London: Aldus Books, 1971. 95. Print.
17. Davies, 107.
18. Barker and Barker, 96–98.
19. Strabo. *Geographica*. Vol. I, Book 4, sec. 2. Trans. Horace Leonard Jones. University of Chicago. n.d. Web. April 2014.
20. Strabo, Vol. II, Book 5, sec. 8
21. Pliny the Elder. *The Natural History*. Book 4, Chap. 30. Perseus Digital Library, Tufts University. n.d. Web. April 2014.
22. Strabo, Vol. IV, Book 5, sec. 5.
23. Pliny, Book 37, Chap. 11.
24. Larsson, Thomas B., and Hans Lundmark. *Approaches to Swedish Prehistory*. Oxford: B.A.R., 1989. 344. Print.
25. Ibid., 345.
26. Ibid., 346.
27. Wefer et al., 285.
28. Jones, 23.
29. Richie, Alexandra. *Faust's Metropolis*. New York: Carroll & Graf, 1998. 3–4. Print.
30. Jones, 23.
31. Richie, 4.

Chapter 6

1. Montelius, Oscar. *The Civilization of Sweden in Heathen Times*. Trans. Francis Henry Woods. New York: Haskell House, 1969. 99. Print.
2. Ibid., 99–103.
3. Ibid.
4. Ibid., 108–9.
5. Ibid., 115–16.
6. Larsson, Lars, Johan Callmer and Berta Stjernquist, eds. *The Archaeology of the Cultural Landscape*. Stockholm: Almquvist & Wiksell International, 1992. 310–26. Print.
7. Ibid., 373.
8. Jones, Gwyn. *A History of the Vikings*. Oxford: Oxford University Press, 1984. 23. Print.
9. Artelius, Tore, and Fredrik Svanberg. *Dealing with the Dead*. Ödenshög, Sweden: National Heritage Board, 2005. 152. Print.
10. Montelius, 117.
11. Ibid., 120.
12. Ibid., 119.
13. Larsson, Thomas B., and Hans Lundmark. *Approaches to Swedish Prehistory*. Oxford: B.A.R., 1989. 67. Print.
14. Larsson, Callmer and Stjernquist, 68.
15. Jones, 24.
16. Mela, Pomponius. *Description of the World*. Book IV. Trans. Frank E. Romer. Ann Arbor: University of Michigan Press, 1998. Chap. 27. 109. Print.
17. Jones, 24.
18. Pliny the Elder. "Chapter 27, The Islands of the Euxine. The Islands of the Northern Ocean." The *Natural History*, Book IV. Plin.Nat. 4.27. Trans. John Bostark and H.T. Riley. Perseus Digital Library, Tufts University. Sec. 13, Par. 3. Web. 30 Nov. 2014.
19. Hutchins, Robert. *The Great Books of the Western World*. Vol. 15: Tacitus. Chicago: Williams Beaton, 1952. v. Print.
20. Tacitus, Publius Cornelius. "Germania." *The Works of Tacitus* (Oxford trans.). New York: Harpers & Brothers, 1874. Chap. 1, Sec. 44. Print.
21. Jones, 24.
22. Tacitus, 44.
23. Ibid., 45.
24. Jones, 25.
25. Hutchins, Vol. 16.
26. Ptolemy, Claudius. *The Geography*. Book II. Trans. Edward Luther Stevenson. University of Chicago. n.d. Sec. 11. Web. Feb. 2012.

Chapter 7

1. Roberts, J.M. *History of the World*. New York: Alfred A. Knopf, 1976. 284. Print.
2. Davies, Norman. *Europe: A History*. Oxford: Oxford University Press, 1996. 232. Print.
3. Wells, H. G. *The Outline of History*. Vol. I. Garden City, NY: Garden City Books, 1956. 408–9. Print.
4. Wolfram, Herwig. *The Roman Empire and Its Germanic People*. Trans. Thomas Dunlap. Berkeley: University of California Press, 1997. 312. Print.
5. Wells, 409.
6. Wolfram, *The Roman Empire and Its Germanic People*, 172.
7. Gibbon, Edward. *The Decline and Fall of the Roman Empire*. Vol. I. Chicago: Encyclopædia Britannica, 1952. 590–91. Print.
8. Ibid.
9. Ibid.
10. Wolfram, *The Roman Empire and Its Germanic People*, XIII.
11. Gibbon, 591.
12. Wolfram, *The Roman Empire and Its Germanic People*, 185–87.
13. Ibid., 44.
14. Burns, Thomas. *A History of the Ostrogoths*. Bloomington: Indiana University Press, 1984. 23–24. Print.
15. Wolfram, *The Roman Empire and Its Germanic People*, 44–45.
16. Ibid.
17. Ibid.
18. Ibid.
19. Burns, 30–31.
20. Wolfram, *The Roman Empire and Its Germanic People*, 76.
21. Ibid., 78.

22. Wolfram, Herwig. *History of the Goths.* Trans. Thomas J. Dunlap. Berkeley: University of California Press, 1979. 57. Print.
23. Wolfram, *The Roman Empire and Its Germanic People*, 79.
24. Ibid., 85.
25. Wolfram, *History of the Goths*, 133.
26. Wolfram, *The Roman Empire and Its Germanic People*, 90–91.
27. Ibid., 95–96.
28. Wolfram, *History of the Goths*, 158–60.
29. Wolfram, *The Roman Empire and Its Germanic People*, 145–47.
30. Ibid.
31. Ibid., 145–58.

Chapter 8

1. Burns, Thomas. *A History of the Ostrogoths.* Bloomington: Indiana University Press, 1984. 44. Print.
2. Wolfram, Herwig. *The Roman Empire and Its Germanic People.* Trans. Thomas Dunlap. Berkeley: University of California Press, 1997. 128–29. Print.
3. Wells, H. G. *The Outline of History.* Vol. I. Garden City, NY: Garden City Books, 1956. 410. Print.
4. Wolfram, *The Roman Empire and Its Germanic People*, 136.
5. Ibid., 137.
6. Gibbon, Edward. *The Decline and Fall of the Roman Empire.* Vol. I. Chicago: Encyclopædia Britannica, 1952. 568. Print.
7. Wolfram, Herwig. *History of the Goths.* Trans. Thomas J. Dunlap. Berkeley: University of California Press, 1979. 261–62. Print.
8. Ibid., 264–65.
9. Ibid., 279.
10. Ibid., 281.
11. Ibid., 283.
12. Ibid., 309.
13. Ibid., 331.
14. Ibid., 338.
15. Ibid., 340.
16. Ibid., 348–49.
17. Ibid., 353–62.
18. Wolfram, *The Roman Empire and Its Germanic People*, 263–64.
19. Ibid., 271.
20. Ibid., 272–73.
21. Ibid., 274.
22. Ibid., 275–78.

Chapter 9

1. Wolfram, Herwig. *The Roman Empire and Its Germanic People.* Trans. Thomas Dunlap. Berkeley: University of California Press, 1997. 28. Print.
2. Wolfram, Herwig. *History of the Goths.* Trans. Thomas J. Dunlap. Berkeley: University of California Press, 1979. 31. Print.
3. Burns, Thomas. *A History of the Ostrogoths.* Bloomington: Indiana University Press, 1984. 23–24. Print.
4. Wolfram, *History of the Goths*, 15.
5. Jordanes. *The Origins and Deeds of the Goths (Getica).* Trans. Charles C. Mierow. Princeton, NJ: Princeton University Press, 1908. Chap. L, Ver. 266. Print.
6. Ibid., Preface, Ver. 1.
7. Ibid., Preface, Ver. 3.
8. Ibid., Chap. I, Ver. 9.
9. Ibid., Chap. IV, Ver. 25–27.
10. Ibid., Chap. IV, Ver. 28.
11. Burns, 60.
12. Jordanes, Chap. IV, Ver. 27–28.
13. Wolfram, *History of the Goths*, 20.
14. Gibbon, Edward. *The Decline and Fall of the Roman Empire.* Vol. I. Chicago: Encyclopædia Britannica, 1952. 97. Print.
15. *National Geographic Atlas of the World.* Seventh edition. Washington, DC: National Geographic Society, 1999. Map 79. Print.
16. Roberts, Michael. *The Early Vasas.* Cambridge: Cambridge University Press, 1968. 26. Print.
17. Jones, Gwyn. *A History of the Vikings.* Oxford: Oxford University Press, 1984. 43. Print.
18. Roberts, Michael. *Gustav Adolf the Great.* New York: Longman, 1992. 72. Print.
19. Wolfram, *History of the Goths*, 21.
20. Jordanes, Chap. III, Ver. 22–23.
21. Wolfram, *History of the Goths*, 22.
22. Ibid., 28.
23. Pliny the Elder. *The Natural History.* Book 37, Chap. 11. Perseus Digital Library, Tufts University. n.d. Web. April 2014.
24. Tacitus, Publius Cornelius. "Germania." *The Works of Tacitus* (Oxford trans.). New York: Harpers & Brothers, 1874. Chap. 1, Sec. 43. Print.
25. Tacitus, Chap. 1, Sec. 44.
26. Ptolemy, Claudius. *The Geography.* Book II. Trans. Edward Luther Stevenson. University of Chicago. n.d. Chap. 10. Web. Feb. 2012.
27. Wolfram, *History of the Goths*, 39.
28. Makiewicz, Tadeusz. *The Archeology of the Transit Gas Pipeline: The Goths in Greater Poland.* Poznán Acheological Museum. n.d. Web. Feb. 2012.
29. Makiewicz; Wolfram, *History of the Goths*, 394.
30. Makiewicz.
31. Ibid.
32. Burns, 21.
33. Ibid., 24–25.
34. Makiewicz.
35. Gibbon, 98.

Chapter 10

1. Wilson, David M. *The Northern World.* New York: Harry N. Abrams, 1980. 145. Print.
2. Jordanes. *The Origins and Deeds of the Goths (Getica).* Trans. Charles C. Mierow. Princeton, NJ: Princeton University Press, 1908. Chap. III. Print.
3. Ibid.
4. Ibid.
5. Ibid.
6. Ibid., Chap. III, Ver. 22.
7. Ibid., Chap. III, Ver. 24.
8. Jones, Gwen. *A History of the Vikings.* Oxford: Oxford University Press, 1984. 26. Print.
9. Wilson, *The Northern World*, 145.
10. Jones, 28.
11. Ibid.
12. Ibid., 29.
13. Procopius. *History of the Wars.* Book VI. Trans. H.B. Dewing. London: William Heinemann, 1971. Chap. XV. Print.
14. Ibid.
15. Wilson, *The Northern World*, 145.
16. Widsith. *Widsith.* Trans. Bella Millett. Wilkins of the Archaeology Department, University of Oxford. n.d. Lines 58–59. Web. May 2014.
17. Ibid.
18. Jones, 34–35.
19. Magnusson, Magnus, Sheila Mackie and Julian Glover. *Beowulf.* Trans. Michael Alexander and Edwin Morgan. Wolfboro: Alan Sutton, 1988. 21. Print.
20. Jones, 35.
21. Ibid., 43.
22. *Beowulf.* Trans. Francis B. Gummere. The Harvard Classics, Vol. 49. New York: P.F. Collier & Son, 1910. Sec. XVIII. Print.
23. Jones, 30.
24. Ibid.
25. Jones, 30; Magnusson, Mackie and Glover, 30.
26. Jones, 36.
27. Ibid., 36–37.
28. *Beowulf*, Sec. XXXI.
29. Ibid.
30. Ibid., Sec. XL.
31. Ibid.
32. Ibid.
33. Ibid., Sec. XLI.
34. Jones, 36–37.
35. *Beowulf*, Sec. XXXIII.
36. Jones, 36–37.
37. Sturluson, Snorri. "The Yn-

glinga Saga," in *Heimskringla*. Trans. Samuel Laing. New York: E. P. Dutton, 1930. Sec. 7. Print.
  38. Jones, 37.
  39. Sturluson.
  40. Ibid., Sec. 12.
  41. Ibid., Sec. 17.
  42. Ibid., Sec. 29.
  43. Jones, 46.
  44. Sturluson, Sec. 34.
  45. Jones, 38.
  46. Wilson, *The Northern World*, 146.
  47. Wilson, David. *The Vikings and Their Origins*. New York: A & W, 1980. 66. Print.
  48. Wilson, *The Northern World*, 146.
  49. Moberg, Vilhelm. *A History of the Swedish People*. Vol. I. Trans. Paul Britten Austin. New York: Dorset Press, 1989. 53. Print.
  50. Ibid., 54–55.

Chapter 11

  1. Jones, Gwen. *A History of the Vikings*. Oxford: Oxford University Press, 1984. 43. Print.
  2. Wilson, David M. *The Northern World*. New York: Harry N. Abrams, 1980. 36–40. Print.
  3. Shepherd, Sandy. *Myths and Legends*. New York: Macmillan, 1995. 70–71. Print.
  4. Almgren, Bertil, Charlotte Blindheim, Yves de Bouard, Torsten Capelle, Arne Emil Christensen, Kristjan Eldjarn, Richard Perkins, Thorkild Ramskou and Peter Sawyer. *The Vikings*. Gothenburg: Crescent Books, 1975. 141–42. Print.
  5. Ibid.
  6. Shepherd, 70–71.
  7. Almgren et al., 141–42.
  8. Shepherd, 70–71.
  9. Adam of Bremen. *History of the Archbishops of Hamburg*. Book 4: "The Temple at Old Uppsala." Trans. Francis J. Tschan. New York: Columbia University Press, 1959. Chap. 26. Print.
  10. Ibid., Chap. 27.
  11. Sturluson, Snorri. "The Ynglinga Saga," in *Heimskringla*. Trans. Samuel Laing. New York: E. P. Dutton, 1930. Sec. 25, 34, 35. Print.
  12. Ibid., Sec. 25.
  13. Ibid., Sec. 35.
  14. Jones, 52.
  15. Ibid., 52–53.
  16. Ibid., 54.
  17. Ibid., 151.
  18. Churchill, Winston. *A History of the English-speaking Peoples*. Vol. I. New York: Barnes & Noble, 1993. 54. Print.
  19. Ibid., 55.
  20. Savage, Anne. *The Anglo-Saxon Chronicles*. New York: Barnes & Noble, 2000. 29. Print.
  21. Ibid.
  22. Bjørklund, Oddvar, Haadon Holmboe, Anders Røhr and Berit Lie. *Historical Atlas of the World*. New York: Barnes & Noble, 1970. Map 32. Print.
  23. Wilson, David. *The Vikings and Their Origins*. New York: A & W, 1980. 65. Print.
  24. Wilson, *The Northern World*, 148–49.
  25. La Fay, Howard. *The Vikings*. Washington, DC: National Geographic Society, 1972. 19. Print.
  26. Wilson, *Vikings*, 70.
  27. La Fay, 17–18.
  28. Moberg, Vilhelm. *A History of the Swedish People*. Vol. I. Trans. Paul Britten Austin. New York: Dorset Press, 1989. 12–29. Print.
  29. Ibid., 16–17.
  30. Wilson, *The Northern World*, 149.
  31. Ibid.
  32. La Fay, 18.
  33. Wilson, *The Northern World*, 146.
  34. Wilson, *Vikings*, 65.
  35. Wilson, *The Northern World*, 148.
  36. Ibid.
  37. Ibid.
  38. Ibid.
  39. Savage, 36.
  40. Ibid., 18.
  41. Ibid., 37.
  42. Wilson, *The Northern World*, 149.
  43. Ibid.
  44. Wilson, *Vikings*, 68–69.
  45. Wilson, *The Northern World*, 149.
  46. Ibid., 150–51.
  47. Ibid., 151.
  48. Ibid., 128.
  49. Ibid., 151–52.
  50. Ibid., 91–94.
  51. Alexander, Caroline. "Magical Mystery Treasure." *National Geographic* (Nov. 2011): 40–61. Print.
  52. *Beowulf*. Trans. Francis B. Gummere. The Harvard Classics, Vol. 49. New York: P.F. Collier & Son, 1910. Prelude. Print.
  53. Ibid.
  54. Wilson, *The Northern World*, 152.
  55. La Fay, 22.
  56. Wilson, *The Northern World*, 152–53.

Chapter 12

  1. La Fay, Howard. *The Vikings*. Washington, DC: National Geographic Society, 1972. 30–31. Print.
  2. There was one incident prior to this in 789, recorded in the Anglo-Saxon Chronicle, concerning a landing of three longships and the killing of a reeve who rode to meet them. Savage, Anne. *The Anglo-Saxon Chronicles*. New York: Barnes & Noble, 2000. 73. Print.
  3. Ibid., 73.
  4. Churchill, Winston S. *A History of the English-speaking Peoples*. Vol. I. New York: Barnes & Noble, 1993. 95–96. Print.
  5. Savage, 76.
  6. Jones, Gwyn. *A History of the Vikings*. Oxford: Oxford University Press, 1984. 212. Print.
  7. Ibid., 198.
  8. Ritchie, Anna. *Viking Scotland*. London: B. T. Batsford, 1993. 10. Print.
  9. Ibid., 21.
  10. Ibid., 18–19.
  11. Wilson, David. *The Northern World*. New York: Harry N. Abrams, 1980. 174. Print.
  12. Jones, 204.
  13. La Fay, 76.
  14. Jones, 204.
  15. Ibid., 205.
  16. Ibid., 206.
  17. La Fay, 74.
  18. Jones, 206.
  19. Wilson, *The Northern World*, 174–75.
  20. Jones, 207.
  21. Ibid.
  22. La Fay, 74.
  23. Jones, 208.
  24. Wilson, *The Northern World*, 95.

Chapter 13

  1. Churchill, Winston S. *A History of the English-speaking Peoples*. Vol. I. New York: Barnes & Noble, 1993. 107. Print.
  2. Ibid., 98.
  3. Savage, Anne. *The Anglo-Saxon Chronicles*. New York: Barnes & Noble, 2000. 83. Print.
  4. Jones, Gwyn. *A History of the Vikings*. Oxford: Oxford University Press, 1984. 210. Print.
  5. Almgren, Bertil, Charlotte Blindheim, Yves de Bouard, Torsten Capelle, Arne Emil Christensen, Kristjan Eldjarn, Richard Perkins, Thorkild Ramskou and Peter Sawyer. *The Vikings*. Gothenburg: Crescent Books, 1975. 74. Print.
  6. Churchill, 98.
  7. Ibid., 99–100.
  8. Savage, 92.
  9. Jones, 219.
  10. Churchill, 100.
  11. Jones, 219–20.
  12. Churchill, 100.
  13. Jones, 219–21.

14. Ibid., 223.
15. Churchill, 113.
16. Jones, 223.
17. Ibid., 226–29.
18. Churchill, 127.
19. Ibid., 128–29.
20. Savage, 119.
21. Jones, 237.
22. *Egil's Saga.* Trans. Hermann Pálsson and Paul Edwards. London: Penguin Books, 1976. 127. Print.
23. Almgen et al., 81.

Chapter 14

1. Davies, Norman. *Europe: A History.* Oxford: Oxford University Press, 1996. 298–302. Print.
2. Almgren, Bertil, Charlotte Blindheim, Yves de Bouard, Torsten Capelle, Arne Emil Christensen, Kristjan Eldjarn, Richard Perkins, Thorkild Ramskou and Peter Sawyer. *The Vikings.* Gothenburg: Crescent Books, 1975. 120. Print.
3. La Fay, Howard. *The Vikings.* Washington, DC: National Geographic Society, 1972. 34. Print.
4. Lie, Berit. *Historical Atlas of the World.* New York: Barnes & Noble, 1970. Map 36. Print.
5. Jones, Gwyn. *A History of the Vikings.* Oxford: Oxford University Press, 1984. 209–10. Print.
6. Ibid., 211.
7. Ibid., 107.
8. Ibid., 212–13.
9. Ibid., 215–16.
10. Ibid., 224–25.
11. Wilson, David. *The Northern World.* New York: Harry N. Abrams, 1980. 171. Print.
12. Brown, R. Allen. *The Normans.* New York: St. Martin's Press, 1984. 14–15. Print.
13. Jones, 229–31.
14. Almgren et al., 122.
15. Ibid.
16. Jones, 213.
17. La Fay, 80.
18. Jones, 213–14.
19. La Fay, 81.
20. Jones, 216.
21. La Fay, 91–92.
22. Jones, 216.
23. La Fay, 92–93.
24. Jones, 216.

Chapter 15

1. Wilson, David M. *The Vikings and Their Origins.* New York: A & W, 1980. 78–79. Print.
2. Jones, Gwyn. *A History of the Vikings.* Oxford: Oxford University Press, 1984. 186. Print.
3. Wilson, *The Vikings and Their Origins*, 79.
4. Jones, 186–87.
5. Ibid., 187.
6. Wilson, *The Vikings and Their Origins*, 78.
7. Jones, 189, 194.
8. Ibid., 189–90.
9. La Fay, Howard. *The Vikings.* Washington, DC: National Geographic Society, 1972. 20. Print.
10. Almgren, Bertil, Charlotte Blindheim, Yves de Bouard, Torsten Capelle, Arne Emil Christensen, Kristjan Eldjarn, Richard Perkins, Thorkild Ramskou and Peter Sawyer. *The Vikings.* Gothenburg: Crescent Books, 1975. 11. Print.
11. Ibid., 13–14.
12. Jones, 193–94.
13. Almgren et al., 14.
14. Jones, 192–94.
15. Almgren et al., 14.
16. Ibid., 11.
17. *Egil's Saga.* Trans. Hermann Pálsson and Paul Edwards. London: Penguin Books, 1976. 79. Print.
18. Ibid.
19. Almgren et al., 24–25.
20. Gibbon, Edward. *The Decline and Fall of the Roman Empire.* Vol. II. Chicago: Encyclopædia Britannica, 1952. 341. Print.

Chapter 16

1. Jones, Gwyn. *A History of the Vikings.* Oxford: Oxford University Press, 1984. 270. Print.
2. Almgren, Bertil, Charlotte Blindheim, Yves de Bouard, Torsten Capelle, Arne Emil Christensen, Kristjan Eldjarn, Richard Perkins, Thorkild Ramskou and Peter Sawyer. *The Vikings.* Gothenburg: Crescent Books, 1975. 96. Print.
3. Jones, 273–75.
4. Ibid.
5. Ibid.
6. Almgren et al., 98–99.
7. Ibid., 102.
8. Ibid., 98–103.
9. Ibid., 105.
10. Ibid., 112–13.
11. La Fay, Howard. *The Vikings.* Washington, DC: National Geographic Society, 1972. 122. Print.
12. Jones, 190–95.
13. Boorstin, Daniel J. *The Discoverers.* New York: Vintage Books, 1985. 211. Print.
14. Ibid.
15. Ibid., 211–12.
16. Ibid.
17. La Fay, 142.
18. Boorstin, 212.
19. Ibid.
20. Jones, 301.
21. Boorstin, 213.
22. Ibid.
23. Ibid., 213–14.
24. La Fay, 140–41.
25. MacDonald, Malcolm Ross. *Encyclopedia of Discovery and Exploration.* Vol. 2. London: Aldus Books, 1971. 59. Print.
26. Boorstin, 214.
27. Jones, 304.
28. Wilson, David. *The Northern World.* New York: Harry N. Abrams, 1980. 181. Print.
29. Jones, 294.
30. Ibid.
31. Schledermann, Peter. "Eskimo and Viking Finds in the High Arctic." *National Geographic* (May 1981). 578. Print.
32. Pringle, Heather. "Vikings and Native Americans." *National Geographic* (Nov. 2012). 80–93. Print.
33. Ibid.
34. Diamond, Jared. *Collapse.* New York: Penguin Books, 2005. 257–58. Print.
35. Jones, 306.
36. Almgren et al., 119.

Chapter 17

1. Shakespeare, William. "Hamlet, Prince of Denmark." *The Plays and Sonnets of William Shakespeare.* Vol. II. Ed. William George Clarke and William Aldis Wright. Chicago: Encyclopædia Britannica, 1952. 54 (Act III, scene III, verse 3). Print.
2. Mabillard, Amanda. "Shakespeare's Sources for Hamlet." *Shakespeare Online*, 2000. Web. July 2014.
3. Jones, Gwyn. *A History of the Vikings.* Oxford: Oxford University Press, 1984. 52. Print.
4. Ibid.
5. Ibid., 53–54.
6. Ibid., 98.
7. La Fay, Howard. *The Vikings.* Washington, DC: National Geographic Society, 1972. 34. Print.
8. Jones, 98–103.
9. Ibid., 105–6.
10. Ibid., 108.
11. Ibid., 108–9.
12. Ibid., 111.
13. Ibid., 113–14.
14. Ibid.
15. Ibid.
16. Ibid., 118.

Chapter 18

1. Jones, Gwyn. *A History of the Vikings.* Oxford: Oxford University Press, 1984. 79–81. Print.
2. Ibid., 82.
3. Ibid., 81–82.
4. Ibid., 84.
5. Ibid., 86.
6. Ibid., 87.
7. Ibid., 88–89.
8. Ibid., 89.

9. *Egil's Saga.* Trans. Gwyn Jones. New York: Twayne, 1960. 35. Print.
10. Jones, 93.
11. Ibid.
12. Ibid., 94–95.
13. Ibid., 118–19.
14. Ibid., 119.
15. Ibid., 121.
16. Ibid., 122–23.
17. Ibid., 125.
18. Ibid., 128.
19. Ibid., 129.
20. Ibid., 129–30.

Chapter 19

1. Churchill, Winston S. *A History of the English-speaking Peoples.* Vol. I. New York: Barnes & Noble, 1993. 130–35. Print.
2. Almgren, Bertil, Charlotte Blindheim, Yves de Bouard, Torsten Capelle, Arne Emil Christensen, Kristjan Eldjarn, Richard Perkins, Thorkild Ramskou and Peter Sawyer. *The Vikings.* Gothenburg: Crescent Books, 1975. 81–83. Print.
3. Ingram, Reverend J. *The Saxon Chronicle.* London: Studio Editions, 1993. 165. Print.
4. Almgren et al., 83.
5. Churchill, 135.
6. Ibid.
7. Ibid.
8. Kipling, Rudyard. "Danegeld." *Poetry Lovers Page.* n.d. Web. July 2012.
9. Ibid.
10. Churchill, 136.
11. Ibid.
12. Ibid., 137.
13. Ingram, 188–89.
14. Jones, Gwyn. *A History of the Vikings.* Oxford: Oxford University Press, 1984. 131. Print.
15. Ibid.
16. Ibid., 132–33.
17. Ibid., 133.
18. Longfellow, Henry Wadsworth. "*Tales of a Wayside Inn* 1863: The Musician's Tale; The Saga of King Olaf II, King Olaf's Return." *Hwlongfellow.org.* n.d. Web. Aug. 2012.
19. Jones, 133–34.
20. Ibid., 134.
21. Ibid., 137.
22. Longfellow, "The Musician's Tale; The Saga of King Olaf XXI, King Olaf's Death-drink."
23. Jones, 140.
24. Ibid., 368.
25. Churchill, 138.
26. Jones, 369–70.
27. Ibid., 371.
28. Churchill, 138.
29. Jones, 371–72.
30. Ibid., 375.
31. Ibid., 376.
32. Ibid., 377–79.
33. Ibid., 380.
34. Ibid., 380–81.
35. Ibid., 398.

Chapter 20

1. Jones, Gwyn. *A History of the Vikings.* Oxford: Oxford University Press, 1984. 386. Print.
2. Ibid., 398.
3. Churchill, Winston S. *A History of the English-speaking Peoples.* Vol. I. New York: Barnes & Noble, 1993. 143–44. Print.
4. Jones, 400.
5. Ibid., 405.
6. Ibid., 406.
7. Ibid., 414.
8. Ibid., 408.
9. Ibid., 410.
10. Ibid., 411.
11. Ibid., 412–13.
12. Savage, Anne. *The Anglo-Saxon Chronicles.* New York: Barnes & Noble, 2000. 194–95. Print.
13. Jones, 413.
14. Churchill, 160.
15. Brown, R. Allen. *The Normans.* New York: St. Martin's Press, 1984. 15–16. Print.
16. Churchill, 142–43.
17. Brown, 43.
18. Ibid., Table 1.
19. Churchill, 153.
20. Ibid., 154.
21. Brown, 54–56.
22. Ibid., 60.
23. Ibid.
24. Ibid., 64.
25. Ibid., 65–66.
26. Coakley, John E., and Robert W. Jessup. *Guide to the Study of Military History.* Washington, DC: Center of Military History, U.S. Army, 1979. 99. Print.
27. Savage, 195.
28. Churchill, 167.
29. Brown, 70.
30. Jones, 414.

Chapter 21

1. Gibbon, Edward. *The Decline and Fall of the Roman Empire.* Vol. II. Chicago: Encyclopædia Britannica, 1952. 350. Print.
2. Brown, R. Allen. *The Normans.* New York: St. Martin's Press, 1984. 81–82. Print.
3. Ibid., 86.
4. Ibid., 86–87.
5. Ibid., 88.
6. Ibid., 90–91.
7. Ibid., 93.
8. Ibid., 96–97.
9. Ibid., 100.
10. Ibid., 102.

Chapter 22

1. Moberg, Vilhelm. *A History of the Swedish People.* Vol. I. Trans. Paul Britten Austin. New York: Dorset Press, 1989. 66. Print.
2. MacDonald, Malcolm Ross. *Encyclopedia of Discovery and Exploration.* Vol. 2. London: Aldus Books, 1971. 35. Print.
3. *Landnámabók.* Trans. Rev. T. Ellwood. Part 3, Chapter XII. New Northvegr Center, 2009. 5. Web. Aug. 2014.
4. Ibid., Part 3, Chapter IX, 4.
5. *The Book of Settlements: Landnámabók.* Trans. Hermann Pálsson and Paul Edwards. Manitoba: University of Manitoba Press, 1972. Chapter 209. Print.
6. *Landnámabók,* Part 3, Chapter XI, 4.
7. Coon, Carleton Stevens. "Iceland." *The Races of Europe,* Chapter IX, Sec. 5. Society for Nordish Physical Anthropology. n.d. Web. Aug. 2014.
8. See chapters 13–20.
9. Jones, Gwyn. *A History of the Vikings.* Oxford: Oxford University Press, 1984. 44. Print.
10. *Rundata* 2.5. Uppsala Universitet, Department of Scandinavian Languages. n.d. DR 337. Web. Aug. 2014.
11. Ibid., Sö 53.
12. Ibid., Sö 62.
13. Ibid., U 668.
14. Ibid., U 344.
15. Ibid., Sö 106.
16. Ibid., Sö 159.
17. Ibid., Sö 164.
18. Peo. "Rune Stones and Other Runic Inscriptions." *Stone-Struck.* 5 Dec. 2010. http://www.runesnruins.com/runes/index.htm. n.d. Vg 61. Web. Aug. 2015.
19. *Rundata,* U 616.
20. Peo, U 812.
21. *Rundata,* U 1181.
22. Peo, Sm 5.
23. Ibid., Sm 101.
24. *Rundata,* Sö 166.
25. Ibid., U 194.
26. Ibid., Sö 14.
27. Peo, Ög 111.
28. *Rundata,* U 16.
29. Ibid., Sm 76.
30. Ibid., Sm 42.
31. Almgren, Bertil, Charlotte Blindheim, Yves de Bouard, Torsten Capelle, Arne Emil Christensen, Kristjan Eldjarn, Richard Perkins, Thorkild Ramskou and Peter Sawyer. *The Vikings.* Gothenburg: Crescent Books, 1975. 122–23. Print.
32. Wilson, David. *The Northern World.* New York: Harry N. Abrams, 1980. 176. Print.

33. Wilson, David M. *The Vikings and Their Origins*. New York: A & W, 1980. 74. Print.
34. Wilson, *The Northern World*, 176.
35. *Rundata*, U 141.
36. Ibid., Sö Fv1954; 22.
37. Ibid., Sö 65.

Chapter 23

1. Jones, Gwyn. *A History of the Vikings*. Oxford: Oxford University Press, 1984. 25. Print.
2. *Egil's Saga*. Trans. Hermann Pálsson and Paul Edwards. London: Penguin Books, 1976. 44. Print.
3. Jones, 2.
4. *Seven Viking Romances*. Trans. Hermann Pálsson and Paul Edwards. London: Penguin Books, 1985. 240. Print.
5. Sturluson, Snorri. "The Ynglinga Saga," in *Heimskringla*. Trans. Samuel Laing. New York: E. P. Dutton, 1930. Sec. 36. Print.
6. Ibid., Sec. 38.
7. *Seven Viking Romances*, 138.
8. Ibid., 144–45.
9. Ibid., 152.
10. Sturluson, Sec. 43.
11. Ibid., Sec. 42.
12. Ibid., Sec. 43.
13. Ibid.
14. Jones, 241.
15. Sturluson, Sec. 45.
16. Savage, Anne. *The Anglo-Saxon Chronicles*. New York: Barnes & Noble, 2000. 40–44. Print.
17. Grammaticus, Saxo. "The Danish History." Ed. Douglas B. Killings. Trans. Oliver Elton. *The Online Medieval & Classical Library*. Release #28b. April 1997. Web. May 2015.
18. Jones, 52–54.
19. *Seven Viking Romances*, 199.
20. Ibid., 227.
21. Jones, 79.
22. Rimbert. "The Life of Anskar, the Apostle of the North, 801–865." Ed. Charles H. Robinson. *Medieval Sourcebook*. Fordham University. n.d. Chap. XI. Web. March 2012.
23. Jones, 107.
24. Ibid.
25. Rimbert, Chap. XIV.
26. Ibid., Chap. XVII.
27. Jones, 107.
28. Ibid., 108.
29. Rimbert, Chap. XIX, Par. 1.
30. Ibid., Chap. XIX, Par. 3.
31. Ibid.
32. Ibid., Chap. XIX, Par. 4.
33. Ibid.
34. Ibid., Chap. XX, Par. 2.
35. Ibid., Chap. XXIV.
36. Ibid., Chap. XXIV, Par. 1.
37. Ibid., Chap. XXVIII.
38. Ibid., Chap. XXXII.
39. Ibid., Chap. XXX.
40. Ibid.
41. Jones, 108.
42. Rimbert, Chap. XXXIII.
43. Ibid.
44. Jones, 109–10.
45. Ibid., 79.
46. Ibid., 128.
47. Ibid.
48. Ibid., 134–38.
49. Moberg, Vilhelm. *A History of the Swedish People*. Vol. I. Trans. Paul Britten Austin. New York: Dorset Press, 1989. Print. 48.
50. Ibid., 48.
51. Grammaticus.
52. Thomas, Wilmer. "A Commented Summary of Adam of Bremen." *Wilmer T. Rev.* 0.3. 19 Sep. 2003. Web. May 2015.

Chapter 24

1. Almgren, Bertil, Charlotte Blindheim, Yves de Bouard, Torsten Capelle, Arne Emil Christensen, Kristjan Eldjarn, Richard Perkins, Thorkild Ramskou and Peter Sawyer. *The Vikings*. Gothenburg: Crescent Books, 1975. 145. Print.
2. Jones, Gwen. *A History of the Vikings*. Oxford: Oxford University Press, 1984. 71. Print.
3. *Egil's Saga*. Trans. Hermann Pálsson and Paul Edwards. London: Penguin Books, 1976. 79. Print.
4. Ibid., 218.
5. "Rigsthula." *The Poetic Edda: Rigsthula*. Trans. Henry Adams Bellows. Sacred-texts. n.d. 205, Vrs. 7. Web. Aug. 2014.
6. Ibid., 210, Vrs. 28.
7. Ibid., 212, Vrs. 34.
8. Jones, 68.
9. "Rigsthula," 201, Intro.
10. Jones, 67.
11. "Rigsthula," 203, Vrs. 1.
12. Ibid., 203, Vrs. 4.
13. Ibid., 203, Vrs. 3.
14. Ibid., 203, Vrs. 4.
15. Ibid., 204, Vrs. 8.
16. Ibid., 204–6.
17. Ibid., 206, Vrs. 12.
18. Gray, A H. "Rigsthula." *A H Gray*, 2014. https://ahgray.wordpress.com/2014/05/18/rigsthula/#more-648. Web. Aug. 2015.
19. "Rigsthula," 209.
20. Ibid., 210.
21. Ibid., 212.
22. Wilson, David M. *The Vikings and Their Origins*. New York: A & W, 1980. 89. Print.
23. Almgren et al., 145.
24. Jones, 150.
25. Almgren et al., 146.
26. Ibid.
27. Ibid.
28. Ibid.
29. Ibid., 164.
30. Ibid., 162.
31. Ibid., 167.
32. Lienhard, John H. "Three Field Crop Rotation." *Engine of Our Ingenuity*, No. 26. Houston Public Media, 1988–1997. Web. Sep. 2014.
33. Almgren et al., 162.
34. "Rigsthula," 204.
35. Ashliman, D.L. "Rígsþula: The Lay of Rig." *Folklore and Mythology Electronic Texts*. Pitt.edu, 2010. Web. Aug. 2015.
36. Wilson, David. *The Northern World*. New York: Harry N. Abrams, 1980. 157. Print.
37. Almgren et al., 169–73.
38. Ibid., 174–79.
39. Ibid., 175–76.
40. Ibid., 179.
41. Ibid., 181.
42. Ibid.
43. Ibid., 189.
44. Ibid., 193.
45. "Brenna-Njáls Saga." Trans. George W. Da-Sent. *Iceland Saga Database*. Chap. 156. Web. Aug. 2014.
46. Almgren et al., 195.
47. Ibid., 193.
48. Ibid., 199.
49. Ibid., 200–201.
50. Ibid., 200–203.
51. Ibid., 204–5.
52. Ibid., 221.
53. Ibid., 217–21.
54. Ibid., 221.
55. La Fay, Howard. *The Vikings*. Washington, DC: National Geographic Society, 1972. 173. Print.
56. Almgren et al., 224–27.
57. Ibid., 221.
58. Ibid., 236–41.
59. Ibid., 248.
60. "Rigsthula," 214.
61. *Egil's Saga*, 190–91.
62. Jones, 419.
63. Ibid., 420.
64. Almgren et al., 148.
65. Jones, 420.
66. Almgren et al., 148.
67. Ibid., 149.
68. La Fay, 71.
69. Ibid., 19.
70. Almgren et al., 24.
71. *Öjebomåla: 1350–1950*. Trans. Marie Peterson MacDonald. Glendive, MT: Gateway Press, 1972. 6–7. Print.
72. Jones, 197.
73. Moberg, 61.
74. Almgren et al., 149.
75. Jones, 202.

Chapter 25

1. *Egil's Saga*. Trans. Hermann Pálsson and Paul Edwards. London: Penguin Books, 1976. 105. Print.

2. Ibid., 106.
3. Ibid.
4. Ibid., 107.
5. Ibid., 108.
6. Sturluson, Snorri. "The Ynglinga Saga," in *Heimskringla*. Trans. Samuel Laing. New York: E. P. Dutton, 1930. Sec. 36. Print.
7. Ibid., Sec. 45.
8. Rimbert. "Life of Anskar, Apostle of the North, 801–865." Ed. Charles H. Robinson. *Medieval Sourcebook*. Chap. XXX. Fordham University. n.d. Web. March 2012.
9. Jones, Gwyn. *A History of the Vikings*. Oxford: Oxford University Press, 1984. 242. Print.
10. Wilson, David. *The Northern World*. New York: Harry N. Abrams, 1980. 171. Print.
11. *Seven Viking Romances*. Trans. Hermann Pálsson and Paul Edwards. London: Penguin Books, 1985. 117. Print.
12. Ibid., 34.

Chapter 26

1. Pares, Bernard. *A History of Russia*. New York: Alfred A. Knopf, 1953. 3–5. Print.
2. Wilson, David. *The Northern World*. New York: Harry N. Abrams, 1980. 194. Print.
3. Lie, Berit. *Historical Atlas of the World*. New York: Barnes & Noble, 1970. Maps 36–39. Print.
4. Gimbutas, Marija. *The Balts*. London: Thames & Hudson, 1963. 21–54. Print.
5. Ibid., 23.
6. Sugar, Peter. *A History of Hungary*. Bloomington: Indiana University Press, 1994. 11. Print.
7. Rootsi, Siiri. "A Counter-Clockwise Northern Route of the Y-Chromosome Haplogroup North from Southeastern Asia towards Europe." *European Journal of Human Genetics* (6 Dec. 2006) 15: 204–11. Kgenfund, 2007. Web. Jan. 2013.
8. Róna-Tas, András. *Hungarians and Europe in the Early Middle Ages*. New York: Central European University Press, 1999. 96. Print.
9. Wilson, *The Northern World*, 184.
10. Davies, Norman. *Europe: A History*. Oxford: Oxford University Press, 1996. 225. Print.
11. Pares, 9.
12. Wilson, *The Northern World*, 184.
13. Ibid., 194.
14. Ibid., 197.
15. Ibid., 201.
16. Pares, 15.
17. Ibid., 14–15.
18. Almgren, Bertil, Charlotte Blindheim, Yves de Bouard, Torsten Capelle, Arne Emil Christensen, Kristjan Eldjarn, Richard Perkins, Thorkild Ramskou and Peter Sawyer. *The Vikings*. Gothenburg: Crescent Books, 1975. 133. Print.
19. Jones, Gwyn. *A History of the Vikings*. Oxford: Oxford University Press, 1984. 249. Print.
20. Pares, 15.
21. "Hungary, Early History." *A Country Study: Hungary*. Federal Research Division, Library of Congress, 1989. Web. Sep. 2014.
22. Pares, 16–17.
23. Ibid.
24. Wells, H.G. *The Outline of History*. Vol. II. Garden City, NY: Garden City Books, 1956. 493–504. Print.
25. Pares, 24.
26. Ibid.
27. Ibid.

Chapter 27

1. Gibbon, Edward. *The Decline and Fall of the Roman Empire*. Vol. II. Chicago: Encyclopædia Britannica, 1952. 341. Print.
2. Pares, Bernard. *A History of Russia*. New York: Alfred A. Knopf, 1953. 33. Print.
3. *The Chronicles of Novgorod, 1064–1471*. Trans. Robert Michell and Nevill Forbes. London: Offices of the Society, 1914. xxii, sec. II. Print.
4. "Excerpts from 'Tales of Times Gone By.'" Kimball Files, http://pages.uoregon.edu/kimball/chronicle.htm. n.d. Sec. 1. Web. Sep. 2014.
5. Jones, Gwyn. *A History of the Vikings*. Oxford: Oxford University Press, 1984. 248. Print.
6. Ibid.
7. Wilson, David. *The Northern World*. New York: Harry N. Abrams, 1980. 194. Print.
8. Jones, 249–50.
9. Jordan, Robert Paul. "Viking Trail East." *National Geographic* (March 1985): 278–317. Print.
10. Jones, 250.
11. Ibid.
12. Hraundal, Thorir Jonsson. "Annales Bertiniani and Ibn Khurradādhbih." *When and How Did the Rūs/Rhos Enter Written Sources*. Center for Medieval Studies, University of Bergen. n.d. Web. Feb. 2013.
13. Jones, 250–51.
14. Jordan, 288–89.
15. Jones, 251–52.
16. Jones, 252; Jordan, 288–89.
17. Almgren, Bertil, Charlotte Blindheim, Yves de Bouard, Torsten Capelle, Arne Emil Christensen, Kristjan Eldjarn, Richard Perkins, Thorkild Ramskou and Peter Sawyer. *The Vikings*. Gothenburg: Crescent Books, 1975. 135. Print.
18. Ibid.

Chapter 28

1. Jones, Gwyn. *A History of the Vikings*. Oxford: Oxford University Press, 1984. 248 Print.
2. Ibid., 242.
3. Ibid.
4. Ibid., 110.
5. Ibid., 242–43.
6. Ibid., 252.
7. Almgren, Bertil, Charlotte Blindheim, Yves de Bouard, Torsten Capelle, Arne Emil Christensen, Kristjan Eldjarn, Richard Perkins, Thorkild Ramskou and Peter Sawyer. *The Vikings*. Gothenburg: Crescent Books, 1975. 51. Print.
8. Ibid.
9. Ibid., 53–54.
10. Ibid., 54.
11. Jones, 168.
12. Almgren et al., 32.
13. Ibid., 34–39.
14. Ibid., 41.
15. Ibid.
16. Jones, 173.
17. Rimbert. "Life of Anskar, Apostle of the North, 801–865." Ed. Charles H. Robinson. *Medieval Sourcebook*. Chap. XI. Fordham University. n.d. Web. March 2012.
18. Ibid., Chap. XIX.
19. Ibid., Chap. XXVII.
20. Jones, 173.
21. Almgren et al., 34–35.
22. Ibid., 32.
23. Jones, 171.
24. Almgren et al., 42–43.
25. Ibid., 35.
26. Ibid., 43.
27. Ibid.
28. Jones, 245.
29. "Excerpts from 'Tales of Times Gone By.'" Kimball Files, http://pages.uoregon.edu/kimball/chronicle.htm. n.d. Sec. 1. Web. Sep. 2014.
30. Ibid.
31. Ibid.
32. *The Chronicles of Novgorod, 1064–1471*. Trans. Robert Michell and Nevill Forbes. London: Offices of the Society, 1914. xxii, Sec. II. Print.
33. Jones, 246–48.
34. Ibid., 274–75.
35. Ibid., 253.
36. Gibbon, Edward. *The Decline and Fall of the Roman Empire*. Vol. II. Chicago: Encyclopædia Britannica, 1952. 341. Print.
37. "Excerpts from 'Tales of Times Gone By,'" Sec. 1.

38. Ibid., Sec. 3.
39. Ibid.
40. Ibid.
41. Pares, Bernard. *A History of Russia*. New York: Alfred A. Knopf, 1953. 19. Print.
42. *The Chronicles of Novgorod*, Sec. II.
43. Pares, 19.
44. *The Chronicles of Novgorod*, Sec. II.
45. Pares, 26.
46. Jordan, Robert Paul. "Viking Trail East." *National Geographic* (March 1985). 282. Print.
47. "Country Study: Hungary." *Library of Congress Country Studies*. Federal Research Division, Library of Congress, 1989. Web. March 2013.
48. Ibid.
49. Pares, 27–28.
50. Jordan, 288.
51. Jones, 174.
52. Almgren et al., 55.
53. Ibid., 57.
54. Jones, 111.
55. Ibid.
56. Almgren et al., 62.
57. Jones, 112.
58. *Rundata* 2.5. Uppsala Universitet, Department of Scandinavian Languages. n.d. DR 2. Web. Aug. 2014.
59. Jones, 112.
60. *Rundata*, DR 4.
61. Jones, 112–13.
62. Almgren et al., 59.
63. Fadlana, Ibn. *The Risālah of Ibn Fadlana*. Trans. James A. McKeithen. Ann Arbor, MI: ProQuest, 2002. Sec. 80–82. Print.
64. Ibid.
65. Fadlan, Ibn. "Risala." Trans. H.M. Smyser. *Viking Answer Lady*. n.d. Sec. 83. Web. Sep. 2014.
66. Ibid., Sec. 83–84.
67. Ibid., Sec. 86.
68. Montgomery, James E. "Ibn Fadlān and the Rūsiyyah." *Journal of Arabic and Islamic Studies* 3 (2000). https://www.library.cornell.edu/colldev/mideast/montgo1.pdf. 15. Web. Aug. 2015.
69. Fadlan, "Risala," Sec. 90.
70. Ibid., Sec. 92.
71. Jordan, 303.
72. Jones, 255.
73. Jones, 248; Jordan, 298.
74. Pares, 27.
75. Ibid.
76. Ibid.
77. Pares, 28.
78. "Excerpts from 'Tales of Times Gone By,'" Sec. 5.
79. Ibid.
80. Ibid.
81. Ibid.
82. Pares, 28.
83. Ibid.
84. Jones, 261–62.
85. Ibid., 261.
86. Ibid.
87. Ibid., 265.
88. Ibid.
89. Almgren et al., 35.
90. Jones, 174.
91. Ibid., 265.
92. Almgren et al., 62.
93. Pares, 28–29.
94. Ibid., 29.
95. Ibid.
96. Ibid.
97. Ibid., 30.
98. Ibid.
99. Gibbon, 341.
100. Pares, 30.
101. *The Russian Primary Chronicles* (Laurentian Text). Trans. Samuel Hazzard Cross and Olgerd P. Sherbowitz-Wetzor. Cambridge: Crimson Printing, 1953. Sec. 6. Print.
102. Ibid.
103. Ibid.
104. Ibid.
105. Ibid.
106. Pares, 32.
107. Jones, 263.
108. Pares, 32–33.
109. Ibid., 32.
110. Ibid., 32–34.
111. Jones, 264.
112. Ibid., 263.
113. Ibid.
114. Pares, 35.
115. Jones, 266.

Chapter 29

1. *Rundata* 2.5. Uppsala Universitet, Department of Scandinavian Languages. n.d. Ög 8. Web. Aug. 2014.
2. Ibid., U 582.
3. Ibid., Vg 181.
4. Ibid., U 346.
5. Ibid., U 533.
6. Ibid., U 698.
7. Ibid., G 319.
8. Ibid., Gs 13.
9. Ibid., Sö 39.
10. Ibid., Sö 198.
11. Peo. "Rune Stones and Other Runic Inscriptions." *Stone-Struck*. 5 Dec. 2010. http://www.runesnruins.com/runes/index.htm. n.d. U 214. Web. Aug. 2015.
12. *Rundata*, Sö 216.
13. Peo, U 154.
14. Ibid., U 153.
15. *Rundata*, U 366.
16. Peo, U 636.
17. *Rundata*, G 220.
18. Ibid., Sö 171.
19. Ibid., U 687.
20. Wilson, David M. *The Vikings and Their Origins*. New York: A & W, 1980. 86–87. Print.
21. *Rundata*, Sö 338.
22. Harlock, Walter E. *Svensk-Engelsk Ordbok*. Stockholm: Svenska Gokförlaget, 1947. 350. Print.
23. Pritsak, Omeljan. *The Origin of Rus': Old Scandinavian Sources Other Than the Sagas*. Cambridge, MA: Harvard University Press, 1981. 367. Print.
24. *Rundata*, G 134.
25. Pritsak, 373.
26. *Rundata*, G 280.
27. Jones, Gwyn. *A History of the Vikings*. Oxford: Oxford University Press, 1984. 259–60. Print.
28. Peo, U 956.
29. Ibid., Sm 92.
30. *Rundata*, Sö 82.
31. Ibid., U 922.
32. Ibid., U 1016.
33. Ibid., U 73.
34. Ibid., G 216.
35. Peo, U 140.
36. *Rundata*, U 270.
37. Ibid., U 374.
38. Ibid., U 446.
39. Ibid., Sö 163.
40. Ibid., Sö 165.
41. Ibid., U 112.
42. Peo, U 792.
43. Jones, 266.
44. Ibid.

Chapter 30

1. Jones, Gwyn. *A History of the Vikings*. Oxford: Oxford University Press, 1984. 267. Print.
2. *Rundata* 2.5. Uppsala Universitet, Department of Scandinavian Languages. n.d. U 661. Web. Aug. 2014.
3. Ibid., U 157.
4. Ibid., Sö 9.
5. Ibid., U 439.
6. Peo. "Rune Stones and Other Runic Inscriptions." *Stone-Struck*. 5 Dec. 2010. http://www.runesnruins.com/runes/index.htm. n.d. U 654. Web. Aug. 2015.
7. *Rundata*, U 778.
8. Peo, Sö 173.
9. *Rundata*, Sö 131.
10. Peo, Sö 179.
11. Ibid., Sö 279.
12. Ibid., Sö 281.
13. Pálsson, Hermann, and Paul Edwards, trans. "Yngvar's Saga." *Vikings in Russia*. Edinburgh: Edinburgh University Press, 1989. 44. Print.
14. Ibid., 56.
15. Tunstall, Peter, trans. "The Saga of Yngvar the Traveler." *oe.eclipse*. 2005. Sec. 3. Web. Oct. 2014.
16. Ibid., Sec. 5.
17. *History of Georgia* (*Kartlis Tskhovreba*). Ed. Stephen Jones.

Trans. Ariane Chanturia, Dimitri Gamkrelidze and Medea Abashidze. Tbilisi: Artanuji, 2008. Print.
  18. Tunstall, Sec. 5.
  19. *History of Georgia.*
  20. Tunstall, Sec. 7.
  21. Ibid., Sec. 8.
  22. *Rundata*, U 1143.
  23. Almgren, Bertil, Charlotte Blindheim, Yves de Bouard, Torsten Capelle, Arne Emil Christensen, Kristjan Eldjarn, Richard Perkins, Thorkild Ramskou and Peter Sawyer. *The Vikings.* Gothenburg: Crescent Books, 1975. 149. Print.
  24. Braun, F., and Ture J. Arne. "Den svenska rustenen från ön Bereanj utanför Dneprmynningen." *Fornvännen.* Swedish National Heritage Board. n.d. 44–48. Web. Oct. 2014.
  25. Jansson, Sven B.F. *Runes of Sweden.* Stockholm: Royal Academy of Letters, 1987. 61. Print.
  26. *Rundata*, X UaFv1914;47.
  27. Braun and Arne, 48.
  28. Almgren et al., 32; Wilson, David. *The Northern World.* New York: Harry N. Abrams, 1980. 173. Print.

Chapter 31

  1. Jones, Gwyn. *A History of the Vikings.* Oxford: Oxford University Press, 1984. 396–97. Print.
  2. Ibid., 394–95.
  3. *The World Book Encyclopedia.* Vol. 10. Chicago: World Book, Inc., 1984. "Icelandic History," 19. Print.
  4. Jones, 306.
  5. Ibid.
  6. Diamond, Jared. *Collapse.* New York: Penguin, 2005. 251. Print.
  7. Ibid., 222.
  8. Ibid., 243–44.
  9. Jones, 307.
  10. Diamond, 258.
  11. Ibid., 241–43.
  12. Jones, 308.
  13. Diamond, 270.
  14. Ibid., 258.
  15. Jones, 308.
  16. Ibid., 309.
  17. Diamond, 261.
  18. Ibid., 270.

Chapter 32

  1. Jones, Gwyn. *A History of the Vikings.* Oxford: Oxford University Press, 1984. 392. Print.
  2. *The World Book Encyclopedia.* Vol. 7. Chicago: World Book, Inc., 1985. 404i. Print.
  3. *World Book Encyclopedia*, Vol. 10, 336.
  4. Ritchie, Ann. *Viking Scotland.* London: B. T. Batsford, 1993. 107–8. Print.
  5. *World Book Encyclopedia*, Vol. 17, 185.
  6. Jones, 392.
  7. Ibid., 393.
  8. Ibid., 389.
  9. Larsson, Lars, Johan Callmer and Berta Stjernquist, eds. *The Archaeology of the Cultural Landscape.* Stockholm: Almquist & Wiksell International, 1992. Print.
  10. Moberg, Vilhelm. *A History of the Swedish People.* Vol. I. Trans. Paul Britten Austin. New York: Dorset Press, 1989. 78–79. Print
  11. Ibid
  12. Ibid., 79–80.
  13. Ibid., 80.
  14. Ibid., 81–82.
  15. Scott, Franklin. *Sweden: The Nation's History.* Carbondale: Southern Illinois University Press, 1988. 25–26 and 47. Print.
  16. Anderson, Ingvar. *A History of Sweden.* Trans. Carolyn Hannay. London: Weidenfeld and Nicolson, 1956. 28. Print.
  17. Moberg, 78.
  18. Scott, 26.
  19. Ibid., 39.
  20. Ibid., 47.
  21. Davies, Norman. *Europe: A History.* Oxford: Oxford University Press, 1996. 358. Print.
  22. Ibid., 362.
  23. Ibid., 362–63.
  24. Ibid., 362.
  25. Moberg, 83.
  26. Ibid., 83–84.
  27. Scott, 66–67.
  28. Ibid., 67.
  29. Ibid., 51.
  30. Davies, 340.
  31. Ibid.
  32. Scott, 52–53.
  33. Davies, 340.
  34. Ibid.
  35. Ibid., 340–41.
  36. Scott, 51.
  37. Davies, 341.
  38. Ibid., 342.
  39. Scott, 66–67.
  40. Moberg, 87.
  41. Ibid., 87–88.
  42. Ibid., 88–89.
  43. Pares, Bernard. *A History of Russia.* New York: Alfred A. Knopf, 1953. 57. Print.
  44. Scott, 67–68.
  45. Moberg, 89–90.
  46. Scott, 47.
  47. Ibid., 67.
  48. Moberg, 90.
  49. Ibid., 90–91.
  50. Scott, 67–68.
  51. Ibid.
  52. Ibid.
  53. Ibid.
  54. Moberg, 82–83.
  55. Scott, 68.
  56. Moberg, 91.
  57. Ibid., 86 and 91.
  58. Scott, 58.
  59. Moberg, 92.
  60. Ibid.
  61. Ibid., 86.
  62. Ibid., 87.
  63. Ibid.
  64. Ibid., 86–95.
  65. Ibid., 93.
  66. Ibid., 94.
  67. Ibid.
  68. Ibid., 95.
  69. Ibid., 96.
  70. Ibid.
  71. Ibid., 97.
  72. Ibid., 98.
  73. Ibid.
  74. Ibid.
  75. Ibid., 99.
  76. Ibid., 100.
  77. Ibid., 103.
  78. Ibid., 104.
  79. Ibid., 107.
  80. Ibid., 104.
  81. Ibid., 106.
  82. Scott, 71–72.
  83. Moberg, 111–12.
  84. Ibid., 110.
  85. Ibid., 112.
  86. Ibid., 114–15.
  87. Diamond, Jared. *Collapse.* New York: Penguin, 2005. 268. Print; Jones, 310.
  88. Moberg, 110–11.
  89. Ibid., 116.
  90. Ibid., 112–13.
  91. Scott, 75.
  92. Moberg, 114–15.

Chapter 33

  1. Pares, Bernard. *A History of Russia.* New York: Alfred A. Knopf, 1953. 64–66. Print.
  2. Ibid., 61.
  3. Ibid., 64.
  4. Ibid., 35–37.
  5. Ibid., 37–38.
  6. Ibid., 39–41.
  7. Morgan, David. *The Mongols.* New York: Basil Blackwell, 1988. 55. Print.
  8. Reischauer, Edwin O., and John K. Fairbank. *East Asia: The Great Tradition.* Boston: Houghton Mifflin, 1960. 266–67. Print.
  9. Morgan, 67.
  10. Ibid.
  11. Chambers, James. *The Devil's Horsemen.* New York: Atheneum, 1985. 2–4. Print.
  12. Ibid., 7–9.
  13. Ibid., 10.
  14. Ibid., 12.
  15. Ibid., 14–16.
  16. Morgan, 71–72.

17. Chambers, 17.
18. Ibid., 16.
19. *National Geographic Atlas of the World*. Seventh edition. Washington, DC: National Geographic Society, 1999. 92. Print.
20. Chambers, 19.
21. Ibid., 20.
22. Ibid., 20–21.
23. Ibid., 23–24.
24. Ibid., 27–28.
25. Ibid., 28.
26. Ibid., 24–29.
27. Ibid., 31.
28. Ibid., 30–31.
29. Ibid., 31.
30. Morgan, 72.
31. Chambers, 47.
32. Morgan, 136–37.
33. Chambers, 49.
34. Ibid., 72–74.
35. Ibid., 81.
36. Ibid., 96–97.
37. Ibid., 98–99.
38. Ibid., 102.
39. Ibid., 106–11.
40. Ibid., 112–13.
41. Ibid., 113.
42. Pares, 56.
43. Chambers, 119–20.
44. Morgan, 142–43.
45. Chambers, 120–21.
46. Ibid., 125.
47. Ibid., 134–35.
48. Ibid., 131.
49. Pares, 57.
50. Ibid., 57–58.

Chapter 34

1. Pares, Bernard. *A History of Russia*. New York: Alfred A. Knopf, 1953. 67. Print.
2. Ibid., 67–68.
3. Ibid., 66–68.
4. Ibid., 78–79.
5. Ibid., 81.
6. Ibid.
7. Ibid., 82–83.
8. Ibid., 70–71.
9. Ibid., 74.
10. Ibid., 74–75.
11. Ibid., 75.
12. Ibid., 72–75.
13. Paul, Michael C. "Archbishop Vasilii Kalika of Novgorod, the Fortress of Orekhov and the Defence of Orthodoxy." *The Clash of Cultures on the Medieval Frontier*. Ed. Alan V. Murray. Farnham: Ashgate, 2009. 253–72. Print.
14. Ibid.
15. Moberg, Vilhelm. *A History of the Swedish People*. Vol. I. Trans. Paul Britten Austin. New York: Dorset Press, 1989. 117. Print.

Chapter 35

1. Moberg, Vilhelm. *A History of the Swedish People*. Vol. I. Trans. Paul Britten Austin. New York: Dorset Press, 1989. 139. Print.
2. Ibid., 123–24.
3. Ibid., 140–41.
4. Ibid., 125–26.
5. *Holy Bible*. King James Version. Philadelphia: John C. Winston, n.d. Revel. 6:8. Print.
6. Moberg, 131–32.
7. Ibid., 133.
8. Ibid., 125.
9. Ibid., 127–28.
10. Ibid., 126.
11. Davies, Norman. *Europe: A History*. Oxford: Oxford University Press, 1996. 411. Print.
12. Moberg, 134–37.
13. Ibid., 144–45.
14. Ibid., 117.
15. Ibid., 141.
16. Ibid.
17. Ibid., 145.
18. Ibid.
19. *Öjebomåla: 1350–1950*. Trans. Marie Peterson MacDonald. Glendive: Gateway Press, 1972. 5–6. Print.
20. Moberg, 117.
21. Ibid., 118.
22. Scott, Franklin. *Sweden: The Nation's History*. Carbondale: Southern Illinois University Press, 1988. 72. Print.
23. Moberg, 118.
24. Scott, 72–73.
25. Ibid., 75.
26. Moberg, 114.
27. Scott, 76.

Chapter 36

1. "Abbey of Vadstena." *New Advent*. Belmont Abbey College. n.d. Web. Nov. 2014.
2. "About the Order." *Birgittasystrarna*. Birgettaskloster Pax Mariae. n.d. Web. Nov. 2014.
3. Ibid.
4. Keller, Theo. "Syon Abbey." *Life in Tudor Times*. Jorge H. Castelli. n.d. Web. Nov. 2014.
5. "Syon Abbey." *Blessed Sacrament Catholic Church*. n.d. Web. Nov. 2014.
6. "About the Order."
7. Ibid.
8. Ibid.
9. "About Us." *Brigittine Monks: Order of the Most Holy Savior*. 2005. Web. April 2010.
10. "St. Bridget's of Sweden Catholic Church." *Lindsborg Little Sweden USA*. n.d. Web. April 2010.
11. *St. Bridget of Sweden Catholic Church* (Lindstrom, Minnesota). n.d. Web. May 2010.
12. "Parish History." *St. Bridget of Sweden Catholic Church* (Lake Balboa, California). 2006. Web. May 2010.
13. Moberg, Vilhelm. *A History of the Swedish People*. Vol. I. Trans. Paul Britten Austin. New York: Dorset Press, 1989. 152. Print.
14. Ibid., 158.
15. Ibid., 153.
16. Ibid.
17. Holbock, Ferdinand. *Married Saints and Blesseds Through the Centuries*. English translation from the second edition of the original German: *Heilige Eheleute: Verheiratete Selige und Heilige aus allen Jahrhunderten*. Salzburg (2001). Trans. Michael J. Miller. San Francisco: Ignatius Press, 2002. Print.
18. Moberg, 154–55.
19. Ibid., 154.
20. Ibid., 117.
21. Ibid., 155–56.
22. Ibid., 168.
23. Ibid., 154.
24. Ibid.

Chapter 37

1. Moberg, Vilhelm. *A History of the Swedish People*. Vol. I. Trans. Paul Britten Austin. New York: Dorset Press, 1989. 121. Print.
2. Scott, Franklin. *Sweden: The Nation's History*. Carbondale: Southern Illinois University Press, 1988. 76. Print.
3. Ibid.
4. Ibid., 80.
5. Moberg, 199.
6. Scott, 80–81.
7. Moberg, 202–3.
8. Ibid., 203.
9. Ibid., 203–4.
10. Scott, 82–83.
11. Moberg, 204–6.
12. Ibid., 204.
13. Ibid.

Bibliography

"Abbey of Vadstena." *New Advent.* Belmont Abbey College. n.d. Web. Nov. 2014.

Aber, James S. "Paleoclimate Reconstruction." *ES 331/767 Lecture 11.* n.d. n.p. Web. Jan. 2014.

"About the Order." *Birgittasystrarna.* Birgettakloster Pax Mariae. n.d. Web. Nov. 2014.

"About Us." *Brigittine Monks: Order of the Most Holy Savior.* 2005. Web. April 2010.

Adam, Jonathan. "Europe during the Last 150,000 Years." Environmental Sciences Division, Oak Ridge National Laboratory. n.d. Web. Jan. 2014.

Adam of Bremen. *History of the Archbishops of Hamburg.* Book 4: "The Temple at Old Uppsala." Trans. Francis J. Tschan. New York: Columbia University Press, 1959. Print.

Alexander, Caroline. "Magical Mystery Treasure." *National Geographic* (Nov. 2011). Print.

Almgren, Bertil, Charlotte Blindheim, Yves De Bouard, Torsten Capelle, Arne Emil Christensen, Kristjan Eldjarn, Richard Perkins, Thorkild Ramskou and Peter Sawyer. *The Vikings.* Gothenburg: Crescent Books, 1975. Print.

Anderson, Ingvar. *A History of Sweden.* Trans. Carolyn Hannay. London: Weidenfeld and Nicolson, 1956. Print.

Artelius, Tore, and Fredrik Svanberg. *Dealing with the Dead.* Ödenshög, Sweden: National Heritage Board, 2005. Print.

Ashliman, D.L. "Rígsþula: The Lay of Rig." *Folklore and Mythology Electronic Texts.* Pitt.edu, 2010. Web. Aug. 2015.

Bailey, Geoff, and Penny Spileins, eds. *Mesolithic Europe.* New York: Cambridge University Press, 2008. Print.

Baldia, Maximilian. "The Corded Ware/Single Grave Culture." *Comp-archaeology*, Version 1.04. The Comparative Archaeology WEB, January 2006. Web. March 2010.

———. "The Funnel Beaker Culture (TRB)." *Comp-archaeology*, Version 4.15. 2009. Web. March 2010.

Barker, Felix, and Anthea Barker. *Encyclopedia of Discovery and Exploration.* Vol. 1. London: Aldus Books, 1971. Print.

Beowulf. Trans. Francis B. Gummere. The Harvard Classics, Vol. 49. New York: P.F. Collier & Son, 1910. Print.

Bjørklund, Oddvar, Haadon Holmboe, Anders Røhr and Berit Lie. *Historical Atlas of the World.* New York: Barnes & Noble, 1970. Print.

The Book of Settlements: Landnámabók. Trans. Hermann Pálsson and Paul Edwards. Manitoba: University of Manitoba Press, 1972. Print.

Boorstin, Daniel J. *The Discoverers.* New York: Vintage Books, 1985. Print.

Braun, F., and Ture J. Arne. "Den svenska rustenen från ön Bereanj utanför Dneprmynningen." *Fornvännen.* Swedish National Heritage Board. n.d. Web. Oct. 2014.

"Brenna-Njáls Saga." Trans. George W. DaSent. *Iceland Saga Database.* Web. Aug. 2014.

Brown, R. Allen. *The Normans.* New York: St. Martin's Press, 1984. Print.

Burenhult, Hans, and Anders Carlsson, eds. "The Alvastra Pile Dwelling." *Theoretical Approaches to Artifacts, Settlement and Society.* Oxford: British Archaeology Reports, 1987. Print.

Burns, Thomas. *A History of the Ostrogoths.* Bloomington: Indiana University Press, 1984. Print.

Chambers, James. *The Devil's Horsemen.* New York: Atheneum, 1985. Print.

The Chronicles of Novgorod, 1064–1471. Trans. Robert Michell and Nevill Forbes. London: Offices of the Society, 1914. Print.

Churchill, Winston. *A History of the English-speaking Peoples.* Vol. I. New York: Barnes & Noble, 1993. Print.

Coakley, John E., and Robert W. Jessup. *Guide to the Study of Military History.* Washington, DC: Center of Military History, US Army, 1979. Print.

Coon, Carleton Stevens. "Iceland." *The Races of Europe.* Society for Nordish Physical Anthropology. n.d. Web. Aug. 2014.

"Country Study: Hungary." *Library of Congress Country Studies.* Federal Research Division, Library of Congress, 1989. Web. March 2013.

Dansgaard, W., J. W. C. White and S. J. Johnsen. "The Abrupt Termination of the Younger Dryas Climate Event." *Nature* (1989) 339: 532–34. doi: 10.1038/33952a0. Web. April 2010.

Davies, Norman. *Europe: A History.* Oxford: Oxford University Press, 1996. Print.

Diamond, Jared. *Collapse.* New York: Penguin, 2005. Print.

Donner, Joakim, *The Quaternary History of Scandinavia*. New York: Cambridge University Press, 1995. Print

Durant, Will. *The History of Civilization*. Vol. 1. New York: Simon & Schuster, 1935. Print.

Egil's Saga. Trans. Hermann Pálsson and Paul Edwards. London: Penguin Books, 1976. Print.

Eriksen, Berit Valentin. "Reconsidering the Geochronological Framework of Lateglacial Hunter-gatherer Colonization of Southern Scandinavia." *Proceedings of a U.I.S.P.P. Symposium, Stockholm, 14–17 October 1999*. Jutland Archaeological Society Publications, Vol. 39. Højbjerg. Web. Jan. 2014.

"Excerpts from 'Tales of Times Gone By.'" Kimball Files, http://pages.uoregon.edu/kimball/chronicle.htm. n.d. Web. Sep. 2014.

Fadlan, Ibn. "Risala." Trans. H.M. Smyser. *Viking Answer Lady*. n.d. Web. Sept. 2014.

Fadlana, Ibn. *The Risālah of Ibn Fadlana*. Trans. James A. McKeithen. Ann Arbor, MI: ProQuest, 2002. Print.

Fenton, Carroll, and Mildred Fenton. *Giants of Geology*. Garden City, NY: Doubleday, 1952. Print.

Fowler, Chris. *The Archaeology of Personhood: An Anthropological Approach*. New York: Routledge, 2004. Print.

Gibbon, Edward. *The Decline and Fall of the Roman Empire*. 2 vols. Chicago: Encyclopædia Britannica, 1952. Print.

Gimbutas, Marija. *The Balts*. London: Thames & Hudson, 1963. Print.

Grammaticus, Saxo. "The Danish History." Ed. Douglas B. Killings. Trans. Oliver Elton. *The Online Medieval & Classical Library*. Release #28b. April 1997. Web. May 2015.

Gray, A H. "Rigsthula." *A H Gray*, 2014. https://ahgray.wordpress.com/2014/05/18/rigsthula/#more-648. Web. Aug. 2015.

Grimm, Sonja, and Mara-Julia Weber. "Dating the Hamburgian in the Context of Lateglacial Chronology." *Academia.edu*. n.d. Web. Feb. 2014.

Gron, Ole. "Mesolithic Dwelling Places in South Scandinavia: Their Definition and Social Interpretation." *The Free Library by Farlex*. Antiquity Publications. 2003. Web. Feb. 2014.

Harding, Anthony. "Amber in the Mycenaean World." British School of Athens, 25 Jan. 2013. From "The Annual of British School of Athens." Vol. 69 (1979). Web. March 2014.

Harlock, Walter E. *Svensk-Engelsk Ordbok*. Stockholm: Svenska Gokförlaget, 1947. Print.

Herm, Gerhard. *The Celts*. New York: St. Martin's Press, 1976. Print.

Hernek, Robert. "New Light on the Sandarna Culture: A Mesolithic Dwelling-site from the Province of Bohuslän." Diss., Göteborg University, 2005. Print.

History of Georgia (*Kartlis Tskhovreba*). Ed. Stephen Jones. Trans. Ariane Chanturia, Dimitri Gamkrelidze and Medea Abashidze. Tbilisi: Artanuji, 2008. Print.

Holbock, Ferdinand. *Married Saints and Blesseds Through the Centuries*. English translation from the second edition of the original German: *Heilige Eheleute: Verheiratete Selige und Heilige aus allen Jahrhunderten*. Salzburg (2001). Trans. Michael J. Miller. San Francisco: Ignatius Press, 2002. Print.

Holloway, Robert. "The Ancient Roots of Milk Consumption and Its Genetic Dependence." Nevada Technical Associates, Inc. n.d. Web. March 2014.

Holy Bible. King James Version. Philadelphia: John C. Winston. n.d. Print.

Hraundal, Thorir Jonsson. "Annales Bertiniani and Ibn Khurradādhbih." *When and How Did the Rūs/Rhos Enter Written Sources*. Center for Medieval Studies, University of Bergen. n.d. Web. Feb. 2013.

"Hungary, Early History." *A Country Study: Hungary*. Federal Research Division, Library of Congress, 1989. Web. Sep. 2014.

Hutchins, Robert. *The Great Books of the Western World*. Vol. 15: *Tacitus*. Chicago: Williams Beaton, 1952. Print.

_____. *The Great Books of the Western World*. Vol. 16: *Ptolemy*. Chicago: Williams Beaton, 1952. Print.

Ingram, Reverend J. *The Saxon Chronicle*. London: Studio Editions, 1993. Print.

Jansson, Sven B.F. *Runes of Sweden*. Stockholm: Royal Academy of Letters, 1987. Print.

Jennbert, Kristina. "Ertebølle Pottery in Southern Sweden: A Question of Handicraft, Networks and Creolisation in a Period of Neolithisation." Lund University Publications, 2011. Web. Feb. 2014.

Johnsen, Sigfús J. "Warm Times/Cold Times: Holocene Climate Variability in the North Atlantic Region." Paper # 48–1, presented at the XVI INQUA Congress, Reno, Nevada, 2003. Web. May 2010.

Jones, Gwyn. *A History of the Vikings*. Oxford: Oxford University Press, 1984. Print.

_____, trans. "Egil's Saga." New York: Twayne, 1960.

Jordan, Robert Paul. "Viking Trail East." *National Geographic* (March 1985): 278–317. Print.

Jordanes. *The Origins and Deeds of the Goths (Getica)*. Trans. Charles C. Mierow. Princeton, NJ: Princeton University Press, 1908. Print.

Karlsson, Andreas, Thomas Wallerström, Anders Götherström and Gunella Holmlaund. "Y-Chromosome Diversity in Sweden: A Long-time Perspective." *European Journal of Human Genetics* (May 2006) 14. National Publishing Group. Web. Jan. 2014.

Keller, Theo. "Syon Abbey." *Life in Tudor Times*. Jorge H. Castelli. n.d. Web. Nov. 2014.

Kipling, Rudyard. "Dane-geld." *Poetry Lovers Page*. n.d. Web. July 2012.

Kobashi, Takuro. "4 + 1.5°C Abrupt Warming 11,270 Years Ago Identified from Trapped Air in Greenland Ice." *Earth and Planetary Science Letters* (2008) 268 (3–4): 397–407. doi:10.1016/j.epsl.foo8.01.032. Web. Jan. 2014.

Kristiansen, Kristian. "What Language Did Neolithic Pots Speak?" *Kristian Kristiansen*, 930 view. Academia.edu (shared research). n.d. Web. March 2014.

La Fay, Howard. *The Vikings*. Washington, DC: National Geographic Society, 1972. Print.

Landnámabók. Trans. Rev. T. Ellwood. New Northvegr Center, 2009. Web. Aug. 2014.

Larsson, Lars. "The Late Palaeolithic in Southern

Sweden: Investigations in a Marginal Region." *Archaeology Data Services* (ADS.UK). n.d. n.p. Web. April 2010.

Larsson, Lars, Johan Callmer and Berta Stjernquist, eds. *The Archaeology of the Cultural Landscape.* Stockholm: Almqvist & Wiksell International, 1992. Print.

Larsson, Thomas, and Hans Lundmark. *Approaches to Swedish Prehistory.* Oxford: BAR International Series 500, 1989. Print.

Lie, Berit. *Historical Atlas of the World.* New York: Barnes & Noble, 1970. Print.

Lienhard, John H. "Three Field Crop Rotation." *Engine of Our Ingenuity*, No. 26. Houston Public Media, 1988–1997. Web. Sep. 2014.

Longfellow, Henry Wadsworth. *"Tales of a Wayside Inn* 1863: The Musician's Tale; The Saga of King Olaf II, King Olaf's Return." *Hwlongfellow.org.* n.d. Web. Aug. 2012.

Mabillard, Amanda. "Shakespeare's Sources for Hamlet." *Shakespeare Online*, 2000. Web. July 2014.

MacDonald, Malcolm Ross. *Encyclopedia of Discovery and Exploration.* Vol. 2. London: Aldus Books, 1971. Print.

Magnusson, Magnus, Sheila Mackie and Julian Glover. *Beowulf.* Trans. Michael Alexander and Edwin Morgan. Wolfboro: Alan Sutton, 1988. Print.

Makiewicz, Tadeusz. *The Archeology of the Transit Gas Pipeline: The Goths in Greater Poland.* Poznán Acheological Museum. n.d. Web. Feb. 2012.

Mallory, J.P., and D.Q. Adams, eds. "TRB Culture." *Encyclopedia of Indo-European Culture.* London: Fitzroy Dearborn, 1997. Print.

Malm, Torben. "Excavating Submerged Stone Age Sites in Denmark: The Tybrind Vig Example." *Abc.se*, 2012. Web. Feb. 2014.

Mela, Pomponius. *Description of the World.* Book IV. Trans. Frank E. Romer. Ann Arbor: University of Michigan Press, 1998. Print.

Moberg, Vilhelm. *A History of the Swedish People.* Vol. I. Trans. Paul Britten Austin. New York: Dorset Press, 1989. Print.

Montelius, Oscar. *The Civilization of Sweden in Heathen Times.* New York: Haskell House, 1969. Print.

Montgomery, James E. "Ibn Fadlān and the Rūsiyyah." *Journal of Arabic and Islamic Studies* 3 (2000). https://www.library.cornell.edu/colldev/mideast/montgo1.pdf. Web. Aug. 2015.

Morgan, David. *The Mongols.* New York: Basil Blackwell, 1988. Print.

Müller, Johannes. "Megaliths and Funnel Beakers: Societies in Change 4100–2700 BC." *Gejouden Voor de Stichting Nederlands Museum.* Academia.edu, 8 April 2011. Web. March 2014.

National Geographic Atlas of the World. Seventh edition. Washington, DC: National Geographic Society, 1999. Print.

Ohlberger, Annesophie. "Distinguished by Culture." MS thesis, Stockholm University. n.d. Web. March 2014.

Öjebomåla: 1350–1950. Trans. Marie Peterson MacDonald. Glendive, MT: Gateway Press, 1972. Print.

Olofsson, Anders. "Pioneering Settlements in the Mesolithic of Northern Sweden." Diss., Umeå University, 2003. Print.

Pálsson, Hermann, and Paul Edwards, trans. "Yngvar's Saga." *Vikings in Russia.* Edinburgh: Edinburgh University Press, 1989. Print.

Pálsson, Hermann, and Snorri Sturluson, trans. "Egil's Saga." Harmondsworth: Penguin Books, 1976.

Pares, Bernard. *A History of Russia.* New York: Alfred A. Knopf, 1953. Print.

"Parish History." *St. Bridget of Sweden Catholic Church* (Lake Balboa, California). 2006. Web. May 2010.

Passarino, Giuseppe, Gianpiero Cavalleri, Alice Lin, Luigi Luca Cavalli-Sforza, Anne-lise Børresen-Dale and Peter Underhill. "Different Genetic Components in the Norwegian Population Revealed by the Analysis of mtDNA and Y Chromosome Polymorphism." *European Journal of Homan Genetics* (Sept. 2002) 10 (9): 521–29. Web. January 2014.

Paul, Michael C. "Archbishop Vasilii Kalika of Novgorod, the Fortress of Orekhov and the Defence of Orthodoxy." *The Clash of Cultures on the Medieval Frontier.* Ed. Alan V. Murray. Farnham: Ashgate, 2009. Print.

Peo. "Rune Stones and Other Runic Inscriptions." *Stone-Struck.* 5 Dec. 2010. http://www.runesnruins.com/runes/index.htm. n.d. Web. Aug. 2015.

Pliny the Elder. *The Natural History.* Perseus Digital Library, Tufts University. n.d. Web. April 2014.

Pringle, Heather. "Vikings and Native Americans." *National Geographic* (Nov. 2012). Print.

Pritsak, Omeljan. *The Origin of Rus': Old Scandinavian Sources Other Than the Sagas.* Cambridge, MA: Harvard University Press, 1981. Print.

Procopius. *History of the Wars.* Book VI. Trans. H.B. Dewing. London: William Heinemann, 1971. Print.

Ptolemy, Claudius. *The Geography.* Book II. Trans. Edward Luther Stevenson. University of Chicago. n.d. Web. Feb. 2012.

Reischauer, Edwin O., and John K. Fairbank. *East Asia: The Great Tradition.* Boston: Houghton Mifflin, 1960. Print.

Richie, Alexandra. *Faust's Metropolis.* New York: Carroll & Graf, 1998. Print.

"Rigsthula." *The Poetic Edda: Rigsthula.* Trans. Henry Adams Bellows. Sacred-texts. n.d. Web. Aug. 2014.

Rimbert. "Life of Anskar, Apostle of the North, 801–865." Ed. Charles H. Robinson. *Medieval Sourcebook.* Fordham University. n.d. Web. March 2012.

Ritchie, Ann. *Viking Scotland.* London: B. T. Batsford, 1993. Print.

Roberts, J.M. *History of the World.* New York: Alfred A. Knopf, 1976. Print.

Roberts, Michael. *The Early Vasas.* Cambridge: Cambridge University Press, 1968. Print.

Roberts, Michael. *Gustav Adolf the Great.* New York: Longman, 1992. Print.

Roberts, N. *The Holocene: An Environmental History.* Second edition. Oxford: Blackwell, 1998. Print.

Roberts, Neil. *The Holocene: An Environmental History.* Oxford: Blackwell, 1989. Print.

Róna-Tas, András. *Hungarians and Europe in the Early Middle Ages.* New York: Central European University Press, 1999. Print.

Rootsi, Siiri. "A Counter-Clockwise Northern Route of the Y-Chromosome Haplogroup North from Southeastern Asia towards Europe." *European Journal of Human Genetics* (6 Dec. 2006) 15: 204–11. Kgenfund, 2007. Web. Jan. 2013.

Rundata 2.5. Uppsala Universitet, Department of Scandinavian Languages. n.d. Web. Aug. 2014.

The Russian Primary Chronicles (Laurentian Text). Trans. Samuel Hazzard Cross and Olgerd P. Sherbowitz-Wetzor. Cambridge: Crimson Printing, 1953. Print.

St. Bridget of Sweden Catholic Church (Lindstrom, Minnesota). n.d. Web. May 2010.

"St. Bridget's of Sweden Catholic Church." *Lindsborg Little Sweden USA*. n.d. Web. April 2010.

Savage, Anne. *The Anglo-Saxon Chronicles*. New York: Barnes & Noble, 2000. Print.

Schledermann, Peter. "Eskimo and Viking Finds in the High Arctic." *National Geographic* (May 1981). Print.

Schmitt, Lou, Stephan Larsson, Corinna Schrum, Irina Alekseeva, Matthias Tomczak and Krister Svedhage. "Why They Came: The Colonization of the Coast of Western Sweden and Its Environmental Context at the End of the Last Glaciation." *Oxford Journal of Archaeology* (Feb. 2006) 25 (1): 1–28. Wiley Social Sciences and Humanities, 2006. Web. Feb. 2014.

Scott, Franklin D. *Sweden: The Nation's History*. Carbondale: Southern Illinois University Press, 1988.

Seven Viking Romances. Trans. Hermann Pálsson and Paul Edwards. London: Penguin Books, 1985. Print.

Shakespeare, William. "Hamlet, Prince of Denmark." *The Plays and Sonnets of William Shakespeare*. Vol. II. Ed. William George Clarke and William Aldis Wright. Chicago: Encyclopædia Britannica, 1952. Print.

Shepherd, Sandy. *Myths and Legends*. New York: Macmillan, 1995. Print.

Skak-Nielsen, N.V. "The Genesis of the Battle Axe Culture: On Klaus Ebbesen's Doctoral Thesis. A Critique and Alternative Conclusion." Trans. Martin Rundkvist. *Fornvänuen* (2006) 101 (4,s): [274]–77. Web. March 2014.

Smith, D.E., and A.G. Dawson. *Shorelines and Isostasy*. London: Academic Press, 1983. Print.

Sørensen, Marie Louise Stig. "Scandinavia in the Bronze Age." *Jrank.org*. n.d. Web. June 2010. From a paper by Oscar Montelius, "Om tidsbestämning inom bronsåldern med särskilt avseende på Skandinavien," 1885.

Stjernquist, Berta. *Acta Archaeologica Lundensia*. Lund: Berlingska Boktryckeriet, 1961. Print.

"The Stone Age." *SNPA.nordish.net/CNIITheStone Age*. Society of Nordish Physical Anthropology. n.d. Web. May 2008.

Strabo. *Geographica*. Trans. Horace Leonard Jones. University of Chicago. n.d. Web. April 2014.

Sturluson, Snorri. "The Ynglinga Saga," in *Heimskringla*. Trans. Samuel Laing. New York: E. P. Dutton, 1930. Print.

Sugar, Peter. *A History of Hungary*. Bloomington: Indiana University Press, 1994. Print.

"Syon Abbey." *Blessed Sacrament Catholic Church*. n.d. Web. Nov. 2014.

Tacitus, Publius Cornelius. "Germania." *The Works of Tacitus* (Oxford trans.). New York: Harpers & Brothers, 1874. Print.

Thomas, Wilmer. "A Commented Summary of Adam of Bremen." *Wilmer T. Rev.* 0.3. 19 Sep. 2003. Web. May 2015.

Thorpe, I.J.N. "Anthropology, Archaeology, and the Origin of Warfare." *World Archaeology* (2005) 35 (1): 155. Web. Jan. 2014.

"Trundholm Sun Chariot." Archeurope.com. n.d. Web. April 2014.

Tunstall, Peter, trans. "The Saga of Yngvar the Traveler." *oe.eclipse*. 2005. Web. Oct. 2014.

Wefer, Gerold, Wolfgang H. Berger, Karl-Ernst Behre and Eystein Jansen. *Climate Development and History of the North Atlantic Realm*. Berlin: Springer, 2002. Print.

Wells, H. G. *The Outline of History*. Vol. I. New York: Doubleday, 1956. Print.

Widsith. *Widsith*. Trans. Bella Millett. Wilkins of the Archaeology Department, University of Oxford. n.d. Web. May 2014.

Wilson, David. *The Vikings and Their Origins*. New York: A & W, 1980. Print.

Wilson, David M. *The Northern World*. New York: Harry N. Abrams, 1980. Print.

Wolfram, Herwig. *History of the Goths*. Trans. Thomas J. Dunlap. Berkeley: University of California Press, 1979. Print.

———. *The Roman Empire and Its Germanic People*. Trans. Thomas Dunlap. Berkeley: University of California Press, 1997. Print.

The World Book Encyclopedia. Chicago: World Book, Inc., 1984. Print.

Yokoyama, Yusuke, Kurt Lambeck, Patrick DeDeckker, Paul Johnston and L. Keith Fifield. "Timing of the Last Glacial Maximum from Observed Sealevel Minima." *Letters to Nature* 406 (16 June 2000): 713–16. Web. Jan. 2014.

Index

Numbers in ***bold italics*** refer to pages with photographs.

Aasa 88, 165
Aattundaland 88
Abalus Isle 46
Abbasid caliphs 199
Åbo 242
Abodrits 131
Abrittus-Hisarlak 58
Achaean Islands 146
Adalbert 171
Adam of Bremen 91, 123, 131–2, 141, 171–2, 211–2
Ad-Din, Ali, Muhammad II of Khwarizm 256
Adils (Athils) 87
Adogit 78
Adrianople 60
Adriatic Sea 56
Aedan 96
Aegean 34, 41, 58
Ælfheah 139
Ælgifu 145
Ælle (Aelle or Ella) 108
Ænglandi 159
Ærø Island 22
Æschere 82
Æsir 90, 137
Aethelferth 96
Æthelred (Ethelred) 139
Æthelstan 138
Aething, Edgar, Earl of Waltheof 150
Africa 48, 115, 116, 117, 199, 233
Agdir 135
Aggersborg 101
Agne 86
Ahrensburg culture 12–4
Aisle of Abalus 74
Akerhus Castle 281
Aki of *Egil's Saga* 191
Åland, Ålanders 205, 220, 221
Alans 59–62, 64, 258
Alaric I 57, 60–1, 62
Alaric II 68–9
Albrecht, duke of Mecklenburg 276
Albrecht of Mecklenburg, king of Sweden 252, 276, 180, 281–2
Alcuin 102
Aldeigjuborg (Staraya Ladoga) 146, 203
al-Din, Jalal 256, 258

Alexander the Great 47
Alexandria 116
Alf 86
Alfred, king of Wessex 120
Alfred the Great of England 108–9, 136, 169
Algaut 88
Algotsson, Duke Bengt 252
Allerød Oscillation 6
Allerød period 12–3
Alps 56
Alric (Eric) 86
Alrik, son of king Eirik of Uppsala 166
Alríka, son of Sigríðr 158
Alsö Decree (barn-lock) 247
al-Tartushi, Ibrahim 212
Althing 123
Altomünster, Germany 278
Alvastra, Östergötland 25, 27
Alvastra Monastery 279
Amal (Amali) 59, 64–5, 68, 72
Amalaric 69–70
Amalasuintha 69
Amazons 161
amber 34
Amber Road 34, 48
Amblothæ (Amleth or Amlethus) 130–1
American Revolutionary War 73
Amu Darya 256
Anastacia, daughter of Yaroslav 220
Ancylus Lake 9
Andcrida 149
Andrew of Chernigov, son of Yaroslav II 264–5
"Angel of Death" 214
Ångermanland 246
Angers 113
Angle 106
Anglia, Angles 94, 96, 103–4, 106, 109–10
Anglo 145
Anglo-Frisian runes 187
Anglo-Irish 208
Anglo-Saxon Chronicle 96, 102, 106, 110, 138–9, 147, 150, 165
Anglo-Saxon England 110, 113
Anglo-Saxons 98, 102, 109, 113, 138, 160, 177, 206

Angoulême 113
Anna of Byzantium 219
Annagassan, County Louth 105
Annales Bertiniani 201
Annals of Lund 92
Annals of Ulster 104
Anne, daughter of Yaroslav 220
Anoundus (Emund) of Sweden 167
L'Anse aux Meadows 125, 127
Ansfrid, Danish missionary to Sweden 168
Anskar, Benedictine monk 167–8, 237
Anthemius 65–6
anti-Magnus party 276
Antonines 77
Antonius Pius 49
Antrim County, Ireland 103
Apollo Grannus 49
Apulia 151, 153
Aputra (Apulia, Apuolé or Pilten) 168, 191, 205
Aquileia 65
Aquitaine 69, 111
Arab caliphate 198
Arabian peninsula 117
Arabian silver 176, 204, 208–9, 216
Arabic 206–7
Arabs 151, 199, 208, 210, 212–3, 233
Aral Sea, 266
Arcadiopolis, Battle of 217
Arctic 46, 118, 162, 212, 225
Arctic Circle 30, 78, 123, 142–3
Arctic pelts 176
Arctic tundra 11
Ardaric 64
Ardgar the hermit 167–8
Arduin 153
Ares 81
Arhus, Denmark 36
Ari the One-eyed 165
Arian 60, 70
Arian Christians 59, 65, 68, 72
Arles 116
Arlette 148
Armagh 104
Arminius 48
Army of the Danube 58

"Army Road" 131
Arrow-Odd 191
Asa gods 237–8, 241
Ascoli 153
Ásfriðr 212
Asgard 91
Asgeir 113
Ashingdon, Essex 142
Asia, Asians 3, 117, 194, 197–9, 233, 254, 264, 272
Asia Minor 44, 58, 60, 146, 197
Askold 209
Astrakhan 258, 269
Astrid 140
Asturia 71
Asturias, Spain 115
Athalaric 69
Athaulf 62
Athelstan 110, 120, 136
Athens, Athenians 61, 187
Atlantic 11, 100, 118, 242
Atterdag, Valdemar, king of Denmark 274, 276, 281
Attila 56–7, 64–5
Augustinian monastery 124
Augustus 57
Aun 87
Austrasia 111
Austria 31, 44, 264
Avaldsnes on Karmøy Island, Vestland 136
Avayalik Island 128
Aversa (near Naples) 153
Azerbaijan 257
Azov Sea 258

Baffin Island 125, 128, 232
Bagaudae 62
Bagdad 2, 3, 198, 203–4, 211–3, 234, 236
Bagrat IV (Jolf), king of Georgia 230, 257
Bahadur, Subedei 256–9, 261–2, 264
Baidar, son of Chagatai 262–3
Balearics 115
Balkan Mountains 60
Balkan Peninsula 58
Balkans 15, 58, 64, 67, 74, 111, 197–8, 217
Balt, Balts 196, 199, 207
Balthic lineage 59
Baltic Ice Lake 9
Baltic language 197
Baltic Sea 1–2, 9, 21–2, 30–1, 38, 44, 48–9, 52–3, 74–5, 77, 92, 95–7, 100–1, 120, 131, 140–1, 143, 168, 177, 189–91, 193–7, 200–1, 203, 205–6, 211, 215, 218, 221–2, 224, 227, 236, 240–2, 245, 253, 269–70, 272, 276, 281, 284
Baltic States 194
Banki (Baggi) 228
Barcelona 70, 111
Bardarson, Ivar 234, 251
Bari 151, 154
Bashi in Georgia 229
Basil, Byzantine emperor 219

Basil I, the Macedonian 199
Basques 70–1
Bath, England 96, 159
Battle Axe culture 28, 30–1, 35
Batu 261–6
Bayeux 113–4
Bayeux Tapestry 177, 183
Beauvais 113
Bedford 109
Bela of Hungry 262–3
Belarus 194, 197, 222
Belgium 12
Belisarius 69, 80, 199
Beloozero 209
Benedictine nunnery 124
Beowulf (epic poem) 81, 84, 87, 92, 94–5, 98, 111, 130
Beowulf (warrior) 82–5
Berezan Island (Island of St. Thomas) 231
Berezan Stone **231**
Bergen, Norway 118, 187–8, 242, 271
Berig 73, 75
Bernicia 109–10
Bible 59
Big-nose, Throndar 165
Bineta on Wollin 167
Birger, Jarl 244–5, 265, 270
Birgersson, Bengt, duke of Finland 246
Birgersson, Erik 246
Birgittine Abbey of Syon, England 277
Birgittine monastery at Vadstena 279
Birgittine order 278
Birka 3, 134, 162, 166–9, 172, 176, 205–8, 211, 215–7, 236–8, 241–2
Birwil the Pale 165
Bithynia 215
Bjarkeyjarréttr (the law of Bjarkey or Björkö) 207
Björkö Island in Lake Mälar 91, 162, 206–7
Björn (IV?), son of Eric (V?) 166–7
Bjørn (war chief) 115–6
Bjorn, king in Uppland 169
Bjorn of Gautland 156
Bjôrn, on Uppland runestone 221
Bjornsdotter, Sigrid of Greenlander 234
Black Death (the Great Death) 4, 270–4, 279
Black Earth 206–7
Black Sea 1, 44, 48, 58, 64, 73, 77, 80, 95, 100, 117, 194, 198, 203, 212, 215, 219, 224–9, 231, 254, 266, 272
Blanche (Blanka) of Namur (Belgium) 251, 277
Blekinge 157, 162, 169, 251, 273
Blessed Virgin Mary 271
"Blood-red Eagle" 108
Bloodaxe, Eirik (Eric) 110, 136, 138, 140
Blot-Sweyn, king of Sweden 240

Blue Spring 274
Bluetooth, Harald 136–7, 141, 169
Boeotia 61
Bohemia 258
Bohuslän 15–6, 27, 53, 258
Boleslav the Pole, king of Wendland 140–1, 169, 196
Boleslaw the Brave, king of Poland 219
Bølling Oscillation 6, 11–2
Bølling Period 11
Bömmel Fjord near Haugesund 276
Book of Itineraries and Kingdoms 203
Book of Revelations 272
Bordeaux 113
Boreal period 5, 15–6
Bornholm 49, 169
Boru, Brian, High King of Ireland 105, 232, 235
Bósi (Bausi) 159
Bosi and Herraud 166
Bosporus 44, 224, 226
Bourgogne 272
Brat the Jute 165
Brattahlid 124, 126
Bravellir, Battle of 131, 165
Bravic War 165
Bråviken, East Gautland 165
Breca 82
Bremen 114, 167
Breslau 242
Brest 266
Bretons 62, 150
Brigittine Monks of Amity, Oregon 278
Britain, British 2, 44–6, 48, 61, 80, 94, 96–8, 103, 111, 121, 155, 187
Britons 94, 96, 103–4
Brittany 94, 149
Brodir of Man 232
Bromme culture 12–4
Bronze Age 3, 31, 33–41, 43–4, 47, 50–1, 75, 90, 180
Bronze Age, Early 30
Bronze Age Greece 39
Bronze Age rock carvings **33**
Bronze Age Weapons **32**
Brothers of the Sword 252
Brunanburh, Battle of 110, 138
Brunswick 242
Brúsi, on runestone 222
Bryansk on the Desna 266
Bryngerd, mother of Fridleif 156
Buda on the Danube 263–4
Bukhārā 255–6
Bulgar, Bulgars 198, 202, 211, 213, 258, 261
Bulgaria, Bulgarians 146, 197, 217
Burgundians 59, 64, 68, 70, 96
Byrhtnoth, earl of Essex 138
Byzantine emperor 146, 220
Byzantine Empire, Byzantium 4, 56, 69, 70, 72, 78, 80–1, 151, 153–4, 160, 162, 182, 198–9, 202–3, 208, 211, 214–5, 217, 219–20, 225–6, 234, 236

Index

Cabo Tres Forcas 115
Caesar, Augustus 48, 53
Caesar, Julius 48
Caesars 56
Caithness 104, 135, 180, 235
Calabria, Cantabrians 151, 153–4
Camargue 115
Cambridge 109, 138
Cantabrians 70
Canterbury 143
Canute IV of Denmark 235
Capet 151
Capetian dynasty 235
Capua (Campania) 153–4
Carcassonne, France 272
Carlingford Lough, County Down 105
Carlscrona 77
Carolinian 207
Carpathian basin 210
Carpathian Mountains 194, 196–7, 211, 262–4, 266
Cartagena 70
Carthage 45, 47, 57
Caspian Sea 194, 198, 203, 209, 211–3, 226–7, 254, 256–7, 268
Castalius 72
Catalaunian Fields 64
Catholic Church 70, 140, 168, 218
Caucasus Mountains 146, 194, 198–9, 227, 254, 257
Cearbhall, king of Leinster 105
Ceawlin 96
Celts 43–4, 45, 94, 96, 103, 123, 181, 149, 174
Cenozoic era 5
Central Asia 64, 197, 199, 254–5, 261
Central Europe 3, 5, 15, 27, 56, 78, 94, 96, 115, 130, 197, 211, 246, 264, 272
central Sweden 9, 11, 22, 31, 36, 46, 90
Centum languages 29
Chacanus, king of Rhos 201
Chaedini 54, 75
Chagatai, son of Genghis Khan 256, 261
Chambers, R.W. 83
Charades 53
Charlemagne 102, 111, 114, 131, 151
Charles the Bald 112–4, 167
Charles the Fat 114
Charles the Simple 114
Chartres 113–4
Cherniakhov culture 77
Chernigov 197, 258, 262
Cherusci tribe 48
Chester 138
Childebert I 70
Chin Empire 255, 261
China, Chinese 3, 162, 196, 204, 211, 215, 254–8, 261, 269, 272
Chinese silk 176, 208–9
Chippenham 109
Chlothar II 111
Chnob 132, 212, 215

Chochilaicus-Huiglancus-Hyglac 84
Christ 59
Christ, Jesus 230
Christian, Christianity 59, 116, 109, 131, 133, 136–7, 140–1, 148, 151, 155, 166–9, 174, 185, 210, 212, 221, 216, 219, 224, 230, 237–8, 240, 248–9, 253
Christian era 186
Christ's example 279
Chronicles of Novgorod 200
Chronicles of the Kings of Lejre 92
Chuds 201, 208
Church of Rome 247
Cimbri 53–4
Cimbrian peninsula (Jutland) 75
Cirencester 96
Civitate, Battle of 154
Claudius II, Roman emperor 59
Clement IV, pope 246
Cleveland 146
The Climate Development of the North Atlantic Realm 10
clinker-built 117
Clonfert 104
Clonmacnois 104
Clontarf, Battle of 105, 232, 235
Clovis I 70, 111
Cniva 58
Codanian Gulf 54
Codanus Bay 53
Codanvia Island 53
Codex Regius 174
Codex Wormanius 174
Colchis 227, 229
Cologne 114
Constans, Ammillius 49
Constantine, Byzantine emperor 219
Constantine of Scotland 110
Constantine, son of Yaroslav II 264
Constantinople (*Miklagård*) 2–3, 57, 60, 65–9, 72, 151, 166, 181, 194, 199, 203, 209–11, 215–7, 219–20, 224, 226, 231, 234, 236
Continental Europe 233
Copenhagen 157, 242, 243
Corbey 166
Corded Ware culture 28, 30, 75, 196
Córdoba 115, 212
Cori (Courlanders) 168, 191
Cork 105
Cornwall 45, 94, 106, 138
Corsairs 200
Cospatric of Northumbria 150
Council 207
Council of Masters (*Sovet gospod*) 269
Council of the Svear 238
Courland 120, 168, 190–1
Cracow (Kraków) 242, 253, 263
Cracow University 253
Crete 226
Crimea, khanate of 269
Croatia 197, 264

Cro-Magnon man 21
Cronian Sea 46
Crusades 233, 240, 262
Cuman (Kipchaks) 254, 257–9, 261–2, 266, 268
Cumbria 140
Curonians 196–7
Cuthwine 96
Cyprus 43
Cyril, Russian Orthodox Metropolitan 268
Czech-Austria 26
Czechs 197

Dacia 48, 58–60
Daegsanstan 96
Daelreodi 96
Dag 86
Dalarna 144
Dalmatia 111, 226, 264
Dalriada 103
Dalsland 84, 90, 249
Danegeld 113, 139–40, 157, 159–60
Danelaw 109–10, 142, 157
Danevirke 111, 131, 133, 137, 211
Dani 80
Danial of Galicia 264
Danish England 108
Danish-English kings 158
Danish History 165
Danish islands 80
Danish kingdoms 97
Danish Mercia 142
Danish-Swedish empire 166
Dantzic 77
Danube basin 43
Danube River 59–60, 64–5, 67, 198, 210–1, 215–7, 263–4
Danubian people 34
Danubian Suebi 64
Danzig 242
Dauciones 54, 75
Daurrud 180
Davis Strait 127
Dazhd-Bog (sun god's son) 218
Decameron by Boccaccio 273
Decius 58
Deild-river, Iceland 156
Deira 108
Demetre (Bjolf), half-brother to Bagrat 230
denarii 49
Denmark, Danes, Danish 3, 5, 9, 12–3, 16–8, 22–3, 25, 27–8, 41, 49–51, 80–4, 86–9, 90, 92, 98, 101–3, 105–9, 111–4, 120–1, 123, 130–3, 137–9, 141–6, 150, 155, 157, 160–2, 165–9, 173, 188–9, 191, 207, 211–2, 217, 226, 235–7, 241–3, 249–50, 253, 245–6, 273–4, 281, 282–4
Derbend 257–8
Derby 108
Description of the Nordic Islands 171
Desna River 197
Diaconus, Leo 216
Diocletian, Roman emperor 56

Dir 209
Dives-sur-Mer 149
Divina dispensatione 241
Dnieper-Don Valley 12
Dnieper River 77, 197–8, 200–3, 208–11, 215, 219, 220, 224–5, 229, 231, 258–9, 264, 266, 268
Dniester River 59, 77, 258, 266
Dobrynya, Novgorod boyar 218–9
Domald 86
Domar 86
Dómisnes (Cape Kolka) 222
Don River 59, 198, 264
Dorestad 113–4, 160
Dorpat 253
Dorset Paleo-Eskimos 125, 128–9, 233
Dorystolon (Silistria) 217
Dover 150
Dregovichi Slavs 198
Drevlyanes (Derevlians) 198, 215–6
Driva 86
Drogo of Hauteville 153
Dubhgall, brother of Sigtrygg Silk-beard 232
Dublin 105, 135, 235
Dublin Vikings 232
Dutch 233
Dvina Bay 193
Dygve 86
Dyrholmen 22

Eadgils 85, 87
Eanmund 85
East Anglia 97, 106–9, 143
East Anglican Danes 109
East Country (Estonia, Latvia and Courland) 165, 191
East Gautland (Gotland) 92, 164–5
Eastern Europe 1–3, 64, 77, 100, 191, 194, 196–7, 199, 200, 204–6, 208, 222, 230–1, 252–3, 255, 257–9, 261, 264, *267*, 269, **295**
Eastern Horn 122
Eastern Orthodox 4, 72, 218
Eastern Roman Empire 60, 64–5, 69
Eastern Slavs 197
Eastfirths 122
Ebbesfleet 94
Ebling 242
Ebo of Rheims 166, 169
Ecgfrith's monastery 102
Ed Stone, from Uppsala 225
Edda of *Rigsthula* 173
Eddas 232
Eddic poem 174, 177
Eddington 109
Eddval, king of Suzdal 192
Edecon 57
Edmond, brother of Athelstan 110
Edmondson, Eric 215
Edmund, king of East Anglia 108
Edmund the Magnificent 138
Edmund the Old 240
Edred 138

Edward, king of England 145–6
Edward of Wessex 109
Edward the Elder 109–10, 138
Edwin, earl of Mercia 146
Egil of *Egil's Saga* 87, 120, 173–4, 185, 190
Egil the One-eye 165
Egill, on runestone 222
Egil's Saga 110, 120, 135, 161, 174, 185, 190
Egilsson, Thorstein of *Egil's Saga* 173
Egypt, Egyptians 41, 43
Eifor (Aifor), cataract on Dnieper 223
Einriði 159
Eirik, king at Uppsala 169
Eirik, king of Norway 120
Eirik of Hladir (Jarl) 142–3
Eirik, son of Jarl Hakon 141
Eiríks Saga 126
Eivísl, on runestone 221
Ejder River 101
Eketorp 97
Elbe 48, 53
Elbing 77
Elder Futhark 186–7
Elin, daughter of Burislaf of Novgorod 156
Elizabeth, daughter of Yaroslav 220
Ellesmere Island 128–9, 232
Emerald Isle 235
Emma, wife of Ethelred and Knut the Great 145, 148–9
England, English 3, 81, 88–9, 92, 96, 98, 100, 102, 104–5, 106–10, 113, 120, 130, 132–3, 136–9, 142–50, 157–60, 162, 165–6, 169, 191, 207, 212, 226–8, 232–3, 235, 237, 243, 249, 278
English Channel 44, 112, 149
Epirus 61, 65
Ereleuva 65
Eric, king in *Ynglinga Tal* 86
Eric of Pomerania, king of the Kalmar Union 281, 283
Erik (Swedish royal house) 240
Erik, bishop of Greenland 232
Erik, king of Svear 215
Erik the Holy, king of Sweden 241
Erik the Red 124–5
Erik XI, the Lame or Lisper 243–4
Erik XIV of Sweden 171
Eriksson, Jarl Hakon (Earl Hákon) 159
Eriksson, Knut, king of Sweden 243
Eriksson, Leif 125–6
Eriksson, Olaf 74
Erimbert 168
Erin 105
Ermanaric 80
Ertebølle culture 16, 18–22, 25
Eruli (Heruli) 81
Essex 106, 109, 138, 142
Estland (Estonia, Latvia, Courland) 88, 162, 191

Estonia, Estonians 1, 88–9, 92, 140, 165, 194, 196–7, 201, 218, 220–1, 227, 241, 253
Estridsson, Svein of Denmark 157, 146, 150, 217, 232, 234–5
Eternal City 278
Ethelfleda 109
Ethelred, king of Wessex 108
Ethelred of English Mercia 109
Ethelred the Unready 138–9, 142–3, 145, 149
Ethelwald 109
Etruscans 43–5, 47, 52, 56
Eufemia 252
Eugenius 110
Euphrates River 48
Euric 57, 66
Europe, European 1, 41, 44, 53, 59, 73, 81, 92, 101, 115, 117–8, 124, 127, 131, 157, 188–9, 199, 221, 232–3, 233–4, 236, 251, 262, 271–3, 277, 284
Eustace, count of Boulogne 149
Evagre 80
Evreux 113
Exeter 139
Exeter Book 81
Eyrathing 136
Eystein 87–8
Eyvind the Eastman 156

Fadlan, Ibn 213–4
Fairhair, Harald 85, 135–6, 139–40, 174, 245
Falan, near Falköping, Västergötland 282
Falster Island 157, 169
Faravid, king of Kvenland 161
Faroe Islands 46, 105, 117, 122–3, 135, 143–4, 236
Favonae 54, 75
Federmesser culture 12
Fedor, posadnik of Novgorod 270
Feletheus-Feva 67
Fellin (Viljandi) 241
Feng (Shakespeare's Claudius) 130–1
Fennic 200
Fensalir 91
Fertile Crescent 194
Filimer, son of Gadaric 73
"Findless Age" 41
Finja 12
Finland, Finish, Finns 1, 4, 6, 18, 26, 40, 54, 80, 86, 92, 96, 173, 188, 196–9, 201, 203, 207, 221–2, 237–8, 241–2, 244, 248, 250, 259, 261
Finnaithae 80
Finnbogi 127
Finni 54, 75
Finnmark 134, 161
Finno-Ugric 27, 196–7, 197–10, 221, 254
Finsta, Uppland 278
Firaesi 54, 75
Fitzhugh, Third Lord of Ravenworth 277
Five Boroughs 108

Fjädrundaland 88, 164
Fjolne 86
Fjords 136
Flintbek 23
Florence 271
Folkung dynasty 244
Forkbeard, Svein of Denmark 137, 139–42, 169
Fosna culture 15, 17
Fosna-Hensbacka 16
Fowler, Henry, German king 115, 212
France, French, Franks 12–3, 63–5, 69–70, 83–4, 90, 96, 105, 107–8, 111, 113–5, 117, 121, 123, 226, 131–2, 134, 140, 143, 148–51, 155, 157–8, 160, 166–8, 182, 196, 207–8, 211, 228, 235–7, 252, 271
Frankfurt 272
Frederick II, Holy Roman emperor 262
French Revolution 277
Frey, fertility god 90–1, 240
Frey (Yngve), from *Ynglinga Tal* 86
Freydis 126–7
Freygeirr, on runestone 222
Freyja 90
Freysteinn (on runestone) 224
Frideric of the Rugians 67
Fridleif, from *Ynglinga Tal* 86
Fridleif, settler of Iceland 156
Fridleifsdale River, Iceland 156
Friesland 120
Frigg 91
Frigidus, Battle of 60
Frikko 91
Frisia, Frisian 83–4, 87, 92, 111–2, 114, 134–5, 160, 181, 207–9, 212, 242
Frisian cog 242
Fritigern 59–60
Frode the Bold of Denmark 87
Frode, Zealand 86
The Frozen Sea 46
Funnel Beaker culture 22–7, 30–1, 34–5
Fyn Island 9, 20, 25, 146, 157
Fyrisvold 86

Gaeta 153
Gaimer IV, prince of Salerno 152
Galicia 220, 254, 259, 262, 268
Galindians 196
Gall-Gaedhil 104
Gallehus, Jutland 95
Gallic Romans 181
Gällivare-Malmberget 6
Gamla Uppland 87
Garda-Ketil the Icelander, with Yngvarr 229
Garðar (land of forts) 222
Garðar (on runestone) 223
Gardar of Sweden 156
Gardarike (land of forts) 197
Garðaríki 205
Garonne River 115
Gåsinge stone from Södermanland 159

Gästrikland, Sweden 222
Gate Fulford, Battle of 146, 149
Gaul 44, 48–9, 57, 62–4, 80
Gautbert, Bishop 166
Gauthigoths 74, 80
Gauthild, daughter of King Algaut 88, 164
Gauti (Gautoi) 81
Gautland 165
Gautr 159
Gautrek, king of West Gotaland (West Gautland, Västergötland) 164
Gautrek the Mild 88
Gauts (Geats or Goths), Gautland 74–5, 81–5, 88–92, 111, 141–2, 160–4, 165–6, 169, 173, 205, 221, 240–1
Gedimin 266
Geek Orthodox 219
Geir the Livonian 165
Geiri 158
Genghis Khan 254–5, 257, 259, 264
Genoa 69
Geography by Ptolemy 54, 74
George IV (Giorgi Lasha—Light of the World) 257–8
Georgia 229, 257–8
Gepids 59, 64–7, 73, 75, 77
Gerar, Palestine 41
German Iron Age 78, 91–2, 94, 161, 182; ships and stones **98**; weapons and armor **99**
Germans, Germany 1, 3–5, 9, 12–3, 16, 23, 27–8, 46, 48, 52, 56–8, 61–2, 74–5, 77–8, 80, 92, 95–6, 111, 115, 137, 151, 154, 160, 171, 196–7, 206–7, 211–2, 217–8, 236, 240, 242, 244, 252–3, 270, 273, 276, 280–1, 282
Gesalec 69
Gesta Danorum 171
Getae 74
Getica 171
Gibbon, Edward 73, 77, 121, 151, 200, 209
Giso 67
Gloucester 96
Gloucestershire 142
Gnezdovo 204
Gnezdovo-Smolensk 203–4
Gnupa 212
Gnupsson, Erik, bishop of Greenland 129
Goa, wife of Hroar 156
Gobi Desert 254
Godfred, king of Denmark 111, 131
Godheim 86
Godwinson, Harold 146–50, 232
Gokstad, Norway 117–8
Golden Fleece 229
Golden Horde 265, 268–9
Good Friday 180
Gorm, of Sweden 156
Gorm, rune master 212
Gorm the Old 132–3

Göta River 9, 248
Göteborg 73
Gothic 69, 71–3, 75, **76**
Gothiscandza 73, 75
Gothones 74
Goths 1, 3, 46, 58–61, 64–5, 67, 69–70, 77–8, 72–5, 80–1, 83, 198, 284
Goths (Gauts) 172
Gotland (Gautland) 88, 164
Gotland Island, Gotlanders 3, 27, 30, 38, 49, 73, 75, 86, 89–90, 92, 96–7, 100, 144, 165, 169, 172, 183, 191, 205–6, 209, 211, 217, 220–1, 224–5, 231, 249, 271, 274, 276, 283
Gottorp Slot 212
Gråborg 97
Grænlands knörr (Greenland carrier) 234, 251
Grænlendinga Saga 126–7
Grammaticus, Saxo 165, 171–2
Grand Prince of Varangian Russia 210
Grani, on Berezan Stone 231
Granmar, king of Södermanland 88, 164
Gratian 60
Gray Monks of Stockholm 248
Great Belt 9
Great Eastern European Plain **192**, 194, 197
Greater Germany 75
Greece, Greeks 43–4, 46–7, 52, 56, 59, 61, 72, 74, 146, 151, 153, 159, 199, 207, 209–10, 218–9, 224–5, 227, 231
Greek fire 215
Greek Orthodox Church 219, 216
Greenland, Greenlanders 2, 6, 46, 105, 117–8, 124, 125–9, 157, 187, 200, 212, 215, 232–6, 251, 283
Gregory IV, pope 166
Gregory IX, pope 262
Gregory of Tours, bishop 84
Grendel 82–3
Greycloak, Harald 136
Griefswald 272
Grikkfara (traveler in Greece) 224
Grikkland (Greece) 225
Grinda, Södermanland 159
Grip, Bo Johnsson 281–2
Grjot River, Iceland 156
Grjótgarðr 159
Grjotgardsson, Hakon, jarl of Hladir 135
Grobin 191, 205
Grud 132
Guadalete River, Battle of 71
Guadalquivir River 115
Guðbjörn 158
Guðlaug 160
Guðmarr 158
Gudmarsson, Ulv of Ulvåsa 278–9
Gudrid 126–7
Gudrod, king of Scania 88, 165

Gudrod, the Hunting King 134
Guðvér 159
Guild of St. John 269
Guildhall of the Gotlanders 210
Gul, Bonde 274
Gulathing 136
Gulf of Bothnia 6, 9, 54, 95, 161, 188, 205, 237
Gulf of Finland 9, 197–8, 203, 205, 211, 221–2, 242, 253
Gulf of Riga 9, 196, 203, 211
Gulf Stream 123
Gunnarr 159
Gunnhild, wife of Eirik Bloodaxe 136
Gunnhild, wife of Pallig 139
Gunni 158–9
Gunnkell 159
Gunnleifr, on runestone 227
Gunthigis (Baza) 72
Gurd 212
Gustav I of Sweden 170, 284
Gustav II of Sweden 74
Guta Saga 205
Gutae (Gautae) 54, 75
Guthfrith of Dublin 110
Guthrum 108–9
Gutones (Gotones) 46, 74–5
Gutthiuda 74
Güyük Khan 264–5
Gyrth, eorl 150

Haddeby Noor 212
Hæthcyn 84–5
Hafrsfjord, Battle of 135
Hagia Sophia in Istanbul 187
Hairy-breeches, Ragnar 107–8
Häkan of Norway 281
Håkan, son of Magnus Smek 251, 274, 276, 280
Håkansson, Olof of Norway 280–1
Hake 86
Hakon, Jarl 169
Hakon Cut-cheek 165
Håkon, king of Norway 249–50
Hakon of Hladir 137, 140
Hakon the Good of Norway 133, 136, 140
Halfdan (Hvitserk) 108
Halfdan, brother to Sigfred 131
Halfdan of Denmark 86
Halfdan of Scania 88
Halfdan the Black, son of Gudrod 135, 174
Halfdan the Generous 134
Halla, wife of Herfinn 156
Halland 31, 54, 80, 157, 162, 251, 271
Hallin 80
Hallstatt culture 31, 41, 44
Halogaland 134–6, 141
Hals, Battle of 136
Hälsinge runes 187
Halstensson, Philip, king of Sweden 240
Hamabek 258
Hamadan, Persia 257
Hamburg 113, 166–7, 242, 245; culture 12

Hamlet 130
Hamlet, Prince of Denmark 130
Hampshire 109
Hann 159
Hanseatic cog 242
Hanseatic League (Hansa) 242–3, 243, 245, 250, 253, 271, 276, 281–3
Har from Aland 165
Harald (built church at Hedeby) 168
Harald, king of Denmark (son of Svein Forkbeard) 142–3
Harald, Norwegian king, burned Hedeby 217
Harald, son of Gorm 133
Haraldsson, Olaf 143–5, 220
Hardangerfjord 140
Hardradi, Harald 144–6, 147–8, 226, 235, 220
Harefoot, Harald 145, 160
Hassmyra 95
Hasteinn 115–6
Hastings 149
Hastings, Battle of 146, 149
Håtuna, near Nyköping, Sweden 248
Håtunaleken (Håtuna Games) 248–9
Heardred 83–5
Hebrides 104, 122–3, 135–6, 140, 155–6, 235
Hedeby 3, 101, 115, 120, 131, 134–5, 160, 162, 167–9, 207, 211–2, 215, 217, 236
Hedemark 134
Hedvig of Holstein 247
Heimdall 174
Heimskringla 169
Helgeå River 143
Helgi (Heiligo), king of Jutland 132, 211
Helgi (to Vinland) 127
Helgi the Lean 156
Helgö 94, 96, 100, 134, 162, 176, 206
Hellerö, Västra Ed Parish, Småland, Sweden 38
Helluland 125
Helsingborg 243
Helsingjaland 135
Hemming 131
Henry, king of France 148
Henry of Silesia 263
Henry III of England 245
Henry IV of England 277
Hensbacka culture 15–7
Heorot 82–3, 87
Herebeald 84
Herfinn, son of Thorgils 156
Hergrim, son of Thorgils 156
Herigar, prefect of Birka 166–8, 207
Herjolf 124
Herjolfsson, Bjarni 124–5
Herraud, son of Hring 166
Herrevad Bridge, Västmanland 244
Heruli (Eruli) 64, 80

Hesselblad, Elizabeth 278
High Middle Ages 252
Hilditonn, Harald 92, 131, 165–6
Hilleviones 54
Historia de omnibus gothorum sueonumque regibus (History of All Kings of Goths and Swedes) 171
Historia Norvegiae 128
Hjalmvigi, with Yngvarr 229
Hjälsta, Uppland 159
Hjalti, Iceland settler 156
Hjorvard 88
Hjôrvarðr 158
Hladir 136
Hogne, king of East Gautland 88, 164
Holderness 146
Hollingstedt 211
Holmgård (Novgorod) 203, 214, 223
Holmgarih 200
Holmgersson, Knut, king of Sweden 243
Holmi 160
Holmr's Sea, near Holmgård (Novgorod) 222
Holocene Epoch 6, 15
Holstein 250
Holt, Iceland 156
Holy Land 151, 240–1, 262
Holy Roman Empire 1, 151, 196, 241, 272
Holy See in Rome 238
Holy Sepulcher 279
Holy Spirit 59
Honorius, western Roman emperor 62, 94
Honorius III, pope 257
Hordaknut 145
Hordaland 136
Horik the Elder, Danish king 131, 167–8
Horik the Younger, king of Denmark 131
Hospitallers 263
Hrafn, on runestone 223
Hrethel 84
Hring of Småland 162
Hring, ruler of Svear and Gauts 92, 165–6
Hring, Sigurd, king of Svear and East Gautland 165, 131
Hróði 159
Hrothgar (Hoögar) 82–3, 130
Hrunting 83
Hsi-Hsia (Tanguts kingdom) 255, 259
Hudson Strait 125
Hugleik 86
Humber River 146
Humphry of Hauteville 153
Hungarians (Magyars), Hungry 196, 216–7, 258, 262–4
Huns 56, 59–62, 64–5, 81, 94, 198
Huntington 109
Husavik, Skjalfandi 122
Hvalsey church on Greenland 234

Hygelac, king of the Geats 8, 83–5, 87, 111

Iberia 15, 44–5, 62, 64, 66, 70, 115, 199
Ice Age 3, 5–6, **8**, 11
Iceland 2, 4, 26–7, 46, 105, 117–9, 120, 122, 123, 124, 126, 135, 138, 140, 155–8, 164, 173, 189, 200, 212, 225, 232–3, 235–7, 251
Icelandic Annals 129, 232
Icelandic gods 90
Icelandic sagas 114, 161, 172, 180, 189, 228, 232
Icelandic Vikings 162
Igor (Ingvar), Grand Prince of Kiev 211, 215
Illyria 61, 68
India, Indians 3, 117, 204, 211, 215, 256, 272
Indians (native Americans) 125–8
Indo-European language 27, 196–7
Indus River 198, 256
Inga 160
Inge the Elder, king of Svear 239
Inge I, the Elder 240
Inge II, the Younger 240
Ingeborg, mother of Magnus Eriksson Smek 249
Ingeborg, wife of Duke Valdemar 249
Ingelheim, near Mainz 201
Ingibjorg, wife of Hring 162
Ingjald the Bad or "The Evil-adviser," 88, 164
Ingjaldr 158
Ingria 1
Ingstad, Anne Stine 127
Ingstad, Helge 127
Inuit 128, 234
Invasion of England **147**
Iona, Scotland 103–4
Ipswich 150
Ireland, Irish 3, 26–7, 44–5, 96, 103–6, 110, 116–7, 120, 122–3, 232, 135, 140, 156, 158, 212, 232, 235
Irish hermit monks 122, 124
Irish Norse 138
Irish Sea 104
Irish wives 123
Iron Age 3, 38, 40–1, 43, 47, 51
Iron Arm (Bras-de-Fer), William of Hauteville 153
Ironside, Bjorn 113–4
Ironside, Edmund 142–3
Irtish River 259
Islam 198
Islamic empire 199
Isle of Athelney 108
Isle of Man 104, 140, 187, 235
Isonzo River 57, 67
Isøre Thing, Zealand 146
Israel 252
Italy and Sicily **152**
Italy, Italians 15, 44, 47, 57, 61–3, 65–9, 72, 80, 96, 111, 116, 151–4, 160, 199, 226
Itil 198, 211, 213
Ivar 92
Ivar of Limerick 105
Ivar of Scania 89
Ivar the Boneless 108
Ivigtut, Greenland (middle settlement) 234
Izborsk 209

Jacob, Onund of Sweden 143, 145–6, 228, 240
Jämtland (Jamtaland) 53, 135
Jarl of Orkney 146
Jarl, son of Fathir and Mothir 175
Jarrow, Northumbria 102, 104
Jason and the Argonauts 229
Jaxartes River (Syr Darya River) 199
Jelling 132
Jend 256
Jerusalem 151, 225
Jews 218, 272
Jochi 256–9, 261
John I of Moscow 268
Jomsborg Vikings 137, 169, 196
Jones, Gwyn 189
Jordanes 68, 72–3, 78, 80–1, 161, 171
Jorund 86
Juno 49
Justinian, eastern Roman emperor 69, 72, 199
Jutland, Jutes 9, 12, 22, 30, 46, 48, 51, 53–4, 75, 80, 88–9, 92, 94, 96, 100–1, 106, 111, 114, 120, 130–3, 136–7, 145, 157, 160, 165, 167, 173, 195, 211–2
Jutta, princess of Denmark 245–6

Kadan, son of Ogedei 262–3
Kænmar, ruler of Kiev 192
Kaffa, Crimea 272
Kainulaists (Kvenir or Kvænir) of Kvenland 54
Kakheti, Georgia 230
Kalka, Battle of 259
Kalmar, Sweden 165, 184, 238, 242, 282
Kalmar *Ledung* (Kalmar Raid) 239
Kalmar Museum 274
Kalmar Union 282–3
Kålsta stone from Uppland 158
Kälvesten runestone 221
Kama River 198, 259
Kamban, Grim 122
Kamenets, near the Dniester 266
Kangli (eastern Cumans) 259
Kangli Khan 259
Karakorum 261, 264–5
Karelia, Karelians 1, 161, 196, 248, 251
Kári 159
Karl, on Berezan Stone 231
Karl, son of Afi and Amma 175
Karl IX 171
Karl XVI of Sweden 171
Karlsefni, Thorfinn 126
Kartlis Tskhovreba (old chronicles of Georgia) 229
Kattegat Sea 53
Kaupang-Skiringssal 134
Kazakhstan 194
Kazan Khanate 269
Kazimir III, the Great of Poland 253
Kent 106, 139, 142
Keril, with Yngvarr 230
Ketill 159
Kettilmundsson, Matts 250
Kettilson, Nils, bishop of Västerås 248
Kexholm 270
Kharkov 194
Khazars 198–9, 202–3, 208–11, 216–8, 258
Kherson 217, 219
Khojend 256
Khordadbeh, Ibn 203
Khurasan 256
Khwarazm-shah (Khwarizmian) Empire 255, 257–8, 261
Kiev 3, 77, 146, 194, 197, 209–11, 215, 217–8, 254, 258, 262, 266, 268–9
Kievan Chronicles (*The Russian Primary Chronicles* or *Tales of Times Gone By*) 200–1
King Gautrek 164
Kingigtorssuaq Island 128
Kipchak Empire 264, 266
Kipchak Turks (Polovtsy, Cumans) 254
Kiruna 6
Kitchen Midden culture 18
Kizil Kum Desert 256
Kjölen Mountains 6
Kjula Runestone from Söderman-land 158
Klak, Harald 131
Knapp, Thord, son of Bjorn of Hang, Iceland 156
Knappstead, Iceland 156
Knights of Georgia 257
Knudson, Erik, king of Sweden 243
Knut the Great 142–5, 149, 158–9, 220
Knutsson, Filip 244
Knutsson, Torgils, Lord High Constable 247–8
Kochu 261
Kolbäck River 244
Kolbein, Iceland settler 156
Kolgrim of Greenlander 234
Kon the Younger 185
Kongemose culture 16, 18, 21
Koningsberg 77
Korea 255, 261
Korshamn 207
Korsør Nor 20
Koten 261
Kotian, chief of the western Cumans 258
Krężnica Jara, Poland 23

Kristina, daughter of Torgils 248
Krivichians 197, 201, 208
Krok the Peasant 165
Kugghamn 207
Kung Bracklös (King Trouserless) 282
Kura River 257
Kurland (Latvia) 165, 205
Kuru 159
Kvalsund, Norway 100
Kván (*Kvæn*) 161
Kvenland 161
Kyrre, Olaf (the Gentle or Peaceful) 148

Labrador 125, 127–9, 232–3
Ladoga-Onega 203
Ladulås (Barn-Locker) 247
lagthings (supra-Things) 136
Lake Helgö 101
Lake Il'men (Ilmen) 200–1, 203, 222
Lake Ladoga 146, 194, 197, 200, 203, 270, 283
Lake Mälar 94, 96, 206
Lake Mjøsa 134, 136
Lake Onega 270
Lake Peipus 196–7, 201, 203
Lake Peipus, Battle of 265
Lambert, count 113
Lambey 104
Landeryd, Östergötland 159
Landnámabók (The Book of Settlement) 156
Långasjö, Värend 274
Langeland 169
Lapps, Lappland 16, 18, 53, 80, 120, 161, 173, 192, 197
Late Dorset 124
Latin 52, 59, 72, 74, 59, 279
Latin alphabet 174, 185, 188
Latin and Filipino Masses 278
Latin Christian Church 4, 57
Latin-Etruscan 268
latitude 120
Latvians (Lettigallians, Letts), Latvia 191, 194, 196–7, 218, 253
Lavello 153
Legendary Kings of Sweden *163*
Leicester 108
Leidre (Lejre, Hleiðra in Zealand) 87
Leifsbudir (Leif's house) 125, 127
Lek 113
Lemovii 74
Lena, Sweden 248
Leo I 65–7
Leo III, the Isaurian 199
Leo IX, pope 153–4
Leo VI, Byzantine emperor 211
Leofwine, eorl 150
Leovigild 70
"Letter of Union" 282
Levoni 54, 75
Liber Historiæ Francorum 84
Liber Monstrorum 84
Liegnitz, Battle of 263

The Life of Anskar by Rimbert 166, 191, 207
Lífland 222
Lihult culture 16, 22, 27
Limerick 105
Limfjord 101
Limoges 113
Lincoln 108
Lindholm Höje, Denmark 177
Lindisfarne 102
Linköping, Sweden 38, 170
Liparit Baghvashi, Georgian general 230
Lisbon, Portugal 115, 278
Lithuania, Lithuanians 1, 191, 194, 196–7, 216, 253, 262, 265–6, 268
Litorina Sea 9, 21
Little Belt 9
Little Ice Age 233
Liuva I 70
Liuva II 70
Livonia (Lífland, Livland), Livonians 165, 196–7, 222
Livonian Brothers of the Sword 241
Lödöse, Sweden 242, 271
Loire, Aquitaine 113
Loire, France 116
Loire River 114
Lokietek, Wladyslaw, (the Dwarf), king of Poland 253
Lolland Island 157, 169
Lombards 59, 80, 94, 151, 153–4, 160
London 109, 142–3, 149, 157, 242
Long Serpent 141
longboat 184, 242
Longfellow, Henry Wadsworth 140–1
longhouse 3, 34–5, 38–9, 43, 46, 51, 125, 177, 179, 237
longitude 120
longships 3, 117–8, *119*, 120
Longsword, William 114, 148
Lords of the Svear 241
Lothair 112
Lothar of France 167
Lough Owel, Westmeath 105
Lough Ree 105
Louis I of France 114
Louis the German 112, 167
Louis the Pious 201
Louis the Stammerer 114
Lovat River 194, 202–3, 224, 268
Lübeck 242, 245, 250, 273
Lugii 74
Luna 116
Lund 25, 120
Lund Cathedral, Denmark 281
Lusatia 241
Lutheran Sweden 277

Macedonia 61
Maelmordha of Leinster 232
Magdeburg 242
Maglemose culture 16, 18, 20
Magnus, Johannes 170–1
Magnus Eriksson Land Law 251

Magnus III if Sweden, Ladulås (Barn-locker) 246–8, 250–1
Magnus III of Norway (Barefoot) 235
Magnus IV of Sweden (Smek), Magnus VII of Norway 4, 234, 249–52, 270–1, 274, 277, 279–80
Magnusson, Birger, king of Sweden 247–50
Magnusson, Erik, father of King Magnus Smek 248–50
Magnusson, Erik, son of King Magnus Smek 251, 276
Magnusson, Knut 244
Magnusson, Valdemar 248–9
Magog, son of Noah 171
Magyars 198, 210–1
Maiden King of Georgia 258
Maine, France 149
Maine, United States 125, 129
"Maine penny" 127
Mainz 1
Mal, prince of the Drevlyanes 215
Mälar 87, 100
Mälaren Lake district 241, 244–5
Malcolm III of Scotland 236
Maldon, Battle of 138
Malmö 12, 252
Manchuria 255
Mangku Khan 265
Manni 157
Mar the Red 165
Mara Mead, Sweden 250
Maragha, Persia 257
Marcomannic runes 187
Margareta, queen of Denmark, Norway and Sweden 280–3
Maritsa River 60
Markgäld (land tax) 249
Markland 125, 129, 232
Marne River 114
Marro, ruler of Muram 192
Mars 91
Märta, wife of King Birger Magnusson 248–9
Mary, daughter of Yaroslav 220
Mary's Heart in Weert, Netherlands 278
Mary's Refuge Abbey in Uden, Netherlands 278
Massilia (Marseille) 44, 62
Mastogloia Sea 9
Mazowiecki, Konrad of Mazovia 241
Meaux 113
Mechtild, wife of Birger Jarl 245
Mecklenburg 77, 241, 280–2
Medelpad, Sweden 187
Medieval Warm Period (MWP) 47, 100, 125, 128, 233
Mediterranean 34, 43–4, 46–7, 51–2, 56, 78, 81, 100, 115–7, 121, 151, 160–1, 226
Meiendorf 6
Melfi 153
Melgaard, Jørgen 127
Melville Bay, Greenland 128

Index

Mentonomon Sea 46, 74
Menved, Erik (Eric), king of Denmark 248–50
Mercia 106, 108–9
Merians 201, 208
Mesolithic 15–7, 18, 23, 40
Mesolithic-Neolithic transition 15
Mesopotamia 226
Mesozoic 5
Meuse River 114
Mexico 278
Michael IV of Byzantium 153, 209
Middle Ages 3, 4, 74, 225, 234, 237, 277, 282
Middle East 23, 48, 71, 81, 198
Middle Europe 30
Midgard 91
Mieszko I of Poland 253
Migration Period 78–81, 92, 94–7, 177
Milan 56, 61, 65
Mindovg 266
Mixi 80
Moberg, Vilhelm 89, 155
Møen Island 157
Moesia 58–60, 66–7
Mogilev on the Dniester 266
Moldavia 59, 263
Møllegabet 22
Möllerod 12
Monastery of the Caves 200
Mongolia, Mongols (Tartars) 4, 255–9, 261–70, 272
Monomakh, Vladimir, Grand Prince of Kiev 254
Montelius, Oscar 31–2
Moors 115–6
Moravians 197, 263
Morcar, earl of Northumbria 146
Moscow 1, 194, 196, 262, 268
Moskva River 268–9
Moster 140
Mstislav, prince of Chernigov 258
Mstislav, prince of Kiev 258–9
Mstislav I, Grand Prince of Kiev 254
Mstislav the Daring 258–9
Munster 104
Muonio River 6
Muslims 69, 71, 152–4, 160, 203, 213, 216, 240, 198–9, 208, 219, 228
Mycenaean Greeks 34

Naddod the Viking 122
Naissus-Nish 59
Nanook 128
Nantes 113
Naples 69
Narbonensis 69
Narbonne 70
Närke 84, 90, 161, 164
Natural History by Pliny the Elder 46
Navarre 116
Nävelsjö stone from Småland 159

Nedao, Battle of 65
Negroes 115
Neolithic 16, 23, 27, 34, 40
Nerike (Närke?) 88
Nero 53
Nestor 200
Netherlands 12, 26–8, 243, 278
Neva, Battle of 244
Neva River 203, 265, 270
Nevsky, Alexander 265
Newfoundland 118, 125, 127, 129
Nicene Creed 59, 72
Nicephorus II of Byzantium 217
Nid River 141
Nidaros (Trondheim), Norway 236
Niflhel 91
Nîmes 116
Nithard 166
Njord 86, 90
Noirmoutier 113
non–Indo-European-speaking peoples 196–7
Norbonne, France 272
Nordic Bronze Age 28, 31–2, 34
Norfolk 109
Noricum 57, 65, 68
Normandy, Normans 114–5, 123, 132, 135, 142, 145, 148–50, 151–4, 157, 160, 183, 226, 235
Norrköping 165
Norrland 6, 40, 53, 161
Norse, Norsemen 100, 102, 104–6, 110, 113–4, 118, 122, 125, 129, 145, 147, 173–4, 191, 193–4, 200, 203, 232, 234–5
North Africa 56–7, 69, 71, 80, 199
North America 2–3, 5, 100, 117, 124–9, 187, 232, 233, 236
North Atlantic 100, 117, 122, 155, 160, 184, 236
North Atlantic islands 2–3, 130
North Cape 251
North Dvina River 192–3
North Pole 120
North Sea 2, 9, 31, 49, 92, 95, 100–1, 122, 131, 177, 211, 236–7, 242, 253, 281
North Sea Empire of Knut 144
North Sea ivory 176
North Star 118
North Wales (Gwynedd, Powys and Dyfed) 106
Northampton 109, 138
Northeastern Europe 203–5, 221, 262
Northern Europe 15, 26–8, 34, 48, 52, 54, **55**, 81, 97, **132**, 196, 241–2, 268
Northmen 115–6, 232
Northumbria 81, 88, 92, 102–3, 106, 108–10, 138, 140, 142–3, 146, 165
Northwest River, Lake Melville, Labrador 127
Northwestern Asia 196
Northwestern Europe 44, 96
Norway, Norwegians 9, 15, 18, 26, 46, 49, 84–5, 88, 90, 92, 95, 102–4, 107, 113–4, 118, 120–4, 127–8, 130, 132–7, 140–2, 143–8, 149, 155–7, 160–2, 165, 169, 172, 183, 188–9, 191, 193, 207, 212, 220, 233–7, 243, 245–6, 249, 251, 276, 280–2
Norwich 139, 150
Nøstvet 16, 27
Nottingham 108
Nova Scotia 125, 129
Novgorod 1, 3, 140, 144, 146, 197, 191, 200, 209–10, 214, 218, 220, 242, 244, 254, 262, 264–6, 268–70, 279, 283
Novgorod-Kiev empire 220
Noyan, Jebe 255–9
Nunguvik 128
Nuremburg 272
Nyköping Banquet 249, 250
Nyköping Castle 248–50
Nyköpingshus fortress 246
Nyland, Finland 246

Ob River 266
Odd of *Arrow-Odd Saga* 191
Odd the Englishman 165
Oddi 158
Oder River 49, 77, 111, 141, 196, 207
Odin 86, 90–1, 136, 141, 218, 240
Oðinkárr 212
Odo, count of Paris 114–5
Odovacar (Odoacer) 57, 63, 66–8
Offa 131
Ogedei Khan 261, 264, 256
Ohthere of Hålgoland 85, 87, 120
Oise River 114
Oissel 114
Öjebomåla 274
Oka River 203, 268
Oksywie culture 75
Olaf (Olof), Swedish king at Birka 168
Olaf (son of Gudrod) 134
Olaf of Dublin 105
Olaf of Hedeby 212
Olaf of Ireland 120
Olaf of Norway 139
Olaf the Holy of Norway 120
Olaf the Keen-eyed, ruler of Næriki (Närke) 164
Olaf the Woodcutter 134
Olaf, son of Sigtrygg 110
Olaf, Swedish ruler at Hedeby 160, 211, 132
Olaf Tree-feller 88
Ólafr, on runestone 221
Óláfs Saga 141
Olafsson, Magnus, of Norway 145–6, 220
Olafsson, Thorstein, captain of last ship to Greenland 234
Olafsson, Tryggvi 139–40
Öland 49, 96–7, 169
Old English 81, 83, 159, 279
Old European language 27
Old Folkung 247

Old Norse 133, 161, 173, 187, 216, 222–3, 225, 228
Old Norse law 179
Old Testament 252
Old Testament Samuel 277
Older Dryas 6, 12
Oldest Dryas 6
Oleg, prince of Kursk 258
Oleg, Rurik's successor 210, 212
Oleg, son of Sviatoslav 218
Óleifa 160
Olga (Helga), Igor's wife 215
Olgerd, son of Gedimin 266
Ölvir 158
Omayyad caliphs 198
On (Ane, Aun) 86
O'Neills of southern Ireland 232
Onela (Ali) 85, 87
Ongentheow 84–5, 87
Onund (Anund) 88
Orda 261
Ordulf of Saxony 145
Øresund Strait 141, 165, 251, 283, 252
The Origins and Deeds of the Goths (Getica), Jordanes 72, 73, 78
Origo Gothic, by Cassiodorus 72
Orkesta, Uppland 158
Orkney Islands 103–4, 135–6, 140, 143–4, 148, 155, 187, 235–6
Orleans 113
Orm of England 165
Orthodox Christians 237, 266, 270
Orthodox Karelians 270
Orthodox Russians 244
Oseberg, Norway 184
Oslo 43, 117, 134, 242, 249, 281
Oslofjord 134
Ospak of Man 232
Österbotten, Finland 246
Östergötland 25, 27, 54, 74, 83–4, 90, 161, 221, 249, 280
Østland 134–6, 140–3
Ostrogoths 57, 59–60, 64–9, 72, 74, 77, 80, 94, 96, 151
Ota 104
Otford 142
Otingis 80
Otrar 256
Ottar 87
Otto II of Germany 137
Ouse River 146
Oxenstierna, Axel, Chancellor of Sweden 1
Oxford 138
Özurr 160

Pacific 117
Paleo-Eskimo cultures 124
Paleolithic 15, 21
Paleozoic era 5
Palermo 69
Palestine 146
Pallig 139
Paltes, ruler of Polotsk 192
Pamplona 116

Pannonia 61, 65–6, 68
Pannonian-Moesian Ostrogoths 67
Pannonian Ostrogoths 66
Papal States 151
Paris 107, 113–5, 235
Parthia 48, 56
Pavia 65
"Pax Romana" 78
Peace of Nöteborg 270
Pelimut 128
Peloponnesian War 47
Pereaslavl (Preslava) 197, 217
Pereiaslav 262
Périgueux 113
Persia 47, 162, 194, 203, 209, 256, 261
Persian Gulf 117, 256
Persson, Birger, governor and lawspeaker of Uppland 278
Perun 218
Pest 263
Petchenegs 198, 210–1, 215, 217–20, 254
Peterson, John 277
petroglyphs **33**, 34
Pettersson, Filip 244
Pevensey, England 148–9
Philip II of France 235
Philippa, daughter of Henry IV of England 283
Philippopolis 217
Phoenicians 43
Photius, patriarch of Constantinople 210
Picenum 69
Picts 94, 96, 103–4, 108, 236
Pilgårds, Gotland 223
Pillars of Hercules (Strait of Gibraltar) 45
Pinsk 266
Piraeus, port of Athens 231
Pisa 116
Pitted Ware culture 25, 27
Placidia, Galla 62
Pleistocene Epoch 5–6, 15
Pliny the Elder 46, 53, 74
Po valley 44
Poetic Edda 184–5
Poland, Poles 28, 75–7, 112, 146, 194, 196–7, 216, 218–9, 220, 241, 253, 258, 262–3
Polotsk 203, 209, 242, 266
Polovcians of Central Asia 223
Polyane Slavs 197
Polynesians 117
Pomerania 1, 75–7
Pomeranian-Mazovian (Wielbark) culture 76
Pomponius Mela 53
Pontus Sea 73
Poznan 23
Prague 1
Pre-Boreal Period 6, 11, 13, 15
Pre-Roman Iron Age 41, 43, 47
pre–Viking 182, 195, 197, 247, 269–70
Procopius of Caesarea 80, 161
Prose Edda 174

Proto-Balto-Slavic languages 29
Proto-Celtic 29
Proto-Germanic languages 29, 30
Proto-Indo-European languages 29
Proto-Italic 29
Prussians 1, 77, 196–7, 241, 243, 253
Prut River 59
Przemysl 262
Przeworsk culture 75–6
Pskov 197, 201, 203, 215, 265
Ptolemy 54–5, 74–5
Punic Wars 47
Pyrenees 62, 70–1, 198
Pytheas of Marseilles 44, **45**, 46, 74

Qara-Khitai Empire of Central Asia 255
Quaternary Period 5
Quentowic 113
Quillanus, ruler of Novgorod 192

Råd 74, 247
Radimichi Slavs 198
Rafarta, wife of Eyvind 156
Ragna 159
Ragnar, attacked Paris 113
Ragni 158
Ragnvaldr, on runestone 225
Rainulf "Drengot" 153–4
Rakkæ 92, 130
Rameses II 41
Ranrike-Bohuslän 142
Rashid, shah of Shirvan 258
Ravenna 56, 61–3, 67–9, 72
Razgard, Bulgaria 58
Reading 139
Reccared I 70
Red Sea 117
Reformation 277–8
Reggio 154
Regnald the Russian 165
Renaissance 74
Reric, Wendland 131
Res gestæ Saxonicæ 212
Reval 242
Revelations of St. Birgitta 252
Reydarfjord 122
Rhaetia 68
Rhine 1, 28, 43, 48, 53, 61, 64, 113–4
Rhineland 207–8
Rhône 44, 115
Rhos 201
Riazan 261–2
Ribe 36, 100
Riccall 146
Richard I of Aversa 153–4
Richard I of Normandy 148
Richard II of Normandy 143, 148
Richard III of Normandy 148
Rig 174
Rig-jarl 185
Riga 241–2, 253, 268
Rigsthula (Rígsþula) 173–4, 177, 185

Index

Rikissa, daughter of Birger Jarl 245
Riksens Råd 247
Rimbert 166–9, 207
Ring, king of Svear 212, 215
Ringerike 135
Ringmere 143
Risala 213
River Shannon 104–5
Roadmaker, Onund, son of Yngvar 162
Robert of Hauteville 153–4
Robert I of Normandy 145, 148
Roberts, Neil 10
Roderic 71
Rodstaff, ruler of Rostof 192
Rofstein (Fufstein), site along Dnieper 223
Roger II, count of Sicily 154
Rognvald, earl of Västergötland 169
Rognvald of York 110
Rognvald the Glorious 85, 135
Rogvolod, king of Polotsk 218
Rollo (Hrolf) of Normandy 114, 148, 151
Roman Catholic 65, 68, 139, 143, 166, 212, 233, 237, 243, 266, 270
Roman coins 49
Roman Empire 1, 3, 48, 56–8, 70, 95, 151, 197, 199, 268
Roman Gaul 111, 96
Roman Iron Age 41, 49–51, 78
Roman Italy 67
Roman legions 94
Roman pontiff 253
Roman world 49
Romania 223
Romanized Thracians 198
Romanus I, Deputy Emperor of Constantinople 215
Rome, Romans 45, 47, 49, 51, 52–4, 56–7, 59–60, 62, 64–8, 69–70, 73, 77–9, 94–6, 106, 116, 149, 151, 166, 179, 199, 206, 237, 241, 243, 246, 278–9, 281
Romulus 57
Romulus Augustus (Augustulus) 57
Roosevelt, Theodore 140
Rorik (Roerik) 114, 209
Rorik of Denmark 131
Roskilde 143
Rostock 242, 272
Rostov 209
Rouen 113–4
Roussell, Aage 127
Rtis 200
Rudolf 114
Rügen 22, 141
Rugians 57, 64, 66–7
Rugii 74, 76
Runes, runestones **52**–3, 157–8, 160, 166, 174, 185, **186**, 187, 212, 221–3, 224, 227, 230–1, 259
Rurik of the Rus 200–1, 204, 208–9, 216

Rurik, took Frisia 160
Rus 2–3, 140, 144–6, 202–3, 209–10, 213–8, 220, 222–3, 226–7, 229, 234, 253, 269
Rus Khaganate 201–4, 208
Rus-Scandinavian connection 220
Russia 1, 3–4, 40, 48, 183, 192, 194, 196–7, 201, 204–5, 209, 215, 219–20, 222–3, 227, 229, 234, 240, 242–3, 253–4, 258–9, 262, 264, 266, 268–9, 270
Russian Primary Chronicles 218
Russian Principalities **260**
Russian steppes 216
Rustah, Ahmad ibn 214–5

Saami (Lapps) 196
Saint Anskar 166
St. Birgitta (St. Bridget of Sweden) 4, 252, 270, 274, 277, 278–9, 281
St. Birgitta Birgersdotter 278–9
St. Brice's Day 139
St. Bridget of Sweden Catholic Church in Lake Balboa, California 278
St. Bridget of Sweden Catholic Church in Lindstrom, Minnesota 278
St. Bridget's of Sweden Catholic Church in Lindsborg, Kansas 278
Saint-Clair-sur-Epte, Treaty of 114, 148
St. Cuthbert 102
St. John's Day 113
St. Katherine, daughter of St. Birgitta 277, 279
St. Lô 114
St. Michael's Day 248
St. Nicholas' Cathedral at Gardar, Greenland 233
St. Sophia, Cathedral of 262, 269
Saint-Valery-sur-Somme 149
Sajo River 263
Salerno 151
Sali the Goth 165
Samarkand 198, 255–6
Samish 40
Sandarna culture 16–7
Sandnes, Greenland 127
Sandwich 150
Saqālibāh 203
Saracen 151–2, 160, 230
Sarai 264–6
Sarmatians 58–9, 64, 66–7, 75
Sarup 25
Sasireti, Georgia, Battle of 230
Satem dialects 29
Saxland (Saxony?) 87–9, 92, 111, 165, 191
Saxo the Splitter 165
Saxony, Saxons 64, 90, 92, 94, 96, 106, 109, 111, 114, 117, 131, 150, 159, 162, 165, 184, 226, 235, 241
Scandia 54, 75
Scandinavia, Scandinavians 3, 5,
9, 20–1, 30, 41, 43–4, 46–9,
51–2, 54–5, 75, 77–9, 84, 80–1,
89, 90, 94–6, 100–2, 105–7,
110, 114, 117–21, 130, 134–5,
146, 148, 151, 158, 173–5, 181–
2, 183, 185, 187–8, 193, 195–7,
200, 203, 205–6, 210–1, 216–7,
219, 221, 223, 226, 233, 235–7,
238, 273–4, 279, 282–3
Scandinavian (Scandes) mountain range 161
Scandinavian peninsula 74, 80, 83, 169
Scandza 73–5, 78, 80
Scania 5–6, 12–3, 15–6, 18, 41, 54, 89–90, 92, 130, 157, 160, 162, 165–6, 176, 251–2, 274, 276
Scarborough 146
Scheldt River 114
Schleifjord 101, 211
Schleswig 236, 283
Schleswig-Holstein 283
Sciri 57, 64–6
Sclavonian 200
Scotland, Scots 44, 46, 96, 103–6, 110, 114, 122, 138, 236, 140, 155, 158
Scots (Irish) 94
Scotti clan 103
Screrefennae 78, 80
Scrithiphini 80
Scyld 82, 99, 130
Scylding (Skjolding) 92, 130
Scylfing (Skilfing, Scylfingas) 85, 92
Scythia (Oium) 73
Sea of Azov 198
Seachlainn, Mael, king of Meath 105
Seeburg (Grobin or Seleburg on the Duna River?) 168, 191
Segebro 12
Seimgalir (Zemgale) in Latvia and Lithuania 222
Seine River 113–4
Selker Noor 212
Selonians 196
Semigalls 253
Semnones 53
Senator, Cassiodorus 68, 72
Serbs 197
Serkland 225, 227–8, 237
Sermermiut at Nordrseta, Greenland 234
Severyane Slavs 197
Seville 115
Shakespeare 130, 250
Sheppey Isle 106, 157
Shetland Islands 46, 103–4, 122–3, 134–6, 143–4, 155, 236
Sicily 47, 57, 62, 68–9, 72, 114, 146, 151–2, 154, 160
Sigerich (ruled Hedeby) 132, 160, 215
Sigfred, king of Denmark 114, 131
Sigrsæll, Eirik, (the Victorious), king of Sweden 17, 137, 169–70, 172, 228, 240

Sigtrygg of York 110
Sigtryggr of Hedeby 212
Sigtuna, Sweden 91, 167, 217, 236
Sigurd of Norway 238
Sigurd of Novgorod 140
Sigurd Snake-eye 108
Sigurd the Stout, 232
Sigviðr, on runestone 223
Silesians 258, 263
Silk Road 162, 272
Simeon, Grand Prince of Russia 268
Sineus 209
Singidunum 66
Single Grave culture 28, 30
Sirius 212
Sirnir of *Arrow-Odd saga* 191
Sitones 54
Sixth Crusade 257–8
Skaldic verse 203
Skalvians 196–7
Skåne 5, 9, 12, 27, 30, 49, 80, 97, 131, 133, 136, 143, 146, 162, 169, 242, 274
Skänninge Assembly 243
Skateholm 20, 22
Skiringssal in Vestfold 135
Skjöldunga Saga 131
Skötkonung, Olaf (Olof) of Sweden 141–2, 169–70, 220, 228, 240
Skraeling Island 128
Skraelings 125–6, 128, 234, 251
Skye 103
Slavic Eastern Europe 200, 236
Slavic, Slavs 145, 165–6, 173, 196–8, 209–10, 216, 218–9, 234, 154, 196–9, 201, 208, 211, 214, 236, 259
Slavic tribes 80, 198
Slettahlid, Iceland 156
Slettu-Bjorn, settler of Iceland 156
Slettubjornstead, Iceland 156
Slovaks 197
Småland Plateau 6
Småland, Smålanders 5, 11–2, 159, 161–2, 205, 224, 238, 250, 271, 273, 280
Smigallians 196
Smolensk 197
Snæ 86
Snör 175
Snorri, first European born in America 127
Söderköping 247
Södermanland 95, 158, 161, 164, 187, 205, 207, 221–2, 224–5, 242, 249
Sofia of Denmark 245
Sogn 136
Soissons 57, 114
Solva (Slveig) of Soleyar, Norway 88
Solve, sea king 88
Solver, king of the Gauts 156
Somerset 108
Somme River 114
Soti, with Yngvarr 229

Sound (Øresund strait) 243
Sound Toll 243
South Danes 81
South Tyrol 44
Southampton 138
Southern Bug 77
Southern Europe 3, 5, 11, 15, 23, 56, 78, 94, 118, 154, 246, 249
Southern Slavs 197
southern Sweden 11, 19, 133
Southern Sweden of the Late Middle Ages *275*
Southwest Asia 261
southwestern Sweden 16–7
Spain 57, 62, 66, 68, 70–1, 96, 111, 115, 143, 199, 277–8
Spanish Caliphate 71
Spanish coast 80
Sparlösa runestone 166
Spjallboði, on runestone 223
Spjót (Spear) 158
Staf (Stafá) River, Iceland 156
Staffordshire, Mercia 98
Stainmore, Northumbria 136
Stamford Bridge, Battle of 146, 149
Staraja Ladoga 231, 191
Staraya Ladoga 197
Starki, Styrbjorn 137, 169
Stävie 25
Stegeborg 250
Stein, Estland 191
Steinselva River 9
Steinunn, a Greenlander 234
Stifla, Iceland 156
Stiklarstadir 144, 220
Stiklarstadir, Battle of 145
Stjerne-Oddi 119
Stockholm 9, 94, 96, 206, 244–5, 248, 280, 284
Stockholm Bloodbath 284
Stockholm Castle 276, 280
Stone Age 3, 91
Stora Bjers, Sweden 22
Stord at Hardangerfjord, Battle of 136
The Story of Burnt Njal 180
Strabain, Awair 205
Strabo 46
Strabo, Theodoric Strabo (The Squinter) 67
Strait of Dover 113
Strait of Gibraltar 115–6
Strait of Messina 62
Stralsund 272
Stralsund, Treaty of 243
Strangford Lough 105
Strasbourg 272
Strathclyde 103, 106, 108, 110
Stribog (god of wind) 218
Sturluson, Snorri 85, 92, 141, 169, 174, 232
Styrbjorn, on runestone 228
Styrkárr 158
Sub-Atlantic Period 6, 11
Sub-Boreal Period 6, 11
Suda River 203
Suebi 62
Suehans (Suetidi, Sviar, Svear, Swedes) 79, 81

Suetidi 80
Suevi 62, 66, 70
Suffolk 109
Suiones 54, 74
sun-board 119
sun-stone 120
Sung Empire 261
Suomusjärvi culture 18
Survey of the Earth, by Pytheas 45
Sussex 106, 149
Sutton Hoo 97
Suzdal 262, 264–5
Svarog (father of Slavic gods) 218
Svavarsson, Gardar 122
Svear (Svéar, Sviar, Svea or Swedes) of Uppland 54, 74, 79–81, 83–7, 90, 92, 95, 97, 141, 160–5, 172–3, 205–6, 209, 215, 220–1, 240–1
Svear-Gotland-Åland Vikings 208
Sveinn, on runestones 157, 159
Sveinsson, Hardegon 132
Sverker (Swedish royal house) 240, 244
Sverker-Erik kings 241
Sverker the Younger, king of Sweden 243
Sverkersson, Johan 243
Sviatoslav, Grand Prince of the Rus 216–8
Svíþjóð 220
Svíþjóð hinn mikla (Sweden the Great) 205
Svyatopolk, son of Vladimir 219
Sweden (Svearland) 165
Sweden, southern tip of 53
Sweden the Great 2, 220, 234
Sweden, west coast of 46, 53
Sweden's Viking Age 161
Swedish Bronze Age 30, 34, 39–40
Swedish Christianization 224
Swedish Finland 268
Swedish geography *7*
Swedish kings 165
Swedish late Mesolithic 19
Swedish lowlands 5
Swedish Mesolithic *17*
Swedish Neolithic Artifacts *29*
Swedish provinces *238*
Swedish Reformation 171
Swedish runestones 189
Swedish Stone Age *13–4*
Swedish Unification *170*
Swedish Uppland 209
Swegde 86
Swerting 84
Switzerland 28, 41, 44
Syas River 203
Sylfa (Solfa) 158
Sylgja, wife of Hring 166
Syon Abby 278
Syr Darya 256
Syracuse 69, 153

Tacitus 54, 74
Tafeistaland (Tavastia), Finland 222

Index

Tale of a Wayside Inn 140
Tamara, queen of Georgia 257
Tanfield Valley 128
Tång, Uppland 159
Tarik 71
Tartars 254, 264, 266, 268–9
Tartars of Crimea 1
Teja 69
Templers 263
Temüchin 254
La Tène industry 41, 44
Tertiary Period 5
Teurnia 65
Teutones 46, 53, 74, 173, 268
Teutonic Knights 241, 253, 263, 265–6, 283
Thames 108
Thanet 138
Thengel the Tall 165
Theodahad 69
Theoderid 64–5
Theodoric the Great 56–7, 65–6, 68–70, 72, 80
Theophanes of Constantinople 215
Theophilus, Byzantine emperor 201, 208
Thetford 138–9
Theudobert 84, 111
Theudoric I of the Franks 84, 111
Things 114, 123, 134, 140, 143, 168, 175, 207
Thir, wife of Þrælll 174
Thirty Years War 1, 243
Thiudimir 56, 64–7
Þjalfi 159
Thjodolf the Learned 85–6, 135
Thor 39, 53, 90–1, 136, 141, 218, 240
Thora, daughter of King Eirek of Upsala 156
Thorberni, Katillus 278
Þorbjörn 158
Thord the Stumbler 165
Thorfinn of *Egil's Saga* 185
Þorgautr (Þorgunn) 157
Thorgils, son of Gorm of Sweden 156
Thorismund 64–5
Thorkell the Tall 142–3, 158
Thorn 77
Thorolf the Thick 161, 165
Thorvald 125
Thrace 58, 60, 215, 217
Thracian Goths 67, 74
Þrælll, son of Ai and Edda 174
Thule 46, 80–1, 128–9
Thule-Inuits 124–5, 128, 233
Thuringians 79
Thyri (or Thyra), wife of Gorm the Old 133
Thyri, wife of Eirik Sigrsæll 169
Thyri, wife of Olaf Tryggvason 141
Thyri, wife of Styrbjorn Starki 137
Tiber 268
Tiflis (Tbilisi) 257
Tigris River 48

Tigris-Euphrates 225
Timboholm, Västergötland 95
Tisza River 211
Tófa 159
Tóla (mother of Yngvarr?) 228
Tóla (on runestone) 158
Toledo 70–1
Tolui 261
Tongue (Tunguá) River, Iceland 156
Tools of the Viking Age *178*
Toregene, mother of Güyük Khan 265
Tornio River 6
Torsås Parish 273
Torzhok 262, 265
Tosti, Skagul 158
Tostig, earl of Northumbria 146, 148
Totila 69
Toulouse 62, 69, 113, 115
Toulouse Visigoths 66
Tours 113
Transcaucasia 257
Transjö, Småland 159
Transoxiana 255–6
Transylvania 1, 263–4
Trave River 242
Treene River 101
Trichterrandbecher (TRB) culture 23
Trier 114
Troia 153
Trojan War 165
Trondelag 134–6, 141, 173
Trondheim 46, 95, 141, 143
Trundholm sun chariot 39
Truso on the Vistula 169
Truvor 209
Tryggvason, Olaf, of Norway 138–9, 140, 169, 196, 228, 240
Tryggvasonar 141
Tufa 67–8
Tumi (Tummi, Dómi) 160
Tunsberg 134
Turgeis 104–5
Turkish 198, 202, 256, 269
Turkish-Slavic Bulgarians 198
Turkoman 264
Turko-Mongolian 254
Turks 199
Tybrind Vig, Denmark 20–1
Tyr 90
Tzimiskes, Johannes 216

Ubbe the Frisian 165
Ubbi (Bjorn Ironside) 108
Ukraine 1, 12, 26, 58, 73, 76–7, 194, 222, 197
Ulf-Krakason, Gunnbjörn 124
Ulf of Denmark, Jarl 143, 145
Ulfilas 59
Ulfr of Uppland 158
Ulfsdotter, Mareta 281
Ulfsson (Estridsson), Svein 145
Ulmerugi 73, 77
Ulster 104
Ulvåsa 279
Unferth 82

United Gotland Travelers of the Holy Roman Empire 242
University of Paris 272
Upernavik, Greenland 128
Uppland 27, 30, 40, 52–3, 78–9, 81, 85, 87, 89–90, 92, 95, 97, 100, 160–2, 165, 169, 172–3, 182, 191, 205, 207, 221–5, 230, 237, 240, 243–4, 250, 273, 280
Uppsala 43, 86–8, 90–1, 224, 240, 247, 250
Ural Mountains 3, 194, 196, 198, 210, 254, 261, 264, 266
Ural River 264

Vadstena Abby in Sweden 277, 281
Væringr 159
Vagoths 80
Valamir 64–6
Valdimar, with Yngvarr 229–30
Valens 60
Valentinian III 57
Val-ès-Dunes, Battle of 148
Valhalla 91, 97, 189
Valia of the Visigoths 62
Valkyries 90, 97
Valleberga, Lund, Scania 157
Valsgärde, Uppland 97
Vandals 57, 59, 61–2, 68–9, 73, 77, 94
Vanir 90
Vanlande 86
Varangian Guard 146, 225–6, 231
Varangian Trade Routes *202*
Varangians 2–3, 200–1, 203–5, 208–11, 215–7, 219–20, 226, 229, 231, 259, 269
Värmland 17, 84, 90, 134, 161, 273
Varus 48
Väsby, Uppland 159
Västerbotten 6
Västergötland 17, 27, 49, 51, 54, 74, 80, 83, 90, 158, 161, 221, 237, 248, 250, 271, 273, 280
Veche 269, 270
Vedbæck 22
Veles (patron of cattle) 218
Velikiye River 203
Vendel Period 78, 92–4, 97, 100, 161, 182
Vendel, Uppland 97
Venedi 76
Venezuela 278
Venice Arsenal 231
Venosa 153
Vepsians 196
Verhansung (commercial boycott) 243
Vermeland (Värmland?) 88
Verona 61, 67
Vestfold, Norway 113, 135–6
Vestland 134–5
Viborg 242, 248, 270
Viborg Thing 145–6
Vidfadmi (Far-reacher), Ivar 131
Vidfavne, Ivar 88, 92, 165, 191
Vidimir 64

Vienna 1, 264
Vífill, on runestone 223
the Vik 134–6, 141–3
Viking Age 53–4, 78, 94, 100–2, 111, 113, 115, 117–8, 150–1, 146, 154–5, 157–8, 161–2, 173, 175–8, 181–7, 194, 196–8, 188, 201, 205–6, 221–2, 224, 232, 234–7, 245–6, 269–70, 274
Viking boat 38
Viking Clothing and Weapons *183*
Viking Expeditions to Europe *112*
Viking Expeditions to North America *126*
Viking period 20, 52, 87, 134
Viking-Rus 201
Viking Ship Museum 117
Viking ships 34, 51
Viking ships and navigation *119*
Viking Sweden 175–6, 223
Vilgerdason, Floki 122
Vinland 118, 125, 127, 129, 232
Virland 221
Visbur 86
Visby 242–3, 271, 274
Visigoth migrations *61*
Visigoths 57, 59–62, 64, 66, 68–9, 70–2, 77, 94, 96
Vistula 48–9, 75, 77, 196–7
Vitebsk on the Dvina 266
Vitigis 69
Vlademar I of Sweden 244–6
Vladimir (Valdimar), duke of Novgorod 140
Vladimir, palatine of Sandomir and Cracow 263
Vladimir I, Grand Prince of the Rus 218–9, 220
Vladimir city 262
Vladimir principality 254, 264–5, 268
Vladimir-Volynsk 266
Voishelk, prince of Lithuania 266
Volga Bend 198
Volga Bulgars 198, 203, 211, 213, 216–8, 257–9
Volga Finns 201
Volga River 28, 194, 197–8, 201–3, 208–9, 211, 113, 254, 259, 261, 268, 270
Volkhov River 194, 197, 200, 203, 269

Volynia 262
von Brunkow, Johan 249
Vrái 159
Vsevolod, son of Yaroslav 220
Vyatichi Slavs 198, 216

Wales 94, 110, 140
Wallachia 223, 263
Wallingford 139
Warrior Kings of Sweden 1
Warsaw 75
Warwickshire 142
Waterford 105
Wedmore 109
Weichsel Glaciation 5–6, 9, 11
Weland 113–4
Welsh 96, 103, 108–10
Wendland, Wends 92, 132, 137, 140, 145, 162, 167, 169, 173, 191, 195–7, 236, 240–1
Wermund 131
Wessex 102, 106, 108–9, 142–3
Wessex-Cornwall 94
West Gautland (Gotland) 89, 164–5
West Wales (Dumnonia) 106, 109
Western Asia 64, 189
Western Dvina River 194, 202–3, 211, 224, 268
Western Europe 41, 64, 100, 102, 115, 117–8, 121, 155, 160, 200, 107–8, 135, 203
western expeditions 2
Western Roman Empire 56–7, 60, 62, 64, 66, 78, 96
Western Settlement, Greenland 234
Western Slavs 196–7
Westminster 150
Wexford 105
"White Christ" 238
White Khanate of Orda 264
White Russia 266
White Sea 193
Widsith 81, 83, 131
Widukind, Saxon chieftain 212, 131
Wielbark culture 75–7
Wiglaf 83
William of Flanders, count 149
William of Normandy (the Conqueror, the Bastard) 148–9, 150, 157, 232, 234–5, 146
Willow Island 128
Wilton 139
Wiltshire 108
Wisconsin Glacial Episode 5
Wismar 242, 272
Wisna, chief of women warriors 165
Wollin 145, 207
Wotan 91
Wulfstan 169

Yaropolk, son of Sviatoslav 218
Yaroslav of Kiev, founded Dorpat 253
Yaroslav, son of Vladimir and Grand Prince of the Rus 144–6, 219, 220, 229, 234, 240, 253–4
Yaroslav the Wise, tomb in Kiev 262
Yaroslav II of Novgorod 264–5
Yaroslav market in Novgorod 269
Yen-Ching 255
Yngling kings 85–6, 88, 143, 238, 240–1, 244
Ynglinga Saga 87, 89–90, 92, 94–5, 111, 115, 162, 171–2. 191
Ynglinga Tal 85–6, 135
Yngvar, from *Ynglinga Tal* 88, 162, 191
Yngvarr (Far Traveled) 227–30, 257
Yngve 86
Yoldia Sea 9
York 108, 110, 113, 120, 136, 146–7, 149, 264
Yorkshire 108
Yorkshire Danes 142
Yotvingians (Sudovians) 196
Younger Dryas 6, 11–3, 15
Younger Futhark 187
Yuri, grand duke of Suzdalia 258
Yury, prince of Moscow 268, 270

Zaragoza 111
Zealand 9, 20, 39, 46, 53, 81, 83, 89, 92, 131, 133, 136, 143, 146, 157, 165
Zeno 57, 67
Zimisces, John 217

www.ingramcontent.com/pod-product-compliance
Ingram Content Group UK Ltd.
Pitfield, Milton Keynes, MK11 3LW, UK
UKHW050542150426
5217IPUK00026B/2041